To my parents, Mila & Gabi

—Itzik Ben-Gan

Table of Contents

What do you think of this book? We want to hear from you!

Microsoft is interested in hearing your feedback so we can continually improve our books and learning resources for you. To participate in a brief online survey, please visit:

www.microsoft.com/learning/booksurvey/

What do you think of this book? We want to hear from you!

Microsoft is interested in hearing your feedback so we can continually improve our books and learning resources for you. To participate in a brief online survey, please visit:

www.microsoft.com/learning/booksurvey/

Foreword

I had met Itzik Ben-Gan briefly a couple of times and knew of his reputation, so I was looking forward to his afternoon session on avoiding cursors in SQL programming at PASS. I was lucky to get there early, as the large room filled up quickly. Itzik took a couple of SQL programming problems and diced them up in the most skillful and entertaining way, showing the elegance and efficiency of set-oriented thinking. The audience loved it—and so did I, except I had a different angle. Having worked on the internals of SQL Server, I could see Itzik touch the product nerves in his demos, and I admired how he turned features into beautiful solutions. After the session, I asked one of the attendees what had been his main takeaway, curious about which of the many techniques would have stood out for him. He looked at me, mildly surprised, and just said, "The man is a genius!" That pretty much sums it up.

This question of cursors is more fundamental than it may appear at first. It points to a deep dichotomy of tremendous practical importance. Most of us were taught to program by chopping up a task into smaller steps that, when executed in sequence, perform a desired computation. But if you approach SQL programming this way, you will get only mediocre results. Your code will be much larger and harder to maintain. It will be less efficient, less flexible, and less tunable. Using SQL effectively is not about an incremental extension of your procedural programming skills or about a specific collection of tricks. Writing SQL well requires approaching problems with a different mind-set—one that is declarative and set oriented, not procedural. This is the dichotomy.

Inside Microsoft SQL Server 2008: T-SQL Querying puts together all the ingredients you need to understand this declarative and set-oriented way of thinking and become a proficient SQL programmer, thus making an important contribution to the SQL Server development community. Its chapters on formal foundations help you understand the basis for the language philosophy and get a sense for its potential. The language itself is covered thoroughly, from the basic operations to the most advanced features, all of them explained in the context of real problem solving. The many examples show you what good SQL looks like, and they cover common patterns you are likely to find when writing applications. A comprehensive chapter on query tuning explains in detail the factors that impact performance in the system, how to go about identifying issues, and how to address them effectively.

Itzik assembled a strong team of collaborators to write this book. Coming from different backgrounds, all of them share a deep expertise in SQL, a passion for database technology, extensive teaching experience, and a recognized track record of contributions to the SQL Server community. Steve Kass is known for his depth of understanding and clarity of thought. Dejan Sarka contributes an extensive knowledge of the relational model and a breadth of database technologies. As for Lubor Kollar, I've had the pleasure of working with him on the definition, design, and implementation of the Query Processing engine of SQL Server for over a decade, and I deeply respect his insight. They make an outstanding team of guides who can help you improve your skills.

SQL is a very powerful language, but I believe only a minority of developers really know how to get the most out of it. Using SQL well can mean code that is 10 times more efficient, more scalable, and more maintainable. *Inside Microsoft SQL Server 2008: T-SQL Querying* tells you how.

César Galindo-Legaria, PhD

Manager of the Query Optimization Team, Microsoft SQL Server

Acknowledgments

Several people contributed to the T-SQL querying and T-SQL programming books, and I'd like to acknowledge their contributions. Some were involved directly in writing or editing the books, while others were involved indirectly by providing advice, support, and inspiration.

To the coauthors of *Inside Microsoft SQL Server 2008: T-SQL Querying*—Lubor Kollar, Dejan Sarka, and Steve Kass—and to the coauthors of *Inside Microsoft SQL Server 2008: T-SQL Programming*—Dejan Sarka, Roger Wolter, Greg Low, Ed Katibah, and Isaac Kunen—it is a great honor to work with you. It is simply amazing to see the level of mastery that you have over your areas of expertise, and it is pure joy to read your texts. Thanks for agreeing to be part of this project.

To Lubor, besides directly contributing to the books, you provide support, advice, and friendship and are a great source of inspiration. I always look forward to spending time with you—hiking, drinking, and talking about SQL and other things.

To Dejko, your knowledge of the relational model is admirable. Whenever we spend time together, I learn new things and discover new depths. I like the fact that you don't take things for granted and don't follow blindly words of those who are considered experts in the field. You have a healthy mind of your own and see things that very few are capable of seeing. I'd like to thank you for agreeing to contribute texts to the books. I'd also like to thank you for your friendship; I always enjoy spending time with you. We need to do the beer list thing again some time. It's been almost 10 years!

To the technical editor of the books, Steve Kass, your unique mix of strengths in mathematics, SQL, and English are truly extraordinary. I know that editing both books and also writing your own chapters took their toll. Therefore, I'd like you to know how much I appreciate your work. I know you won't like my saying this, but it is quite interesting to see a genius at work. It kept reminding me of Domingo Montoya's work on the sword he prepared for the six-fingered man from William Goldman's *The Princess Bride*.

To Umachandar Jayachandran (UC), many thanks for helping out by editing some of the chapters. Your mastery of T-SQL is remarkable, and I'm so glad you could join the project in any capacity. I'd also like to thank Bob Beauchemin for reviewing the chapter on Spatial Data.

To Cesar Galindo-Legaria, I feel honored that you agreed to write the foreword for the T-SQL querying book. The way you and your team designed SQL Server's optimizer is simply a marvel. I'm constantly trying to figure out and interpret what the optimizer does, and whenever I manage to understand a piece of the puzzle, I find it astonishing what a piece of software is capable of. Your depth of knowledge, your pleasant ways, and your humility are an inspiration.

To the team at Microsoft Press: Ken Jones, the product planner: I appreciate the personal manner in which you handle things and always look forward to Guinness sessions with you. I think that you have an impossible job trying to make everyone happy and keep projects moving, but somehow you still manage to do it.

To Sally Stickney, the development editor, thanks for kicking the project off the ground. I know that the T-SQL querying book was your last project at Microsoft Press before you started your new chosen path in life and am hopeful that it left a good impression on you. I wish you luck and happiness in your new calling.

To Denise Bankaitis, the project editor, you of all people at Microsoft Press probably spent most time working on the books. Thanks for your elegant project management and for making sure things kept flowing. It was a pleasure to work with you.

I'd also like to thank DeAnn Montoya, the project manager for the vendor editorial team, S4Carlisle Publishing Services, and Becka McKay, the copy editor. I know you spent countless hours going over our texts, and I appreciate it a lot.

To Solid Quality Mentors, being part of this amazing company and group of people is by far the best thing that happened to me in my career. It's as if all I did in my professional life led me to this place where I can fulfill my calling, which is teaching people about SQL. To Fernando Guerrero, Brian Moran, and Douglas McDowell: the company grew and matured because of your efforts, and you have a lot to be proud of. Being part of this company, I feel a part of something meaningful and that I'm among family and friends—among people whom I both respect and trust.

I'd like to thank my friends and colleagues from the company: Ron Talmage, Andrew J. Kelly, Eladio Rincón, Dejan Sarka, Herbert Albert, Fritz Lechnitz, Gianluca Hotz, Erik Veerman, Jay Hackney, Daniel A. Seara, Davide Mauri, Andrea Benedetti, Miguel Egea, Adolfo Wiernik, Javier Loria, Rushabh Mehta, Greg Low, Peter Myers, Randy Dyess, and many others. I'd like to thank Jeanne Reeves for making many of my classes possible and all the back-office team for their support. I'd also like to thank Kathy Blomstrom for managing our writing projects and for your excellent edits.

I'd like to thank the members of the SQL Server development team who are working on T-SQL and its optimization: Michael Wang, Michael Rys, Eric Hanson, Umachandar Jayachandran (UC), Tobias Thernström, Jim Hogg, Isaac Kunen, Krzysztof Kozielczyk, Cesar Galindo-Legaria, Craig Freedman, Conor Cunningham, and many others. For better or worse, what you develop is what we have to work with, and so far the results are outstanding! Still, until we get a full implementation of the OVER clause, you know I won't stop bothering you. ;-)

I'd like to thank Dubi Lebel and Assaf Fraenkel from Microsoft Israel and also Ami Levin, who helps me run the Israeli SQL Server users group.

To the team at *SQL Server Magazine*: Megan Bearly, Sheila Molnar, Mary Waterloo, Michele Crockett, Mike Otey, Lavon Peters, and Anne Grubb: Being part of this magazine is a great privilege. Congratulations on the 10th anniversary of the magazine! I can't believe that 10 years passed so quickly, but that's what happens when you have fun.

To my fellow SQL Server MVPs: Erland Sommarskog, Alejandro Mesa, Aaron Bertrand, Tibor Karaszi, Steve Kass, Dejan Sarka, Roy Harvey, Tony Rogerson, Marcello Poletti (Marc), Paul Randall, Bob Beauchemin, Adam Machanic, Simon Sabin, Tom Moreau, Hugo Kornelis, David Portas, David Guzman, and many others: Your contribution to the SQL Server community is remarkable. Much of what I know today is thanks to our discussions and exchange of ideas.

To my fellow SQL Server MCTs: Tibor Karaszi, Chris Randall, Ted Malone, and others: We go a long way back, and I'm glad to see that you're all still around in the SQL teaching community. We all share the same passion for teaching. Of anyone, you best understand the kind of fulfillment that teaching can bestow.

To my students: Without you, my work would be meaningless. Teaching is what I like to do best, and the purpose of pretty much everything else that I do with SQL—including writing these books—is to support my teaching. Your questions make me do a lot of research, and therefore I owe much of my knowledge to you.

To my parents, Emilia and Gabriel Ben-Gan, and to my siblings, Ina Aviram and Michael Ben-Gan, thanks for your continuous support. The fact that most of us ended up being teachers is probably not by chance, but for me to fulfill my calling, I end up traveling a lot. I miss you all when I'm away, and I always look forward to our family reunions when I'm back.

To Lilach, you're the one who needs to put up with me all the time and listen to my SQL ideas that you probably couldn't care less about. It's brainwashing, you see—at some point you will start asking for more, and before you know it, you will even start reading my books. Not because I will force you but because you will want to, of course. That's the plan at least. Thanks for giving meaning to what I do and for supporting me through some rough times of writing.

Introduction

This book and its sequel—*Inside Microsoft SQL Server 2008: T-SQL Programming*—cover advanced T-SQL querying, query tuning, and programming in Microsoft SQL Server 2008. They are designed for experienced programmers and DBAs who need to write and optimize code in SQL Server 2008. For brevity, I'll refer to the books as *T-SQL Querying* and *T-SQL Programming*, or just as *these books*.

Those who read the SQL Server 2005 edition of the books will find plenty of new materials covering new subjects, new features, and enhancements in SQL Server 2008, plus revisions and new insights about the existing subjects.

These books focus on practical common problems, discussing several approaches to tackle each. You will be introduced to many polished techniques that will enhance your toolbox and coding vocabulary, allowing you to provide efficient solutions in a natural manner.

These books unveil the power of set-based querying and explain why it's usually superior to procedural programming with cursors and the like. At the same time, they teach you how to identify the few scenarios where cursor-based solutions are superior to set-based ones.

This book—*T-SQL Querying*—focuses on set-based querying and query tuning, and I recommend that you read it first. The second book—*T-SQL Programming*—focuses on procedural programming and assumes that you read the first book or have sufficient querying background.

T-SQL Querying starts with five chapters that lay the foundation of logical and physical query processing required to gain the most from the rest of the chapters in both books.

The first chapter covers logical query processing. It describes in detail the logical phases involved in processing queries, the unique aspects of SQL querying, and the special mind-set you need to adopt to program in a relational, set-oriented environment.

The second chapter covers set theory and predicate logic—the strong mathematical foundations upon which the relational model is built. Understanding these foundations will give you better insights into the model and the language. This chapter was written by Steve Kass, who was also the main technical editor of these books. Steve has a unique combination of strengths in mathematics, computer science, SQL, and English that make him the ideal author for this subject.

The third chapter covers the relational model. Understanding the relational model is essential for good database design and helps in writing good code. The chapter defines relations and tuples and operators of relational algebra. Then it shows the relational model from a different perspective called *relational calculus*. This is more of a business-oriented perspective, as the logical model is described in terms of predicates and propositions. Data integrity is crucial for transactional systems; therefore, the chapter spends time discussing all kinds of constraints. Finally, the chapter introduces normalization—the formal process of improving database design. This chapter was written by Dejan Sarka. Dejan is one of the people with the deepest understanding of the relational model that I know.

The fourth chapter covers query tuning. It introduces a query tuning methodology we developed in our company (Solid Quality Mentors) and have been applying in production systems. The chapter also covers working with indexes and analyzing execution plans. This chapter provides the important background knowledge required for the rest of the chapters in both books, which as a practice discuss working with indexes and analyzing execution plans. These are important aspects of querying and query tuning.

The fifth chapter covers complexity and algorithms and was also written by Steve Kass. This chapter particularly focuses on some of the algorithms used often by the SQL Server engine. It gives attention to considering worst-case behavior as well as average case complexity. By understanding the complexity of algorithms used by the engine, you can anticipate, for example, how the performance of certain queries will degrade when more data is added to the tables involved. Gaining a better understanding of how the engine processes your queries equips you with better tools to tune them.

The chapters that follow delve into advanced querying and query tuning, addressing both logical and physical aspects of your code. These chapters cover the following subjects: subqueries, table expressions, and ranking functions; joins and set operations; aggregating and pivoting data; TOP and APPLY; data modification; querying partitioned tables; and graphs, trees, hierarchies, and recursive queries.

The chapter covering querying partitioned tables was written by Lubor Kollar. Lubor led the development of partitioned tables and indexes when first introduced in the product, and many of the features that we have today are thanks to his efforts. These days Lubor works with customers who have, among other things, large implementations of partitioned tables and indexes as part of his role in the SQL Server Customer Advisory Team (SQL CAT).

Appendix A covers logic puzzles. Here you have a chance to practice logical puzzles to improve your logic skills. SQL querying essentially deals with logic. I find it important to practice pure logic to improve your query problem-solving capabilities. I also find these puzzles fun and challenging, and you can practice them with the entire family. These puzzles are a compilation of the logic puzzles that I covered in my T-SQL column in *SQL Server Magazine*. I'd like to thank *SQL Server Magazine* for allowing me to share these puzzles with the book's readers.

The second book—*T-SQL Programming*—focuses on programmatic T-SQL constructs and expands its coverage to treatment of XML and XQuery and the CLR integration. The book's chapters cover the following subjects: views; user-defined functions; stored procedures; triggers; transactions and concurrency; exception handling; temporary tables and table variables; cursors; dynamic SQL; working with date and time; CLR user-defined types; temporal support in the relational model; XML and XQuery (including coverage of open schema); spatial data; change data capture, change tracking, and auditing; and Service Broker.

The chapters covering CLR user-defined types, temporal support in the relational model, and XML and XQuery were written by Dejan Sarka. As I mentioned, Dejan is extremely knowledgeable in the relational model and has very interesting insights into the model itself and the way the constructs that he covers in his chapters fit in the model when used sensibly.

The chapter about spatial data was written by Ed Katibah and Isaac Kunen. Ed and Isaac are with the SQL Server development team and led the efforts to implement spatial data support in SQL Server 2008. It is a great privilege to have this chapter written by the designers of the feature. Spatial data support is new to SQL Server 2008 and brings new data types, methods, and indices. This chapter is not intended as an exhaustive treatise on spatial data or as an encyclopedia of every spatial method that SQL Server now supports. Instead, this chapter will introduce core spatial concepts and provide the reader with key programming constructs necessary to successfully navigate this new feature to SQL Server.

The chapter about change data capture, change tracking, and auditing was written by Greg Low. Greg is a SQL Server MVP and the managing director of SolidQ Australia. Greg has many years of experience working with SQL Server—teaching, speaking, and writing about it—and is highly regarded in the SQL Server community. The technologies that are the focus of this chapter track access and changes to data and are new in SQL Server 2008. At first glance, these technologies can appear to be either overlapping or contradictory, and the best-use cases for each might be far from obvious. This chapter explores each technology, discusses the capabilities and limitations of each, and explains how each is intended to be used.

The last chapter, which covers Service Broker (SSB), was written by Roger Wolter. Roger is the program manager with the SQL Server development team and led the initial efforts to introduce SSB in SQL Server. Again, there's nothing like having the designer of a component explain it in his own words. The "sleeper" feature of SQL Server 2005 is now in production in a wide variety of applications. This chapter covers the architecture of SSB and how to use SSB to build a variety of reliable asynchronous database applications. The SQL 2008 edition adds coverage of the new features added to SSB for the SQL Server 2008 release and includes lessons learned and best practices from SSB applications deployed since the SQL Server 2005 release. The major new features are Queue Priorities, External Activation, and a new SSB troubleshooting application that incorporates lessons the SSB team learned from customers who have already deployed applications.

Hardware and Software Requirements

To practice all the material in these books and run all code samples, it is recommended that you use Microsoft SQL Server 2008 Developer or Enterprise Edition and Microsoft Visual Studio 2008 Professional or Database Edition. If you have a subscription to MSDN, you can download SQL Server 2008 and Visual Studio 2008 from *http://msdn.microsoft.com*. Otherwise, you can download a 180-day free SQL Server 2008 trial software from *http://www.microsoft.com/sqlserver/2008/en/us/trial-software.aspx* and a 90-day free Visual Studio 2008 trial software from *http://msdn.microsoft.com/en-us/vstudio/aa700831.aspx*.

You can find system requirements for SQL Server 2008 at *http://msdn.microsoft.com/en-us/library/ms143506.aspx* and for Visual Studio 2008 at *http://msdn.microsoft.com/en-us/vs2008/products/bb894726.aspx*.

Companion Content and Sample Database

These books feature a companion Web site that makes available to you all the code used in the books, the errata, additional resources, and more. The companion Web site is *http://www.insidetsql.com*.

For each of these books the companion Web site provides a compressed file with the book's source code, a script file to create the books' sample database, and additional files that are required to run some of the code samples.

After downloading the source code, run the script file TSQLFundamentals2008.sql to create the sample database InsideTSQL2008, which is used in many of the books' code samples. The data model of the InsideTSQL2008 database is provided in Figure I-1 for your convenience.

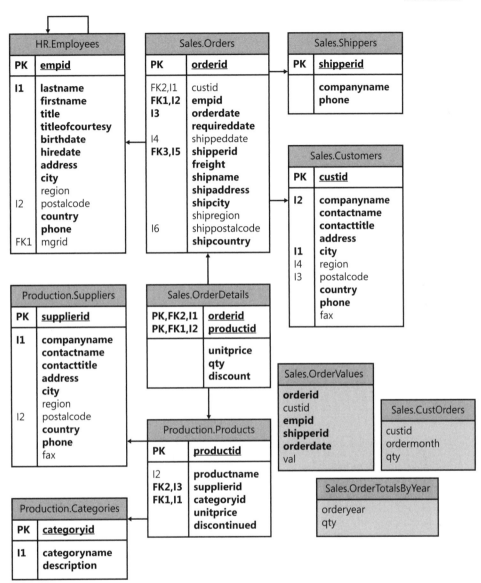

FIGURE I-1 Data model of the TSQLFundamentals2008 database

Find Additional Content Online

As new or updated material becomes available that complements your books, it will be posted online on the Microsoft Press Online Windows Server and Client Web site. The type of material you might find includes updates to books content, articles, links to companion content, errata, sample chapters, and more. This Web site is available at *http://microsoftpresssrv .libredigital.com/serverclient/* and is updated periodically.

Support for These Books

Every effort has been made to ensure the accuracy of these books and the contents of the companion Web site. As corrections or changes are collected, they will be added to a Microsoft Knowledge Base article.

Microsoft Press provides support for books at the following Web site:

http://www.microsoft.com/learning/support/books

Questions and Comments

If you have comments, questions, or ideas regarding the books or questions that are not answered by visiting the sites above, please send them to me via e-mail to

itzik@SolidQ.com

or via postal mail to

Microsoft Press

Attn: Inside Microsoft SQL Server 2008: T-SQL Querying and Inside Microsoft SQL Server 2008: T-SQL Programming Editor

One Microsoft Way

Redmond, WA 98052-6399.

Please note that Microsoft software product support is not offered through the above addresses.

Chapter 1
Logical Query Processing

Observing true experts in different fields, you find a common practice that they all share—mastering the basics. One way or another, all professions deal with problem solving. All solutions to problems, complex as they may be, involve applying a mix of fundamental techniques. If you want to master a profession, you need to build your knowledge upon strong foundations. Put a lot of effort into perfecting your techniques, master the basics, and you'll be able to solve any problem.

This book is about Transact-SQL (T-SQL) querying—learning key techniques and applying them to solve problems. I can't think of a better way to start the book than with a chapter on the fundamentals of logical query processing. I find this chapter the most important in the book—not just because it covers the essentials of query processing but also because SQL programming is conceptually very different than any other sort of programming.

Transact-SQL is the Microsoft SQL Server dialect of, or extension to, the ANSI and ISO SQL standards. Throughout the book, I'll use the terms *SQL* and *T-SQL* interchangeably. When discussing aspects of the language that originated from ANSI SQL and are relevant to most dialects, I'll typically use the term *SQL*. When discussing aspects of the language with the implementation of SQL Server in mind, I'll typically use the term *T-SQL*. Note that the formal language name is *Transact-SQL,* although it's commonly called *T-SQL*. Most programmers, including myself, feel more comfortable calling it T-SQL, so I made a conscious choice to use the term *T-SQL* throughout the book.

> ## Origin of SQL Pronunciation
>
> Many English-speaking database professionals pronounce *SQL* as *sequel,* although the correct pronunciation of the language is *S-Q-L* ("ess kyoo ell"). One can make educated guesses about the reasoning behind the incorrect pronunciation. My guess is that there are both historical and linguistic reasons.
>
> As for historical reasons, in the 1970s, IBM developed a language named SEQUEL, which was an acronym for Structured English QUEry Language. The language was designed to manipulate data stored in a database system named System R, which was based on Dr. Edgar F. Codd's model for relational database management systems (RDBMS). The acronym SEQUEL was later shortened to SQL because of a trademark dispute. ANSI adopted SQL as a standard in 1986, and ISO did so in 1987. ANSI declared that the official pronunciation of the language is "ess kyoo ell," but it seems that this fact is not common knowledge.
>
> As for linguistic reasons, the *sequel* pronunciation is simply more fluent, mainly for English speakers. I often use it myself for this reason.

> **More Info** The coverage of SQL history in this chapter is based on an article from Wikipedia, the free encyclopedia, and can be found at *http://en.wikipedia.org/wiki/SQL.*

SQL programming has many unique aspects, such as thinking in sets, the logical processing order of query elements, and three-valued logic. Trying to program in SQL without this knowledge is a straight path to lengthy, poor-performing code that is difficult to maintain. This chapter's purpose is to help you understand SQL the way its designers envisioned it. You need to create strong roots upon which all the rest will be built. Where relevant, I'll explicitly indicate elements that are specific to T-SQL.

Throughout the book, I'll cover complex problems and advanced techniques. But in this chapter, as mentioned, I'll deal only with the fundamentals of querying. Throughout the book, I'll also focus on performance. But in this chapter, I'll deal only with the logical aspects of query processing. I ask you to make an effort while reading this chapter not to think about performance at all. You'll find plenty of performance coverage later in the book. Some of the logical query processing phases that I'll describe in this chapter might seem very inefficient. But keep in mind that in practice, the actual physical processing of a query might be very different than the logical one.

The component in SQL Server in charge of generating the actual work plan (execution plan) for a query is the *query optimizer*. The optimizer determines in which order to access the tables, which access methods and indexes to use, which join algorithms to apply, and so on. The optimizer generates multiple valid execution plans and chooses the one with the lowest cost. The phases in the logical processing of a query have a very specific order. In contrast, the optimizer can often make shortcuts in the physical execution plan that it generates. Of course, it will make shortcuts only if the result set is guaranteed to be the correct one—in other words, the same result set you would get by following the logical processing phases. For example, to use an index, the optimizer can decide to apply a filter much sooner than dictated by logical processing.

For the aforementioned reasons, it's important to make a clear distinction between logical and physical processing of a query.

Without further ado, let's delve into logical query processing phases.

Logical Query Processing Phases

This section introduces the phases involved in the logical processing of a query. I'll first briefly describe each step. Then, in the following sections, I'll describe the steps in much more detail and apply them to a sample query. You can use this section as a quick reference whenever you need to recall the order and general meaning of the different phases.

Listing 1-1 contains a general form of a query, along with step numbers assigned according to the order in which the different clauses are logically processed.

LISTING 1-1 Logical query processing step numbers

```
(5) SELECT (5-2) DISTINCT (5-3) TOP(<top_specification>) (5-1) <select_list>
(1) FROM (1-J) <left_table> <join_type> JOIN <right_table> ON <on_predicate>
     | (1-A) <left_table> <apply_type> APPLY <right_table_expression> AS <alias>
     | (1-P) <left_table> PIVOT(<pivot_specification>) AS <alias>
     | (1-U) <left_table> UNPIVOT(<unpivot_specification>) AS <alias>
(2) WHERE <where_predicate>
(3) GROUP BY <group_by_specification>
(4) HAVING <having_predicate>
(6) ORDER BY <order_by_list>;
```

Figure 1-1 contains a flow diagram representing logical query processing phases in detail. Throughout the chapter I'll refer to the step numbers that appear in the diagram.

The first noticeable aspect of SQL that is different from other programming languages is the order in which the code is processed. In most programming languages, the code is processed in the order in which it is written. In SQL, the first clause that is processed is the FROM clause, while the SELECT clause, which appears first, is processed almost last.

Each step generates a virtual table that is used as the input to the following step. These virtual tables are not available to the caller (client application or outer query). Only the table generated by the final step is returned to the caller. If a certain clause is not specified in a query, the corresponding step is simply skipped. The following section briefly describes the different logical steps.

Logical Query Processing Phases in Brief

Don't worry too much if the description of the steps doesn't seem to make much sense for now. These are provided as a reference. Sections that come after the scenario example will cover the steps in much more detail.

- **(1) FROM**   The FROM phase identifies the query's source tables and processes table operators. Each table operator applies a series of subphases. For example, the phases involved in a join are (1-J1) Cartesian Product, (1-J2) ON Filter, (1-J3) Add Outer Rows. The FROM phase generates virtual table VT1.

- **(1-J1) Cartesian Product**   This phase performs a Cartesian product (cross join) between the two tables involved in the table operator, generating VT1-J1.

- **(1-J2) ON Filter**   This phase filters the rows from VT1-J1 based on the predicate that appears in the ON clause (<*on_predicate*>). Only rows for which the predicate evaluates to TRUE are inserted into VT1-J2.

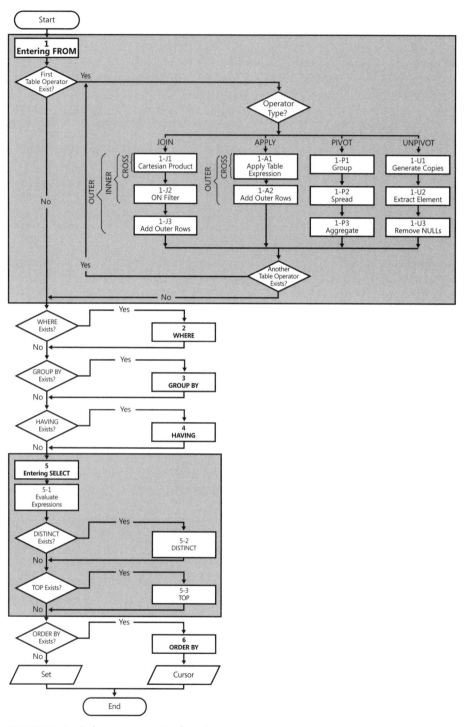

FIGURE 1-1 Logical query processing flow diagram

- **(1-J3) Add Outer Rows**   If OUTER JOIN is specified (as opposed to CROSS JOIN or INNER JOIN), rows from the preserved table or tables for which a match was not found are added to the rows from VT1-J2 as outer rows, generating VT1-J3.

- **(2) WHERE**   This phase filters the rows from VT1 based on the predicate that appears in the WHERE clause (<*where_predicate*>). Only rows for which the predicate evaluates to TRUE are inserted into VT2.

- **(3) GROUP BY**   This phase arranges the rows from VT2 in groups based on the column list specified in the GROUP BY clause, generating VT3. Ultimately, there will be one result row per group.

- **(4) HAVING**   This phase filters the groups from VT3 based on the predicate that appears in the HAVING clause (<*having_predicate*>). Only groups for which the predicate evaluates to TRUE are inserted into VT4.

- **(5) SELECT**   This phase processes the elements in the SELECT clause, generating VT5.

- **(5-1) Evaluate Expressions**   This phase evaluates the expressions in the SELECT list, generating VT5-1.

- **(5-2) DISTINCT**   This phase removes duplicate rows from VT5-1, generating VT5-2.

- **(5-3) TOP**   This phase filters the specified top number or percentage of rows from VT5-2 based on the logical ordering defined by the ORDER BY clause, generating the table VT5-3.

- **(6) ORDER BY**   This phase sorts the rows from VT5-3 according to the column list specified in the ORDER BY clause, generating the cursor VC6.

Sample Query Based on Customers/Orders Scenario

To describe the logical processing phases in detail, I'll walk you through a sample query. First run the following code to create the dbo.Customers and dbo.Orders tables, populate them with sample data, and query them to show their contents:

```
SET NOCOUNT ON;
USE tempdb;

IF OBJECT_ID('dbo.Orders') IS NOT NULL DROP TABLE dbo.Orders;
IF OBJECT_ID('dbo.Customers') IS NOT NULL DROP TABLE dbo.Customers;
GO

CREATE TABLE dbo.Customers
(
  customerid  CHAR(5)      NOT NULL PRIMARY KEY,
  city        VARCHAR(10) NOT NULL
);
```

```
CREATE TABLE dbo.Orders
(
  orderid    INT      NOT NULL PRIMARY KEY,
  customerid CHAR(5)      NULL REFERENCES Customers(customerid)
);
GO

INSERT INTO dbo.Customers(customerid, city) VALUES('FISSA', 'Madrid');
INSERT INTO dbo.Customers(customerid, city) VALUES('FRNDO', 'Madrid');
INSERT INTO dbo.Customers(customerid, city) VALUES('KRLOS', 'Madrid');
INSERT INTO dbo.Customers(customerid, city) VALUES('MRPHS', 'Zion');

INSERT INTO dbo.Orders(orderid, customerid) VALUES(1, 'FRNDO');
INSERT INTO dbo.Orders(orderid, customerid) VALUES(2, 'FRNDO');
INSERT INTO dbo.Orders(orderid, customerid) VALUES(3, 'KRLOS');
INSERT INTO dbo.Orders(orderid, customerid) VALUES(4, 'KRLOS');
INSERT INTO dbo.Orders(orderid, customerid) VALUES(5, 'KRLOS');
INSERT INTO dbo.Orders(orderid, customerid) VALUES(6, 'MRPHS');
INSERT INTO dbo.Orders(orderid, customerid) VALUES(7, NULL);

SELECT * FROM dbo.Customers;
SELECT * FROM dbo.Orders;
```

This code generates the following output:

```
customerid city
---------- ----------
FISSA      Madrid
FRNDO      Madrid
KRLOS      Madrid
MRPHS      Zion

orderid    customerid
---------- ----------
1          FRNDO
2          FRNDO
3          KRLOS
4          KRLOS
5          KRLOS
6          MRPHS
7          NULL
```

I'll use the query shown in Listing 1-2 as my example. The query returns customers from Madrid who placed fewer than three orders (including zero orders), along with their order counts. The result is sorted by order count, from smallest to largest.

LISTING 1-2 Query: Madrid customers with fewer than three orders

```
SELECT C.customerid, COUNT(O.orderid) AS numorders
FROM dbo.Customers AS C
  LEFT OUTER JOIN dbo.Orders AS O
    ON C.customerid = O.customerid
WHERE C.city = 'Madrid'
GROUP BY C.customerid
HAVING COUNT(O.orderid) < 3
ORDER BY numorders;
```

This query returns the following output:

```
customerid numorders
---------- -----------
FISSA      0
FRNDO      2
```

Both FISSA and FRNDO are customers from Madrid who placed fewer than three orders. Examine the query and try to read it while following the steps and phases described in Listing 1-1, Figure 1-1, and the section "Logical Query Processing Phases in Brief." If this is your first time thinking of a query in such terms, you might be confused. The following section should help you understand the nitty-gritty details.

Logical Query Processing Phase Details

This section describes the logical query processing phases in detail by applying them to the given sample query.

Step 1: The FROM Phase

The FROM phase identifies the table or tables that need to be queried, and if table operators are specified, this phase processes those operators from left to right. Each table operator operates on one or two input tables and returns an output table. The result of a table operator is used as the left input to the next table operator—if one exists—and as the input to the next logical query processing phase otherwise. Each table operator has its own set of processing subphases. For example, the subphases involved in a join are (1-J1) Cartesian Product, (1-J2) ON Filter, (1-J3) Add Outer Rows. Here I will provide a description of the subphases involved in a join; later in the chapter, under "Table Operators," I'll describe the other table operators. The FROM phase generates virtual table VT1.

Step 1-J1: Perform Cartesian Product (Cross Join)

This is the first of three subphases that are applicable to a join table operator. This subphase performs a Cartesian product (a cross join, or an unrestricted join) between the two tables involved in the join and, as a result, generates virtual table VT1-J1. This table contains one row for every possible choice of a row from the left table and a row from the right table. If the left table contains n rows and the right table contains m rows, VT1-J1 will contain $n \times m$ rows. The columns in VT1-J1 are qualified (prefixed) with their source table names (or table aliases, if you specified them in the query). In the subsequent steps (step 1-J2 and on), a reference to a column name that is ambiguous (appears in more than one input table) must be table-qualified (for example, *C.customerid*). Specifying the table qualifier for column names that appear in only one of the inputs is optional (for example, *O.orderid* or just *orderid*).

Apply step 1-J1 to the sample query (shown in Listing 1-2):

```
FROM dbo.Customers AS C ... JOIN dbo.Orders AS O
```

As a result, you get the virtual table VT1-J1 (shown in Table 1-1) with 28 rows (4×7).

TABLE 1-1 Virtual Table VT1-J1 Returned from Step 1-J1

C.customerid	C.city	O.orderid	O.customerid
FISSA	Madrid	1	FRNDO
FISSA	Madrid	2	FRNDO
FISSA	Madrid	3	KRLOS
FISSA	Madrid	4	KRLOS
FISSA	Madrid	5	KRLOS
FISSA	Madrid	6	MRPHS
FISSA	Madrid	7	NULL
FRNDO	Madrid	1	FRNDO
FRNDO	Madrid	2	FRNDO
FRNDO	Madrid	3	KRLOS
FRNDO	Madrid	4	KRLOS
FRNDO	Madrid	5	KRLOS
FRNDO	Madrid	6	MRPHS
FRNDO	Madrid	7	NULL
KRLOS	Madrid	1	FRNDO
KRLOS	Madrid	2	FRNDO
KRLOS	Madrid	3	KRLOS
KRLOS	Madrid	4	KRLOS
KRLOS	Madrid	5	KRLOS
KRLOS	Madrid	6	MRPHS
KRLOS	Madrid	7	NULL
MRPHS	Zion	1	FRNDO
MRPHS	Zion	2	FRNDO
MRPHS	Zion	3	KRLOS
MRPHS	Zion	4	KRLOS
MRPHS	Zion	5	KRLOS
MRPHS	Zion	6	MRPHS
MRPHS	Zion	7	NULL

Step 1-J2: Apply ON Filter (Join Condition)

The ON filter is the first of three possible filters (ON, WHERE, and HAVING) that can be specified in a query. The predicate in the ON filter is applied to all rows in the virtual table returned by the previous step (VT1-J1). Only rows for which the *<on_predicate>* is TRUE become part of the virtual table returned by this step (VT1-J2).

Three-Valued Logic

Allow me to digress a bit to cover some important aspects of SQL related to this step. The possible values of a predicate (logical expression) in SQL are TRUE, FALSE, and UNKNOWN. This is referred to as *three-valued logic* and is unique to SQL. Logical expressions in most programming languages can be only TRUE or FALSE. The UNKNOWN logical value in SQL typically occurs in a logical expression that involves a *NULL* (for example, the logical value of each of these three expressions is UNKNOWN: *NULL > 42; NULL = NULL; X + NULL > Y*). The mark NULL represents a missing value. When comparing a missing value to another value (even another NULL), the logical result is always UNKNOWN.

Dealing with UNKNOWN logical results and NULLs can be very confusing. While *NOT* TRUE is FALSE, and NOT FALSE is TRUE, the opposite of UNKNOWN (NOT UNKNOWN) is still UNKNOWN.

UNKNOWN logical results and NULLs are treated inconsistently in different elements of the language. For example, all query filters (ON, WHERE, and HAVING) treat UNKNOWN like FALSE. A row for which a filter is UNKNOWN is eliminated from the result set. On the other hand, an UNKNOWN value in a CHECK constraint is actually treated like TRUE. Suppose you have a CHECK constraint in a table to require that the salary column be greater than zero. A row entered into the table with a NULL salary is accepted because (*NULL > 0*) is UNKNOWN and treated like TRUE in the CHECK constraint.

A comparison between two NULLs in a filter yields UNKNOWN, which, as I mentioned earlier, is treated like FALSE—as if one NULL is different than another.

On the other hand, for UNIQUE constraints, set operators (such as UNION and EXCEPT), and sorting or grouping operations, NULLs are treated as equal:

- You cannot insert into a table two rows with a NULL in a column that has a UNIQUE constraint defined on it. T-SQL violates the standard on this point.

- A GROUP BY clause groups all NULLs into one group.

- An ORDER BY clause sorts all NULLs together.

- Set operators treat NULLs as equal when comparing rows from the two sets.

In short, to spare yourself some grief it's a good idea to be aware of the way UNKNOWN logical results and NULLs are treated in the different elements of the language.

Apply step 1-J2 to the sample query:

```
ON C.customerid = O.customerid
```

The first column of Table 1-2 shows the value of the logical expression in the ON filter for the rows from VT1-J1.

TABLE 1-2 Logical value of ON Predicate for Rows from VT1-J1

Logical Value	C.customerid	C.city	O.orderid	O.customerid
FALSE	FISSA	Madrid	1	FRNDO
FALSE	FISSA	Madrid	2	FRNDO
FALSE	FISSA	Madrid	3	KRLOS
FALSE	FISSA	Madrid	4	KRLOS
FALSE	FISSA	Madrid	5	KRLOS
FALSE	FISSA	Madrid	6	MRPHS
UNKNOWN	FISSA	Madrid	7	NULL
TRUE	FRNDO	Madrid	1	FRNDO
TRUE	FRNDO	Madrid	2	FRNDO
FALSE	FRNDO	Madrid	3	KRLOS
FALSE	FRNDO	Madrid	4	KRLOS
FALSE	FRNDO	Madrid	5	KRLOS
FALSE	FRNDO	Madrid	6	MRPHS
UNKNOWN	FRNDO	Madrid	7	NULL
FALSE	KRLOS	Madrid	1	FRNDO
FALSE	KRLOS	Madrid	2	FRNDO
TRUE	KRLOS	Madrid	3	KRLOS
TRUE	KRLOS	Madrid	4	KRLOS
TRUE	KRLOS	Madrid	5	KRLOS
FALSE	KRLOS	Madrid	6	MRPHS
UNKNOWN	KRLOS	Madrid	7	NULL
FALSE	MRPHS	Zion	1	FRNDO
FALSE	MRPHS	Zion	2	FRNDO
FALSE	MRPHS	Zion	3	KRLOS
FALSE	MRPHS	Zion	4	KRLOS
FALSE	MRPHS	Zion	5	KRLOS
TRUE	MRPHS	Zion	6	MRPHS
UNKNOWN	MRPHS	Zion	7	NULL

Only rows for which the *<on_predicate>* is TRUE are inserted into VT1-J2, shown in Table 1-3.

TABLE 1-3 Virtual Table VT1-J2 Returned from Step 1-J2

Logical Value	C.customerid	C.city	O.orderid	O.customerid
TRUE	FRNDO	Madrid	1	FRNDO
TRUE	FRNDO	Madrid	2	FRNDO
TRUE	KRLOS	Madrid	3	KRLOS
TRUE	KRLOS	Madrid	4	KRLOS
TRUE	KRLOS	Madrid	5	KRLOS
TRUE	MRPHS	Zion	6	MRPHS

Step 1-J3: Add Outer Rows

This step occurs only for an outer join. For an outer join, you mark one or both input tables as *preserved* by specifying the type of outer join (LEFT, RIGHT, or FULL). Marking a table as preserved means that you want all of its rows returned, even when filtered out by the *<on_predicate>*. A left outer join marks the left table as preserved, a right outer join marks the right one, and a full outer join marks both. Step 1-J3 returns the rows from VT1-J2, plus rows from the preserved table(s) for which a match was not found in step 1-J2. These added rows are referred to as *outer rows*. NULLs are assigned to the attributes (column values) of the nonpreserved table in the outer rows. As a result, virtual table VT1-J3 is generated.

In our example, the preserved table is Customers:

```
Customers AS C LEFT OUTER JOIN Orders AS O
```

Only customer FISSA did not yield any matching orders (and thus wasn't part of VT1-J2). Therefore, a row for FISSA is added to VT1-J2, with NULLs for the Orders attributes. The result is virtual table VT1-J3 (shown in Table 1-4). Because the FROM clause of the sample query has no more table operators, the virtual table VT1-J3 is also the virtual table VT1 returned from the FROM phase.

TABLE 1-4 Virtual Table VT1-J3 (also VT1) Returned from Step 1-J3

C.customerid	C.city	O.orderid	O.customerid
FRNDO	Madrid	1	FRNDO
FRNDO	Madrid	2	FRNDO
KRLOS	Madrid	3	KRLOS
KRLOS	Madrid	4	KRLOS
KRLOS	Madrid	5	KRLOS
MRPHS	Zion	6	MRPHS
FISSA	Madrid	NULL	NULL

Note If multiple table operators appear in the FROM clause, they are processed from left to right. The result of each table operator is provided as the left input to the next table operator. The final virtual table will be used as the input for the next step.

Step 2: The WHERE Phase

The WHERE filter is applied to all rows in the virtual table returned by the previous step. Those rows for which *<where_predicate>* is TRUE make up the virtual table returned by this step (VT2).

Caution Because the data is not yet grouped, you cannot use aggregates here—for example, you cannot write *WHERE orderdate = MAX(orderdate)*. Also, you cannot refer to column aliases created by the SELECT list because the SELECT list was not processed yet—for example, you cannot write *SELECT YEAR(orderdate) AS orderyear ... WHERE orderyear > 2008*.

Apply the filter in the sample query:

```
WHERE C.city = 'Madrid'
```

The row for customer MRPHS from VT1 is removed because the city is not Madrid, and virtual table VT2, which is shown in Table 1-5, is generated.

TABLE 1-5 Virtual Table VT2 Returned from Step 2

C.customerid	C.city	O.orderid	O.customerid
FRNDO	Madrid	1	FRNDO
FRNDO	Madrid	2	FRNDO
KRLOS	Madrid	3	KRLOS
KRLOS	Madrid	4	KRLOS
KRLOS	Madrid	5	KRLOS
FISSA	Madrid	NULL	NULL

A confusing aspect of queries containing an OUTER JOIN clause is whether to specify a logical expression in the ON filter or in the WHERE filter. The main difference between the two is that ON is applied before adding outer rows (step 1-J3), while WHERE is applied afterwards. An elimination of a row from the preserved table by the ON filter is not final because step 1-J3 will add it back; an elimination of a row by the WHERE filter, by contrast, is final. Bearing this in mind should help you make the right choice.

For example, suppose you want to return certain customers and their orders from the Customers and Orders tables. The customers you want to return are only Madrid customers—both those who placed orders and those who did not. An outer join is designed exactly for such a request. You perform a left outer join between Customers and Orders, marking the Customers table as the preserved table. To be able to return customers who placed no orders, you must specify the correlation between Customers and Orders in the ON clause (*ON C.customerid = O.customerid*). Customers with no orders are eliminated in step 1-J2 but added back in step 1-J3 as outer rows. However, because you want to return only Madrid customers you must specify the city filter in the WHERE clause (*WHERE C.city = 'Madrid'*). Specifying the city filter in the ON clause would cause non-Madrid customers to be added back to the result set by step 1-J3.

> **Tip** This logical difference between the ON and WHERE clauses exists only when using an outer join. When you use an inner join, it doesn't matter where you specify your logical expressions because step 1-J3 is skipped. The filters are applied one after the other with no intermediate step between them.

Step 3: The GROUP BY Phase

The GROUP BY phase associates rows from the table returned by the previous step to groups according to the <group_by_specification>. I will discuss this specification in detail in Chapter 8,

"Aggregating and Pivoting Data," but for now, assume that it specifies a single list of attributes to group by. This list is called the *grouping set*.

In this phase, the rows from the table returned by the previous step are arranged in groups. Each unique combination of values of the attributes that belong to the grouping set identifies a group. Each base row from the previous step is associated to one and only one group. Virtual table VT3 consists of the rows of VT2 arranged in groups (the *raw* information) along with the group identifiers (the *groups* information).

Apply step 3 to the sample query:

```
GROUP BY C.customerid
```

You get the virtual table VT3 shown in Table 1-6.

TABLE 1-6 Virtual Table VT3 Returned from Step 3

| Groups | Raw | | | |
C.customerid	C.customerid	C.city	O.orderid	O.customerid
FRNDO	FRNDO	Madrid	1	FRNDO
	FRNDO	Madrid	2	FRNDO
KRLOS	KRLOS	Madrid	3	KRLOS
	KRLOS	Madrid	4	KRLOS
	KRLOS	Madrid	5	KRLOS
FISSA	FISSA	Madrid	NULL	NULL

Eventually, a query that contains a GROUP BY clause will generate one row per group (unless filtered out). Consequently, when GROUP BY is specified in a query, all subsequent steps (HAVING, SELECT, and so on) can specify only expressions that have a scalar (singular) value per group. These expressions can include columns or expressions from the GROUP BY list—such as *C.customerid* in the sample query here—or aggregate functions, such as *COUNT(O.orderid)*.

Examine VT3 in Table 1-6 and think what the query should return for customer FRNDO's group if the SELECT list you specified had been *SELECT C.customerid, O.orderid*. There are two different *orderid* values in the group; therefore, the answer is not a scalar. SQL doesn't allow such a request. On the other hand, if you specify *SELECT C.customerid, COUNT(O.orderid) AS numorders*, the answer for FRNDO is a scalar: it's 2.

This phase considers NULLs as equal. That is, all NULLs are grouped into one group, just like a known value.

Step 4: The HAVING Phase

The HAVING filter is applied to the groups in the table returned by the previous step. Only groups for which the *<having_predicate>* is TRUE become part of the virtual table returned by this step (VT4). The HAVING filter is the only filter that applies to the grouped data.

Apply this step to the sample query:

```
HAVING COUNT(O.orderid) < 3
```

The group for KRLOS is removed because it contains three orders. Virtual table VT4, which is shown in Table 1-7, is generated.

TABLE 1-7 Virtual Table VT4 Returned from Step 4

C.customerid	C.customerid	C.city	O.orderid	O.customerid
FRNDO	FRNDO	Madrid	1	FRNDO
	FRNDO	Madrid	2	FRNDO
FISSA	FISSA	Madrid	NULL	NULL

Note It is important to specify *COUNT(O.orderid)* here and not *COUNT(*)*. Because the join is an outer one, outer rows were added for customers with no orders. *COUNT(*)* would have added outer rows to the count, undesirably producing a count of one order for FISSA. *COUNT(O.orderid)* correctly counts the number of orders for each customer, producing the desired value 0 for FISSA. Remember that *COUNT(<expression>)* ignores NULLs just like any other aggregate function.

Note An aggregate function does not accept a subquery as an input—for example, *HAVING SUM((SELECT ...)) > 10.*

Step 5: The SELECT Phase

Though specified first in the query, the SELECT clause is processed only at the fifth step. The SELECT phase constructs the table that will eventually be returned to the caller. This phase involves three subphases: (5-1) Evaluate Expressions, (5-2) Apply DISTINCT Clause, (5-3) Apply TOP Option.

Step 5-1: Evaluate Expressions

The expressions in the SELECT list can return base columns and manipulations of base columns from the virtual table returned by the previous step. Remember that if the query is an aggregate query, after step 3 you can refer to base columns from the previous step only if they are part of the groups section (GROUP BY list). If you refer to columns from the raw section, they must be aggregated. Base columns selected from the previous step maintain their column names unless you alias them (for example, *col1 AS c1*). Expressions that are not base columns should be aliased to have a column name in the result table—for example, *YEAR(orderdate) AS orderyear.*

> **Important** Aliases created by the SELECT list cannot be used by earlier steps—for example, in the WHERE phase. In fact, expression aliases cannot even be used by other expressions within the same SELECT list. The reasoning behind this limitation is another unique aspect of SQL; many operations are all-at-once operations. For example, in the following SELECT list, the logical order in which the expressions are evaluated should not matter and is not guaranteed: *SELECT c1 + 1 AS e1, c2 + 1 AS e2*. Therefore, the following SELECT list is not supported: *SELECT c1 + 1 AS e1, e1 + 1 AS e2*. You're allowed to use column aliases only in steps following the SELECT phase, such as the ORDER BY phase—for example, *SELECT YEAR(orderdate) AS orderyear ... ORDER BY orderyear*.
>
> The concept of an all-at-once operation can be hard to grasp. For example, in most programming environments, to swap values between variables you use a temporary variable. However, to swap table column values in SQL, you can use:
>
> ```
> UPDATE dbo.T1 SET c1 = c2, c2 = c1;
> ```
>
> Logically, you should assume that the whole operation takes place at once. It is as if the table is not modified until the whole operation finishes and then the result replaces the source. For similar reasons, the following UPDATE would update all of T1's rows, adding to c1 the maximum c1 value from T1 when the update started:
>
> ```
> UPDATE dbo.T1 SET c1 = c1 + (SELECT MAX(c1) FROM dbo.T1);
> ```
>
> Don't be concerned that the maximum c1 value might keep changing as the operation proceeds; it does not because the operation occurs all at once.

Apply this step to the sample query:

```
SELECT C.customerid, COUNT(O.orderid) AS numorders
```

You get the virtual table VT5-1, which is shown in Table 1-8. Because no other subphases (DISTINCT and TOP) of the SELECT phase are applied in the sample query, the virtual table VT5-1 returned by this subphase is also the virtual table VT5 returned by the SELECT phase.

TABLE 1-8 Virtual Table VT5-1 (also VT5) Returned from Step 5

C.customerid	numorders
FRNDO	2
FISSA	0

Step 5-2: Apply the DISTINCT Clause

If a DISTINCT clause is specified in the query, duplicate rows are removed from the virtual table returned by the previous step, and virtual table VT5-2 is generated.

> **Note** SQL deviates from the relational model by allowing a table to have duplicate rows (when a primary key or unique constraint is not enforced) and a query to return duplicate rows in the result. A relation in the relational model represents a set from set theory, and a set (as opposed to a multiset) has no duplicates. Using the DISTINCT clause you can ensure that a query returns unique rows and in this sense conform to the relational model.

Step 5-2 is skipped in our example because DISTINCT is not specified in the sample query. In our particular example, it would remove no rows.

Step 5-3: Apply the TOP Option

The TOP option is a feature specific to T-SQL that allows you to specify a number or percentage of rows (rounded up) to return. The specified number of rows is selected based on the query's ORDER BY clause. Traditionally, and according to the ANSI SQL standard, ORDER BY is supposed to serve a presentation purpose. However, when the TOP option is specified, the ORDER BY clause also serves a logical purpose— answering the question "top according to what order?" Table VT5-3 is generated.

As mentioned, this step relies on the query's ORDER BY clause to determine which rows are considered the "first" requested number of rows. If an ORDER BY clause with a unique ORDER BY list is specified in a query, the result is deterministic. That is, only one correct result is possible, containing the first requested number of rows based on the specified order. Similarly, when an ORDER BY clause is specified with a non-unique ORDER BY list but the TOP option is specified WITH TIES, the result is also deterministic. SQL Server inspects the last row that was returned and returns all other rows from the table that have the same sort values as the last row.

However, when a non-unique ORDER BY list is specified without the WITH TIES option, or ORDER BY is not specified at all, a TOP query is nondeterministic. That is, the rows returned are the ones that SQL Server happened to access first, and there might be different results that are considered correct. If you want to guarantee determinism, a TOP query must have either a unique ORDER BY list or the WITH TIES option.

Step 5-3 is skipped in our example because TOP is not specified.

Step 6: The Presentation ORDER BY Phase

The rows from the previous step are sorted according to the column list specified in the ORDER BY clause, returning the cursor VC6. The ORDER BY clause is the only step where column aliases created in the SELECT phase can be reused.

If DISTINCT is specified, the expressions in the ORDER BY clause have access only to the virtual table returned by the previous step (VT5). If DISTINCT is not specified expressions in the ORDER BY clause can access both the input and the output virtual tables of the SELECT phase. That is, in the ORDER BY clause you can specify any expression that would have been allowed in the SELECT clause. Namely, you can sort by expressions that you don't end up returning in the final result set.

There is a reason for not allowing access to expressions you're not returning if DISTINCT is specified. When adding expressions to the SELECT list, DISTINCT can potentially change the number of rows returned. Without DISTINCT, of course, changes in the SELECT list don't affect the number of rows returned.

In our example, because DISTINCT is not specified, the ORDER BY clause has access to both VT4, shown in Table 1-7, and VT5, shown in Table 1-8.

In the ORDER BY clause, you can also specify ordinal positions of result columns from the SELECT list. For example, the following query sorts the orders first by customerid and then by orderid:

```
SELECT orderid, customerid FROM dbo.Orders ORDER BY 2, 1;
```

However, this practice is not recommended because you might make changes to the SELECT list and forget to revise the ORDER BY list accordingly. Also, when the query strings are long, it's hard to figure out which item in the ORDER BY list corresponds to which item in the SELECT list.

> **Important** This step is different than all other steps in the sense that it doesn't return a valid table; instead, it returns a cursor. Remember that SQL is based on set theory. A set doesn't have a predetermined order to its rows: It's a logical collection of members, and the order of the members shouldn't matter. A query with a presentation ORDER BY clause returns an object with rows organized in a particular order. ANSI calls such an object a *cursor*. Understanding this step is one of the most fundamental steps to correctly understanding SQL.

When describing the contents of a table, most people (including me) routinely depict the rows in a certain order. However, a table represents a set (or multiset if duplicates exist), and a set has no order, so such depiction can cause some confusion by implying a certain order. Figure 1-2 shows an example for depicting the content of tables in a more correct way that doesn't imply order.

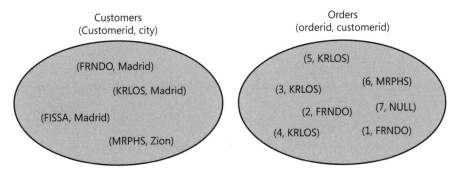

FIGURE 1-2 Customers and Orders sets

> **Note** Although SQL doesn't assume any given order to a table's *rows,* it does maintain ordinal positions for *columns* based on creation order. Specifying *SELECT ** (although a bad practice for several reasons that I'll describe later in the book) guarantees the columns would be returned in creation order. In this respect SQL deviates from the relational model.

Because this step doesn't return a table (it returns a cursor), a query with a presentation ORDER BY clause cannot be used to define a table expression—that is, a view, an inline table-valued function, a derived table, or a common table expression (CTE). Rather, the result must be returned to the client application that can consume cursor records one at a time, in order. For example, the following derived table query is invalid and produces an error:

```
SELECT *
FROM (SELECT orderid, customerid
      FROM dbo.Orders
      ORDER BY orderid DESC) AS D;
```

 Similarly, the following view is invalid:

```
CREATE VIEW dbo.VSortedOrders
AS

SELECT orderid, customerid
FROM dbo.Orders
ORDER BY orderid DESC;
GO
```

In SQL, no query with an ORDER BY clause is allowed in a table expression. In T-SQL, there is an exception to this rule—when the TOP option is also specified. This exception has to do with a problematic aspect of the design of the TOP option that causes a lot of confusion. The TOP option is logically processed as part of the SELECT phase (step 5-3), before the Presentation ORDER BY phase (step 6). Its purpose is to filter the requested number or percentage of rows based on a logical definition of order. Unfortunately, the TOP option is not designed with its own ORDER BY clause; rather, its logical ordering is based on the same ORDER BY clause that is normally used for presentation purposes. This fact makes the TOP option restricted in the sense that you cannot define one order for the TOP option and another for presentation. Also, things can get quite confusing when you try to figure out the nature of the result of a TOP query. Is it a table (no guaranteed order) or a cursor? Because no standard defines TOP, it's a matter of what the SQL Server developers envisioned. When a TOP query is specified as the outermost query rather than defining a table expression, the ORDER BY clause serves two different purposes. One is to define logical precedence among rows for the TOP option in step 5-3, and the other is to define presentation order in step 6 in the result cursor. Consider the following query as an example:

```
SELECT TOP (3) orderid, customerid
FROM dbo.Orders
ORDER BY orderid DESC;
```

You're guaranteed to get the three rows with the highest order IDs, and you're also guaranteed to get them sorted in the output based on orderid descending. Here's the output of this query:

```
orderid     customerid
----------- ----------
11077       RATTC
11076       BONAP
11075       RICSU
```

However, if a TOP query with an ORDER BY clause is used to define a table expression, it's supposed to represent a table with no guaranteed order. Therefore, in such a case the ORDER BY clause is only guaranteed to define logical order for the TOP option, while presentation order is not guaranteed. For example, the following query does not guarantee presentation order:

```
SELECT *
FROM (SELECT TOP (3) orderid, customerid
      FROM dbo.Orders
      ORDER BY orderid DESC) AS D;
```

Of course, SQL Server has no reason to change the order of the rows in the output if it scans them in index order or sorts them to filter the requested number of rows, but the point I'm trying to make is that in this case presentation order in the output is not guaranteed. Programmers who don't understand this point—or the difference between a table and a cursor—try to exploit the TOP option in absurd ways, for example, by trying to create a sorted view:

```
CREATE VIEW dbo.VSortedOrders
AS

SELECT TOP (100) PERCENT orderid, customerid
FROM dbo.Orders
ORDER BY orderid DESC;
GO
```

A view is supposed to represent a table, and a table has no guaranteed order. SQL Server allows the use of the ORDER BY clause in a view when TOP is also specified, but because the query is used to define a table expression, the only guarantee that you get is that the ORDER BY clause will serve the logical meaning for TOP; you don't get a guarantee for presentation order. Therefore, if you run the following code, you're not guaranteed to get the rows in the output sorted by orderid descending:

```
SELECT orderid, customerid FROM dbo.VSortedOrders;
```

So remember, don't assume any particular order for a table's rows. Conversely, don't specify an ORDER BY clause unless you really need the rows sorted or need to describe the ordering for a TOP option. Sorting has a cost—SQL Server needs to perform an ordered index scan or apply a sort operator.

The ORDER BY clause considers NULLs as equal. That is, NULLs are sorted together. ANSI leaves the question of whether NULLs are sorted lower or higher than known values up to implementations, which must be consistent. T-SQL sorts NULLs as lower than known values (first).

Apply this step to the sample query:

```
ORDER BY numorders
```

You get the cursor VC6 shown in Table 1-9.

TABLE 1-9 Cursor VC6 Returned from Step 6

C.customerid	numorders
FISSA	0
FRNDO	2

Further Aspects of Logical Query Processing

This section covers further aspects of logical query processing, including table operators (JOIN, APPLY, PIVOT, and UNPIVOT), the OVER clause, and set operators (UNION, EXCEPT, and INTERSECT). Note that I could say much more about these language elements besides their logical query processing aspects, but that's the focus of this chapter. Also, if a language element described in this section is completely new to you (for example, PIVOT, UNPIVOT, or APPLY), it might be a bit hard to fully comprehend its meaning at this point. Later in the book I'll conduct more detailed discussions including uses, performance aspects, and so on. You can then return to this chapter and read about the logical query processing aspects of that language element again to better comprehend its meaning.

Table Operators

SQL Server 2008 supports four types of table operators in the FROM clause of a query: JOIN, APPLY, PIVOT, and UNPIVOT.

> **Note** APPLY, PIVOT, and UNPIVOT are not ANSI operators; rather, they are extensions specific to T-SQL.

I covered the logical processing phases involved with joins earlier and will also discuss joins in more detail in Chapter 7, "Joins and Set Operations." Here I'll briefly describe the other three operators and the way they fit in the logical query processing model.

Table operators get one or two tables as inputs. Call them *left input* and *right input* based on their position in respect to the table operator keyword (*JOIN, APPLY, PIVOT, UNPIVOT*). Just like joins, all table operators get a virtual table as their left input. The first table operator that appears in the FROM clause gets a table expression as the left input and returns a virtual table as a result. A table expression can stand for many things: a real table, a temporary table, a table variable, a derived table, a CTE, a view, or a table-valued function.

> **More Info** For details on table expressions, please refer to Chapter 6, "Subqueries, Table Expressions, and Ranking Functions."

The second table operator that appears in the FROM clause gets as its left input the virtual table returned from the previous table operation.

Each table operator involves a different set of steps. For convenience and clarity, I'll prefix the step numbers with the initial of the table operator (J for JOIN, A for APPLY, P for PIVOT, and U for UNPIVOT).

Following are the four table operators along with their elements:

```
(J) <left_table_expression>
      {CROSS | INNER | OUTER} JOIN <right_table_expression>
      ON <on_predicate>

(A) <left_table_expression>
      {CROSS | OUTER} APPLY <right_table_expression>

(P) <left_table_expression>
      PIVOT (<aggregate_func(<aggregation_element>)> FOR
        <spreading_element> IN(<target_col_list>))
        AS <result_table_alias>

(U) <left_table_expression>
      UNPIVOT (<target_values_col> FOR
        <target_names_col> IN(<source_col_list>))
        AS <result_table_alias>
```

As a reminder, a join involves a subset (depending on the join type) of the following steps:

1. J1: Apply Cartesian Product

2. J2: Apply ON Filter

3. J3: Add Outer Rows

APPLY

The APPLY operator (depending on the apply type) involves one or both of the following two steps:

1. A1: Apply Right Table Expression to Left Table Rows

2. A2: Add Outer Rows

The APPLY operator applies the right table expression to every row from the left input. The right table expression can refer to the left input's columns. The right input is evaluated once for each row from the left. This step unifies the sets produced by matching each left row with the corresponding rows from the right table expression, and this step returns the combined result.

Step A1 is applied in both CROSS APPLY and OUTER APPLY. Step A2 is applied only for OUTER APPLY. CROSS APPLY doesn't return an outer (left) row if the inner (right) table expression returns an empty set for it. OUTER APPLY will return such a row, with NULLs as placeholders for the inner table expression's attributes.

For example, the following query returns the two orders with the highest order IDs for each customer:

```
SELECT C.customerid, C.city, A.orderid
FROM dbo.Customers AS C
  CROSS APPLY
    (SELECT TOP (2) O.orderid, O.customerid
     FROM dbo.Orders AS O
     WHERE O.customerid = C.customerid
     ORDER BY orderid DESC) AS A;
```

This query generates the following output:

```
customerid city        orderid
---------- ----------  -----------
FRNDO      Madrid      2
FRNDO      Madrid      1
KRLOS      Madrid      5
KRLOS      Madrid      4
MRPHS      Zion        6
```

Notice that FISSA is missing from the output because the table expression A returned an empty set for it. If you also want to return customers who placed no orders, use OUTER APPLY as follows:

```
SELECT C.customerid, C.city, A.orderid
FROM dbo.Customers AS C
  OUTER APPLY
    (SELECT TOP (2) O.orderid, O.customerid
     FROM dbo.Orders AS O
     WHERE O.customerid = C.customerid
     ORDER BY orderid DESC) AS A;
```

This query generates the following output:

```
customerid city        orderid
---------- ----------  -----------
FISSA      Madrid      NULL
FRNDO      Madrid      2
FRNDO      Madrid      1
KRLOS      Madrid      5
KRLOS      Madrid      4
MRPHS      Zion        6
```

 More Info For more details on the APPLY operator, refer to Chapter 9, "TOP and APPLY."

PIVOT

The PIVOT operator allows you to rotate, or pivot, data between columns and rows, performing aggregations along the way.

Suppose you wanted to query the Sales.OrderValues view in the InsideTSQL2008 sample database (see the book's introduction for details on the sample database) and return the total value of orders handled by each employee for each order year. You want the output to have a row for each employee, a column for each order year, and the total value in the intersection of each employee and year. The following PIVOT query allows you to achieve this:

```
USE InsideTSQL2008;

SELECT *
FROM (SELECT empid, YEAR(orderdate) AS orderyear, val
      FROM Sales.OrderValues) AS OV
  PIVOT(SUM(val) FOR orderyear IN([2006],[2007],[2008])) AS P;
```

This query generates the following output:

empid	2006	2007	2008
3	18223.96	108026.17	76562.75
6	16642.61	43126.38	14144.16
9	9894.52	26310.39	41103.17
7	15232.16	60471.19	48864.89
1	35764.52	93148.11	63195.02
4	49945.12	128809.81	54135.94
2	21757.06	70444.14	74336.56
5	18383.92	30716.48	19691.90
8	22240.12	56032.63	48589.54

Don't get distracted by the subquery that generates the derived table OV. As far as you're concerned, the PIVOT operator gets a table expression called OV as its left input, with a row for each order, with the employee ID (*empid*), order year (*orderyear*), and order value (*val*). The PIVOT operator involves the following three logical phases:

1. **P1: Grouping**

2. **P2: Spreading**

3. **P3: Aggregating**

The first phase (P1) is tricky. You can see in the query that the PIVOT operator refers to two of the columns from OV as input arguments (*val* and *orderyear*). The first phase implicitly groups the rows from OV based on all columns that weren't mentioned in PIVOT's inputs, as though a hidden GROUP BY were there. In our case, only the *empid* column wasn't mentioned anywhere in PIVOT's input arguments. So you get a group for each employee.

> **Note** PIVOT's implicit grouping phase doesn't affect any explicit GROUP BY clause in a query. The PIVOT operation will yield a virtual result table for input to the next logical phase, be it another table operation or the WHERE phase. And as I described earlier in the chapter, a GROUP BY phase might follow the WHERE phase. So when both PIVOT and GROUP BY appear in a query, you get two separate grouping phases—one as the first phase of PIVOT (P1) and a later one as the query's GROUP BY phase.

PIVOT's second phase (P2) spreads values of <spreading_col> to their corresponding target columns. Logically, it uses the following CASE expression for each target column specified in the IN clause:

```
CASE WHEN <spreading_col> = <target_col_element> THEN <expression> END
```

In this situation, the following three expressions are logically applied:

```
CASE WHEN orderyear = 2006 THEN val END,
CASE WHEN orderyear = 2007 THEN val END,
CASE WHEN orderyear = 2008 THEN val END
```

> **Note** A CASE expression with no ELSE clause has an implicit ELSE NULL.

For each target column, the CASE expression will return the value (val column) only if the source row had the corresponding order year; otherwise, the CASE expression will return NULL.

PIVOT's third phase (P3) applies the specified aggregate function on top of each CASE expression, generating the result columns. In our case, the expressions logically become the following:

```
SUM(CASE WHEN orderyear = 2006 THEN val END) AS [2006],
SUM(CASE WHEN orderyear = 2007 THEN val END) AS [2007],
SUM(CASE WHEN orderyear = 2008 THEN val END) AS [2008]
```

In summary, the previous PIVOT query is logically equivalent to the following query:

```
SELECT empid,
  SUM(CASE WHEN orderyear = 2006 THEN val END) AS [2006],
  SUM(CASE WHEN orderyear = 2007 THEN val END) AS [2007],
  SUM(CASE WHEN orderyear = 2008 THEN val END) AS [2008]
FROM (SELECT empid, YEAR(orderdate) AS orderyear, val
      FROM Sales.OrderValues) AS OV
GROUP BY empid;
```

> **More Info** For more details on the PIVOT operator, refer to Chapter 8.

UNPIVOT

UNPIVOT is the inverse of PIVOT, rotating data from columns to rows.

Before I demonstrate UNPIVOT's logical phases, first run the following code, which creates and populates the dbo.EmpYearValues table and queries it to present its content:

```
SELECT *
INTO dbo.EmpYearValues
FROM (SELECT empid, YEAR(orderdate) AS orderyear, val
      FROM Sales.OrderValues) AS OV
  PIVOT(SUM(val) FOR orderyear IN([2006],[2007],[2008])) AS P;
```

```
UPDATE dbo.EmpYearValues
  SET [2006] = NULL
WHERE empid IN(1, 2);

SELECT * FROM dbo.EmpYearValues;
```

This code returns the following output:

```
empid       2006        2007        2008
----------- ----------- ----------- -----------
3           18223.96    108026.17   76562.75
6           16642.61    43126.38    14144.16
9           9894.52     26310.39    41103.17
7           15232.16    60471.19    48864.89
1           NULL        93148.11    63195.02
4           49945.12    128809.81   54135.94
2           NULL        70444.14    74336.56
5           18383.92    30716.48    19691.90
8           22240.12    56032.63    48589.54
```

I'll use the following query as an example to describe the logical processing phases involved with the UNPIVOT operator:

```
SELECT empid, orderyear, val
FROM dbo.EmpYearValues
  UNPIVOT(val FOR orderyear IN([2006],[2007],[2008])) AS U;
```

This query unpivots (or splits) the employee yearly values from each source row to a separate row per order year, generating the following output:

```
empid       orderyear   val
----------- ----------- -----------
3           2006        18223.96
3           2007        108026.17
3           2008        76562.75
6           2006        16642.61
6           2007        43126.38
6           2008        14144.16
9           2006        9894.52
9           2007        26310.39
9           2008        41103.17
7           2006        15232.16
7           2007        60471.19
7           2008        48864.89
1           2007        93148.11
1           2008        63195.02
4           2006        49945.12
4           2007        128809.81
4           2008        54135.94
2           2007        70444.14
2           2008        74336.56
5           2006        18383.92
5           2007        30716.48
5           2008        19691.90
8           2006        22240.12
8           2007        56032.63
8           2008        48589.54
```

The following three logical processing phases are involved in an UNPIVOT operation:

1. **U1:** Generating Copies
2. **U2:** Extracting Elements
3. **U3:** Removing Rows with NULLs

The first step (U1) generates copies of the rows from the left table expression provided to UNPIVOT as an input (EmpYearValues, in our case). This step generates a copy for each column that is unpivoted (appears in the IN clause of the UNPIVOT operator). Because there are three column names in the IN clause, three copies are produced from each source row. The resulting virtual table will contain a new column holding the source column names as character strings. The name of this column will be the one specified right before the IN clause (*orderyear,* in our case). The virtual table returned from the first step in our example is shown in Table 1-10.

TABLE 1-10 **Virtual Table Returned from UNPIVOT's First Step**

empid	2006	2007	2008	orderyear
3	18223.96	108026.17	76562.75	2006
3	18223.96	108026.17	76562.75	2007
3	18223.96	108026.17	76562. 75	2008
6	16642.61	43126.38	14144.16	2006
6	16642.61	43126.38	14144.16	2007
6	16642.61	43126.38	14144.16	2008
9	9894.52	26310.39	41103.17	2006
9	9894.52	26310.39	41103.17	2007
9	9894.52	26310.39	41103.17	2008
7	15232.16	60471.19	48864.89	2006
7	15232.16	60471.19	48864.89	2007
7	15232.16	60471.19	48864.89	2008
1	NULL	93148.11	63195.02	2006
1	NULL	93148.11	63195.02	2007
1	NULL	93148.11	63195.02	2008
4	49945.12	128809.81	54135.94	2006
4	49945.12	128809.81	54135.94	2007
4	49945.12	128809.81	54135.94	2008
2	NULL	70444.14	74336.56	2006
2	NULL	70444.14	74336.56	2007
2	NULL	70444.14	74336.56	2008
5	18383.92	30716.48	19691.90	2006
5	18383.92	30716.48	19691.90	2007
5	18383.92	30716.48	19691.90	2008

TABLE 1-10 Virtual Table Returned from UNPIVOT's First Step

empid	2006	2007	2008	orderyear
8	22240.12	56032.63	48589.54	2006
8	22240.12	56032.63	48589.54	2007
8	22240.12	56032.63	48589.54	2008

The second step (U2) extracts the value from the source column corresponding to the unpivoted element that the current copy of the row represents. The name of the target column that will hold the values is specified right before the FOR clause (*val* in our case). The target column will contain the value from the source column corresponding to the current row's order year from the virtual table. The virtual table returned from this step in our example is shown in Table 1-11.

TABLE 1-11 Virtual Table Returned from UNPIVOT's Second Step

empid	val	orderyear
3	18223.96	2006
3	108026.17	2007
3	76562.75	2008
6	16642.61	2006
6	43126.38	2007
6	14144.16	2008
9	9894.52	2006
9	26310.39	2007
9	41103.17	2008
7	15232.16	2006
7	60471.19	2007
7	48864.89	2008
1	NULL	2006
1	93148.11	2007
1	63195.02	2008
4	49945.12	2006
4	128809.81	2007
4	54135.94	2008
2	NULL	2006
2	70444.14	2007
2	74336.56	2008
5	18383.92	2006
5	30716.48	2007
5	19691.90	2008
8	22240.12	2006
8	56032.63	2007
8	48589.54	2008

UNPIVOT's third and final step (U3) is to remove rows with NULLs in the result value column (*val*, in our case). The virtual table returned from this step in our example is shown in Table 1-12.

TABLE 1-12 Virtual Table Returned from UNPIVOT's Third Step

empid	val	orderyear
3	18223.96	2006
3	108026.17	2007
3	76562.75	2008
6	16642.61	2006
6	43126.38	2007
6	14144.16	2008
9	9894.52	2006
9	26310.39	2007
9	41103.17	2008
7	15232.16	2006
7	60471.19	2007
7	48864.89	2008
1	93148.11	2007
1	63195.02	2008
4	49945.12	2006
4	128809.81	2007
4	54135.94	2008
2	70444.14	2007
2	74336.56	2008
5	18383.92	2006
5	30716.48	2007
5	19691.90	2008
8	22240.12	2006
8	56032.63	2007
8	48589.54	2008

When you're done experimenting with the UNPIVOT operator, drop the EmpYearValues table:

```
DROP TABLE dbo.EmpYearValues;
```

More Info For more details on the UNPIVOT operator, refer to Chapter 8.

OVER Clause

The OVER clause allows you to request window-based calculations. You can use this clause with aggregate functions (both built-in and custom common language runtime [CLR]-based aggregates), and it is a required element for the four analytical ranking functions (*ROW_NUMBER*, *RANK*, *DENSE_RANK*, and *NTILE*). The OVER clause defines the window of rows over which the aggregate or ranking function is calculated.

I won't discuss applications of windows-based calculations here, nor will I go into detail about exactly how these functions work; I'll only explain the phases in which the OVER clause is applicable. I'll cover the OVER clause in more detail in Chapters 6 and 8.

The OVER clause is applicable only in one of two phases: the SELECT phase (5) and the ORDER BY phase (6). This clause has access to whichever virtual table is provided to that phase as input. Listing 1-3 highlights the logical processing phases in which the OVER clause can be used.

LISTING 1-3 OVER clause in logical query processing

```
(5) SELECT (5-2) DISTINCT (5-3) TOP(<top_specification>) (5-1) <select_list>
(1) FROM (1-J) <left_table> <join_type> JOIN <right_table> ON <on_predicate>
        | (1-A) <left_table> <apply_type> APPLY <right_table_expression> AS <alias>
        | (1-P) <left_table> PIVOT(<pivot_specification>) AS <alias>
        | (1-U) <left_table> UNPIVOT(<unpivot_specification>) AS <alias>
(2) WHERE <where_predicate>
(3) GROUP BY <group_by_specification>
(4) HAVING <having_predicate>
(6) ORDER BY <order_by_list>;
```

You specify the OVER clause following the function to which it applies in either the *select_list* or the *order_by_list*.

Even though I didn't really explain in detail how the OVER clause works, I'd like to demonstrate its use in both phases where it's applicable. In the following example, an OVER clause is used with the *COUNT* aggregate function in the SELECT list:

```
USE InsideTSQL2008;

SELECT orderid, custid,
  COUNT(*) OVER(PARTITION BY custid) AS numorders
FROM Sales.Orders
WHERE shipcountry = N'Spain';
```

This query produces the following output:

```
orderid     custid      numorders
----------- ----------- -----------
10326       8           3
10801       8           3
10970       8           3
```

10928	29	5
10568	29	5
10887	29	5
10366	29	5
10426	29	5
10550	30	10
10303	30	10
10888	30	10
10911	30	10
10629	30	10
10872	30	10
10874	30	10
10948	30	10
11009	30	10
11037	30	10
11013	69	5
10917	69	5
10306	69	5
10281	69	5
10282	69	5

The PARTITION BY clause defines the window for the calculation. The *COUNT(*)* function counts the number of rows in the virtual table provided to the SELECT phase as input, where the *custid* value is equal to the one in the current row. Remember that the virtual table provided to the SELECT phase as input has already undergone WHERE filtering—that is, only customers from Spain have been filtered.

You can also use the OVER clause in the ORDER BY list. For example, the following query sorts the rows according to the total number of output rows for the customer (in descending order):

```
SELECT orderid, custid,
  COUNT(*) OVER(PARTITION BY custid) AS numorders
FROM Sales.Orders
WHERE shipcountry = N'Spain'
ORDER BY COUNT(*) OVER(PARTITION BY custid) DESC;
```

This query generates the following output:

orderid	custid	numorders
10550	30	10
10303	30	10
10888	30	10
10911	30	10
10629	30	10
10872	30	10
10874	30	10
10948	30	10
11009	30	10
11037	30	10
11013	69	5
10917	69	5
10306	69	5

10281	69	5
10282	69	5
10928	29	5
10568	29	5
10887	29	5
10366	29	5
10426	29	5
10326	8	3
10801	8	3
10970	8	3

More Info For details on using the OVER clause with aggregate functions, please refer to Chapter 8. For details on using the OVER clause with analytical ranking functions, please refer to Chapter 6.

Set Operators

SQL Server 2008 supports four set operators: UNION ALL, UNION, EXCEPT, and INTERSECT. These SQL operators correspond to operators defined in mathematical set theory. Listing 1-4 contains a general form of a query applying a set operator, along with numbers assigned according to the order in which the different elements of the code are logically processed.

LISTING 1-4 General form of a query applying a set operator

```
(1) query1
(2) <set_operator>
(1) query2
(3) [ORDER BY <order_by_list>]
```

Set operators compare complete rows between the two inputs. UNION ALL returns one result set with all rows from both inputs. UNION returns one result set with the distinct rows from both inputs (no duplicates). EXCEPT returns distinct rows that appear in the first input but not in the second. INTERSECT returns the distinct rows that appear in both inputs. I could say much more about these set operators, but here I'd just like to focus on the logical processing steps involved in a set operation.

An ORDER BY clause is not allowed in the individual queries because the queries are supposed to return sets (unordered). You are allowed to specify an ORDER BY clause at the end of the query, and it will apply to the result of the set operation.

In terms of logical processing, each input query is first processed separately with all its relevant phases. The set operator is then applied, and if an ORDER BY clause is specified, it is applied to the result set.

Take the following query as an example:

```
USE InsideTSQL2008;

SELECT region, city
FROM Sales.Customers
WHERE country = N'USA'

INTERSECT

SELECT region, city
FROM HR.Employees
WHERE country = N'USA'

ORDER BY region, city;
```

This query generates the following output:

```
country          region           city
---------------  ---------------  ---------------
USA              WA               Kirkland
USA              WA               Seattle
```

First, each input query is processed separately following all the relevant logical processing phases. The first query returns locations (region, city) of customers from the United States. The second query returns locations of employees from the United States. The set operator INTERSECT returns distinct rows that appear in both inputs—in our case, locations that are both customer locations and employee locations. Finally, the ORDER BY clause sorts the rows by *region* and *city*.

As another example for logical processing phases of a set operation, the following query returns customers that have made no orders:

```
SELECT custid FROM Sales.Customers
EXCEPT
SELECT custid FROM Sales.Orders;
```

The first query returns the set of customer IDs from Customers, and the second query returns the set of customer IDs from Orders. The set operation returns the set of rows from the first set that do not appear in the second set. Remember that a set has no duplicates; the EXCEPT set operator returns distinct occurrences of rows from the first set that do not appear in the second set.

The result set's column names are determined by the set operator's first input. Columns in corresponding positions must match in their data types or be implicitly convertible. Finally, an interesting aspect of set operations is that they treat NULLs as equal.

More Info You can find a more detailed discussion about set operators in Chapter 7.

Conclusion

Understanding logical query processing phases and the unique aspects of SQL is important to get into the special mind set required to program in SQL. By being familiar with those aspects of the language, you can produce efficient solutions and explain your choices. Remember, the idea is to master the basics.

Chapter 2
Set Theory and Predicate Logic

Steve Kass

This chapter contains a brief introduction to two cornerstones of mathematics: set theory and predicate logic, which are intimately connected to the world of databases. Database tables represent sets of facts, and database queries produce result sets based on query predicates.

The objects of study in logic are propositions—statements of fact that are either true or false—and propositional functions, which are open statements with one or more unspecified values. Database tables hold representations of statements of fact, and query predicates are propositional functions.

Later in this book, you'll use logical set-based thinking to write a T-SQL SELECT query to return the following result set: "all customers for whom every employee from the USA has handled at least one order."

Your query won't tell the Microsoft SQL Server engine how to produce the desired result; instead, it will simply describe the result, in sharp contrast to how you'd use a procedural programming language, such as C# or Fortran, to produce the same result. The more you understand about set theory and logic, the easier SQL will be for you.

An Example of English-to-Mathematics Translation

I'll begin this chapter by describing "all customers for whom every employee from the USA has handled at least one order" not in SQL, as you will see in Chapter 6, "Subqueries, Table Expressions, and Ranking Functions," but in the mathematical language of set theory. Turning English into mathematics, by the way, is much harder than doing mathematics or speaking English, and this example will highlight some of the mathematical ideas that are particularly useful to SQL programmers. Some of the set theory notation in this section will be defined later. Don't worry if it's unfamiliar.

First of all, let's give the result set we're after a name.

> ### Definition of the set S (in English)
> Let S be the set of all customers for whom every employee from the USA has handled at least one order.

By naming this set of customers (even by referring to it as a set, so that we can talk about having named it!), we've made an implicit assumption that the description has a clear *meaning*—it describes something unambiguously.

The definition mentions customers, employees, and orders, and to talk about these categories of things mathematically, we should think of them as sets and name them: Let Customers, Employees, and Orders be the sets of customers, employees, and orders, respectively. To describe S mathematically, we don't have to understand what these terms mean; we only have to name them.

One meaningful term in the description doesn't represent a kind of thing: *handled*. Again, we don't need to know what it means from a business point of view for an employee to handle an order for a customer, but we do need to understand that, given appropriate details, *has handled* is either true or false. We also have to be clear what details it's true or false about. If we dissect how *handled* is used in the description, we see that it has to do with three details: an employee, an order, and a customer.

It's especially useful to be able to write down the *handled* fact in a particular case. Given a particular employee e, a particular order o, and a particular customer c, this fact (employee e handled order o for customer c) is either true or false. In other words, it's a *predicate*. Using function notation, write **handled(e,o,c)** to represent the truth value of "employee e handled order o for customer c." Depending on the values of e, o, and c, $handled(e,o,c)$ has a truth value: it's true or it's false.

> **Note** You might have interpreted *handled* as involving only two details: an employee and an order, ending up with $handled(e,o)$ for "employee e handled order o." That's not wrong, and in fact it might be the best way to begin if we were designing a database to support queries to return S. To define S mathematically, however, the three-detail notion is closer to what defines S as a set of customers: whether a particular customer c is in the set S. It's harder to express S mathematically with the two-detail interpretation.

The last element in the description we need notation for is *from the USA*. Being from the USA or not is a property of employees, and we'll write **fromUSA(e)** to represent the truth value of "employee e is from the USA." To make things a bit simpler to write down at first, let *USAEmployees* be the set of employees from the USA or, mathematically, let *USAEmployees* = $\{e \in Employees : fromUSA(e)\}$.

Now that we've named everything we might need, we turn to the question of describing membership in S in terms of the objects we've defined.

Question　In terms of the sets Customers, USAEmployees, and Orders and the function $handled(e,o,c)$, when is a particular customer c in S?

Answer　The customer c is in S if and only if for every (employee) e in the set USAEmployees, there is at least one (order) o in the set Orders for which $handled(e,o,c)$.

Using mathematical notation only, here's what we get:

Definition of the Set S (in Mathematics)

Let *USAEmployees* = {*e* ∈ *Employees* : *fromUSA(e)*}. Then define the set

S = {*c* ∈ *Customers* : ∀*e* ∈ *USAEmployees* (∃*o* ∈ *Orders* : (*handled(e,o,c)*))}

At the end of this chapter, we'll revisit this set.

Well-Definedness

In nonmathematical language, we describe something as well-defined if it has a distinct boundary or outline. In mathematics, *well-defined* has a different meaning. Mathematicians call something well-defined if it's defined unambiguously. Read the following terms and descriptions and decide which terms are defined unambiguously.

Provinces   The set of Canadian provinces

Numerator   The numerator of the number 0.2 written as a fraction

Low Temp   The lowest temperature ever recorded in Russia

Big Number   The largest number that can be described with fewer than 20 words

Contact List   The name and a phone number for each of this book's authors, alphabetized by author's last name

Shortest Book   The book in the Library of Congress that has the fewest pages

Square x^2

Letter   The letter B

Let's see if we agree on which of these are well-defined.

Provinces   This is a well-defined set: One way of denoting this set is {Alberta, British Columbia, Manitoba, New Brunswick, Newfoundland and Labrador, Nova Scotia, Ontario, Prince Edward Island, Quebec, Saskatchewan}.

Numerator   This number isn't well-defined because we have many ways to write 0.2 as a fraction, and they don't all have the same numerator.

Low Temp   This is well-defined, even though we might not know the value.

Big Number   Although this may appear to be a valid definition, it's not. Consider the number "*N* plus one, where *N* is the largest number that can be described with fewer than 20 words." This is a variation on the *Berry Paradox*.

Contact List   This isn't well-defined if any of the authors has more than one phone number because it doesn't specify how we choose phone numbers for the list.

Shortest Book   Although the minimum number of pages is well-defined (assuming a standard procedure for counting pages), more than one book might have the minimum number of pages. As a result, we can't be sure there is a single shortest book.

Square   We don't know the value of x, so x^2 isn't a well-defined number. On the other hand, it is a well-defined algebraic expression.

Letter   This defines a particular letter of the English alphabet but not a specific example of that letter in, say, a copy of this book.

These simple examples offer a number of lessons, but I'll mention just one in particular: *English can easily mislead*. For example, two words that indicate uniqueness—the definite article *the* and the superlative *shortest*—were used to describe something that wasn't in fact unique.

Later in this chapter, I'll be more specific about the notion of well-definedness as it applies to sets.

Definitions

The elements of mathematical language, like English words, have meanings—at least most of them do. The definition of an English word is typically a written record of a preexisting meaning. In mathematics, however, an object's definition typically *establishes* its meaning. Definitions in mathematics come in several forms; here are a few examples of definitions. These particular definitions aren't needed elsewhere in the chapter; they're only here for illustration.

Sample Definitions

For any real number x, let $\lfloor x \rfloor$ be the unique integer in the half-open interval $[x, x+1)$. The function $x \mapsto \lfloor x \rfloor$ is called the *greatest integer function*.

Let T be the set of continuous bijective involutions on the unit interval.

Let $S = \{(n, n+1) : n$ is a positive integer$\}$

An integer n is *prime* if $n > 1$ and n has no integer divisors d between 2 and $n - 1$.

The *Fibonacci sequence* is the sequence of integers F_i defined recursively as follows: $F_1 = F_2 = 1; F_n = F_{n-1} + F_{n-2}$, for $n > 2$.

Undefined Terms

Any mathematical framework—set theory, logic, geometry, and so on—begins with some undefined terms and unproven axioms—usually these are simple objects or accepted notions, such as point or set, or that two numbers equal to the same number are themselves equal.

Equality, Identity, and Sameness

One of the most frequently used symbols in mathematics is the equal sign (=). Informally, it's the symbol for *is*, as in *one plus one is two*. The equal sign is used in mathematics in many ways to represent some notion of equality, sameness, or nondistinctness. Roughly speaking (which is all we can do without a major detour into deep questions of philosophy), it's safe to substitute one mathematical quantity for another one if the two are equal.

Don't assume, however, that $x=y$ means that x and y are *identical* in every possible way. Although no one would dispute that alligator=alligator, we can still distinguish the two. A molecule of pigment in one of them is certainly not also in the other, and I can point to one of them, let's say the one on the left, and describe it as *this* alligator, and you know that the other one is a different alligator. If you have the slightest inkling that someone might be using the equal sign imprecisely, a good question to ask is "equal *as what?*" The two alligators in alligator=alligator are equal *as animal names* or equal *as words* and probably equal *as character strings* (though not if one of them ends up hyphenated when this book is printed). The two alligators are decidedly not, on the other hand, equal *as arrangements of pigment molecules.*

While it might seem unnecessary to spend even this short amount of time splitting hairs, as it were, we'll see some practical implications later.

Mathematical Conventions

Every now and then in my beginning programming classes, a student—usually a good one—will name variables with an extra dose of creativity, and I'll be confronted with something I call the *penguin* dialect of programming, as shown in Listing 2-1.

LISTING 2-1 Bubble sort, written in the *penguin* dialect

```
for(int penguin = 0; penguin < tiger-1; ++penguin) {
  for(int Betty = 0; Betty < tiger-penguin-1; ++Betty) {
    if (abba[Betty+1] < abba[Betty]) {
      int Whoops = abba[Betty];
      abba[Betty] = abba[Betty+1];
      abba[Betty+1] = Whoops;
    }
  }
}
```

In contrast, a textbook author might express the same algorithm this way, in what I call the *ijk* dialect, as shown in Listing 2-2.

LISTING 2-2 Bubble sort, written in the *ijk* dialect

```
for(int i = 0; i < n-1; ++i) {
  for(int j = 0; j < n-i-1; ++j) {
    if (a[j+1] < a[j]) {
      int t = a[j];
      a[j] = a[j+1];
      a[j+1] = t;
    }
  }
}
```

Yet another category of programmer might create this version of the algorithm. Making no attempt to hide my own personal bias, I call this the *usefulNames* dialect, as shown in Listing 2-3.

LISTING 2-3 Bubble sort, written in the *usefulNames* dialect

```
for(int passNo = 0; passNo < arrSize-1; ++passNo) {
  for(int position = 0; position < arrSize-passNo-1; ++position) {
    if (arr[position+1] < arr[position]) {
      int temp = arr[position];
      arr[position] = arr[position+1];
      arr[position+1] = temp;
    }
  }
}
```

The creative student chose names such as *penguin* and *Betty* in part because she wasn't yet familiar with the naming conventions of programming and in part because experience hadn't yet taught her the importance of conventions. The author of the second version chose the names *i* and *j* because she was accustomed to an accepted system of naming conventions: the *ijk* dialect. The third author, I would venture, understands the importance of naming conventions and knows from experience how those conventions affect the ability to understand and develop correct code.

The *ijk* dialect rose to prominence in mathematics for good reasons. Formulas are easier to fit on a page (not to mention the back of an envelope or a napkin) if notation is concise. Conciseness was important, too, in the early days of computing, when statements had to fit on 80-column punch cards.

I won't abandon the venerable conventions of mathematics, but I'll try to be aware of the barrier to understanding they can create. Where appropriate, I'll point out some of the specific conventions, which may be useful if you decide to delve more deeply into the subjects of this chapter.

Numbers

There are many kinds of numbers in theoretical mathematics, but in most practical settings, numbers mean *real numbers*, from the familiar number line, which, like the x-axis of coordinate geometry, extends forever in both directions from zero. Numbers to the left of zero are negative; numbers to the right are positive.

The real number system is fundamentally intuitive because it corresponds to familiar concepts from geometry: length, line, point, ray. In fact, the real numbers are important because they are the numbers with which we express things that we can measure. They also provide the basis for nearly all kinds of calculation or computation, through the operations of arithmetic.

Real numbers and arithmetic "play well together," you might say. If we add some numbers in one order—for example, we add 3.4 and 18—and then we add 30.1 to the result, we get the same answer as if we started by adding 18 and 30.1. The nice properties real numbers have with respect to arithmetic are taught in school: the associative law, the distributive laws, the commutative law, and so on.

Other important properties of the real numbers are a little less familiar but include these: Given two positive real numbers x and y, with x the smaller, there's a whole number n for which y lies between nx and $(n+1)x$. For any two real numbers x and y, again with x the smaller, there is another real number (in fact infinitely many) strictly between x and y.

Like most programming languages, T-SQL provides a data type intended to represent real numbers. In fact, it provides two: REAL and FLOAT. However, neither these types nor SQL Server's other number types (some of which are termed *exact* types) are faithful representations of the real number system from mathematics.

Hold onto that thought. We'll come back to it.

Context

The correct interpretation of language depends on context. In some cases, the context for interpreting a word is adjacent, as is the context for interpreting the word "floor" differently in the following two sentences: "This will floor you" and "The floor is dirty." In other cases, the context is more general, as in the context for interpreting the remark "Watch the batter!" differently when at an baseball game and when in a cooking class. Every natural language depends on context to clarify meaning, and it's a fact of life we tend to accommodate naturally, for the most part.

Mathematical expressions depend on context also, but we don't grow to learn the details and implications of mathematical context as naturally as we do for our native tongue. Table 2-1 presents a few examples from arithmetic and algebra where the same expression can have more than one interpretation, depending on the context.

TABLE 2-1 Expressions and Possible Meanings in Different Contexts

Expression	Possible Meaning	A Context for This Meaning
$c(a+b)$	The application of the function c to the argument $a+b$	The symbol c has been defined as a function.
$c(a+b)$	The product of the numbers c and $a+b$	The symbol c has been defined as a number.
$b = A^{-1}$	The reciprocal of A: $b = 1/A$	The symbol A represents a number.
$b = A^{-1}$	The inverse function of A: if $A(x) = y$, b satisfies the equation $b(y) = x$	The symbol A represents a function.
iy	The product of i and y	The symbol i was defined as an integer.
iy	An imaginary number	The surrounding discussion is about complex numbers.

It's possible to define a system of notation far less dependent on context than the familiar language of mathematics. Such a system would be cumbersome to learn and use, however, because reusing symbols to mean different things in different contexts provides economy and convenience.

Dates

The importance of context is not restricted to the interpretation of expressions. The interpretation of individual literal values can depend on context as well.

The concept of a calendar date is a good example of this. There's no one "right" way to denote calendar dates, but to communicate, we have to denote them. A character string that represents a specific value is called a *literal*. Table 2-2 presents some literal date values and the meanings they would have in some of SQL Server's supported languages.

TABLE 2-2 Date Literals with Culture-Dependent Meanings

Date literal	Possible meaning	A language where this is the meaning
3 listopad 2008	The 3rd day of the 11th month of the year 2008	Polish
3 listopad 2008	The 3rd day of the 10th month of the year 2008	Croatian
13-12-09	The 12th day of the 13th month of the year 2009	US English
13-12-09	The 13th day of the 12th month of the year 2009	German
13-12-09	The 9th day of the 12th month of the year 2013	Swedish

Depending on the server's *two-year date cutoff* setting, which provides yet additional context for the interpretation of dates, the date literal string 13-12-09 could be interpreted with the year 1909 or 1913, depending on language.

Fortunately, you can specify dates in culture-independent ways, and one that works well for SQL Server is the string YYYYMMDD. (In code, be sure to surround it with quotes, as in *'20071112'*, so that it isn't interpreted as an integer!)

Alphabetical Order

Later in this chapter, I'll discuss the notion of order in more detail. At this point, I'll simply mention that alphabetical order is another notion that depends on context. In a Spanish dictionary from the early twentieth century, you'll find the word *llama* after the word *lobo* because Spanish traditionally considered the word *llama* to begin with the letter (yes, *letter*, not *letters*) *ll*, which comes after the letter *l*. In an English dictionary, *llama* begins with *l*; thus, *llama* appears before *lobo*.

Functions, Parameters, and Variables

I'll assume you're familiar with the language of mathematical *functions*, such as $f(x)=x^2$, and I'll address any tricky concepts when they arise. The word *parameter* is worth a few remarks. This term may mean a number of things: in the function definition $f(x) = x^2$, x is a placeholder (or more precisely, a formal parameter or free variable). If we apply the definition of the same function and write $f(9) = 81$, the number 9 is also called a parameter (an actual parameter). Roughly speaking, a parameter is a placeholder for a value, a value that fills such a placeholder, or a value that might be a different value. In this chapter, the term *parameter* will mean formal parameter or placeholder.

Ideally, for every parameter in an expression, a well-defined set of values can be substituted in its place. This set is called the parameter's *domain*. If the domain of x in the expression $f(x) = x^2$ is the set of real numbers, we can also call x a real-valued parameter. An expression with a parameter, such as x^2, is called a *parameterized* expression.

> **Note** Parameter domains often go unstated. They may be implied by conventions mathematicians follow when they choose symbols and names: the names x, y, s, and t are typically used for real-valued parameters; z, and sometimes w, are good choices for complex-valued parameters; p, q, and r are typical rational-valued parameter names; and letters near the middle of the alphabet, including i, j, k, m, and n, more often than not represent integer-valued parameters.
>
> In programming languages, domains correspond to types, and parameters correspond to variables. In T-SQL, a variable's type must be specified.

To set the stage for what comes later, consider the real-valued parameter x in the parameterized, real-valued expression x^2. Despite being named real valued, neither x nor x^2 has any value at all, at least not until x is specified. If we supply a value—for example, 3—for x, the expression x^2 then has a value, which in this case is 9. Supplying the value 3 for the parameter x is informally called *plugging 3 in for x* or, formally, *binding x to the value 3*. We can be sure an expression represents a specific value when all of its parameters have been bound.

Instructions and Algorithms

The topics of this chapter, set theory and logic, are mathematical frameworks for describing things and facts, respectively, both of which are most easily considered static. While a computer program—source code—is static, the execution of a program is dynamic. If the program is useful, the execution is almost certainly nondeterministic. In most programming languages, the code describes the process of execution.

A rigorous mathematical treatment of program code is more straightforward than one of program execution. At the least, the mathematical tools for describing execution are further removed from the mathematical foundations of set theory and logic. The beauty of SQL, though, is that its code can describe results directly, without having to express algorithms and describe the process of execution. Not surprisingly, the inspiration that led to SQL was set theory.

Set Theory

Itzik Ben-Gan is one of this book's authors. That's a fact, and database systems like SQL Server 2008 help us identify facts and separate them from fiction. Here are some other facts about who is and who isn't one of this book's authors: Dejan Sarka is one; Bill Gates is not.

In the language of sets, we can describe the set of authors of this book, and we can use the language of set theory to express facts.

If we name the set of authors of this book A, we can write A = {Itzik Ben-Gan, Lubor Kollar, Dejan Sarka, Steve Kass}. We call A a set, and we call the four authors *elements*, or *members*, of A. The statement that Itzik is one of the book's authors can be expressed as Itzik∈A.

> **Note** As we'll soon see, there should always be some universal context for a given set's elements *and its nonelements*. For the preceding set A, the context might be people, and we could describe *the set* A *of people*, not just *the set* A, to be the authors of this book. We won't always allude to or specify this universal context, but wherever we see or say *set*, we should be prepared to answer *set of what*?

> ## Definition of the Set Membership Operator
> The symbol ∈ is the *set membership operator*. If A is a set and x is a potential member of A, we write $x{\in}A$ to mean that x is a member of A, and we write $x{\notin}A$ to mean that x is not a member of A.

> **Note** For given values of x and A three scenarios are possible:
>
> x **is an element of A** In this scenario, $x{\in}A$ is true, and $x{\notin}A$ is false. For example, this scenario would hold if x were the number -12 and A were the set of even integers.
>
> x **is not an element of A** $x{\in}A$ is false, and $x{\notin}A$ is true. For example, this scenario would hold if x were the state of Maine and A were the set of Canadian provinces as of the year 2008.
>
> **The expressions $x{\in}A$ and $x{\notin}A$ are (both) not valid propositions** For example, this scenario would hold if x were the state of Maine and A were the set of ingredients in *coq au vin*. In this case, A is a set of some food ingredients, and Maine is not a food ingredient. This scenario would also hold if A were not a set.

Set theory is the fundamental underpinning of mathematics, and the fundamental concept of set theory is the notion of *membership*.

Notation for Sets

Braces, like I used earlier when I wrote A = {Itzik Ben-Gan, Lubor Kollar, Dejan Sarka, Steve Kass}, are standard notation in mathematics for sets. Put some things between braces, and you have a set. You can even put nothing between the braces, like this: {}, and it's a set, known for obvious reasons as the empty set.

Enumeration

If we list a set's elements—separated by commas and between braces—we've enumerated the elements of the set. *Enumeration* of elements is a simple way to denote a set if the set doesn't contain many elements. If the set is large but the elements have a pattern, we can describe the set using an *ellipsis* (. . .). If we need to and the intent is clear, we can use more than one ellipsis and (in a pinch) semicolons to separate sublisted groups of elements in patterns, as shown in Table 2-3.

TABLE 2-3 Sets Described Using Enumeration

Set (notation)	Set (English)
{1,2,3,4, . . .}	The positive integers
{0, −1, 1, −2, 2, −3, 3, −4, 4, . . .}	The integers
{. . ., −3, −2, −1, 0, 1, 2, 3, . . .}	The integers
{A, B, C, . . ., Z}	The letters of the English alphabet
{A, B, C, . . ., Z, a, b, c, . . ., z}	Uppercase and lowercase English letters
{0; 0.0, 0.1, 0.2, . . ., 0.9; 0.01, 0.02, . . ., 0.99; . . .}	The decimal numbers at least 0 but less than 1

Set-Builder Notation

Set-builder notation also uses braces, but it avoids listing every element explicitly without resorting to ellipses. Set-builder notation has two common variations. In one, the elements of a set are described as those elements from another set that satisfy a condition. Here is how you could write the set E of positive even integers with this kind of set-builder notation: $E = \{n \in \mathbb{Z} : n > 0 \text{ and } (n/2) \in \mathbb{Z}\}$. In the other variation, set-builder notation describes the elements of a set as those "built" from the elements of another set by a formula. Here is a way to do that for the same set E: $E = \{2n : n \in \mathbb{Z}^+\}$.

Note In the definition of the set E, / is the division operator of arithmetic, which is the inverse of multiplication. In particular, 1/2 equals one-half. In T-SQL and many strongly typed programming languages, 1/2 equals zero because integer division yields the integer result of truncating the quotient towards zero.

The symbol $\mathbb{Z}$ is standard mathematical notation for the set of integers, as is $\mathbb{Z}^+$ for the positive integers.

Well-Definedness of Sets

The word *set* is usually left undefined, but particular sets, such as the set of this book's authors, are defined as needed. One way to be sure S is well-defined is to verify the following two conditions:

- There is a universal set U or domain of discourse for S, whether explicitly stated or understood from context. The set U contains precisely the elements of S together with the nonelements of S.

- The definition of S is sufficient to answer the question "Is *x* an element of S?" for any element *x* in U.

Not all authors insist on the first requirement, but it's extremely useful. It's also appropriate to the context of learning about a typed programming language (T-SQL) and the fundamentals of databases, where universal sets are important.

Domains of Discourse

Recall the earlier example from this chapter where we represented the statement "employee *e* handled order *o* for customer *c*" as *handled(e,o,c)*. Given a particular employee *e*, order *o*, and customer *c*, the statement, or equivalently the expression *handled(e,o,c)*, has a truth value of either true or false. These two values, true and false, were the only possible values of the expression *handled(e,o,c)*.

On the other hand, I used this example without any indication of what possible values the input variables *e, o,* and *c* could equal. What are the possible ways in which the variable *e* can represent "a particular employee," *o* can represent "a particular order," and *c* can represent "a particular customer"?

At first, you might think this is a needlessly picky question. As long as *o* is an order, what's the problem? But if I'm charged with writing the code to implement the evaluation of *handled(e,o,c)*, I need to know the possible values of the variable *o*. Without knowing, I can't be sure my implementation is valid. The architect whose model required an implementation of *handled()* also has to know to be able to validate the model.

Without a well-defined domain for the variable *e*, representing "all possible employees," we'll never be able to validate a model that uses the notion of employee, let alone that tries to represent notions such as *handled*. Notions like that of *employee* are central to the effective use of databases. Let me give you a concrete example of where you might find domains of discourse in the business world and why careful attention to them is important: forms.

Domains and Bad Data

At some point in your life you've had to fill out a form with details like your name, your date of birth, your address, and so on—phone number, e-mail, citizenship—the list is endless. Whether it was a paper form or something you filled out online, your answers had to fit. (Even if you could "attach additional pages as needed," your answers had to fit in the envelope or mailbox!) Furthermore, if the information you provided was destined for a well-designed database, the information had to fit not only the form but also (after interpretation by a data entry clerk, a software interface, or another intermediary) the constraints of the database design.

For this example, suppose that the forms we're thinking about are receipts from individual sales and that these forms have a place for, among other things, the date of the sale and the tax paid on the sale. Down the road, these forms are entered into a database, and the data may be used to generate a report—perhaps a report of tax receipts by month. To produce the report, the sales data has to be partitioned, or grouped, into months, according to the sale date, and the tax receipts have to be added up for each month. However the data is represented, we have to be able to figure out a month and a number from each receipt.

Because you're reading this book, it's probably safe to assume that you've had to think about this kind of process. You've probably had to get your hands dirty in it. More likely than not, you've also had the experience of seeing or worrying about information that looks like the information in Table 2-4.

TABLE 2-4 Sale Dates and Tax Received for Some Sales

Receipt Number	Sale Date	Tax Collected	Customer Name
1	Jul 3	$1.24	Mark Hassall
2	Sunday, 10/3	exempt	Torstonen
3	Sunday, 10/3	Carole Poland	$2.56
6	10/12/2007	N/A	CAROLE POLAND
	10-13-2007	$3.00	POLAND
11	10-13-2007	$1.24	Yao-Chiang
11	Febuary '07		Did not provide
12	February 11	$18.24	katrin
13	Feb 13	3.10	FRNDO
14	2/13/07	.41	Jim Wickam (sp?)
#17	14 Feb	2.25	Sittichai
18	Carole Poland	5	blank

Not even the most talented programmer can write procedures to report tax receipts by month from data like this—well, not procedures that produce *correct* reports. The requirement is incompatible with the data, and one or the other has to be bent.

Let's assume the data is bent into shape, and instead of the unmanageable information in Table 2-4, the data appears as shown in Table 2-5.

TABLE 2-5 Sale Dates and Tax Received for Some Sales

Receipt Number	Sale Date	Tax Collected	Customer Name
1	7/3/2007	1.24	Mark Hassall
2	10/3/2007	exempt	Torsten Arndt
3	10/3/2007	2.56	Yao-Qiang Cheng
6	10/12/2007	0	Carole Poland
7	10/13/2007	3.00	Carole Poland
11	10/13/2007	1.24	Yao-Qiang Cheng
11	2/25/2007		NULL
12	2/15/2007	18.24	Katrin Gulbis
13	2/29/2007	3.10	Nkenge McLin
14	3/13/2007	0.41	Jim Wickham
17	3/16/2007	2.25	Sittichai Tuntisangaroon
18	3/12/2007	5	blank

If you looked closely, you may have noticed something strange about receipt 13's sale date. In the row containing 13 in the Receipt Number column, the Sale Date column contains 2/29/2007, which doesn't represent a date. The Sale Date column still contains strings, not dates. While most of the values this time do represent dates, not all of them do. Whether we use strings, numbers, or another data type, we need a column that holds faithful, unambiguous representations of dates.

> **Note** Wish as we might, someone, if not us, has to accommodate the receipt that has an illegible or missing date. Recognizing the value of a column to hold faithful, unambiguous representations of dates—when they existed, which might not be always—those responsible for SQL provided for nullable column declarations. I won't have too much to say about NULL, I'm afraid. The mathematics becomes much harder—some might say intractable—if you attempt to accommodate NULLs.

Dates and literal date strings aren't the same, literal date strings and strings aren't the same, and the interpretation of literal date strings isn't invariant from culture to culture, epoch to epoch, or system to system.

The best we can do is document and define categories (such as dates), identify one or more faithful representations of them (such as date strings in a particular format), and understand and record as much as we can about the representations and concepts, their cultural interpretations, and what universe of potential values serves as the domain of discourse for a category.

The data in Tables 2-4 and 2-5 contain other properties that will make it hard to create a tax report. I won't say anything about them, but I encourage you to think about why, mathematically, they cause problems.

Domains and Modeling

Now return to this chapter's first example. As a mathematical object, *fromUSA* is a function. It takes one input value (an employee *e*) and yields (more precisely, associates to that value) a unique output from the set {true, false} of logical truth values. In mathematics, *function* doesn't belong to a well-defined category, nor does the more specific *functions of one variable that return truth values as output*. To work with functions mathematically, we need to be precise about the function's domain.

Because notions such as *employee* simply fail to admit a well-defined universal set of any reasonable description, we choose properties or surrogates that work. We may not be able to describe "all employees," but we can decide that employees, when we need to refer to them in questions or assertions of fact, must be identified unambiguously by a specific group of properties (such as the combination of name, phone number, and birth date) or by an identifier of some kind. We can then define the universal domain of employees as the universe of such identifiers.

Once we specify a domain for employees (or values that represent employees), we can be precise about what kind of mathematical object handled is: a Boolean-valued function of one variable, with domain the set of employee identifiers.

Whether we choose to represent an object by a surrogate, as we might represent an order by an order number, or by one or more properties, as we might represent a person by birth date and some DNA measurements, we expect the surrogate to represent the object faithfully.

Faithfulness

As you know by now, we may think about concepts, but in practice, we must work with representations of concepts. As best we can, we choose representations of concepts that don't mislead us or to be more precise, that don't require us to sacrifice our ability to answer questions.

> ### Definition of a Faithful Representation
>
> Let X and S be sets, and let $\mathcal{F}$ be a collection of functions. (Think of X as your objects of interest; think of S as the strings, numbers, or other objects you hope to use to represent elements of X. Think of $\mathcal{F}$ as the tools you need to answer questions about elements of X for some larger purpose.)
>
> In addition, let $\mathcal{R} : X \rightarrow S$ be a function that associates to each $x \in X$ a representation $\mathcal{R}(x)$ in S. The function $\mathcal{R}$ is called a representation of X, and it is *faithful* for $\mathcal{F}$ if there is a collection of functions $\mathcal{F}_{\mathcal{R}}$ that refer to S instead of X, and to $\mathcal{R}(x)$ instead of x, but that correctly perform every calculation that was possible in $\mathcal{F}$ before the substitution of S for X and $\mathcal{R}(x)$ for x.

Informally, a representation is a naming scheme, and a faithful representation is a naming scheme that works. A naming scheme for things can work if the names alone allow you to keep track of what you need to keep track of.

Suppose X is the set of US dollar-denominated bills manufactured by the United States Bureau of Engraving and Printing (BEP). If you were a shop owner, you might need to answer just one or two kinds of questions about elements of X: how much is a particular bill worth, and how many of each denomination are "here" (where "here" might refer to a customer's hand or your cash drawer).

> **Note** Another question you might think of is "Is this bill genuine, as opposed to counterfeit?" That's not a question about elements of X, however, because X is the set of dollar-denominated bills manufactured by the United States Bureau of Engraving and Printing. That agency doesn't manufacture counterfeit bills!

A system that represented bills in X as strings such as $1, $10, $2, and so on would serve your purposes, as long as the strings correctly reflected the bill's face value. This way to represent the elements of X would be *faithful* to your needs. This same system of representing the bills in X might not be faithful to the needs of a bank, however. You can imagine that a bank's theft-insurance contract might require it to keep track of the individual large-denomination bills it handled. Fortunately, the BEP prints identifying numbers on each bill it prints, and those numbers are unique[1] within each denomination and series of issue; representing bills by their series of issue, serial number, and denomination would work for the bank's purpose because it fully distinguishes every individual element of X from every other.

A representation can still be faithful even if it doesn't reflect everything directly. We'll see this in the next example.

Let C be the set of automobiles manufactured in North America since 1980.

One can imagine the need to keep track of many things about cars, but consider just two: the year of manufacture and the amount of gasoline in the car's tank at a particular moment in time. Each can be thought of as a function on the set C: let *year_made(c)* be the year in which car c was made, and let *gas_level(c)* be the function of time that gives us the amount of gasoline in the tank of car c at time *t*, where *t* is between the time the car rolled off the assembly line and now. For actual calculations with numbers, though we'll do none here, we would also indicate the units of measurement, which might be US gallons for an amount of gasoline and coordinated universal time (or UTC) for a moment in time.

These two functions, *year_made* and *gas_level*, are well-defined functions of a car. For a particular car c, the meaning of *year_made(c)* is well-defined. For a given car c, *gas_level(c)* is

---

[1] This is true by design and, let's assume, in practice. In theory, however, the BEP presses can malfunction, and bills could be printed with nonunique, illegible, or multiple serial numbers.

also well-defined. It may be impossible in 2009 to discover the exact value of "the amount of gasoline in this car at midnight on April 9, 2004," but that phrase unambiguously describes a value nonetheless.

Many representations for the set C are faithful for the functions *year_made* and *gas_level*. The VIN, or vehicle identification number, which by law (most) vehicles must have, is one. Another is the car's owner and license plate number. While neither would make *gas_level easy* to calculate, the point is that they would not make it *impossible*. On the other hand, we couldn't use a representation that failed to distinguish every car from every other, as we could for bills.

Note that the representation (owner, license plate number) doesn't reflect the identity of each car directly, in the sense that we can't discover the representation details by studying a car. This indirectness of representation doesn't translate to unfaithfulness, however.

No REAL Faithfulness

Earlier in this chapter, I asked you to hold onto a thought, and we'll return to it now. I said earlier that the data types SQL Server provides for numbers don't faithfully represent the real number system of mathematics. We can now be precise. Here's a simple demonstration in code that the REAL type doesn't represent real number faithfully:

```
DECLARE @a REAL = 0.001;
DECLARE @b REAL = 9876543;
DECLARE @c REAL = 1234567;

SELECT
    @a * (@b * @c) as [a(bc)],
    (@a * @b) * @c as [(ab)c]
```

This code produces the following result:

```
a(bc)          (ab)c
-------------  -------------
1.219325E+10   1.219326E+10
```

Notice that the two result values, which are the results of multiplying the same three numbers in different orders, are slightly different. In other words, while in the "real" real numbers and arithmetic, $a(bc) = (ab)c$, it's not true for SQL Server's representation of the real numbers and arithmetic. This is no slight against SQL Server, and the result conforms to the important IEEE standard for floating-point arithmetic. But computer representations of numbers aren't faithful to arithmetic, and while they suit most needs, they don't answer all questions with the "correct" mathematical answers.

To the extent that degrees of faithfulness exist, SQL Server represents mathematical sets and their operations with a considerable degree of faithfulness, more than it (or most any other programming language) does for numbers and arithmetic.

Russell's Paradox

In about 1901, Bertrand Russell discovered that the informal notion of *set* in mathematics was logically flawed. The informal notion of set takes as axioms (fundamental propositions) that any collection of things is a set and that any criterion can serve to define membership in a set. Russell showed that these axioms were inconsistent because they lead to a contradiction.

> **Note** Russell's discovery doesn't mean the axioms of set theory are false, only that they are incapable of serving to found a consistent mathematical theory.

Russell reasoned as follows: Let U be the set of all sets. Since U is a set and at the same time every set is an element of U, then $U \in U$. Recognizing that the property $U \in U$ was curious, Russell considered the collection of *all* curious sets—sets that contain themselves as elements. Call this set of all curious sets C; we can express C as $\{x \in U : x \in x\}$. Similarly, consider everything else (the set of noncurious sets) NC. Every set is either curious (in which case $x \in x$), or it's not curious (in which case $x \notin x$). Thus, NC = $\{x \in U : x \notin x\}$.

No contradiction so far—sets are either curious or they aren't. But Russell wondered which kind of set NC was. Is NC a curious set, or is it a noncurious set? Because there are only two possibilities, we can explore each one.

Let's explore the possibility first that NC is a curious set. If so, it belongs to the set of all curious sets, which we've called C. In other words, NC$\in$C. But at the same time, if NC is a curious set, it contains itself as an element (that's what *curious* means), so NC$\in$NC. This can't be; NC can't be an element of both C and NC because no set can be both curious and not curious. This possibility led to a contradiction.

Now let's explore the possibility that NC is not a curious set. It's the only possibility left, by the way. Reasoning much as before, if NC is not a curious set, it doesn't contain itself (otherwise, it would be curious). Therefore, NC$\notin$NC. But if NC is not an element of NC, it's not noncurious, which makes it curious. This possibility also led to a contradiction.

Russell's argument has become known as Russell's Paradox. By itself, it's not really a paradox at all; it's a valid demonstration that the informal approach to sets (nowadays called *naïve set theory*) is inconsistent. What does remains something of a paradox is whether a correct theoretical foundation for mathematics exists.

For us, Russell's Paradox underlines the importance of working within a well-defined universal set.

Ordered Pairs, Tuples, and Cartesian Products

An important concept in mathematics—and one that is central to database programming—is that of an ordered pair (a,b). To include ordered pairs in a rigorous treatment of mathematics, there must be a universal set of ordered pairs. This is the Cartesian product.

Ordered Pairs and *k*-Tuples

We will consider *ordered pair* to be a new undefined term, like set. Recall that a particular set is defined by its members and nonmembers; a particular ordered pair is defined by its first part and its second part. We also accept without definition the term *tuple*, or *k-tuple*, for an object that, like an ordered pair, has parts but where there are k parts. An ordered pair is a tuple—in particular, a 2-tuple; (x,y,z,w) is also a tuple—and, in particular, a 4-tuple.

Notation and Definitions for Ordered Pairs and Tuples

If s and t are elements of some domains, (s,t) is called the *ordered pair* with *first part* (or coordinate) s and *second part* (or coordinate) t. Two ordered pairs (s,t) and (x,y) with matching domains are *equal* if their corresponding parts are equal: $s=x$ and $t=y$.

If $s, t, \ldots, r$ are (k-many) elements of some domains, $(s,t,\ldots,r)$ is called an ordered k-tuple. Reference to the parts of $(s,t,\ldots,r)$ and equality for k-tuples follow the analogues for ordered pairs.

Subscript notation is used for the parts of ordered pairs and tuples, when the tuple itself is represented by a single symbol. It's especially convenient when all the parts have a common domain. If r is a k-tuple of real numbers and j is an integer between 1 and k, r_j is a real number and denotes the jth part of r.

The most familiar example of ordered pairs in mathematics, and perhaps the original one, is the usual notation for points in the coordinate plane: (x,y), where x and y are real numbers. The seventeenth-century mathematician René Descartes used this notation, which is now called the Cartesian coordinate system in his honor.

Naming the points in the plane (x,y) works. In the sense we described earlier, this notation faithfully represents the essence of points. Thus, nothing is lost by saying "the point (x,y)" instead of "the point represented by (x,y)."

The set of *all* points in the plane is P = $\{(x,y) : x \in \mathbb{R}$ and $y \in \mathbb{R}\}$. A more compact way to write the set P is $\mathbb{R} \times \mathbb{R}$, which mathematicians understand to mean the same thing and which is called the Cartesian product of $\mathbb{R}$ and $\mathbb{R}$.

The Cartesian Product

A Cartesian product is the domain of discourse for ordered pairs or tuples. Here's the general definition.

Definition of Cartesian Product

Let S and T be sets. The *Cartesian product* of S and T, denoted S×T, is the set {(s,t) : s∈S and t∈T}. If no confusion arises, the terms *S-coordinate* and *T-coordinate* can be used in place of *first coordinate* and *second coordinate*, respectively, for the parts of elements of S×T. The sets S and T are called *factors* (and if needed, the first and second factors, respectively) of S×T.

Cartesian products with more than two factors are defined analogously as sets of tuples, with no distinction made between, for example, *(A×B)×C*, which contains elements of the form *((a,b),c)*, and *A×B×C*, which contains elements of the form *(a,b,c)*.

Note In the definitions for ordered pairs, equality of ordered pairs was defined as coordinate-wise equality on the coordinate parts. Any operation defined on a Cartesian product's factors can similarly be "lifted," or imparted to the elements of S×T. When this is done, the operation is said to be a coordinate-wise operation. In the Cartesian plane, for example, a "coordinate-wise +" operation combines the points *(x,y)* and *(s,t)* to obtain *(x+s,y+t)*. With the exception of the = operator, don't assume a familiar symbol represents a coordinate-wise operation on ordered pairs (or tuples). For example, although |s| means the absolute value of the number s, |(s,t)| does not represent (|s|,|t|).

The Cartesian product is not commutative: *A×B* and *B×A* are not the same when *A* and *B* are different.

The Empty Set(s)

The empty set contains no elements, but what is its universe? If imagining a set of all sets gets us into trouble, a set of all possible elements can only be worse because sets can be elements of sets. As we've seen before, using the word *the* doesn't make something unique. The empty set of integers is the set whose elements are (there are none) and whose nonelements comprise all integers. On the other hand, the empty set of English words is the set whose elements are (there are none) and whose nonelements comprise all English words.

How many empty sets are there? Perhaps my insistence that sets have well-defined domains has backfired and buried us in empty sets! Fortunately, we can declare the question invalid. Our framework only defines equality of things and questions such as "how many?" within some universal set *U*, and no universal set contains "all the empty sets." We do want to know how to interpret any sentence containing the phrase "the empty set," and that we can know.

Definition of the Symbol $\varnothing$

The symbol $\varnothing$ represents the empty set. When the domain of discourse is the universe U, $\varnothing$ represents the subset of U for which $x \in \varnothing$ is false for every x in U.

Note One attempt to resolve Russell's Paradox is to create a tower of universal sets, where the depth of set-within-set-within-set-within-set… nesting is controlled. The nth universal set can only contain elements from the previous universal set, and this prevents any universal set from containing itself.

The Characteristic Function of a Set

Set theory, functions, and logic are intimately connected, and one connection among them is the notion of the characteristic function of a set.

Definition of the Characteristic Function of a Set

If S is a set with universe U, the *characteristic function* of S, denoted $\mathbf{1}_S$, is the function of U, whose value is 1 for elements in S and 0 for elements not in S.[2] As a consequence, the statements $x \in$ S and $\mathbf{1}_S(x) = 1$ are logically equivalent and interchangeable. Similarly, the statement $x \notin$ S is logically equivalent to the statement $\mathbf{1}_S(x) = 0$.

The characteristic function of a set S completely characterizes S. Its domain is the universe U, and the elements of S are precisely the elements x of U for which $\mathbf{1}_S(x) = 1$. As a result, we can define a set by specifying its characteristic function, and this turns out to be particularly useful in some cases.

We now have several ways to describe a set: by description, by enumeration or set-builder notation, by condition, and by characteristic function. For a moment, assume that the domain of discourse is the integers. Here are four definitions of the same subset of the integers.

Description   S is the set of positive even integers.

Enumeration and Set Builder   S = {2, 4, 6, 8, 10, …}, or S = {$2k : k \in \mathbb{Z}^+$}

Condition   S = {$n : n > 0$ and n is an integer multiple of 2}

Characteristic Function   S is the set whose characteristic function is $f(n)$, where $f(n)$ is defined for integers n as follows: If n is negative, odd, or zero, $f(n) = 0$; otherwise, $f(n) = 1$.

---

[2] Another common notation for the characteristic function of S is χ_S, using the Greek letter chi.

Cardinality

Informally, the *cardinality* of a set is the number of elements in the set. For example, the cardinality of {134, −11, 33} is three because there are three elements in the set. Similarly, the cardinality of {} is zero, and the cardinality of {Itzik, Lubor, Dejan, Steve} is four. We have several ways to express the cardinality of a set in words:

The cardinality of S *is four.*

The set S *has cardinality four.*

S *contains four elements.*

Earlier in this chapter, we were careful to point out that sets and depictions of sets are different things. We also noted that it's important to know what the universe is. These details are still important. As sets of integers, {1+1, 5−2, 2+1}, {2, 3, 3}, and {3, 2} all denote the same set: the set containing the two integers 2 and 3, which has cardinality two. As sets of arithmetic expressions, however, they aren't the same; the first contains three elements (because it contains three different expressions), whereas the second and third each contain two elements.

Mathematicians use the shorthand notation $|S|$ for the cardinality of the set S. It's identical to the notation for the absolute value, and context clears up the meaning: if S is a number, $|S|$ is the absolute value of S, and if S is a set, $|S|$ is the cardinality of S.

Formal and Constructive Definitions of Cardinality

Most formal definitions of cardinality use the idea of a one-to-one correspondence. If the elements of S can be put into one-to-one correspondence, or matched up, with the integers from 1 up to k, S is said to be finite and have cardinality k. This works in part because of the rather obvious (but nontrivial to prove) fact that the elements of a set can be matched up with the integers from 1 to k for at most one value of k. The formal definition of cardinality in terms of correspondence lends itself to an effective treatment of infinite sets.

For finite sets, we can give a constructive definition of cardinality in terms of characteristic functions. Recall that every set S is characterized by a function $\mathbf{1}_S$ (the characteristic function or membership function or S), where $\mathbf{1}_S(x)$ is defined and equal to either 0 or 1 for each x in the universe for S.

Definition: Let S be a finite set with universe U. The cardinality of S is defined to be the sum of the values $\mathbf{1}_S(x)$. In other words, $|S| := \sum_{x \in U} \mathbf{1}_S(x)$

A number of useful results about cardinality follow from this definition and earlier results about characteristic functions.

> ## A Simple Result about Cardinality
> The cardinality of the empty set is zero: $|\varnothing| = 0$. Recall that $\mathbf{1}_{\varnothing}(x)$ always equals zero. Therefore, $|\varnothing|$ is a sum of zeros and equals zero.

Order

If I asked you to put the numbers 12.4, 5.2, 16.0, and 0.7 into numerical order, you'd list them this way: 0.7, 5.2, 12.4, 16.0. Similarly, if I asked you to alphabetize the names Itzik, Steve, Dejan, and Lubor, you'd list them in the following order: Dejan, Itzik, Lubor, Steve. In each case, you can do this because given two different names (or numbers), it's always the case that one of them precedes the other, and you know the rule.

A set of values can be put into order when we have an appropriate notion of *is less than*, *comes before*, or *precedes*. In this section, we'll investigate notions of precedence, and in particular, we'll identify what properties allow us to use a given definition of precedence to put things in order. Mathematically, *precedes* (for a given universe, such as numbers or names) is a Boolean-valued function of two variables, where the domain of each variable is the given universe.

Numerical Order

When we talk about numerical order, *precedes* means *is less than*, and *x is less than y* is usually written as $x<y$. With regard to real numbers, everyone agrees on the meaning of $<$. We say $x<y$ if and only if $y-x$ is a positive number.

> **Note** The astute reader might catch the fact that this definition of $<$ is problematic because we haven't defined the term *positive*. In fact, we haven't defined a lot of things, such as what the number 5.2 means, for example. Fortunately, as long as you and I agree on the rules of arithmetic and simple notions like *positive*, we'll be fine. A thorough development of the real number system is well beyond the scope of this chapter.

Alphabetical Order

When we talk about alphabetical order, the meaning of precedes is culture dependent. In most programming languages, the precedes operator for strings is denoted $<$, just like it is for numbers. And in most programming languages and cultures, alphabetical order would provide that Dejan $<$ Itzik, Itzik $<$ Lubor, and Lubor $<$ Steve. However, there's often no consensus among cultures about alphabetical order, and it's often not obvious what cultural rules the < operator is using. In T-SQL, you can sometimes apply cultural rules explicitly by specifying a *collation*, as I've done in the following example:

```
DECLARE @Names TABLE (
  name VARCHAR(20)
);

INSERT INTO @Names VALUES
  ('DeSzmetch'),('DESZMETCH'),('DESZMETCK'),('DesZmetch'),('deszmetch');

SELECT
  name,
  RANK() OVER (ORDER BY name COLLATE Latin1_General_BIN) AS [Lat...BIN],
  RANK() OVER (ORDER BY name COLLATE Traditional_Spanish_CI_AS) AS [Tra...CI_AS],
  RANK() OVER (ORDER BY name COLLATE Latin1_General_CS_AS) AS [Lat...CS_AS],
  RANK() OVER (ORDER BY name COLLATE Latin1_General_CI_AS) AS [Lat...CI_AS],
  RANK() OVER (ORDER BY name COLLATE Hungarian_CI_AS) AS [Hun..._CI_AS]
FROM @Names
ORDER BY name COLLATE Latin1_General_BIN;
```

This is the output:

```
name        Lat...BIN   Tra...CI_AS Lat...CS_AS Lat...CI_AS Hun..._CI_AS
----------  ----------- ----------- ----------- ----------- ------------
DESZMETCH   1           2           4           1           2
DESZMETCK   2           1           5           5           5
DeSzmetch   3           2           3           1           2
DesZmetch   4           2           2           1           1
deszmetch   5           2           1           1           2
```

As you can see from the output, there's no single correct way to rank the names DeSzmetch, DESZMETCH, DESZMETCK, DesZmetch, and deszmetch in alphabetical order.

Note in particular that alphabetical order doesn't necessarily order strings in a character-by-character fashion. In the language of T-SQL, understand that you cannot expect these two ORDER BY clauses to produce the same results, even though for some collations they will:

```
ORDER BY string;

ORDER BY
  SUBSTRING(string,1,1),
  SUBSTRING(string,2,1),
  ...
```

Trichotomy

Given two real numbers x and y, x is either less than, equal to, or greater than y. This fundamental property of the real numbers, that exactly one of $x<y$, $x=y$, and $x>y$ is always true, is known as the *law of trichotomy*.

Induced Order

The comparison operator < is what allows us to put real numbers into order—to sort them. Another way to say this is to say that the usual ordering of the real numbers is the ordering *induced* by the < operator.

By this point, you should be suspicious every time I use the word *the*, and I used it in the previous sentence in *the ordering*. Not every comparison operator on a set of things induces a well-defined ordering, or an ordering at all, but less-than for numbers does.

A Trichotomous > That Doesn't Induce an Ordering

In the game rock-paper-scissors, the rules say that rock beats scissors, paper beats rock, and scissors beat paper. The idea of *beats* is a comparison, so we could define the > operator on the set {rock, paper, scissors} to mean *beats*, according to the game's rules. It shouldn't take you long to realize that it's not possible to order rock, paper, and scissors from "best to worst" according to the > operator. In this case, then, "the ordering induced by the > operator" is not well-defined.

The < operator for real numbers induces what mathematicians call a *total order*. To induce a total order, a comparison operator not only has to be trichotomous but also has to be antisymmetric and transitive. We'll take a look at these properties later.

Ordinal Numbers

Earlier, I defined cardinality for finite sets. In particular, I observed that cardinality was well-defined. The question "The set S contains how many elements?" asks for a well-defined answer, which might be "The set S contains 10 elements." Notice how this question about cardinality and the sentence that answered it follow the pattern illustrated in Table 2-6.

TABLE 2-6 A Question Answered by a Cardinal Number

Description	Sentence
Question sentence	The set S contains how many elements?
Question-word identified	The set S contains *how many* elements?
Question-word replaced by a fill-in-the-blank	The set S contains _____ elements?
Blank filled in to produce the answer sentence	The set S contains 47 elements.
Mathematical version of the question	Solve for n: $|S| = n$.

Given a set S, the question in this case ("The set S contains how many elements?") has a well-defined right answer. That's because the cardinality function, which answers "how many elements" questions about sets, is a well-defined function. Numbers that answer a *how many* question are called *cardinal numbers* in mathematics because they express the cardinality of a set. The finite cardinal numbers are exactly the nonnegative integers, by the way, although there are many different infinite cardinal numbers. Infinite sets are not all infinite in the same way, one could say. Unfortunately, we won't have a chance to look into that fascinating corner of mathematics here.

Table 2-7 offers the same analysis of a similar question and its answer.

TABLE 2-7 A Question Answered by an Ordinal Number

Description	Sentence
Question sentence	The number x appears in the list L in what position?
Question-word identified	The number x appears in the list L in *what* position?
Question-word replaced by a fill-in-the-blank	The number x appears in the list L in _____ position?
Blank filled in to produce the answer sentence	The number x appears in the list L in the 47th position.
Mathematical version of the question	None (explanation to follow).

In the answer I gave, the number 47 (or the word *47th*) is an *ordinal number*. In mathematics, an ordinal number is a number that can represent a position in order (as opposed to a cardinality). In the finite realm, the ordinal numbers and the cardinal numbers are the same, but we still have a reason to look at them separately.

Whichth One?

An easier way to ask for the position of x in the list L is this:

Whichth number in L *is x?*

The only problem is this: *whichth* isn't a word. But what a useful word it (and *whenth*) would be! If a new acquaintance mentioned that she had six siblings, you could ask *whichth* oldest she was. You could ask some one *whenth* they arrived at work this morning, if you wanted to find out if they arrived first, second, third, or so on, as opposed to what time they arrived. Or in *whichth* place their daughter's team finished in the soccer league this season.

You can ask these questions directly in Chinese, it turns out, because (roughly speaking) there's a word for *th*: 第. Just as you can find out how many of something there are by asking "how many" (几个?) there are, you can find out the position of something by asking whichth (第几个?) one it is. It's amazing that English has no word for whichth.

Notice that I didn't give a mathematical version of the ordinal number question, nor have I defined a notation for the ordinal number representing x's position in L. The cardinal number question about S had a simple answer $|S|$. One reason we have no "ordinality" function is that the notion isn't well-defined. While x may indeed appear in the 47th position of the list L, it may also appear in the 46th position. Other values of x may not appear in the list at all. Cardinality is well-defined but not "ordinality," at least not in a way that's simply analogous.

SQL, however, provides functions for both cardinality (COUNT) and ordinal position (ROW_NUMBER, RANK, and DENSE_RANK). If the elements of L are ordered by their *xCol* value, and @*x* is one of the values in the column *xCol*, all of @*x*'s position(s) in L can be retrieved with this query:

```
WITH T AS (
  SELECT
    ROW_NUMBER() OVER (ORDER BY xCol) as rn,
    xCol
  FROM L
)
  SELECT rn
  FROM T
  WHERE xCol = @x
```

The two rank functions answer a more precise question, and that question, unlike the question "What is the row number of *x*?," is well-defined.

Set Operators

Arithmetic operators such as $+$, $\geq$, and $-$ are surely familiar to you. Some of them, like $+$, combine numbers and give a numerical result as in the expression $4+11$ (which equals 15). Others, like $\geq$, express relationships. When these operators appear between numbers, the resulting expression yields a truth value, not another number. For example, $\geq$ expresses the relationship "greater than or equal to." The value of the expression $5\geq5$ is true, and $-8\geq-5$ is false.

The algebra of sets includes its own collection of useful operators. Like the operators of arithmetic, some of the set operators combine two sets and yield a set, while others express relationships and yield a truth value. I'll define the most important set operators in this section, and because the notation for these operators isn't universal, as it is for the operators of arithmetic, I'll mention alternate notations or definitions when they exist.

Definition of Subset

Let A and B be sets with the same universe *U*. The set A is called a *subset* of B (denoted $A \subseteq B$) if every element of A is an element of B. Either of the following can also be used as the definition:

$A \subseteq B$ if and only if $\mathbf{1}_A(x) \leq \mathbf{1}_B(x)$.

$A \subseteq B$ if and only if for every $x \in U$, $(x \in A \rightarrow x \in B)$.

Note The subset relation is sometimes denoted as $\subset$, but for some authors, $A \subset B$ means something different: that A is a *proper* subset of B (a subset of B that is not equal to B).

The following results follow from the definition of subset:

- The empty set is a subset of any set: For any set S, $\varnothing \subseteq S$. This follows easily from the fact that $\mathbf{1}_\varnothing(x) = 0$ for all $x \in U$.

- If $A \subseteq B$, then $|A| \leq |B|$. From earlier results about characteristic functions, the terms in the sum for $|B|$ are each less than or equal to the corresponding term in the sum for $|A|$. Note that conversely, $|A| \leq |B|$ does *not* imply that $A \subseteq B$.

Definition of Set Complement

Let S be a set with universe U. The *complement* of S, denoted S^C, is the set containing those elements of U that are not elements of S. Either of the following properties of the complement of S can also be used as the definition:

The characteristic function of S^C is the function $f(x) = 1 - \mathbf{1}_S(x)$.

$S^C = \{x \in U : x \notin S\}$.

> **Note** The complement of S is sometimes denoted as S' or $\overline{S}$.

Several results follow from the definition of the complement:

- Every element of U is an element of S or an element of S^C but not both.

- The complement of the complement of S is S: $(S^C)^C = S$.

- The complement of the entire domain of discourse U is the empty set: $U^C = \varnothing$, and the complement of the empty set is the entire domain of discourse U: $\varnothing^C = U$.

Union and Intersection

Given two sets with the same universe, we may need to consider the single set of elements contained in either set. This is the union of the sets. Similarly, we may wish to consider the set of elements contained in both sets. This is the intersection of the sets.

Definitions of Union and Intersection

Let A and B be sets with the same universe U.

The *union* of A and B, denoted $A \cup B$, is the set containing those elements of U that are either elements of A or elements of B (or elements of both). Either of the following can also be used as the definition:

$\mathbf{1}_{A \cup B}(x) = max(\mathbf{1}_A(x), \mathbf{1}_B(x))$.

$A \cup B = \{x \in U : x \in A \text{ or } x \in B\}$.

Let A and B be sets with the same universe U.

The *intersection* of A and B, denoted A∩B, is the set containing those elements of U that are both elements of A and elements of B. Either of the following can also be used as the definition:

$$\mathbf{1}_{A\cap B}(x)= min(\mathbf{1}_A(x),\mathbf{1}_B(x)).$$

$A∩B = \{x \in U : x \in A \text{ and } x \in B\}.$

Set Difference

Sometimes, we may wish to consider those elements of a set that are *not* elements of a second set. The set difference operator gives us the result.

Definition of Set Difference

Let A and B be sets with the same universe U.

The *set difference* of A and B, denoted A\B, is the set containing those elements of U that both elements of A and non-elements of B. Either of the following are equivalent and can be used as the definition:

$$\mathbf{1}_{A\backslash B}(x)= max(0,\mathbf{1}_A(x)-\mathbf{1}_B(x)).$$

$A\backslash B = A∩B^c.$

$A\backslash B = \{x \in U : x \in A \text{ and } x \notin B\}.$

Set Partitions

Given a set S with universal set U, and an element $x \in U$, x is either in S or S^C, but not both. The two sets S and S^C are said to *partition* U, and $\{S,S^C\}$ is called a *partition* of U. Note that the word partition is used both as a verb and as a noun. More generally, a collection of sets partitions S if every element of S is in exactly one of the sets.

Definition of Set Partition

Let S be a set, and let $A_1, A_2, \ldots, A_k$ be subsets of S. The sets $A_1, A_2, \ldots, A_k$ partition S, and $\{A_1, A_2, \ldots, A_k\}$ is a *partition* of S, if the following two conditions hold:

The union of the sets A_i is S.

The sets A_i and A_j are disjoint whenever $i \neq j$.

Sets with the latter property are called *pairwise disjoint*.

If $\{A_1, A_2, ..., A_k\}$ is a partition of S, the answer to "In which A_i is the element x?" is well-defined.

We've already seen one example of a partition: Given a set S with universe U, the sets S and S^C partition U.

Generalizations of Set Theory

An understanding of basic set theory is a great help, but it's important to recognize its limitations in describing the world, and in the case of this book, T-SQL querying. I've already addressed some of the ways in which mathematics fails to represent the world precisely, but one generalization of set theory is particularly relevant to databases.

Multiset Theory

It's a mathematical fact that the sets {2, 8, 4, −4}, {−4, 8, 4, 2}, and {2, 4, 2, 8, −4, 8, 2, 4, −4} are equal, but you would probably agree that the last set listed "contains three twos." Of course, a set S of numbers can't "contain three twos." It can either contain a two or not contain a two. If it contains a two, $\mathbf{1}_S(2) = 1$. If it doesn't, $\mathbf{1}_S(2) = 0$, and nothing else is possible.

It's possible to accommodate the idea of "multiple membership" in set theory, except that it would no longer be set theory, it would be *multiset theory*, sometimes known as the *theory of bags*. The simplest way to begin developing a theory of multisets is by generalizing the characteristic function.

> ### The Multiplicity Function of a Bag
>
> If B is a bag (or multiset) with universe U, the *multiplicity function* of B, denoted $\mathbf{M}_B$, is the function on U that tells how many copies of an element B contains.

Many definitions from set theory extend almost unchanged to bag theory if the characteristic function is replaced by the multiplicity function. For example, the multiplicity function of an intersection can be taken to be the minimum of the multiplicity functions. Other notions are far more problematic. It's not clear how to define a multiset's complement, for example. Should universal sets contain an unlimited number of each of their elements, and should the complement of any finite multiset be infinite? Because set cardinalities have more than one "size" of infinity, which size should be used for multisets?

The problems with multiset theory often lead database theoreticians to outlaw duplicate rows within a table—for example, by requiring primary key constraints. It's harder to prevent result sets from containing duplicates, however. This would require changing the meaning of SELECT to what is now written as SELECT DISTINCT, and this would create other complications, particularly with aggregates. T-SQL, like most SQL dialects, supports multisets in most places but not everywhere. T-SQL, for example, doesn't support EXCEPT ALL and INTERSECT ALL, only EXCEPT DISTINCT and INTERSECT DISTINCT.

Predicate Logic

Predicate logic is a mathematical framework for representing and manipulating expressions that are true or false: facts and falsehoods.

Logic-Like Features of Programming Languages

T-SQL, like many programming languages, incorporates true-false expressions and logical operators in several places, not all of which are, strictly speaking, related to predicate logic.

> **Note** A true-false expression is called a *Boolean* expression (after the logician George Boole). Boolean logic begins with the study of Boolean expressions.

The Keyword IF in Control-of-Flow Statements

Although the focus of this book is on T-SQL's query language, and SQL's central (or at least most interesting) paradigm is set based, "regular" programming based on decision and repetition is also implemented. For example, many of this book's code samples begin with a conditional statement to delete an object if it already exists. You encountered this statement in Chapter 1, "Logical Query Processing":

```
IF OBJECT_ID('dbo.Orders') IS NOT NULL DROP TABLE dbo.Orders;
```

This is a valid T-SQL statement, and it conforms to the syntax SQL Server Books Online gives for an IF...ELSE statement:

```
IF Boolean_expression { sql_statement | statement_block }
[ELSE { sql_statement | statement_block } ]
```

The Boolean expression is *OBJECT_ID('dbo.Orders') IS NOT NULL,* and the *sql_statement* is *DROP TABLE dbo.Orders.*

The way in which a program implements decision making or repetition is often referred to as the program's *logic.* Formal logic, however, isn't about what happens when a program runs, nor is it about the way in which programs implement algorithms to solve problems.

In particular, the expression *if <this> then <that>* in formal logic bears nothing more than a superficial resemblance to the statement *IF <this> THEN <that>* in a programming language. The former is a sentence that in its entirety is either true or false; the latter is an instruction to produce behavior that depends on whether *<this>* (not the entire statement) is true or false.

While formal logic might not have anything to say about an IF statement in SQL, it has plenty to say about one particular element of an IF statement: the part that SQL Server Books Online calls the *Boolean_expression* and that I called *<this>* in the preceding paragraph. Boolean expressions appear in other control-of-flow structures, such as SQL's WHILE loop. Additionally, logic provides a framework that allows us to validate programs—to determine whether they in fact express the desired intent and produce the correct control-of-flow.

Propositions and Predicates

Propositions and predicates are types of Boolean expressions: expressions that evaluate to one of the two truth values in Boolean logic: True or False.

> ### Definitions of Proposition and Predicate
>
> A *proposition* is a statement that is either true or false. A *predicate* is a proposition that contains one or more variables or parameters; in other words, a predicate is a parameterized proposition. Both propositions and predicates are Boolean expressions.

For example, "12 + 7 = 21" is a proposition (it happens to be false). "It is raining" is also a proposition, although its truth value depends on context and interpretation. "It is raining" answers the question "Is it raining?" For the question to have an answer of yes or no, context must provide the answers to "Where?" and "When?", and the interpretation of "raining" must be specific enough to yield a clear yes or no answer.

> **Note** In fact, the truth value of "12 + 7 = 21" also depends on context and interpretation. It depends on the interpretation of the symbols 12, +, 7, =, and 21. If this statement were made in the context of a lecture on octal arithmetic, the interpretations of 12 and 21 would be ten and seventeen, respectively, and the statement would be true. Alternatively, if 12 + 7 = 21 were part of a logic puzzle about an alternate universe where mathematical symbols were interpreted differently, the truth value might be different.
>
> Don't forget the importance of context. I've seen plenty of unwelcome T-SQL surprises from propositions like *(OrderDate > '12/01/04')*. In the United States, *'12/01/04'* represents December 1, 2004, but in most of the rest of the world, it represents January 4, 2012. If you need to express the 2004 date in a context-free way, this is one option: *'2004-12-01T00:00:00.000'*.

Some propositions, while clearly true or false, may depend on more than one fact. For example, "Panama and Norway are members of the United Nations" is true because Panama is a member of the United Nations and Norway is a member of the United Nations. The proposition "Either the earth travels around the sun or the sun travels around the earth" is true because the earth travels around the sun.

Other propositions assert the existence or universality of facts in a collection. For example, "Every order has been shipped" asserts many facts at once. "Someone is logged into the system" asserts the existence of at least one fact. Database programming languages such as SQL are well equipped to handle these kinds of statements, though some can be expressed more directly than others. As a tool, formal logic helps us express assertions like these precisely, construct SQL statements to evaluate them, and build confidence in our code's correctness.

Boolean Expressions in T-SQL

Boolean expressions appear in the syntax of several T-SQL statements. Most important, Boolean expressions follow the keywords WHERE, ON, and HAVING to help filter a query's result set and in CHECK constraints to provide data integrity. Boolean expressions also follow the keywords IF and WHILE to control program flow and repetition, and they appear in the CASE WHEN expression.

Proposition or Predicate?

I defined a *proposition* as a statement that has a specific truth value. The expression $x<3$ contains a variable and has no fixed truth value and is therefore a predicate, not a proposition. On the other hand, the expression $x<3+x$ also contains a variable, but it does have a fixed truth value, or at least it seems to in the context of real numbers. Unlike for $x<3$, the truth of $x<3+x$ doesn't depend on the value of x. Does this make $x<3+x$ a proposition?

The name doesn't really matter. It's more important to understand what things mean, not what to call them. When we say that $x<3+x$ is true, we mean that it's true *for all x-values*. We could also consider whether $x<3$ is true *for all x-values*, and our conclusion would be that it's not. In the same sense that $x<3+x$ is true, then $x<3$ is false, but we aren't usually so quick to assign a single truth value to the expression $x<3$. New terms are sometimes used to distinguish situations like this: $x<3+x$ might be called an *identity*, and $x<3$ might be called an *equation* or *inequality*. These words can be useful, but they aren't easy to define rigorously.

No matter how we name expressions, recognizing things that are implied or hidden—such as *for all x-values*—is useful and sometimes crucial. Perhaps the most ubiquitous example of something hidden or implied is a dependence on time. As I type this sentence, I can say truthfully that George W. Bush is the president of the United States. As you read the sentence, however, my assertion is not true. There is a hidden dependence on time, and an understanding that adds "right now" to the proposition.

Creating Propositions from Predicates

It's important to understand that any predicate with one variable x can be transformed into a proposition by preceding it with "For every x in the universe of discourse, ..." The process of taking the open sentence $P(x)$ and turning it into "For every x in the domain of discourse, $P(x)$

is true" is called *universal quantification*. Although there's an *x* in "For every *x* in the domain of discourse, *P(x)* is true," the truth value of the sentence doesn't depend on a value of *x*. In fact, you can't even plug in a value of *x*.

Universal quantification is one of three important ways to create a proposition from an open sentence. Another is *existential quantification*, preceding the proposition with "There exists at least one value of *x* in the domain of discourse for which." The following quantified statement is true: "There exists at least one real number *x* for which *x* < 3."

A third way to create a proposition out of an open sentence is to provide a specific value for the variable. If *P(x)* is the statement *x*<3, then *P(2.5)* is the statement "2.5<3", and is true. *P(8)*, however, is false.

Ways to Give a Truth Value to a Predicate

Let *P(x)* be a predicate, and let *U* be the universe of discourse for values of *x*. Also let *z* be a particular element of *U*. Then each of the following is a proposition:

- *P(x)* is true for every *x*∈*U*. This is notated as: ∀*x*∈*U*, *P(x)*.

- *P(x)* is true for at least one *x*∈*U*. This is notated as: ∃*x*∈*U* such that *P(x)*.

- *P(z)*

The formalism doesn't prevent mathematicians and others from asserting the truth of something like *x*<*x*+3. But when a mathematician asserts the truth of *x*<*x*+3, it's understood that she means ∀*x*∈*U*, *x*<*x*+3.

It's also common practice not to specify the quantifier in the case of if-then statements. If the universe of discourse is the set of integers, the statement "If *n* is positive, then $n^2 > n$" is understood to mean this: For all integers *n*, (*n* is positive → $n^2 > n$).

The Law of Excluded Middle

The law of excluded middle requires that every well-formed proposition is either true or false—that there are two truth values and no more. The word *middle* means some middle ground on the true-false scale that is neither true nor false. We take the law of excluded middle as a principle of logic.

The law of excluded middle is what allows mathematicians to prove theorems with the technique known as *proof by contradiction*.

And, Or, and Not

If *P* and *Q* are propositions, they can be combined using logical operators to form other propositions. For example, the logical expression *P*∧*Q* (spoken as *P and Q*) is also a proposition, and its truth value depends on the truth values of P and Q. This operator, *logical and*, is one of four basic logical operators.

Definitions of the Basic Logical Operators

Let P and Q be propositions. The three most basic logical operators are defined in Table 2-8.

TABLE 2-8 Definitions of Logical Operators

Operator	Notation	Meaning	True if and Only if:	Alternate Name
Not	$\neg P$	Not P	P is false.	Negation
And	$P \wedge Q$	P and Q	Both P and Q are true.	Conjunction
Or	$P \vee Q$	P or Q (or both)	At least one of P and Q is true.	Disjunction

---

Note that conjunction and disjunction are commutative operators: the positions of P and Q can be interchanged without changing the truth value.

What Not Is Not

Combining and transforming mathematical sentences with logical operators is important, and generally straightforward. However, as is often the case in life, what seems simplest is what causes the most trouble because we tend to be less careful about it. Applying the logical operator *not*, or negating propositions, is not something to do lightly. All too often, it seems right (but isn't) to negate a proposition by negating everything in sight or by using an invalid generalization. Here's one example: the negation of the proposition $x<3$ is $x \geq 3$. On the other hand, the negation of $-1<x<3$ is *not* $-1 \geq x \geq 3$. (What is the correct negation?)

When And Means Or

In English and other natural languages, the words *and* and *or* are used in a wide variety of situations. In some of these situations they have meanings that seem to contradict their meanings as logical operators. Because of this, you should never be hasty when you attempt to express a real-world notion logically.

In the WHERE clause of a query, combining conditions with AND serves to make the number of rows in the result set smaller. However, the English *and* often corresponds not to the AND of a query's WHERE clause but to the logical operator OR or the set operator UNION.

Consider the following English request:

Please bring me the latest invoices for customer 45 and customer 17.

This doesn't translate into the query predicate *custid=45 AND custid=17.* Instead, it probably translates into the query predicate *custid=45 OR custid=17.* On the other hand, this English request doesn't follow the same pattern:

Please bring me the latest recipes for ham and eggs.

Exclusive Or

In English, when *or* doesn't mean *and*, it still doesn't always mean the same thing as logical *or*. Logical *or* means one or the other or possibly both. Sometimes the English word means one or the other *but not both*, which in a mathematical discussion is distinguished by the name *exclusive or*. An example of this can be found on many restaurant menus in the phrase "includes soup or salad."

Logical Equivalence

Two value expressions of any kind are considered equal if they have the same value: 3+3 equals 6. Expressions that contain variables are considered equal if they are equal for any particular variable values: Regardless of what x, y, and z happen to be, $\{x,y,z\} = \{a,x,y,z\} \cap \{b,x,y,z\}$. Predicates, which are logical propositions containing variables, are said to be logically equivalent if they have the same truth value for any particular values of their variables. Several different symbols are used to represent logical equivalence and some very similar notions. I won't get into any of the subtleties, and from among the possible symbols, which include $\equiv$, $\leftrightarrow$, and $\Leftrightarrow$, I'll use the last one, the bidirectional double arrow.

DeMorgan's Laws

Logical expressions can be rewritten as equivalent logical expressions in a number of ways. Two of the most useful and important identities provide ways to rewrite negations, and they are called DeMorgan's Laws, after Augustus DeMorgan.

Statement of DeMorgan's Laws

Let P and Q be propositions. Then the following equivalences hold:

$\neg(P \vee Q) \Leftrightarrow (\neg P) \wedge (\neg Q)$.

$\neg(P \wedge Q) \Leftrightarrow (\neg P) \vee (\neg Q)$.

Logical Implication

Mathematical logic was developed largely as an attempt to justify the way in which mathematicians prove theorems through inference and deduction. One of the most important rules of inference is called *modus ponens*. Modus ponens is the rule of inference that allows us to infer the truth of one proposition Q from the truth of another proposition P when it's known that P implies Q. An argument using modus ponens might go like this: "The law is clear: if you drive faster than 55 miles per hour on this highway, you have broken the law. You were driving faster than 55 miles per hour, therefore you have broken the law."

Logical inference isn't the focus of this chapter, but we will take a moment to consider propositions that take the form of logical implication.

If *P*, Then *Q*

Suppose *P* and *Q* are valid logical propositions. Then *if P, then Q* is a valid logical proposition. The proposition *if P, then Q* is denoted $P \rightarrow Q$, and its truth value depends on the truth values of *P* and *Q* as follows.

> ### Definition of $P \rightarrow Q$
>
> The proposition $P \rightarrow Q$, read *P implies Q* or *if P, then Q*, is true when either *P* is false or *Q* is true (or both). The proposition $P \rightarrow Q$ is false when *P* is true and *Q* is false. More concisely, $(P \rightarrow Q) \Leftrightarrow (\neg P \vee Q)$.

There is more than one way to express an implication in words, and in mathematical logic, the following expressions are taken to have the precise meanings shown:

1. *P* unless *Q* means $(\neg Q) \rightarrow P$.
2. *P* only if *Q* means $P \rightarrow Q$.
3. *P*, if *Q* means $Q \rightarrow P$.

Note that unlike the logical operators $\wedge$ and $\vee$, the operator $\rightarrow$ is not commutative. The truth values of $P \rightarrow Q$ and $Q \rightarrow P$ are not necessarily the same.

The Contrapositive

The definition $(P \rightarrow Q) \Leftrightarrow (\neg P \vee Q)$, together with DeMorgan's law for negating conjunctions, yields the following fact: $(P \rightarrow Q) \Leftrightarrow (\neg Q \rightarrow \neg P)$. The implication *If not Q, then not P* is called the contrapositive of *If P then Q*. In mathematics, it's often easier to discover rules of inference that validate the contrapositive form of an implication, and doing so is called *proof by contrapositive*.

Vacuous Truths

According to the definition of logical implication, the statement $P \rightarrow Q$ holds except when *P* is true and *Q* is false. In particular, it holds whenever *P* is false, regardless of the truth value of *Q*. As a result, some if-then statements are logically true but may sound false or seem puzzling. For example, these propositions are both true:

If 1=0, the moon is made of cheese.

If the real number x is negative and positive, then x equals 11.

In both propositions, the *if* part of the implication is false, so the entire if-then statement is true. Because implications figure prominently in logical inference, we're accustomed to encountering implications in a context where the *if* part is true, and the implication allows the *then* part to be deduced. This isn't the case in the preceding statements. No inference is possible, and the statements provide no information about the truth value of the *then* part.

An implication $P \to Q$ is called *vacuously true* if P is false. Similarly, the quantified statement $\forall x \in U\ (P(x) \to Q(x))$ is called vacuously true if $P(x)$ is false for all values of x in its domain of discourse. The reason for this terminology is simple: the statement $\forall x \in U\ (P(x) \to Q(x))$ asserts that $Q(x)$ holds whenever $P(x)$ holds. If $P(x)$ never holds, the statement asserts nothing at all.

Quantification

Statements that assert either the universality or the existence of some fact over a universe of discourse are called *quantified statements*. Here's an example of each kind. The words in italic are the ones that indicate quantification.

Universally quantified statement   The Philharmonic has performed *every* Haydn symphony.

Existentially quantified statement   The Philharmonic Orchestra has performed *a* Haydn symphony.

Negating Quantified Statements

The ability to negate quantified statements is a valuable skill for programmers, especially SQL programmers. As Itzik shows later in this book, some problems are easier to solve when analyzed using reverse logic. Instead of finding all the answers to a question, find everything that *isn't not* an answer.

Earlier in the chapter, I warned you that to negate a proposition, you can't simply negate everything in sight. The logical opposite of an advertising claim that "all our books are discounted" is not "all our books are not discounted," nor is it "none of our books are discounted," nor is it "all our nonbooks are discounted." The actual logical opposite—which expresses simply that the claim is false—is "it is not true that all our books are discounted," or equivalently, "at least one of our books is not discounted." While we might also say this more simply as "not all our books are discounted," this use of "not all" invites misinterpretation or at least mistranslation when translated into a computer program.

Two general principles concern the negation of quantified statements. Universally quantified statements are false if there is one exception to the universal claim they make. Existentially quantified statements are false if there are no examples of the existence they claim.

Generally, universal statements may be hard to prove (because their validity must be verified universally) but easy to disprove (because one exception violates the universality). On the other hand, existential statements may be easy to prove (only one valid example is enough) but hard to disprove (because everything must be proven invalid).

Here are the rules for negating quantified propositions, using notation. Recall that $\forall$ means *for all*, and $\exists$ means *there exists*.

Rules for negating quantified predicates

Let *P(x)* and *Q(x)* be predicates, where *U* is the domain for *x*.

$\neg(\forall x \in U, P(x)) \Leftrightarrow \exists x \in U$ for which $\neg P(x)$

$\forall x \in U, P(x) \Leftrightarrow \neg(\exists x \in U$ for which $\neg P(x))$

$\neg(\exists x \in U$ for which $P(x)) \Leftrightarrow \forall x \in U, \neg P(x)$

$\exists x \in U$ for which $P(x) \Leftrightarrow \neg(\forall x \in U, \neg P(x))$

These rules generalize DeMorgan's Laws. If $U=\{a,b,c,...\}$, to say that *P(x)* is true for all elements of *U* is to say that *P(a)*, *P(b)*, *P(c)*, ... are all true, or equivalently, that the conjunction $P(a) \wedge P(b) \wedge P(c) \wedge ...$ is true. Similarly, to say that there exists at least one value *x* in *U* for which *P(x)* is true is to say that either *P(a)* or *P(b)* or *P(c)* or ... is true, or equivalently, that $P(a) \vee P(b) \vee P(c) \vee ...$ is true.

Multiple Quantification

This chapter's first example contained two quantifiers. The membership condition for the set *S* was $\forall e \in USAEmployees$ ($\exists o \in Orders : (handled(e,o,c)))$, hence the condition for *c* not to be a member of *S* was this: $\neg(\forall e \in USAEmployees$ ($\exists o \in Orders : (handled(e,o,c))))$.

The rules for negating quantified propositions allow us to rewrite this condition as follows:

$\neg(\forall e \in USAEmployees$ ($\exists o \in Orders : (handled(e,o,c))))$

$\Leftrightarrow \exists e \in USAEmployees$ for which $\neg(\exists o \in Orders : (handled(e,o,c)))$

$\Leftrightarrow \exists e \in USAEmployees$ for which ($\forall o \in Orders, \neg handled(e,o,c))$

Each version gives the condition for not returning a particular customer *c*, and the last one can be expressed in English this way: There is some employee *e* from the USA for whom we can say this about every order *o* of the company: it is not the case that *o* was handled by employee *e* for customer *c*.

Alternatives and Generalizations

There a number of alternatives and generalizations to predicate logic. Some model true-false statements differently, and others handle more general notions of truth. In this section, I'll briefly mention one alternative framework and two generalizations to predicate logic.

Boolean Algebra

It's possible—and for many purposes very useful—to place logic into a framework where the truth values True and False are associated with the numbers 1 and 0, respectively. In fact, SQL Server's integer data type BIT is often used for logical calculations. SQL Server provides several integer operators, &, ~, ^, and |, that apply calculations bitwise, or separately on the individual bits that make up the integer's internal representation. Loosely, these four operators correspond to *and*, *not*, *exclusive or*, and *or*, respectively. As you might guess, T-SQL's ^ operator is easily confused with the operator ∧, which is used in logic to mean *and*. In addition (no pun intended), the bitwise operator & is easily confused with arithmetic's + operator.

Three-Valued Logic

In the real world, not every important question can be answered. In this very brief treatment of three-valued logic, we'll see what happens if we abandon the law of excluded middle and allow a third truth value in addition to the Boolean values True and False.

T-SQL supports Boolean values only for predicates in SQL statements, not as persisted data in a table. However, T-SQL, like most database query languages, supports three truth values: True, False, and UNKNOWN.

To some extent, a third truth value representing UNKNOWN can be accommodated in propositional logic. Recall the law of excluded middle. It states that for any proposition P, the proposition (P is true or P is false) holds. The law of excluded middle doesn't address the discoverability of P's truth value; it only asserts that P has one. In the real world, however, the discoverability of truth matters, and the need for a third truth value comes up in the context of missing information.

Missing information can cause havoc in a business setting. Suppose you find an empty folder among your customer files; you know a customer file should be there, but the file is missing, and you have no way to identify the missing customer.

All at once, it becomes impossible to answer a multitude of questions: How many customers are in arrears? Is Maria Cameron already a customer (assuming she isn't found in any of the nonmissing files)? These questions have an answer, but until the missing file is found, the answer will remain unknown. Accommodating UNKNOWN as a truth value in predicate logic is much more complicated than in propositional logic. The following example suggests that at best, the waters are murky when UNKNOWN is in the picture.

Recall that set theory and logic were linked via the idea of the characteristic function of a set. If the truth value of propositions can be unknown, the truth value of set membership can also be unknown, and a third value (a value other than 0 or 1) is needed for $\mathbf{1}_S(x)$. Before long, however, you'll find yourself needing to distinguish "the value is definitely unknown" from "we don't know whether the value is true, false, or unknown."

Fuzzy Logic

If you thought three-valued logic was a significant departure from the world of True and False, fuzzy logic is a further departure. The premise of fuzzy logic is that absolute truths or falsehoods aren't all we care about or know. We may decide to include a fact in our model that we are relatively certain of, but not absolutely so. In fuzzy logic, the discrete values False and True are replaced by the continuum of numbers from zero to one. A zero is an absolute falsehood, a one is an absolute truth, and in between are the shades of gray.

A system can operate according to a threshold. You might only want to consider facts that are 99.5 percent likely to be true. Someone else might be willing to deal with 90 percent likelihood. Creating a rigorous mathematical framework for fuzzy logic is a serious challenge.

Relations

Operators such as = and <, which compare two elements of the same kind and yield a truth value as a result, are called *relations*. A relation ~ on elements of a set U can be considered as the set $\{(u,v) \in U \times U : u \sim u\}$ of pairs of elements that satisfy the relation. Alternatively, ~ can be considered as a predicate with two variables, each of which has U as its domain.

The Reflexive, Symmetric, and Transitive Properties

The definition of > in the earlier rock-scissors-paper example wasn't typical. Most directional or bidirectional comparison operators in mathematics, such as <, ≥, and =, are transitive. Here's a precise definition of the transitive property and some other useful properties a relation can have.

Properties of Relations

Let ~ be a relation on the universal set U. In other words, let $u \sim v$ have a well-defined truth value whenever u and v are elements of U. The relation ~ is said to be reflexive, irreflexive, symmetric, antisymmetric, or transitive according to the following definitions:

- **Reflexive**   The relation ~ is reflexive if $x \sim x$ is true for every x in U.

- **Irreflexive**   The relation ~ is irreflexive if $x \sim x$ is false for every x in U.

- **Symmetric**   The relation ~ is symmetric if $x \sim y$ and $y \sim x$ always have the same truth value, when x and y are elements of U.

- **Antisymmetric**   The relation ~ is antisymmetric if $x \sim y$ and $y \sim x$ always have the opposite truth value, when x and y are elements of U.

- **Transitive**   The relation ~ is transitive if whenever $x \sim y$ and $y \sim z$ are true, $x \sim z$ is also true, when x, y, and z are elements of U.

Although the names might suggest otherwise, it's *not* the case that every relation is either reflexive or irreflexive (or either symmetric or antisymmetric). An example of a relation that is neither reflexive nor irreflexive is the relation "is the reverse of" on words. There are words *w* for which *w* is the reverse of *w*, such as *radar*, but there are also words for which *w* is not the reverse of *w*, like *sonar*.

Not All < Operators Were Created Equal

Just as it was important to know a set's universe *U*, it's important to know a relation's universe—it's part of what defines the relation. The symbol < can appear between numbers or strings in SQL, but the relation < between numbers is not the same thing as the relation < between strings. If you aren't careful, as the following T-SQL example shows, you can run into trouble or at least what looks like trouble:

```
DECLARE @x VARCHAR(10);
DECLARE @y INT;
DECLARE @z VARCHAR(10);

SET @x = '1000';
SET @y = '2000';
SET @z = '+3000';

SELECT
    CASE WHEN @x < @y THEN 'TRUE' ELSE 'FALSE' END AS [x<y?],
    CASE WHEN @y < @z THEN 'TRUE' ELSE 'FALSE' END AS [y<z?],
    CASE WHEN @x < @z THEN 'TRUE' ELSE 'FALSE' END AS [x<z?]
```

This produces the following output, which appears to contradict the transitivity of the T-SQL operator <.

```
x<y?  y<z?  x<z?
----- ----- -----
TRUE  TRUE  FALSE
```

There's no contradiction because technically "the T-SQL operator <" is ambiguous. The code sample has two different less than operators: the < operator for numbers, which we might call $<_n$, and the < operator for strings, which we might call $<_s$. The rules of T-SQL require that the expression *<string> < <number>* be evaluated as *CAST(<string> AS <number>) < <number>*.

This T-SQL batch shows what's going on:

```
DECLARE @x VARCHAR(10);
DECLARE @y INT;
DECLARE @z VARCHAR(10);

SET @x = '1000';
SET @y = '2000';
SET @z = '+3000';
```

```
SELECT
   CASE WHEN @x < @y THEN 'TRUE' ELSE 'FALSE' END AS [CAST(x)<y?],
   CASE WHEN @y < @z THEN 'TRUE' ELSE 'FALSE' END AS [y<CAST(z)?],
   CASE WHEN @x < @z THEN 'TRUE' ELSE 'FALSE' END AS [x<z?],
   CASE WHEN CAST(@x AS INT) < CAST(@z AS INT)
        THEN 'TRUE' ELSE 'FALSE' END AS [CAST(x)<CAST(z)?]
```

A Practical Application

At the beginning of this chapter, we considered a set S—the set of all customers for whom every employee from the USA has handled at least one order. We'll finish the chapter by considering the set S once again, from a different perspective, and turn the result into a query. I'll also show you how to represent the characteristic function of a set in SQL.

Run the following T-SQL batch to set the database context for this section's queries:

```
USE InsideTSQL2008;
GO
```

In set-builder notation, we were able to write S in this way:

$S = \{c \in Customers : \forall e \in USAEmployees \, (\exists o \in Orders : (handled(e,o,c)))\}$

Consider the overall form of this definition in the following way: S is the set of customers for which something is true for every USA employee. If just a few employees are from the USA, let's say e_1, e_2, and e_3, we can write the *for every USA employee* part as *for employee e_1, for employee e_2, and for employee e_3.*

Still assuming there are only these three USA employees, this would be true: S is the set of customers c for which the following three conditions hold:

1. Employee e_1 handled an order for customer c.
2. Employee e_2 handled an order for customer c.
3. Employee e_3 handled an order for customer c.

Equivalently, S is the set of customers c in all three of the following sets:

1. The set C1 of customers for whom employee e_1 handled an order
2. The set C2 of customers for whom employee e_2 handled an order
3. The set C3 of customers for whom employee e_3 handled an order

Do you see where this is leading? The set S can be written as an intersection of three sets: $S = C1 \cap C2 \cap C3$.

From this, we can express $\mathbf{1}_S$, the characteristic function of S: $\mathbf{1}_S = \min(\mathbf{1}_{C1}, \mathbf{1}_{C2}, \mathbf{1}_{C3})$. We can generalize this to the case in which we have any number of USA employees: in general, $\mathbf{1}_S = \min(\mathbf{1}_{C(e)})$, where $C(e)$ is the set of customers for whom employee e handled an order.

For an employee e, the function $\mathbf{1}_{C(e)}$ is easy to describe. It's a characteristic function for a set of customers, so it has a value of 0 or 1 for each customer. Its value for a particular customer c is 0 if employee e never handled an order for customer c and 1 otherwise (if employee e did handle an order for customer c).

Here's how to express the characteristic function $\mathbf{1}_{C(e)}$ in SQL, if the *empid* value of employee e is *@empid*. The following query's result set is the set of ordered pairs $(c, \mathbf{1}_{C(e)}(c))$, one pair for each customer:

```
SELECT
  custid,
  CASE WHEN custid IN (
      SELECT custid
      FROM Sales.Orders AS O
      WHERE O.empid = @empid
    ) THEN 1 ELSE 0 END AS charfun
FROM Sales.Customers AS C
```

The result set of this query contains one row for each customer, and the *charfun* value in that row is the value of the characteristic function of the set of customers served by the employee whose ID is *@empid* on the customer in the row: $\mathbf{1}_{C(e)}(c)$.

If for each customer c we want to find the minimum value of $\mathbf{1}_{C(e)}(c)$ for all USA employees, we first want a virtual table that contains for each customer a row for each characteristic function. We can do this by replacing *@empid* with the column value *empid* from the table HR.Employees. Then we can group by customer and find the minimum among the characteristic function values. Here's the query:

```
WITH TheseEmployees AS (
  SELECT empid
  FROM HR.Employees
  WHERE country = 'USA'
), CustomerCharacteristicFunctions AS (
  SELECT
    custid,
    CASE WHEN custid IN (
        SELECT custid
        FROM Sales.Orders AS O
        WHERE O.empid = E.empid
      ) THEN 1 ELSE 0 END AS charfun
  FROM Sales.Customers AS C
  CROSS JOIN TheseEmployees AS E
)
  SELECT
    custid, MIN(charfun) as mincharfun
  FROM CustomerCharacteristicFunctions
  GROUP BY custid
  ORDER BY custid;
```

This query produces the following result (abbreviated):

```
custid       mincharfun
-----------  -----------
1            0
2            0
3            0
4            0
5            1
6            0
7            0
8            0
9            1
...
```

When the minimum value of $\mathbf{1}_{C(e)}(c)$ for all USA employees equals 1, customer c is in the set S. This observation leads us to the query in Listing 2-4, which produces the list of customers for whom every employee from the USA has handled at least one order. Listing 2-4 also includes the code to create and drop a supporting index for this query.

LISTING 2-4 Query to find customers who were served by every USA employee

```
CREATE INDEX sk_custid_empid ON Sales.Orders(custid,empid);
GO

WITH TheseEmployees AS (
  SELECT empid
  FROM HR.Employees
  WHERE country = 'USA'
), CharacteristicFunctions AS (
  SELECT
    custid,
    CASE WHEN custid IN (
        SELECT custid
        FROM Sales.Orders AS O
        WHERE O.empid = E.empid
      ) THEN 1 ELSE 0 END AS charfun
  FROM Sales.Customers AS C
  CROSS JOIN TheseEmployees AS E
)
  SELECT
    custid
  FROM CharacteristicFunctions
  GROUP BY custid
  HAVING MIN(charfun) = 1
  ORDER BY custid;
GO

DROP INDEX Sales.Orders.sk_custid_empid;
```

This query produces the following result, which correctly lists the customers in *S*:

```
Custid
-----------
5
9
20
24
34
35
37
38
39
41
46
47
48
51
55
63
65
71
80
83
84
87
89
```

The query plan, shown in Figure 2-1, is surprisingly efficient. The warning symbol on the Nested Loops operator signals a join without a join predicate. This warning always appears when there is a CROSS JOIN operator in the query, and it's nothing to be alarmed about.

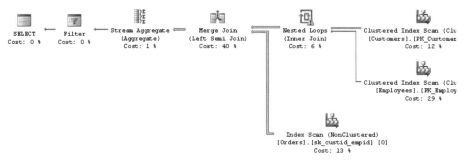

FIGURE 2-1 Execution plan for the query in Listing 2-4 based on characteristic functions

Whether this approach leads to efficient queries depends on the details of the problem and the characteristics of the actual data. However, we can't deny that this is a flexible query. By changing the HAVING predicate, the query can easily be modified to answer similar questions. Here is one example: To obtain those customers for whom at least one USA employee, but not every one of them, has handled at least one order, use the same query with a different HAVING clause: *HAVING MAX(charfun) = 1 AND MIN(charfun) = 0.*

Conclusion

This chapter contained a brief introduction to two foundations of modern mathematics and computer science: set theory and predicate logic. Set theory and logic are particularly important to understanding SQL and relational databases. Along the way, you learned some specific techniques, such as how to negate quantified predicates, and some alternate ways to characterize sets and express logical propositions. One particular tool, the characteristic function of a set, provided a valuable and flexible key programming technique.

Chapter 3
The Relational Model

Databases are central to information systems—they are the heart of applications. The structure of a database, called a *data model* (or *schema*, also *database design*), specifies a database. One of the most important models used for modern databases is the relational model. Although it is not the only data model, it is probably the most important one. The relational model is used mainly for transactional databases—where an enterprise's data is first stored—as opposed to warehouse databases, which serve as a repository for historical data. Compared to other contemporary data models, the relational model is particularly useful for transactional databases because data integrity can be declared and enforced by the model. Data integrity is the conformance of data to business rules. If your data is wrong the first time it enters your enterprise, it has a negative impact on your complete business. For example, analytical systems would not help you improve your operations because of the common concept *garbage in – garbage out*. Another advantage to the relational model is that it is mathematically defined. Therefore, when modeling, you are not guided by best practices only; you can evaluate your design and firmly ascertain whether it is good or bad.

Relational database management systems (RDBMS), including Microsoft SQL Server, store data in relational format. Although the physical implementation varies by vendor, the relational model provides a consistent user perception of the data for all RDBMS. In this chapter, I'll introduce the main concepts of the relational model. This knowledge will help you understand later chapters when you explore advanced queries.

Introduction to the Relational Model

The relational model was conceived in the 1960s by Edgar F. Codd, who worked for IBM. It is a simple yet rigorously defined conceptualization of how users perceive and work with data. It addresses the three major aspects of data processing in the following way, according to *An Introduction to Database Systems, 8th edition* by C. J. Date (Addison-Wesley, 2003):

- **Structural**   The data is perceived by the user as tables and nothing but tables.
- **Manipulative**   Users manipulate the data with an open-ended set of relational operators. The operators constitute the *relational algebra*.
- **Integrity**   The tables must satisfy defined integrity constraints.

The structural aspect can also be expressed by the Information Principle, which states that all information in a relational database is expressed in one (and only one) way as explicit values in columns within rows of a table.

In the relational model, a table is called a relation, and a row is called a tuple. In the next section, I'll introduce relations and tuples in more detail.

Relations, Tuples and Types

A *relation* is the mathematical object that represents what database practitioners call a table. The elements of a particular relation, like the rows of a table, represent instances of some real-world entity, like person, place, thing, or event. The relation is the set of these elements, which are—mathematically—*tuples*. I'll start by defining a tuple: A tuple is the set of its attributes, each of which is represented by three things: the attribute's name, the attribute's type, and the attribute's value.

> **Note** The relational model uses more general notions of relation and tuple than those introduced in Chapter 2, "Set Theory and Predicate Logic." In Chapter 2, you learned about *ordered* tuples, which had well-defined positional parts: first, second, and so on. Here, tuples still have well-defined parts, but those parts are *unordered*, and they are identified by attribute names instead of ordinal positions. In Chapter 2, a relation was a set of ordered pairs from a Cartesian product. Here, a relation is a set of unordered tuples that have the same *heading*. The notions used in the relational model are more abstract, and making them mathematically precise is never intuitive.

The set of attribute names and types of a tuple, taken together, are called the *heading* of a tuple. You can think of the heading of a tuple as a form to be filled out; the form has attribute names with blank spaces for values to be filled in. A tuple is a filled-in copy of a heading form. Tuple properties include the following:

- Every attribute of a tuple contains exactly one value of the appropriate type for each of its attribute names. Again thinking of a tuple as a filled-in copy of a heading form, there is exactly one value in each blank space (and it is of the appropriate type for the particular attribute).

- The attributes have no ordering (just as the elements of a set have no ordering). Consequently, every attribute must have a distinct name because you cannot refer to an attribute using its position in a tuple. In terms of forms, the way in which the attribute names are arranged on the heading form is irrelevant; only the names of the attributes matter, and, consequently, those names must be distinct.

- A subset of a tuple is a tuple (with fewer attributes). Again using the form analogy, one section of a form, viewed by itself, is still a form, but it may have fewer items.

Although it is possible to define operators from relational algebra on tuples, you do not manipulate individual tuples in a relational database. Operations are performed only on sets of tuples, that is, on relations. Tuples not only make up relations but also help define them. A relation consists of a set of tuples with the same heading, and we can call the heading of these tuples the relation's heading and vice versa. Similarly, we can think of relations as having attributes. Relations with different headings are different *types* of relations. The data types of attributes, as opposed to the heading types of relations, are sometimes called *domains* in the relational model to avoid overusing the word *type*.

Just as the contents of a database table might change, a relation should be able to contain different sets of tuples at different times. The relations of the relational model are actually variables—sometimes called relational variables, or relvars, and the value of a relational variable of some type is a set of tuples of that type. We won't always distinguish relations from relational variables of the same type, following common practice in other areas of mathematics. We often write *"n* is an integer" when we should more correctly write *"n* is an integer variable," for example. The fact that a relation is a set of tuples has the following important consequences:

- As is the case for tuples, the attributes of a relation have no ordering.

- Every attribute of a relation has one strongly defined data type. Every tuple of a relation contains exactly one value of this type for each attribute.

- A *projection* of a relation is a relation, where a projection is an operation that selects a specific subset of attributes from a relation (and from all of its tuples). Projection is one of the most important operators in relational algebra.

- A relation has no duplicate tuples. This is a consequence of the fact that a relation is a set, and sets contain distinct elements. Because a relation's tuples are distinct, they can be distinguished by some or all of their attribute values. A minimal subset of attributes that for any value of the relvar suffices to distinguish tuples is called a *key*.

- The order of tuples is insignificant. Again, this comes from set theory: the elements of a set are not ordered. This means that in a relation, terms such as first, next, prior, last, and *n*th tuple are undefined.

I've now used the term *type* multiple times, tacitly assuming that you understand what a type is. Here's a somewhat formal definition of a type: A type, which is also called a *data type* or a *domain*, is a finite set of values, such as a finite set of integers. Although in mathematics, universal sets (for example, the integers) can be infinite, in a computer system, you always hit a limitation. Therefore, a set of possible values of a type is finite. Every value has exactly one *most specific* type. When I say "most specific," I consider the possibility of type inheritance (although type inheritance is not implemented in SQL Server yet). For example, the value 3 can be considered a real number, an integer, or a natural number; natural number is the most specific type for it. In short, you can safely say that every value in a relational database has one type only.

A type consists of the following:

- A name
- One or more named possible representations:
    - One is physically stored.
    - At least one is declared to the users.
- A set of operators permissible on the type's values
- Type constraints

Every variable and every attribute has an explicit type, every operator returns a result of some explicit type, every parameter of every operator has an explicit type, and every expression is implicitly of some type. Physical storage is not exposed to users; it is system dependent. A type constrains possible values in different ways: with explicit constraints and with operators defined. For example, for integer type, you can define the operators Plus, Minus, and Multiply. The operator Divide is not defined as an integer for all pairs of integers because the result can fall out of the integer domain. The natural numbers are the integers with a constraint—the number must be positive (or, according to some authors, nonnegative). Operators and constraints are interleaved. Notice that the Minus operator is not defined within the natural numbers, even though it was for the integers.

For a type to be useful, it has to implement at least two operators: a *mutator* operator, which allows updating variables and attributes of the type, and a *selector* operator, which allows retrieving values of the type. Other operators can be defined by the creator of a type as appropriate to the intended use of the type. Note that a type can have multiple presentations and thus can have multiple selector operators. For example, a point in a plane can be represented in Cartesian or polar coordinate systems.

An important concept is whether a type is *scalar* or *nonscalar*. A nonscalar type has a set of user-visible and directly accessible components; a scalar type does not. Scalar types are also called *atomic* or *encapsulated* types. This description is somewhat vague. Is it clear whether a point in the coordinate plane is scalar? Both Cartesian and polar presentations have user-visible components. However, if you operate on only whole points and never on the individual coordinates, an individual point is indivisible and is therefore scalar. What about the type *car*? It definitely has user-visible components; still, you normally treat it as indivisible and therefore scalar. Let me try to give a precise definition. A value is scalar as long as you operate on it only with operators defined for its type. Operators might retrieve or update a single coordinate of a point, but as long as those operators are defined on points (as opposed to numbers), a point is still scalar. A collection of points stored in a string is nonscalar if you need to operate with points retrieved from the string. If you use this collection as a string and operate on it with string operators only, then this value is scalar. How about a collection of points that defines a polygon? If you define a polygon type explicitly, this is a scalar type. If you operate with points that define corners of the polygon through operations defined on the polygon type, values of this type are still scalar. Note that this reflects the real world. Sometimes you treat a value as a scalar of some type and sometimes as a collection of components where each component has its own type. For example, you drive a car as if it is a scalar value. When you take your car to a mechanic, however, the mechanic may treat your car as a nonscalar collection of components.

In relations, only scalar (or atomic) attributes are allowed. This doesn't mean that points in a plane cannot be attribute values of a relation; however, the values of the attribute have to be stored using the most specific type for the points—in other words, the point type and not as a string of coordinates. Which is the most specific type of a value? That depends on the intended use. If you are developing a human-resources application, a picture of an employee can probably be treated as scalar value of some binary type, and you would model a Subjects relation using a single attribute Picture. If you are developing a face-recognition application and need to analyze the picture using some vector graphics, you would model a Subjects relation using an associated Pictures relation that has its own, more detailed attributes (or, alternatively, a Subjects relation with detailed attributes of a picture instead of a single Picture attribute).

At any rate, the relational model is not limited to using a few specific types; it supports all possible types. Some of the most common types are supplied by an RDBMS. These are called *system* types. In addition, an RDBMS should allow you to extend the set of system types with *user-defined* types. SQL Server allows the creation of user-defined types in versions 2005 and later.

The Meaning of Relations

As I already mentioned, each relation represents some real-world entity, such as a person, place, thing, or event. An *entity* is a thing that can be distinctly identified and is of business interest. The term *entity class* can be used instead of *entity* for a kind of thing (like "person") as opposed to a specific example or representation (like "Steve Kass," which represents a specific person). Each representation of an entity can be uniquely identified, a fact that makes it possible to use a relation to represent an entity. Each representation of an entity plays an important role in the application or system it is represented in. This is the concept of *abstraction*: in a database, you only have entity classes (and attributes of those entities) that have a reason to be there. Each representation of an entity can be described by one or more attributes. *Relationships* are associations between entities. A relation is a subset of the cross products of the entity sets involved in the relationship. Attributes give some information about entities that is of interest for the application.

The previous paragraph defines the meaning of relations in terms of entities and the relationships among them, as defined by Peter Chen in his famous paper "The Entity-Relationship Model—Toward a Unified View of Data," referenced by most data-modeling books. The entity-relationship (ER) approach is also the most widely used approach to relational database modeling—find entities, relationships, and their attributes. However, there is another approach to understanding what relations mean. I actually prefer the second approach because it is more natural. In this approach, you describe relations in terms of *propositions* and *predicates*.

In Chapter 2, you learned the definition of propositions and predicates. What does this definition have to do with a relation? In natural language we make assertions about entities of interest by statements of fact—or, in logic, by *propositions*. For example, this is a proposition: The employee with ID number 17 is named Fernando, works in department D1, and was hired on July 19th, 2003. Generalized forms of propositions are *predicates*. For example, this is a predicate: The employee with ID number (Emp#) is named (Name), works in department (Dept#), and was hired on (Hiredate). The four terms in parentheses are placeholders or parameters that correspond to the four values in the preceding proposition. When you substitute parameters with specific values, a predicate reduces to an individual proposition. Here are the values for the parameters that reduce the predicate above to the proposition that precedes it:

(17; Fernando; D1; July 19th, 2003)

You can see that the parameters form a tuple. I wanted you to see that tuples in a relation actually represent propositions. Just as tuples represent propositions, relation headers represent the predicates for those propositions. I like this approach because it is very close to natural language. Just describe a business problem, find predicates, and write them down—you have your data model. Of course, you need a tool that converts predicates to relations. This natural language approach to modeling is called object-role modeling. It is described in *Information Modeling and Relational Databases, 2nd edition* by Terry Halpin and Tony Morgan (Morgan Kaufmann, 2008).

But this is not a modeling book. You just need to understand what relations mean. You can think of them as containers of real-world entities or as predicates and propositions from natural language. Note that for the predicates I've mentioned so far, there are no constraints on the tuple values that turn them into propositions, except that they must be values of the attribute types. I will deal with constraints shortly; for now, let me offer an informal, generic statement of the kind of rule you enforce with constraints: A proposition that evaluates false for the relation predicate (header) cannot be a part of the relation at any time.

Views (and Other Virtual Relations)

Views are an important part of a relational database. Also, an important part of queries in an application are temporary relations (or *rowsets* in SQL Server terminology). A view is a virtual relation; it is actually a stored query that is evaluated at run time when needed. A database user, application developer, or application should not be able to distinguish a view from a table. This is an important principle—*the principle of interchangeability*, which states that there should be no distinction between actual (sometimes called *base*) relations and virtual relations. This principle provides logical data independence in a relational database. Logical data independence can help you a lot with two problems: growth and restructuring. If a table in a database grows too large, resulting in poor performance, you can subdivide it manually into several new tables, then unite those tables into a view whose name is the original table name. The new tables can even be in separate databases or on separate servers. If you need to restructure a table and cannot change an application that uses it, you can create a view that returns the original structure to the application. An application uses a view without knowing it is a virtual relation. However, views cannot provide total data independence. If you cannot hide all the changes of a table's structure from an application with a view, you have to change the application as well. For example, you might need to add an attribute that has to be inserted by end users manually.

This concept of interchangeability can be extended further to table expressions—queries that return relations inside outer queries. You probably already know about derived tables and common table expressions; you'll learn how to use them efficiently in Chapter 6, "Subqueries, Table Expressions, and Ranking Functions."

Naming Conventions

Naming conventions help you make more intuitive designs and write clearer code. Your choice of convention is not as important as choosing a convention and using it consistently; I do not want to force a particular one on you. Conventions are a matter of history, taste, system limitations, and so on. Database designers tend to get really passionate about naming conventions.

I like the predicate-and-propositions approach to the meaning of relations. For example, I am repeating the proposition I already mentioned: "The employee with ID number 17 is named Fernando, works in department D1, and was hired on July 19th, 2003." I suggest that you should always be able to re-create the predicates and the propositions. A tuple that represents this proposition is written in a relation with values only, like (17, Fernando, D1, 2003-07-19). It is easy to recreate this proposition if its predicate, i.e. table structure, has meaningful names for table itself and for columns, like Employees(EmployeeId, EmployeeName, DepartmentId, HireDate). However, if the table and the columns would be named Table1(column1, column2, column3, column4). In short, you should be able to read your database. This makes it simpler to determine whether your database serves your business problem well and whether your data is in accordance with business rules. It also makes it much simpler to familiarize a new programmer with the database design and makes the task of data interchange with other systems easier.

The only naming convention I really do not like for a relational database is the one called Hungarian notation, in which you use prefixes to denote object types. Hungarian notation uses names like tblEmployees for an employee table and vwCustomerOrders for a customer orders view; such names contradict the principle of interchangeability, which is one of the most important principles in the relational model.

The Relational Model: A Quick Summary

The relational model is background independent, which means it does not depend on any specific presumption. I will return to this fact multiple times. To begin, let me state explicitly that the relational model is not type dependent. There are no prescribed "relational" types, and there are no "beyond relational" types. The relational model allows any type at all. In fact, it is completely valid to define a relation with a single attribute of a quite complex type; this would be a typed relation. However, system-supplied types are usually easier to use because database developers already know how to use them and, of course, don't have to develop them from scratch.

To summarize, the relational model consists of the following components:

- An open-ended collection of scalar types

- A way to define types—in other words, a type generator

- A way to define relation types—in other words, a relation type generator

- A way to generate relational variables and assign values (sets) to them

- Relational algebra: an open-ended collection of relational operators

Tables represent relations, and all information in a relational database is stored in tables. A relation represents an entity from the real world. In addition, tuples of a relation represent propositions, and a relation header represents a predicate.

The relational model is not dependent on naming conventions, either. Again, it is background independent. This means it is your responsibility to use a naming convention descriptive enough to make it possible to re-create predicates and propositions from your database.

Relational Algebra and Relational Calculus

To manipulate relations (relational variables), you need some operators. Relations and operators on relations form what is called *relational algebra*. The collection of relational operators is open ended, but some operators are considered basic. Although the basic operators are somewhat intuitive, I'll introduce them for the sake of completeness.

Basic Operators

As for simple types, we need at least two operators on relation types: one to store a set of tuples in a relational variable and one to retrieve a variable's value. These correspond to the familiar notions of assignment and evaluation. The relational selector operator (corresponding to evaluation) returns a table from a relational variable, and the relational assignment operator assigns a table value to a relational variable.

A set of basic Boolean operators on relations and tuples is obviously needed as well:

- $=$ (equals)

- $\neq$ (not equals)

- $\subseteq$ (subset of)

- $\supseteq$ (superset of)

- $\in$ (element of)

- $=\varnothing$ (is empty)

The first four operators listed here accept two relations as parameters. The fifth one checks whether a tuple is a member of a relation—in other words, it accepts a tuple as the left parameter and a relation as the right parameter. Finally, the last operator in the list accepts a single relation as a parameter and checks whether it is empty. If you wish, you can define additional operators for convenience, such as proper subset of (to mean subset of and not equal to) and proper superset of (superset of and not equal to). I want to mention one other specific operator that helps greatly with the tabular presentation of a relation—the Order By <attribute_1,attribute_2,...,attribute_n> operator.

The Order By operator does not return an unordered result; thus, it does not return a set or relation, which are unordered. You can think of the return value of the Order By operator as a sorted table. Sorting is not predefined for relations and tuples, however; therefore, supporting the Order By operator for a particular relation requires that at least one attribute of the relation support ordering and the following operators:

- $>$ (greater than)
- $\geq$ (greater than or equal to)
- $\leq$ (less than or equal to)
- $<$ (less than)

The table returned by the Order By operator is sorted according to values of one or more attributes, all of which must be of data types that support the listed type operators.

Relational Algebra

Relational algebra is a collection of operators that accept relations as input parameters and return relations. The fact that the result of any relational operation is a relation is referred as the relational *closure* property of the relational algebra. Codd originally defined eight relational operators—four of them are based on traditional set operators, and four of them are special relational operators. These eight are Restrict, Project, Product, Union, Intersect, Minus, Join, and Divide.

Relational algebra is not closed; you can define additional operators as long as they respect the relational closure property. I'll introduce a handful of useful operators in addition to Codd's original eight. Of course, because the collection of relational operators is open ended, my list is not complete. I deliberately selected the operators that I find most useful and that are used in the Transact-SQL language later in this book.

Codd's Eight Original Operators

The Restrict operator filters tuples of a relation. The result of this operator is a relation with fewer tuples than (or the same number as) the original relation. The heading type of the relation returned is the same as the heading type of the original relation. The restriction is based on a Boolean expression (called the *restriction expression*) comparing values of attributes to literals, variables, other attributes, or expressions. The Restrict operator's output relation contains exactly those tuples from the original relation for which the restriction expression evaluates to True.

The Restrict operator filters a relation horizontally; in contrast, the Project operator filters a relation vertically. The Project operator is much simpler: in addition to a relation, the Project operator takes, as input, a list of attributes needed for the resulting relation. Note that the proper projection should include unique tuples only; otherwise, the result is not a relation. Nevertheless, RDBMS do not enforce this rule because it is more practical to allow a multiset (or a bag) as the result to send it directly to a client application or to store it temporarily.

Figure 3-1 shows the Restrict and the Project operators graphically. Imagine that the right rectangle showing the Project operator represents the relation Employees, with attributes ID, Name, HireDate, DepartmentID, and BirthDate. The Project operator returns a relation with ID, HireDate, and DepartmentID as its attributes, and these attributes are indicated by the darker shading in the figure.

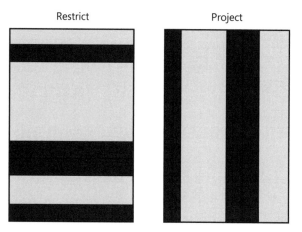

FIGURE 3-1 The Restrict and Project operators

The Product operator is based on the Cartesian product from mathematics. You already know from Chapter 2 that the Cartesian product of two sets is a set of ordered pairs *(x,y)*, where *x* comes from the first set and *y* from the second set. However, in the relational model, tuples are not ordered, and the Product operator should respect the relational closure property and return a set of unordered tuples, not a set of ordered pairs. Thus, in relational algebra, the Product operator is generalized. Instead of returning ordered pairs *(x,y)* of tuples (where *x* is a tuple from the first input to Product and *y* a tuple from the second), the Product operator returns tuples that are the union of the original two tuples. *Union* is used here in its set theory sense—it means that the final tuple has as its attributes the union of the attributes of the two original tuples. Union of course means distinct union, and therefore, if an attribute appears in both input relations, only one occurrence is preserved in the output of the Product operator. What happens if the two original relations include an attribute with the same name and you want to preserve both of them? Clearly, the Product operator is not complete; we need an additional operator that allows the renaming of an attribute. Such an operator is not a part of Codd's original algebra, so I will introduce after this section that deals with the original eight operators.

The Union relational operator is based on the set Union operator. However, the relational Union operator again differs from its mathematical counterpart because of the closure property of relational algebra. Because the result must be a relation and a relation can have tuples of only one heading type, the relational union must either be restricted to input relations of the same type or implicitly project each input relation onto the attributes that are common to both input relations. Figure 3-2 shows the Product and the Union operators. For the Union operator, a projection on each of the two relations is used to limit the union to attributes that the relations have in common only. The result of Union has the same heading type as both inputs (or their projections onto the common attributes) and contains distinct tuples.

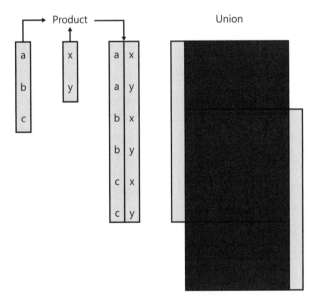

FIGURE 3-2 The Product and Union operators

The relational Intersect operator is, analogously to the relational Union operator, based on the set theory Intersect operator, and like Union has the restriction that the operands (relations) be of the same type or that an implicit projection is preapplied to the operands. The result is the set of distinct tuples that appear in both input relations (or in their projections onto the common attributes).

Another relational operator, the Minus (or Difference) operator, is based on the equivalent operator of set theory, again with an understood projection to make the operands have the same type. The result of the relational Minus operator is a relation that includes only tuples from the left operand that do not appear in the right operand. Figure 3-3 shows the Intersect and the Minus operators.

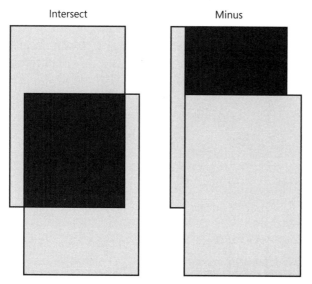

FIGURE 3-3 The Intersect and Minus operators

There are many varieties of the *Join* relational operator; however, the most important one is the Natural Join operator, which is illustrated in Figure 3-4. The Natural Join needs two relations with at least one attribute in common; the result is a relation with tuples for which the attributes in common have equal values. These common attributes come from only one of the joined relations and with the union of other attributes from both relations. Union is here again used in set theory sense, meaning a union of distinct attributes from the original relations. Like the Product operator, the Join operator would be much more useful with an operator that would allow renaming an attribute. As mentioned, Figure 3-4 shows the Natural Join operator. Imagine that the left input relation is the Employees relation with employee ID number and Department ID number attributes and that the right input relation is the Departments relation with Department ID number and Department Name attributes. The Natural Join operator uses the Department ID number common attribute to match the employees with their departments based on equality of the Department ID number. Note that in the resulting relation, the Department ID number appears only once. In addition, the result contains only tuples arising from a match based on Department ID numbers in both input relations. Finally, also note that a single department (y2 in Figure 3-4) is matched with more than one employee.

Not all joins are natural joins, and not all joins are based on the equality operator. General joins (joins that don't necessarily use the equality operator as the matching condition for tuples) are called Θ (*theta*) joins. If the operator for matching tuples is the equality operator, then the join is called *equi-join*. A natural join is just a special case of equi-join.

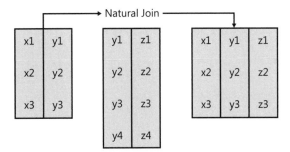

FIGURE 3-4 The Natural Join operator

Probably the most poorly understood relational operator is the Divide operator. A *divisor* relation is used to partition a *dividend* relation and produce a *quotient* relation. The quotient relation is made up of those values of one column from the dividend table for which the second column contains all of the values in the divisor.

Although this is a theoretical chapter, I am going to use code to explain the Divide operator and a problem you can meet if you divide with an empty set, a zero divide problem. I'll use an example that you saw in Chapter 2 and that you'll see again in Chapter 6. The problem, which refers to the InsideTSQL2008 database, asks you to return all customers for whom every employee from the USA has handled at least one order. In this case, you divide the set of all orders by the set of all employees from the USA, and you expect the set of matching customers back. T-SQL has no Divide operator. To show the problem, I'll rephrase the problem as it appears in Chapter 6:

```
Return customers
for whom you cannot find
  any employee
  from the USA
  for whom you cannot find
    any order
    placed for the subject customer
    and by the subject employee
```

The query for this problem is quite intuitive:

```
USE InsideTSQL2008;

SELECT custid FROM Sales.Customers AS C
WHERE NOT EXISTS
  (SELECT * FROM HR.Employees AS E
   WHERE country = N'USA'
     AND NOT EXISTS
       (SELECT * FROM Sales.Orders AS O
        WHERE O.custid = C.custid
          AND O.empid = E.empid));
```

This query returns 23 rows, which means there are 23 customers for whom every employee from the USA has handled at least one order. Let's ask the same question with a different country: How many customers are there for whom every employee from Israel has handled at least one order? Here is the same query with one changed parameter:

```
SELECT custid FROM Sales.Customers AS C
WHERE NOT EXISTS
  (SELECT * FROM HR.Employees AS E
   WHERE country = N'IL'
     AND NOT EXISTS
       (SELECT * FROM Sales.Orders AS O
        WHERE O.custid = C.custid
          AND O.empid = E.empid));
```

This query returns 91 rows, representing all customers. This might not be the result you expected, given that there are no employees from Israel in the HR.Employees table. This is the way the Divide operator was defined originally. Because the HR.Employees table has no employee from Israel, the condition that a customer was served by all employees from Israel is true for every customer (it is *vacuously* true). In other words, every customer was served by *every* employee from Israel. However, something else is also true: every customer was served by *no* employees from Israel. Note that there is no preferred truth here; the one you take depends on the problem you are solving. Do we have something like Russell's Paradox here (which you remember from Chapter 2)? Not really. The problem is that we did not think through the possibility of having no employees from Israel. If the original question's "customers ... for whom ... at least one order" was intended to mean there were in fact some orders, we can answer the question by simply adding a condition to the predicate requiring to return customers served by all employees from Israel if there is at least one employee from Israel:

```
Return customers
for whom you cannot find
  any employee
  from Israel
  for whom you cannot find
    any order
    placed for the subject customer
    and by the subject employee
  if there is at least one employee from Israel
```

The query now looks like this:

```
SELECT custid FROM Sales.Customers AS C
WHERE
 NOT EXISTS
  (SELECT * FROM HR.Employees AS E
   WHERE country = N'IL'
     AND NOT EXISTS
       (SELECT * FROM Sales.Orders AS O
        WHERE O.custid = C.custid
          AND O.empid = E.empid))
 AND EXISTS
  (SELECT * FROM HR.Employees AS E
   WHERE country = N'IL');
```

This query returns zero rows, as you might have expected when you originally posed the question. The formula for the Divide operator includes three relations:

a Divide By b Per c,

where *a* is the dividend, *b* is the divisor, and *c* is the mediator relation. Let relation a have attributes A and relation b attributes B. The Divide operator returns a relation that includes of all tuples from divisor such that a tuple {A, B} appears in the mediator relation for all tuples from divisor relation. In the examples I have shown, the dividend is the Customers relation, the divisor is the relation that includes employees from a specific country (USA or Israel on examples), and the mediator is the Orders relation. However, in order to avoid the zero divide problem, I used a fourth temporary relation (SELECT * FROM HR.Employees AS E WHERE country = N'IL'). You can express the predicate requiring to return customers served by all employees from the USA if there is at least one employee from the USA in yet another way, that is, by finding distinct customers (represented with *custid*) from orders served by employees from the USA having the number of distinct USA employees that served a customer equal to the total number of employees from the USA (again, as you'll find in Chapter 6):

```
SELECT custid
FROM Sales.Orders
WHERE empid IN
  (SELECT empid FROM HR.Employees
   WHERE country = N'USA')
GROUP BY custid
HAVING COUNT(DISTINCT empid) =
  (SELECT COUNT(*) FROM HR.Employees
   WHERE country = N'USA');
```

This query returns the result for the second version of the division for both USA and Israel employees and is also much shorter. To conclude the eight original relational algebra operators, Figure 3-5 shows the extended Divide operator (with mediator relation) graphically.

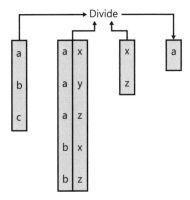

FIGURE 3-5 The extended Divide operator

Additional Relational Algebra Operators

As I already stated, relational algebra has an open-ended set of operators; I'm focusing on some of the most useful ones.

I already pointed out how the Rename operator is useful. Without it, any nonunary operators—operators that accept more than one relation as parameters—would be very limited. The Rename operator assigns an alias to an attribute or to a relation in a query. Note that it is practical to have aliases for relations as well as for attributes because a single query can refer to the same relation more than once.

A language that supports relational algebra is said to be *relationally complete*; however, this doesn't mean that it is *computationally complete* as well. I haven't yet introduced an operator that would return a computed attribute in the resulting relation. The Extend operator is the operator that adds a named expression (which evaluates to a scalar value) to the resulting relation. Note that this expression is not limited to computations between attributes of a single tuple only; the expression can also work on multiple tuples if it aggregates multiple input values to a single output value. Figure 3-6 shows the Rename and the Extend operators, with aliased and added attributes in darker color with pattern.

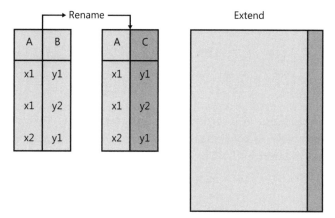

FIGURE 3-6 The Rename and Extend operators

The Extend operator does horizontal, or tuple-wise, computations. We need an operator for vertical, or attribute-wise, computations as well. The operator that does vertical computations is the Summarize operator (shown in Figure 3-7); it combines a projection on attributes over which the vertical computation is made with an extension of the resulting relation to include aggregate computations.

Semi joins are joins that return tuples from one relation based on the existence of related tuples in the other relation. A left Semijoin operator (shown in Figure 3-8) returns tuples from the left relation, and a right Semijoin operator returns tuples from the right relation.

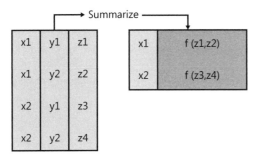

FIGURE 3-7 The Summarize operator

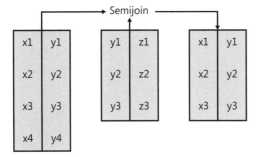

FIGURE 3-8 The (left) Semijoin operator

Graph theory is one of the most powerful theories in mathematics. It was developed by Leonhard Euler when he was studying a famous historical mathematical problem called The Seven Bridges of Königsberg. Here's a short description of the problem from Wikipedia:

> *The city of Königsberg in Prussia (now Kaliningrad, Russia) was set on both sides of the Pregel River, and included two large islands which were connected to each other and the mainland by seven bridges.*

> *The problem was to find a walk through the city that would cross each bridge once and only once.*

In graph theory, a *graph* is a set of items (called nodes or vertices) and connections (called edges) between pairs of items. The nodes are abstract static items, and the edges can represent associations or relationships between nodes. A road system, for example, can be represented with a graph: cities are nodes, and roads are edges. Trees and hierarchies are special cases of graphs. In a relation, we commonly model a graph with the *adjacency list* model. In this model, we consider the graph's edges as *directed edges* from one vertex to another, and we represent these directed edges as tuples. The nodes connected by an edge (which can be viewed as *adjacent* by virtue of the edge connecting them) are represented by attributes of the edge tuple. Only nodes with a connection are represented. The problem with the adjacency list model comes when you have to query it. For example, if you need to find all possible paths from city A to city B in the road system, your query must involve some kind of loop. (The loop can be hidden in a recursive common table expression, but it's still a loop.) To make such queries faster and simpler, we can use a new relational operator, the

TClose operator. This unary operator returns the *transitive closure* of the original relation. The result is a relation with the same heading type as the original relation, but it includes tuples for all pairs of nodes with unbroken paths between them. Querying such a resulting relation is much simpler. You'll learn more about graphs, trees, hierarchies, and also how to compute the transitive closure of a graph in Chapter 12, "Graphs, Trees, Hierarchies, and Recursive Queries." For now, just look at the graphical representation of the operator in Figure 3-9.

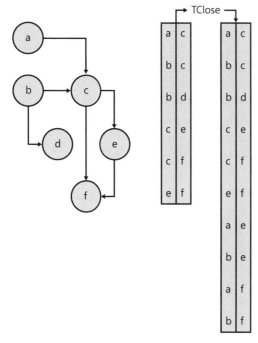

FIGURE 3-9 The (left) TClose operator

For the sake of completeness, I'll add two more well-known operators that deal with relations with temporal data: Unpack and Pack. Although this book does not deal with temporal problems, many books do, such as *Inside Microsoft SQL Server 2008: T-SQL Programming* by Itzik Ben-gan et al. (Microsoft Press, 2009).

Imagine that each tuple in a relation has an attribute representing the time interval for which the tuple is valid. Pretend that you have a time-interval type in your type collection, either system defined or user defined. A tuple with such a *validity interval* might look like this:

{A, d4:d6}

Without explicitly defining the header of this tuple, let's say the proposition here says that supplier A is under contract (is a valid supplier) during the period from the point in time d4 to the point in time d6 and that points in time are discrete: d1, d2, d3, and so on, like calendar days, for example. You could also have additional tuples for the same supplier, like so:

{A, d5:d7}

{A, d8:d8}

Here, the three tuples for supplier A have overlapping and abutting validity intervals. How can you find the number of distinct time points supplier A was under a contract? How can you combine tuples with adjacent and overlapping intervals into a single tuple that represents that supplier A was under contract continuously for one longer interval without interruptions?

Let's define the Unpack operator as a unary relational operator that returns a relation with all distinct valid time points projected over a set of input operators, the way the Summarize operator projects over input attributes. However, Unpack is doing the opposite of Summarize in terms of tuples returned; the relation returned is exploded to include tuples for all distinct valid time points. In the case of propositions from the example, the only input attribute for which time points can be unpacked is the supplier. The Pack operator does the opposite: it returns a relation with input attributes for which intervals are packed and intervals that are a union of all intervals from the source tuples for the same input attributes that overlap or meet. Note that *union* here is not a relational Union operator; it is an interval union, defined only for intervals that overlap or meet. Figure 3-10 shows the Unpack and Pack operators graphically.

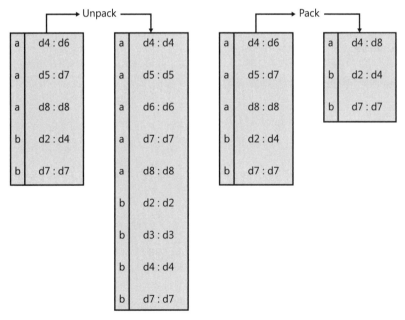

FIGURE 3-10 The Unpack and Pack operators

Primitive Relational Algebra Operators

Maybe you've already noticed that many of the relational operators defined so far can be expressed with other relational operators. In fact, most of the operators mentioned so far are just shortcuts that make relational expressions simpler and shorter. In fact, even Codd's original eight operators are not all primitive; some can be expressed with others. An RDBMS Query Optimizer component can utilize this fact when optimizing a query; it can rewrite a query to its logical equivalent using different operators, which might be implemented with faster physical operators than other relational operators in a specific RDBMS. For example, you might notice that sometimes SQL Server uses the Merge Join physical operator when you use the Union logical (relational) operator.

Note also that the relational operators that are based on set operators differ from the original set operators.

Relational Calculus

Relational algebra provides an open-ended set of relational operators. You use them to construct the desired relation that results from a query; you are prescribing a system of how to get the resulting relation. Relational algebra is *prescriptive*. Relational calculus is an alternative way to obtain a desired resulting relation from a system. With relational calculus, you describe the resulting relation. Therefore, relational calculus is *descriptive*.

How do you describe the resulting relation you need? Once again we use predicates. You describe the resulting relation with a constrained predicate. For example, when I described the Divide relational operator, I tacitly used relational calculus to introduce the problem: Return all customers for whom every employee from the USA has handled at least one order. The more detailed description is the following:

```
Return customers
for whom you cannot find
  any employee
  from the USA
  for whom you cannot find
    any order
    placed for the subject customer
    and by the subject employee
```

Relational calculus exists in two flavors: *tuple calculus* and *domain calculus*. In tuple calculus, you specify a query's result by describing tuple membership conditions for the resulting relation. In domain calculus, you specify the resulting relation by constraining the domains of attributes. Although there is a strict mathematical difference between tuple calculus and domain calculus, for the purposes of this book we can treat that difference as a nuance. The difference was important in the past because different languages—languages that were serious competitors to SQL—evolved based on tuple and domain calculus. For tuple calculus, QUEL (Query Language) was developed; domain calculus was supported by QBE (Query by Example) language.

To explain the difference between relational algebra and relational calculus, let me give an example. Imagine two relations: Customers with attributes *CustomerId*, *CustomerName*, and *City* and Orders with attributes *OrderId*, *CustomerId*, and *OrderDate*. The query you are solving is "Get the *CustomerId* and *CustomerName* attribute values of the distinct customers from Paris that have placed at least one order." A prescriptive, algebraic formulation of the query could be the following:

1. Join Customers and Orders over *CustomerId*.

2. Restrict the result to tuples for City Paris.

3. Summarize the result over *CustomerId* and *CustomerName* to get distinct customers.

4. Project the result over *CustomerId* and *CustomerName*.

A descriptive, calculus formulation of the query would be the following:

Return *CustomerId* and *CustomerName* for customers from Paris for which exists some order.

The description of a query's result is very similar in tuple and domain calculus. In both cases, it includes a description of the resulting header (also called a *proto-tuple*) and a description of constraints in terms of a predicate that uses a quantified expression. In the example, CustomerId and CustomerName define the proto-tuple, the header of the resulting relation. The predicate in the example uses an existentially quantified statement "for customers from Paris for which exists some order." The word *exists* indicates quantification. You create the predicate by combining logical expressions using the standard logical operators ¬ (Not), ∧ (And), and ∨ (Or). In addition, quantified expressions are necessary for relational calculus. Therefore, the existential quantifier ∃ (Exists) and the universal quantifier ∀ (For all) are an indispensable part of relational calculus.

SQL allows you to express the desired result of a query in nearly human language. It supports both logical operators and quantifiers. Itzik has pointed out many times in this book that some problems are easier to solve when rephrased with a different predicate or are analyzed using reverse logic. Now you can see that what this often means is that you are actually using relational calculus.

Relational calculus and relational algebra are equivalent; they both have the same expressivity. Therefore, it is really up to you to select the most suitable way for expressing the desired resulting relation; how you express a query (using relational algebra or relational calculus) and how you understand the meaning of a relation (entity or predicate and propositions) are similar.

T-SQL Support

I mentioned that SQL is not the only language used for manipulating relations. In fact, the relational model is not language dependent; this is another aspect of background independence of the relational model. SQL is just one possible language. However, there is an existing ANSI standard for SQL. And while it's not perfect, SQL is the most widely used contemporary language for manipulating relations. Transact-SQL (T-SQL) is SQL Server's dialect of standard SQL.

T-SQL supports most of the operators of relational algebra. You manipulate relations with Data Manipulation Language (DML) statements, namely, SELECT, INSERT, UPDATE, DELETE, and MERGE. The Product operator is expressed with CROSS JOIN. The Restrict operator is supported in the WHERE and HAVING clauses and implicitly in the ON clause of a JOIN operation if the join is not a CROSS JOIN, as other joins filter the result of a CROSS JOIN. The Project operator is supported in the SELECT part of a query, where you list attributes explicitly. The Union, Intersect, and Minus relational operators have counterparts in the T-SQL UNION, INTERSECT, and EXCEPT operators. All kinds of Join operators—theta joins, equi-joins, semi joins, and natural joins—are supported with the JOIN operator. The Rename operator is expressed in T-SQL with the AS clause, which can appear in a query's SELECT list for renaming attributes and in a query's FROM part for renaming relations. The Extend operator is expressed in the SELECT list, which can include named calculated expressions in addition to original attributes. The Summarize operator translates to the T-SQL GROUP BY clause. The Divide, TClose, Unpack, and Pack relational operators have no directly equivalent T-SQL operators.

Relational calculus is supported by the SELECT part of a query, where you describe the proto-tuple, and in the WHERE and HAVING clauses, where you constrain the resulting relation with a predicate. Of course, T-SQL supports all standard logical operators: ¬ (Not), ∧ (And), and ∨ (Or) and both the existential quantifier ∃ (Exists) and the universal quantifier ∀ (For all) in expressions that constrain the resulting relation.

Given all of this information, we can say that T-SQL is relationally complete.

Data Integrity

I already mentioned that data integrity is crucial for a relational database. Actually, data integrity rules are an important part of a relational database. An RDBMS has to enforce the rules. By making the rules part of a database, you inform the system what those rules are. With declarative constraints, how they are enforced is up to the system; with procedural code, you define how to implement them. In both cases, you express constraints in terms of predicates.

Relation headers—physical table and view definitions including attribute type definitions, together with declarative and procedural constraints—form a database schema. Now we can summarize what exactly a database schema is. A database schema represents *constrained predicates* that describe a business scenario. You can get the constrained predicates from relation headers and constraints defined in the database. A database predicate can be defined as an aggregation of all relation and constraint predicates. Data integrity rules can be expressed with a single rule: *there must be no value in a database at any time that would violate its constrained predicate.*

Constraints can be classified into basic constraints that define *entity, referential,* and *domain* integrity and business rules. Basic integrity rules are expressible with declarative constraints. Most business rules need programmatic code in SQL Server. Business rules can be anything, such as cardinality or frequency rules (how many tuples can exist in a relation at any time), data derivation rules (how you calculate state from events), subset rules (a relation can have a subset of tuples from another relation only), inclusion rules (a period when a supplier has supplied a product must be included in a period when the supplier had valid contract), process rules (which event should happen first), and much more. It is up to the database and application designer to decide where to implement the rules. I strongly advocate having at least declarative constraints in your relational database. After all, if you do not use them, why do you use an RDBMS?

Constraints can be classified in other ways as well. For example, they can be classified according to which kind of object they constrain: type, attribute, relation, and database constraints. They can also be classified as immediate or deferred, based on when they are enforced: immediately or at the end of the current transaction. Note that according to the rule that "there must be no value in a database at any time that would violate its constrained predicate," only immediate constraints should work inside a relational database. This means that constraints must be enforced at a single DML statement boundary, not at the end of a transaction or even later. A single DML statement is treated in an RDBMS as an atomic operation even if it modifies multiple rows; therefore, during the statement execution you could get rows that violate some constraint but never after the statement is finished. Note that immediate constraints only cannot guarantee that a database would reflect a valid state of affairs in real-world environment at all times. For example, although transferring money from one account to another is intended as an atomic operation, it involves two updates in a database. Both updates must finish successfully, or none should be performed. Therefore, we clearly need some other means to make databases consistent with the real world at any time. This can be done with *transactions*. A transaction is a logical unit of work that extends a statement-level notion of atomicity. Although transactions play an important role in an RDBMS, I am not going to explain them more in detail here; to learn more about them, please refer to *Inside Microsoft SQL Server 2008: T-SQL Programming*.

ANSI standard SQL allows deferred constraints. SQL Server does not implement them. However, they can be implemented in procedural code for advanced checks and searches for incorrect data. *Correctness* is a stricter term than *consistency*; an RDBMS can enforce data consistency but not correctness. Consistency means that data is in accordance with business rules declared and known to the system; correctness is defined outside the system by users of the system.

Declarative Constraints

Because declarative constraints are the most important way of implementing business rules in a relational database, I'll discuss them in more detail than other constraints.

Entity Integrity

Tables in a database are physical representation of relations, and the rows of a table represent tuples; relations consist of unique tuples. This is what entity integrity is about—uniquely identifying rows in a table. You must have a combination of columns (which physically represent attributes) that uniquely identify a row. The minimal set of columns that still uniquely identify each row is called a *key*. Each table can have multiple unique column combinations— in other words, multiple *candidate keys*. It is up to you to select one of them as your *primary reference* for each row and call it the *primary key*. SQL Server has two constraints for entity integrity: the *Unique* constraint for candidate keys and the *Primary Key* constraint for primary keys. You can have multiple Unique constraints and one Primary Key constraint per table.

You know that every table should have a key. You also know that SQL Server does not enforce this; you can create a table without a Primary Key or Unique constraint. The reason for this is purely practical. Imagine you need to import data from a text file. If you had a key defined, you would have to cleanse the data in your text file before the import. Cleansing text files is much less practical than cleansing data in a SQL Server table. Nevertheless, in production, all your tables should have a key defined for each table.

Each key has two required and two desired properties (D. Sarka, 2008). Uniqueness and applicability are required; stability and minimality are desired. Uniqueness means the key identifies each tuple uniquely. Applicability means the key has to be applicable for all tuples in a relation, it has to be known, and it should not consist of attributes that are meaningless for some tuples. (See the section "Generalization and Specialization" later in this chapter.) Stability means the key should not change, if possible. Minimality means the key should consist of the fewest columns possible and the fewest bytes possible. Nevertheless, because of physical problems, you should search for keys with all four properties. To track changes for an entity over time, such as in data warehousing scenarios, stability becomes a necessary property. And minimal keys provide the best performance.

There is an old debate about keys and which are better: *natural* or *surrogate*. A natural key is a subset of the attributes that define an entity. A surrogate key is a key the designer creates and adds to the attributes of an entity; typically it is a sequential number. Personally, I avoid participating in this old debate. You cannot strictly distinguish between natural and surrogate keys. Is a Social Security ID (SSID) a natural or surrogate key? Somebody could add it to the attributes of Person entity. Let me try to express a definition of a natural key: a key is natural if the attribute it represents is used for identification independently of the database. If you have something unique, applicable, stable, and short in your table, use it. If you don't, add a sequential number for the primary reference, and you will have all required and desired properties for your primary key.

If a key is applicable, its values must be known. SQL Server enforces this rule by prohibiting columns that allow NULLs from participating in Primary Key constraints; however, it allows nullable columns in Unique constraints. I'll come back to NULL, which is the marker for something unknown, later in this chapter. For now, I'll simply advise you not to use nullable columns for keys.

Referential Integrity

A *foreign key* is a set of columns whose values match some key of another table—in other words, a copy of a key from another relation. Foreign keys denote associations between relations; they are the glue that keeps relations in a database together. The rule foreign keys enforce can be expressed briefly: *There must be no unmatched foreign keys in a database at any time.* Foreign keys maintain references between relations—in other words, they enforce referential integrity.

The foreign key rule can be maintained during update and delete operations in different ways. In SQL Server, four possibilities exist for enforcing the foreign key rule, and each possibility consists of two pairs of rules. One pair of rules deals with the primary (*parent*) table, and one pair deals with the secondary (*child*) table. The pair of rules for the child table is immutable; the rules are always the same for all four possibilities of implementing a foreign key:

- You cannot insert a row in the child table if it has no related row in the parent table.

- You cannot update the foreign key columns in the child table in a way that would leave them without a related row in the parent table.

The two rules for the parent table differ with each of the four possible implementations. The four standard possibilities and the implementation of the two rules for the parent table are the following:

- No Action implementation

    - You cannot delete a row in the parent table if it has related rows in the child table.

    - You cannot update the key columns in the parent table if they have related rows in the child table that would become orphaned.

- Cascade implementation

    - If you delete a row in the parent table, you have to delete all related rows in the child table.

    - If you update a primary key in the parent table, you have to update foreign keys in all related child tables to the same new value.

- Set Null implementation

    - If you delete a row in the parent table, you have to set to unknown (NULL) all foreign keys of related rows in the child table.

    - If you update a primary key in the parent table, you have to set to unknown (NULL) all foreign keys of related rows in the child table.

- Set Default implementation

    - If you delete a row in the parent table, you have to set to a predefined default value all foreign keys of related rows in the child table.

    - If you update a primary key in the parent table, you have to set to a predefined default value all foreign keys of related rows in the child table.

In short, whatever you do, never leave rows in the child table orphaned. You would normally use the No Action implementation. You should use the Cascade implementation for deletes only in case you want to implement a strong relationship between the parent and the child table. In such a relationship the child table rows make no sense without parent rows. A classical example is orders and order line items: order line items cannot exist without an order. If you delete an order, you should delete all of its line items as well. I do not like to use Cascade updates. Cascade updates indicate that your key in the parent table is not stable, and stability is one of the desired properties of a key. The Set Null and Set Default rules are useful for maintaining history of the child table; for example, an order with unknown customer gives you information that something was ordered and when it was ordered but not who ordered it. Nevertheless, today history is commonly maintained in a data warehouse, and you usually do not need these rules.

A foreign key constraint must reference a key in the parent table. The parent table can be the same as the child table; a foreign key can refer to the table itself. This is how you can represent graphs, trees, and hierarchies using the adjacency list model.

Domain Integrity

Domain integrity limits the domain of possible values of an attribute. Of course, an attribute's type already constrains the possible values of the attribute. Another standard way to limit the domain of an attribute in a relational database is with a *check constraint.*

A check constraint is a logical expression that returns true, false, or unknown—it is another predicate. An RDBMS enforces it whenever a tuple is inserted or updated. The tuple's attribute values replace the predicate's parameters, making the predicate a proposition. A tuple is rejected if the proposition evaluates to false. The syntax of a check constraint expression is similar to the syntax of expressions in a WHERE clause.

Check constraints can be as simple as checking a range of values. However, what do you do when you don't know the allowed range in advance—when you have to maintain the values to the allowed range dynamically? What do you do when the list of possible values is very long or even infinite? A check constraint expression would consist of an enormous list of values connected with logical OR operators, and you would have to change the constraint whenever the list of possible values changed. In such a case, it's simpler to use lookup tables. You connect the attribute(s) you are constraining to a lookup table with a foreign key. Therefore, foreign key constraints can serve as domain integrity mechanisms as well.

All the constraints I've mentioned—keys, foreign keys, and check constraints—play an important role in query optimization. They give information to an RDBMS, and this helps find an optimal execution plan. Keys give information that you're searching for a single value; this value is unique. Therefore, the search is very narrow, and the system can use an index seek. Foreign keys give information that a parent row always exists, which helps to find the most efficient join algorithm. Check constraints give information about range, which means (for example) that searching for a value that is out of range returns zero rows, and the system doesn't even have to read the data to return the correct result set. You'll learn more about query tuning in Chapter 4, "Query Tuning."

Other Means of Enforcing Integrity

As I've already mentioned, explicit constraints are not the only means of enforcing data integrity. Data types are constraints as well; they constrain with type-defined constraints and with sets of operations allowed. An attribute is constrained with its data type. You can also define whether a column of a table allows NULLs. Finally, the definitions of tables constrain as well: if you don't have a place to insert a value, you cannot insert it. I will explain this a bit more in the normalization section of this chapter.

You cannot implement all business rules by using declarative means. Some constraints are too complex, and some span a database boundary. A foreign key, for example, is limited to associating tables in the same database only. Some constraints have to be implemented programmatically. You can put your constraining code in a client application, in the middle tier, in the data access layer, in stored procedures in a database, or anywhere you have some code. However, if you want your RDBMS to enforce complex constraints automatically, you have to use triggers.

Triggers are special stored procedures that an RDBMS executes, or fires, automatically. You can use Data Modification Language (DML) triggers to enforce data modification rules and Data Definition Language (DDL) triggers to enforce schema modification rules. Triggers can fire before or after the statement that is modifying the state of a database. SQL Server 2008 supports two kinds of DML triggers: INSTEAD OF and AFTER triggers; only one kind of DDL trigger is supported: the AFTER. INSTEAD OF triggers are not actually ANSI-standard BEFORE triggers; they do fire before the statement, but they also intercept the statement, and then you can do whatever you want in the body of the trigger. If you want the statement to execute, you have to write it explicitly in the body of the trigger.

In theory, you should always be able to use a view instead of a base relation. However, not all views are updatable. For example, a view can summarize some attributes of a base table; an RDBMS doesn't know how to distribute a value from a single row from a view over multiple base rows. INSTEAD OF triggers are especially meant for making views updatable.

SQL Server 2008 also has a built-in XML system type. The XML type enforces some integrity rules by itself: it allows well-formed XML only. In addition, you can validate XML values against a predefined schema from a schema collection you create inside a SQL Server database. Details of triggers and XML validations are beyond scope of this chapter; for more, please refer to *Inside Microsoft SQL Server 2008: T-SQL Programming*.

You can also use some elements of a database that don't really enforce data integrity but instead help users insert correct values. Defaults can help insert a value when it is not explicitly listed in the INSERT statement. SQL Server 2008 has also a Timestamp type; SQL Server inserts and updates values of this type automatically and guarantees that values in columns of this type are unique across a database. The IDENTITY property of a column can help you insert sequential numbers.

One important thing you need to know is the order in which the system enforces constraints. You probably noticed that I switched from discussing a general (and theoretical) implementation to a SQL Server 2008–specific implementation. The details of constraints are quite system specific, and it seems more appropriate to switch to the system that this book is about—namely, Microsoft SQL Server 2008. Therefore, the order of execution in SQL Server is as follows:

1. Schema is checked (whether an update is valid for the table schema).

2. Data types are checked.

3. INSTEAD OF triggers fire instead of the actual statement.

4. *Default* constraints are applied.

5. Nullability is checked.

6. *Primary Key* and *Unique* constraints are checked.

7. *Foreign Key* and *Check* constraints are enforced.

8. Statement is executed.

9. AFTER triggers fire.

What this order tells you is that declarative constraints are enforced before the actual statement, and they prevent improper updates, while AFTER triggers fire after the statement, and you have to roll back an improper modification discovered by the statement's AFTER trigger. This means that using declarative constraints is more efficient than using AFTER triggers, and you should opt for using declarative constraints whenever possible. Don't forget another advantage in using declarative constraints: they can help in query optimization.

The Good, the Bad, and the . . . Unknown!

The last question I want to touch on regarding data integrity is whether you should allow NULLs in your database. In an ideal world, your database should represent true propositions only; if something is NULL and you do not know what that NULL means, you cannot say it is true. Therefore, from a strict point of view, you should not allow any NULLs.

However, in the real world, you always have some missing information, at least temporarily. In addition, you really can experience Russell's Paradox, as described in Chapter 2. In addition to the theoretical description, I'd like to offer an example I found in *Fermat's Last Theorem* by Simon Singh (HarperPerennial, 2005), showing Russell's Paradox in real life. This is the problem of the meticulous librarian.

This library has two kinds of catalogs (of whatever you want); some list themselves in references, and some don't. The librarian wants to make two new catalogs: one that lists all catalogs that do list themselves and one that lists all catalogs that do not list themselves.

The problem is with the latter catalog: should it list itself? If it does list itself, by definition it should not be listed. If it does not list itself, by definition it should be listed. Imagine you have to insert these two catalogs in a database, and in a table describing catalogs, you have an attribute that is a flag showing whether a catalog lists itself. What would you insert in this attribute for the catalog that lists all catalogs that do not list themselves? I think that NULL is quite all right, showing that you cannot have anything meaningful there.

Of course, in real life, you will encounter missing information because of many reasons other than Russell's Paradox. Nevertheless, you have to find a way to deal with missing information.

ANSI standard prescribes and SQL Server implements NULLs for denoting missing values. Note that NULL is not a value; it is just a marker. NULL doesn't even have the privilege to be equal to itself. Some authors (Date, Pascal) strictly forbid NULLs, others explicitly allow them (Codd), and others (Halpin) do not discuss them—they just show how to model and use them. Which is correct?

If NULLs were not allowed, you'd still have to implement some special values denoting missing information. The advantage of this approach is that you could use standard Boolean operators in your queries, and there would be no need for special operators that handle NULLs. The disadvantage is that there is no single, standard, special value accepted worldwide. In addition, a single special value would not be sufficient; we would actually need one for each data type. Using NULLs means using a standard that is already accepted; however, it also means introducing three-valued logic, where *not true* is not the same as *false*. Three-valued logic makes queries more complicated.

After considering many pros and cons, my personal conclusion is that NULLs are here to stay, and they are implemented by all major RDBMS; therefore, I prefer using them to inventing special values. You'll learn a lot about writing efficient three-valued logic queries in this book. Nevertheless, some NULLs can be avoided—namely, NULLs that are there because an attribute is not applicable for a particular tuple of a relation. This is a matter of design. A good schema constrains—in other words, excludes—NULLs that represent "not applicable." Therefore, the time has come to define a good schema!

Normalization and Other Design Topics

I need to clarify something immediately. This is not a modeling book; it is a practical book with a couple of introductory chapters that explain the theory behind the practice. The theory helps you understand why some things in SQL Server are implemented as they are implemented. This book will help you better understand what you are doing when you create and maintain a relational database as well as help you find different ways of expressing queries, find more optimized queries, and so on. Therefore, I won't talk about how to model; I'll talk about what you need to achieve with your models.

Many modeling books are on the market; I don't need to advertise them. I will mention a couple of books I really like just to make this chapter more complete. Personally, I prefer the object-role modeling (ORM) approach, and *Information Modeling and Relational Databases, 2nd edition* by Terry Halpin and Tony Morgan (Morgan Kauffman, 2008) is the bible of ORM. For the most popular modeling approach, the ER approach, I like *Data Modeling Essentials, 3rd edition* by Graeme Simsion and Graham Witt (Morgan Kauffman, 2004), where you can find a lot on the modeling process and finding information about business rules. Finally, if you are developer and you already use Unified Modeling Language (UML) for modeling, *Database Design for Smarties: Using UML for Data Modeling* by Robert J. Muller (Morgan Kauffman, 1999) could be a good resource for you.

What you need to achieve in order to create a good relational model is mathematically described with *normalization* and *specialization*. Because normalization is more complex, I'll spend more time on it, although both parts are important for a good design. But before I start with normalization, let me repeat a very simple yet important sentence about good design: A relational database is well designed if you can reconstruct the predicates (and propositions) used to describe the business problem.

Normal Forms Dealing with Functional Dependencies

Tables are normalized when they represent propositions about entities of one type—in other words, when they represent a single set. This means that entities do not overlap in tables and that tables are orthogonal or normal in mathematical terms. When a table meets a certain prescribed set of conditions, it is said to be in a particular *normal form*. A database is normalized when all tables are normalized. You can create fully normalized database models with ORM or with the ER approach.

Normalization is a redesign process to unbundle the entities. The process involves decomposition but not decomposition that leads to a loss of information. After the normalization process, all the original information must be obtainable with queries that involve relational operators such as Join and others. The normalization is achieved by applying a sequence of rules to create what are called normal forms. The goal is to eliminate redundancy and incompleteness. Note that the latter is often overlooked; however, normalization eliminates incompleteness in addition to eliminating redundancy.

Many normal forms are defined. The most important ones are first, second, third, Boyce-Codd, fourth, and fifth normal forms. If a database is in fifth normal form, it is said to be fully normalized. If a database is not fully normalized, you can experience data manipulation anomalies.

I'll start with the first four normal forms, which deal with functional dependencies. A dependent variable is *functionally dependent* on an independent one when exactly one value of the dependent variable exists for each value of independent variable. This means that if we know the value of the independent variable, we know the value of the dependent variable as well. In a relation, nonkey attributes are functionally dependent on keys; if you know the key value, you can find the nonkey attribute value. This is what functional dependency in a relation means.

First Normal Form

Imagine a real-world scenario with customers that order products. Customers, orders, and products are entities you discovered when you got the description of the business scenario. Initially, you model everything in a single table called Orders. Table 3-1 shows an imaginary Orders table. Columns that are part of the key are shaded (*OrderId* only in this example).

TABLE 3-1 A Table Before 1NF

OrderId	CustomerId	CustomerName	OrderDate	Items
1	1	Company ABC	2008-10-22	Ap Apples q=5, Ch Cherries q=10
2	1	Company ABC	2008-10-24	Ba Bananas q=12
3	2	Company ABC	2008-09-15	Ap Apples q=3, Ba Bananas q=3

This design is, of course, problematic. Some possible data manipulation anomalies are the following:

- Insert
    - How do you insert a customer without an order? (By the way, can you see the incompleteness problem?)
- Update
    - If item Ba is renamed, how do you perform an update? You can easily miss some row you should update. This occurs because of redundancy.
- Delete
    - If order 3 is deleted, the data for customer 2 is lost. This is also a problem of incompleteness.
- Select
    - How do you calculate the total quantity of bananas? This is the problem with a nonscalar column. The *Items* column is a collection.

The first normal form (1NF) says that *a table is in first normal form if all columns are atomic*. No multivalued columns are allowed. Note that the 1NF definition simply states that a table must represent a relation.

Decomposition has to start with the Items column. You need a single row per item in an order, and every atomic piece of data of a single item (*ProductId, ProductName, Quantity*) must get its own column. However, after the decomposition, you get multiple rows for a single order. *OrderId* by itself cannot be the key anymore. The new key is composed of the *OrderId* and *ProductId* columns. If you allow multiple products on a single order—for example, each time with a different discount—you would not be able to use the *ProductId* as a part of the key. You would probably add *ItemId* attribute and use it as a part of the new key. A decomposed table in 1NF would look like Table 3-2.

TABLE 3-2 A Table in 1NF

OrderId	CustomerId	CustomerName	OrderDate	ItemID	ProductId	Quantity	Product Name
1	1	Company ABC	2008-10-22	1	Ap	5	Apples
1	1	Company ABC	2008-10-22	2	Ch	10	Cherries
2	1	Company ABC	2008-10-24	1	Ba	12	Bananas
3	2	XYZ	2008-09-15	1	Ap	3	Apples
3	2	XYZ	2008-09-15	2	Ba	3	Bananas

Before I start with 2NF, let me point out one common misconception with 1NF. You'll often read about repeating group of columns. Take, for example, the Employees table design shown in Figure 3-11.

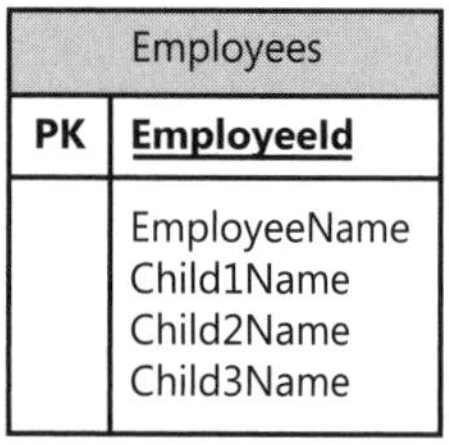

Employees	
PK	**EmployeeId**
	EmployeeName Child1Name Child2Name Child3Name

FIGURE 3-11 The Employees table

You probably feel uncomfortable with this table. It has a repeating group of columns with a similar name—*ChildXName*. Child1Name means the name of the oldest child, Child2Name means the name of the second oldest, and Child3Name means the name of the third oldest (disregarding twins). Of course, the question is, what if an employee has more than three children? You'd probably create a new table. You might think that you are normalizing the Employees table.

You know that the relational model does not depend on names. Let's rename the table and all of the columns and get a table shown in Figure 3-12.

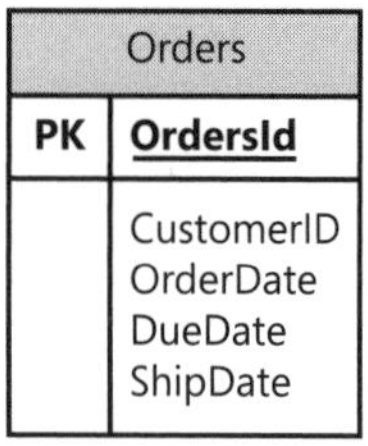

Orders	
PK	**OrdersId**
	CustomerID OrderDate DueDate ShipDate

FIGURE 3-12 The Orders table (the Employees table renamed)

You probably feel more comfortable with this design, and this table seems perfectly normalized. The Employees table was in 1NF as well, but the problem is that a constraint is built into both tables. The first constraint says we have employees with three (or at most three if the columns allow NULLs) children; the second constraint says an order has three dates. Of course, the first constraint makes no sense in real world, and the first design was bad anyway. However, it was normalized. Remember that you can constrain with the data model itself with table design. Often a repeating group of columns with similar names really represents a hidden collection; however, don't decompose such groups automatically. Check the business rules—the constrained predicates—first.

Second Normal Form

After achieving 1NF, as you saw in Table 3-2, you still have many updating anomalies:

- Insert
  - How do you insert a customer without an order? (Incompleteness)
- Update
  - If a customer changes the order date for an order, how do you perform the update? (Redundancy)
- Delete
  - If you delete order 3, the data for customer 2 is lost. (Incompleteness)

To achieve second normal form (2NF), a table must be in 1NF (do you see the linear progression?), and *every nonkey column must be functionally dependent on the entire key*. This means that no nonkey column can depend on a part of the key only. In Table 3-2, you need *OrderId* only to get *CustomerId* and *OrderDate*; you don't need *ItemId*, which is also part of the key. For the normal forms beyond 1NF, decomposition means creating new tables, not just new rows like in 1NF. To achieve 2NF, you need to decompose the table into two tables, like Tables 3-3 and 3-4 show.

TABLE 3-3 The Orders Table in 2NF

OrderId	CustomerId	CustomerName	OrderDate
1	1	Company ABC	2008-10-22
2	1	Company ABC	2008-10-24
3	2	XYZ	2008-09-15

TABLE 3-4 The OrderDetails Table in 2NF

OrderId	ItemId	ProductId	Quantity	ProductName
1	1	Ap	5	Apples
1	2	Ch	10	Cherries
2	1	Ba	12	Bananas
3	1	Ap	3	Apples
3	2	Ba	3	Bananas

You make the split so that you leave attributes that depend on *OrderId* only in the Orders table, and you introduce a new table, OrderDetails, with the other attributes. 2NF deals with the relationship between columns that are part of a key and other columns that are not part of a key.

To gain nonloss decomposition, you have to be able to join the two new tables back to produce the original table. Therefore, you need some common value in both tables. Of course, this is the *OrderId* column from the Orders table, which is, as you already know, the foreign key column in the OrderDetails table.

Third Normal Form

With 2NF, we've resolved the order date update anomaly because of redundancy. However, many issues remain:

- Insert
  - ❑ How do you insert a customer without an order? (Incompleteness)
- Update
  - ❑ If a customer or a product is renamed, how do you perform the update? (Redundancy)
- Delete
  - ❑ If you delete order 3, the data for customer 2 is lost. (Incompleteness)

To achieve third normal form (3NF), a table must be in 2NF, and *every nonkey column must be nontransitively dependent on every key*. In other words, nonkey columns must be mutually independent. For example, in Table 3-3, from *OrderId*, you can find *CustomerId*, and from *CustomerId*, you can transitively find the *CustomerName* value. Try to find a similar problem in Table 3-4 (of course, *ProductId* and *ProductName* are not mutually independent).

To achieve 3NF, you must create new tables for dependencies between nonkey columns, as shown in Tables 3-5 through 3-8.

TABLE 3-5 The Customers Table in 3NF

CustomerId	CustomerName
1	Company ABC
2	XYZ

TABLE 3-6 The Orders Table in 3NF

OrderId	CustomerId	OrderDate
1	1	2008-10-22
2	1	2008-10-24
3	2	2008-09-15

TABLE 3-7 **The OrderDetails Table in 3NF**

OrderId	ItemId	ProductId	Quantity
1	1	Ap	5
1	2	Ch	10
2	1	Ba	12
3	1	Ap	3
3	2	Ba	3

TABLE 3-8 **The Products Table in 3NF**

ProductId	ProductName
Ap	Apples
Ch	Cherries
Ba	Bananas

When you reach 3NF, you usually get rid of all data manipulation anomalies. Usually when you normalize up to 3NF, the result satisfies BCNF, 4NF, and 5NF as well. Higher normal forms violations are rare. To make this overview complete, however, I'll describe the higher normal forms and give a couple of practical tips on how to recognize the possibility of violating them.

Boyce-Codd Normal Form

The first question you might ask yourself is why the next NF is not called 4NF. The fact is that Mr. Codd actually wanted to replace 3NF with the one we now know as Boyce-Codd normal form (BCNF). Because it is stricter than 3NF, 3NF did not disappear, and consequently we have somewhat inconsistent numbering.

I'll show how you can violate BCNF. Imagine for a moment we have the Orders table, without the *OrderId* column and with a single order per customer per day allowed. Also, each order has a standard ship time, and therefore *OrderDate* gives you the expected *DueDate*. Table 3-9 shows this example. To make the dependency clear, the *DueDate* is always a day after the *OrderDate*.

TABLE 3-9 **The Imaginary Orders Table**

CustomerId	OrderDate	DueDate	OtherOrderColumns
1	2008-10-22	2008-10-23	…
1	2008-10-24	2008-10-25	…
2	2008-09-15	2008-09-16	…

This table has two composite candidate keys: {*CustomerId, OrderDate*} and {*CustomerId, DueDate*}. The candidate keys overlap on the *CustomerId* column (which is shaded with a darker color to show that it is used twice). It is in 3NF because all nonkey columns intransitively depend on each key. However, a specific data manipulation anomaly is possible:

- Update

  - If a customer changes *OrderDate*, you should not forget to update the *DueDate* as well. (Redundancy)

You can violate BCNF only in the rare situation that a table has more than one composite candidate key and the candidate keys overlap. It would be possible to decompose the Table 3-9 into two new tables based on two candidate keys, for the sake of brevity in short notation, showing table headings only:

OrdersOrderDate {CustomerId, OrderDate, OtherOrderColumns}

OrdersDueDate {CustomerId, DueDate, OtherOrderColumns}

However, your common sense tells you this decomposition is not something you'd want in your model. In addition, there is some hidden redundancy among the two new tables—other nonkey columns repeat. It is not possible to solve this problem with normalization rules only. (You already know that common sense can help you.) I'll return to this problem with a formal solution later when I describe the Principle of Orthogonal Design.

I did not define BCNF yet. BCNF says that *every determinant must be a key*. The independent part of a functional dependency is called the determinant. A key attribute must be a determinant—it must not be determined. In Table 3-9, *OrderDate* determined *DueDate* and vice versa, and both are key attributes (precisely, part of some key). In other words, to achieve BCNF, you must have no functional dependencies between key attributes.

You can achieve BCNF without decomposition by using common sense. Tables 3-10 and 3-11 show the two possibilities to achieve BCNF in Table 3-9.

TABLE 3-10 **The Orders Table in BCNF: First Solution**

CustomerId	OrderDate	StandardShippingTimeDays	OtherOrderColumns
1	2008-10-22	1	...
1	2008-10-24	1	...
2	2008-09-15	1	...

TABLE 3-11 **The Orders Table in BCNF: Second Solution**

OrderId	CustomerId	OrderDate	DueDate	OtherOrderColumns
1	1	2008-10-22	2008-10-23	...
2	1	2008-10-24	2008-10-25	...
3	2	2008-09-15	2008-09-16	...

Note that the solution shown in Table 3-11 does not define pairs (*CustomerId, OrderDate*) and (*CustomerId, DueDate*) as keys anymore. Therefore, it is not really a solution if the two pairs still determine orders. However, I introduced it here because it is closer to real-world scenarios; a customer can submit more than one order per day.

Higher Normal Forms

Higher normal forms, namely, the fourth and the fifth normal forms, do not deal with functional dependencies; they deal with multivalued and join dependencies. I'll now introduce the fourth and the fifth normal forms.

Fourth Normal Form

As I mentioned earlier, violations of fourth and fifth normal forms are very rare, and they can usually be avoided with common sense. To begin with, violations can occur only in a table that consists of columns that together compose a key, with no nonkey column, and with at least three key columns. The following examples of 4NF and 5NF violations, as well as the solutions, are based on examples in *Practical Issues in Database Management* by Fabian Pascal (Addison-Wesley, 2000).

Let me start by describing an example of a business problem. A fictitious company works on projects. Employees are assigned to these projects. Each employee has a set of skills. If an employee is assigned to a project, that employee performs all activities that he or she can perform. Table 3-12 shows this example. Although not shown here, imagine there are separate Employees, Projects, and Activities tables in the database.

TABLE 3-12 The Employees-Projects-Activities Table

Employee	Project	Activity
1	Proj 111	ABC
1	Proj 111	DEF
1	Proj 222	ABC
1	Proj 222	DEF
2	Proj 111	ABC
2	Proj 111	XYZ

You'll notice some redundancy. The following data manipulation anomalies are possible:

- Insert
    - How do you assign an employee to a project if the employee has no skills yet? (Incompleteness)
- Update
    - If an employee is reassigned from one project to another, how do you manage to update all rows needed? (Redundancy)

- Delete

  ❏ If you delete all project assignments for an employee, information regarding the skills of this employee is lost. (Incompleteness)

The information about projects and activities repeats for each employee. We could avoid this problem if we allow multivalued columns, as shown in Table 3-13.

TABLE 3-13 The Employees-Projects-Activities Table with Multivalued Columns

Employee	Project	Activity
1	Proj 111	ABC
	Proj 222	DEF
2	Proj 111	ABC
		XYZ

This situation indicates that there is something called multivalued dependency between employees and projects and activities. Multivalued dependencies are a generalization of functional dependencies. Fourth normal form (4NF) says that *there must be no nontrivial multivalued dependencies that are not functional dependencies*. To achieve this, you have to decompose Table 3-12, as shown in Tables 3-14 and 3-15.

TABLE 3-14 The Employees-Projects Table

Employee	Project
1	Proj 111
1	Proj 222
2	Proj 111

TABLE 3-15 The Employees-Activities Table

Employee	Activity
1	ABC
1	DEF
2	ABC
2	XYZ

Fifth Normal Form

I'll now change the business problem description slightly. If an employee is assigned to a project, that employee doesn't have to perform all activities that he or she has skills to perform on this project; in fact, a project might not need some of the activities the assigned employees has skills to perform. However, if a project includes an activity, an employee is assigned to a project, and the employee assigned performs the aforementioned activity, the employee must perform that activity on that project. An example is shown in Table 3-16.

TABLE 3-16 The Employees-Projects-Activities Table

Employee	Project	Activity
1	Proj 111	ABC
1	Proj 111	DEF
1	Proj 222	ABC
2	Proj 111	ABC
2	Proj 111	XYZ

Without decomposition, the possible data manipulation anomalies are similar to the anomalies mentioned in the 4NF section. After decomposition in two tables, as you saw in Tables 3-14 and 3-15, you try to join the decomposed tables to get back the original Table 3-16. What happens is that you get an additional, spurious tuple:

{1, Proj 222, DEF}

With the decomposition of Table 3-16 into two tables that are actually projections of the original table, you got a spurious row if you joined the two new tables. The problem lies in the fact that the original table violated so-called *join dependency* constraint. A relation satisfies join dependency if every legal value of relation is equal to the join of its projections. Join dependencies are a generalization of multivalued dependencies. To solve the problem, you need decomposition to three tables. In addition to the Employees-Projects and Employees-Activities tables, you need also a Projects-Activities table, as shown in Table 3-17.

TABLE 3-17 The Projects-Activities Table

Project	Activity
Proj 111	ABC
Proj 111	DEF
Proj 222	ABC
Proj 111	XYZ

If there is no join dependency violation, a table is in 5NF. A more formal definition says that *every nontrivial join dependency in the table is implied by the keys of the table.*

Finally, let me return to that common sense I mentioned a couple of times. What happens if a project includes an activity, an employee is assigned to a project, and the assigned employee performs the aforementioned activity, but the employee does not have to perform that activity on that project? Then you need four tables, which is a design that you would probably create initially. You need the Employees-Projects table, which shows which employees are assigned to which project; the Employees-Activities table, which shows which activities employees can perform; the Projects-Activities table, which shows which activities are needed in which project; and, finally, the Employees-Projects-Activities table, which shows which activity is performed by which employee on which project.

Additional Normal Forms

Before introducing fourth and fifth normal forms, let me briefly mention domain-key normal form (DKNF). In DKNF, all constraints come from domains (types) and keys (candidate keys and foreign keys). A table in DKNF is free of violating entity, referential, and domain integrity rules, as described previously. It is in fifth normal form as well and thus fully normalized. However, DKNF is a more theoretical than practical normal form. To achieve it, you would have to create many, many different types. This is a nearly impossible mission, especially if your types need to be widely accepted and your type constraints need to be agreed on. In addition, users of your types (the database and other developers) would have to learn a lot just to start using your types.

C. J. Date also proposed sixth normal form—a normal form that solves possible temporal data anomalies. However, to solve temporal data problems, I would also have to introduce the *Interval* data type, implement the Pack and Unpack operators, and solve some other problems as well. Refer to *Inside Microsoft SQL Server 2008: T-SQL Programming* to find a deeper discussion of temporal data and suggested solutions for temporal problems.

Denormalization

You should always try to reach at least 3NF when designing a database. However, sometimes you have to turn the process around and, after fully normalizing a database, start denormalizing it. The two main reasons for denormalization are performance and history, as explained in *Designing Database Solutions by Using Microsoft SQL Server 2005* by Dejan Sarka, Andy Leonard, Javier Loria, and Adolfo Wiernik (Microsoft Press, 2007).

A classic business question is, how much of a product is currently in stock? You can calculate quantities on stock by summarizing shipments and subtracting deliveries. States and levels can always be calculated from events. However, this question could be very frequent. Therefore, it makes sense to aggregate events to levels and states and maintain these aggregates with every new event. In addition, you could speed joins by replicating a foreign key from the first child table to the second one. This way queries might involve fewer tables to join. In both cases, you denormalized to improve performance.

Imagine another example. An invoicing application uses a fully normalized database design. A customer's address is stored in the Customers table only. If a customer moves, you update that customer's address with the new one. Let's say that after the update, the customer asks you to reprint an old invoice. Now you have a problem because you didn't store the old address. You can solve this problem by maintaining a copy of the customer address on the invoice date in the Invoices table. (I should mention that this might not be treated as denormalization—you probably just missed that *InvoiceAddress* attribute when analyzing the business problem!) Figure 3-13 shows the fully normalized Invoices database.

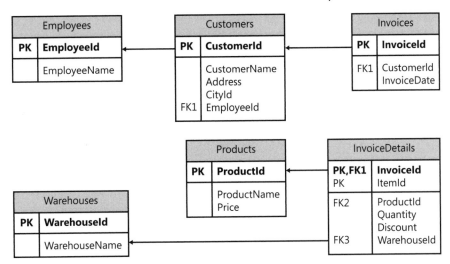

FIGURE 3-13 Normalized Version of Invoices Database

You can denormalize in multiple places. For example, you might transfer the *EmployeeId* column to the Invoices table to avoid a join to the Customers table when you are analyzing invoices over employees only. You could include the *CustomerName* and *CustomerAddress* columns in the Invoices table to maintain history. You could maintain aggregates, such as stock level per warehouse (in a separate table), total stock level per product, year-to-date sales per customers, and more. Figure 3-14 shows a denormalized version of the invoices database.

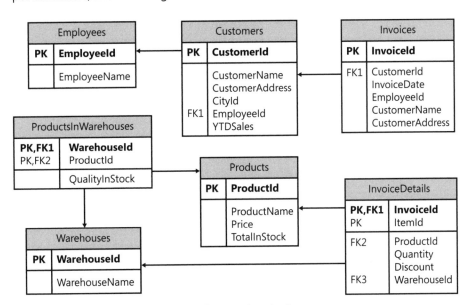

FIGURE 3-14 The denormalized version of the invoices database

Remember to denormalize very deliberately. After denormalization, you introduce possible update anomalies back to the database. You have to maintain redundant data in user-defined transactions. If you insert a new event, for example, take care to update the level or the state derived from events in the same transaction. Triggers are especially useful for maintaining denormalized data. With triggers, which are automatically part of a transaction, you transfer the burden of maintaining the denormalized data on your RDBMS.

Generalization and Specialization

Let's return to the NULLs problem. Remember that you can have NULLs when an attribute is not applicable for some tuples. You can eliminate the need to use NULLs in this way by means of *specialization* by introducing *subtypes*. The problem could also be turned around; remember the decomposition for resolving BCNF violation earlier in this chapter:

OrdersOrderDate {CustomerId, OrderDate, OtherOrderColumns}

OrdersDueDate {CustomerId, DueDate, OtherOrderColumns}

These two relations have many attributes in common, and this is a kind of redundancy. You can solve this redundancy by means of *generalization* by introducing *supertypes*.

Two entities are of distinct, or *primitive,* types if they have no attributes in common. Some relations can have both common and distinct attributes. If they have a common identifier (that is, a common primary identification schema or a common primary key), we can talk about a special supertype/subtype relationship. Supertypes and subtypes are helpful for representing different levels of generalization or specialization. In a business problem description, the verb *is* (or explicitly *is a kind of*) leads to a supertype/subtype relationship. For example, a customer is a partner, and a supplier is a partner as well. Obviously, customers and suppliers have something in common.

In the preceding example, partners are a supertype of customers and suppliers. If you start with subtypes and find a supertype, you're using a bottom-up approach. The top-down approach is the opposite. Whether you generalize or specialize, the same problem arises: where to stop? This question can be answered easily with the top-down approach. Stop specializing (in other words, stop introducing) subtypes when there are no additional interesting attributes for another level of subtypes. The opposite technique is more problematic; after all, you could finish with just a few entities, such as subjects, objects, and events. One possible stopping condition is when you reach abstract objects, or objects that do not exist in the real world. Abstract objects are not part of a relational database. However, sometimes it is practical to introduce a supertype just to share a common identification schema even between disjoint entities. From experience, I suggest a practical approach that works quite well for me: stop when you have a problem naming the supertype (when you reach names like *thing*). If you cannot name it immediately, you are probably trying to generalize disjoint entities.

Here is some additional practical advice for generalization and specialization. If you have a table with few known values and many NULLs in some column, it's probably a candidate for specialization. Check whether those NULLs represent unknown values or attributes that are nonapplicable for the rows in which they appear. You can get rid of NULLs for attributes that are not applicable if you introduce subtypes. For the bottom-up approach, tables that have many columns with similar or even the same names probably need a supertype table. Note that you are again dependent on a good naming convention.

Figure 3-15 shows entities that need generalization.

CustomersOriginal	
PK	**CustomerId**
	CompanyName Address DiscountCode

SuppliersOriginal	
PK	**SupplierId**
	CompanyName Address URL

FIGURE 3-15 Before generalization

Let me mention a big issue with generalization. What if your system with the design from Figure 3-15 is already in production with a lot of data already inserted? In that case, generalization is not that simple. Not only do you have to introduce a generalized model like the one shown in Figure 3-16, but you also have to take care of the data. You need to merge and de-duplicate customers and suppliers in the case of a customer who is also a supplier.

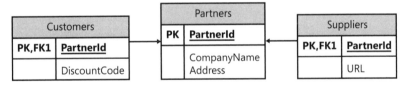

FIGURE 3-16 After generalization

I gave you a lot of practical advice on how to find supertypes and subtypes. I also mentioned a formal rule regarding when to stop specializing: when you no longer have any attributes to add to a subtype. However, to make this topic consistent with the rest of this theoretical chapter, we need a formal definition for when you have to stop generalizing.

Principle of Orthogonal Design

You find the most general supertypes when *no two relations are be defined in such a way that they can represent the same facts*. A more formal definition says that your database should be in accordance with the Principle of Orthogonal Design, as stated in *An Introduction to Database Systems, 8th edition* by C. J. Date (Addison-Wesley, 2003):

> *Let A and B be distinct base relvars. Then there must not exist nonloss decompositions of A and B into A1, A2, …, Am and B1, B2, …, Bn (respectively) such that some projection Ai in set A1, A2, …, Am and some projection Bj in set B1, B2, …, Bn have overlapping meanings.*

Let me finish this topic with couple of words of explanation. The term *relvar* is used here for relation, which is probably the correct term, as a relation is actually a relational variable. The term *orthogonal* means that relations must have mutually independent meanings, and this is exactly what we wanted for primitive types. You might notice that the principle is just formalized common sense. While normalization reduces redundancy within relations, generalization (or orthogonal design) reduces redundancy across relations. Finally, specialization reduces the need to use the NULL value for an attribute that is not applicable. Note also that the Principle of Orthogonal Design also prevents unnecessary horizontal decompositions based on nonoverlapping restrictions of the original relation, as you would again get some projections of the new decomposed relations with overlapping meanings. The implication of the orthogonal design is that even if relations A and B have the same heading type, the following must hold:

A Union B   : is a disjoint union

A Intersect B   : is empty

A Minus B   : is equal to A

You can use these equations for checking whether you have relations with non-overlapping meaning.

Conclusion

This chapter was an introduction to the relational model. Basic terms such as *type, tuple, relation,* and *attribute* were explained. The meaning of a relation should be now clear to you, and you should recognize that you can treat a relation like a business entity or understand it like a predicate with propositions. You can also use this dual approach when manipulating relations; you can be prescriptive, by using relational algebra, or descriptive, by using relational calculus. The importance of data integrity and the means to maintain data integrity were emphasized. Namely, constraints were explained comprehensively. The problem of NULLs was discussed. The chapter concluded with a set of formal rules and principles for achieving a good design, including normalization and orthogonal design. Many times a good naming convention was pointed out as crucial for a good design. All the theoretical knowledge found in this chapter and Chapter 2 should help you understand the advanced queries you'll encounter in the following chapters.

Chapter 4
Query Tuning

This chapter lays the foundation of query tuning knowledge required for both this book and *Inside Microsoft SQL Server 2008: T-SQL Programming*. (For brevity, I'll refer to the programming book as *Inside T-SQL Programming* and to both this book and *Inside T-SQL Programming* as "these books.") Here you will be introduced to a tuning methodology, acquire tools for query tuning, learn how to analyze execution plans and perform index tuning, and learn the significance of preparing good sample data and the importance of using set-based solutions.

When building the table of contents for this book, I faced quite a dilemma with regard to the query tuning chapter, a dilemma that I've also faced when teaching advanced T-SQL—should this material appear early or late? On one hand, the chapter provides important background information that is required for the rest of the book; on the other hand, some techniques used for query tuning involve advanced queries—sort of a chicken-and-egg quandary. I decided to incorporate the chapter early in the book, but I wrote it as an independent unit that can be used as a reference. My recommendation is that you read this chapter before the rest of the book, and when a query uses techniques that you're not familiar with yet, just focus on the conceptual elements described in the text. Some queries will use techniques that are described later in the book (for example, pivoting, running aggregations, the OVER clause, CUBE, CTEs, and so on) or in *Inside T-SQL Programming* (for example, temporary tables, cursors, routines, CLR integration, compilations, and so on). Don't be concerned if the techniques are not clear. Feel free, though, to jump to the relevant chapter if you're curious about a certain technique. When you finish reading these books, I suggest that you return to this chapter and revisit any queries that were not clear at first to make sure you fully understand their mechanics.

Credits go to the mentors within the company I work for—Solid Quality Mentors—for their contribution to this chapter, especially to Andrew J. Kelly and Eladio Rincón.

Sample Data for This Chapter

Throughout the chapter, I will use the Performance database and its tables in my examples. Run the code in Listing 4-1 to create the database and its tables and populate them with sample data. Note that it will take a few minutes for the code to finish.

LISTING 4-1 Creation script for sample database and tables

```
SET NOCOUNT ON;
USE master;
IF DB_ID('Performance') IS NULL
  CREATE DATABASE Performance;
GO
USE Performance;
GO

-- Creating and Populating the Nums Auxiliary Table
SET NOCOUNT ON;
IF OBJECT_ID('dbo.Nums', 'U') IS NOT NULL
  DROP TABLE dbo.Nums;
CREATE TABLE dbo.Nums(n INT NOT NULL PRIMARY KEY);

DECLARE @max AS INT, @rc AS INT;
SET @max = 1000000;
SET @rc = 1;

INSERT INTO dbo.Nums(n) VALUES(1);
WHILE @rc * 2 <= @max
BEGIN
  INSERT INTO dbo.Nums(n) SELECT n + @rc FROM dbo.Nums;
  SET @rc = @rc * 2;
END

INSERT INTO dbo.Nums(n)
  SELECT n + @rc FROM dbo.Nums WHERE n + @rc <= @max;
GO

-- Drop Data Tables if Exist
IF OBJECT_ID('dbo.EmpOrders', 'V') IS NOT NULL
  DROP VIEW dbo.EmpOrders;
GO
IF OBJECT_ID('dbo.Orders', 'U') IS NOT NULL
  DROP TABLE dbo.Orders;
GO
IF OBJECT_ID('dbo.Customers', 'U') IS NOT NULL
  DROP TABLE dbo.Customers;
GO
IF OBJECT_ID('dbo.Employees', 'U') IS NOT NULL
  DROP TABLE dbo.Employees;
GO
IF OBJECT_ID('dbo.Shippers', 'U') IS NOT NULL
  DROP TABLE dbo.Shippers;
GO

-- Data Distribution Settings
DECLARE
  @numorders   AS INT,
  @numcusts    AS INT,
  @numemps     AS INT,
  @numshippers AS INT,
  @numyears    AS INT,
  @startdate   AS DATETIME;
```

```
SELECT
  @numorders   =    1000000,
  @numcusts    =      20000,
  @numemps     =        500,
  @numshippers =          5,
  @numyears    =          4,
  @startdate   = '20050101';

-- Creating and Populating the Customers Table
CREATE TABLE dbo.Customers
(
  custid    CHAR(11)     NOT NULL,
  custname  NVARCHAR(50) NOT NULL
);

INSERT INTO dbo.Customers(custid, custname)
  SELECT
    'C' + RIGHT('000000000' + CAST(n AS VARCHAR(10)), 10) AS custid,
    N'Cust_' + CAST(n AS VARCHAR(10)) AS custname
  FROM dbo.Nums
  WHERE n <= @numcusts;

ALTER TABLE dbo.Customers ADD
  CONSTRAINT PK_Customers PRIMARY KEY(custid);

-- Creating and Populating the Employees Table
CREATE TABLE dbo.Employees
(
  empid     INT          NOT NULL,
  firstname NVARCHAR(25) NOT NULL,
  lastname  NVARCHAR(25) NOT NULL
);

INSERT INTO dbo.Employees(empid, firstname, lastname)
  SELECT n AS empid,
    N'Fname_' + CAST(n AS NVARCHAR(10)) AS firstname,
    N'Lname_' + CAST(n AS NVARCHAR(10)) AS lastname
  FROM dbo.Nums
  WHERE n <= @numemps;

ALTER TABLE dbo.Employees ADD
  CONSTRAINT PK_Employees PRIMARY KEY(empid);

-- Creating and Populating the Shippers Table
CREATE TABLE dbo.Shippers
(
  shipperid   VARCHAR(5)   NOT NULL,
  shippername NVARCHAR(50) NOT NULL
);

INSERT INTO dbo.Shippers(shipperid, shippername)
  SELECT shipperid, N'Shipper_' + shipperid AS shippername
  FROM (SELECT CHAR(ASCII('A') - 2 + 2 * n) AS shipperid
        FROM dbo.Nums
        WHERE n <= @numshippers) AS D;
```

```
ALTER TABLE dbo.Shippers ADD
  CONSTRAINT PK_Shippers PRIMARY KEY(shipperid);

-- Creating and Populating the Orders Table
CREATE TABLE dbo.Orders
(
  orderid   INT        NOT NULL,
  custid    CHAR(11)   NOT NULL,
  empid     INT        NOT NULL,
  shipperid VARCHAR(5) NOT NULL,
  orderdate DATETIME   NOT NULL,
  filler    CHAR(155)  NOT NULL DEFAULT('a')
);

INSERT INTO dbo.Orders(orderid, custid, empid, shipperid, orderdate)
  SELECT n AS orderid,
    'C' + RIGHT('000000000'
            + CAST(
                1 + ABS(CHECKSUM(NEWID())) % @numcusts
                AS VARCHAR(10)), 10) AS custid,
    1 + ABS(CHECKSUM(NEWID())) % @numemps AS empid,
    CHAR(ASCII('A') - 2
          + 2 * (1 + ABS(CHECKSUM(NEWID())) % @numshippers)) AS shipperid,
      DATEADD(day, n / (@numorders / (@numyears * 365.25)), @startdate)
        -- late arrival with earlier date
        - CASE WHEN n % 10 = 0
            THEN 1 + ABS(CHECKSUM(NEWID())) % 30
            ELSE 0
          END AS orderdate
  FROM dbo.Nums
  WHERE n <= @numorders
  ORDER BY CHECKSUM(NEWID());

CREATE CLUSTERED INDEX idx_cl_od ON dbo.Orders(orderdate);

CREATE NONCLUSTERED INDEX idx_nc_sid_od_i_cid
  ON dbo.Orders(shipperid, orderdate)
  INCLUDE(custid);

CREATE UNIQUE INDEX idx_unc_od_oid_i_cid_eid
  ON dbo.Orders(orderdate, orderid)
  INCLUDE(custid, empid);

ALTER TABLE dbo.Orders ADD
  CONSTRAINT PK_Orders PRIMARY KEY NONCLUSTERED(orderid),
  CONSTRAINT FK_Orders_Customers
    FOREIGN KEY(custid)    REFERENCES dbo.Customers(custid),
  CONSTRAINT FK_Orders_Employees
    FOREIGN KEY(empid)     REFERENCES dbo.Employees(empid),
  CONSTRAINT FK_Orders_Shippers
    FOREIGN KEY(shipperid) REFERENCES dbo.Shippers(shipperid);
GO
```

The Orders table is the main data table, and it's populated with 1,000,000 orders spanning four years beginning in 2005. The Customers table is populated with 20,000 customers, the Employees table with 500 employees, and the Shippers table with five shippers. Note that I distributed the order dates, customer IDs, employee IDs, and shipper IDs in the Orders table with random functions. You might not get the same numbers of rows that I'll be getting in my examples back from the queries, but statistically they should be fairly close.

The Nums table is an auxiliary table of numbers, containing only one column, called *n*, populated with integers in the range 1 through 1,000,000.

The code in Listing 4-1 creates the following indexes on the Orders table:

- *idx_cl_od*   Clustered index on *orderdate*

- *PK_Orders*   Unique nonclustered index on *orderid*, created implicitly by the primary key

- *idx_nc_sid_od_i_cid*   Nonclustered index on *shipperid*, *orderdate*, with included column *custid*

- *idx_unc_od_oid_i_cid_eid*   Unique nonclustered index on *orderdate*, *orderid*, with included columns *custid*, *empid*

Index structures and their properties will be explained later in the "Index Tuning" section.

Tuning Methodology

This section describes a tuning methodology that should help you detect performance bottlenecks in your system. I will briefly discuss general performance bottlenecks, but keep in mind that the focus of this chapter—and this book—is query tuning.

So, when your system suffers from performance problems, how do you start to solve the problems?

The answer to this question reminds me of a programmer and an IT manager at a company I worked for years ago. The programmer had to finish writing a component and deploy it, but his code had a bug he couldn't find. He produced a printout of the code (which was pretty thick) and went to the IT manager, who was in a meeting. The IT manager was extremely good at detecting bugs, which is why the programmer sought him. The IT manager took the thick printout, opened it, and immediately pointed to a certain line of code. "Here's your bug," he said. "Now go." After the meeting was over, the programmer asked the IT manager how he found the bug so fast. The IT manager replied, "I knew that anywhere I pointed there would be a bug."

You can point anywhere in the database and find room for tuning. But is it worth it? For example, would it be worthwhile to tune the concurrency aspects of the system if blocking contributes only to 1 percent of the waits in the system as a whole? It's important to follow a path or methodology that leads you through a series of steps to the main problem areas or bottlenecks in the system—those that contribute to most of the waits. This section will introduce such a methodology.

Before you continue, drop the existing clustered index from the Orders table:

```
USE Performance;
GO
DROP INDEX dbo.Orders.idx_cl_od;
```

Suppose your system suffers from performance problems as a whole—users complain that "everything is slow." Listing 4-2 contains a sampling of queries that run regularly in your system.

LISTING 4-2 Sample queries

```
SET NOCOUNT ON;
USE Performance;
GO
SELECT orderid, custid, empid, shipperid, orderdate, filler
FROM dbo.Orders
WHERE orderid = 3;
GO
SELECT orderid, custid, empid, shipperid, orderdate, filler
FROM dbo.Orders
WHERE orderid = 5;
GO
SELECT orderid, custid, empid, shipperid, orderdate, filler
FROM dbo.Orders
WHERE orderid = 7;
GO
SELECT orderid, custid, empid, shipperid, orderdate, filler
FROM dbo.Orders
WHERE orderdate = '20080212';
GO
SELECT orderid, custid, empid, shipperid, orderdate, filler
FROM dbo.Orders
WHERE orderdate = '20080118';
GO
SELECT orderid, custid, empid, shipperid, orderdate, filler
FROM dbo.Orders
WHERE orderdate = '20080828';
GO
SELECT orderid, custid, empid, shipperid, orderdate, filler
FROM dbo.Orders
WHERE orderdate >= '20080101'
  AND orderdate < '20080201';
GO
SELECT orderid, custid, empid, shipperid, orderdate, filler
FROM dbo.Orders
WHERE orderdate >= '20080401'
  AND orderdate < '20080501';
GO
```

```
SELECT orderid, custid, empid, shipperid, orderdate, filler
FROM dbo.Orders
WHERE orderdate >= '20080201'
  AND orderdate < '20090301';
GO
SELECT orderid, custid, empid, shipperid, orderdate, filler
FROM dbo.Orders
WHERE orderdate >= '20080501'
  AND orderdate < '20080601';
GO
```

Restart your SQL Server instance and then run the code in Listing 4-2 several times (try 10). SQL Server will internally record performance information you will rely on later. Restarting your instance will reset some of the counters.

When dealing with performance problems, database professionals tend to focus on the technical aspects of the system, such as resource queues, resource utilization, and so on. However, users perceive performance problems simply as waits—they make a request and have to wait to get the results back. A response that takes longer than three seconds to arrive after an interactive request is typically perceived by users as a performance problem. They don't really care how many commands wait on average on each disk spindle or what the cache hit ratio is, and they don't care about blocking, CPU utilization, average page life expectancy in cache, and so on. They care about waits, and that's where performance tuning should start.

The tuning methodology I recommend applies a top-down approach. It starts by investigating waits at the instance level and then drills down through a series of steps until the processes/ components that generate the bulk of the waits in the system are identified. Once you identify the offending processes, you can focus on tuning them. Following are the main steps of the methodology:

1. Analyze waits at the instance level

2. Correlate waits with queues

3. Determine a course of action

4. Drill down to the database/file level

5. Drill down to the process level

6. Tune indexes/queries

In the following sections I cover in detail each step in the tuning methodology. I describe some of the objects that you need to query to get performance information. In some cases I give recommendations to automate the collection of certain performance data using your own manual scheduled jobs. Where relevant I explain how the data can be analyzed graphically using graphs that you manually create in tools like Microsoft Office Excel.

Note that SQL Server 2008 introduces a component called the *data collector* that collects different sets of data (performance and other) from different sources and stores it in a relational data warehouse known as the *management data warehouse*. The data collector installs three *system data collection sets* that collect disk usage, server activity, and query statistics information. The new data collection platform helps you automate the collection of performance and other information and also analyze it graphically with preconfigured reports. The system data collection sets are already configured to query many of the objects that I will describe in the following sections. So naturally, if you're relying on the data collector to collect such data, you won't necessarily need to configure your own manual jobs. Please refer to SQL Server Books Online under "System Data Collection Sets" for specifics about the information collected by those collection sets, the objects that are queried, and even the specific queries used to query those objects.

Analyze Waits at the Instance Level

The first step in the tuning methodology is to identify at the instance level which types of waits contribute most to the waits in the system. This is done by querying a dynamic management view (DMV) called *sys.dm_os_wait_stats*. This DMV contains more than 400 wait types, most of which are documented in SQL Server Books Online with at least a short description. If you think about it, this is a manageable number that is convenient to work with as a starting point. Some other performance tools give you too much information to start with and create a situation in which you can't see the forest for the trees.

Run the following query to return the waits in your system sorted by type:

```
SELECT
  wait_type,
  waiting_tasks_count,
  wait_time_ms,
  max_wait_time_ms,
  signal_wait_time_ms
FROM sys.dm_os_wait_stats
ORDER BY wait_type;
```

Here's an abbreviated version of the results I got when I ran this query on my system:

wait_type	waiting _tasks _count	wait _time _ms	max _wait _time _ms	signal _wait _time _ms
...				
ASYNC_IO_COMPLETION	3	1710	658	0
ASYNC_NETWORK_IO	288785	176144	959	21377
AUDIT_GROUPCACHE_LOCK	0	0	0	0
...				
CXPACKET	50281	195552	3482	20132
CXROWSET_SYNC	0	0	0	0

```
DAC_INIT                 1       1       1     0
...
IO_COMPLETION            652     40492   1598  165
IO_RETRY                 0       0       0     0
IOAFF_RANGE_QUEUE        0       0       0     0
...
LCK_M_S                  24      25429   9065  9
LCK_M_SCH_M              18      166     34    5
LCK_M_SCH_S              1       654     654   0
...
PAGELATCH_SH             448     269     142   64
PAGELATCH_UP             15      14      4     7
PARALLEL_BACKUP_QUEUE    0       0       0     0
...
WRITELOG                 5325    28738   309   2453
XACT_OWN_TRANSACTION     0       0       0     0
XACT_RECLAIM_SESSION     0       0       0     0
...
```

> **Note** Of course, you shouldn't draw conclusions about production systems from the output that I got. Needless to say, my personal computer or your test computer or personal test environment won't necessarily reflect a real production environment. I'm just using this output for illustration purposes. I'll mention later which types of waits are typically predominant in production environments.

The DMV accumulates values since the server was last restarted. If you want to reset its values, run the following code (but don't run it now):

```
DBCC SQLPERF('sys.dm_os_wait_stats', CLEAR);
```

The DMV *sys.dm_os_wait_stats* contains the following attributes:

- *wait_type*
- *waiting_tasks_count*   The number of waits on this wait type
- *wait_time_ms*   The total wait time for this wait type in milliseconds (including *signal_wait_time_ms*)
- *max_wait_time_ms*
- *signal_wait_time_ms*   The difference between the time the waiting thread was signaled and when it started running

The meaning of most attributes should be simple enough to understand, except for the last one, perhaps. A thread enters a wait state when the resource it is waiting for is not available. Once the resource becomes available, the waiting thread is signaled. However, the CPU might be busy at this point serving other threads. The attribute *signal_wait_time_ms* indicates the time it took from the moment the thread is signaled that the resource is available until the thread gets CPU time and starts using the resource. As you can imagine, high values in this attribute typically indicate CPU problems.

Among the various types of waits, you will find ones related to locks, latches, I/O (including I/O latches), parallelism, the transaction log, memory, compilations, OLEDB (linked servers and other OLEDB components), and so on. Typically, you will want to ignore some types of waits—for example, sleep wait types that occur when a thread is suspended doing nothing, queue wait types that occur when a worker is idle waiting for a task to be assigned, or wait types described specifically in SQL Server Books Online as not indicating a problem, such as CLR_AUTO_EVENT, REQUEST_FOR_DEADLOCK_SEARCH, and others. Make sure you filter out irrelevant waits so that they do not skew your calculations.

In many cases you'll find I/O-related waits are among the most common types of waits (for example, IOLATCH waits), for several reasons. I/O is typically the most expensive resource involved with data-manipulation activities. Also, when queries or indexes are not designed and tuned well, the result is typically excessive I/O. Also, when customers think of "strong" computers, they usually focus their attention on CPU and memory, and they don't always pay adequate attention to the I/O subsystem. Database systems need strong I/O subsystems.

High values in network-related waits (for example, ASYNC_NETWORK_IO) may indicate a network problem, though they may also indicate that the client is not consuming the data sent to it by SQL Server fast enough.

Some systems don't necessarily access large portions of data; instead, these systems involve processes that access small portions of data very frequently. Such is typically the case with online transaction processing (OLTP) environments, which have stored procedures and queries that access small portions of data but are invoked very frequently. In such environments, compilations and recompilations of the code might be the main cause of a bottleneck, in which case you will likely see high values in signal waits (related to CPU). Lots of use of ad-hoc queries instead of stored procedures and prepared statements may lead to flooding the memory with ad-hoc plans, in which case you will typically see high values in the CMEMTHREAD wait type, which occurs when a task is waiting on a thread-safe memory object.

You may also have issues with parallel query plans that use too many threads. This may result in long waits of threads that wait for other threads to finish their work (CXPACKET wait) before they can continue; the system as a whole might not provide optimal throughput. Such systems may benefit from lowering the max degree of parallelism. Note, though, that sometimes the CXPACKET wait type is only a symptom caused by other reasons—for example, excessive I/O resulting from lack of important indexes—in which case you will also see high values in I/O-related waits.

OLTP systems also involve a lot of data modification in small portions, and the transaction log often becomes a bottleneck in such environments. When SQL Server cannot write fast enough to the log, you typically see high values in the WRITELOG wait type.

The tempdb database can also be a serious bottleneck because all temporary tables, whether created implicitly by an execution plan or explicitly, are created in tempdb. SQL Server also uses tempdb's space to perform other activities. Performance problems in tempdb may cause high values in I/O-related waits and others. High values in latch waits (for example, PAGE_LATCH_UP) may indicate contention on internal structures such as IAM, GAM, SGAM, and PFS pages. The cause might be frequent allocations of pages for temporary tables, heavy inserts to heaps, and other causes. Improper file layout may lead to such contention.

The OLEDB wait type represents waits related to linked servers, BULK INSERT, Full Text, and others. However, note that an OLEDB call cannot yield; therefore, the wait state starts when the call starts and ends when the call ends. This means that high values in this wait type don't necessarily indicate a performance problem.

Occasionally, you also find systems with concurrency-related (blocking) problems, in which case lock waits (LCK) will be high.

I gave a few examples for performance problems and the common types of waits that are associated with them. This coverage is not complete and is provided just to give you a sense of how wait stats information can be analyzed.

Isolating Top Waits

Let's get back to the wait information that you receive from the DMV. You probably won't find it convenient to browse all wait types and try to manually figure out which are the most substantial. You want to isolate the top waits—those that in total accumulate to some threshold percentage of the total waits in the system. You can use a number like 80 percent because typically a small number of wait types contributes to the bulk of the waits in the system.

The following query isolates the top waits that accumulate in total to 80 percent of the wait time in the system, returning no fewer than five waits:

```
WITH Waits AS
(
  SELECT
    wait_type,
    wait_time_ms / 1000. AS wait_time_s,
    100. * wait_time_ms / SUM(wait_time_ms) OVER() AS pct,
    ROW_NUMBER() OVER(ORDER BY wait_time_ms DESC) AS rn,
    100. * signal_wait_time_ms / wait_time_ms as signal_pct
  FROM sys.dm_os_wait_stats
  WHERE wait_time_ms > 0
    AND wait_type NOT LIKE N'%SLEEP%'
    AND wait_type NOT LIKE N'%IDLE%'
    AND wait_type NOT LIKE N'%QUEUE%'
    AND wait_type NOT IN(  N'CLR_AUTO_EVENT'
                         , N'REQUEST_FOR_DEADLOCK_SEARCH'
                         , N'SQLTRACE_BUFFER_FLUSH'
                         /* filter out additional irrelevant waits */ )
)
```

```
SELECT
  W1.wait_type,
  CAST(W1.wait_time_s AS NUMERIC(12, 2)) AS wait_time_s,
  CAST(W1.pct AS NUMERIC(5, 2)) AS pct,
  CAST(SUM(W2.pct) AS NUMERIC(5, 2)) AS running_pct,
  CAST(W1.signal_pct AS NUMERIC(5, 2)) AS signal_pct
FROM Waits AS W1
  JOIN Waits AS W2
    ON W2.rn <= W1.rn
GROUP BY W1.rn, W1.wait_type, W1.wait_time_s, W1.pct, W1.signal_pct
HAVING SUM(W2.pct) - W1.pct < 80 -- percentage threshold
    OR W1.rn <= 5
ORDER BY W1.rn;
```

This query generates (on my system) the following output:

```
wait_type          wait_time_s    pct     running_pct  signal_pct
------------------ -------------- ------  ------------ -----------
PAGEIOLATCH_SH     2305.85        34.50   34.50        1.68
CXPACKET           1630.89        24.40   58.89        18.22
ASYNC_NETWORK_IO   1572.81        23.53   82.42        10.86
PAGEIOLATCH_EX     368.67         5.52    87.94        0.78
WRITELOG           160.28         2.40    90.34        11.53
```

This query uses techniques to calculate running aggregates, which I'll explain later in the book. Remember, focus for now on the concepts rather than on the techniques used to achieve them. This query returns the top waits that accumulate to 80 percent of the waits in the system, after filtering out irrelevant wait types. Of course, you can adjust the threshold and filter out other irrelevant waits to your analysis. To see at least *n* rows in the output (let's say *n* = 5), the expression *OR W1.rn <= 5* is specified in the HAVING clause. With each wait type, the query returns the following:

- The total wait time in seconds that processes waited on that wait type since the system was last restarted or the counters were cleared

- The percentage of the wait time of this type out of the total

- The running percentage from the top-most wait type until the current one

- The percentage of the signal wait time out of the wait time (remember that *wait_time_ms* includes *signal_wait_time_ms*)

> **Note** In the *sys.dm_os_wait_stats* DMV, *wait_time_ms* represents the total wait time of all processes that waited on this type, even if multiple processes were waiting concurrently. Still, these numbers would typically give you a good sense of the main problem areas in the system.

Examining the top waits, you can identify several potential problem areas: read-related I/O, parallelism, and network. Waits related to write-related I/O and writes to the transaction log also appear in the output, but those seem minor compared to the others. With this information in hand, you are ready for the next step.

Collecting Wait Information

I also find it handy to collect wait information in a table and update it at regular intervals (for example, once an hour). By doing this, you can analyze the distribution of waits during the day and identify peak periods. Note that if you enabled data collection and the system collection set "Server Activity", wait-stats information is automatically collected for you in the management data warehouse. You can then analyze waits over time via the report Server Activity History (found in SQL Server Management Studio by right-clicking Data Collection under Management in Object Explorer and choosing Reports). In this section I describe what you need to define in case you're not using the data collector to collect wait stats.

Run the following code to create the WaitStats table:

```
USE Performance;
IF OBJECT_ID('dbo.WaitStats', 'U') IS NOT NULL DROP TABLE dbo.WaitStats;

CREATE TABLE dbo.WaitStats
(
  dt                    DATETIME      NOT NULL DEFAULT (CURRENT_TIMESTAMP),
  wait_type             NVARCHAR(60)  NOT NULL,
  waiting_tasks_count   BIGINT        NOT NULL,
  wait_time_ms          BIGINT        NOT NULL,
  max_wait_time_ms      BIGINT        NOT NULL,
  signal_wait_time_ms   BIGINT        NOT NULL
);

CREATE UNIQUE CLUSTERED INDEX idx_dt_type ON dbo.WaitStats(dt, wait_type);
CREATE INDEX idx_type_dt ON dbo.WaitStats(wait_type, dt);
```

Define a job that runs on regular intervals and uses the following code to load the current data from the DMV:

```
INSERT INTO Performance.dbo.WaitStats
    (wait_type, waiting_tasks_count, wait_time_ms,
     max_wait_time_ms, signal_wait_time_ms)
  SELECT
    wait_type, waiting_tasks_count, wait_time_ms,
    max_wait_time_ms, signal_wait_time_ms
  FROM sys.dm_os_wait_stats
  WHERE wait_type NOT IN (N'MISCELLANEOUS');
```

Remember that the wait information in the DMV is cumulative. To get the waits that took place within each interval, you need to apply a self-join between two instances of the table—one representing the current samples and the other representing the previous samples. The join condition will match each current row to the row representing the previous sampling for the same wait type. Then you can subtract the cumulative wait time of the previous sampling from the current, thus producing the wait time during the interval. The following code creates the *IntervalWaits* function, which implements this logic:

```
IF OBJECT_ID('dbo.IntervalWaits', 'IF') IS NOT NULL
  DROP FUNCTION dbo.IntervalWaits;
GO
```

Roger K. Hodgkiss
1 Seminole Drive
Nashua, NH 03063

```
CREATE FUNCTION dbo.IntervalWaits
  (@fromdt AS DATETIME, @todt AS DATETIME)
RETURNS TABLE
AS

RETURN
  WITH Waits AS
  (
    SELECT dt, wait_type, wait_time_ms,
      ROW_NUMBER() OVER(PARTITION BY wait_type
                        ORDER BY dt) AS rn
    FROM dbo.WaitStats
  )
  SELECT Prv.wait_type, Prv.dt AS start_time,
    CAST((Cur.wait_time_ms - Prv.wait_time_ms)
          / 1000. AS NUMERIC(12, 2)) AS interval_wait_s
  FROM Waits AS Cur
    JOIN Waits AS Prv
      ON Cur.wait_type = Prv.wait_type
      AND Cur.rn = Prv.rn + 1
      AND Prv.dt >= @fromdt
      AND Prv.dt < DATEADD(day, 1, @todt)
GO
```

The function accepts the date boundaries of a period that you want to analyze. For example, the following query returns the interval waits for the period '20090212' through '20090213' (inclusive), sorted by the totals for each wait type in descending order, wait type, and start time:

```
SELECT wait_type, start_time, interval_wait_s
FROM dbo.IntervalWaits('20090212', '20090213') AS F
ORDER BY SUM(interval_wait_s) OVER(PARTITION BY wait_type) DESC,
  wait_type, start_time;
```

I find Microsoft Office Excel PivotTables or Analysis Services cubes extremely handy in analyzing such information graphically. These tools allow you to easily see the distribution of waits graphically. For example, suppose you want to analyze the waits over the period '20090212' through '20090213' using Excel PivotTables. Prepare the following IntervalWaitsSample view, which will be used as the external source data for the PivotTable:

```
IF OBJECT_ID('dbo.IntervalWaitsSample', 'V') IS NOT NULL
  DROP VIEW dbo.IntervalWaitsSample;
GO

CREATE VIEW dbo.IntervalWaitsSample
AS

SELECT wait_type, start_time, interval_wait_s
FROM dbo.IntervalWaits('20090212', '20090215') AS F;
GO
```

Create a PivotTable and pivot chart in Excel and specify the *IntervalWaitsSample* view as the PivotTable's external source data. Figure 4-1 shows what the PivotTable looks like with my sample data, after filtering only the top waits.

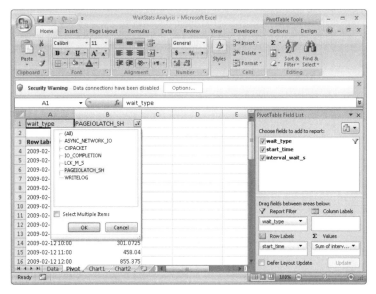

FIGURE 4-1 PivotTable in Excel

Figure 4-2 has a pivot chart, showing graphically the distribution of the PAGEIOLATCH_SH wait type over the input period.

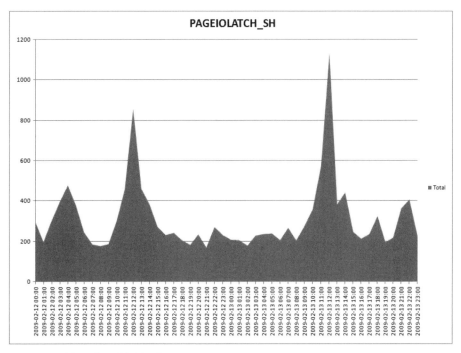

FIGURE 4-2 Pivot chart 1 in Excel

The PAGEIOLATCH_SH wait type indicates waits on I/O for read operations. You can clearly see that, in our case, dramatic peaks occur every day around noon.

Figure 4-3 has a pivot chart showing graphically the distribution of all top wait types.

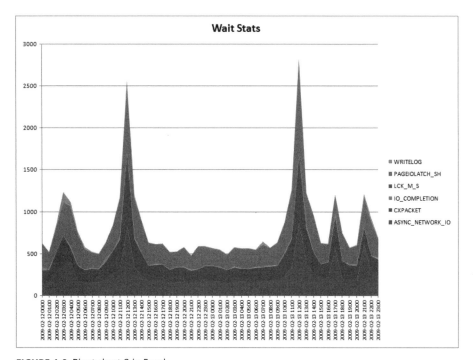

FIGURE 4-3 Pivot chart 2 in Excel

Again, you can see that most waits occur around noon daily.

As an example of how handy the analysis of interval waits can be, in one of my tuning projects I found high peaks of I/O latches every four hours that lasted for quite a while (almost the whole four hours) and then dropped. Naturally, in such a case you look for activities that run on a scheduled basis. Sure enough, the "criminal" was isolated: a scheduled job that invoked the *sp_updatestats* stored procedure against every database every four hours and ran for almost four hours. This stored procedure is used to update statistics globally at the database level. Statistics are histograms maintained for columns that the optimizer uses to determine selectivity of queries, density of joins, and so on. Apparently, in this case some years prior a query didn't perform well because of a lack of up-to-date statistics on a particular indexed column. The customer got a recommendation back then to refresh statistics, and running the stored procedure seemed to solve the problem. Since then, the customer had been running *sp_updatestats* globally every four hours.

Note that SQL Server automatically creates and updates statistics. Typically, the automatic maintenance of statistics is sufficient, and you should intervene manually only in special cases. And if you do intervene manually, do not use *sp_updatestats* globally! The *sp_updatestats* stored procedure is useful mainly to refresh statistics globally after an upgrade of the product or after attaching a database from an earlier version of the product or service pack level.

Ironically, when we found the problem, the query that was the trigger for creating the job was not even used anymore in the system. We simply removed the job and let SQL Server use its automatic maintenance of statistics. Naturally, the graph of I/O latches simply flattened, and the performance problem vanished.

Correlate Waits with Queues

After you identify the top waits at the instance level, you should correlate them with queues to identify the problematic resources. You mainly use Performance Monitor counters for this task. For example, if you identified I/O-related waits in the previous step, you would check the different I/O queues, cache hit ratios, and memory counters. Fewer than two I/O commands should be waiting on an I/O queue on average per spindle (disk). Cache hit ratios should be as high as possible.

As for memory, it is tightly related to I/O because the more memory you have, the more time pages (data and execution plans) can remain in cache, reducing the need for physical I/O. However, if you have I/O issues, how do you know if adding memory will really help? You need to be familiar with the tools that would help you make the right choice. For example, the counter *SQL Server:Buffer Manager – Page life expectancy* will tell you how many seconds on average a page is expected to remain in cache without reference. Low values indicate that adding memory will allow pages to remain longer in cache, while high values indicate that adding memory won't help you much in this respect. The actual numbers depend on your expectations and the frequency with which you run queries that rely on the same data/execution plans. Typically, numbers greater than several hundred indicate a good state of memory.

But let's say that you have very low values in the counter. Does this mean that you have to add memory? Adding memory in such a case would probably help, but some queries lack important indexes on the source tables and end up performing excessive I/O that could be avoided with a better index design. With less I/O and less memory pressure, the problem can be eliminated without investing in hardware. Of course, if you continue your analysis and realize that your indexes and queries are tuned well, you would then consider hardware upgrades.

Similarly, if you identified other types of waits as the top ones, you would check the relevant queues and resource utilization. For example, if the waits involve compilations/recompilations, you would check the compilations/recompilations, CPU utilization, context switching counters, and so on.

SQL Server 2008 collects important performance counters (both generic operating system counters and SQL Server instance counters) as part of the "Server Activity" collection set (assuming it's enabled). If you prefer to collect such information yourself, you can use the Windows Performance Monitor/System Monitor. SQL Server 2008 also provides you with a DMV called *sys.dm_os_performance_counters* containing all the SQL Server instance object-related counters that you can find in Performance Monitor. Unfortunately, this DMV doesn't give you the more generic operating system counters, such as CPU utilization, I/O queues, and so on. You have to analyze those externally.

For example, when I ran the following query on my system, I got the output shown (in abbreviated form) in Table 4-1:

```
SELECT
  object_name,
  counter_name,
  instance_name,
  cntr_value,
  cntr_type
FROM sys.dm_os_performance_counters;
```

TABLE 4-1 **Contents of *sys.dm_os_performance_counters* in Abbreviated Form**

object_name	counter_name	instance_name	cntr_value	cntr_type
MSSQL$SQL08:Buffer Manager	Buffer cache hit ratio		153	537003264
MSSQL$SQL08:Buffer Manager	Buffer cache hit ratio base		153	1073939712
MSSQL$SQL08:Buffer Manager	Page lookups/sec		36230931	272696576
MSSQL$SQL08:Buffer Manager	Free list stalls/sec		0	272696576
MSSQL$SQL08:Buffer Manager	Free pages		164	65792
MSSQL$SQL08:Buffer Manager	Total pages		69472	65792
MSSQL$SQL08:Buffer Manager	Target pages		187769	65792
MSSQL$SQL08:Buffer Manager	Database pages		58627	65792
MSSQL$SQL08:Buffer Manager	Reserved pages		0	65792
MSSQL$SQL08:Buffer Manager	Stolen pages		10681	65792
...				

You might find the ability to query these performance counters in SQL Server useful because you can use query manipulation to analyze the data. As with wait information, you can collect performance counters in a table on regular intervals and then use queries and tools such as PivotTables to analyze the data over time.

Determine Course of Action

The next step—after you have identified the main types of waits and resources involved—represents a junction in the tuning process. Based on your discoveries thus far, you will determine a course of action for further investigation. In our case, we need to identify the causes of I/O, parallelism, network-related waits, and transaction log–related waits (minor); we will then continue with a route based on our findings. But if the previous steps had identified blocking problems, compilation/recompilation problems, or others, you would need to proceed with a completely different course of action.

The I/O-related waits (including I/O latches and write log waits) require us at this point to drill down to the database level. I explain how this is done in the next section.

As I mentioned earlier, the parallelism waits (CXPACKET) occur in parallel query plans when threads wait for an exchange packet from other threads before they can continue work. High values in this wait type might indicate that CPU resources are not utilized optimally, especially in OLTP environments where many requests run simultaneously. The problem may be mitigated by lowering the maximum degree of parallelism in the server. Note that even when queries are restricted to use only one CPU, it doesn't mean that SQL Server cannot utilize more than one CPU; rather, a single query will not be processed with a parallel query plan. High values in the CXPACKET wait type can also be caused by using hyperthreading. Note that high values in CXPACKET wait type do not always represent a direct cause of a problem; instead, they can be a symptom, in which case you will typically see high values in other wait types (for example, I/O latches). Also, it is quite natural in parallel query plans for threads to wait for other threads to finish work. So even when you have high values in this wait type, you won't always be able to improve the system's throughput by lowering the maximum degree of parallelism.

High values in network waits might indicate network bandwidth problems, but they may also indicate other problems. For example, the client application may have been written inefficiently and can't consume the data fast enough from the moment it made the request. This can happen, for example, when the client uses server-side cursors and in between each fetch of a row it does a lot of processing. Also, some things that seem obvious to most programmers are not necessarily obvious to everyone. This might surprise you, but occasionally we find applications that do not do any filtering in the database as part of their queries—instead, they do the filtering in the application. This, of course, can put an enormous load on the network.

I discuss some of the other performance problems later in these books.

Drill Down to the Database/File Level

The next step in our tuning process is to drill down to the database/file level. You want to isolate the databases that involve most of the cost. Within the database, you want to drill down to the file type (data/log) because the course of action you take depends on the file type. One of the tools that allows you to analyze I/O information at the database/file level is a dynamic management function (DMF) called *sys.dm_io_virtual_file_stats*. The function accepts a database ID and file ID as inputs and returns I/O information about the input database file. You specify NULLs in both to request information about all databases and all files.

The function returns the following attributes:

- *database_id*
- *file_id*
- *sample_ms* (the number of milliseconds since the instance of SQL Server has started and can be used to compare different outputs from this function)
- *num_of_reads*
- *num_of_bytes_read*
- *io_stall_read_ms* (the total time, in milliseconds, that the users waited for reads issued on the file)
- *num_of_writes*
- *num_of_bytes_written*
- *io_stall_write_ms*
- *io_stall* (the total time, in milliseconds, that users waited for I/O to be completed on the file)
- *size_on_disk_bytes* (in bytes)
- *file_handle* (the Microsoft Windows file handle for this file)

Note The measurements are reset when SQL Server starts, and they indicate only physical I/O against the files and not logical I/O.

At this point, we want to figure out which databases involve most of the I/O and I/O stalls in the system and, within the database, which file type (data/log). The following query will give you this information, sorted in descending order by the I/O stalls:

```
WITH DBIO AS
(
  SELECT
    DB_NAME(IVFS.database_id) AS db,
    MF.type_desc,
    SUM(IVFS.num_of_bytes_read + IVFS.num_of_bytes_written) AS io_bytes,
    SUM(IVFS.io_stall) AS io_stall_ms
  FROM sys.dm_io_virtual_file_stats(NULL, NULL) AS IVFS
    JOIN sys.master_files AS MF
      ON IVFS.database_id = MF.database_id
      AND IVFS.file_id = MF.file_id
  GROUP BY DB_NAME(IVFS.database_id), MF.type_desc
)
```

```
SELECT db, type_desc,
  CAST(1. * io_bytes / (1024 * 1024) AS NUMERIC(12, 2)) AS io_mb,
  CAST(io_stall_ms / 1000. AS NUMERIC(12, 2)) AS io_stall_s,
  CAST(100. * io_stall_ms / SUM(io_stall_ms) OVER()
      AS NUMERIC(10, 2)) AS io_stall_pct,
  ROW_NUMBER() OVER(ORDER BY io_stall_ms DESC) AS rn
FROM DBIO
ORDER BY io_stall_ms DESC;
```

This query generates (on my system) the following output:

db	type_desc	io_mb	io_stall_s	io_stall_pct	rn
Performance	ROWS	26002.09	14364.84	86.77	1
MDW	ROWS	1495.23	834.43	5.04	2
AdventureWorks2008	ROWS	99.82	311.11	1.88	3
Performance	LOG	121.43	275.64	1.66	4
MDW	LOG	625.91	177.80	1.07	5
tempdb	ROWS	107.40	147.05	0.89	6
Northwind	ROWS	38.39	117.32	0.71	7
msdb	LOG	64.63	104.98	0.63	8
master	ROWS	58.13	100.44	0.61	9
msdb	ROWS	149.90	89.24	0.54	10
Generic	LOG	1.05	12.25	0.07	11
model	ROWS	8.52	3.66	0.02	12
tempdb	LOG	7.34	3.54	0.02	13
pubs	ROWS	4.57	2.64	0.02	14
InsideTSQL2008	ROWS	4.50	2.35	0.01	15
Generic	ROWS	4.32	1.74	0.01	16
master	LOG	1.07	1.61	0.01	17
AdventureWorks2008	LOG	0.23	1.59	0.01	18
Northwind	LOG	0.07	1.30	0.01	19
InsideTSQL2008	LOG	0.12	1.09	0.01	20
pubs	LOG	0.41	0.96	0.01	21
model	LOG	0.56	0.40	0.00	22

The output shows the database name, file type, total I/O (reads and writes) in megabytes, I/O stalls in seconds, I/O stalls in percent of the total for the whole system, and a row number indicating a position in the sorted list based on I/O stalls. Of course, if you want, you can calculate a percentage and row number based on I/O as opposed to I/O stalls, and you can also use running aggregation techniques to calculate a running percentage, as I demonstrated earlier. You might also be interested in a separation between the reads and writes for your analysis. In this output, you can clearly identify the main element involving most of the system's I/O stalls—the data portion of Performance, which scores big time (86 percent of the stalls), and the data portion of MDW, which also incurs a large percent (5 percent of the stalls). I enabled the data collector in my system and the three system collection sets, which store the information in this management data warehouse. By default, the collection frequency is 60 seconds. Behind, with about 1 to 2 percent each, are the data portions of AdventureWorks2008 and tempdb and the log portions of Performance and MDW. Obviously, you should focus on these elements, paying special attention to data activity against the Performance database.

Regarding the bulk of our problem—I/O against the data portion of the Performance database—you now need to drill down to the process level to identify the processes that involve most of the waits.

If high waits are associated with the transaction log, you can identify the problematic databases by using the *sys.dm_io_virtual_file_stats* DMF. This wasn't a significant issue in any of the databases in my system, but let's assume it was. You first need to check whether the log is configured adequately, that is, whether it is placed on its own disk drive with no interference and, if so, whether the disk drive is fast enough. If the log happens to be placed on a slow disk drive, you might want to consider dedicating a faster disk for it. Once the logging activity exceeds the throughput of the disk drive, you start getting waits and stalls. You might be happy dedicating a faster disk drive for the log, but then again, you might not have the budget, or you might have already assigned the fastest disk you could for it. Keep in mind that the transaction log is written sequentially, so striping it over multiple disk drives won't help, unless you also have activities that read from the log (such as backups and transactional replication). You might also be able to optimize the processes that cause intensive logging by reducing their amount of logging. I'll elaborate on minimally logged operations in Chapter 10, "Data Modification."

As for tempdb, many activities—both explicit and implicit—might cause tension in tempdb to the point where it can become a serious bottleneck in the system. The tempdb database is used by SQL Server to store explicitly created temporary tables and table variables and implicitly created worktables. It is also used as a temporary storage area for many other internal activities. Several features that rely on row versioning keep their version store in tempdb, including snapshot isolations, triggers, online index operations, and multiple active result sets (MARS). Typically you'll have a lot of room for optimizing tempdb, and you should definitely give that option adequate attention. I'll elaborate on tempdb and on row versioning in *Inside T-SQL Programming* in the chapters that cover temporary tables, triggers, and transactions.

Note that two system collection sets collect I/O-related information (if enabled). The "Server Activity" collection set collects some I/O-related performance counters and queries the *sys.dm_io_virtual_file_stats* DMV. The "Disk Usage" collection set collects information about data and log files from the catalog views sys.database_files, sys.partitions, sys.allocation_ units, and sys.internal_tables and the command DBCC SQLPERF (LOGSPACE). You also get preconfigured reports called Server Activity History and Disk Usage Summary (in Object Explorer, right-click Data Collection under Management and choose Reports), allowing you to graphically analyze I/O information stored in the management data warehouse.

For our demonstration, let's focus on solving the I/O problems related to the data portion of the Performance database.

Drill Down to the Process Level

Now that you know which databases (in our case, one) involve most of the performance problem, you want to drill down to the process level, namely, identify the processes (stored procedures, queries, and so on) that need to be tuned. For this task, you will find SQL Server's built-in tracing capabilities extremely powerful. You need to trace a workload representing the typical activities in the system against the databases you need to focus on, analyze the trace data, and isolate the processes that need to be tuned.

Before I talk about the specific trace you need to create for such tuning purposes, I'd first like to point out a few important tips regarding working with traces in SQL Server in general.

Traces have an impact on the performance of the system, and you should put effort into reducing their impact. My good friend Brian Moran once compared the problematic aspect of measuring performance to the Heisenberg Uncertainty Principle in quantum mechanics. The principle was formulated by Werner Heisenberg in 1927. Very loosely speaking, when you measure something, a factor of uncertainty is caused by your measurement. The more precise the measure of something's position, the more uncertainty there is regarding its momentum (loosely, velocity and direction). So the more precisely you know one thing, the less precisely you can know some parallel quantity. On the scale of atoms and elementary particles, the effect of the uncertainty principle is very important. There's no proof to support the uncertainty principal, but the theory is mathematically sound and supported by experimentation.

Going back to our traces, you don't want your tracing activity to cause a performance problem itself. You can't avoid its effect altogether—that's impossible—but you can definitely do much to reduce it by following some important guidelines:

- Don't trace with the SQL Server Profiler GUI; instead, use the T-SQL code that defines the trace. When you trace with Profiler, you're actually running two traces—one that directs the output to the target file and one that streams the trace information to the client running Profiler. You can define the trace graphically with Profiler and then script the trace definition to T-SQL code using the menu item File | Export | Script Trace Definition | For SQL Server 2005 - 2008. You can then make slight revisions to the code depending on your needs. I like to encapsulate the code in a stored procedure that accepts as arguments elements that I want to make variable—for example, the database ID I use as a filter in the trace definition.

- Do not trace directly to a table, as this will have a significant performance impact. Tracing to a file on a local disk is the fastest option (tracing to a network share is bad as well). You can later load the trace data to a table for analysis using the *fn_trace_gettable* function, using a BULK operation such as SELECT INTO.

- Tracing can produce enormous amount of data and excessive I/O activity. Make sure the target trace file does not reside on disk drives that contain database files (such as data, log, and tempdb). Ideally, dedicate a separate disk drive for the target trace files.

- Be selective in your choices of event classes and data columns—only trace what you need, removing all default and unnecessary ones. Of course, don't be too selective; make sure that all relevant event classes and data columns are included. Be aware that if you trace individual statement event classes (for example, *SP:StmtCompleted*, *SQL:StmtCompleted*), those tend to produce large amounts of trace data because each individual statement within a procedure/batch produces a trace event. Unless you really need to trace the individual statements, consider tracing at the procedure/batch level (for example, *SP:Completed*, *SQL:BatchCompleted*).

- Use the trace filtering capabilities to filter only the relevant events. For example, when tuning a particular database, make sure you filter events only for the relevant database ID.

With these important guidelines in mind, let's proceed to the trace that we need for our tuning purposes.

Trace Performance Workload

You now need to define a trace that will help you identify processes that need to be tuned in the Performance database. When faced with such a need, DBAs tend to trace slow-running processes by filtering events where the Duration data column is greater than or equal to some value (say, 3,000 milliseconds). Though such a trace can be very interesting, it won't necessarily reveal all important queries that should be tuned. Think of the following: You have a query that runs for about 30 seconds a couple of times a day and another query that runs for a about half a second 40,000 times a day. Which would you say is more important to tune? Obviously, the latter is more important, but if you filter only events that run for at least three seconds, you'll filter out the more important query to tune.

In short, for our purposes you don't want to filter based on Duration at all. Of course, this means that you might get enormous amounts of trace data, so make sure you follow the guidelines I suggested earlier. You do want to filter only the databases that are relevant to your tuning process.

As for event classes, if most activities in your system are invoked by stored procedures and each stored procedure invokes a small or limited number of activities, trace the *SP:Completed* event class. You will then be able to aggregate the data by the procedure. Similarly, if most of the activities are invoked by batches with a small number of activities, trace the *SQL:BatchCompleted* event class. However, if each procedure invokes many activities, you want to trace the *SP:StmtCompleted* event class to capture each individual statement invoked from each stored procedure. If you have activities that are submitted as ad-hoc batches (as in our case), trace the *SQL:StmtCompleted* event class. Remember, though, that tracing individual statement event classes can produce a lot of trace information and have an impact on the traced SQL Server instance. As much as possible, try to limit such tracing to short periods to collect a representative workload. Finally, if you have activities submitted as remote procedure calls, trace the *RPC:Completed* event class. Notice that all event classes are *Completed* ones as opposed to the respective *Starting* event classes. Only the *Completed* event classes carry performance information such as Duration, CPU, Reads, and Writes because, naturally, these values are unknown when the respective event starts.

As for data columns, you mainly need the TextData column that will carry the actual T-SQL code and the relevant performance-related counters—for example, the Duration column. Remember that users perceive waits as the performance problem, and Duration stands for the elapsed time it took the event to run. If you're specifically targeting I/O-related problems, you may want to analyze the Reads and Writes columns. I also like to trace the RowCounts data column, especially when looking for network-related problems. Queries returning the result set to the client with large numbers in this counter would indicate potential pressure on the network. Other than that, you might want additional data columns based on your needs. For example, if you later want to analyze the data by host, application, login, and so on, make sure you also include the corresponding data columns.

You can define a trace following these guidelines and then script its definition to T-SQL code. I did so and encapsulated the code in a stored procedure called *PerfworkloadTraceStart*.

The stored procedure accepts a database ID and file name as input parameters. It defines a trace using the specified database ID as a filter and the given file name as the target for the trace data; it starts the trace and returns the newly generated trace ID via an output parameter. Run the following code to create the *PerfworkloadTraceStart* stored procedure:

```
SET NOCOUNT ON;
USE master;
GO

IF OBJECT_ID('dbo.PerfworkloadTraceStart', 'P') IS NOT NULL
   DROP PROC dbo.PerfworkloadTraceStart;
GO

CREATE PROC dbo.PerfworkloadTraceStart
   @dbid      AS INT,
   @tracefile AS NVARCHAR(245),
   @traceid   AS INT OUTPUT
AS

-- Create a Queue
DECLARE @rc          AS INT;
DECLARE @maxfilesize AS BIGINT;

SET @maxfilesize = 5;

EXEC @rc = sp_trace_create @traceid OUTPUT, 0, @tracefile, @maxfilesize, NULL
IF (@rc != 0) GOTO error;

-- Set the events
DECLARE @on AS BIT;
SET @on = 1;

-- RPC:Completed
exec sp_trace_setevent @traceid, 10, 15, @on;
exec sp_trace_setevent @traceid, 10, 8, @on;
exec sp_trace_setevent @traceid, 10, 16, @on;
exec sp_trace_setevent @traceid, 10, 48, @on;
exec sp_trace_setevent @traceid, 10, 1, @on;
exec sp_trace_setevent @traceid, 10, 17, @on;
exec sp_trace_setevent @traceid, 10, 10, @on;
exec sp_trace_setevent @traceid, 10, 18, @on;
exec sp_trace_setevent @traceid, 10, 11, @on;
```

```
exec sp_trace_setevent @traceid, 10, 12, @on;
exec sp_trace_setevent @traceid, 10, 13, @on;
exec sp_trace_setevent @traceid, 10, 6, @on;
exec sp_trace_setevent @traceid, 10, 14, @on;

-- SP:Completed
exec sp_trace_setevent @traceid, 43, 15, @on;
exec sp_trace_setevent @traceid, 43, 8, @on;
exec sp_trace_setevent @traceid, 43, 48, @on;
exec sp_trace_setevent @traceid, 43, 1, @on;
exec sp_trace_setevent @traceid, 43, 10, @on;
exec sp_trace_setevent @traceid, 43, 11, @on;
exec sp_trace_setevent @traceid, 43, 12, @on;
exec sp_trace_setevent @traceid, 43, 13, @on;
exec sp_trace_setevent @traceid, 43, 6, @on;
exec sp_trace_setevent @traceid, 43, 14, @on;

-- SP:StmtCompleted
exec sp_trace_setevent @traceid, 45, 8, @on;
exec sp_trace_setevent @traceid, 45, 16, @on;
exec sp_trace_setevent @traceid, 45, 48, @on;
exec sp_trace_setevent @traceid, 45, 1, @on;
exec sp_trace_setevent @traceid, 45, 17, @on;
exec sp_trace_setevent @traceid, 45, 10, @on;
exec sp_trace_setevent @traceid, 45, 18, @on;
exec sp_trace_setevent @traceid, 45, 11, @on;
exec sp_trace_setevent @traceid, 45, 12, @on;
exec sp_trace_setevent @traceid, 45, 13, @on;
exec sp_trace_setevent @traceid, 45, 6, @on;
exec sp_trace_setevent @traceid, 45, 14, @on;
exec sp_trace_setevent @traceid, 45, 15, @on;

-- SQL:BatchCompleted
exec sp_trace_setevent @traceid, 12, 15, @on;
exec sp_trace_setevent @traceid, 12, 8, @on;
exec sp_trace_setevent @traceid, 12, 16, @on;
exec sp_trace_setevent @traceid, 12, 48, @on;
exec sp_trace_setevent @traceid, 12, 1, @on;
exec sp_trace_setevent @traceid, 12, 17, @on;
exec sp_trace_setevent @traceid, 12, 6, @on;
exec sp_trace_setevent @traceid, 12, 10, @on;
exec sp_trace_setevent @traceid, 12, 14, @on;
exec sp_trace_setevent @traceid, 12, 18, @on;
exec sp_trace_setevent @traceid, 12, 11, @on;
exec sp_trace_setevent @traceid, 12, 12, @on;
exec sp_trace_setevent @traceid, 12, 13, @on;

-- SQL:StmtCompleted
exec sp_trace_setevent @traceid, 41, 15, @on;
exec sp_trace_setevent @traceid, 41, 8, @on;
exec sp_trace_setevent @traceid, 41, 16, @on;
exec sp_trace_setevent @traceid, 41, 48, @on;
exec sp_trace_setevent @traceid, 41, 1, @on;
exec sp_trace_setevent @traceid, 41, 17, @on;
exec sp_trace_setevent @traceid, 41, 10, @on;
exec sp_trace_setevent @traceid, 41, 18, @on;
exec sp_trace_setevent @traceid, 41, 11, @on;
```

```
exec sp_trace_setevent @traceid, 41, 12, @on;
exec sp_trace_setevent @traceid, 41, 13, @on;
exec sp_trace_setevent @traceid, 41, 6, @on;
exec sp_trace_setevent @traceid, 41, 14, @on;

-- Set the Filters

-- Application name filter
EXEC sp_trace_setfilter @traceid, 10, 0, 7, N'SQL Server Profiler%';
-- Database ID filter
EXEC sp_trace_setfilter @traceid, 3, 0, 0, @dbid;

-- Set the trace status to start
EXEC sp_trace_setstatus @traceid, 1;

-- Print trace id and file name for future references
PRINT 'Trace ID: ' + CAST(@traceid AS VARCHAR(10))
  + ', Trace File: ''' + @tracefile + '.trc''';

GOTO finish;

error:
PRINT 'Error Code: ' + CAST(@rc AS VARCHAR(10));

finish:
GO
```

Note that for demonstration purposes I included both proc/batch-level and statement-level event classes, even though in my case it would have been enough to trace just the *SQL:StmtCompleted* event class. In practice, you should include only the event classes that you need.

Run the following code to start the trace, filtering events against the Performance database and sending the trace data to the file 'c:\temp\Perfworkload 20090212.trc':

```
DECLARE @dbid AS INT, @traceid AS INT;
SET @dbid = DB_ID('Performance');

EXEC master.dbo.PerfworkloadTraceStart
  @dbid      = @dbid,
  @tracefile = 'c:\temp\Perfworkload 20090212',
  @traceid   = @traceid OUTPUT;
```

If you were to assume that the newly generated trace ID is 2, you would get the following output:

```
Trace ID: 2, Trace File: 'c:\temp\perfworkload 20090212.trc'
```

You need to keep the trace ID aside, as you will use it later to stop the trace and close it.

Next, run the sample queries from Listing 4-2 several times. When done, stop the trace and close it by running the following code (assuming the trace ID is 2):

```
EXEC sp_trace_setstatus 2, 0;
EXEC sp_trace_setstatus 2, 2;
```

Of course, you should specify the actual trace ID you got for your trace. If you lost the scrap of paper you wrote the trace ID on, query the sys.traces view to get information about all running traces.

When tracing a workload in a production environment for tuning purposes, make sure you trace a sufficiently representative one. In some cases, this might mean tracing for only a couple of hours, while in other cases it can be a matter of days.

The next step is to load the trace data to a table and analyze it. Of course, you can open it with Profiler and examine it there; however, typically such traces generate a lot of data, and you can't do much with Profiler to analyze the data. In our case, we have a small number of sample queries. Figure 4-4 shows what the trace data looks like when loaded in Profiler.

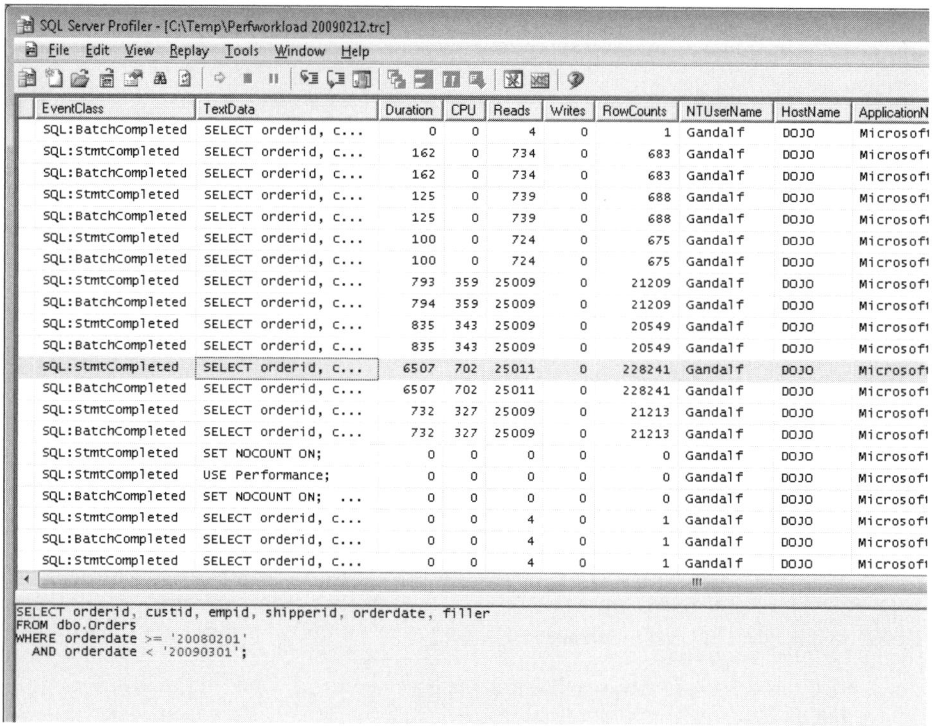

FIGURE 4-4 Performance workload trace data

Examining the trace data, you can clearly see some long-running queries that generate a lot of I/O. These queries use range filters based on the *orderdate* column and seem to consistently incur about 25,000 reads. The Orders table currently contains 1,000,000 rows and resides on about 25,000 pages. This tells you that these queries are causing full table scans to acquire the data and are probably missing an important index on the *orderdate* column. The missing index is probably the main cause of the excessive I/O in the system.

Also, you can find some queries that return a very large number of rows in the result set—several thousand and, in some cases, hundreds of thousands of rows. You should check whether filters and further manipulation are applied in the server when possible rather than bringing everything to the client through the network and performing filtering and further manipulation there. These queries are probably the main cause of the network issues in the system.

Of course, such graphical analysis with Profiler is feasible only with tiny traces such as the one we're using for demonstration purposes. In production environments, it's just not realistic; you need to load the trace data to a table and use queries to analyze the data.

Analyze Trace Data

As I mentioned earlier, you use the *fn_trace_gettable* function to return the trace data in table format. Run the following code to load the trace data from our file to the Workload table:

```
USE Performance;
IF OBJECT_ID('dbo.Workload', 'U') IS NOT NULL DROP TABLE dbo.Workload;
GO

SELECT CAST(TextData AS NVARCHAR(MAX)) AS tsql_code,
  Duration AS duration
INTO dbo.Workload
FROM sys.fn_trace_gettable('c:\temp\Perfworkload 20090212.trc', NULL) AS T
WHERE Duration > 0
  AND EventClass IN(41, 45);
```

Note that this code loads only the TextData (T-SQL code) and Duration data columns to focus particularly on query run time. Typically, you would want to also load other data columns that are relevant to your analysis—for example, the I/O and CPU counters, row counts, host name, application name, and so on. Also, because in this case I want to analyze individual statements, I'm filtering event classes 41 (*SQL:StmtCompleted*) and 45 (*SP:StmtCompleted*).

Remember that it is important to aggregate the performance information by the query or T-SQL statement to figure out the overall performance impact of each query with its multiple invocations. The following code attempts to do just that, and it generates the output shown in abbreviated form in Table 4-2:

```
SELECT
  tsql_code,
  SUM(duration) AS total_duration
FROM dbo.Workload
GROUP BY tsql_code;
```

TABLE 4-2 Aggregated Duration by Query in Abbreviated Form

tsql_code	duration
SELECT orderid, custid, empid, shipperid, orderdate, filler FROM dbo.Orders WHERE orderdate = '20080118';	1326071
SELECT orderid, custid, empid, shipperid, orderdate, filler FROM dbo.Orders WHERE orderdate = '20080212';	1519084
SELECT orderid, custid, empid, shipperid, orderdate, filler FROM dbo.Orders WHERE orderdate = '20080828';	1083055
SELECT orderid, custid, empid, shipperid, orderdate, filler FROM dbo.Orders WHERE orderdate >= '20080101' AND orderdate < '20080201';	7998453
SELECT orderid, custid, empid, shipperid, orderdate, filler FROM dbo.Orders WHERE orderdate >= '20080201' AND orderdate < '20090301';	65186723
...	

But we have a problem. You can see in the aggregated data that some queries that are logically the same or follow the same pattern ended up in different groups. That's because they happened to be using different values in their filters. Only query strings that are completely identical were grouped together. As an aside, you wouldn't be facing this problem had you used stored procedures, each invoking an individual query or a very small number of queries. Remember that in such a case you would have traced the *SP:Completed* event class, and then you would have received aggregated data by the procedure. But that's not the case here.

A simple but not very accurate way to deal with the problem is to extract a substring of the query strings and aggregate by that substring. Typically, the left portion of query strings that follow the same pattern is the same, while somewhere to the right you have the arguments that are used in the filter. You can apply trial and error, playing with the length of the substring that you will extract; with luck, the substring will be long enough to allow grouping queries following the same pattern together and small enough to distinguish queries of different patterns from each other. This approach, as you can see, is tricky and would not guarantee accurate results. Essentially, you pick a number that seems reasonable, close your eyes, and hope for the best.

For example, the following query aggregates the trace data by a query prefix of 100 characters and generates the output shown in Table 4-3:

```
SELECT
  SUBSTRING(tsql_code, 1, 100) AS tsql_code,
  SUM(duration) AS total_duration
FROM dbo.Workload
GROUP BY SUBSTRING(tsql_code, 1, 100);
```

TABLE 4-3 **Aggregated Duration by Query Prefix**

tsql_code	total_duration
SELECT orderid, custid, empid, shipperid, orderdate, filler FROM dbo.Orders WHERE orderdate = '200	3928210
SELECT orderid, custid, empid, shipperid, orderdate, filler FROM dbo.Orders WHERE orderdate >= '20	89089077
SELECT orderid, custid, empid, shipperid, orderdate, filler FROM dbo.Orders WHERE orderid = 5;	2000
SELECT orderid, custid, empid, shipperid, orderdate, filler FROM dbo.Orders WHERE orderid = 7;	1000

In our case, this prefix length did the trick for some queries, but it wasn't very successful with others. With more realistic trace data, you won't have the privilege of looking at a tiny number of queries and being able to play with the numbers so easily. But the general idea is that you adjust the prefix length by applying trial and error.

The following code uses a prefix length of 94 and generates the output shown in Table 4-4:

```
SELECT
    SUBSTRING(tsql_code, 1, 94) AS tsql_code,
    SUM(duration) AS total_duration
FROM dbo.Workload
GROUP BY SUBSTRING(tsql_code, 1, 94);
```

TABLE 4-4 **Aggregated Duration by Query Prefix, Adjusted**

tsql_code	total_duration
SELECT orderid, custid, empid, shipperid, orderdate, filler FROM dbo.Orders WHERE orderdate	93017287
SELECT orderid, custid, empid, shipperid, orderdate, filler FROM dbo.Orders WHERE orderdate	93017287

Now you end up with overgrouping. In short, finding the right prefix length is a tricky process, and its accuracy and reliability are questionable.

A much more accurate approach is to parse the query strings and produce a *query signature* for each. A query signature is a query template that is the same for queries following the same pattern. After creating these, you can then aggregate the data by query signatures instead of by the query strings themselves. SQL Server 2008 provides you with the *sp_get_query_template* stored procedure, which parses an input query string and returns the query template and the definition of the arguments via output parameters.

For example, the following code invokes the stored procedure, providing a sample query string as input:

```
DECLARE @my_templatetext AS NVARCHAR(MAX);
DECLARE @my_parameters   AS NVARCHAR(MAX);
```

```
EXEC sp_get_query_template
  N'SELECT * FROM dbo.T1 WHERE col1 = 3 AND col2 > 78',
  @my_templatetext OUTPUT,
  @my_parameters OUTPUT;

SELECT @my_templatetext AS querysig, @my_parameters AS params;
```

This code generates the following output:

```
querysig                                                 params
-------------------------------------------------------  --------------
select * from dbo . T1 where col1 = @0 and col2 > @1     @0 int,@1 int
```

The problem with this stored procedure is that you need to use a cursor to invoke it against every query string from the trace data, and this can take quite a while with large traces. The stored procedure also (by design) returns an error in some cases (see SQL Server Books Online for details), which could compromise its value. It would be much more convenient to have this logic implemented as a function, allowing you to invoke it directly against the table containing the trace data. Fortunately, such a function exists; it was written by Stuart Ozer, who is with the Microsoft SQL Server Customer Advisory Team (SQL CAT). I would like to thank him for allowing me to share the code with the readers of this book. Here's the function's definition:

```
IF OBJECT_ID('dbo.SQLSig', 'FN') IS NOT NULL
  DROP FUNCTION dbo.SQLSig;
GO

CREATE FUNCTION dbo.SQLSig
  (@p1 NTEXT, @parselength INT = 4000)
RETURNS NVARCHAR(4000)

--
-- This function is provided "AS IS" with no warranties,
-- and confers no rights.
--Use of included script samples are subject to the terms specified at
-- http://www.microsoft.com/info/cpyright.htm
--
-- Strips query strings
AS
BEGIN
  DECLARE @pos AS INT;
  DECLARE @mode AS CHAR(10);
  DECLARE @maxlength AS INT;
  DECLARE @p2 AS NCHAR(4000);
  DECLARE @currchar AS CHAR(1), @nextchar AS CHAR(1);
  DECLARE @p2len AS INT;

  SET @maxlength = LEN(RTRIM(SUBSTRING(@p1,1,4000)));
  SET @maxlength = CASE WHEN @maxlength > @parselength
                        THEN @parselength ELSE @maxlength END;
  SET @pos = 1;
  SET @p2 = '';
  SET @p2len = 0;
  SET @currchar = '';
  set @nextchar = '';
  SET @mode = 'command';
```

```
   WHILE (@pos <= @maxlength)
   BEGIN
     SET @currchar = SUBSTRING(@p1,@pos,1);
     SET @nextchar = SUBSTRING(@p1,@pos+1,1);
     IF @mode = 'command'
     BEGIN
       SET @p2 = LEFT(@p2,@p2len) + @currchar;
       SET @p2len = @p2len + 1 ;
       IF @currchar IN (',','(',' ','=','<','>','!')
         AND @nextchar BETWEEN '0' AND '9'
       BEGIN
         SET @mode = 'number';
         SET @p2 = LEFT(@p2,@p2len) + '#';
         SET @p2len = @p2len + 1;
       END
       IF @currchar = ''''
       BEGIN
         SET @mode = 'literal';
         SET @p2 = LEFT(@p2,@p2len) + '#''';
         SET @p2len = @p2len + 2;
       END
     END
     ELSE IF @mode = 'number' AND @nextchar IN (',',')',' ','=','<','>','!')
       SET @mode= 'command';
     ELSE IF @mode = 'literal' AND @currchar = ''''
       SET @mode= 'command';

     SET @pos = @pos + 1;
   END
   RETURN @p2;
END
GO
```

The function accepts as inputs a query string and the length of the code you want to parse.
The function returns the query signature of the input query, with all parameters replaced
by a number sign (#). Note that this is a fairly simple function and might need to be tailored
to particular situations. Run the following code to test the function:

```
SELECT dbo.SQLSig
  (N'SELECT * FROM dbo.T1 WHERE col1 = 3 AND col2 > 78', 4000);
```

You get the following output:

```
SELECT * FROM dbo.T1 WHERE col1 = # AND col2 > #
```

Of course, you could now use the function and aggregate the trace data by query signature.
However, keep in mind that although T-SQL is very efficient with data manipulation, it is slow
in processing iterative/procedural logic. This is a classic example where a common language
run-time (CLR) implementation of the function makes more sense. The CLR is much faster
than T-SQL for iterative/procedural logic and string manipulation. SQL Server 2008 allows
you to develop .NET routines based on the CLR.

Listing 4-3 has the definition of a CLR-based, user-defined function called *RegexReplace* using C# code.

LISTING 4-3 *RegexReplace* functions

```csharp
using Microsoft.SqlServer.Server;
using System.Data.SqlTypes;
using System.Text.RegularExpressions;

public partial class RegExp
{
  [SqlFunction(IsDeterministic = true, DataAccess = DataAccessKind.None)]
  public static SqlString RegexReplace(
    SqlString input, SqlString pattern, SqlString replacement)
  {
    return (SqlString)Regex.Replace(
      input.Value, pattern.Value, replacement.Value);
  }
}
```

The function merely calls the *Replace* method of the *Regex* object, exposing replacement and parsing capabilities based on regular expressions. The function exposes generic pattern-based string replacement capabilities using regular expressions.

> **Note** I didn't bother checking for NULL inputs in the CLR code because T-SQL allows you to specify the option RETURNS NULL ON NULL INPUT when you register the functions, as I will demonstrate later. This option means that when a NULL input is provided, SQL Server doesn't invoke the function at all; rather, it simply returns a NULL output.

If you're familiar with developing CLR routines in SQL Server, deploy these functions in the Performance database. If you're not, just follow these steps:

1. Create a new Microsoft Visual C# Class Library project in Microsoft Visual Studio 2008 (File | New | Project… | Visual C# | Class Library).

2. In the New Project dialog box, name the project and solution **RegExp**, specify C:\ as the location, and confirm.

3. Rename the file Class1.cs to **RegExp.cs** and within it paste the code from Listing 4-3, overriding its current content.

4. Build the assembly by choosing the Build | Build RegExp menu item. A file named C:\RegExp\RegExp\bin\Debug\RegExp.dll containing the assembly is created.

5. At this point, you go back to SQL Server Management Studio (SSMS) and apply a couple of additional steps to deploy the assembly in the Performance database

and then register the *RegexReplace* function. But first, you need to enable CLR in SQL Server (which is disabled by default) by running the following code:

```
EXEC sp_configure 'clr enabled', 1;
RECONFIGURE;
```

6. Load the intermediate language (IL) code from the .dll file into the Performance database by running the following code:

```
USE Performance;
CREATE ASSEMBLY RegExp
FROM 'C:\RegExp\RegExp\bin\Debug\RegExp.dll';
```

7. Register the *RegexReplace* function by running the following code:

```
CREATE FUNCTION dbo.RegexReplace(
  @input       AS NVARCHAR(MAX),
  @pattern     AS NVARCHAR(MAX),
  @replacement AS NVARCHAR(MAX))
RETURNS NVARCHAR(MAX)
WITH RETURNS NULL ON NULL INPUT
EXTERNAL NAME RegExp.RegExp.RegexReplace;
GO
```

You're done. At this point, you can start using the function like you do any other user-defined function.

You can now use the *RegexReplace* function to produce a query signature for query strings by using a regular expression that has the right parsing logic. For example, the following code shows how to use the function in a query against the Workload table to produce query signatures for the query strings stored in the *tsql_code* attribute:

```
SELECT
  dbo.RegexReplace(tsql_code,
    N'([\s,(=<>!](?![^\]]+[\]]))(?:(?:(?:(?#     expression coming
      )(?:([N])?('')(?:[^'']|'''')*(''))(?#       character
      )|(?:0x[\da-fA-F]*)(?#                       binary
      )|(?:[-+]?(?:(?:[\d]*\.[\d]*|[\d]+)(?#       precise number
      )(?:[eE]?[\d]*)))(?#                         imprecise number
      )|(?:[~]?[-+]?(?:[\d]+))(?#                  integer
      ))(?:[\s]?[\+\-\*\/\%\&\|\^][\s]?)?)+(?#     operators
      ))',
    N'$1$2$3#$4') AS sig,
  duration
FROM dbo.Workload;
```

This regular expression covers cases that the T-SQL function overlooks, and it can be easily enhanced to support more cases if you need it to. In case you're curious, producing query signatures with the *RegexReplace* function is faster than producing them with the T-SQL function by a factor of 10.

This query generates the output shown in Table 4-5 in abbreviated form.

TABLE 4-5 Trace Data with Query Signatures in Abbreviated Form

sig	duration
...	
SELECT orderid, custid, empid, shipperid, orderdate, filler FROM dbo.Orders WHERE orderdate = '#';	162009
SELECT orderid, custid, empid, shipperid, orderdate, filler FROM dbo.Orders WHERE orderdate = '#';	125007
SELECT orderid, custid, empid, shipperid, orderdate, filler FROM dbo.Orders WHERE orderdate = '#';	100005
SELECT orderid, custid, empid, shipperid, orderdate, filler FROM dbo.Orders WHERE orderdate >= '#' AND orderdate < '#';	793045
SELECT orderid, custid, empid, shipperid, orderdate, filler FROM dbo.Orders WHERE orderdate >= '#' AND orderdate < '#';	835047
SELECT orderid, custid, empid, shipperid, orderdate, filler FROM dbo.Orders WHERE orderdate >= '#' AND orderdate < '#';	6507372
SELECT orderid, custid, empid, shipperid, orderdate, filler FROM dbo.Orders WHERE orderdate >= '#' AND orderdate < '#';	732041
SELECT orderid, custid, empid, shipperid, orderdate, filler FROM dbo.Orders WHERE orderdate = '#';	143008
SELECT orderid, custid, empid, shipperid, orderdate, filler FROM dbo.Orders WHERE orderdate = '#';	181010
SELECT orderid, custid, empid, shipperid, orderdate, filler FROM dbo.Orders WHERE orderdate = '#';	102005
...	

As you can see, you get back query signatures, which you can use to aggregate the trace data. Keep in mind, though, that query strings can get lengthy, and grouping the data by lengthy strings is slow and expensive. Instead, you might prefer to generate an integer checksum for each query string by using the T-SQL *CHECKSUM* function. For example, the following query generates a checksum value for each query string from the Workload table:

```
SELECT
  CHECKSUM(dbo.RegexReplace(tsql_code,
    N'([\s,(=<>!](?![^\]]+[\]]))(?:(?:(?:(?#    expression coming
    )(?:([N])?('')(?:[^'']|'''')*(''))(?#       character
    )|(?:0x[\da-fA-F]*)(?#                       binary
    )|(?:[-+]?(?:(?:[\d]*\.[\d]*|[\d]+)(?#       precise number
    )(?:[eE]?[\d]*)))(?#                         imprecise number
    )|(?:[~]?[-+]?(?:[\d]+))(?#                  integer
    ))(?:[\s]?[\+\-\*\/\%\&\|\^][\s]?)?)+(?#     operators
    ))',
    N'$1$2$3#$4')) AS cs,
  duration
FROM dbo.Workload;
```

This query generates the following output, shown here in abbreviated form:

```
cs           duration
-----------  --------------------
-184235228   162009
-184235228   125007
-184235228   100005
368623506    793045
368623506    835047
368623506    6507372
368623506    732041
-184235228   143008
-184235228   181010
-184235228   102005
...
```

Use the following code to add to the Workload table a computed persisted column called *cs* that calculates the checksum of the query signatures and create a clustered index on the *cs* column:

```
ALTER TABLE dbo.Workload ADD cs AS CHECKSUM(dbo.RegexReplace(tsql_code,
    N'([\s,(=<>!](?![^\]]+[\]]))(?:(?:(?:(?#    expression coming
    )(?:([N])?('')(?:[^'']|'''')*(''))(?#       character
    )|(?:0x[\da-fA-F]*)(?#                       binary
    )|(?:[-+]?(?:(?:[\d]*\.[\d]*|[\d]+)(?#       precise number
    )(?:[eE]?[\d]*)))(?#                         imprecise number
    )|(?:[~]?[-+]?(?:[\d]+))(?#                  integer
    ))(?:[\s]?[\+\-\*\/\%\&\|\^][\s]?)?)+(?#     operators
    ))',
    N'$1$2$3#$4')) PERSISTED;

CREATE CLUSTERED INDEX idx_cl_cs ON dbo.Workload(cs);
```

Run the following code to return the new contents of the Workload table, shown in abbreviated form in Table 4-6:

```
SELECT tsql_code, duration, cs
FROM dbo.Workload
```

TABLE 4-6 **Contents of Table Workload**

tsql_code	duration	cs
...		
SELECT orderid, custid, empid, shipperid, orderdate, filler FROM dbo.Orders WHERE orderdate = '20080118';	128007	-184235228
SELECT orderid, custid, empid, shipperid, orderdate, filler FROM dbo.Orders WHERE orderdate = '20080828';	102005	-184235228
SELECT orderid, custid, empid, shipperid, orderdate, filler FROM dbo.Orders WHERE orderdate = '20080212';	187010	-184235228
SELECT orderid, custid, empid, shipperid, orderdate, filler FROM dbo.Orders WHERE orderdate = '20080118';	119006	-184235228

TABLE 4-6 **Contents of Table Workload**

tsql_code	duration	cs
SELECT orderid, custid, empid, shipperid, orderdate, filler FROM dbo.Orders WHERE orderdate = '20080828';	118006	-184235228
SELECT orderid, custid, empid, shipperid, orderdate, filler FROM dbo.Orders WHERE orderdate >= '20080101' AND orderdate < '20080201';	923052	368623506
SELECT orderid, custid, empid, shipperid, orderdate, filler FROM dbo.Orders WHERE orderdate >= '20080401' AND orderdate < '20080501';	879050	368623506
SELECT orderid, custid, empid, shipperid, orderdate, filler FROM dbo.Orders WHERE orderdate >= '20080201' AND orderdate < '20090301';	6340362	368623506
SELECT orderid, custid, empid, shipperid, orderdate, filler FROM dbo.Orders WHERE orderdate >= '20080501' AND orderdate < '20080601';	745042	368623506
SELECT orderid, custid, empid, shipperid, orderdate, filler FROM dbo.Orders WHERE orderdate >= '20080101' AND orderdate < '20080201';	812046	368623506
...		

At this point, you want to aggregate the data by the query signature checksum. It would also be very useful to get running aggregates of the percentage of each signature's duration of the total duration. This information can help you easily isolate the query patterns that you need to tune. Remember that typical production workloads can contain a large number of query signatures. It would make sense to populate a temporary table with the aggregate data and index it and then run a query against the temporary table to calculate the running aggregates.

Run the following code to populate the temporary table #AggQueries with the total duration per signature checksum, including the percentage of the total, and a row number based on the duration in descending order:

```
IF OBJECT_ID('tempdb..#AggQueries', 'U') IS NOT NULL DROP TABLE #AggQueries;

SELECT cs, SUM(duration) AS total_duration,
  100. * SUM(duration) / SUM(SUM(duration)) OVER() AS pct,
  ROW_NUMBER() OVER(ORDER BY SUM(duration) DESC) AS rn
INTO #AggQueries
FROM dbo.Workload
GROUP BY cs;

CREATE CLUSTERED INDEX idx_cl_cs ON #AggQueries(cs);
```

Run the following code to return the contents of the temporary table:

```
SELECT cs, total_duration, pct, rn
FROM #AggQueries
ORDER BY rn;
```

This code generates the following output:

```
cs           total_duration  pct                 rn
-----------  --------------- ------------------- ---
368623506    89089077        95.773814372342239  1
-184235228   3928210         4.222960524729406   2
-1872968693  3000            0.003225102928353   3
```

Use the following query to return the running aggregates of the percentages, filtering only those rows where the running percentage accumulates to a certain threshold that you specify:

```
SELECT AQ1.cs,
  CAST(AQ1.total_duration / 1000000.
    AS NUMERIC(12, 2)) AS total_s,
  CAST(SUM(AQ2.total_duration) / 1000000.
    AS NUMERIC(12, 2)) AS running_total_s,
  CAST(AQ1.pct AS NUMERIC(12, 2)) AS pct,
  CAST(SUM(AQ2.pct) AS NUMERIC(12, 2)) AS run_pct,
  AQ1.rn
FROM #AggQueries AS AQ1
  JOIN #AggQueries AS AQ2
    ON AQ2.rn <= AQ1.rn
GROUP BY AQ1.cs, AQ1.total_duration, AQ1.pct, AQ1.rn
HAVING SUM(AQ2.pct) - AQ1.pct <= 80 -- percentage threshold
--  OR AQ1.rn <= 5
ORDER BY AQ1.rn;
```

In our case, if you use 80 percent as the threshold, you get only one row. For demonstration purposes, I uncommented the part of the expression in the HAVING clause and got the following output from the query:

```
cs           total_s  running_total_s  pct     run_pct  rn
-----------  -------  ---------------  ------  -------- ---
368623506    89.09    89.09            95.77   95.77    1
-184235228   3.93     93.02            4.22    100.00   2
-1872968693  0.00     93.02            0.00    100.00   3
```

You can see at the top that one query pattern accounts for 95.77 percent of the total duration. Based on my experience, a handful of query patterns typically cause most of the performance problems in a given system.

To get back the actual queries that you need to tune, you should join the result table returned from the preceding query with the Workload table, based on a match in the checksum value (*cs* column), like so:

```
WITH RunningTotals AS
(
  SELECT AQ1.cs,
    CAST(AQ1.total_duration / 1000.
      AS DECIMAL(12, 2)) AS total_s,
    CAST(SUM(AQ2.total_duration) / 1000.
      AS DECIMAL(12, 2)) AS running_total_s,
```

```
      CAST(AQ1.pct AS DECIMAL(12, 2)) AS pct,
      CAST(SUM(AQ2.pct) AS DECIMAL(12, 2)) AS run_pct,
      AQ1.rn
    FROM #AggQueries AS AQ1
      JOIN #AggQueries AS AQ2
        ON AQ2.rn <= AQ1.rn
    GROUP BY AQ1.cs, AQ1.total_duration, AQ1.pct, AQ1.rn
    HAVING SUM(AQ2.pct) - AQ1.pct <= 90 -- percentage threshold
--    OR AQ1.rn <= 5
)
SELECT RT.rn, RT.pct, W.tsql_code
FROM RunningTotals AS RT
  JOIN dbo.Workload AS W
    ON W.cs = RT.cs
ORDER BY RT.rn;
```

You will get the output shown in abbreviated form in Table 4-7.

TABLE 4-7 Top Slow Queries in Abbreviated Form

rn	pct	tsql_code
1	95.77	SELECT orderid, custid, empid, shipperid, orderdate, filler FROM dbo.Orders WHERE orderdate >= '20080101' AND orderdate < '20080201';
1	95.77	SELECT orderid, custid, empid, shipperid, orderdate, filler FROM dbo.Orders WHERE orderdate >= '20080401' AND orderdate < '20080501';
1	95.77	SELECT orderid, custid, empid, shipperid, orderdate, filler FROM dbo.Orders WHERE orderdate >= '20080201' AND orderdate < '20090301';
...		

Of course, with a more realistic workload you might get a large number of queries back, but you're really interested in the query pattern that you need to tune. So instead of joining back to the Workload table, use the APPLY operator to return only one row for each query signature with the query pattern and a single sample per pattern out of the actual queries like so:

```
WITH RunningTotals AS
(
  SELECT AQ1.cs,
    CAST(AQ1.total_duration / 1000000.
      AS NUMERIC(12, 2)) AS total_s,
    CAST(SUM(AQ2.total_duration) / 1000000.
      AS NUMERIC(12, 2)) AS running_total_s,
    CAST(AQ1.pct AS NUMERIC(12, 2)) AS pct,
    CAST(SUM(AQ2.pct) AS NUMERIC(12, 2)) AS run_pct,
    AQ1.rn
  FROM #AggQueries AS AQ1
    JOIN #AggQueries AS AQ2
      ON AQ2.rn <= AQ1.rn
  GROUP BY AQ1.cs, AQ1.total_duration, AQ1.pct, AQ1.rn
  HAVING SUM(AQ2.pct) - AQ1.pct <= 80 -- percentage threshold
)
```

```
SELECT RT.rn, RT.pct, S.sig, S.tsql_code AS sample_query
FROM RunningTotals AS RT
  CROSS APPLY
    (SELECT TOP(1) tsql_code, dbo.RegexReplace(tsql_code,
        N'([\s,(=<>!](?![^\]]+[\]]))(?:(?:(?:(?#     expression coming
        )(?:([N])?('')(?:[^'']|'''')*(''))(?#     character
        )|(?:0x[\da-fA-F]*)(?#                     binary
        )|(?:[-+]?(?:(?:[\d]*\.[\d]*|[\d]+)(?#     precise number
        )(?:[eE]?[\d]*)))(?#                       imprecise number
        )|(?:[~]?[-+]?(?:[\d]+))(?#                integer
        ))(?:[\s]?[\+\-\*\/\%\&\|\^][\s]?)?)+(?#   operators
        ))',
        N'$1$2$3#$4') AS sig
      FROM dbo.Workload AS W
      WHERE W.cs = RT.cs) AS S
ORDER BY RT.rn;
```

You will get the output shown in Table 4-8.

TABLE 4-8 Signature and Sample of the Top Slow Queries

rn	pct	sig	sample_query
1	95.77	SELECT orderid, custid, empid, shipperid, orderdate, filler FROM dbo.Orders WHERE orderdate >= '#' AND orderdate < '#';	SELECT orderid, custid, empid, shipperid, orderdate, filler FROM dbo.Orders WHERE orderdate >= '20080101' AND orderdate < '20080201';

Now you can focus your tuning efforts on the query patterns that you got back—in our case, only one. Of course, in a similar manner you can identify the query patterns that generate the largest result sets, most of the I/O, and so on.

Query Statistics

SQL Server 2008 provides a DMV called *sys.dm_exec_query_stats* that aggregates query performance information for queries whose plans are in cache. Unlike the trace approach, this DMV won't report any information for queries whose plans are not in cache (for example, when procedures or queries use the RECOMPILE option). However, for queries whose plans are in cache, you get very interesting performance information that is aggregated since the query plan was cached. Needless to say, if the plan is removed from cache, this information is gone. Note, though, that if you enable the system collection set "Query Statistics," it collects information from this DMV on regular intervals based on the collection frequency defined for it and stores the information in the management data warehouse. You can also analyze this information graphically with the preconfigured report Query Statistics History. (In Object Explorer, right-click Data Collection under Management and choose Reports.) Of course, if you want, you can also create your own jobs to collect information from this DMV with your own queries.

The information that this view provides for each cached query plan includes, among other things, the following:

- A SQL handle that you can provide as input to the function *sys.dm_exec_sql_text* to get the text of the parent query or batch of the current query. You also get the start and end offsets of the query that the current row represents so that you can extract it from the full parent query or batch text. Note that the offsets are zero based and are specified in bytes, although the text is Unicode (meaning two bytes of storage per character).

- A plan handle that you can provide as input to the function *sys.dm_exec_query_plan* to get the XML form of the plan.

- Creation time and last execution time.

- Execution count.

- Performance information including worker (CPU) time, physical reads, logical reads, CLR time, and elapsed time. For each performance counter, you get the total for all invocations of the plan, last, minimum and maximum.

- A binary query hash and a binary plan hash. The former allows you to identify queries with the same query signature, similar to the checksum value I suggested creating earlier for traced data. The latter allows you to identify similar query execution plans. Note that the query hash and plan hash values (*query_hash* and *query_plan_hash* attributes) were introduced in SQL Server 2008, while all other attributes were also available in SQL Server 2005.

For example, the following code identifies the five query patterns in the Performance database with the highest total duration and returns the output shown in Table 4-9 in my system:

```
SELECT TOP (5)
  MAX(query) AS sample_query,
  SUM(execution_count) AS cnt,
  SUM(total_worker_time) AS cpu,
  SUM(total_physical_reads) AS reads,
  SUM(total_logical_reads) AS logical_reads,
  SUM(total_elapsed_time) AS duration
FROM (SELECT
        QS.*,
        SUBSTRING(ST.text, (QS.statement_start_offset/2) + 1,
          ((CASE statement_end_offset
              WHEN -1 THEN DATALENGTH(ST.text)
              ELSE QS.statement_end_offset END
                - QS.statement_start_offset)/2) + 1
        ) AS query
      FROM sys.dm_exec_query_stats AS QS
        CROSS APPLY sys.dm_exec_sql_text(QS.sql_handle) AS ST
        CROSS APPLY sys.dm_exec_plan_attributes(QS.plan_handle) AS PA
      WHERE PA.attribute = 'dbid'
        AND PA.value = DB_ID('Performance')) AS D
GROUP BY query_hash
ORDER BY duration DESC;
```

TABLE 4-9 **Top Slow Queries Based on Query Stats**

sample_query	cnt	cpu	reads	logical_ reads	duration
SELECT orderid, custid, empid, shipperid, orderdate, filler FROM dbo.Orders WHERE orderdate >= '20080501' AND orderdate < '20080601';	665	1926343195	47873	16606308	2786190354
SELECT orderid, custid, empid, shipperid, orderdate, filler FROM dbo.Orders WHERE orderdate = '20080828';	501	129140379	1920	376180	195947201
select dbo.SQLSig (N'select * from t1 where col1 = ' + cast(n as nvarchar(11)), 4000) from dbo.nums where n <= 25000;	4	31001772	1	120	31179782
INSERT INTO Performance.dbo.WaitStats (wait_type, waiting_tasks_count, wait_ time_ms, max_wait_time_ms, signal_wait_ time_ms) SELECT DISTINCT RTRIM(wait_type) AS wait_type, waiting_tasks_count, wait_time_ms, max_wait_time_ms, signal_ wait_time_ms FROM sys.dm_os_wait_stats;	62	996056	400	158352	25149438
SELECT [orderid],[custid],[empid], [shipperid],[orderdate],[filler] FROM [dbo].[Orders] WHERE [orderid]=@1	504	121006	360	2016	14790845

Of course, you could use techniques I showed earlier to calculate running percents and filter query patterns based on those.

Tune Indexes and Queries

Now that you know which patterns you need to tune, you can start with a more focused query-tuning process. The process might involve index tuning or query code revisions, and we will practice it thoroughly throughout the book. Or you might realize that the queries are already tuned pretty well, in which case you would need to inspect other aspects of the system (for example, hardware, database layout, and so on).

In our case, the tuning process is fairly simple. You need to create a clustered index on the *orderdate* column:

```
CREATE CLUSTERED INDEX idx_cl_od ON dbo.Orders(orderdate);
```

Later in the chapter, I'll cover index tuning and explain why a clustered index is adequate for query patterns such as the ones that our tuning process isolated.

To see the effect of adding the index, run the following code to start a new trace:

```
DECLARE @dbid AS INT, @traceid AS INT;
SET @dbid = DB_ID('Performance');

EXEC dbo.PerfworkloadTraceStart
  @dbid      = @dbid,
  @tracefile = 'c:\temp\Perfworkload 20090212 - Tuned',
  @traceid   = @traceid OUTPUT;
```

When I ran this code, I got the following output showing that the trace ID generated is 2:

```
Trace ID: 2, Trace File: 'c:\temp\Perfworkload 20090212 - Tuned.trc'
```

Run the sample queries from Listing 4-2 again and then stop the trace:

```
EXEC sp_trace_setstatus 2, 0;
EXEC sp_trace_setstatus 2, 2;
```

Figure 4-5 shows the trace data loaded with Profiler.

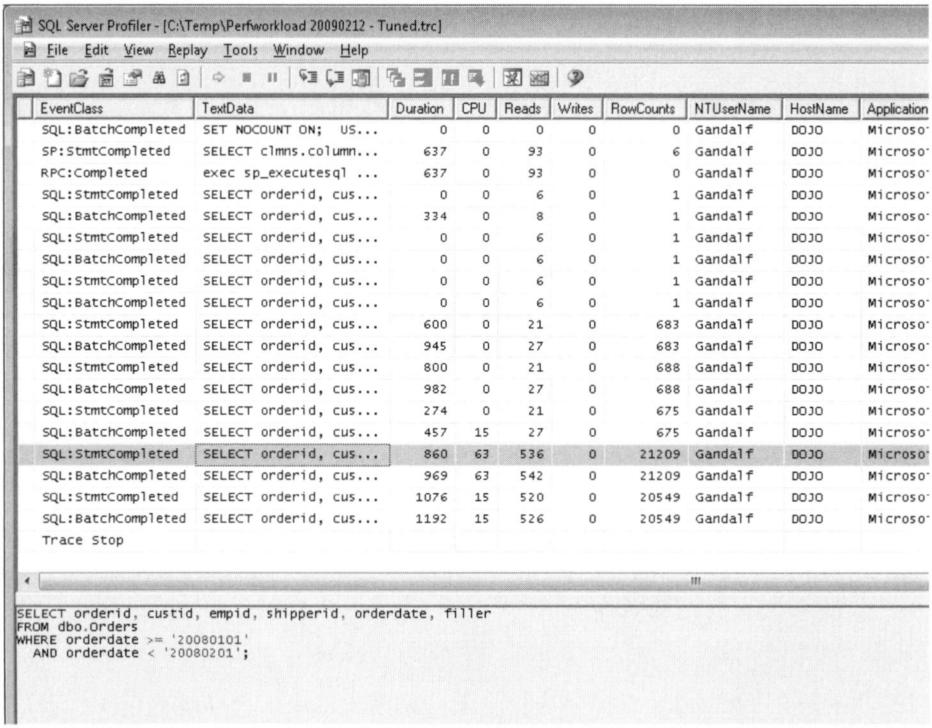

FIGURE 4-5 Performance workload trace data after adding index

You can see that the duration and I/O involved with the query pattern we tuned are greatly reduced. Still, some queries generate a lot of network traffic. With those, you might want to check whether some of the processing of their result sets could be achieved at the server side, thus reducing the amount of data submitted through the network.

Tools for Query Tuning

This section provides an overview of the query-tuning tools that will be used throughout these books, and it will focus on analyzing execution plans.

Cached Query Execution Plans

SQL Server 2008 provides several objects that you can query to analyze the behavior of cached query execution plans:

- The *sys.dm_exec_cached_plans* DMV contains information about the cached query execution plans, with a row per each cached plan.

- The *sys.dm_exec_plan_attributes* DMF contains one row per attribute associated with the plan, whose handle is provided as input to the DMF.

- The *sys.dm_exec_sql_text* DMF returns the text associated with the query, whose handle is provided as input to the DMF.

- The *sys.dm_exec_query_plan* DMF provides the XML form of the execution plan of the query, whose handle is provided as input to the DMF.

SQL Server 2008 also provides you with a compatibility view called *sys.syscacheobjects* that exposes cached query plan information the way it did in previous versions of SQL Server.

Clearing the Cache

When analyzing query performance, you sometimes need to clear the cache. SQL Server provides you with tools to clear both data and execution plans from the cache. To clear data from the cache globally, use the following command:

```
DBCC DROPCLEANBUFFERS;
```

To clear execution plans from the cache globally, use the following command:

```
DBCC FREEPROCCACHE;
```

To clear execution plans of a particular database, use the following command:

```
DBCC FLUSHPROCINDB(<db_id>);
```

Note that the DBCC FLUSHPROCINDB command is undocumented.

To clear execution plans of a particular cache store, use the following command:

```
DBCC FREESYSTEMCACHE(<cachestore>);
```

You can specify the following values as input: *'ALL'*, *pool_name*, *'Object Plans'*, *'SQL Plans'*, *'Bound Trees'*. Note that the last three options are undocumented. The *'ALL'* option indicates that you want to clear all supported caches. The *pool_name* value indicates the name of a Resource Governor pool cache that you want to clear. For the undocumented options, specify *'Object Plans'* to clear object plans (plans for stored procedures, triggers, and user-defined functions). Specify *'SQL Plans'* to clear plans for ad-hoc statements, including prepared statements. Specify *'Bound Trees'* to clear plans for views, constraints, and defaults.

> **Caution** Consider carefully before using these commands in production environments. Obviously, clearing the cache has a performance impact on the system. After clearing the data cache, SQL Server needs to physically read pages accessed for the first time from disk. After clearing execution plans from the cache, SQL Server needs to generate new execution plans for queries. Also, be sure that you are aware of the impact of clearing the cache even when doing so in development or test environments.

Dynamic Management Objects

SQL Server 2005 introduced for the first time support for dynamic management objects, including DMVs and DMFs. SQL Server 2008 added new objects and in some cases added new attributes to existing objects. These contain extremely useful information about the server that you can use to monitor SQL Server, diagnose problems, and tune performance. Much of the information provided by these views and functions has never before been available. Studying them in detail is time very well spent. In these books, I make use of the ones that are relevant to my discussions, but I urge you to take a close look at others as well. You can find information about them in SQL Server Books Online.

STATISTICS IO

STATISTICS IO is a session option used extensively throughout these books. It returns I/O-related information about the statements that you run. To demonstrate its use, first clear the data cache:

```
DBCC DROPCLEANBUFFERS;
```

Then run the following code to turn the session option on and invoke a query:

```
SET STATISTICS IO ON;

SELECT orderid, custid, empid, shipperid, orderdate, filler
FROM dbo.Orders
WHERE orderdate >= '20060101'
  AND orderdate < '20060201';
```

You should get output similar to the following:

```
Table 'Orders'. Scan count 1, logical reads 536, physical reads 3, read-ahead reads 548, lob
logical reads 0, lob physical reads 0, lob read-ahead reads 0.
```

The output tells you how many times the table was accessed in the plan (*Scan count*); how many reads from cache were involved (*logical reads*); how many reads from disk were involved (*physical reads* and *read-ahead reads*); and similarly, how many logical and physical reads related to large objects were involved (*lob logical reads, lob physical reads, lob read-ahead reads*).

Run the following code to turn the session option off:

```
SET STATISTICS IO OFF;
```

Measuring the Run Time of Queries

STATISTICS TIME is a session option that returns the net CPU and elapsed clock time information about the statements that you run. It returns this information for both the time it took to parse and compile the query and the time it took to execute it. To demonstrate the use of this session option, first clear both the data and execution plans from cache:

```
DBCC DROPCLEANBUFFERS;
DBCC FREEPROCCACHE;
```

Run the following code to turn the session option on:

```
SET STATISTICS TIME ON;
```

Then invoke the following query:

```
SELECT orderid, custid, empid, shipperid, orderdate, filler
FROM dbo.Orders
WHERE orderdate >= '20060101'
  AND orderdate < '20060201';
```

You will get output similar to the following:

```
SQL Server parse and compile time:
   CPU time = 0 ms, elapsed time = 64 ms.
SQL Server parse and compile time:
   CPU time = 0 ms, elapsed time = 1 ms.

 SQL Server Execution Times:
   CPU time = 31 ms,   elapsed time = 711 ms.
```

The output tells you the net CPU time and elapsed clock time for parsing and compiling the query and also the time it took to execute it. Run the following code to turn the option off:

```
SET STATISTICS TIME OFF;
```

This tool is convenient when you want to analyze the performance of an individual query interactively. When you run benchmarks in batch mode, the way to measure the run time of queries is different. Store the value of the SYSDATETIME function in a variable directly before the query. Directly after the query, issue an INSERT statement into the table where you collect performance information, subtracting the value stored in the variable from the current value of SYSDATETIME. Note that SYSDATETIME returns a DATETIME2 value, which has an accuracy level of 100 nanoseconds; however, the actual accuracy of the function depends on the computer hardware and version of Windows your SQL Server instance is running on. That's because the SYSDATETIME function internally invokes the *GetSystemTimeAsFileTime()* Windows API, which is hardware and operating system dependent. When measuring the time statistics of queries for which the accuracy level of this function is insufficient, run the queries repeatedly in a loop and divide run time for the entire loop by the number of iterations.

Analyzing Execution Plans

An execution plan is the "work plan" the optimizer generates to determine how to process a given query. The plan contains operators that are generally applied in a specific order. Some operators can be applied while their preceding operator is still in progress. Some operators might be applied more than once. Also, some branches of the plan are invoked in parallel if the optimizer chose a parallel plan. In the plan, the optimizer determines the order in which to access the tables involved in the query, which indexes to use and which access methods to use to apply to them, which join algorithms to use, and so on. In fact, for a given query the optimizer considers multiple execution plans, and it chooses the plan with the lowest cost out of the ones that were generated. Note that SQL Server might not generate all possible execution plans for a given query. If it always did, the optimization process could take too long. SQL Server will calculate thresholds for the optimization process based on the sizes of the tables involved in the query, among other things. One threshold is time based. SQL Server won't spend longer than the time threshold on optimization. Another threshold is cost based. That is, if a plan is found with a lower cost than the cost threshold, it is considered "good enough," in which case optimization stops and that plan is used.

Throughout these books, I'll frequently analyze execution plans of queries. This section and the one that follows ("Index Tuning") should give you the background required to follow and understand the discussions involving plan analysis. Note that the purpose of this section is not to familiarize you with all possible operators; instead, it is to familiarize you with the techniques to analyze plans. The "Index Tuning" section will familiarize you with index-related operators, and later in the book I'll elaborate on additional operators—for example, join-related operators will be described in Chapter 7, "Joins and Set Operations."

Graphical Execution Plans

Graphical execution plans are used extensively throughout these books. SSMS allows you both to get an estimated execution plan (by pressing Ctrl+L) and to include an actual one (by pressing Ctrl+M) along with the output of the query you run. Note that both will typically give you the same plan; remember that an execution plan is generated before the query is run. However, when you request an estimated plan, the query is not run at all. Obviously, some measures can be collected only at run time (for example, the actual number of rows returned from each operator and the number of executions of the operator). In the estimated plan, you will see estimations for measures that can be collected only at run time, while the actual plan will show the actuals and also some of the same estimates.

To demonstrate a graphical execution plan analysis, I will use the following query:

```
SELECT custid, empid, shipperid, COUNT(*) AS numorders
FROM dbo.Orders
WHERE orderdate >= '20080201'
  AND orderdate < '20080301'
GROUP BY CUBE(custid, empid, shipperid);
```

The query returns aggregated counts of orders for all possible grouping sets that can be defined based on the attributes *custid*, *empid*, and *shipperid*. I'll discuss the CUBE subclause of the GROUP BY clause in detail in Chapter 8, "Aggregating and Pivoting Data."

Note I did some graphical manipulation on the execution plans that appear in this chapter to fit images in the printed pages and for clarity.

As an example, if you request an estimated execution plan for the preceding query, you will get the plan shown in Figure 4-6.

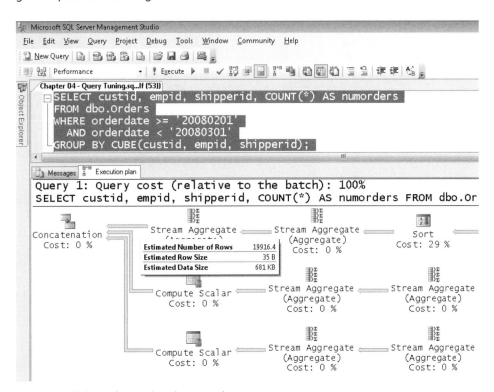

FIGURE 4-6 Estimated execution plan example

Notice that when you place your mouse pointer over an arrow that goes out of an operator (for example, the one going out of the second Stream Aggregate operator), you get an estimated number of rows. By the way, a nice aspect of the arrows representing data flow is that their thickness is proportional to the number of rows returned by the source operator. You want to keep an eye especially on thick arrows, as these might indicate a performance issue.

Next, turn on the Include Actual Execution Plan option and run the query. You will get both the output of the query and the actual plan, as shown in Figure 4-7.

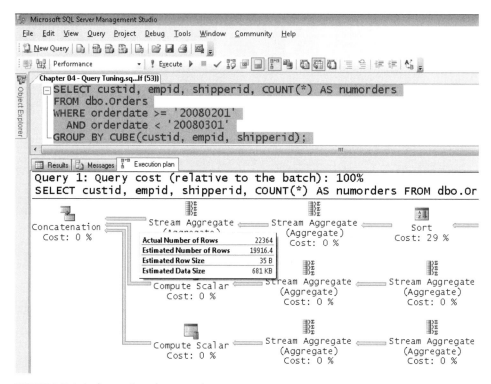

FIGURE 4-7 Actual execution plan example

Notice that now you get the actual number of rows returned by the source operator.

When you get elaborated plans like this one that do not fit in one screen, you can use a really cool zooming feature. Press the plus sign (+) button that appears at the bottom right corner of the execution plan pane, and you will get a rectangle that allows you to navigate to a desired place in the plan, as shown in Figure 4-8.

Figure 4-9 shows the full execution plan for our query—that's after some graphical manipulation for clarity and to make it fit in one screen.

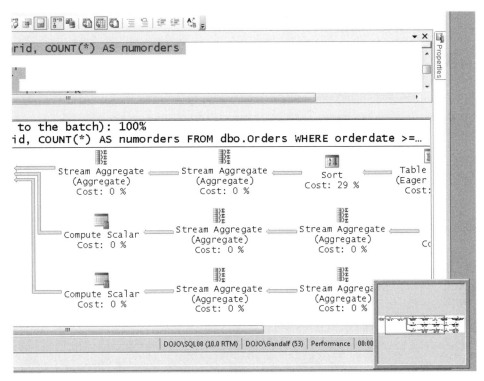

FIGURE 4-8 Zooming feature in graphical showplan

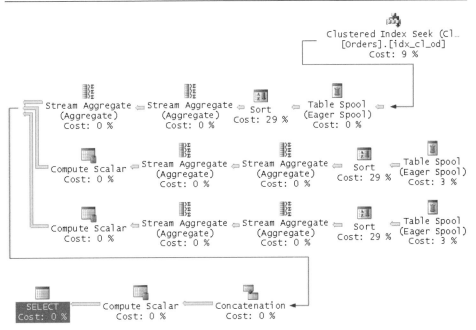

FIGURE 4-9 Execution plan for CUBE query

I shifted the position of some of the operators and added arrows to denote the original flow. Also, I included the full object names where relevant. In the original plan, object names are truncated if they are long.

A plan is a tree of operators. Data flows from a child operator to a parent operator. The tree order of graphical plans that you get in SSMS is expressed from right to left and from top to bottom. That's typically the order in which you should analyze a plan to figure out the flow of activity. In our case, the Clustered Index Seek operator is the first operator that starts the flow, yielding its output to the next operator in the tree—Table Spool (Eager Spool)—and so on.

Notice the cost percentage associated with each operator. This value is the percentage of the operator's cost out of the total cost of the query, as estimated by the optimizer. You want to keep an eye especially on operators that involve high-percentage values and focus your tuning efforts on those operators. When you place your mouse pointer over an operator, you will get a yellow information box. One of the measures you will find there is called *Estimated Subtree Cost*. This value represents the cumulative estimated cost of the subtree, starting with the current operator (all operators in all branches leading to the current operator). The subtree cost associated with the root operator (topmost, leftmost) represents the estimated cost of the whole query, as shown in Figure 4-10.

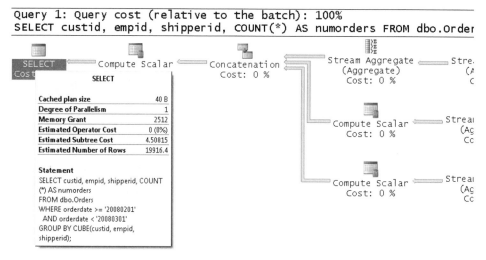

FIGURE 4-10 Subtree cost

Note that you shouldn't expect a direct correlation between a query's subtree cost and its actual run time. The query cost value is used by the optimizer to compare with other query plans. Given two query plans that the optimizer generates, it tries to come up with a lower-cost value for the plan that is supposed to run faster.

Another nice feature of graphical execution plans is that you can easily compare the costs of multiple queries. You can use this feature to compare the costs of different queries that produce the same result. For example, suppose you want to compare the costs of the following queries:

```
SELECT custid, orderid, orderdate, empid, filler
FROM dbo.Orders AS O1
WHERE orderid =
  (SELECT TOP (1) O2.orderid
   FROM dbo.Orders AS O2
   WHERE O2.custid = O1.custid
   ORDER BY O2.orderdate DESC, O2.orderid DESC);

SELECT custid, orderid, orderdate, empid, filler
FROM dbo.Orders
WHERE orderid IN
(
  SELECT
    (SELECT TOP (1) O.orderid
     FROM dbo.Orders AS O
     WHERE O.custid = C.custid
     ORDER BY O.orderdate DESC, O.orderid DESC) AS oid
  FROM dbo.Customers AS C
);

SELECT A.*
FROM dbo.Customers AS C
  CROSS APPLY
    (SELECT TOP (1)
        O.custid, O.orderid, O.orderdate, O.empid, O.filler
     FROM dbo.Orders AS O
     WHERE O.custid = C.custid
     ORDER BY O.orderdate DESC, O.orderid DESC) AS A;

WITH C AS
(
  SELECT custid, orderid, orderdate, empid, filler,
    ROW_NUMBER() OVER(PARTITION BY custid
                      ORDER BY orderdate DESC, orderid DESC) AS n
  FROM dbo.Orders
)
SELECT custid, orderid, orderdate, empid, filler
FROM C
WHERE n = 1;
```

You highlight the queries that you want to compare and request a graphical execution plan (estimated or actual, as needed). In our case, you get the plans shown in Figure 4-11.

At the top of each plan, you get the percentage of the estimated cost of the query out of the whole batch. For example, in our case, you get 37% for Query 1, 19% for Query 2, 30% for Query 3, and 14% for Query 4.

When you place your mouse pointer over an operator, you get a yellow ToolTip box with information about the operator, as shown in Figure 4-12.

Query 1: Query cost (relative to the batch): 37%
SELECT custid, orderid, orderdate, empid, filler FROM dbo.Orders AS C

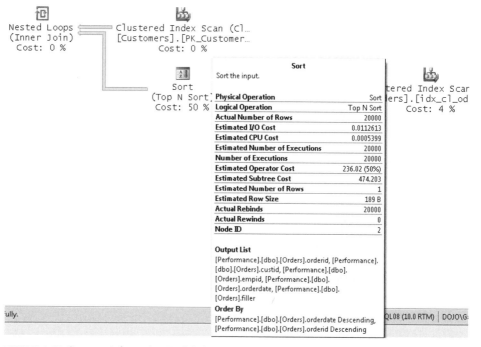

```
[SELECT]        [Filter]           [Nested Loops]        [Clustered Index Scan (Cl...
 SELECT          Filter             (Inner Join)          [Orders].[idx_cl_od] [O1]
 Cost: 0 %       Cost: 0 %          Cost: 1 %             Cost: 2 %
```

Query 2: Query cost (relative to the batch): 19%
SELECT custid, orderid, orderdate, empid, filler FROM dbo.Orders WHER

```
[SELECT]        [Parallelism]         [Nested Loops]        [Nested Loops]
 SELECT          Parallelism           Nested Loops          Nested Loops
 Cost: 0 %      (Gather Streams)      (Inner Join)          (Inner Join)        (I
```

Query 3: Query cost (relative to the batch): 30%
SELECT A.* FROM dbo.Customers AS C CROSS APPLY (SELECT TOP (1) O.cust

```
[SELECT]        [Nested Loops]        [Clustered Index Scan (Cl...
 SELECT          Nested Loops          [Customers].[PK_Customer...
 Cost: 0 %      (Inner Join)          Cost: 0 %
                 Cost: 0 %
```

Query 4: Query cost (relative to the batch): 14%
WITH C AS (SELECT custid, orderid, orderdate, empid, filler, ROW_NUM

```
[SELECT]        [Parallelism]         [Filter]        [Parallelism]              [Sequ
 SELECT          Parallelism           Filter          Parallelism                (Con
 Cost: 0 %      (Gather Streams)      Cost: 0 %       (Distribute Streams)
                 Cost: 0 %                             Cost: 8 %
```

FIGURE 4-11 Comparing costs of execution plans

```
[Nested Loops]          [Clustered Index Scan (Cl...
 Nested Loops            [Customers].[PK_Customer...
 (Inner Join)            Cost: 0 %
 Cost: 0 %
```

	Sort	
	Sort the input.	
Sort	**Physical Operation**	Sort
(Top N Sort	**Logical Operation**	Top N Sort
Cost: 50 %	**Actual Number of Rows**	20000
	Estimated I/O Cost	0.0112613
	Estimated CPU Cost	0.0005399
	Estimated Number of Executions	20000
	Number of Executions	20000
	Estimated Operator Cost	236.02 (50%)
	Estimated Subtree Cost	474.203
	Estimated Number of Rows	1
	Estimated Row Size	189 B
	Actual Rebinds	20000
	Actual Rewinds	0
	Node ID	2

Output List
[Performance].[dbo].[Orders].orderid, [Performance].
[dbo].[Orders].custid, [Performance].[dbo].
[Orders].empid, [Performance].[dbo].
[Orders].orderdate, [Performance].[dbo].
[Orders].filler

Order By
[Performance].[dbo].[Orders].orderdate Descending,
[Performance].[dbo].[Orders].orderid Descending

(right side:)
```
tered Index Scar
ers].[idx_cl_od
 Cost: 4 %
```

fully.

QL08 (10.0 RTM) | DOJO\G:

FIGURE 4-12 Operator information ToolTip box

The information box gives you the following information:

- The operator's name and a short description of its function.

- **Physical Operation**   The physical operation that will take place in the engine.

- **Logical Operation**   The logical operation according to Microsoft's conceptual model of query processing. For example, for a join operator you get the join algorithm used as the physical operation (Nested Loops, Merge, Hash) and the logical join type used as the logical operation (Inner Join, Outer Join, Semi Join, and so on). When no logical operation is associated with the operator, this measure will have the same value as shown in the physical operation.

- **Actual Number of Rows**   The actual number of rows returned from the operator (shown only for actual plans).

- **Estimated I/O Cost, and Estimated CPU Cost**   The estimated part of the operator's cost associated with that particular resource (I/O or CPU). These measures help you identify whether the operator is I/O or CPU intensive. For example, you can see that the current Sort operator is mainly I/O bound.

- **Estimated Number of Executions and Number of Executions**   The number of times this operator is estimated to be executed and the number of times this operator was executed in practice. These measures are important because they can help you identify suboptimal choices made by the optimizer when you find big differences between the two. These measures were available in the graphical execution plans provided by SQL Server 2000 Query Analyzer but were not provided by SSMS 2005. Fortunately, they were added back in SSMS 2008.

- **Estimated Operator Cost**   The cost associated with the particular operator.

- **Estimated Subtree Cost**   As described earlier, the cumulative cost associated with the whole subtree up to the current node.

- **Estimated Number of Rows**   The number of rows estimated to be returned from this operator. In some cases, you can identify costing problems related to insufficient statistics or to other reasons by observing a discrepancy between the actual number of rows and the estimated number.

- **Estimated Row Size**   You might wonder why an actual value for this number is not shown in the actual query plan. The reason is that you might have dynamic-length attribute types in your table with rows that vary in size.

- **Actual Rebinds and Actual Rewinds**   These measures are relevant only to certain operators (Nonclustered Index Spool, Remote Query, Row Count Spool, Sort, Table Spool, Table-valued Function, and in some cases Assert and Filter). Also, with those operators, these measures are applicable only when they appear as the inner side of a Nested Loops join; otherwise, Rebinds will show 1, and Rewinds will show 0. These measures refer to the number of times that an internal *Init* method is called. The sum of the number of rebinds and rewinds should be equal to the number of rows processed on the outer side of the join.

A rebind means that one or more of the correlated parameters of the join changed and the inner side must be reevaluated. A rewind means that none of the correlated parameters changed and that the prior inner result set might be reused.

- **Bottom part of the information box**   Shows other aspects related to the operator, such as the associated object name, output, arguments, and so on.

You can get more detailed coverage of the properties of an operator in the Properties window (by pressing F4), as shown in Figure 4-13.

Coverage of graphical execution plans continues in the "Index Tuning" section when I discuss index access methods.

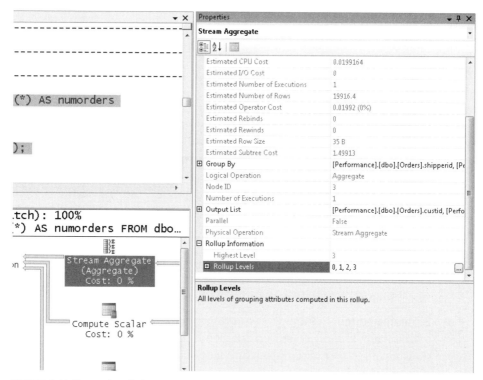

FIGURE 4-13 Properties window

Textual Showplans

SQL Server gives you tools in the form of SET options to get an execution plan as text. Note, though, that those SET options are scheduled for deprecation in a future version of SQL Server and are provided in SQL Server 2008 for backward compatibility. You should start getting used to using the SET options that provide the plan information in XML form instead; I'll describe those options in the next section. For the sake of completeness I will describe the textual showplan options as well. For example, if you turn the SHOWPLAN_TEXT session option on, when you run a query, SQL Server doesn't process it. Rather, it just generates an execution plan and returns it as text. To demonstrate this session option, turn it on by running the following code:

```
SET SHOWPLAN_TEXT ON;
```

Then invoke the query in Listing 4-4:

LISTING 4-4 Sample query to test showplan options

```
SELECT orderid, custid, empid, shipperid, orderdate, filler
FROM dbo.Orders
WHERE orderid = 280885;
```

You will get the following output:

```
|--Nested Loops(Inner Join, OUTER REFERENCES:([Uniq1002],
   [Performance].[dbo].[Orders].[orderdate]))
  |--Index Seek(OBJECT:([Performance].[dbo].[Orders].[PK_Orders]),
     SEEK:([Performance].[dbo].[Orders].[orderid]=[@1]) ORDERED FORWARD)
  |--Clustered Index Seek(OBJECT:([Performance].[dbo].[Orders].[idx_cl_od]),
     SEEK:([Performance].[dbo].[Orders].[orderdate]=
           [Performance].[dbo].[Orders].[orderdate]
     AND [Uniq1002]=[Uniq1002]) LOOKUP ORDERED FORWARD)
```

To analyze the plan, you "read" or "follow" branches in inner levels before outer ones (bottom to top) and branches that appear in the same level from top to bottom. As you can see, you get only the operator names and their basic arguments. Run the following code to turn the session option off:

```
SET SHOWPLAN_TEXT OFF;
```

If you want more detailed information about the plan that is similar to what the graphical execution plan gives you, use the SHOWPLAN_ALL session option for an estimated plan and the STATISTICS PROFILE session option for the actual one. SHOWPLAN_ALL will produce a table result, with the information provided by SHOWPLAN_TEXT, and also the following measures: *StmtText, StmtId, NodeId, Parent, PhysicalOp, LogicalOp, Argument, DefinedValues, EstimateRows, EstimateIO, EstimateCPU, AvgRowSize, TotalSubtreeCost, OutputList, Warnings, Type, Parallel,* and *EstimateExecutions.*

To test this session option, turn it on:

```
SET SHOWPLAN_ALL ON;
```

Run the query in Listing 4-4 and examine the result. When you're done, turn it off:

```
SET SHOWPLAN_ALL OFF;
```

The STATISTICS PROFILE option produces an actual plan. The query runs, and its output is produced. You also get the output returned by SHOWPLAN_ALL. In addition, you get the attributes *Rows* and *Executes*, which hold actual values as opposed to estimated ones. To test this session option, turn it on:

```
SET STATISTICS PROFILE ON;
```

Run the query in Listing 4-4 and examine the result. When you're done, turn it off:

```
SET STATISTICS PROFILE OFF;
```

XML Showplans

If you want to develop your own code that parses and analyzes execution plan information or if you want to analyze execution plan information sent to you by a customer or a colleague, you will find the information returned by the textual showplan options very hard to work with. SQL Server 2008 provides two session options that allow you to get estimated and actual execution plan information in XML format; XML data is much more convenient for an application code to parse and work with. Also, when clicking an XML value produced by one of the XML showplan options in SSMS 2008 or when opening a file with an XML showplan saved with a .sqlplan extension, SSMS parses the information and presents it as a graphical execution plan. The SHOWPLAN_ XML session option will produce an XML value with the estimated plan information, and the STATISTICS XML session option will produce a value with actual plan information.

To test SHOWPLAN_XML, turn it on by running the following code:

```
SET SHOWPLAN_XML ON;
```

Then run the query in Listing 4-4. You will get the XML form of the estimated execution plan.

To have SSMS parse and present the XML information graphically, simply click the XML value. Figure 4-14 shows an example of graphical depiction of the XML showplan.

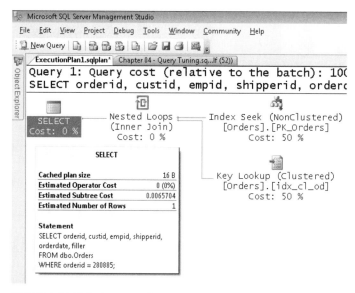

FIGURE 4-14 XML plan example

Run the following code to turn the session option off:

```
SET SHOWPLAN_XML OFF;
```

As I mentioned earlier, to get an XML value with information about the actual execution plan, use the STATISTICS XML session option as follows:

```
SET STATISTICS XML ON;
GO
SELECT orderid, custid, empid, shipperid, orderdate, filler
FROM dbo.Orders
WHERE orderid = 280885;
GO
SET STATISTICS XML OFF;
```

If you want customers or colleagues to send you an estimated or actual showplan, instruct them to save the XML value in a file with the extension .sqlplan, and when you open this file in SSMS, it automatically parses and presents it graphically.

Note also that the XML showplans provide the richest form of execution plan information. Some attributes of the plan appear only in this form and not in the textual or graphical forms, including information about missing indexes, whether the plan is trivial, the actual degree of parallelism used by the query, actual memory grant, and more.

Hints

Hints allow you to override the default behavior of SQL Server in different respects, and SQL Server will comply with your request when technically possible. The term *hint* is a misnomer because it's not a kind gesture that SQL Server might or might not comply with; rather, you're forcing SQL Server to apply a certain behavior when it's technically possible. Syntactically, there are three types of hints: join hints, query hints, and table hints. Join hints are specified between the keyword representing the join type and the *JOIN* keyword (for example, *INNER MERGE JOIN*). Query hints are specified in an OPTION clause following the query itself (for example, *SELECT ... OPTION (OPTIMIZE FOR (@od = '99991231')*). Table hints are specified right after a table name or alias in a WITH clause (for example, *FROM dbo.Orders WITH (index = idx_unc_od_oid_i_cid_eid)*).

Hints can be classified in different categories based on their functionality, including index hints, join hints, parallelism, locking, compilation, and others. Keep in mind that performance-related hints, such as forcing the usage of a certain index, make that particular aspect of the optimization static. When data distribution in the queried tables changes, the optimizer doesn't consult statistics to determine whether it is worthwhile to use the index because you forced it to always use it. You lose the benefit in cost-based optimization that SQL Server's optimizer gives you. Make sure that you use performance-related hints in production code only after exhausting all other means, including query revisions, ensuring that statistics are up to date, have a sufficient sampling rate, and so on.

I consider the USE PLAN query hint to be the ultimate hint. This hint allows you to provide an XML value holding complete execution plan information to force the optimizer to use the plan that you provided. You can use the SHOWPLAN_XML or STATISTICS XML session options to generate an XML plan in a controlled environment and then specify the XML value under the USE PLAN hint like so:

```
<query> OPTION(USE PLAN N'<xml_plan_goes_here>');
```

As an example, run the following code to produce an XML showplan for a query in a controlled environment:

```
SET SHOWPLAN_XML ON;
GO
SELECT orderid, custid, empid, shipperid, orderdate
FROM dbo.Orders
WHERE orderid >= 2147483647;
GO
SET SHOWPLAN_XML OFF;
```

Then run the query, providing the XML plan value in the USE PLAN hint like so:

```
DECLARE @oid AS INT;
SET @oid = 1000000;

SELECT orderid, custid, empid, shipperid, orderdate
FROM dbo.Orders
WHERE orderid >= @oid
OPTION (USE PLAN N'<xml_plan_goes_here>');
```

SQL Server 2008 also supports a plan guide feature that allows you to associate an XML plan or other hints to a query when you cannot or do not want to change the query's text directly by adding hints. You use the stored procedure *sp_create_plan_guide* to produce a plan guide for a query. You can find more details about this in SQL Server Books Online. I will use hints in several occasions in these books and explain them in context.

Traces/Profiler

The tracing capabilities of SQL Server give you extremely powerful tools for tuning and for other purposes as well. One of the great benefits tracing has over other external tools is that you get information about events that took place within the server in various components. Tracing allows you to troubleshoot performance problems, application behavior, deadlocks, audit information, and so much more. I demonstrated using traces for collecting performance workload data earlier in the book. Make sure you go over the guidelines for tracing that I provided earlier. I'll also demonstrate tracing to troubleshoot deadlocks in *Inside T-SQL Programming*.

Database Engine Tuning Advisor

The Database Engine Tuning Advisor (DTA) is a tool that can give you physical design recommendations (indexes, partitioning) based on an analysis of a workload that you give it as input. The input can be a trace file or table, a script file containing T-SQL queries, or an XML input file. One benefit of DTA is that it uses SQL Server's optimizer to make cost estimations—the same optimizer that generates execution plans for your queries. DTA generates statistics and hypothetical indexes, which it uses in its cost estimations. SQL Server 2008 introduces support for filtered indexes that I'll discuss later in the chapter. Besides providing recommendations for regular indexes, indexed views, and partitioning, DTA in SQL Server 2008 also provides recommendations for filtered indexes, among other enhancements. Note that you can run DTA in batch mode by using the dta.exe command-line utility.

Data Collection and Management Data Warehouse

As I mentioned earlier in the chapter, SQL Server 2008 introduces a data collection platform that enables you to collect performance and other information and store it in a management data warehouse for later analysis. One of the main components of the data collection platform is the data collector, which collects data from a variety of sources that are defined as data collection targets and stores it in the management data warehouse. The data collector installs three system data collection sets that collect performance-related information including disk usage, server activity, and query statistics information. Object Explorer in SSMS has a folder called Management through which you can configure the management data warehouse, enable data collection and the system collection sets, and analyze the collected performance information using predefined reports.

Using SMO to Clone Statistics

Query performance problems can evolve because of inaccurate selectivity estimates made by the optimizer based on the existing distribution statistics (histograms). However, you can't always duplicate the production data in your test environment to try to reproduce the problems. In such a case you will probably find it convenient to be able to clone the production statistics into your test environment without cloning the data. You can achieve this by using the scripting capabilities of the SQL Server Management Objects (SMO) API, specifically, the *ScriptingOptions.OptimizerData* property.

Index Tuning

This section covers index tuning, which is an important facet of query tuning. Indexes are sorting and searching structures. They reduce the need for I/O when looking for data and for sorting when certain elements in the plan need or can benefit from sorted data. While some aspects of tuning can improve performance by a modest percentage, index tuning can often improve query performance by orders of magnitude. Hence, if you're in charge of tuning, learning about indexes in depth is time well spent.

I'll start by describing table and index structures that are relevant for our discussions. Then I'll describe index access methods used by the optimizer and conclude the section with an analysis of indexing strategies.

Table and Index Structures

Before delving into index access methods, you need to familiarize yourself with table and index structures. This section describes pages and extents, heaps, clustered indexes, and nonclustered indexes.

Pages and Extents

A page is an 8-KB unit where SQL Server stores data. It can contain table or index data, bitmaps for allocation, free space information, and so on. A page is the smallest I/O unit that SQL Server can read or write. In older versions of SQL Server (prior to 2005) a row could not span multiple pages and was limited to 8,060 bytes gross (aside from large object data). The limitation was because of the page size (8,192 bytes), which was reduced by the header size (96 bytes), a pointer to the row maintained at the end of the page (2 bytes), and a few additional bytes reserved for future use. Starting with SQL Server 2005, a feature called *row-overflow data* relaxes the limitation on row size for columns of types VARCHAR, NVARCHAR, VARBINARY, SQL_VARIANT, or CLR user-defined types. When the row exceeds 8,060 bytes, values of such types can be moved to what are known as row overflow pages, and a 24-byte pointer to the off-row data is maintained in the original page. This way, a row can end up spanning multiple pages. In-row data is still limited to 8,060 bytes. A value of one of the aforementioned types can be moved to row-overflow pages provided that the value size doesn't exceed 8,000 bytes. If the size exceeds 8,000 bytes, the value is stored internally as a large object, and a 16-byte pointer to the large object value is maintained in the original row.

Keep in mind that a page is the smallest I/O unit that SQL Server can read or write. Even if SQL Server needs to access a single row, it has to load the whole page to the cache and read it from there. Queries that involve primarily data manipulation are typically bound mainly by their I/O cost. Of course, a physical read of a page is much more expensive than a logical read of a page that already resides in cache. It's hard to come up with a number that would represent the performance ratio between them because several factors are involved in the cost of a read, including the type of access method used, the fragmentation level of the data, and other factors. Therefore, I strongly advise against relying on any number as a rule of thumb.

Extents are units of eight contiguous pages. When a table or index needs more space for data, SQL Server allocates a full extent to the object. The single exception applies to small objects: if the object is smaller than 64 KB, SQL Server typically allocates an individual page when more space is needed, not a full extent. That page can reside within a mixed extent whose eight pages belong to different objects. Some activities of data deletion—for example, dropping a table and truncating a table—deallocate full extents. Such activities are minimally logged; therefore, they are very fast compared to the fully logged DELETE statement. Also, some read activities—such as read-ahead reads, which are typically applied for large table or index scans—can read data at the extent level, or even bigger blocks. The most expensive part of an I/O operation is the movement of the disk arm, while the actual magnetic read or write operation is much less expensive; therefore, reading a page can take almost as long as reading a full extent.

Table Organization

A table can be organized in one of two ways—either as a heap or as a B-tree. Technically the table is organized as a B-tree when you create a clustered index on the table and as a heap when you don't. Because a table must be organized in one of these two ways—heap or B-tree—the table organization is known as HOBT. Regardless of how the table is organized, it can have zero or more nonclustered indexes defined on it. Nonclustered indexes are always organized as B-trees. The HOBT, as well as the nonclustered indexes, can be made of one or more units called partitions. Technically, the HOBT and each of the nonclustered indexes can be partitioned differently. Each partition of each HOBT and nonclustered index stores data in collections of pages known as allocation units. The three types of allocation units are known as IN_ROW_DATA, ROW_OVERFLOW_DATA, and LOB_DATA. IN_ROW_DATA holds all fixed-length columns and also variable-length columns as long as the row size does not exceed the 8,060-byte limit. ROW_OVERFLOW_DATA holds VARCHAR, NVARCHAR, VARBINARY, SQL_VARIANT, or CLR user-defined typed data that does not exceed 8,000 bytes but was moved from the original row because it exceeded the 8,060-row size limit. LOB_DATA holds large object values (VARCHAR(MAX), NVARCHAR(MAX), VARBINARY(MAX) that exceed 8,000 bytes, XML, or CLR UDTs). The system view *sys.system_internals_allocation_units* holds the anchors pointing to the page collections stored in the allocation units. In the following sections I describe the heap, clustered index, and nonclustered index structures. For simplicity's sake, I'll assume that the data is nonpartitioned; but if it is partitioned, the description is still applicable to a single partition.

Heap

A *heap* is a table that has no clustered index. The structure is called a heap because the data is not organized in any order; rather, it is laid out as a bunch of extents. Figure 4-15 illustrates how our Orders table might look like when organized as a heap.

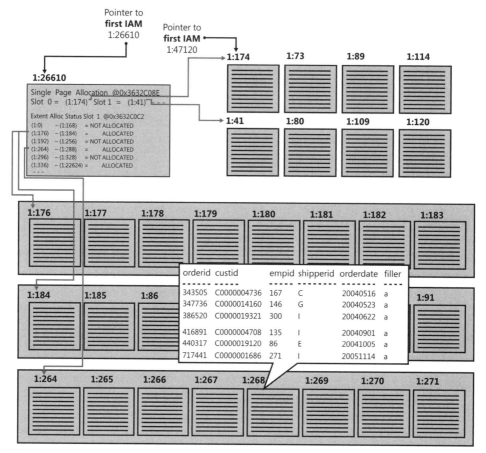

FIGURE 4-15 Heap

The only structure that keeps track of the data belonging to a heap is a bitmap page (or a series of pages if needed) called the Index Allocation Map (IAM). This bitmap has pointers to the first eight pages allocated from mixed extents and a representative bit for each extent in a range of 4 GB in the file. The bit is 0 if the extent it represents does not belong to the object owning the IAM page and 1 if it does. If one IAM is not enough to cover all the object's data, SQL Server will maintain a chain of IAM pages. SQL Server uses IAM pages to move through the object's data when the object needs to be scanned. SQL Server loads the object's first IAM page and then directs the disk arm sequentially to fetch the extents by their file order. As long as there's no file system fragmentation of the data files, the scan is done in a sequential manner on disk.

As you can see in Figure 4-15, SQL Server maintains internal pointers to the first IAM page and the first data page of a heap. Those pointers can be found in the system view *sys.system_internals_allocation_units*.

Because a heap doesn't maintain the data in any particular order, new rows that are added to the table can go anywhere. SQL Server uses bitmap pages called Page Free Space (PFS) to keep track of free space in pages so that it can quickly find a page with enough free space to accommodate a new row or allocate a new one if no such page exists.

When a row expands as a result of an update to a variable-length column and the page has no room for the row to expand, SQL Server moves the expanded row to a page with enough space to accommodate it and leaves behind what's known as a *forwarding pointer* that points to the new location of the row. The purpose of forwarding pointers is to avoid the need to modify pointers to the row from nonclustered indexes when data rows move.

I didn't yet explain a concept called a *page split* (because page splits can happen only in B-trees), but suffice to say for now that heaps do not incur page splits. The relevance of this fact will become apparent later in the chapter.

Clustered Index

All indexes in SQL Server are structured as *B-trees*, which are a special case of *balanced trees*. The definition of a balanced tree (adopted from *www.nist.gov*) is "a tree where no leaf is much farther away from the root than any other leaf."

> **More Info** If you're interested in the theoretical algorithmic background for balanced trees, please refer to *http://www.nist.gov/dads/HTML/balancedtree.html* and to *The Art of Computer Programming, Volume 3: Sorting and Searching (2nd Edition)* by Donald E. Knuth (Addison-Wesley Professional, 1998).

A *clustered index* is structured as a balanced tree, and it maintains the entire table's data in its leaf level. The clustered index is not a copy of the data; rather, it *is* the data. I'll describe the structure of a clustered index in SQL Server through the illustration shown in Figure 4-16.

The figure shows an illustration of how the Orders table might look when organized in a clustered index where the *orderdate* column is defined as the index's key column. Throughout these books, I'll refer to a table that has a clustered index as a *clustered table*. As you can see in the figure, the full data rows of the Orders table are stored in the index *leaf level*. The data rows are organized in the leaf in a sorted fashion based on the index key columns (*orderdate* in our case). A doubly linked list maintains this logical order, but note that depending on the fragmentation level of the index, the file order of the pages might not match the logical order maintained by the linked list.

Also notice that with each leaf row, the index maintains a value called an *uniquifier* (abbreviated to *unq* in the illustration). This value enumerates rows that have the same key value, and it is used together with the key value to uniquely identify rows when the index's key columns are not unique. Later, when discussing nonclustered indexes, I'll elaborate on the reasoning behind this architecture and the need to uniquely identify a row in a clustered index.

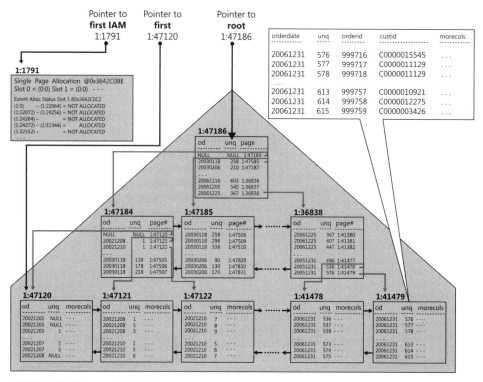

FIGURE 4-16 Clustered table/index

The rest of the discussion in this section is relevant to both clustered and nonclustered indexes unless explicitly stated otherwise. When SQL Server needs to perform ordered scan (or ordered partial scan) operations in the leaf level of the index, it does so by following the linked list. Note that in addition to the linked list, SQL Server also maintains an IAM page (or pages) to map the data stored in the index by file order. SQL Server may use the IAM pages when it needs to perform unordered scans of the index's leaf level. This type of scan based on IAM pages is known as an *allocation order scan*. A scan that is done in index order is known as an *index order scan*. The performance difference between the two types of scans depends on the level of fragmentation in the index. Remember that the most expensive part of an I/O operation is the movement of the disk arm (that's at least the case with traditional disk drives that have moving parts, as opposed to solid-state disks). An index order scan in an index with no fragmentation at all performs similarly to an allocation ordered scan, while an index order scan will be substantially slower in an index with a high level of fragmentation.

Fragmentation (known as logical scan fragmentation) evolves mainly because of splits of pages at the leaf level of the index. A split of a leaf page occurs when a row needs to be inserted into the page (because of the insert of a new row or an update of an existing row) and the target page does not have room to accommodate the row. Remember that an index maintains the data in an ordered fashion based on index key order. A row must enter a certain page based on its key value. If the target page is full, SQL Server will split the page. That is, it will allocate a new page, then move half the rows from the original page to the new one, then insert the new row either to the original or to the new page based on its key value, and then adjust the linked list to reflect the right logical order of the pages. The new page is not guaranteed to come right after the one that split—it could be somewhere later in the file, and it could also be somewhere earlier in the file. Logical scan fragmentation is measured as the percentage of the out-of-order pages in the leaf level of the index with respect to the total number of pages. An out-of-order page is a page that appears logically after a certain page according to the linked list but before it in the file.

Note one exception to the rule that an insert to a full index leaf page will cause a split: When the inserted row has a higher key than the highest key in the index, the rightmost index leaf page is not split. Instead, a new empty page is allocated, and the new row is inserted into that page. This architecture is designed to avoid costly splits and empty space that will not be reclaimed in ever-increasing indexes.

On top of the leaf level of the index, the index maintains additional levels, each summarizing the level below it. Each row in a nonleaf index page points to a whole page in the level below it. The row contains two elements: the key column value of the first row in the pointed index page and a 6-byte pointer to that page. The pointer holds the file number in the database and the page number in the file. When SQL Server builds an index, it starts from the leaf level and adds levels on top. It stops as soon as a level contains a single page, also known as the *root* page.

SQL Server always starts with the root page when it needs to navigate to a particular key at the leaf, using an access method called an *index seek*, which I'll elaborate on later in the chapter. The seek operation will jump from the root to the relevant page in the next level, and it will continue jumping from one level to the next until it reaches the page containing the sought key at the leaf. Remember that all leaf pages are the same distance from the root, meaning that a seek operation will cost as many page reads as the number of levels in the index. The I/O pattern of these reads is *random I/O*, as opposed to sequential I/O, because naturally the pages read by a seek operation will seldom reside next to each other.

In terms of our performance estimations, it is important to know the number of levels in an index because that number will be the cost of a seek operation in terms of page reads, and some execution plans invoke multiple seek operations repeatedly (for example, a Nested Loops join operator). For an existing index, you can get this number by invoking the INDEXPROPERTY function with the *IndexDepth* property. But for an index that you haven't created yet, you need to be familiar with the calculations that allow you to estimate the number of levels that the index will contain.

The operands and steps required for calculating the number of levels in an index (call it *L*) are as follows (remember that these calculations apply to clustered and nonclustered indexes unless explicitly stated otherwise):

- **The number of rows in the table (call it *num_rows*)**   This is 1,000,000 in our case.

- **The average gross leaf row size (call it *leaf_row_size*)**   In a clustered index, this is actually the data row size. By "gross," I mean that you need to take the internal overhead of the row and the 2-byte pointer stored at the end of the page—pointing to the row. The row overhead typically involves a few bytes. In our Orders table, the gross average data row size is roughly 200 bytes.

- **The average leaf page density (call it *page_density*)** This value is the average percentage of population of leaf pages. Reasons for pages not being completely full include data deletion, page splits caused by insertion of rows to full pages, having very large rows, and explicit requests not to populate the pages in full by specifying a *fillfactor* value when rebuilding indexes. In our case, we created a clustered index on the Orders table after populating it with the data, we did not add rows after creating the clustered index, and we did not specify a *fillfactor* value. Therefore, *page_density* in our case is close to 100 percent.

- **The number of rows that fit in a leaf page (call it *rows_per_leaf_page*)** The formula to calculate this value is *(page_size - header_size) * page_density / leaf_row_size*. Note that if you have a good estimation of *page_density*, you don't need to floor this value because the fact that a row cannot span pages (with the aforementioned exceptions) is already accounted for in the *page_density* value. In such a case, you want to use the result number as is even if it's not an integer. On the other hand, if you just estimate that *page_density* will be close to 100 percent, as it is in our case, omit the *page_density* operand from the calculation and floor the result. In our case, *rows_per_leaf_page* amount to *floor((8192 - 96) / 200) = 40*.

- **The number of pages maintained in the leaf (call it *num_leaf_pages*)** This is a simple formula: *num_rows / rows_per_leaf_page*. In our case, it amounts to *1,000,000 / 40 = 25,000*.

- **The average gross nonleaf row size (call it *non_leaf_row_size*)** A nonleaf row contains the key columns of the index (in our case, only *orderdate*, which is 8 bytes); the 4-byte *uniquifier* (which exists only in a clustered index that is not unique); the page pointer, which is 6 bytes; a few additional bytes of internal overhead, which total 5 bytes in our case; and the row offset pointer at the end of the page, which is 2 bytes. In our case, the gross nonleaf row size is 25 bytes.

- **The number of rows that can fit in a nonleaf page (call it *rows_per_non_leaf_page*)** The formula to calculate this value is similar to calculating *rows_per_leaf_page*. For the sake of simplicity, I'll ignore the nonleaf page density factor and calculate the value as *floor((page_size - header_size) / non_leaf_row_size)*, which in our case amounts to *floor((8192 - 96) / 25) = 323*.

- **The number of levels above the leaf (call it *L-1*)** This value is calculated with the following formula: $ceiling(log_{rows\_per\_non\_leaf\_page}(num\_leaf\_pages))$. In our case, L-1 amounts to $ceiling(log_{323}(25000)) = 2$. Obviously, you simply need to add 1 to get *L*, which in our case is 3.

This exercise leads me to a very important point that I will rely on in my performance discussions. You can play with the formula and see that with up to about several thousand rows, our index will have two levels. Three levels would have up to about 4,000,000 rows, and four levels would have up to about 4,000,000,000 rows. With nonclustered indexes, the formulas are identical—it's just that you can fit more rows in each leaf page, as I will describe later. So with nonclustered indexes, the upper bound for each number of levels covers even more rows in the table. The point is that in our table all indexes have three levels, which is the cost you have to consider in your performance estimation when measuring the cost of a seek operation. And in general, with small tables most indexes will typically have up to two levels, and with large tables, they will typically have three or four levels, unless the total size of the index keys is large. Keep these numbers in mind for our later discussions.

Nonclustered Index on a Heap

A nonclustered index is also structured as a B-tree and in many respects is similar to a clustered index. The only difference is that a leaf row in a nonclustered index contains only the index key columns and a *row locator* value pointing to a particular data row. The content of the row locator depends on whether the table is a heap or a clustered table. This section describes nonclustered indexes on a heap, and the following section will describe nonclustered indexes on a clustered table.

Figure 4-17 illustrates the nonclustered index created by our primary key constraint (*PK_Orders*) defining the *orderid* column as the key column.

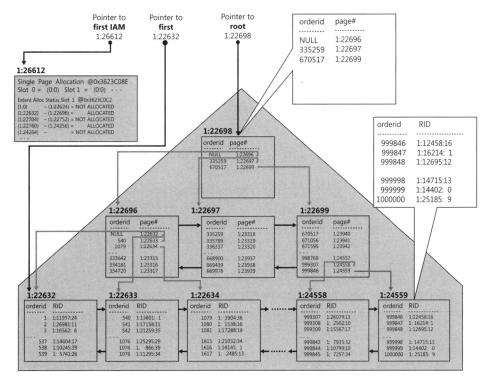

FIGURE 4-17 Nonclustered index on a heap

The row locator used by a nonclustered index leaf row to point to a data row is an 8-byte physical pointer called *RID*. It consists of the file number in the database, the target page number in the file, and the row number in the target page (zero based). When looking for a particular data row through the index, SQL Server has to follow the seek operation with a *RID lookup* operation, which translates to reading the page that contains the data row. Therefore, the cost of a RID lookup is one page read. For a single lookup or a very small number of lookups, the cost is not high, but for a large number of lookups, the cost can be very high because SQL Server ends up reading one whole page per sought row. For range queries that use a nonclustered index and a series of lookups—one per qualifying key—the cumulative cost of the lookup operations typically makes up the bulk of the cost of the query. I'll demonstrate this point in the "Index Access Methods" section. As for the cost of a seek operation, remember that the formulas I provided earlier are just as relevant to nonclustered indexes. It's just that the *leaf_row_size* is smaller, and therefore the *rows_per_leaf_page* will be higher. But the formulas are the same.

Nonclustered Index on a Clustered Table

Nonclustered indexes created on a clustered table are architected differently than on a heap. The only difference is that the row locator in a nonclustered index created on a clustered table is a value called a *clustering key*, as opposed to being an RID. The clustering key consists of the values of the clustered index keys from the pointed row and the *uniquifier* (if present). The idea is to point to a row "logically" as opposed to "physically." This architecture was designed mainly for OLTP systems, where clustered indexes often suffer from many page splits upon data insertions and updates. If nonclustered indexes pointed to RIDs of rows, all pointers to the data rows that moved would have to be changed to reflect their new RIDs—and that's true for all relevant pointers in all nonclustered indexes. Instead, SQL Server maintains logical pointers that don't change when data rows move.

Figure 4-18 illustrates what the *PK_Orders* nonclustered index might look like; the index is defined with the *orderid* as the key column, and the Orders table has a clustered index defined with the *orderdate* as the key column.

A seek operation looking for a particular key in the nonclustered index (some *orderid* value) will end up reaching the relevant leaf row and have access to the row locator. The row locator in this case is the clustering key of the pointed row. To actually grab the pointed row, a lookup operation will need to perform a whole seek within the clustered index based on the acquired clustering key. This type of lookup is known as a *key lookup*, as opposed to a RID lookup. I will demonstrate this access method later in the chapter. The cost of each lookup operation here (in terms of the number of page reads) is as high as the number of levels in the clustered index (3 in our case). That's compared to a single page read for a RID lookup when the table is a heap. Of course, with range queries that use a nonclustered index and a series of lookups, the ratio between the number of logical reads in a heap case and a clustered table case will be close to *1:L*, where *L* is the number of levels in the clustered index. Before you worry too much about this point and remove all clustered indexes from your

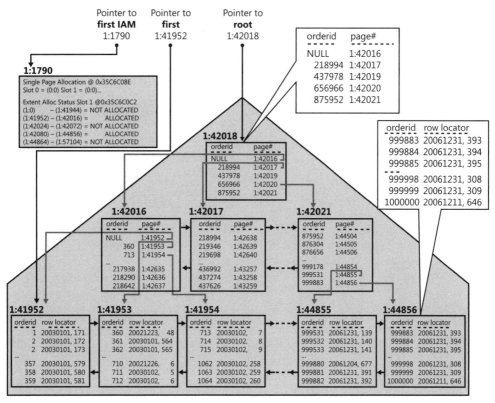

FIGURE 4-18 Nonclustered index on a clustered table

tables, keep in mind that with all lookups going through the clustered index, the nonleaf levels of the clustered index will typically reside in cache. Typically, most of the physical reads in the clustered index will be against the leaf level. Therefore, the additional cost of lookups against a clustered table compared to a heap is usually a small portion of the total query cost. Now that the background information about table and index structures has been covered, the next section will describe index access methods.

Index Access Methods

This section provides a technical description of the various index access methods; it is designed to be used as a reference for discussions in these books involving analysis of execution plans. Later in this chapter, I'll describe an analysis of indexing strategies that demonstrates how you can put this knowledge into action.

If you want to follow the examples in this section, rerun the code in Listing 4-1 to re-create the sample tables in our Performance database along with all the indexes. I'll be discussing some access methods to use against the Orders table, both when it's structured as a heap and when it's structured as a clustered table. Therefore, I'd also suggest that you run the code in Listing 4-1 against another database (say, Performance2), after renaming the database name in the script accordingly and commenting out the statement that creates the clustered index on Orders.

When I discuss an access method involving a clustered table, run the code against the Performance database. When the discussion is about heaps, run it against Performance2. Also remember that Listing 4-1 uses randomization to populate the customer IDs, employee IDs shipper IDs, and order dates in the Orders table. This means that your results will probably slightly differ from mine.

Table Scan/Unordered Clustered Index Scan

A *table scan* or an *unordered clustered index scan* involves a scan of all data pages belonging to the table. The following query against the Orders table structured as a heap would require a table scan:

```
SELECT orderid, custid, empid, shipperid, orderdate
FROM dbo.Orders;
```

Figure 4-19 shows the graphical execution plan produced by the relational engine's optimizer for this query, and Figure 4-20 shows an illustration of the way this access method is processed by the storage engine.

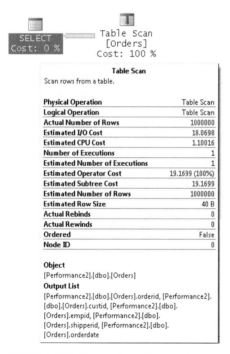

Table Scan	
Scan rows from a table.	
Physical Operation	Table Scan
Logical Operation	Table Scan
Actual Number of Rows	1000000
Estimated I/O Cost	18.0698
Estimated CPU Cost	1.10016
Number of Executions	1
Estimated Number of Executions	1
Estimated Operator Cost	19.1699 (100%)
Estimated Subtree Cost	19.1699
Estimated Number of Rows	1000000
Estimated Row Size	40 B
Actual Rebinds	0
Actual Rewinds	0
Ordered	False
Node ID	0

Object
[Performance2].[dbo].[Orders]
Output List
[Performance2].[dbo].[Orders].orderid, [Performance2].
[dbo].[Orders].custid, [Performance2].[dbo].
[Orders].empid, [Performance2].[dbo].
[Orders].shipperid, [Performance2].[dbo].
[Orders].orderdate

FIGURE 4-19 Table scan (execution plan)

Allocation Order Scan

FIGURE 4-20 Table scan

An instruction of the optimizer in the execution plan to perform a table scan can be carried out by the storage engine only in one way—using an allocation order scan. That is, SQL Server uses the table's IAM pages to scan the extents belonging to the table by their file order. As long as there's no file system fragmentation, the activity is done as a sequential activity in the disk drives. The number of logical reads should be similar to the number of pages the table consumes (around 25,000 in our case). Note that in such scans SQL Server typically uses a very efficient read-ahead strategy that can read the data in larger chunks than 8 KB. When I ran this query on my system, I got the following performance measures from STATISTICS IO, STATISTICS TIME:

- Logical reads 24391

- Physical reads 3

- Read-ahead reads 24368

- CPU time 951 ms

- Elapsed time 23935 ms

- Estimated subtree cost 19.1699

Of course, the run times I got are not an indication of the run times you would get in an average production system. But I wanted to show them for illustration and comparison purposes.

If the table has a clustered index, the access method that will be applied will be an unordered clustered index scan (that is, a Clustered Index Scan operator, with the property *Ordered: False*). Figure 4-21 shows the execution plan that the optimizer will produce for this query. Notice that the *Ordered* property of the Clustered Index Scan operator indicates False. Figure 4-22 shows an illustration of the two ways that the storage engine can carry out this access method.

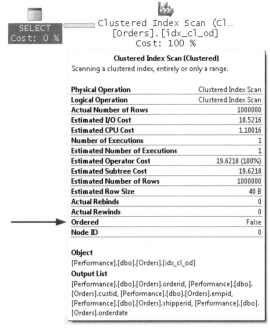

FIGURE 4-21 Unordered clustered index scan (execution plan)

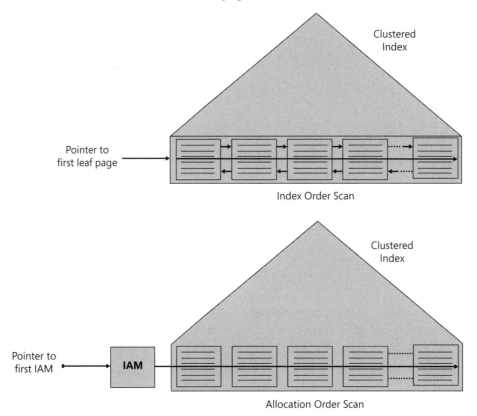

FIGURE 4-22 Unordered clustered index scan

The fact that the *Ordered* property of the Clustered Index Scan operator indicates False means that as far as the relational engine is concerned, the data does not need to be returned from the operator ordered. This doesn't mean that it is a problem if it is returned ordered; instead, it means that any order would be fine. This leaves the storage engine with some maneuvering space in the sense that it is free to choose between two types of scans: an index order scan (scan of the leaf of the index following the linked list) and an allocation order scan (scan based on IAM pages). The factors that the storage engine takes into consideration when choosing which type of scan to employ include performance and data consistency. I'll provide more details about the storage engine's decision-making process after I describe ordered index scans (Clustered Index Scan and Index Scan operators with the property *Ordered: True*).

Here are the performance measures I got for this query:

- Logical reads 25081
- Physical reads 5
- Read-ahead reads 25073
- CPU time 889 ms

- Elapsed time 24025 ms

- Estimated subtree cost 19.6218

Unordered Covering Nonclustered Index Scan

An *unordered covering nonclustered index scan* is similar in concept to an unordered clustered index scan. The concept of a *covering index* means that a nonclustered index contains all columns specified in a query. In other words, a covering index is not an index with special properties; rather, it becomes a covering index with respect to a particular query. SQL Server can find all the data it needs to satisfy the query by accessing solely the index data, without the need to access the full data rows. Other than that, the access method is the same as an unordered clustered index scan, only, obviously, the leaf level of the covering nonclustered index contains fewer pages than the leaf of the clustered index because the row size is smaller and more rows fit in each page. I explained earlier how to calculate the number of pages in the leaf level of an index (clustered or nonclustered).

As an example for this access method, the following query requests all *orderid* values from the Orders table:

```
SELECT orderid
FROM dbo.Orders;
```

Our Orders table has a nonclustered index on the *orderid* column (*PK_Orders*), meaning that all the table's order IDs reside in the index's leaf level. The index covers our query. Figure 4-23 shows the graphical execution plan you would get for this query, and Figure 4-24 illustrates the two ways in which the storage engine can process it.

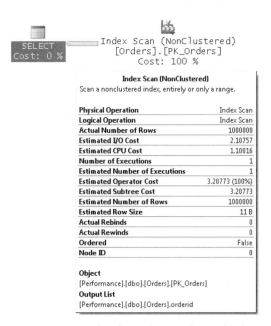

FIGURE 4-23 Unordered covering nonclustered index scan (execution plan)

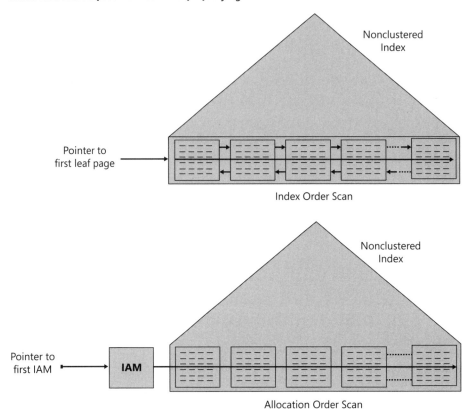

FIGURE 4-24 Unordered covering nonclustered index scan

The leaf level of the *PK_Orders* index contains fewer than 3,000 pages, compared to the 25,000 data pages in the table. Here are the performance measures I got for this query:

- Logical reads 2850
- Physical reads 2
- Read-ahead reads 2580
- CPU time 327 ms
- Elapsed time 16649 ms
- Estimated subtree cost 3.20773

Ordered Clustered Index Scan

An *ordered clustered index scan* is a full scan of the leaf level of the clustered index guaranteeing that the data will be returned to the next operator in index order. For example, the following query, which requests all orders sorted by *orderdate,* will get such an access method in its plan:

```
SELECT orderid, custid, empid, shipperid, orderdate
FROM dbo.Orders
ORDER BY orderdate;
```

You can find the execution plan for this query in Figure 4-25 and an illustration of how the storage engine carries out this access method in Figure 4-26.

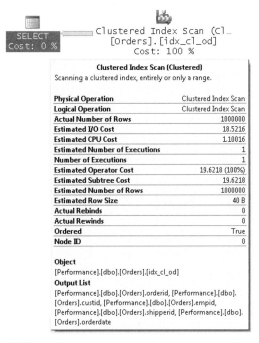

FIGURE 4-25 Ordered clustered index scan (execution plan)

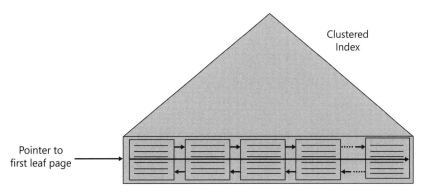

FIGURE 4-26 Ordered clustered index scan

Notice in the plan that the *Ordered* property is True. This indicates that the data needs to be returned from the operator ordered. When the operator has the property *Ordered: True,* the scan can be carried out by the storage engine only in one way—by using an index order scan (scan based on index linked list), as shown in Figure 4-26. Unlike an allocation order scan, the performance of an index order scan depends on the fragmentation level of the index. With no fragmentation at all, the performance of an index order scan should be very close to the performance of an allocation order scan because both will end up reading the data in file order sequentially. However, as the fragmentation level grows higher, the performance difference will be more substantial, in favor of the allocation order scan, of course. The natural deductions are that you shouldn't request the data sorted if you don't need it sorted, to allow the potential for using an allocation order scan, and that you should resolve fragmentation issues in indexes that incur large index order scans. I'll elaborate on fragmentation and its treatment later. Here are the performance measures that I got for this query:

- Logical reads 25081

- Physical reads 5

- Read-ahead reads 25073

- CPU time 983 ms

- Elapsed time 25192 ms

- Estimated subtree cost 19.6218

Note that the optimizer is not limited to ordered-forward activities. Remember that the linked list is a doubly linked list, where each page contains both a *next* and a *previous* pointer. Had you requested a descending sort order, you would have still gotten an ordered index scan, only ordered backward (from tail to head) instead of ordered forward (from head to tail). SQL Server also supports descending indexes, but these are not needed in simple cases like getting descending sort orders. Rather, descending indexes are valuable when you create an index on multiple key columns that have opposite directions in their sort requirements—for example, sorting by *col1, col2* DESC.

Ordered Covering Nonclustered Index Scan

An *ordered covering nonclustered index scan* is similar in concept to an ordered clustered index scan, with the former performing the access method in a nonclustered index—typically when covering a query. The cost is, of course, lower than a clustered index scan because fewer pages are involved. For example, the *PK_Orders* index on our clustered Orders table happens to cover the following query, even though it might not seem so at first glance:

```
SELECT orderid, orderdate
FROM dbo.Orders
ORDER BY orderid;
```

Keep in mind that on a clustered table, nonclustered indexes will use clustering keys as row locators. In our case, the clustering keys contain the *orderdate* values, which can be used for covering purposes as well. Also, the first (and, in our case, the only) key column in the nonclustered index is the *orderid* column, which is the column specified in the ORDER BY clause of the query; therefore, an ordered index scan is a natural access method for the optimizer to choose.

Figure 4-27 shows the query's execution plan, and Figure 4-28 illustrates the way the storage engine processes the access method.

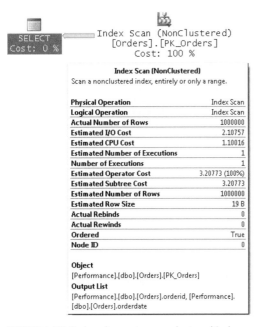

FIGURE 4-27 Ordered covering nonclustered index scan (execution plan 1)

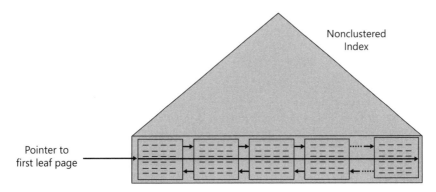

FIGURE 4-28 Ordered covering nonclustered index scan

Notice in the plan that the *Ordered* property of the Index Scan operator in the yellow information box shows *True*.

Here are the performance measures that I got for this query:

- Logical reads 2850

- Physical reads 2

- Read-ahead reads 2850

- CPU time 592 ms

- Elapsed time 18153 ms

- Estimated subtree cost 3.20733

An ordered index scan is used not only when you explicitly request the data sorted but also when the plan uses an operator that can benefit from sorted input data. This can be the case when processing GROUP BY, DISTINCT, joins, and other requests. This can also happen in less obvious cases. For example, check out the execution plan shown in Figure 4-29 for the following query:

```
SELECT orderid, custid, empid, orderdate
FROM dbo.Orders AS O1
WHERE orderid =
  (SELECT MAX(orderid)
   FROM dbo.Orders AS O2
   WHERE O2.orderdate = O1.orderdate);
```

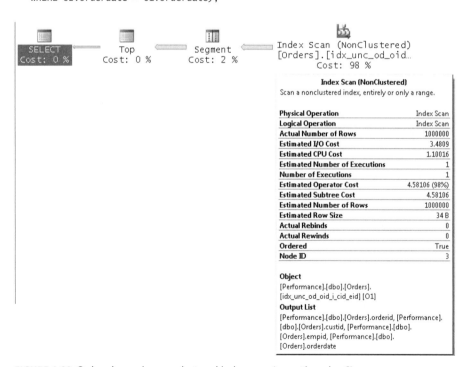

FIGURE 4-29 Ordered covering nonclustered index scan (execution plan 2)

The Segment operator arranges the data in groups and emits a group at a time to the next operator (Top in our case). Our query requests the orders with the maximum *orderid* per *orderdate*. Fortunately, we have a covering index for the task (*idx_unc_od_oid_i_cid_eid*), with the key columns being (*orderdate, orderid*) and included nonkey columns being (*custid, empid*). I'll elaborate on included nonkey columns later in the chapter. The important point for our discussion is that the segment operator organizes the data by groups of orderdate values and emits the data, a group at a time, where the last row in each group is the maximum *orderid* in the group; because *orderid* is the second key column right after *orderdate*. Therefore, the plan doesn't need to sort the data; rather, the plan just collects it with an ordered scan from the covering index, which is already sorted by *orderdate* and *orderid*. The Top operator has a simple task of just collecting the last row (TOP 1 descending), which is the row of interest for the group. The number of rows reported by the Top operator is 1491, which is the number of unique groups (*orderdate* values), each of which got a single row from the operator. Because our nonclustered index covers the query by including in its leaf level all other columns that are mentioned in the query (*custid, empid*), there's no need to look up the data rows; the query is satisfied by the index data alone. Here are the performance measures I got for this query:

- Logical reads 4717

- Physical reads 8

- Read-ahead reads 4696

- CPU time 468 ms

- Elapsed time 2157 ms

- Estimated subtree cost 4.68121

The number of logical reads that you see is similar to the number of pages that the leaf level of the index holds.

The Storage Engine's Treatment of Scans

This section is applicable to all versions of SQL Server from 7.0 through to 2008.

Before I continue the coverage of additional index access methods, I'm going to explain the way the storage engine treats the relational engine's instructions to perform scans. The relational engine is like the brains of SQL Server; it includes the optimizer that is in charge of producing execution plans for queries. The storage engine is like the muscles of SQL Server; it needs to carry out the instructions provided to it by the relational engine in the execution plan and perform the actual row operations. Sometimes the optimizer's instructions leave the storage engine with some room for maneuvering, and then the storage engine determines the best of several possible options based on factors such as performance and consistency.

When the plan shows a Table Scan operator, the storage engine has only one option—to use an allocation order scan. When the plan shows an Index Scan operator (clustered or nonclustered) with the property *Ordered: True*, the storage engine can use only an index order scan.

Allocation Order Scans vs. Index Order Scans   When the plan shows an Index Scan operator with *Ordered: False*, the relational engine doesn't care in what order the rows are returned. In this case there are two options to scan the data—allocation order scan and index order scan. It is up to the storage engine to determine which to employ. Unfortunately, the storage engine's actual choice is not indicated in the execution plan, or anywhere else. I will explain the storage engine's decision-making process, but it's important to understand that what the plan shows is the relational engine's instructions and not what the storage engine did.

The performance of an allocation order scan is not affected by logical fragmentation in the index because it's done in file order anyway. However, the performance of an index order scan is affected by fragmentation—the higher the fragmentation, the slower the scan. Therefore, as far as performance is concerned, the storage engine considers the allocation order scan the preferable option. The exception is when the index is very small (up to 64 pages), the cost of interpreting IAM pages becomes significant with respect to the rest of the work, in which case the storage engine considers the index order scan to be preferable. Small tables aside, in terms of performance the allocation order scan is considered preferable.

However, performance is not the only aspect that the storage engine needs to take into consideration; it also needs to account for data consistency expectations based on the effective isolation level. When there's more than one option to carry out a request, the storage engine opts for the fastest option that meets the consistency requirements.

In certain circumstances, scans can end up returning multiple occurrences of rows or even skip rows. Allocation order scans are more prone to such behavior than index order scans. I'll first describe how such a phenomenon can happen with allocation order scans and in which circumstances. Then I'll explain how it can happen with index order scans.

Allocation Order Scans   Figure 4-30 demonstrate in three steps how an allocation order scan can return multiple occurrences of rows.

Step 1 shows an allocation order scan in progress, reading the leaf pages of some index in file order (not index order). Two pages were already read (keys 50, 60, 70, 80, 10, 20, 30, 40). At this point, before the third page of the index is read, someone inserts a row into the table with key 25.

Step 2 shows a split that took place in the page that was the target for the insert since it was full. As a result of the split, a new page was allocated—in our case later in the file at a point that the scan did not yet reach. Half the rows from the original page move to the new page (keys 30, 40), and the new row with key 25 was added to the original page because of its key value.

Step 3 shows the continuation of the scan: reading the remaining two pages (keys 90, 100, 110, 120, 30, 40) including the one that was added because of the split. Notice that the rows with keys 30 and 40 were read a second time.

Allocation Order Scan: Getting Multiple Occurrences of Rows

Step 1:

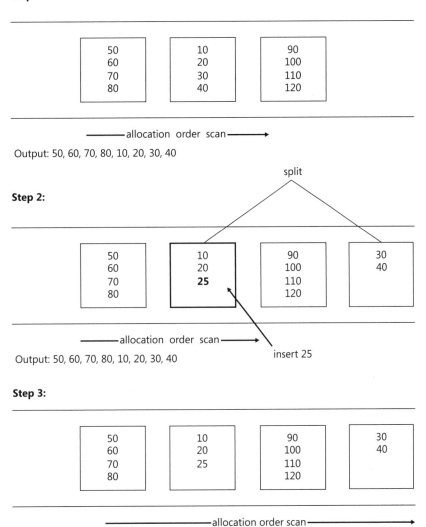

Output: 50, 60, 70, 80, 10, 20, 30, 40

Step 2:

Output: 50, 60, 70, 80, 10, 20, 30, 40

Step 3:

Output: 50, 60, 70, 80, 10, 20, **30**, **40**, 90, 100, 110, 120, **30**, **40**

FIGURE 4-30 Allocation order scan: getting multiple occurrences of rows

Of course, in a very similar fashion, depending on how far the scan reaches by the point this split happens and where the new page is allocated, the scan might end up skipping rows. Figure 4-31 demonstrates how this can happen in three steps.

Step 1 shows an allocation order scan in progress that manages to read one page (keys 50, 60, 70, 80) before the insert takes place.

Allocation Order Scan: Skipping Rows

Step 1:

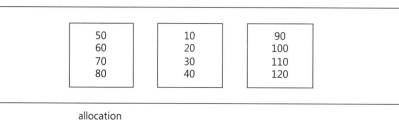

Output: 50, 60, 70, 80

Step 2:

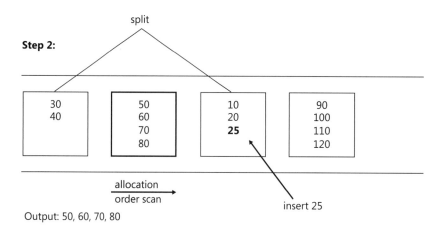

Output: 50, 60, 70, 80

Step 3:

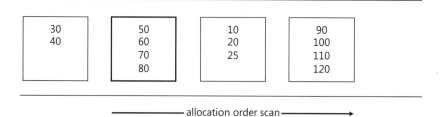

Output: 50, 60, 70, 80, 10, 20, 25, 90, 100, 110, 120,

FIGURE 4-31 Allocation order scan: skipping rows

Step 2 shows the split of the target page, only this time the new page is allocated earlier in the file at a point that the scan already passed. Like in the previous split example, the rows with keys 30 and 40 move to the new page, and the new row with key 25 is added to the original page.

Step 3 shows the continuation of the scan: reading the remaining two pages (keys 10, 20, 25, 90, 100, 110, 120). As you can see, the rows with keys 30 and 40 were completely skipped.

In short, an allocation order scan can return multiple occurrences of rows and skip rows resulting from splits that take place during the scan. A split can take place because of an insert of a new row, an update of an index key causing the row to move, or an update of a variable-length column causing the row to expand. Remember that splits only take place in indexes; heaps do not incur splits. Therefore, such phenomena cannot happen in heaps.

An index order scan is safer in the sense that it won't read multiple occurrences of the same row or skip rows because of splits. Remember that an index order scan follows the index linked list in order. If a page that the scan hasn't yet reached splits, the scan ends up reading both pages; therefore, it won't skip rows. If a page that the scan already passed splits, the scan doesn't read the new one; therefore, it won't return multiple occurrences of rows.

The storage engine is well aware of the fact that allocation order scans are prone to such inconsistent reads because of splits, while index order scans aren't. It will carry out an Index Scan *Ordered: False* with an allocation order scan in one of two categories of cases that I will refer to as the unsafe and safe categories.

The unsafe category is when the scan can actually return multiple occurrences of rows or skip rows because of splits. The storage engine opts for this option when the index size is greater than 64 pages and the request is running under the read uncommitted isolation level (for example, when you specify NOLOCK in the query). Most people's perception of read uncommitted is simply that the query does not request a shared lock and therefore that it can read uncommitted changes (dirty reads). This perception is true, but unfortunately most people don't realize that in the eyes of the storage engine, read uncommitted is also an indication that pretty much all bets are off in terms of consistency. In other words, it will opt for the faster option even at the cost of returning multiple occurrences of rows or skipping rows. When the query is running under the default read committed isolation level or higher, the storage engine will opt for an index order scan to prevent such phenomena from happening because of splits. To recap, the storage engine employs allocation order scans of the unsafe category when all of the following are true:

- The index size is greater than 64 pages.

- The plan shows Index Scan, *Ordered: False*.

- The query is running under the read uncommitted isolation level.

- Changes are allowed to the data.

In terms of the safe category, the storage engine also opts for allocation order scans with higher isolation levels than read uncommitted when it knows that it is safe to do so without sacrificing the consistency of the read (at least as far as splits are concerned). For example, when you run the query using the TABLOCK hint, the storage engine knows that no one can change the data while the read is in progress. Therefore, it is safe to use an allocation order scan. Of course this comes at the cost of requests for modifications being blocked during the read. Another example where the storage engine knows that it is safe to employ an allocation order scan is when the index resides in a read-only filegroup or database. To summarize, the storage engine will use an allocation order scan of the safe category when the index size is greater than 64 pages and the data is read-only (because of the TABLOCK hint, read-only filegroup, or database).

Keep in mind that logical fragmentation has an impact on the performance of index order scans but not on that of allocation order scans. And based on the preceding information, you should realize that the storage engine will sometimes use index order scans to process an Index Scan operator with the *Ordered: False* property.

The next section will demonstrate both unsafe and safe allocation order scans.

Run the following code to create a table called T1:

```
SET NOCOUNT ON;
USE tempdb;
GO

-- Create table T1
IF OBJECT_ID('dbo.T1', 'U') IS NOT NULL DROP TABLE dbo.T1;

CREATE TABLE dbo.T1
(
  cl_col UNIQUEIDENTIFIER NOT NULL DEFAULT(NEWID()),
  filler CHAR(2000) NOT NULL DEFAULT('a')
);
GO
CREATE UNIQUE CLUSTERED INDEX idx_cl_col ON dbo.T1(cl_col);
GO
```

A unique clustered index is created on *cl_col*, which will be populated with random GUIDs by the default expression *NEWID()*. Populating the clustered index key with random GUIDs should cause a high level of splits, which in turn should cause a high level of logical fragmentation in the index.

Run the following code to insert rows into the table using an infinite loop and stop it after a few seconds (say 5, to allow more than 64 pages in the table):

```
SET NOCOUNT ON;
USE tempdb;

TRUNCATE TABLE dbo.T1;

WHILE 1 = 1
  INSERT INTO dbo.T1 DEFAULT VALUES;
```

Run the following code to check the fragmentation level of the index:

```
SELECT avg_fragmentation_in_percent FROM sys.dm_db_index_physical_stats
(
  DB_ID('tempdb'),
  OBJECT_ID('dbo.T1'),
  1,
  NULL,
  NULL
);
```

When I ran this code in my system, I got more than 98 percent fragmentation, which of course is very high. If you need more evidence to support the fact that the order of the pages in the linked list is different from their order in the file, you can use the undocumented DBCC IND command, which gives you the B-tree layout of the index:

```
DBCC IND('tempdb', 'dbo.T1', 0);
```

I prepared the following piece of code to spare you from having to browse through the output of DBCC IND in attempt to figure out the index leaf layout:

```
CREATE TABLE #DBCCIND
(
  PageFID INT,
  PagePID INT,
  IAMFID INT,
  IAMPID INT,
  ObjectID INT,
  IndexID INT,
  PartitionNumber INT,
  PartitionID BIGINT,
  iam_chain_type VARCHAR(100),
  PageType INT,
  IndexLevel INT,
  NextPageFID INT,
  NextPagePID INT,
  PrevPageFID INT,
  PrevPagePID INT
);

INSERT INTO #DBCCIND
  EXEC ('DBCC IND(''tempdb'', ''dbo.T1'', 0)');

CREATE CLUSTERED INDEX idx_cl_prevpage ON #DBCCIND(PrevPageFID, PrevPagePID);

WITH LinkedList
AS
(
  SELECT 1 AS RowNum, PageFID, PagePID
  FROM #DBCCIND
  WHERE IndexID = 1
    AND IndexLevel = 0
    AND PrevPageFID = 0
    AND PrevPagePID = 0
```

```
UNION ALL

SELECT PrevLevel.RowNum + 1,
  CurLevel.PageFID, CurLevel.PagePID
FROM LinkedList AS PrevLevel
  JOIN #DBCCIND AS CurLevel
    ON CurLevel.PrevPageFID = PrevLevel.PageFID
    AND CurLevel.PrevPagePID = PrevLevel.PagePID
)
SELECT
  CAST(PageFID AS VARCHAR(MAX)) + ':'
  + CAST(PagePID AS VARCHAR(MAX)) + ' ' AS [text()]
FROM LinkedList
ORDER BY RowNum
FOR XML PATH('')
OPTION (MAXRECURSION 0);

DROP TABLE #DBCCIND;
```

The code stores the output of DBCC IND in a temp table, then it uses a recursive query to follow the linked list from head to tail, and then it uses a technique using the *FOR XML PATH* option to concatenate the addresses of the leaf pages into a single string in linked list order. I got the following output on my system, shown here in abbreviated form:

```
1:3672 1:1245 1:1460 1:670 1:3046 1:1994 1:1856 1:386 1:2903 1:1167 1:2785 1:663...
```

It's easy to observe logical fragmentation here. For example, page 1:3672 points to the page 1:1245, which is earlier in the file.

Next, run the following code to query T1:

```
SELECT SUBSTRING(CAST(cl_col AS BINARY(16)), 11, 6) AS segment1, *
FROM dbo.T1;
```

The last 6 bytes of a *UNIQUEIDENTIFIER* value represent the first segment that determines ordering; therefore, I extracted that segment with the *SUBSTRING* function so that it would be easy to see whether the rows are returned in index order. The execution plan of this query indicates a Clustered Index Scan, *Ordered: False*. However, because the environment is not read-only and the isolation is the default read committed, the storage engine uses an index order scan. This query returns the rows in the output in index order. For example, here's the output that I got on my system, shown in abbreviated form:

```
segment1           cl_col                                    filler
---------------    --------------------------------------    -------
0x0001EDAA3379     870FE202-4216-4BD2-9CF0-0001EDAA3379      a
0x000403806831     6F247C4D-A317-450F-B596-000403806831      a
0x0009A1FB7D6A     5EA6CC99-948C-4A10-8C37-0009A1FB7D6A      a
0x000B6712B99C     1D545D02-6887-4F8A-A95F-000B6712B99C      a
0x0021719D7298     38B2E138-E6F4-4B32-8E7D-0021719D7298      a
0x002BD242E426     1A22523F-0046-4A83-AD4A-002BD242E426      a
0x002FAFA27D1B     890693F4-0E5A-4120-8D8F-002FAFA27D1B      a
```

```
0x006F682B4B92    2F1F94D1-0597-4755-87D8-006F682B4B92    a
0x007141F248CC    D0125167-03DC-4790-8EF9-007141F248CC    a
0x007980632C84    368F5CE4-413C-46B9-9AB3-007980632C84    a
...
```

Query the table again, this time with the NOLOCK hint:

```
SELECT SUBSTRING(CAST(cl_col AS BINARY(16)), 11, 6) AS segment1, *
FROM dbo.T1 WITH (NOLOCK);
```

This time the storage engine employs an allocation order scan of the unsafe category. Here's the output I got from this code on my system:

```
segment1           cl_col                                 filler
---------------    ------------------------------------   -------
0x014764C5D8EE     4F3B1F56-E906-4604-BEFD-014764C5D8EE    a
0x01562FB6BA4F     F806B778-4B95-4C83-8CD1-01562FB6BA4F    a
0x01602D85E409     10812BEE-00C9-46E4-86E0-01602D85E409    a
0x656D2B798163     361A0DB6-BDF6-4B93-8D02-656D2B798163    a
0x65A8EB2A6C4E     CFCCCBB7-8BBD-4BED-9F6E-65A8EB2A6C4E    a
0x65AF86168CA8     007CC2B4-3B4A-416F-ACCA-65AF86168CA8    a
0x4A4BA14669E8     DE40A86F-B83A-4BC8-BC42-4A4BA14669E8    a
0xF27FCD39F328     71DFA3CA-3C15-40B5-8393-F27FCD39F328    a
0xF2871A254745     5483FEAC-52CC-4554-B1C4-F2871A254745    a
0x7BB93E98B826     36690994-2ED8-4DB6-98E4-7BB93E98B826    a
...
```

Notice that this time the rows are not returned in index order. If splits occur while such a read is in progress, the read might end up returning multiple occurrences of rows and skipping rows.

As an example for an allocation order scan of the safe category, run the query with the TABLOCK hint:

```
SELECT SUBSTRING(CAST(cl_col AS BINARY(16)), 11, 6) AS segment1, *
FROM dbo.T1 WITH (TABLOCK);
```

Here, even though the code is running under the read committed isolation, the storage engine knows that it is safe to use an allocation order scan because no one can change the data during the read. I got the following output back from this query:

```
segment1           cl_col                                 filler
---------------    ------------------------------------   -------
0x014764C5D8EE     4F3B1F56-E906-4604-BEFD-014764C5D8EE    a
0x01562FB6BA4F     F806B778-4B95-4C83-8CD1-01562FB6BA4F    a
0x01602D85E409     10812BEE-00C9-46E4-86E0-01602D85E409    a
0x656D2B798163     361A0DB6-BDF6-4B93-8D02-656D2B798163    a
0x65A8EB2A6C4E     CFCCCBB7-8BBD-4BED-9F6E-65A8EB2A6C4E    a
0x65AF86168CA8     007CC2B4-3B4A-416F-ACCA-65AF86168CA8    a
0x4A4BA14669E8     DE40A86F-B83A-4BC8-BC42-4A4BA14669E8    a
0xF27FCD39F328     71DFA3CA-3C15-40B5-8393-F27FCD39F328    a
0xF2871A254745     5483FEAC-52CC-4554-B1C4-F2871A254745    a
0x7BB93E98B826     36690994-2ED8-4DB6-98E4-7BB93E98B826    a
...
```

Next I'll demonstrate how an unsafe allocation order scan can return multiple occurrences of rows. Open two connections (call them Connection 1 and Connection 2). Run the following code in Connection 1 to insert rows into T1 in an infinite loop, causing frequent splits:

```
SET NOCOUNT ON;
USE tempdb;

TRUNCATE TABLE dbo.T1;

WHILE 1 = 1
  INSERT INTO dbo.T1 DEFAULT VALUES;
```

Run the following code in Connection 2 to read the data in a loop while Connection 1 is inserting data:

```
SET NOCOUNT ON;
USE tempdb;


WHILE 1 = 1
BEGIN
  SELECT * INTO #T1 FROM dbo.T1 WITH(NOLOCK);

  IF EXISTS(
    SELECT cl_col
    FROM #T1
    GROUP BY cl_col
    HAVING COUNT(*) > 1) BREAK;

  DROP TABLE #T1;
END

SELECT cl_col, COUNT(*) AS cnt
FROM #T1
GROUP BY cl_col
HAVING COUNT(*) > 1;

DROP TABLE #T1;
```

The SELECT statement uses the NOLOCK hint, and the plan shows Clustered Index Scan, *Ordered: False*, meaning that the storage engine will likely use an allocation order scan of the unsafe category. The SELECT INTO statement stores the output in a temporary table so that it will be easy to prove that rows were read multiple times. In each iteration of the loop, after reading the data into the temp table, the code checks for multiple occurrences of the same GUID in the temp table. This can happen only if the same row was read more than once. If duplicates are found, the code breaks from the loop and returns the GUIDs that appear more than once in the temp table. When I ran this code, after a few seconds I got the following output in Connection 2 showing all the GUIDs that were read more than once:

```
cl_col                                cnt
------------------------------------- -----------
8DB22EB6-A2CF-4390-9402-CC4A7D92A174  2
B26AE864-EC15-481A-938C-9CC31288CE13  2
```

```
DD564EEE-C669-44A3-AB5B-46D010F6F9CF    2
EFB70510-C818-49AE-A889-46D0158A3BAD    2
48AA6FF8-D4BF-4628-8AFD-61ABC6361C65    2
59B1FBB5-0571-4EF2-9A96-EBAC9E51CF78    2
C21F5696-7B9C-4B8A-BB16-61A8F0F84CD8    2
E9BFB860-F720-493C-AF15-EBAC959BEA0D    2
DF75BFDA-772B-48CE-B048-CC494D57C489    2
DACE0814-9D15-4077-AB59-9CC0831DE9F2    2
5362C689-AC26-495E-8C4B-B442EF28BA9F    2
```

At this point you can stop the code in Connection 1.

If you want, you can rerun the test without the NOLOCK hint and see that the code in Connection 2 doesn't stop because duplicate GUIDs are not found.

Next I'll demonstrate an unsafe allocation order scan that skips rows. Run the following code to create the tables T1 and Sequence:

```
-- Create table T1
SET NOCOUNT ON;
USE tempdb;

IF OBJECT_ID('dbo.T1', 'U') IS NOT NULL DROP TABLE dbo.T1;

CREATE TABLE dbo.T1
(
  cl_col UNIQUEIDENTIFIER NOT NULL DEFAULT(NEWID()),
  seq_val INT NOT NULL,
  filler CHAR(2000) NOT NULL DEFAULT('a')
);
CREATE UNIQUE CLUSTERED INDEX idx_cl_col ON dbo.T1(cl_col);

-- Create table Sequence
IF OBJECT_ID('dbo.Sequence', 'U') IS NOT NULL DROP TABLE dbo.Sequence;

CREATE TABLE dbo.Sequence(val INT NOT NULL);
INSERT INTO dbo.Sequence(val) VALUES(0);
```

The table T1 is similar to the one used in the previous demonstration, but this one has an additional column called *seq_val* that will be populated with sequential integers. The table Sequence holds the last used sequence value (populated initially with 0), which will be incremented by 1 before each insert to T1. To prove that a scan skipped rows, you simply need to show that the output of the scan has gaps between contiguous values in the *seq_val* column. To demonstrate this behavior, open two connections (again, call them Connection 1 and Connection 2). Run the following code from Connection 1 to insert rows into T1 in an infinite loop, incrementing the sequence value by 1 in each iteration:

```
SET NOCOUNT ON;
USE tempdb;

UPDATE dbo.Sequence SET val = 0;
TRUNCATE TABLE dbo.T1;
```

```
DECLARE @nextval AS INT;

WHILE 1 = 1
BEGIN
  UPDATE dbo.Sequence SET @nextval = val = val + 1;
  INSERT INTO dbo.T1(seq_val) VALUES(@nextval);
END
```

Run the following code in Connection 2 while the inserts are running in Connection 1:

```
SET NOCOUNT ON;
USE tempdb;

DECLARE @max AS INT;
WHILE 1 = 1
BEGIN
  SET @max = (SELECT MAX(seq_val) FROM dbo.T1);
  SELECT * INTO #T1 FROM dbo.T1 WITH(NOLOCK);
  CREATE NONCLUSTERED INDEX idx_seq_val ON #T1(seq_val);

  IF EXISTS(
    SELECT *
    FROM (SELECT seq_val AS cur,
            (SELECT MIN(seq_val)
             FROM #T1 AS N
             WHERE N.seq_val > C.seq_val) AS nxt
          FROM #T1 AS C
          WHERE seq_val <= @max) AS D
    WHERE nxt - cur > 1) BREAK;

  DROP TABLE #T1;
END

SELECT *
FROM (SELECT seq_val AS cur,
        (SELECT MIN(seq_val)
         FROM #T1 AS N
         WHERE N.seq_val > C.seq_val) AS nxt
      FROM #T1 AS C
      WHERE seq_val <= @max) AS D
WHERE nxt - cur > 1;

DROP TABLE #T1;
```

This code runs an infinite loop that in each iteration reads the data using NOLOCK into a temp table and breaks from the loop as soon as contiguous values with a gap between them are found in the *seq_val* column. The code then presents the pairs of contiguous values that have a gap between them. After a few seconds I got the following output in Connection 2, shown here in abbreviated form:

```
cur         nxt
----------- -----------
53          55
620         622
792         794
```

803	805
838	840
1202	1204
1600	1602
1643	1645
1647	1649
1788	1791
. . .	

You can stop the code in Connection 1.

You can run the test again without the NOLOCK hint, in which case the storage engine will use an index order scan. The code in Connection 2 should not break from the loop because gaps won't be found.

Index Order Scans   If you think that index order scans are safe from phenomena such as returning multiple occurrences of rows or skipping rows, think again. It is true that index order scans are safe from such phenomena because of page splits, but page splits are not the only reason for data to move around in the index leaf. Another cause of movement in the leaf is update of an index key. If an index key is modified after the row was read by an index order scan and the row is moved to a point in the leaf that the scan hasn't reached yet, the scan will read the row a second time. Similarly, if an index key is modified before the row is read by an index order scan and the row is moved to a point in the leaf that the scan has already passed, the scan will never reach that row.

For example, suppose you have an Employees table that currently has four employee rows (employee A with a salary of 2000, employee B with a salary of 4000, employee C with a salary of 3000, and employee D with a salary of 1000). A clustered index is on the salary column. Figure 4-32 shows in three steps how an index order scan can return multiple occurrences of the same row because of an update that takes place during the read.

You issue a query against the table and the storage engine uses an index order scan. Remember that an index order scan is always used when the plan shows Index Scan: *Ordered: True* (for example, when the query has an ORDER BY clause), but also when the *Ordered* property is *False*, the environment is read-write, and the isolation is not read uncommitted.

Step 1 shows that the scan already read the first page in the leaf level and returned the rows for employees D, A, and C. If the query is running under read uncommitted, no shared locks are acquired on the rows. If the query is running under read committed, shared locks are acquired, but they are released as soon as the query is done with the resource (for example, a row or page), even though the query hasn't finished yet. This means that at the point in time that the scan is done with the page, in both isolations no locks are held on the rows that were read.

Step 2 shows an update of the row for employee D, increasing the salary from 1000 to 5000. The row moves to the second page in the leaf level because of the index key change.

Index Order Scan: Getting Multiple Occurrences of Rows
Step 1:

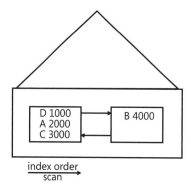

Output: D 1000, A 2000, C 3000

Step 2:

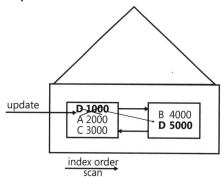

Output: D 1000, A 2000, C 3000

Step 3:

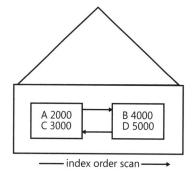

Output: **D 1000,** A 2000, C 3000, B 4000, **D 5000**

FIGURE 4-32 Index order scan: getting multiple occurrences of rows

Step 3 shows the continuation of the scan, reading the second page in the leaf of the index, returning the rows for employees B and D. Note that employee D was returned a second time.

The first time, the row was returned with salary 1000 and the second time with salary 5000. Note that this phenomenon cannot happen in higher isolation levels than read committed because higher isolations keep shared locks until the end of the transaction. This phenomenon cannot happen also under the two isolation levels that are based on row versioning—read committed snapshot and snapshot.

Similarly, an index order scan can skip rows. Figure 4-33 shows how this can happen in three steps.

Index Order Scan: Skipping Rows

Step 1:

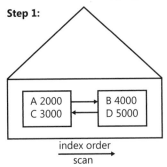

Output A 2000, C 3000

Step 2:

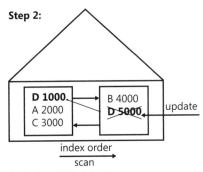

Output A 2000, C 3000

Step 3:

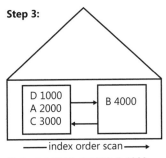

Output A 2000, C 3000, B 4000

FIGURE 4-33 Index order scan: skipping rows

Employee D starts with salary 5000 this time, and its row resides in the second index leaf page. Step 1 shows that the scan already read the first page in the leaf level and returned the rows for employees A and C.

Step 2 shows an update of the row for employee D, decreasing the salary from 5000 to 1000. The row moves to the first page in the leaf level because of the index key change.

Step 3 shows the continuation of the scan, reading the second page in the leaf of the index, returning the rows for employee B. Note that the row for employee D was not returned at all—neither with the salary 5000 nor with 1000. Note that this phenomenon can happen in read uncommitted, read committed, and even repeatable read because the update was done to a row that was not yet read. This phenomenon cannot happen in serializable isolation level or in the snapshot-based isolations.

To see both phenomena with your own eyes, you can run a simple test. First, execute the following code to create and populate the Employees table:

```
USE tempdb;
IF OBJECT_ID('dbo.Employees', 'U') IS NOT NULL  DROP TABLE dbo.Employees;

CREATE TABLE dbo.Employees
(
  empid VARCHAR(10) NOT NULL,
  salary MONEY NOT NULL,
  filler CHAR(2500) NOT NULL DEFAULT('a')
);

CREATE CLUSTERED INDEX idx_cl_salary ON dbo.Employees(salary);
ALTER TABLE dbo.Employees
  ADD CONSTRAINT PK_Employees PRIMARY KEY NONCLUSTERED(empid);

INSERT INTO dbo.Employees(empid, salary) VALUES
  ('D', 1000.00),('A', 2000.00),('C', 3000.00),('B', 4000.00);
```

Open two connections. Run the following code in Connection 1 to run an infinite loop that in each iteration updates the salary of employee D from its current value to 6000 minus its current value (switching between the values 1000 and 5000):

```
SET NOCOUNT ON;
USE tempdb;

WHILE 1=1
  UPDATE dbo.Employees
    SET salary = 6000.00 - salary
  WHERE empid = 'D';
```

This code causes the row for employee D to keep moving between the two index leaf pages. Run the following code in Connection 2:

```
SET NOCOUNT ON;
USE tempdb;
```

```
WHILE 1 = 1
BEGIN
  SELECT * INTO #Employees FROM dbo.Employees;

  IF @@rowcount <> 4 BREAK; -- use =3 for skipping, =5 for multi occur

  DROP TABLE #Employees;
END

SELECT * FROM #Employees;

DROP TABLE #Employees;
```

The code runs an infinite loop that reads the contents of the Employees table into a temp table. Because the code doesn't specify the NOLOCK hint and the environment is read-write, the storage engine uses an index order scan. The code breaks from the loop when the number of rows read is different than the expected number (four). In case the scan reads the same row twice, this code returns five rows in the output:

```
empid      salary                 filler
---------- ---------------------- ------
D          1000.00                a
A          2000.00                a
C          3000.00                a
B          4000.00                a
D          5000.00                a
```

In cases where the scan skips a row, this code returns three rows in the output:

```
empid      salary                 filler
---------- ---------------------- ------
A          2000.00                a
C          3000.00                a
B          4000.00                a
```

You can change the filter to = 3 to wait for a case where the row is skipped, and you can change it to = 5 to wait for a case where the row is read twice.

I hope this section gave you a better understanding of how the storage engine handles scans and, most important, the implications of running your code under the read uncommitted isolation level. The next sections continue the coverage of index access methods.

Nonclustered Index Seek + Ordered Partial Scan + Lookups

The access method *nonclustered index seek + ordered partial scan + lookups* is typically used for small-range queries (including a point query) using a nonclustered index scan that doesn't cover the query. To demonstrate this access method, I will use the following query:

```
USE Performance;

SELECT orderid, custid, empid, shipperid, orderdate
FROM dbo.Orders
WHERE orderid BETWEEN 101 AND 120;
```

We don't have a covering index because the first key column is the filtered column *orderid*, but we do have a noncovering one—the *PK_Orders* index. If the query is selective enough, the optimizer would use the index. *Selectivity* is defined as the percentage of the number of rows returned by the query out of the total number of rows in the table. The term *high selectivity* refers to a small percentage, while *low selectivity* refers to a large percentage. Our access method first performs a seek within the index to find the first key in the sought range (*orderid = 101*). The second part of the access method is an ordered partial scan in the leaf level from the first key in the range until the last (*orderid = 120*). The third and last part involves lookups of the corresponding data row for each key. Note that the third part doesn't have to wait for the second part to finish. For each key found in the range, SQL Server can already apply a lookup. Remember that a lookup in a heap (a RID lookup) translates to a single page read, while a lookup in a clustered table (a key lookup) translates to as many reads as the number of levels in the clustered index (three in our case).

It is vital for making performance estimations to understand that with this access method, the part involving the lookups typically incurs most of the query's cost; this is because it involves most of the I/O activity. Remember that the lookup translates to a whole page read or one whole seek within the clustered index per sought row, and the lookups are always random I/O (as opposed to sequential ones).

To estimate the I/O cost of such a query, you can typically focus on the cost of the lookups. If you want to make more accurate estimations, also taking into consideration the seek within the index and the ordered partial scan, feel free to do so, but these parts will be negligible as the range grows larger. The I/O cost of a seek operation is three reads in our case (the number of levels in the index). The I/O cost of the ordered partial scan depends on the number of rows in the range (20 in our case) and the number of rows that fit in an index page (more than 300 in our case). For our query, no additional read is actually involved for the partial scan because all the keys in the range we are after reside in the leaf page that the seek reached, or they might span an additional page if the first key appears close to the end of the page. The I/O cost of the lookup operations will be the number of rows in the range (20 in our case), multiplied by one if the table is a heap or multiplied by the number of levels in the clustered index (3 in our case) if the table is clustered. So you should expect around 23 logical reads in total if you run the query against a heap and around 63 logical reads if you run it against a clustered table. Remember that the nonleaf levels of the clustered index typically reside in cache because of all the lookup operations going through it; you shouldn't concern yourself too much with the seemingly higher cost of the query in the clustered table scenario.

Figure 4-34 shows the execution plan for the query over a heap, and Figure 4-35 shows an illustration of the access method.

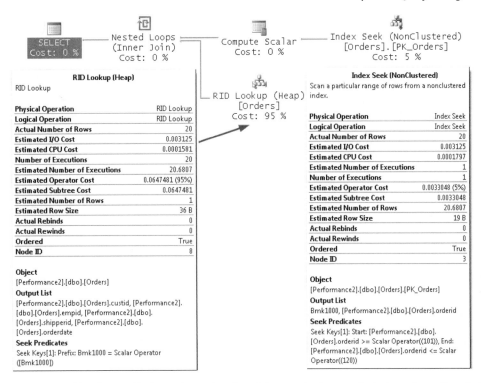

RID Lookup (Heap)	
RID Lookup	
Physical Operation	RID Lookup
Logical Operation	RID Lookup
Actual Number of Rows	20
Estimated I/O Cost	0.003125
Estimated CPU Cost	0.0001581
Number of Executions	20
Estimated Number of Executions	20.6807
Estimated Operator Cost	0.0647481 (95%)
Estimated Subtree Cost	0.0647481
Estimated Number of Rows	1
Estimated Row Size	36 B
Actual Rebinds	0
Actual Rewinds	0
Ordered	True
Node ID	8

Object
[Performance2].[dbo].[Orders]
Output List
[Performance2].[dbo].[Orders].custid, [Performance2].
[dbo].[Orders].empid, [Performance2].[dbo].
[Orders].shipperid, [Performance2].[dbo].
[Orders].orderdate
Seek Predicates
Seek Keys[1]: Prefix: Bmk1000 = Scalar Operator
([Bmk1000])

Index Seek (NonClustered)	
Scan a particular range of rows from a nonclustered index.	
Physical Operation	Index Seek
Logical Operation	Index Seek
Actual Number of Rows	20
Estimated I/O Cost	0.003125
Estimated CPU Cost	0.0001797
Estimated Number of Executions	1
Number of Executions	1
Estimated Operator Cost	0.0033048 (5%)
Estimated Subtree Cost	0.0033048
Estimated Number of Rows	20.6807
Estimated Row Size	19 B
Actual Rebinds	0
Actual Rewinds	0
Ordered	True
Node ID	3

Object
[Performance2].[dbo].[Orders].[PK_Orders]
Output List
Bmk1000, [Performance2].[dbo].[Orders].orderid
Seek Predicates
Seek Keys[1]: Start: [Performance2].[dbo].
[Orders].orderid >= Scalar Operator((101)), End:
[Performance2].[dbo].[Orders].orderid <= Scalar
Operator((120))

FIGURE 4-34 Nonclustered index seek + ordered partial scan + lookups against a heap (execution plan)

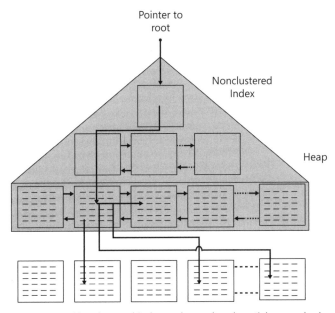

FIGURE 4-35 Nonclustered index seek + ordered partial scan + lookups against a heap

Note that in the execution plan you won't explicitly see the partial scan part of the access method; rather, it's hidden in the Index Seek operator. You can deduce it from the Seek Predicates shown in the information box for the operator and from the fact that it shows *True* in the *Ordered* property.

Here are the performance measures I got for the query:

- Logical reads 23

- Physical reads 22

- CPU time 0 ms

- Elapsed time 437 ms

- Estimated subtree cost 0.0681393

Figure 4-36 shows the execution plan of the query over a clustered table, and Figure 4-37 shows an illustration of the access method.

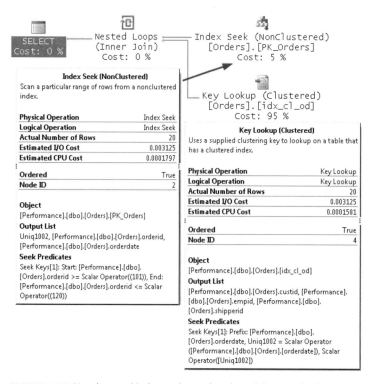

FIGURE 4-36 Nonclustered index seek + ordered partial scan + lookups against a clustered table (execution plan)

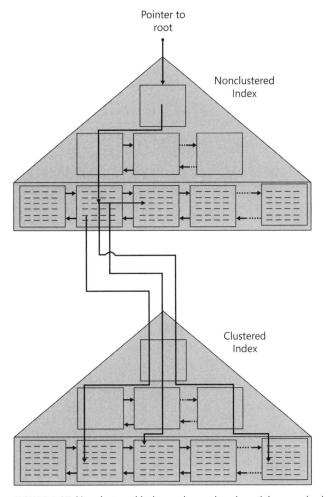

FIGURE 4-37 Nonclustered index seek + ordered partial scan + lookups against a clustered table

Here are the performance measures I got for the query in this case:

- Logical reads 63
- Physical reads 7
- CPU time 0 ms
- Elapsed time 189 ms
- Estimated subtree cost 0.0681399

Notice that the graphical execution plans distinguish between a RID lookup and a key lookup. The latter is a seek within the clustered index.

This access method is efficient only when the query is very selective (a point query or a small range). Feel free to play with the range in the filter, increasing it gradually, and see how dramatically the cost increases as the range grows larger. That will happen up to the point at which the optimizer figures that it would simply be more efficient to apply a table scan rather than using the index. I'll demonstrate such an exercise later in the chapter, in the section "Analysis of Indexing Strategies."

Unordered Nonclustered Index Scan + Lookups

The optimizer typically uses the *unordered nonclustered index scan + lookups* access method when the following conditions are in place:

- The query is selective enough.

- The optimal index for a query does not cover it.

- The index doesn't maintain the sought keys in order.

For example, such is the case when you filter a column that is not the first key column in the index. The access method will involve an unordered full scan of the leaf level of the index, followed by a series of lookups. As I mentioned, the query must be selective enough to justify this access method; otherwise, with too many lookups it will be more expensive than simply scanning the whole table. To figure out the selectivity of the query, SQL Server needs statistics on the filtered column (a histogram with the distribution of values). If such statistics do not exist, SQL Server creates them, provided that the database property *AUTO_CREATE_STATISTICS* is turned on.

For example, the following query uses such an access method against the index *idx_nc_sid_od_i_cid*, created on the key columns (*shipperid, orderdate*) *and the included column* (*custid*); what's important about this index is that the *custid* column appears in the index leaf rows but not as the first key column:

```
SELECT orderid, custid, empid, shipperid, orderdate
FROM dbo.Orders
WHERE custid = 'C0000000001';
```

Figure 4-38 shows the execution plan for the query over a heap, and Figure 4-39 illustrates the access method.

The Parallelism operators indicate that the plan is a parallel query plan utilizing multiple threads to process the query. The Repartition Streams operator produces multiple streams of records, while the Gather Streams operator consumes multiple input streams and produces a single output stream.

```
Query 1: Query cost (relative to the batch): 100%
SELECT [orderid],[custid],[empid],[shipperid],[orderdate] FROM [dbo].
Missing Index (Impact 99.244): CREATE NONCLUSTERED INDEX [<Name of Mi
```

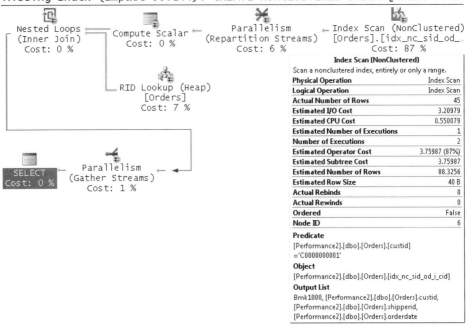

Nested Loops
(Inner Join)
Cost: 0 %

Compute Scalar
Cost: 0 %

Parallelism
(Repartition Streams)
Cost: 6 %

Index Scan (NonClustered)
[Orders].[idx_nc_sid_od_..
Cost: 87 %

RID Lookup (Heap)
[Orders]
Cost: 7 %

SELECT
Cost: 0 %

Parallelism
(Gather Streams)
Cost: 1 %

Index Scan (NonClustered)	
Scan a nonclustered index, entirely or only a range.	
Physical Operation	Index Scan
Logical Operation	Index Scan
Actual Number of Rows	45
Estimated I/O Cost	3.20979
Estimated CPU Cost	0.550079
Estimated Number of Executions	1
Number of Executions	2
Estimated Operator Cost	3.75987 (87%)
Estimated Subtree Cost	3.75987
Estimated Number of Rows	88.3256
Estimated Row Size	40 B
Actual Rebinds	0
Actual Rewinds	0
Ordered	False
Node ID	6

Predicate
[Performance2].[dbo].[Orders].[custid]
='C0000000001'
Object
[Performance2].[dbo].[Orders].[idx_nc_sid_od_i_cid]
Output List
Bmk1000, [Performance2].[dbo].[Orders].custid,
[Performance2].[dbo].[Orders].shipperid,
[Performance2].[dbo].[Orders].orderdate

FIGURE 4-38 Unordered nonclustered index scan + lookups against a heap (execution plan)

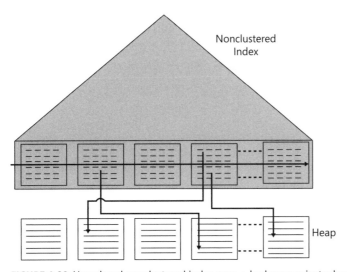

FIGURE 4-39 Unordered nonclustered index scan + lookups against a heap

The I/O cost of this query involves the cost of the unordered scan of the leaf of the index (see the section "The Storage Engine's Treatment of Scans" for details about how scans are processed) plus the cost of the lookups (random I/O). In terms of logical reads, the scan will cost as many page reads as the number of pages in the leaf of the index. As described earlier, the cost of the lookups is the number of qualifying rows multiplied by 1 in a heap and multiplied by the number of levels in the clustered index (3 in our case) if the table is clustered. Here are the measures I got for this query against a heap:

- Logical reads 4460

- Physical reads 94

- Read-ahead reads 4706

- CPU time 141 ms

- Elapsed time 2105 ms

- Estimated subtree cost 4.31519

Figure 4-40 shows the execution plan for the query over a clustered table, and Figure 4-41 illustrates the access method.

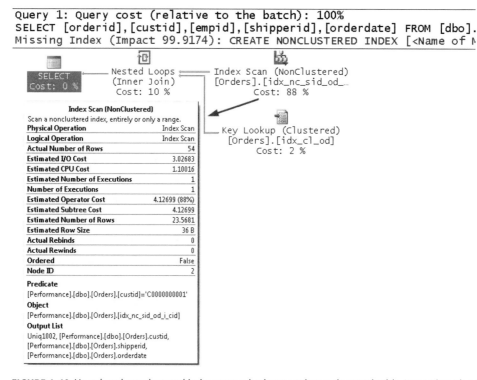

FIGURE 4-40 Unordered nonclustered index scan + lookups against a clustered table (execution plan 1)

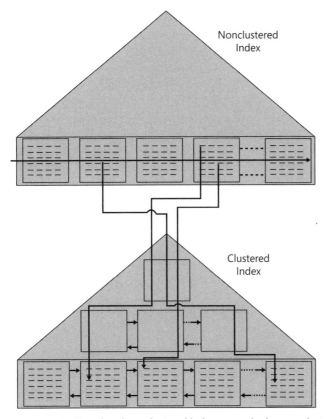

FIGURE 4-41 Unordered nonclustered index scan + lookups against a clustered table

Here are the measures I got for this query against a clustered table:

- Logical reads 4262
- Physical reads 70
- Read-ahead reads 4099
- CPU time 202 ms
- Elapsed time 2732 ms
- Estimated subtree cost 4.68131

As you can see in Figure 4-40, in this case SQL Server decided not to use a parallel query plan.

Remember that SQL Server needs statistics on the *custid* column to determine the selectivity of the query. The following query will tell you which statistics SQL Server created automatically on the Orders table:

```
SELECT name
FROM sys.stats
WHERE object_id = OBJECT_ID('dbo.Orders')
  AND auto_created = 1;
```

You should get statistics with a name similar to _WA_Sys_00000002_7A672E12, which SQL Server created automatically for this purpose.

You may have noticed in both Figure 4-38 and Figure 4-40 that SSMS indicates a missing index, with an estimated impact (improvement) of more than 99 percent. When the optimizer optimized this query, it looked for what it considers to be an optimal index, and because it did not find it, it reported the missing index. The XML showplan of the query reports missing index information in the *MissingIndexes* attribute; SSMS parses this information and displays it graphically. Similar information was also available in the XML showplan in SQL Server 2005, but SSMS 2005 did not present it graphically as part of the graphical execution plan the way SSMS 2008 does. If you right-click the missing index information and choose Missing Index Detail, SSMS opens a new query window with the CREATE INDEX statement for the recommended index. In our case, you get the following code:

```
/*
Missing Index Details from SQLQuery1.sql - DOJO\SQL08.Performance (DOJO\Gandalf (51))
The Query Processor estimates that implementing the following index could improve the query
cost by 99.9174%.
*/

/*
USE [Performance]
GO
CREATE NONCLUSTERED INDEX [<Name of Missing Index, sysname,>]
ON [dbo].[Orders] ([custid])
INCLUDE ([orderid],[empid],[shipperid],[orderdate])
GO
*/
```

SQL Server also records such missing index information internally and exposes it through the dynamic management objects *sys.dm_db_missing_index_details*, *sys.dm_db_missing_index_group_stats*, *sys.dm_db_missing_index_groups*, and *sys.dm_db_missing_index_columns*. Query those objects to get missing index information that was collected since SQL Server was last restarted.

Let's return to the access method that is the focus of this section. A similar access method can be used when you apply pattern-matching filters with the LIKE predicate, even when the pattern starts with a wildcard. SQL Server internally maintains cardinality information on substrings within string columns. Therefore, it can estimate the selectivity of a query for such filters.

To demonstrate this capability, SQL Server will be able to estimate the selectivity of the following query, which produces the plan shown in Figure 4-42:

```
SELECT orderid, custid, empid, shipperid, orderdate
FROM dbo.Orders
WHERE custid LIKE '%9999';
```

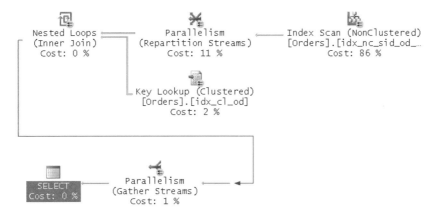

FIGURE 4-42 Unordered nonclustered index scan + lookups against a clustered table (execution plan 2)

Here are the performance measures that I got for this query:

- Logical reads 4634
- Physical reads 90
- Read-ahead reads 4819
- CPU time 811 ms
- Elapsed time 2667 ms
- Estimated subtree cost 4.13886

Clustered Index Seek + Ordered Partial Scan

The optimizer typically uses the access method *clustered index seek + ordered partial scan* for range queries where you filter based on the first key columns of the clustered index. This access method first performs a seek operation to the first key in the range, and then it applies an ordered partial scan at the leaf level from the first key in the range until the last. The main benefit of this method is that no lookups are involved. Remember that lookups are very expensive with large ranges. The performance ratio between this access method—which doesn't involve lookups—and one that uses a nonclustered index and lookups becomes larger and larger as the range grows.

The following query, which looks for all orders placed on a given *orderdate*, uses the access method, which is the focus of this discussion:

```
SELECT orderid, custid, empid, shipperid, orderdate
FROM dbo.Orders
WHERE orderdate = '20080212';
```

Note that even though the filter uses an equality operator, it is in essence a range query because there are multiple qualifying rows. Either way, a point query can be considered a special case of a range query. The I/O cost of this access method will involve the cost of the seek operation (3 random reads in our case) and the cost of the ordered partial scan within the leaf (in our case, 19 page reads). In total, you get 22 logical reads. Note that the ordered scan typically incurs the bulk of the cost of the query because it involves most of the I/O. Remember that with index order scans, logical index fragmentation plays a crucial role. When fragmentation is at a minimum (as in our case), physical reads are close to sequential. However, as the fragmentation level grows higher, the disk arm has to move frantically to and fro, degrading the performance of the scan.

Figure 4-43 shows the execution plan for the query, and Figure 4-44 illustrates the access method.

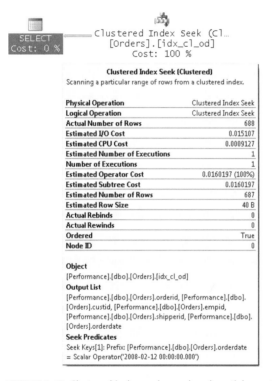

FIGURE 4-43 Clustered index seek + ordered partial scan (execution plan)

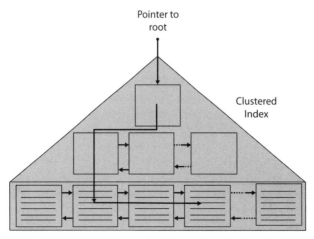

FIGURE 4-44 Clustered index seek + ordered partial scan

Here are the performance measures I got for this query:

- Logical reads 22

- Physical reads 3

- Read-ahead reads 19

- CPU time 0 ms

- Elapsed time 148 ms

- Estimated subtree cost 0.0160197

Note that this plan is trivial for the optimizer to generate. That is, the plan is not dependent on the selectivity of the query. Rather, it will always be used regardless of the size of the sought range, unless, of course, you have an even better index for the query to begin with.

Covering Nonclustered Index Seek + Ordered Partial Scan

The access method *covering nonclustered index seek + ordered partial scan* is almost identical to the previously described access method. The only difference is that the former uses a covering nonclustered index instead of the clustered index. Of course, to use this method the filtered columns must be the first key columns in the index. The benefit of this access method over the previous one lies in the fact that a nonclustered index leaf page naturally can fit more rows than a clustered index one; therefore, the bulk cost of the plan, which is the partial scan cost of the leaf, is lower. The cost is lower because fewer pages need to be scanned for the same size of the range. Of course, here as well, index fragmentation plays an important performance role because the partial scan is ordered.

As an example, the following query looking for a range of *orderdate* values for a given *shipperid* uses this access method against the covering index *idx_nc_sid_od_i_cid*, created on the key list (*shipperid, orderdate*) and included list (*custid*):

```
SELECT shipperid, orderdate, custid
FROM dbo.Orders
WHERE shipperid = 'C'
  AND orderdate >= '20080101'
  AND orderdate < '20090101';
```

> **Note** To have the partial scan read the minimum required pages, the first index key columns must be *shipperid, orderdate,* in that order. If you swap their order, the partial scan will end up also scanning rows that meet the date range also for other shippers, requiring more I/O.

Figure 4-45 shows the execution plan for the query, and Figure 4-46 illustrates the access method.

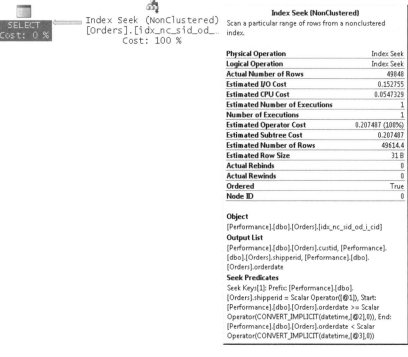

Index Seek (NonClustered)	
Scan a particular range of rows from a nonclustered index.	
Physical Operation	Index Seek
Logical Operation	Index Seek
Actual Number of Rows	49848
Estimated I/O Cost	0.152755
Estimated CPU Cost	0.0547329
Estimated Number of Executions	1
Number of Executions	1
Estimated Operator Cost	0.207487 (100%)
Estimated Subtree Cost	0.207487
Estimated Number of Rows	49614.4
Estimated Row Size	31 B
Actual Rebinds	0
Actual Rewinds	0
Ordered	True
Node ID	0

Object
[Performance].[dbo].[Orders].[idx_nc_sid_od_i_cid]
Output List
[Performance].[dbo].[Orders].custid, [Performance].
[dbo].[Orders].shipperid, [Performance].[dbo].
[Orders].orderdate
Seek Predicates
Seek Keys[1]: Prefix: [Performance].[dbo].
[Orders].shipperid = Scalar Operator([@1]), Start:
[Performance].[dbo].[Orders].orderdate >= Scalar
Operator(CONVERT_IMPLICIT(datetime,[@2],0)), End:
[Performance].[dbo].[Orders].orderdate < Scalar
Operator(CONVERT_IMPLICIT(datetime,[@3],0))

FIGURE 4-45 Covering nonclustered index seek + ordered partial scan (execution plan)

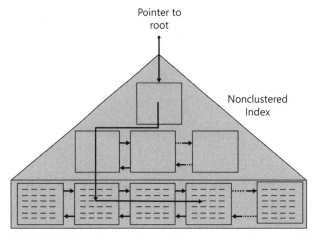

FIGURE 4-46 Covering nonclustered index seek + ordered partial scan

Here are the performance measures I got for this query:

- Logical reads 211

- CPU time 16 ms

- Elapsed time 1195 ms

- Estimated subtree cost 0.207487

Note that this plan is also a trivial plan that is not based on the query's selectivity.

Remember, the main benefit of this access method is that no lookups are involved because the index covers the query. Also, you read fewer pages than in a similar access method against a clustered index.

Also note that when you create covering indexes, the index columns serve two different functions. Columns that you filter or sort by are required as key columns that will be maintained in all levels of the balanced tree, and they also determine the sort order at the leaf. Other index columns might be required only for covering purposes. If you include all index columns in the index's key column list, bear the cost in mind. SQL Server needs to keep the tree balanced, and it will have to apply physical movement of data and adjustments in the tree when you modify key column values in the table. That's just a waste with columns that are required only for covering purposes and not for filtering or sorting.

To tackle this need, SQL Server supports the concept of *included nonkey columns* in the index. When you create an index, you separately specify which columns will make the key list and which will be included just for covering purposes—only at the leaf level of the index.

For example, our last query relied only on *shipperid* and *orderdate* for filtering and sorting purposes, while it relied on *custid* only for covering purposes. Therefore, the index that was defined to support this query (*idx_nc_sid_od_i_cid*) specified the *custid* attribute in the INCLUDE clause. Here's the original index definition:

```
CREATE NONCLUSTERED INDEX idx_nc_sid_od_i_cid
  ON dbo.Orders(shipperid, orderdate)
  INCLUDE(custid);
```

Recall that earlier I discussed the following query:

```
SELECT orderid, custid, empid, shipperid, orderdate
FROM dbo.Orders
WHERE custid = 'C0000000001';
```

The plan that the optimizer created for it was an *unordered nonclustered index scan + lookups* since no better index was in place. The optimizer reported a missing index, and the index it recommended was on *custid* as the key and all other columns as included columns. Run the following code to create such an index:

```
CREATE INDEX idx_nc_cid_i_oid_eid_sid_od
  ON dbo.Orders(custid)
  INCLUDE(orderid, empid, shipperid, orderdate);
```

Run the query and notice how this time the number of logical reads drops to 3! Remember that without the index the number of logical reads was more than 4,000.

Run the following code to remove the index:

```
DROP INDEX dbo.Orders.idx_nc_cid_i_oid_eid_sid_od;
```

Run the query again and notice how the number of logical reads goes back to over 4,000.

Note that the key list is limited to 16 columns and 900 bytes. An added bonus with included nonkey columns is that they are not bound by the same limitations. In fact, they can even include large objects such as variable-length columns defined with the *MAX* specifier and *XML* columns.

Index Intersection

So far, I've focused mainly on the performance benefit you get from indexes when reading data. Keep in mind, though, that indexes incur a cost when you modify data. Any change of data (deletes, inserts, updates) must be reflected in the indexes that hold a copy of that data, and it might cause page splits and adjustments in the balanced trees, which can be very expensive. Therefore, you cannot freely create as many indexes as you like, especially in systems that involve intensive modifications, such as OLTP environments. You want to prioritize and pick the more important indexes. This is especially a problem with covering indexes because different queries can benefit from completely different covering indexes, and you might end up with a very large number of indexes that your queries could benefit from.

Fortunately, the problem is somewhat reduced because the optimizer supports a technique called *index intersection*, where it intersects data obtained from two indexes and, if required, then intersects the result with data obtained from another index and so on. For example, the optimizer will use index intersection for the following query, producing the plan shown in Figure 4-47:

```
SELECT orderid, custid
FROM dbo.Orders
WHERE shipperid = 'A';
```

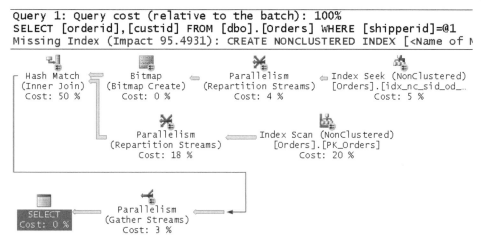

FIGURE 4-47 Execution plan with index intersection

I will elaborate on join operators in Chapter 7. The optimal index here would be one where *shipperid* is defined as the key column and *orderid* and *custid* are defined as included nonkey columns but no such index is on the table. Rather, the index *idx_nc_sid_od_i_cid* defines the *shipperid* as the key column and also contains the *custid* column, and the index *PK_Orders* contains the *orderid* column. The optimizer used the access method *nonclustered index seek + ordered partial scan* to obtain the relevant data from *idx_nc_sid_od_i_cid*, and it used an unordered nonclustered index scan to obtain the relevant data from *PK_Orders*. It then inter- sected the two sets based on the row locator values; naturally, row locator values pointing to the same rows will be matched. You can think of index intersection as an internal join based on a match in row locator values.

Here are the performance measures that I got for this query:

- Scan count 6
- Logical reads 3771
- Physical reads 84
- Read-ahead reads 672
- CPU time 1248 ms
- Elapsed time 4357 ms
- Estimated subtree cost 13.0864

Filtered Indexes and Statistics

SQL Server 2008 introduces support for filtered indexes and statistics. A filtered index is an index on a subset of rows defined based on a predicate. Filtered indexes are cheaper to create and to maintain compared to nonfiltered ones because only modifications to the relevant subset of rows need to be reflected in the index. Also, filtered distribution statistics (histograms)—whether created on the first index key column or otherwise—are more accurate than nonfiltered statistics. That's because the maximum number of steps in a histogram is limited, and with filtered statistics that number is used to represent a smaller set of rows.

I'll provide several scenarios in which you may find filtered indexes useful. The first scenario involves queries that filter data based on a column that has a large percentage of NULLs. When filtering rows based on a predicate in the form <column> <operator> <value>, the filter eliminates rows with a NULL in that column. The optimizer is well aware of this fact. Therefore, if you create an index on this column excluding rows where the column is NULL, the optimizer will still consider using the index for such predicates. The following example demonstrates this capability.

Run the following code to create an index on the Sales.SalesOrderHeader table in the AdventureWorks2008 database with *CurrencyRateID* as the key and a filter based on the predicate *CurrencyRateID IS NOT NULL*:

```
USE AdventureWorks2008;

CREATE NONCLUSTERED INDEX idx_currate_notnull
  ON Sales.SalesOrderHeader(CurrencyRateID)
  WHERE CurrencyRateID IS NOT NULL;
```

Run the following query and notice in its execution plan (shown in Figure 4-48) that the index was used:

```
SELECT *
FROM Sales.SalesOrderHeader
WHERE CurrencyRateID = 4;
```

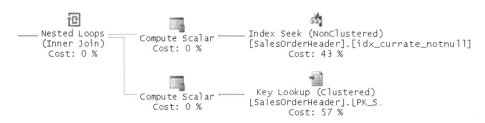

FIGURE 4-48 Execution plan with filtered index idx_currate_notnull

Another scenario for using filtered indexes is to support queries that use a range filter against a certain column, and the ranges requested by users are typical. For example, suppose that when users query orders and filter the orders based on a range of freight values, they tend to be interested in cases where the freight is worth more than $5,000. In such a case, it makes sense to create the following filtered index where the *Freight* attribute is greater than or equal to $5,000:

```
CREATE NONCLUSTERED INDEX idx_freight_5000_or_more
  ON Sales.SalesOrderHeader(Freight)
  WHERE Freight >= $5000.00;
```

The optimizer would then consider using the index even when the query filter is after a subinterval of the index filter. For example, run the following query and notice in its execution plan (shown in Figure 4-49) that the index is used:

```
SELECT *
FROM Sales.SalesOrderHeader
WHERE Freight BETWEEN $5500.00 AND $6000.00;
```

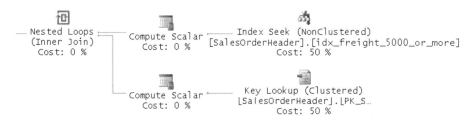

FIGURE 4-49 Execution plan with filtered index idx_freight_5000_or_more

Filtered indexes support the INCLUDE clause. For example, run the following code to create an index on the Sales.SalesOrderHeader table, with the attribute *OrderDate* as the key, the attributes *SalesOrderID, CustomerID, TotalDue* as included columns, and a filter based on the predicate *TerritoryID = 5*:

```
CREATE NONCLUSTERED INDEX idx_territory5_orderdate
  ON Sales.SalesOrderHeader(OrderDate)
  INCLUDE(SalesOrderID, CustomerID, TotalDue)
  WHERE TerritoryID = 5;
```

This index covers the following query:

```
SELECT SalesOrderID, CustomerID, OrderDate, TotalDue
FROM Sales.SalesOrderHeader
WHERE TerritoryID = 5;
```

The plan for this query is shown in Figure 4-50.

FIGURE 4-50 Execution plan 1 with filtered index idx_territory5_orderdate

All index rows are needed by the query because the query's filter is based on the same predicate as the index filter; therefore, the optimizer chooses a full scan of the index. If your query asks to further filter the rows based on a range of order dates, the optimizer would use a seek followed by a partial scan in the index. The following query demonstrates such a request, and its plan is shown in Figure 4-51:

```
SELECT SalesOrderID, CustomerID, OrderDate, TotalDue
FROM Sales.SalesOrderHeader
WHERE TerritoryID = 5
  AND OrderDate >= '20040101';
```

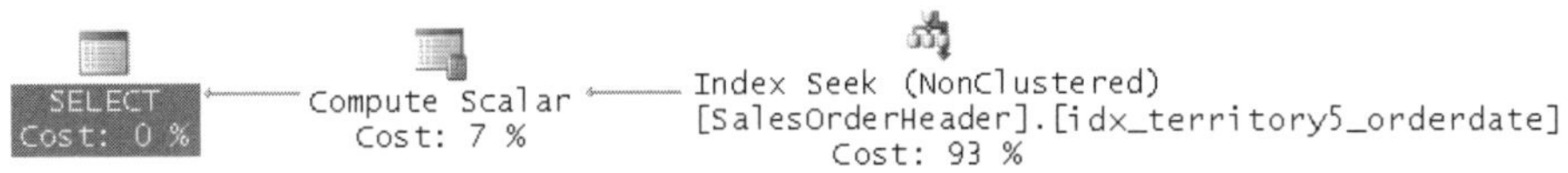

FIGURE 4-51 Execution plan 2 with filtered index idx_territory5_orderdate

SQL Server automatically creates distribution statistics on the first index key column. Naturally, when creating filtered indexes you also get filtered statistics. SQL Server also allows you to create filtered statistics manually, as the following example shows:

```
CREATE STATISTICS stats_territory4_orderdate
  ON Sales.SalesOrderHeader(OrderDate)
  WHERE TerritoryID = 4;
```

You can also use filtered indexes to solve a common request related to enforcing data integrity. The *UNIQUE* constraint supported by SQL Server treats two NULLs as equal for the purposes of enforcing uniqueness. This means that if you define a *UNIQUE* constraint on a NULLable column, you are allowed only one row with a NULL in that column. In some cases, though, you might need to enforce the uniqueness only of nonNULL values but allow multiple NULLs. ANSI SQL does support such a kind of *UNIQUE* constraint, but SQL Server never implemented it. Now, with filtered indexes, it's quite easy to handle this need. Simply create a unique filtered index based on a predicate in the form *WHERE <column> IS NOT NULL*. As an example, run the following code to create a table called T1 with such a filtered index on the column *col1*:

```
IF OBJECT_ID('dbo.T1', 'U') IS NOT NULL DROP TABLE dbo.T1;
CREATE TABLE dbo.T1(col1 INT NULL, col2 VARCHAR(10) NOT NULL);
GO
CREATE UNIQUE NONCLUSTERED INDEX idx_col1_notnull
  ON dbo.T1(col1)
  WHERE col1 IS NOT NULL;
```

Run following code twice in an attempt to insert two rows with the same non-NULL *col1* value:

```
INSERT INTO dbo.T1(col1, col2)
  VALUES(1, 'a');
```

The second run of this code will fail with the following error:

```
Msg 2601, Level 14, State 1, Line 1
Cannot insert duplicate key row in object 'dbo.T1' with unique index 'idx_col1_notnull'.
The statement has been terminated.
```

Run the following code twice in an attempt to insert two rows with NULL *col1* value:

```
INSERT INTO dbo.T1(col1, col2)
  VALUES(NULL, 'a');
```

And this time both rows are inserted.

When you're done experimenting with filtered indexes, run the following code for cleanup:

```
DROP INDEX Sales.SalesOrderHeader.idx_currate_notnull;
DROP INDEX Sales.SalesOrderHeader.idx_freight_5000_or_more;
DROP INDEX Sales.SalesOrderHeader.idx_territory5_orderdate;
DROP STATISTICS Sales.SalesOrderHeader.stats_territory4_orderdate;
DROP TABLE dbo.T1;
```

Indexed Views

This section briefly describes and demonstrates the concept of *indexed views* for the sake of completeness. I won't conduct a lengthy discussion on the subject here. I'll provide a bit more details in *Inside T-SQL Programming*.

SQL Server allows you to create indexes on views—not just on tables. Normally, a view is a virtual object, and a query against it ultimately queries the underlying tables. However, when you create a clustered index on a view, you materialize all of the view's contents within the clustered index on disk. After creating a clustered index, you can also create multiple nonclustered indexes on the view as well. The data in the indexes on the view will be kept in sync with the changes in the underlying tables as with any other index.

Indexed views are beneficial mainly in reducing I/O costs and expensive processing of data. Such costs are especially apparent in aggregation queries that scan large volumes of data and produce small result sets and in expensive join queries.

For example, the following code creates an indexed view that is designed to tune aggregate queries that group orders by *empid* and *YEAR(orderdate)*, returning the count of orders for each group:

```
USE Performance;

IF OBJECT_ID('dbo.EmpOrders', 'V') IS NOT NULL
  DROP VIEW dbo.EmpOrders;
GO
CREATE VIEW dbo.EmpOrders
  WITH SCHEMABINDING
AS

SELECT empid, YEAR(orderdate) AS orderyear, COUNT_BIG(*) AS numorders
FROM dbo.Orders
GROUP BY empid, YEAR(orderdate);
GO

CREATE UNIQUE CLUSTERED INDEX idx_ucl_eid_oy
  ON dbo.EmpOrders(empid, orderyear);
```

Query the view, and you will get the execution plan shown in Figure 4-52, showing that the clustered index on the view was scanned:

```
SELECT empid, orderyear, numorders
FROM dbo.EmpOrders;
```

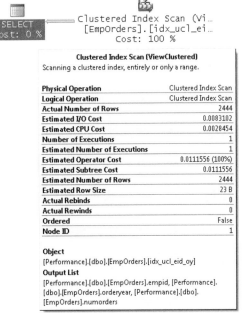

FIGURE 4-52 Execution plan for query against indexed view

The view contains a very small number of rows (around a couple of thousand) compared to the number of rows in the table (a million). The leaf of the index contains only about 10 pages. Hence, the I/O cost of the plan would be about 10 page reads.

Here are the performance measures I got for this query:

- Logical reads 10

- CPU time 0 ms

- Elapsed time 144 ms

- Estimated subtree cost 0.0111556

Interestingly, if you work with an Enterprise (or Developer) edition of SQL Server, the optimizer will consider using indexes on the view even when querying the underlying tables directly. For example, the following query produces a similar plan to the one shown in Figure 4-52, with the same query cost:

```
SELECT empid, YEAR(orderdate) AS orderyear, COUNT_BIG(*) AS numorders
FROM dbo.Orders
GROUP BY empid, YEAR(orderdate);
```

If you're not working with an Enterprise edition, you have to query the view directly and also specify that you do not want the optimizer to expand its optimization choices beyond the scope of the view. You do so by specifying the NOEXPAND table hint: *FROM <view_name> WITH (NOEXPAND).*

Analysis of Indexing Strategies

Recall the earlier discussion about the tuning methodology. When you perform index tuning, you do so with respect to the query patterns that incur the highest cumulative costs in the system. For a given query pattern, you can build an index optimization scale that would help you make the right design choices. I will demonstrate this process through an example. To follow the demonstrations, before you continue, drop the view created earlier and all the indexes on the Orders table except for the clustered index. Alternatively, you can rerun the code in Listing 4-1 after commenting or removing all index and primary key creation statements on Orders, keeping only the clustered index.

In our example, suppose that you need to tune the following query pattern:

```
SELECT orderid, custid, empid, shipperid, orderdate
FROM dbo.Orders
WHERE orderid >= value;
```

Remember that the efficiency of some access methods depends on the selectivity of the query, while the efficiency of others doesn't. For access methods that depend on selectivity, assume that the query pattern is typically fairly selective (around 0.1 percent selectivity, or around 1000 qualifying rows). Use the following query in your tuning process when aiming at such selectivity:

```
SELECT orderid, custid, empid, shipperid, orderdate
FROM dbo.Orders
WHERE orderid >= 999001;
```

I'll progress in the index optimization scale from the worst-case scenario to the best, using this query as a reference, but I'll also describe what would happen when the selectivity of the query changes.

Table Scan (Unordered Clustered Index Scan)

The worst-case scenario for our query pattern with fairly high selectivity is when you have no good index. You will get the execution plan shown in Figure 4-53, using a table scan (unordered clustered index scan).

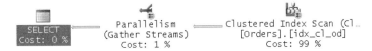

```
                       Parallelism            Clustered Index Scan (Cl...
    SELECT            (Gather Streams)          [Orders].[idx_cl_od]
    Cost: 0 %              Cost: 1 %                Cost: 99 %
```

FIGURE 4-53 Execution plan with table scan (unordered clustered index scan)

Even though you're after a fairly small number of rows (1,000 in our case), the whole table is scanned. I got the following performance measures for this query:

- Logical reads 25175

- CPU time 249 ms

- Elapsed time 8605

- Estimated subtree cost 19.3423

This plan is trivial and not dependent on selectivity—that is, you get the same plan regardless of the selectivity of the query.

Unordered Covering Nonclustered Index Scan

The next step in the optimization scale would be to create a covering nonclustered index where the filtered column (*orderid*) is not the first index column:

```
CREATE NONCLUSTERED INDEX idx_nc_od_i_oid_cid_eid_sid
  ON dbo.Orders(orderdate)
  INCLUDE(orderid, custid, empid, shipperid);
```

This index yields an access method that uses a full unordered scan of the leaf of the index, as shown in Figure 4-54.

FIGURE 4-54 Execution plan with unordered covering nonclustered index scan

The row size in the covering index is about a fifth of the size of a full data row, and this will be reflected in the query's cost and run time. Here are the performance measures I got for this query:

- Logical reads 5142

- CPU time 140 ms

- Elapsed time 2543 ms

- Estimated subtree cost 4.58245

As with the previous plan, this plan is also trivial and not dependent on selectivity.

> **Note** The run times you will get for your queries will vary based on what portion of the data is cached. If you want to make credible performance comparisons in terms of run times, make sure that the caching environment in both cases reflects what you would have in your production environment. That is, if you expect most pages to reside in cache in your production environment (warm cache), run each query twice and measure the run time of the second run. If you expect most pages not to reside in cache (cold cache), in your tests clear the cache before you run each query.

Before you proceed, drop the index that you just created:

```
DROP INDEX dbo.Orders.idx_nc_od_i_oid_cid_eid_sid;
```

Unordered Nonclustered Index Scan + Lookups

The next step in our index optimization scale is to create a smaller nonclustered index that doesn't cover the query and that contains the filtered column (*orderid*), but not as the first key column:

```
CREATE NONCLUSTERED INDEX idx_nc_od_i_oid
  ON dbo.Orders(orderdate)
  INCLUDE(orderid);
```

You get an unordered nonclustered index scan + lookups, as shown in Figure 4-55.

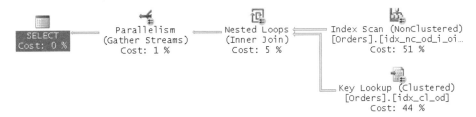

FIGURE 4-55 Execution plan with unordered nonclustered index scan + lookups

Note that the efficiency of this plan compared to the previous one depends on the selectivity of the query. As the selectivity of the query gets lower (low selectivity means a high percentage of rows), the more substantial the cost is of the lookups here. In our case, the query is fairly selective, so this plan is more efficient than the previous two; however, with low selectivity, this plan will be less efficient than the previous two.

Here are the performance measures that I got for this query:

- Logical reads 6501

- CPU time 109 ms

- Elapsed time 1534 ms

- Estimated subtree cost 5.23753

Note that even though the number of logical reads and the query cost seem higher than in the previous plan, you can see that the run times are lower. Remember that the lookup operations here traverse the clustered index, and the nonleaf levels of the clustered index are most likely to reside in cache.

Before you continue, drop the new index:

```
DROP INDEX dbo.Orders.idx_nc_od_i_oid;
```

Nonclustered Index Seek + Ordered Partial Scan + Lookups

You can get the next level of optimization in the scale by creating a nonclustered noncovering index on *orderid*:

```
CREATE UNIQUE NONCLUSTERED INDEX idx_unc_oid
  ON dbo.Orders(orderid);
```

This index yields a nonclustered index seek + ordered partial scan + lookups, as shown in Figure 4-56.

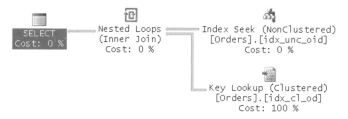

FIGURE 4-56 Execution plan with nonclustered index seek + ordered partial scan + lookups

Instead of performing the full index scan as the previous plan did, this plan performs a seek to the first key in the sought range, followed by an ordered partial scan of only the relevant range. Still, you get as many lookups as previously, which in our case amounts to a big chunk of the query cost. As the range grows larger, the contribution of the lookups to the query's cost becomes more substantial, and the costs of these two plans grows closer and closer.

Here are the performance measures for this query:

- Logical reads 3976

- CPU time 0 ms

- Elapsed time 545 ms

- Estimated subtree cost 3.22853

Determining the Selectivity Point

Allow me to digress a bit to expand on a subject I started discussing earlier—plans that are dependent on the selectivity of the query. The efficiency of the last plan is dependent on selectivity because you get one whole lookup per sought row. At some selectivity point, the optimizer would realize that a table scan is more efficient than using this plan. You might find it surprising, but that selectivity point is a pretty small percentage. Even if you have no clue about how to calculate this point, you can practice a trial-and-error approach, where you apply a binary algorithm, shifting the selectivity point to the left or right based on the plan that you get. You can invoke a range query, where you start with 50 percent selectivity by invoking the following query:

```
SELECT orderid, custid, empid, shipperid, orderdate
FROM dbo.Orders
WHERE orderid >= 500001;
```

Examine the estimated execution plan (no need for actual here) and determine whether to proceed in the next step to the left or to the right of this point, based on whether you got a table scan (clustered index scan) or an index seek. With the median key, you get the plan shown in Figure 4-57, showing a table scan.

FIGURE 4-57 Estimated plan showing a table scan

This tells you that 50 percent is not selective enough to justify using the nonclustered index. So you go to the right, to the middle point between 50 percent and a 100 percent. Following this logic, you would end up using the following keys: 750001, 875001, 937501, 968751, 984376, 992189, and 996095. The last key yields a plan where the nonclustered index is used. So now you go to the left, to the point between the keys 992189 and 996095, which is 994142. You will find that the nonclustered index is still used, so you keep on going left, to the point between the keys 992189 and 994142. You continue this process, going left or right according to your findings, until you reach the first selectivity point where the nonclustered index is used. You will find that this point is the key 993347, producing the plan shown in Figure 4-58.

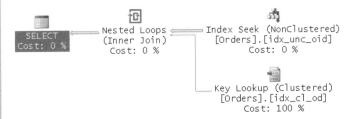

FIGURE 4-58 Estimated plan showing the index is used

You can now calculate the selectivity, which is the number of qualifying rows (6,654) divided by the number of rows in the table (1,000,000), which amounts to 0.6654 percent.

In our query pattern's case, with this selectivity or higher (lower percentage), the optimizer uses the nonclustered index, while with a lower selectivity, it opts for a table scan. As you can see, in our query pattern's case, the selectivity point is even lower than 1 percent. Some database professionals might find this number surprisingly small, but if you make performance estimations like the ones we did earlier, you will find it reasonable. Don't forget that page reads are the only factor that you should take into consideration. You should also consider the access pattern (random/sequential) and other factors as well. Remember that random I/O is much more expensive than sequential I/O. Lookups use random I/O, while a table scan can potentially use sequential I/O.

Before you proceed, drop the index used in the previous step:

```
DROP INDEX dbo.Orders.idx_unc_oid;
```

Clustered Index Seek + Ordered Partial Scan

You can get the next level of optimization by creating a clustered index on the *orderid* column. Because a clustered index is already on the Orders table, drop it first and then create the desired one:

```
DROP INDEX dbo.Orders.idx_cl_od;
CREATE UNIQUE CLUSTERED INDEX idx_cl_oid ON dbo.Orders(orderid);
```

You will get a trivial plan that uses a seek to the first key matching the filter, followed by an ordered partial scan of the sought range, as shown in Figure 4-59.

```
       SELECT          ⟵——————  Clustered Index Seek (Cl…
       Cost: 0 %                    [Orders].[idx_cl_oid]
                                        Cost: 100 %
```

FIGURE 4-59 Execution plan with clustered index seek + ordered partial scan

The main benefit of this plan is that no lookups are involved. As the selectivity of the query goes lower, this plan becomes more and more efficient compared to a plan that does apply lookups. The I/O cost involved with this plan is the cost of the seek (3 in our case), plus the number of pages that hold the data rows in the filtered range (25 in our case). For the most part, the main cost of such a plan is typically the cost of the ordered partial scan, unless the range is really tiny (for example, a point query). Remember that the performance of an index order scan depends to a great extent on the fragmentation level of the index. Here are the performance measures that I got for this query:

- Logical reads 28
- CPU time 0 ms
- Elapsed time 236 ms
- Estimated subtree cost 0.130601

Before proceeding to the next step, restore the original clustered index:

```
DROP INDEX dbo.Orders.idx_cl_oid;
CREATE  CLUSTERED INDEX idx_cl_od ON dbo.Orders(orderdate);
```

Covering Nonclustered Index Seek + Ordered Partial Scan

The optimal level in our scale is a nonclustered covering index defined with the *orderid* column as the key and all the other columns as included nonkey columns:

```
CREATE UNIQUE NONCLUSTERED INDEX idx_unc_oid_i_od_cid_eid_sid
  ON dbo.Orders(orderid)
  INCLUDE(orderdate, custid, empid, shipperid);
```

The plan's logic is similar to the previous one, except that here the ordered partial scan ends up reading fewer pages. That, of course, is because more rows fit in a leaf page of this index than data rows do in a clustered index page. You get the plan shown in Figure 4-60.

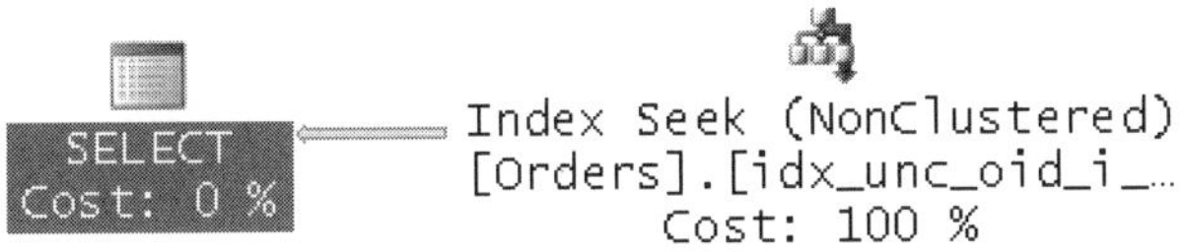

FIGURE 4-60 Execution plan with covering nonclustered index seek + ordered partial scan

And here are the performance measures I got for this query:

- Logical reads 9
- CPU time 0 ms
- Elapsed time 230 ms
- Estimated subtree cost 0.0080857

Again, this is a trivial plan. And the performance of the ordered partial scan varies depending on the fragmentation level of the index. As you can see, the cost of the query dropped from 19.621100 in the lowest level in the scale to 0.008086 and the elapsed time from more than 8 seconds to 230 milliseconds. Such a drop in run time is common when tuning indexes in an environment with poor index design.

When done, drop the last index you created:

```
DROP INDEX dbo.Orders.idx_unc_oid_i_od_cid_eid_sid;
```

Summary of Analysis of Indexing Strategy

Remember that the efficiency of several plans in our index optimization scale was based on the selectivity of the query. If the selectivity of a query you're tuning varies significantly between invocations of the query, make sure that in your tuning process you take this into account. For example, you can prepare tables and graphs with the performance measurements versus selectivity and analyze such data before you make your index design choices. Table 4-10 shows a summary of logical reads versus selectivity of the different levels in the scale for the sample query pattern under discussion against the sample Orders table.

TABLE 4-10 Logical Reads vs. Selectivity for Each Access Method

Access Method	1 0.0001%	1,000 0.1%	10,000 1%	100,000 10%	200,000 20%	500,000 50%	1,000,000 100%	Rows Selectivity
Table Scan/ Unordered Clustered Index Scan	25,391	25,391	25,391	25,383	25,355	25,271	25,081	
Unordered Covering Nonclustered Index Scan	5,158	5,158	5,158	5,158	5,158	5,150	5,096	
Unordered Nonclustered Index Scan + Lookups	2,857	5,963	33,990	312,009	618,250	1,536,956	3,065,577	
Nonclustered Index Seek + Ordered Partial Scan + Lookups	6	3,078	31,131	312,613	621,680	1,554,822	3,069,871	
Clustered Index Seek + Ordered Partial Scan	4	28	249	2,447	4,890	12,220	24,434	
Covering Nonclustered Index Seek + Ordered Partial Scan	4	9	54	512	1,021	2,546	5,089	

Note To apply a certain execution plan in a case where the optimizer would normally opt for another plan that is more efficient, I had to use a table hint to force using the relevant index.

Of course, logical reads shouldn't be the only indication you rely on. Remember that different I/O patterns have different performance and that physical reads are much more expensive than logical reads. But when you see a significant difference in logical reads between two options, it is usually a good indication of which option is faster. Figure 4-61 has a graphical depiction of the information from Table 4-10.

You can observe many interesting things when analyzing the graph. For example, you can clearly see which plans are based on selectivity and which aren't. You can also see the selectivity point at which one plan becomes better than another.

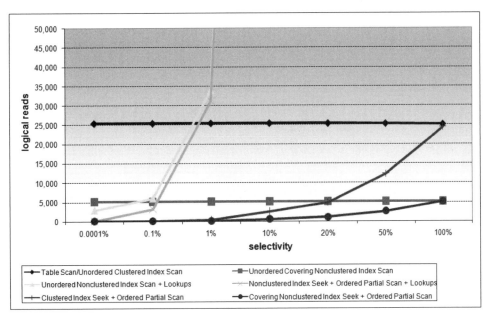

FIGURE 4-61 Graph of logical reads versus selectivity

Similarly, Table 4-11 shows summary performance statistics of the query cost versus selectivity.

Figure 4-62 shows a graph based on the data in Table 4-11.

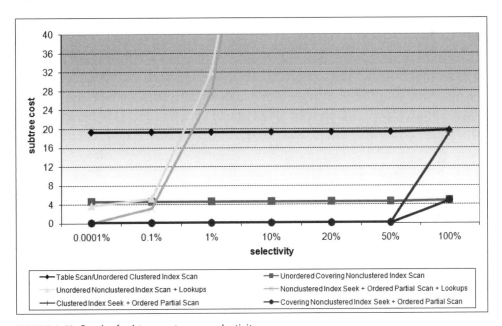

FIGURE 4-62 Graph of subtree cost versus selectivity

TABLE 4-11 Estimated Subtree Costs vs. Selectivity for Each Access Method

Access Method	Rows						
	1	1,000	10,000	100,000	200,000	500,000	1,000,000
	Selectivity						
	0.0001%	0.1%	1%	10%	20%	50%	100%
Table Scan/ Unordered Clustered Index Scan	19.3423	19.3423	19.3423	19.3423	19.3423	19.3423	19.6218
Unordered Covering Nonclustered Index Scan	4.58245	4.58245	4.58245	4.58245	4.58245	4.58245	4.86402
Unordered Nonclustered Index Scan + Lookups	3.69101	5.23753	32.0467	96.3647	113.061	160.825	244.096
Nonclustered Index Seek + Ordered Partial Scan + Lookups	0.0065704	3.22853	27.4126	97.121	119.371	182.763	289.656
Clustered Index Seek + Ordered Partial Scan	0.130601	0.130601	0.130601	0.130601	0.130601	0.130601	19.1699
Covering Nonclustered Index Seek + Ordered Partial Scan	0.0080857	0.0080857	0.0080857	0.0080857	0.0080857	0.0080857	4.86328

You can observe a striking resemblance between the two graphs. When you think about it, this makes sense because most of the cost involved with our query pattern is because of I/O. Naturally, in plans where a more substantial portion of the cost is related to CPU, you will get different results.

Of course, you also want to generate similar statistics and graphs for the actual run times of the queries in your benchmarks. At the end of the day, run time is what the user cares about.

I also find it valuable to visualize performance information in another graphical way, as shown in Figure 4-63.

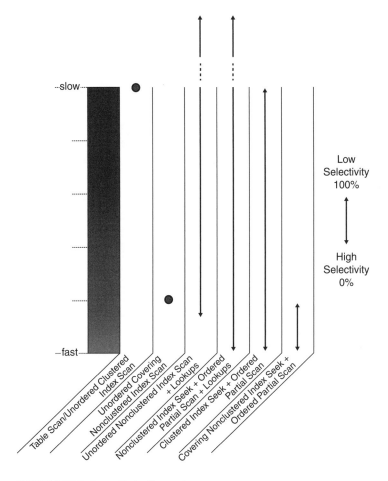

FIGURE 4-63 Index optimization scale

You might find it easier with this illustration to identify plans that are based on selectivity versus plans that aren't (represented as a dot) and also to make comparisons between the performance of the different levels of optimization in the scale.

> **Note** For simplicity's sake, all statistics and graphs shown in this section were collected against the Performance database I used in this chapter, where the level of fragmentation of indexes was minimal. When you conduct benchmarks and performance tests, make sure you introduce the appropriate levels of fragmentation in the indexes in your test system so that they reflect the fragmentation levels of the indexes in your production system adequately. The performance of index order scans might vary significantly based on the level of fragmentation of your indexes. Remember that the storage engine uses index order scans to carry out requests from the relational engine to process full ordered index scans, partial ordered index scans, and in some cases also unordered index scans. (See the section "The Storage Engine's Treatment of Scans" earlier in the chapter for details.) Similarly, you also need to examine the average page densities in your production system and introduce similar page densities in the test system.

Besides having the ability to design good indexes, it is also important to be able to identify which indexes are used more heavily and which are rarely or never used. You don't want to keep indexes that are rarely used because they do have negative performance effects on modifications.

SQL Server collects index usage information in the background and enables you to query this information through dynamic management objects. You get a DMF called *dm_db_index_operational_stats* and a DMV called *dm_db_index_usage_stats*. The *dm_db_index_operational_stats* DMF gives you low-level I/O, locking, latching, and access method activity information. You provide the function with database ID, object ID, index ID (or 0 for a heap), and partition ID. You can also request information about multiple entities by specifying a NULL in the relevant argument. For example, to get information about all objects, indexes, and partitions in the Performance database, you would invoke the function as follows:

```
SELECT *
FROM sys.dm_db_index_operational_stats(
  DB_ID('Performance'), null, null, null);
```

The *dm_db_index_usage_stats* DMV gives you usage counts of the different index operations:

```
SELECT *
FROM sys.dm_db_index_usage_stats;
```

These dynamic management objects make the analysis of index usage simple and accurate.

Fragmentation

I referred to index fragmentation on multiple occasions in this chapter. When I mentioned fragmentation, I referred to a type known as *logical scan fragmentation* or *average fragmentation in percent* or *external fragmentation*. As I mentioned earlier, this type reflects the percentage of out-of-order pages in the index in terms of their file order versus their logical order in the linked list. Remember that this fragmentation can have a substantial impact on ordered scan operations in indexes. It has no effect on operations that do not rely on the index's linked list—for example, seek operations, lookups, allocation order scans, and so on.

You want to minimize the fragmentation level of indexes for queries with a substantial portion of their cost involved with ordered scans. You do so by rebuilding or reorganizing indexes.

Another type of fragmentation that you typically care about is what I referred to as average page density. Some database professionals refer to this type of fragmentation as *internal fragmentation*, but to avoid confusion I consciously didn't use this term earlier. Although logical scan fragmentation is never a good thing, average page density has two facets. A low percentage (low level of page population) has a negative impact on queries that read data because they end up reading more pages than they could potentially if the pages were better populated. The positive impact of having some free space in index pages is that insertions of rows to such pages would not cause page splits, which are very expensive. As you can guess, free space in index pages is bad in systems that involve mostly reads (for example, data warehouses) and good for systems that involve many inserts (for example, OLTP systems). You might even want to introduce some free space in index pages by specifying a *fillfactor* value when you rebuild your indexes.

To determine whether you need to rebuild or reorganize your indexes, you need information about both types of fragmentation. You can get this information by querying the DMF *dm_db_index_physical_stats*. For example, the following query will return fragmentation information about the indexes in the Performance database:

```
SELECT *
FROM sys.dm_db_index_physical_stats(
  DB_ID('Performance'), NULL, NULL, NULL, 'SAMPLED');
```

The fragmentation types I mentioned show up in the attributes *avg_fragmentation_in_percent* and *avg_page_space_used_in_percent*, and as you can see, the attribute names are self-explanatory.

As I mentioned earlier, to treat both types of fragmentation you need to rebuild or reorganize the index. Rebuilding an index has the optimal defragmentation effect. The operation makes its best attempt to rebuild the index such that the file order of the pages is as close as possible to their order in the linked list and to make the pages as contiguous as possible. Also, remember that you can specify a fillfactor to introduce some free space in the index leaf pages. Note that if your computer has multiple CPUs and SQL Server uses parallel index rebuilds (Enterprise edition only), the operation will finish faster than with a single thread but is likely to result in more logical fragmentation. You can restrict the operation to a single CPU with the MAXDOP hint—this way, at the cost of a longer index rebuild, you will likely get less fragmentation. Also, SQL Server needs space for sorting in the filegroup where the index resides. If the filegroup files have only a little free space, some logical fragmentation in the index at the end of the operation is likely. To minimize fragmentation, ensure that you have sufficient free space in the files or use the option *SORT_IN_TEMPDB* to request that the index rebuild use space from the tempdb database for sorting.

By default, index rebuilds are offline operations. Rebuilding a clustered index acquires an exclusive lock for the whole duration of the operation, meaning that other processes can neither read nor write to the table. Rebuilding a nonclustered index acquires a shared lock, meaning that writes are blocked against the table, and obviously, the index cannot be used during the operation. SQL Server Enterprise supports *online index operations* by request (you need to specify *ON* in the option *ONLINE*) that allow you to create, rebuild, and drop indexes online. In addition, these operations allow users to interact with the data while the operation is in progress. Online index operations use row-versioning technology. When an index is rebuilt online, SQL Server actually maintains two indexes behind the scenes, and when the operation is done, the new one overrides the old one.

For example, the following code rebuilds the *idx_cl_od* index on the Orders table online:

```
ALTER INDEX idx_cl_od ON dbo.Orders REBUILD WITH (ONLINE = ON);
```

Note that online index operations need sufficient space in the database and overall are slower than offline operations. If you can spare a maintenance window for the activity to work offline, you had better do so. Even when you do perform the operations online, they have a performance impact on the system while they are running, so it's best to run them during off-peak hours.

Instead of rebuilding an index, you can also reorganize it. Reorganizing an index involves a bubble sort algorithm to sort the index pages in the file according to their order in the index's linked list. The operation does not attempt to make the pages more contiguous (reduce gaps). As you can guess, the defragmentation level that you get from this operation is not as optimal as fully rebuilding an index. Also, this operation performs more logging than an index rebuild overall and therefore is typically slower.

So why use this type of defragmentation? First, in non-Enterprise editions of SQL Server it is the only online defragmentation utility. The operation grabs short-term locks on a pair of pages at a time to determine whether they are in the correct order, and if they are not, it swaps them. Second, an index rebuild must run as a single transaction, and if it's aborted while in process, the whole activity is rolled back. This is unlike an index reorganize operation, which can be interrupted as it operates on a pair of pages at a time. When you later run the reorganize activity again, it will pick up where it left off earlier.

Here's how you reorganize the *idx_cl_od* index:

```
ALTER INDEX idx_cl_od ON dbo.Orders REORGANIZE;
```

Partitioning

SQL Server supports native partitioning of tables and indexes. Partitioning your objects means that they are internally split into multiple physical units that together make the object (table or index). Partitioning is virtually unavoidable in medium to large environments. By partitioning your objects, you improve the manageability and maintainability of your system, and you improve the performance of activities such as purging historic data, data loads, and others. Partitioning in SQL Server is native—that is, you have built-in tools to partition the tables and indexes, while, logically, to the applications and users they appear as whole units. You need to know some important details about querying and query tuning when your tables and indexes are partitioned. Chapter 11, "Querying Partitioned Tables," covers the subject in detail.

Preparing Sample Data

When conducting performance tests, it is vital that the sample data you use be well prepared so that it reflects the production system as closely as possible, especially with respect to the factors you are trying to tune. Typically, it's not realistic to just copy all the data from the production tables, at least not with the big ones. However, you should make your best effort to have an adequate representation that reflects similar data distribution, density of keys, cardinality, and so on. You also want your queries against the test system to have similar selectivity to the queries against the production system. Performance tests can be skewed when the sample data does not adequately represent the production data.

In this section, I'll provide an example of skewed performance testing results resulting from inadequate sample data. I'll also discuss the TABLESAMPLE option.

Data Preparation

When I prepared the sample data for this chapter's demonstrations, I didn't need to reflect a specific production system, so preparing sample data was fairly simple. I needed it mainly for the "Tuning Methodology" and "Index Tuning" sections. I could express most of my points through simple random distribution of the different attributes that were relevant to our discussions. But our main data table, Orders, does not accurately reflect an average production Orders table. For example, I produced a fairly even distribution of values in the different attributes, while typically in production systems, different attributes have different types of distribution (some uniform, some standard). Some customers place many orders, and others place few. Some customers are also more active during certain periods of time and less active during others. Depending on your tuning needs, you might or might not need to reflect such things in your sample data, but you definitely need to consider them and decide whether they do matter.

When you need large tables with sample data, the easiest thing to do is to generate some small table and duplicate its content (save the key columns) many times. This can be fine if, for example, you want to test the performance of a user-defined function invoked against every row or a cursor manipulation iterating through many rows. But such sample data in some cases can yield completely different performance than what you would get with sample data that more adequately reflects your production data. To demonstrate this, I'll walk you through an example that I cover in much more depth in *Inside T-SQL Programming*. I often give this exercise in class and ask students to prepare a large amount of sample data without giving any hints.

The exercise has to do with a table called Sessions, which you create and populate by running the following code:

```
SET NOCOUNT ON;
USE Performance;

IF OBJECT_ID('dbo.Sessions', 'U') IS NOT NULL DROP TABLE dbo.Sessions;

CREATE TABLE dbo.Sessions
(
  keycol    INT          NOT NULL IDENTITY,
  app       VARCHAR(10) NOT NULL,
  usr       VARCHAR(10) NOT NULL,
  host      VARCHAR(10) NOT NULL,
  starttime DATETIME     NOT NULL,
  endtime   DATETIME     NOT NULL,
  CONSTRAINT PK_Sessions PRIMARY KEY(keycol),
  CHECK(endtime > starttime)
);
GO

INSERT INTO dbo.Sessions VALUES
  ('app1', 'user1', 'host1', '20090212 08:30', '20090212 10:30'),
  ('app1', 'user2', 'host1', '20090212 08:30', '20090212 08:45'),
  ('app1', 'user3', 'host2', '20090212 09:00', '20090212 09:30'),
  ('app1', 'user4', 'host2', '20090212 09:15', '20090212 10:30'),
  ('app1', 'user5', 'host3', '20090212 09:15', '20090212 09:30'),
  ('app1', 'user6', 'host3', '20090212 10:30', '20090212 14:30'),
  ('app1', 'user7', 'host4', '20090212 10:45', '20090212 11:30'),
  ('app1', 'user8', 'host4', '20090212 11:00', '20090212 12:30'),
  ('app2', 'user8', 'host1', '20090212 08:30', '20090212 08:45'),
  ('app2', 'user7', 'host1', '20090212 09:00', '20090212 09:30'),
  ('app2', 'user6', 'host2', '20090212 11:45', '20090212 12:00'),
  ('app2', 'user5', 'host2', '20090212 12:30', '20090212 14:00'),
  ('app2', 'user4', 'host3', '20090212 12:45', '20090212 13:30'),
  ('app2', 'user3', 'host3', '20090212 13:00', '20090212 14:00'),
  ('app2', 'user2', 'host4', '20090212 14:00', '20090212 16:30'),
  ('app2', 'user1', 'host4', '20090212 15:30', '20090212 17:00');

CREATE INDEX idx_nc_app_st_et ON dbo.Sessions(app, starttime, endtime);
```

The Sessions table contains information about user sessions against different applications. The request is to calculate the maximum number of concurrent sessions per application—that is, the maximum number of sessions that were active at any point in time against each application.

The following query, followed by its output, produces the requested information:

```
SELECT app, MAX(concurrent) AS mx
FROM (SELECT app,
        (SELECT COUNT(*)
         FROM dbo.Sessions AS S
         WHERE T.app = S.app
           AND T.ts >= S.starttime
           AND T.ts < S.endtime) AS concurrent
      FROM (SELECT app, starttime AS ts FROM dbo.Sessions) AS T) AS C
GROUP BY app;
```

```
app          mx
----------   -----------
app1         4
app2         3
```

The derived table T contains the application name (*app*) and session start time (*starttime as ts*) pairs. For each row of T, a subquery counts the number of sessions that were active for the application *T.app* at time *T.ts*. The outer query then groups the data by *app* and returns the maximum count for each group. SQL Server's optimizer generates the execution plan shown in Figure 4-64 for this query.

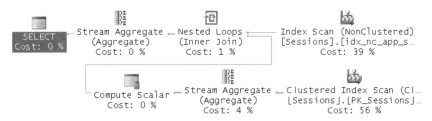

FIGURE 4-64 Execution plan for query against the Sessions table

The script that creates the Sessions table also creates the covering index *idx_nc_app_st_et* based on the key list (*app, starttime, endtime*), which is the optimal index for this query. In the plan, this index is fully scanned (Index Scan operator) to return all rows. As rows are streamed out from the Index Scan operator, a Nested Loops operator invokes a series of activities (Clustered Index Scan, followed by Stream Aggregate) to calculate the count of active sessions for each row. Because the Sessions table is so tiny (only one page of data), the optimizer simply decides to scan the whole table (unordered clustered index scan) to calculate each count. With a larger data set, instead of scanning the table, the plan would perform a seek and ordered partial scan of the covering index to obtain each count. Finally, another Stream Aggregate operator groups the data by *app* to calculate the maximum count for each group.

Now that you're familiar with the problem, suppose you were asked to prepare sample data with 1,000,000 rows in the source table (call it BigSessions) such that it would represent a realistic environment. Ideally, you should be thinking about realistic distribution of session start times, session duration, and so on. However, people often take the most obvious approach, which is to duplicate the data from the small source table many times; in our case, such an approach would drastically skew the performance compared to a more realistic representation of production environments.

Now run the following code to generate the BigSessions table by duplicating the data from the Sessions table many times. You will get 1,000,000 rows in the BigSessions table:

```
IF OBJECT_ID('dbo.BigSessions', 'U') IS NOT NULL DROP TABLE dbo.BigSessions;

SELECT ROW_NUMBER() OVER(ORDER BY (SELECT 0)) AS keycol,
  app, usr, host, starttime, endtime
INTO dbo.BigSessions
FROM dbo.Sessions AS S
  CROSS JOIN Nums
WHERE n <= 62500;
```

```
CREATE UNIQUE CLUSTERED INDEX idx_ucl_keycol
  ON dbo.BigSessions(keycol);
CREATE INDEX idx_nc_app_st_et
  ON dbo.BigSessions(app, starttime, endtime);
```

Run the following query against BigSessions:

```
SELECT app, MAX(concurrent) AS mx
FROM (SELECT app,
        (SELECT COUNT(*)
          FROM dbo.BigSessions AS S
          WHERE T.app = S.app
            AND T.ts >= S.starttime
            AND T.ts < S.endtime) AS concurrent
      FROM (SELECT app, starttime AS ts FROM dbo.BigSessions) AS T) AS C
GROUP BY app;
```

Note that this is the same query as before (but against a different table). The query will finish in a few seconds, and you will get the execution plan shown in Figure 4-65.

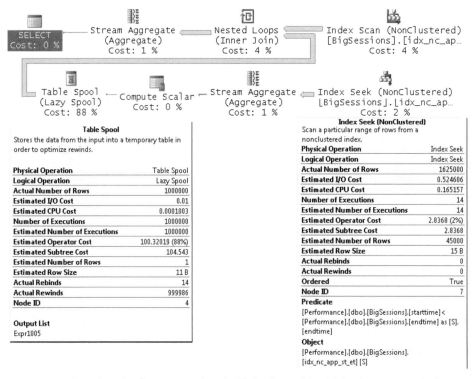

FIGURE 4-65 Execution plan for query against the BigSessions table with inadequate sample data

Here are the performance measures I got for this query:

- Logical reads 212102
- CPU time 3463 ms
- Elapsed time 4064 ms
- Estimated subtree cost 113.904

At first glance it might seem like the lower branch of the plan is executed once for each of the rows returned from the Index Scan operator. The Index Scan operator returns 1,000,000 rows. The lower branch of the plan seems to do quite significant work per outer row—scanning all rows with the same *app* value as in the outer row and *starttime* smaller than or equal to the one in the outer row. Given such a plan and such a large number of rows involved, it is quite inconceivable that the query would finish in a matter of only four seconds. The fact that there's a performance skew here because of bad sample data is elusive. The derived table T has only 14 distinct rows (with *app, ts* values). Observe in Figure 4-65 that the *Number of Executions* property of the Index Seek operator is 14. The optimizer is smart enough to realize that it can reuse the information obtained for one row for all other rows with the same *app* and *ts* values. Therefore, it invoked the Index Scan operator that scans the relevant range of rows and the Stream Aggregate operator that counts them only 14 times!

Observe the Table Spool operator as well, which represents a temporary table holding the session count for each distinct combination of *app* and *starttime* values. Notice the number of rebinds (14) and the number of rewinds (999,986). Remember that a rebind means that one or more correlated parameters of the join operator changed and that the inner side must be reevaluated. That happens 14 times, once for each distinct pair of *app* and *starttime*—meaning that the actual count activity preceding the operator took place only 14 times. A rewind means that none of the correlated parameters changed and that the prior inner result set can be reused; this happened 999,986 times (1,000,000 – 14 = 999,986).

That's why the query finished in only a few seconds. A production environment might have only a few applications, but so few distinct start times would be unlikely. Naturally, with more realistic data distribution for our scenario, the count activity will take place many more times than 14, and you will get a much slower query. It was a mistake to prepare the sample data by simply copying the rows from the small Sessions table many times. The distribution of values in the different columns should represent production environments more realistically.

Run the following code to populate BigSessions with more adequate sample data:

```
IF OBJECT_ID('dbo.BigSessions', 'U') IS NOT NULL DROP TABLE dbo.BigSessions;

SELECT
  ROW_NUMBER() OVER(ORDER BY (SELECT 0)) AS keycol,
  D.*,
  DATEADD(
    second,
```

```
     1 + ABS(CHECKSUM(NEWID())) % (20*60),
     starttime) AS endtime
INTO dbo.BigSessions
FROM
(
  SELECT
    'app' + CAST(1 + ABS(CHECKSUM(NEWID())) % 10 AS VARCHAR(10)) AS app,
    'user1' AS usr,
    'host1' AS host,
    DATEADD(
      second,
      1 + ABS(CHECKSUM(NEWID())) % (30*24*60*60),
      '20090101') AS starttime
  FROM dbo.Nums
  WHERE n <= 1000000
) AS D;

CREATE UNIQUE CLUSTERED INDEX idx_ucl_keycol
  ON dbo.BigSessions(keycol);
CREATE INDEX idx_nc_app_st_et
  ON dbo.BigSessions(app, starttime, endtime);
```

I populated the table with sessions that start at random times over a period of one month and last up to 20 minutes. I also distributed 10 different application names randomly. Now request an estimated execution plan for the original query, and you will get the plan shown in Figure 4-66.

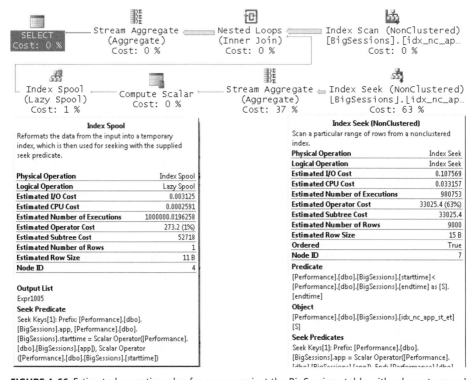

FIGURE 4-66 Estimated execution plan for query against the BigSessions table with adequate sample data

The cost of the query is now 52,727. Trust me: You don't want to run it to see how long it really takes. Or, if you like, you can start running it and come back the next day hoping that it finished.

Now that the sample data is more realistic, you can see that the set-based solution presented in this section is slow—unlike what you might be led to believe when using inadequate sample data. In short, you can see how vital it is to put some thought into preparing good sample data. Of course, the tuning process only starts now; you might want to consider query revisions, cursor-based solutions, revisiting the model, and so on. But here I wanted to focus the discussion on bad sample data. I'll conduct a more thorough tuning discussion related to the problem at hand in *Inside T-SQL Programming*.

TABLESAMPLE

SQL Server supports a feature that allows you to sample data from an existing table. The tool is a clause called TABLESAMPLE that you specify after the table name in the FROM clause along with some options. Here's an example for using TABLESAMPLE to request 1,000 rows from the Orders table in the Performance database:

```
SELECT *
FROM dbo.Orders TABLESAMPLE (1000 ROWS);
```

Note that if you run this query you probably won't get exactly 1,000 rows. I'll explain why shortly.

You can specify TABLESAMPLE on a table-by-table basis. Following the TABLESAMPLE keyword, you can optionally specify the sampling method to use. Currently, SQL Server supports only the *SYSTEM* method, which is also the default if no method is specified. In the future, we might see additional algorithms. Per ANSI, the SYSTEM keyword represents an implementation-dependent sampling method. This means you will find different algorithms implemented in different products when using the *SYSTEM* method. In SQL Server, the *SYSTEM* method implements the same sampling algorithm used to sample pages to generate distribution statistics.

You can use either the ROWS or the PERCENT keyword to specify how many rows you would like to get back. Based on your inputs, SQL Server calculates random values to figure out whether a page should be returned. Note that the decision of whether to read a portion of data is done at the page level. This fact, along with the fashion in which SQL Server determines whether to pick a page based on a random factor, means that you won't necessarily get the exact number of rows that you asked for; rather, you'll get a fairly close value. The more rows you request, the more likely you are to get a result set size close to what you requested.

Here's an example for using the TABLESAMPLE clause in a query against the Orders table, requesting 1,000 rows:

```
SELECT *
FROM dbo.Orders TABLESAMPLE SYSTEM (1000 ROWS);
```

I ran this query three times and got a different number of rows every time: 880, 1200, and 920.

An important benefit you get with the *SYSTEM* sampling method is that only the chosen pages (those that SQL Server picked) are scanned. So even if you query a huge table, you will get the results pretty fast—as long as you specify a fairly small number of rows. As I mentioned earlier, you can also specify a percentage of rows. Here's an example requesting 0.1 percent, which is equivalent to 1,000 rows in our table:

```
SELECT *
FROM dbo.Orders TABLESAMPLE (0.1 PERCENT);
```

When you use the ROWS option, SQL Server internally first converts the specified number of rows to a percentage. Remember that you are not guaranteed to get the exact number of rows that you requested; rather, you'll get a close value determined by the number of pages that were picked and the number of rows on those pages (which may vary).

To make it more likely that you'll get the exact number of rows you are after, specify a higher number of rows in the TABLESAMPLE clause and use the TOP option to limit the upper bound that you will get, like so:

```
SELECT TOP (1000) *
FROM dbo.Orders TABLESAMPLE (2000 ROWS);
```

There's still a chance that you will get fewer rows than the number you requested, but you're guaranteed not to get more. By specifying a higher value in the TABLESAMPLE clause, you increase the likelihood of getting the number of rows you are after.

If you need to get repeatable results, use a clause called REPEATABLE, which was designed for this purpose, providing it with the same seed in all invocations. For example, running the following query multiple times yields the same result, provided that the data in the table has not changed:

```
SELECT *
FROM dbo.Orders TABLESAMPLE (1000 ROWS) REPEATABLE(42);
```

Note that with small tables you might not get any rows at all. For example, run the following query multiple times, requesting a single row from the Production.ProductCostHistory table in the AdventureWorks2008 database:

```
SELECT *
FROM AdventureWorks2008.Production.ProductCostHistory TABLESAMPLE (1 ROWS);
```

You only occasionally get any rows back. I witnessed a very interesting discussion in a technical SQL Server forum. Someone presented such a query and wanted to know why he didn't get any rows back. Steve Kass, a friend and coauthor of mine and the ingenious technical editor of these books, provided the following illuminating answer and kindly allowed me to quote him here:

> *"As documented in Books Online ("Limiting Results Sets by Using TABLESAMPLE"), the sampling algorithm can only return full data pages. Each page is selected or skipped with probability [desired number of rows]/[rows in table].*
>
> *The Production.ProductCostHistory table fits on 3 data pages. Two of those pages contain 179 rows, and one contains 37 rows. When you sample for 10 rows (1/40 of the table), each of the 3 pages is returned with probability 1/40 and skipped with probability 39/40. The chance that no rows are returned is about (39/40)^3, or about 93%. When rows are returned, about 2/3 of the time you will see 179 rows, and about 1/3 of the time you will see 37 rows. Very rarely, you will see more rows, if two or more pages are returned, but this is very unlikely.*
>
> *As BOL suggests, SYSTEM sampling (which is the only choice) is not recommended for small tables. I would add that if the table fits on N data pages, you should not try to sample fewer than 1/N-th of the rows, or that you should never try to sample fewer rows than fit on at least 2 or 3 data pages.*
>
> *If you were to sample roughly two data pages worth of rows, say 263 rows, the chance of seeing no rows would be about 3.7%. The larger (more data pages) the table, the smaller the chance of seeing no rows when at least a couple of pages worth are requested. For example, if you request 300 rows from a 1,000,000-row table that fits on 10,000 data pages, only in 5% of trials would you see no rows, even though the request is for far less than 1% of the rows.*
>
> *By choosing the REPEATABLE option, you will get the same sample each time. For most seeds, this will be an empty sample in your case. With other seeds, it will contain 37, 179, 216, 358, or 395 rows, depending on which pages were selected, with the larger numbers of rows returned for very few choices of seed.*
>
> *That said, I agree that the consequences of returning only full data pages results in very confusing behavior!"*

With small tables, you might want to consider other sampling methods. You don't care too much about scanning the whole table because you consider these techniques against small tables anyway. For example, the following query will scan the whole table, but it guarantees that you get a single random row:

```
SELECT TOP(1) *
FROM AdventureWorks2008.Production.ProductCostHistory
ORDER BY CHECKSUM(NEWID());
```

Note that other database platforms, such as DB2, implement additional algorithms—for example, the Bernoulli sampling algorithm. You can implement it in SQL Server by using the following query, provided by Steve Kass:

```
SELECT *
FROM AdventureWorks2008.Production.ProductCostHistory
WHERE ABS((ProductID%ProductID)+CHECKSUM(NEWID()))/POWER(2.,31) < 0.01
```

The constant 0.01 is the desired probability (in this case, 1 percent) of choosing a row. The expression *ProductID%ProductID* was included to make the WHERE clause correlated and force its evaluation on each row of ProductCostHistory. Without it, the value of the WHERE condition would be calculated just once, and either the entire table would be returned or no rows would be returned. Note that this technique requires a full table scan and can take a while with large tables. You can test it against our Orders table and see for yourself.

An Examination of Set-Based vs. Iterative/Procedural Approaches and a Tuning Exercise

Thus far in the chapter, I focused mainly on index tuning for given queries. However, in large part, query tuning involves query revisions. That is, with different queries or different T-SQL code you can sometimes get substantially different plans, with widely varying costs and run times. In a perfect world, the ideal optimizer would always figure out exactly what you are trying to achieve, and for any form of query or T-SQL code that attempts to achieve the same thing, you would get the same plan—and only the best plan, of course. But alas, we're not there yet. You still have many performance improvements to gain merely from changing the way you write your code. This will be demonstrated thoroughly throughout these books. Here, I'll demonstrate a typical tuning process based on code revisions by following an example.

Note that set-based queries are typically superior to solutions based on iterative/procedural logic—such as ones using cursors, loops, and the like. Besides the fact that set-based solutions usually require much less code, they also usually involve less overhead than cursors. A lot of overhead is incurred with the record-by-record manipulation of cursors. You can make simple benchmarks to observe the performance differences. Run a query that simply selects all rows from a big table, discarding the results in the graphical tool so that the time it takes to display the output won't be taken into consideration. Also run cursor code that simply scans all table rows one at a time. Even if you use the fastest available cursor—FAST_ FORWARD (forward only, read only)—you will find that the set-based query runs dozens of times faster. You can express the cost of processing n rows in a table using a set-based query as n and then processing the same number of rows with a cursor that can be expressed as $n + n \times o$, where o represents the overhead associated with a single row manipulation with the cursor. Besides the overhead involved with a cursor, you'll also have an issue with the execution plans. When using a cursor, you apply a very rigid physical approach to accessing the data because your code focuses a lot on how to achieve the result. A set-based query, on the other hand, focuses logically on *what* you want to achieve rather than *how* to achieve it. Typically, set-based queries leave the optimizer with much more room for maneuvering and leeway to do what it is good at—optimization.

That's the rule of thumb. However, I'm typically very careful with adopting rules of thumb, especially with regard to query tuning—because optimization is such a dynamic world, and there are always exceptions. In fact, as far as query tuning is concerned, my main rule of thumb is to be careful about adopting rules of thumb.

You will encounter cases where it is very hard to beat cursor code, and you need to be able to identify them; but these cases are the minority. I'll discuss the subject at length in Chapter 8, "Cursors," of *Inside T-SQL Programming*.

To demonstrate a tuning process based on code revisions, I'll use our Orders and Shippers tables. The request is to return shippers that used to be active but do not have any activity as of 2004. That is, a qualifying shipper is one for whom you cannot find an order on or after 2004. You don't care about shippers who have made no orders at all.

Before you start working, remove all indexes from the Orders table and make sure that you have only the clustered index defined on the *orderdate* column and the primary key (nonclustered) defined on the *orderid* column.

If you rerun the code in Listing 4-1, make sure that for the Orders table, you keep only the following index and primary key definitions:

```
CREATE CLUSTERED INDEX idx_cl_od ON dbo.Orders(orderdate);
ALTER TABLE dbo.Orders ADD
  CONSTRAINT PK_Orders PRIMARY KEY NONCLUSTERED(orderid);
```

Next, run the following code to add a few shippers to the Shippers table and a few orders to the Orders table:

```
INSERT INTO dbo.Shippers(shipperid, shippername) VALUES
  ('B', 'Shipper_B'),
  ('D', 'Shipper_D'),
  ('F', 'Shipper_F'),
  ('H', 'Shipper_H'),
  ('X', 'Shipper_X'),
  ('Y', 'Shipper_Y'),
  ('Z', 'Shipper_Z');

INSERT INTO dbo.Orders(orderid, custid, empid, shipperid, orderdate) VALUES
  (1000001, 'C0000000001', 1, 'B', '20030101'),
  (1000002, 'C0000000001', 1, 'D', '20030101'),
  (1000003, 'C0000000001', 1, 'F', '20030101'),
  (1000004, 'C0000000001', 1, 'H', '20030101');
```

You're supposed to get the shipper IDs B, D, F, and H in the result. These are the only shippers that were active at some point but not as of 2004.

In terms of index tuning, it's sometimes hard to figure out what the optimal indexes are without having an existing query to tune. But in our case, index tuning is rather simple and possible without having the solution code first. Obviously, you will want to search for the maximum *orderdate* value for each *shipperid*, so naturally the optimal index would be a nonclustered covering index defined with *shipperid* and *order*date as the key columns, in that order:

```
CREATE NONCLUSTERED INDEX idx_nc_sid_od
  ON dbo.Orders(shipperid, orderdate);
```

I suggest that at this point you try to come up with the best-performing solution that you can and then compare it with the solutions that I will demonstrate.

As the first solution, I'll start with the following cursor-based code:

```
DECLARE
  @sid     AS VARCHAR(5),
  @od      AS DATETIME,
  @prevsid AS VARCHAR(5),
  @prevod  AS DATETIME;

DECLARE ShipOrdersCursor CURSOR FAST_FORWARD FOR
  SELECT shipperid, orderdate
  FROM dbo.Orders
  ORDER BY shipperid, orderdate;

OPEN ShipOrdersCursor;

FETCH NEXT FROM ShipOrdersCursor INTO @sid, @od;

SELECT @prevsid = @sid, @prevod = @od;

WHILE @@fetch_status = 0
BEGIN
  IF @prevsid <> @sid AND @prevod < '20040101' PRINT @prevsid;
  SELECT @prevsid = @sid, @prevod = @od;
  FETCH NEXT FROM ShipOrdersCursor INTO @sid, @od;
END

IF @prevod < '20040101' PRINT @prevsid;

CLOSE ShipOrdersCursor;

DEALLOCATE ShipOrdersCursor;
```

This code implements a straightforward data-aggregation algorithm based on sorting. The cursor is defined on a query that sorts the data by *shipperid* and *orderdate*, and it scans the records in a forward-only, read-only manner—the fastest scan you can get with a cursor. For each shipper, the code inspects the last row found—which happens to hold the maximum *orderdate* for that shipper—and if that date is earlier than '20040101', the code emits the *shipperid* value. This code ran on my computer for 28 seconds. Imagine the run time in a larger Orders table that contains millions of rows.

The next solution (call it *set-based solution 1*) is a natural GROUP BY query that many programmers would come up with:

```
SELECT shipperid
FROM dbo.Orders
GROUP BY shipperid
HAVING MAX(orderdate) < '20040101';
```

You just say what you want rather than spending most of your code describing how to get it. The query groups the data by *shipperid*, and it returns only shippers with a maximum *orderdate* that is earlier than '20040101'.

This query ran for about one second on my computer. The optimizer produced the execution plan shown in Figure 4-67 for this query.

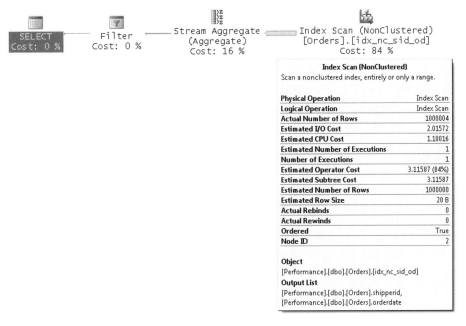

FIGURE 4-67 Execution plan for set-based solution 1

The plan shows that our covering index was fully scanned in order. The maximum *orderdate* was isolated for each *shipperid* by the Stream Aggregate operator. Then the filter operator filtered only shippers for whom the maximum *orderdate* was before '20040101'.

Here are the vital performance measures I got for this query:

- Logical reads 2736

- CPU time 562 ms

- Elapsed time 1224 ms

Note that you might get slightly different performance measures. At this point, you need to ask yourself if you're happy with the result and, if you're not, whether you have potential for optimization at all.

Of course, this solution is a big improvement over the cursor-based one in terms of both performance and code readability and maintenance. However, a run time of close to one second for such a query might not be satisfactory. Keep in mind that an Orders table in some production environments can contain far more than one million rows.

If you determine that you want to tune the solution further, you now need to figure out whether you have potential for optimization. Remember that in the execution plan for the last query, the leaf level of the index was fully scanned to obtain the latest *orderdate* for each shipper. That scan required 2,736 page reads. Our Shippers table contains 12 shippers. Your gut feeling should tell you that you must be able to find a way to obtain the data with far fewer reads. In our index, the rows are sorted by *shipperid* and *orderdate*. This means that in some groups of rows—a group for each *shipperid*—the last row in each group contains the latest *orderdate* that you want to inspect. Alas, the optimizer currently doesn't have the logic within it to "zigzag" between the levels of the index, jumping from one shipper's latest *orderdate* to the next. If it did, the query would have incurred substantially less I/O. By the way, such zigzagging logic can be beneficial for other types of requests—for example, requests involving filters on a nonfirst index column and others as well. But I won't digress.

Of course, if you request the latest *orderdate* for a particular shipper, the optimizer can use a seek directly to the last shipper's row in the index. Such a seek would cost three reads in our case. Then the optimizer can apply a TOP operator going one step backward, returning the desired value—the latest *orderdate* for the given shipper—to a Stream Aggregate operator.

The following query demonstrates acquiring the latest *orderdate* for a particular shipper, producing the execution plan shown in Figure 4-68:

```
SELECT MAX(orderdate) FROM dbo.Orders WHERE shipperid = 'A';
```

FIGURE 4-68 Execution plan for a query handling a particular shipper

This plan incurs only three logical reads. Now, if you do the math for 12 shippers, you will realize that you can potentially obtain the desired result with substantially less I/O than 2,736 reads. Of course, you could scan the Shippers rows with a cursor and then invoke such a query for each shipper, but it would be counterproductive and a bit ironic to beat a cursor solution with a set-based solution that you then beat with another cursor.

Realizing that what you're after is invoking a seek operation for each shipper, you might come up with the following attempt as a step toward the solution (prior to filtering):

```
SELECT shipperid,
  (SELECT MAX(orderdate)
   FROM dbo.Orders AS O
   WHERE O.shipperid = S.shipperid) AS maxod
FROM dbo.Shippers AS S;
```

You query the Shippers table, and for each shipper, a subquery acquires the latest *orderdate* value (aliased as *maxod*).

But strangely enough, you get the plan shown in Figure 4-69, which looks surprisingly similar to the previous one in the sense that a full ordered scan of the index on the Orders table is used to calculate the MAX aggregate.

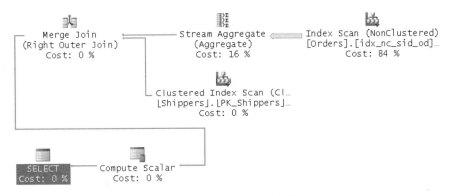

FIGURE 4-69 Execution plan for query with subquery and MAX

You may have expected the optimizer to first scan the 12 shippers from the Shippers table and then use a loop that for each shipper applies a seek operation in the index to pull the max *orderdate* for that shipper. Of course, without access to the optimizer's code it would be hard to tell why you didn't get the plan you expected. Fortunately, I got an explanation from Cesar Galindo-Legaria, who does have such access. It appears that this query fell victim to an attempt the optimizer made to improve the query performance, while in practice it ended up hurting it. The optimizer unnested the correlated subquery, converting it internally to a join. The reason that the optimizer applies such rearrangements is that the join form tends to be optimized better (enables better cardinality estimates and navigational strategies from both sides). However, the join form prevents the special scalar aggregate optimization over an index that we want to see here. The reason that the optimizer doesn't reintroduce the correlation (that would allow the scalar aggregate optimization) is that the exploration space explodes easily. As a result the current plan is far from ideal. This query incurred 2,736 logical reads against the Orders table and ran for close to one second on my computer. It seems that the optimizer got too sophisticated this time.

The situation seems to be evolving into a battle of wits with the optimizer—not a battle to the death, of course; there won't be any iocane powder involved here, just I/O. The optimizer pulls a trick on you; now pull your best trick. One attempt before considering a complete rewrite of the solution is to use a logically equivalent query but with the TOP option instead of MAX. The reasoning behind trying this trick is that from observations of many plans, it appears that the optimizer does not unnest subqueries when you use TOP.

You issue the following query, close your eyes, and hope for the best:

```
SELECT shipperid,
  (SELECT TOP (1) orderdate
   FROM dbo.Orders AS O
   WHERE O.shipperid = S.shipperid
   ORDER BY orderdate DESC) AS maxod
FROM dbo.Shippers AS S;
```

And when you open your eyes, voilà! You see the plan you wished for, as shown in Figure 4-70.

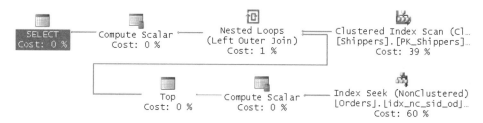

FIGURE 4-70 Execution plan for query with subquery and TOP

The Shippers table is scanned, and for each of the 12 shippers, a Nested Loops operator invokes a similar activity to the one you got when invoking a query for a particular shipper. This plan incurs only 2 logical reads against Shippers and 36 logical reads against Orders. The net CPU time is not even measurable with STATISTICS TIME (shows up as 0), and I got about 100 milliseconds of elapsed time. You can now slightly revise the code to have the subquery in the WHERE clause and filter only the shippers with a maximum order date that is before 2004, like so (call it *set-based solution 2*):

```
SELECT shipperid
FROM dbo.Shippers AS S
WHERE
  (SELECT TOP (1) orderdate
   FROM dbo.Orders AS O
   WHERE O.shipperid = S.shipperid
   ORDER BY orderdate DESC) < '20040101';
```

The plan is very similar to the one you got prior to filtering, but with an additional filter operator, as you can see in Figure 4-71.

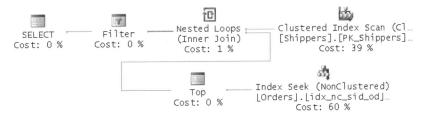

FIGURE 4-71 Execution plan for set-based solution 2

Once you get over the excitement of outwitting the optimizer, you start having some troubling thoughts. Why is it that the optimizer doesn't unnest subqueries when using TOP? In some cases it makes sense not to unnest—when there's the possibility that the nested and unnested forms would yield different results. But there are cases, like in our query, where both forms would yield the same results. The SQL Server developers know that many programmers and DBAs use the TOP option as a way to force the optimizer not to unnest subqueries and therefore are reluctant to change this optimizer's behavior. But it's hard to say how long the developers would keep restraining the optimizer in this manner. What if in a future version of SQL Server or perhaps a future service pack the developers won't restrain the optimizer anymore? Then SQL Server could internally translate our TOP query to the logically equivalent MAX or MIN version, and then you would get the inefficient plan for the aforementioned reasons.

And if this is not confusing enough, see what happens if you make slight revisions (logically meaningless ones, mind you) to the MAX version of the solution:

```
SELECT shipperid
FROM dbo.Shippers AS S
WHERE
  (SELECT DISTINCT MAX(orderdate)
   FROM dbo.Orders AS O
   WHERE O.shipperid = S.shipperid) < '20040101';

SELECT shipperid
FROM dbo.Shippers AS S
WHERE
  (SELECT TOP (1) MAX(orderdate)
   FROM dbo.Orders AS O
   WHERE O.shipperid = S.shipperid) < '20040101';
```

In both cases you get the more efficient plan that first scans the 12 shippers and in a loop pulls the maximum order date with a seek against the index on the Orders table.

In short, I'd be reluctant to rely on any of the preceding variations just because of the big impact that the slight revisions have on the way the query is optimized. In this sense I'd consider the optimization of this general form of the solution unstable. I'd keep looking for alternatives that are more stable.

If you look hard enough, you will find this one (call it *set-based solution 3*):

```
SELECT shipperid
FROM dbo.Shippers AS S
WHERE NOT EXISTS
  (SELECT * FROM dbo.Orders AS O
   WHERE O.shipperid = S.shipperid
     AND O.orderdate >= '20040101')
  AND EXISTS
  (SELECT * FROM dbo.Orders AS O
   WHERE O.shipperid = S.shipperid);
```

This solution is natural and in fact is quite a literal translation of the English phrasing of the request. You query the Shippers table and filter shippers for whom you cannot find an order on or past '20040101' and for whom you can find at least one order. You get the plan shown in Figure 4-72.

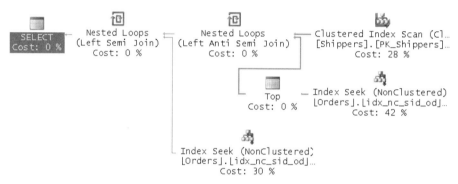

FIGURE 4-72 Execution plan for set-based solution 3

The Shippers table is scanned, yielding 12 rows. For each shipper, a Nested Loops operator invokes a seek against our covering index to check whether an *orderdate* of '20040101' or later exists for the shipper. If the answer is no, another seek operation is invoked against the index to check whether an order exists at all. The I/O cost against the Orders table is 59 reads—slightly higher than the previous solution. However, in terms of simplicity and naturalness, this solution wins big time! Therefore, I would stick to it.

As you probably realize, index tuning alone is not enough; you can do much with the way you write your queries. Being a *Matrix* fan, I'd like to believe that it's not the spoon that bends; it's only your mind.

Conclusion

This chapter covered a tuning methodology, index tuning, the importance of sample data, and query tuning by query revisions. So much is involved in tuning, and knowledge of the product's architecture and internals plays a big role in doing it well. But knowledge is not enough. I hope this chapter gave you the tools and guidance that will allow you to put your knowledge into action as you progress in these books—and, of course, in your production environments.

Chapter 5
Algorithms and Complexity

Steve Kass

This chapter contains a brief introduction to a central topic in computer science: algorithms and complexity. In theory, modern computers can solve nearly any problem that can be expressed precisely. In practice, however, we encounter two considerable obstacles: No computer can solve problems without valid strategies or methods for solving them, and valid problem-solving strategies and methods are useful only if they yield answers within a reasonable amount of time.

Strategies and methods for solving particular problems, given arbitrary input, are called *algorithms*. The computational *complexity* of a problem-solving algorithm measures the way in which the resources needed to execute the algorithm depend on the input for which the problem is to be solved.

Some algorithms require—for correctness, efficiency, or both—data to be organized in a particular way. A *data structure* is a scheme for organizing data to support efficient algorithms, and most algorithms assume—either implicitly or explicitly—particular data structures.

In some respects, database programmers need to know considerably less about algorithms and complexity than other programmers, such as systems programmers. Recall that SQL is a fourth-generation, declarative programming language. An SQL program describes the desired result, and the RDBMS implementation analyzes the description and then chooses and implements an efficient algorithm to produce the result. The mere fact that correct implementations of SQL exist is remarkable; the fact, that there exist astoundingly good implementations, like Microsoft's, is nothing short of miraculous. The modern RDBMS is not only a testament to its creators; it's also a testament to the foundations of computer science, which provided the mathematical framework for conceiving, developing, and validating such a complex system.

Many excellent books on algorithms and complexity are available, and they typically include a catalog of important algorithms and analyses of their complexity. In this chapter, I will instead describe some real-world problems that serve as good analogies to get you thinking about some of algorithms Microsoft SQL Server implements. These problems, which for small input are hand solvable, demonstrate some fundamental patterns of complexity, and they illustrate in a concrete way several factors that affect the running time and space requirements of important algorithms.

Do You Have a Quarter?

Many of you probably have a change jar somewhere—a container full of coins. From time to time, you might dig into your change jar to find a quarter,[1] and the process of doing so is probably second nature. Partly because it's so familiar, the process of retrieving a quarter from a change jar will be a useful example for the discussion of algorithms and complexity. While a coin isn't exactly data, retrieving a quarter is much like executing this T-SQL SELECT query:

```
SELECT TOP (1) Coin
FROM ChangeJar
WHERE Denomination = 0.25
ORDER BY (SELECT NULL);
```

How to Retrieve a Quarter from a Coin Jar

I'm sure you know more than one algorithm for executing this task—to retrieve a quarter from a coin jar. Most of the time, you look into the jar, spot a quarter at the top, and pull it out. Every now and then, however, there's no quarter at the top, and you have to dig deeper. When this happens, you might shake the jar or stick your hand into it and mix the coins up, expecting to find a quarter at the top again after the mixing. If you still can't find a quarter, you might empty the coins onto your kitchen counter and spread them out so that you can hunt through your coins more quickly than you can when they're all in the jar. This last strategy, of course, requires you have a kitchen counter (or other flat surface) nearby that you can clear off before emptying the coins onto it. If you try to do this right before suppertime, you might have to wait a little while or abandon the strategy.

You can see from this example that how—and how quickly—you can find a quarter in a coin jar depends on many things: what's in the jar, how the jar's contents are distributed, how you go about looking, and what other tools (like a table) are at your disposal, just to name a few. More obscure factors, too, can affect both your strategy and its efficiency: how bright the room lights are, how big your hands are compared to the size of the jar's mouth, how full the jar is (because shaking a full jar doesn't do a good job of mixing up its contents), and whether someone else is also retrieving a quarter from of the same jar (or preparing dinner) at the same time as you. How many other factors can you think of?

The various strategies for retrieving a quarter, as well as the factors that affect how well each strategy works, all have analogs both in the abstract study of algorithms and complexity and in the practical matter of executing queries in a SQL Server database. For example, the kitchen counter corresponds to both the abstract notion of space and the real SQL Server data cache. Shaking the coin jar corresponds to randomizing the distribution of values in the algorithm's input or changing the SQL Server statistics for an index or table.

---

[1] A quarter is the largest commonly circulating US coin, and it is worth 25 cents, or one-quarter dollar. If digging for quarters isn't something you do often enough to have a "feel" for it, use an analogous scenario, with any common coin instead of quarters.

Sometimes the Jar Has No Quarters

Just because you need a quarter doesn't mean you have a quarter, and it's certainly possible your jar is full of pennies, nickels, and dimes—and perhaps a few buttons and some pocket lint—but no quarters. If you run into this situation too often, you might consider rethinking your coin storage strategy and devise a system that will let you know right away that you've run out of quarters. For example, you might replace your change jar with two jars: one for quarters and one for everything else. You won't be able to empty your pockets as quickly because you'll have to separate the quarters from the rest of the change, but when you go looking for change, you'll know right away whether you have any quarters.

> **Note**   If you're like me, the two-jar solution won't really work. After a long day, I'd throw all my change, quarters included, into the nonquarters jar. Integrity constraints like CHECK (denomination <> 0.25) are one reason an RDBMS is better than a room full of jars!

I've described two coin storage setups: a one-jar setup, which optimizes the task of storing coins, and a two-jar setup, which optimizes the task of retrieving single quarters (whether this task is successful or not). The abstract analog in this case is the idea of a *data structure*, and the practical analog is the design of a database—choosing how to represent real-world information using database tables and how to arrange the information in tables with *indexes*. To analyze and design computer programs that are effective and efficient, it's important (and rewarding) to understand the complex and beautiful interplay between data structures, algorithms, and complexity. If you enjoy it, I can guarantee it will never bore you.

Pay close attention to day-to-day problem-solving tasks like digging for change. If you do, you'll develop insight into the algorithms and complexity of more abstract problem-solving tasks like those that come up in database management.

How Algorithms Scale

The jargon of database management uses the word *scale* in phrases such as *scale out*, *scale up*, and *scalable solution*. To talk about how a system or algorithm *scales* is to talk about how the system or algorithm is affected by changes (usually increases) in the amount of input data.

A naïve expectation about scaling is to expect this behavior: if there's twice as much data, it will take twice as long to process the data. While some systems and algorithms behave that way, many don't. Some tasks take the same amount of time regardless of the amount of data. For these tasks, if there's twice as much data, it will take no longer to process the data. An example is the task of retrieving a quarter from a jar of quarters. No matter how full the jar is, it takes one simple step to retrieve a quarter from the jar (or, if the jar is empty, to fail at the task). For other tasks, it might take four times as long to process twice as much data. For some kinds of tasks, twice as much data might take so much longer to process that you'd never live to see the result!

An Example of Quadratic Scaling

One of my first encounters with a real-world scaling problem and with naïve expectations about scaling took place in 1969 in my eighth-grade metalworking class. One of the projects was to build a 5-by-7-inch folder out of sheet metal, hinged at the top. I wanted to build a folder twice as big (10-by-14 inch) so that I could use it for standard notebook paper. Shop class students had to pay for the materials they used, and for this project, that meant three pieces of metal (two pieces of sheet metal for the front and back of the folder and one length of hinged metal for the shorter side) and a few rivets or screws. The teacher agreed to let me build a double-sized folder, as long as I paid double for the materials. Of course my folder needed more than twice as much metal.

Let's do the actual calculation, assuming the flat metal cost $0.01/square inch and the hinge cost $0.10/inch, ignoring the cost of the rivets and screws. The details for several different sizes of notebook, including the two sizes mentioned here, are shown in Table 5-1.

TABLE 5-1 Cost of Materials for Metal Folders

Folder size	5" by 7"	10" by 14"	50" by 70"	100" by 140"
Sheet metal required	70 sq. in.	280 sq. in.	7,000 sq. in	28,000 sq. in.
Cost of sheet metal	$0.70	$2.80	$70.00	$280.00
Length of hinge required	5 inches	10 inches	50 inches	100 inches
Cost of hinge	$0.50	$1.00	$5.00	$10.00
Total cost of materials	$1.20	$3.80	$75.00	$290.00

The cost of materials for my double-sized 10-by-14-inch folder was about 3.17 times the cost of materials for the 5-by-7-inch folder. Note that doubling the dimensions doesn't always increase the cost of materials by a factor of 3.17. The materials for a 100-by-140-inch folder cost about 3.87 times as much as for a 50-by-70-inch folder.

The relationship between notebook size and materials cost in this example is called quadratic. We'll see why a bit later in the chapter.

An Algorithm with Linear Complexity

Recall that the way in which an algorithm's cost depends on its input size is called the algorithm's *complexity*. When an algorithm's complexity agrees with the naïve expectation (twice the input requires twice the cost), the algorithm is said to have *linear* complexity because the graph of cost as a function of input size in this case is (or more precisely, approaches) a straight line.

One algorithm with linear complexity is the algorithm for finding the largest number in an unordered list as follows: allocate a variable to keep track of one number, initialize that variable to the value of the first item in the list, and then inspect the remaining items in the list one by one, overwriting the value of the variable each time a larger value is found in the list. Of course, if the numbers in the list are in order, you can find the largest number in the list much more quickly: just look at the end of the list, where the largest number must be. The trade-off is that you must maintain the ordering of the list.

Exponential and Superexponential Complexity

As the input size grows, some algorithms become more expensive at a truly astonishing rate. Unfortunately, for many important problems the only known algorithms exhibit *exponential* or *superexponential* complexity, and these problems are effectively unsolvable for all but the very smallest inputs.

One problem with superexponential complexity is the minimum bin packing problem, where the goal is to pack a collection of items into the fewest possible number of bins of fixed capacity.

The Minimum Bin Packing Problem

Given a collection of n items with weights $w_1, w_2, \ldots, w_n$ and an unlimited supply of empty bins, each with capacity C, where C is no smaller than the weight of the heaviest item, what is the smallest number of bins into which the items can be distributed without exceeding the bin capacity?

All known algorithms for solving the bin packing problem effectively consider every possible arrangement of the items, and this requires a number of computational steps that grows exponentially with the number of items n.

Fortunately, there are efficient ways to solve the bin packing problem approximately that will require no more than 1¼ times the optimal number of bins.

The Factorial Function

As I pointed out in the sidebar, all known algorithms for solving the bin packing problem effectively consider every possible arrangement of the n input items. How many arrangements is that? For a small number of items, it's easy to list all the arrangements and count them. Three items, A, B, and C, can be arranged in six ways: ABC, ACB, BAC, BCA, CAB, and CBA. Four items can be arranged in 24 ways—there are six ways to arrange the items A, B, and C, and for each one, there are four different places to "drop in" item D. For example, you can drop item D into the arrangement BAC in these four ways: ^{D}BAC, B^{D}AC, BA^{D}C, and BAC^D. Increasing the number of items from three to four therefore quadrupled (multiplied by four) the number of arrangements—from 6 to 24. In the same way, increasing the number of items from four to five will quintuple the number of arrangements—from 24 to 120.

There's a simple mathematical pattern to these numbers 6, 24, and 120: $6 = 3 \times 2 \times 1$, $24 = 4 \times 3 \times 2 \times 1$, and $120 = 5 \times 4 \times 3 \times 2 \times 1$. The pattern continues, and the number of arrangements of n items is the product of the integers 1 through n. The notation $n!$, called the *factorial function* of n or n *factorial*, represents the product of the integers from 1 through n.

Because there are $n!$ arrangements to consider, it takes at least $n!$ computational steps to solve the minimum bin packing problem for n input items. Later in this chapter, you'll see why the growth rate of $n!$ as a function of n is called superexponential, and you'll also see why problems like this one are considered unsolvable.

Sublinear Complexity

By necessity, if you want to determine something about data, you have to inspect the data. For example, to determine the lowest salary among an organization's employees, you need to inspect each employee's salary. This suggests that there are never algorithms that can handle n items in less than n operations or that n is the most efficient complexity possible. An algorithm that handles input size n with complexity better than n is called a sublinear algorithm. Are there any algorithms with sublinear complexity?

Yes, there are. We saw one such algorithm earlier. The quarter-retrieval problem can be solved in a single operation, regardless of the number of coins, if the coins are organized in two jars—one for quarters and one for other coins. At first, you might consider this strategy for achieving sublinear performance to be a bit of a cheat. After all, it takes at least n steps to organize n coins, so even if the retrieval of a quarter can be accomplished in one step, the entire workload of organizing n coins, then retrieving a quarter, takes at least n steps. However, you need to organize the coins only once. Once you've organized the coins into two jars, you can retrieve quarters repeatedly using the fast algorithm (take a coin from the quarters jar).

If you can solve a problem in sublinear time, it must be the case that you don't need to inspect all the data to solve the problem. Later in this chapter, we'll see examples of problems that can be answered without looking at all the data. In some cases, it's obvious this is possible; in other cases, it's not, and the algorithms are surprisingly clever.

Binary Search

When data is well maintained, many tasks are easier to solve. For example, the binding of this book maintains the book's pages in order. Page 50 comes right before page 51 and so on. If I asked you to turn to page 273, you could do so relatively quickly—not immediately in a single step but quickly—and probably in a dozen or fewer steps. If the book were twice as long, it's unlikely it would take more than one extra step to find a given page. Chances are you would use a variation on *binary search*. The binary search algorithm allows you to find a target value in an ordered list of n items in $\log_2 n$ time as follows. Go to the middle item of the list. If the target item equals this item, you're done. If not, compare the target item with the middle item to decide which half of the list you need to search. Next, inspect the middle item of the half you're searching and repeat the strategy. Each inspection narrows your search to half as many items as the previous step, so the number of items you have to inspect equals the number of times you can divide n by 2 and get a result greater than 1. You can do this $\log_2 n$ times (give or take one).

Constant Complexity

An algorithm is said to have constant complexity if it can be executed in a number of steps that's independent of the input size. The algorithm to find a quarter in a jar of quarters is an example of an algorithm with constant complexity. The algorithm that answers the question "Are there any customers?" by scanning a Customers table also has constant complexity.

Technical Definitions of Complexity

Most algorithms require some fixed overhead costs regardless of input. For example, an algorithm to count the number of rows in a table might require overhead to allocate space for and initialize an integer variable to be incremented for each row. When the input is large, fixed overhead is likely to be insignificant relative to the total execution cost. Comparing execution costs for large inputs provides more insight into the essence of an algorithm's computational complexity. In the metal notebook example, doubling the size of a large notebook increased the cost of materials by a factor of about 3.87, and you can check that doubling the size of an extremely large notebook increases the cost of materials by a factor of almost exactly 4.0. The relationship between hinge length (in inches) and materials cost (in dollars) for notebooks having the same proportions as a 5-by-7-inch notebook can be expressed mathematically as *MaterialsCost(h)* = $0.1h + 0.028h^2$. This cost function is a quadratic polynomial.

Complexity is often expressed by the relationship between input size and cost for inputs large enough that fixed overhead costs don't matter. Technically, this is the *asymptotic complexity*. For large values of *h* in the preceding example, the quadratic term $0.028h^2$ dominates the cost, and doubling the input size approximately quadruples the cost. The single expression h^2 characterizes this doubling-quadrupling behavior, and the cost in this case is said to have asymptotic order h^2.

Big Oh and related notations

Complexity is often expressed using *Big Oh notation*. In Big Oh notation—which uses not only the big oh symbol *O* but also big theta (Θ), little oh (*o*), big omega (Ω), and others—the asymptotic cost in the previous example can be expressed this way: *MaterialsCost(n)* $\in \Theta(n^2)$, or "the cost function is in big theta of *n*-squared." You can also say the cost "is *n*-squared" or "grows like *n*-squared."

For many algorithms that depend on more than the size of the input, it may be possible to express the minimum and maximum possible costs as functions of the input size. These are called the *best-case complexity* and *worst-case complexity*, respectively. It may also be possible to determine lower and upper bounds on complexity. Big Oh notation is useful in describing these various properties of complexity as well as other asymptotic properties of an algorithm's complexity.

I won't define the Big Oh notations here; the definitions are quite technical. However, I will point out that you're more likely to hear someone mention Big Oh than Big Theta, which I used earlier. If you hear students of computer science refer to Big Oh, they are almost certainly talking about algorithmic complexity, but they could mean Big Anything because the meanings of the various notations are frequently confused.

The Big Oh family of notations are generally attributed to the late-nineteenth- and early-twentieth-century number theorists Landau and Bachmann. Although they look like real-valued functions, the expressions $\Theta(n^2)$, $O(n)$, $o(\log n)$, and so on are not real-valued functions. Instead, they are sets of functions, whence the preceding language "*in* $\Theta(n^2)$".

Unfortunately, this notation is used in a number of confusing (some might say careless, sloppy, or wrong) ways. In particular, $f = O(g)$ is commonly written to mean not that f equals $O(g)$ but that f equals some element of $O(g)$.

> **Note** The abuse of notation here is similar to that used when describing indefinite integrals in calculus. Neither side of the expression $\int x^3 dx = \frac{1}{4}x^4 + C$ is a function.

Despite a few shortcomings, Big Oh notation is useful because it captures important aspects of the relationship between input size and cost. For example every function in $\Theta(n^2)$ exhibits the "twice the input, four times the cost" behavior once n is large enough. The complexity class $\Theta(n^2)$ also contains all quadratic polynomials, and every function in $\Theta(n^2)$ is called quadratically complex.

Big Oh notation also makes it possible to describe cost "functions" that aren't in fact deterministic functions. In the coin jar example, the time required to find a quarter wasn't a well-defined function of the number of coins in the jar. The time depended in part on the number of coins in the jar but also on other features of the input, such as the proportion of quarters and how the quarters were distributed in the jar, to name two. Although *QuarterRetrievalTime(n)* isn't a function, we know that the time required to retrieve a quarter (or fail to retrieve a quarter, if there are no quarters) is at worst proportional to n. In Big Oh notation, this is easy to say: *QuarterRetrievalTime(n)* = $O(n)$.

Polynomial and Nonpolynomial Complexity

As we saw earlier, the cost functions $0.028n^2$ and n^2 are both in the complexity class $\Theta(n^2)$ because they both exhibit the "twice the input, four times the cost" behavior for large inputs. On the other hand, the behavior of the cost function n^3 is "twice the input, eight times the cost," and n^3 is not in the class $\Theta(n^2)$. In general, if the asymptotic behavior of a cost function $C(n)$ is "twice the input, k times the cost" for some positive constant k, $C(n)$ is in the complexity class $\Theta(n^p)$, where $p = \log_2 k$. The complexity classes $\Theta(n^p)$ for different values of p are distinct, but if $C(n)$ is in $\Theta(n^p)$ for any value of $p \geq 0$, $C(n)$ is said to have *polynomial complexity*. The class of functions with polynomial complexity is called P. Many real-world problems have complexity n^p—typically for p-values between 0 and 4.

The cost function for the minimum bin packing problem, $n!$, and, unfortunately, the cost functions for quite a few important real-world problems, have *nonpolynomial* complexity because they grow too quickly to belong in P. Functions with nonpolynomial complexity include 2^n (which is the number of subsets of an n-element set), 3^n (the number of ways to assign a truth value of True, False, or Unknown to each of n propositions), $n!$ (the number of arrangements of n items), $2^{n \times n}$ (the number of distinct binary relations on an n-element set), and n^n (the number of ways to match the elements of one n-element set to the elements of another).

If an algorithm has polynomial complexity, it's generally possible to accommodate an increase in input size with additional resources. On the other hand, if an algorithm has nonpolynomial complexity, it's generally impossible to use it for all but very small inputs, and scaling may be out of the question. Problems for which the only known algorithms have nonpolynomial complexity are called *intractable*. They aren't *unsolvable* because there are algorithms to solve them, but for all practical purposes, they might as well be unsolvable—for large input, the algorithms won't come up with a solution in anyone's lifetime.

Comparing Complexities

The central processing unit (CPU) of a typical computer today can execute a few billion[2] low-level instructions per second. Higher-level operations like those expressed as statements in a language like C# or Fortran require multiple machine instructions, and a reasonable benchmark to use for comparing complexities is a million steps per second. The sidebar "Sorting a Million Numbers" describes a quick test that affirms this benchmark.

Sorting a Million Numbers

In Chapter 6, "Subqueries, Table Expressions, and Ranking Functions," you'll find the code to create Nums, a million-row table of integers. The query below sorts the 1,000,000 integers in Nums according to the value of *REVERSE(n)*, for which there's no supporting index. This query took 21 seconds to execute on my single-core home computer. You don't have to jump to Chapter 6 and find the definition of Nums. You can use any million-row table you might have handy. Select one column and order it by an expression that isn't indexed.

```
USE InsideTSQL2008;
GO

SELECT n
FROM dbo.Nums
ORDER BY REVERSE(n);
```

---

[2] In this book, billion means 10^9. In the UK and Australia, the word *billion* (or a linguistic cognate) historically described the larger number 10^{12}. If confusion is possible, it's safe to describe 10^9 as a thousand million.

According to the estimated (nonparallel) execution plan for this query, 97 percent of the cost goes to the Sort operator. The complexity of SQL Server's sorting algorithm is $n \log_2 n$. For n=1,000,000, $n \log_2 n$ microseconds is about 19.9 seconds, which is very close to 97 percent of the actual elapsed time.

Note Before running the query, I selected the option Discard Results after Query Executes in Management Studio for both text and grid results. You can find it by choosing Query Options from the shortcut menu of the query editor. This way, the elapsed time corresponded to the time it took to sort the results, not the time it took to present them.

Using this benchmark, Table 5-2 compares the running time of algorithms that take $\log n$, n, $n \log n$, n^2, n^3, and 2^n steps to process input of size n for various values of n from 10 to 10^{10} (10 billion). Times well below a millisecond are denoted by *negligible*, and other times are rounded and expressed in the most meaningful units.

TABLE 5-2 Running Times for Various Input Sizes and Complexities

Complexity	$n = 10$	$n = 20$	$n = 100$	$n = 1000$	$n = 10^6$	$n = 10^9$	$n = 10^{10}$
$\log n$	negligible	negligible	negligible	negligible	negligible	negligible	negligible
n	negligible	negligible	negligible	1 ms	1 second	15 min.	3 hours
$n \log n$	negligible	negligible	1 ms	10 ms	20 secs.	8 hours	4 days
n^2	negligible	negligible	10 ms	1 second	12 days	310 centuries	3 million years
n^3	1 ms	8 ms	1 second	20 min.	310 centuries	forever	forever*
2^n	1 ms	15 min.	forever*	forever	forever	forever	forever

Lest you think forever is an exaggeration, the two entries marked with an asterisk—not the longest times in the table—are each about 40 billion billion years, and yes, that's *40 billion billion*, not just 40 billion.

What may be more surprising than the things that take forever is how much longer it takes to use an n^2 algorithm than an $n \log n$ algorithm for large n.

Classic Algorithms and Algorithmic Strategies

Before the middle of the twentieth century, computing technology wasn't powerful enough to handle what we consider fundamental computational tasks today—searching and sorting, network optimization, data compression, encryption, and so on—at least not on a large scale. Consequently, few people had put their energy into finding algorithms for these tasks.

In this section we'll look at a few algorithms and strategies that are now considered classic, although in many cases they were developed within the last 50 years. You can find many excellent books and online sources that describe and analyze these and other algorithms in detail. One of my favorites is *Introduction to Algorithms, Second Edition*, by Cormen, Leiserson, Rivest (for whom the R in RSA encryption stands), and Stein.

Algorithms for Sorting

Arranging data in a prescribed order is a fundamental data processing task: alphabetizing a list of names, arranging books on a shelf or in a bookstore or library, listing businesses by their proximity to a consumer, or numbering search results by relevance—these are all examples of sorting. Often, data needs to be sorted for it to be searched efficiently.

In this section, I'll describe several important sorting algorithms for the general problem of putting items into a specified order. Some are valid for data stored in an array, and some are valid for data stored in a (linked) list, and some work in either case.

Arrays and Lists

An array is a data structure that allows single-step access to any item given its current ordinal position. In other words, if you need to inspect the 328th item, you can access it directly, without having to start at the first item and move 327 steps forward. This kind of access to the items is called *random access*. If an array is named *A*, the item in ordinal position *j* is usually called *A[j]*.

A *list* is a data structure that, like an array, keeps data in order but where items can be accessed only from the beginning (or from either the beginning or the end). This kind of access is called *sequential access*. If a list is called *L*, the first element of the list is usually called the *head* item of the list, and the last item is called the *tail* item. If *x* is one of the items in *L*, the item before *x* is called its predecessor, and the item after *L* is called its successor. There's no standard notation for the item in ordinal position *j* of a list *L* because it can't be accessed directly.

While arrays are optimized for random access, lists are typically optimized for inserting and deleting data. If the 219th item of a 1,000-item array is deleted, the last 781 items must be moved: the item that was 220th must be moved to the 219th position, the 221st to the 220th position, and so on. If an item is deleted from a list, its predecessor can simply consider its successor to come next.

Note It's also possible to store data in order and suffer the worst aspects of both arrays and lists. Magnetic tape drives are like lists in that they only allow sequential access, but they are like arrays in that they are nonoptimized for inserting and deleting information. Sorting data on magnetic tape drives is called *external sorting* and requires algorithms different from those described here.

Quadratic Sorting Algorithms

When you arrange a handful of playing cards or alphabetize a few dozen folders in a file cabinet, you're probably applying a quadratic sorting algorithm like *insertion sort* or *selection sort*.

Insertion sort　To sort a list of items with insertion sort, begin with the second item. If it belongs before the first item, exchange it with the first item. Then look at the third item and move it up zero, one, or two slots so that the first three items are in order. Look at the fourth item and move it up zero, one, two, or three slots so the first four items are in order. Proceed in this manner until you have looked at the last item and moved it into the correct place. If insertion sort is used for an array and newly considered items must frequently be moved many slots up, a great deal of data movement may be needed.

Insertion sort has worst-case complexity $O(n^2)$. On the other hand, if the data is already in order (and, trust me, this often happens), insertion sort is linear. Insertion sort is relatively easy to implement correctly, and when n is small, it's a good choice.

Selection sort　Selection sort resembles insertion sort, but it's better than insertion sort for data in an array because data is swapped into position instead of squeezed into position. To sort a list of items with selection sort, first scan the items to find the one that should be placed first. Swap that item with the first item. Then scan items 2 through n to find the one belonging first (of those n-1 items). Swap it with the second item. Continue in this manner until you have scanned the final two items, found which one goes before the other, and swapped them if needed.

An important aspect of these sorts is that you can be specific about what is true if you quit before you finish the process. If you carry out insertion sort only through the 10th item, you can be sure that the first 10 items are in order. They may not, however, be the 10 items that ultimately belong in the first 10 positions. If you quit selection sort after the 10th item, you can be sure that the first 10 items are in order *and* that they are the 10 items that ultimately belong in the first 10 positions. If you think about the sorts this way, you might conclude that selection sort is better. However, if you think about it, you'll realize that handling each successive item in insertion sort gets more difficult and that handling each successive item in selection sort gets less difficult. If there are many items, it will take you longer to handle the first 10 with selection sort. It's no surprise, then, that you get more accomplished.

O(*n* log *n*) Sorting Algorithms

The two most commonly used sorting algorithms have complexity $O(n \log n)$. Both of them rely on a valuable strategy for solving large problems: divide and conquer, and they are most easily implemented using recursion.

Merge sort　It's easy to describe merge sort, though you wouldn't likely use it to sort cards or files by hand. To sort the items in a list or array with merge sort, first check to see if you have only one item. If so, you're done sorting! Otherwise, see if you have only two items. If so, compare the two items and swap them if necessary. Otherwise, you have more than two items to sort, and you must do three things: sort the first half of the items (using merge sort), sort the second half of the items, and merge the two (now sorted) halves into a single list that is in order. Merging two sorted lists to obtain a single sorted list takes only $O(n)$ time when there are a total of n items. However, each item participates in roughly log n merge operations, so the complexity of the entire sorting algorithm is $O(n \log n)$. Merge sort is reliably fast because its best-case, worst-case, and average-case complexities are all the same. The downside of merge sort is that simple implementations require space for the merge operation.

Quick sort   Quick sort, like merge sort, is easiest to describe and implement recursively. Here's how it works: To sort the items in a list or array with quick sort, begin by setting aside the first item of the list. Its value is called the *pivot*. Then divide the remaining items from the second item to the last item into two separate lists—one to the left of the pivot item and containing the items that come before the pivot and the other to the right of the pivot item and containing items that come after the pivot value. Then sort each of these two lists (using quick sort). That's it. One advantage to quick sort is that it can easily be implemented with very modest space requirements. On the other hand, it has a worst-case complexity of $O(n^2)$, which ironically occurs when the list is already sorted! Fortunately, if the algorithm is modified slightly, and the pivot item is chosen at random, the worst-case scenario is not the already-sorted scenario, and quick sort is very unlikely to be slow.

Faster Sorting Algorithms

Comparison-based swapping sorts are sorts that rearrange elements only by swapping, and the decision to swap or not swap elements is made by comparing the elements. Comparison-based swapping sorts cannot have complexity better than $O(n \log n)$. However, there are other ways to sort items.

Ultra sort   Ultra sort requires a staging area that will receive the data as it's scanned, and the preparation of the staging area depends on the type of data to be sorted. Suppose you're sorting numbers from 1 to 1,000. First allocate and initialize to zero an array A containing 1,000 items: $A[1]$, $A[2]$, through $A[1000]$. This setup takes $O(1)$ time. Now scan the data to be sorted. When you encounter a 17, increment the value of $A[17]$. When you encounter a 36, increment $A[36]$, and so on. When you've gone through the entire list, you have an array A that recorded the number of 1s, of 2s, and so on in your original list. To return the original list in sorted order, step through the array A. When you get to $A[63]$, for example, and find that it equals 3, return 63 to the user 3 times. Then go to $A[64]$. This sort required $O(n)$ time and $O(1)$ space. Unfortunately, if you were sorting integers, the size of your $O(1)$ space would be about 16 billion bytes, and while 16 billion is technically $O(1)$, it's the dominant term, and quick sort or merge sort will probably be an improvement.

String Searching

Another common data processing task is to find a string within a longer string, for example, to find a particular word in a word processing document. If I want to find the word *particular* in the previous sentence, how long does it take?

Not long, if I mean I want to find it "as a word" and not as consecutive letters ignoring spaces, for example. However, suppose I want to find a particular computer virus signature on my hard drive. Is there a quick way to do it?

Searching for a Virus Signature in a Gigabyte BLOB

Suppose 0x00010001000100010001000100010001000100010001 is a dangerous virus signature and you need to find it if it exists as a substring of gigabyte BLOB (Binary Large Object). Surprisingly, there is an algorithm to search for it that will inspect considerably fewer than all the bytes of the BLOB. Here is the procedure:

Algorithm to search for 0x00010001000100010001000100010001000100010001

1. Inspect the 20th byte of the BLOB, which would be the last byte of the signature if the signature appeared at the beginning of the BLOB. If the 20th byte is not 0x00 or 0x01, the virus signature cannot begin at any one of the first 20 bytes of the BLOB. As a result, the leftmost position where the virus signature can begin is the 21st byte.

2. Inspect the 40th byte, which is where the virus signature would end if it began at the 21st byte. If that byte is not 0x00 or 0x01, proceed to the next step.

3. Inspect the 60th byte and so on.

Once in a while, you will inspect a byte that is 0x00 or 0x01, and you'll have to follow different rules that don't let you jump ahead by 20 bytes, but you can still rule out many starting points if the byte you inspect is preceded closely by a byte that isn't 0x00 or 0x01. It's quite likely that you have to inspect only one or two bytes out of every 20 in your BLOB, and you'll often determine that the virus signature is absent after inspecting only 5 to 10 percent of the BLOB bytes.

This clever algorithm was described by Boyer and Moore in 1977 and provides an example of a sublinear complexity algorithm that requires no preorganization of the data.

A Practical Application

In the final section of this chapter, I'll describe a real-world process control problem I encountered about 10 years ago and was able to solve with an efficient algorithm that had only recently been published in a mathematics journal. This real-world problem concerns the identification of a *trend marker* in a series of measurements of toxin levels. In the following description, I've simplified the scenario but not the algorithm, which eventually received governmental certification and was used for environmental monitoring.

Identifying Trends in Measurement Data

The ongoing debate about global warming underlines the fact that there is no simple criterion for identifying an increasing trend in a series of measurements. Many industries use statistical process control (SPC) software to identify trends, and these software programs can be configured to identify many different kinds of patterns called *trend markers* in a series of measurements. A simple trend marker is a *record high* measurement: a measurement higher than any previously recorded value. Another trend marker is the occurrence of seven consecutive above-average measurements. Yet another is the occurrence of two consecutive measurements at or above the 98th percentile of all previous measurements. A number of commercial SPC programs include these trend markers.

Increasing Subsequences

One useful trend marker not typically included in commercial software packages is an *increasing subsequence* of a particular length. Here's an example of a sequence of measurements that includes a length-four increasing subsequence. The four numbers in bold form an increasing subsequence—increasing because they increase from left to right and subsequence because the values come from the original sequence.

*3.894, 4.184, **3.939**, **4.050**, 3.940, **4.140**, 3.914, **4.156**, 4.143, 4.035, 4.097*

The subsequence identified in bold isn't the only increasing subsequence of length four, nor is it the longest increasing subsequence in the original sequence.

The problem we'll solve in T-SQL is that of finding the length of the longest increasing subsequence.

Longest Increasing Subsequence Length Problem (LISLP)

Input: A sequence X of n numbers: $x_1, x_2, \ldots, x_n$.

Output: The largest integer k for which there is a length-k increasing subsequence of X.

The Algorithmic Complexity of LISLP

One way to solve this problem is to enumerate all the subsequences of X and check each one to see if its values form an increasing sequence. If X is a very short sequence, this works reasonably well. For example, if X contains 6 elements, there are only 57 subsequences of length at least two. (Note that a subsequence can't really be increasing if it doesn't contain at least two items.)

How Many Subsequences Are There?

Unfortunately, the number of subsequences of X grows exponentially with the length of X. If X contains not six but 26 elements, there are more than 67 million subsequences. If X contains 60 elements, there are more than a billion billion. A billion billion nanoseconds is about 31 years. Don't try enumerating this many subsequences at home! If the sequence X contains n items, there's a subsequence of X for every subset of the set of item positions {1, 2, 3, ..., n}, or 2^n subsequences in all. There are n one-item subsequences and one zero-item subsequence, leaving us with $2^n - (n+1)$ subsequences of length at least two. Although in practice you might not need to consider all these subsequences—for example, as soon as you find one increasing subsequence, you can skip all the unchecked subsequences of the same length—enumerating subsequences is not the way to solve LISLP.

An Algorithm for LISLP with $\Theta(n \log n)$ Complexity

The algorithmic complexity of enumerating all subsequences of a length-n sequence is $\Theta(2^n)$, which, as we've seen, makes the problem impossible to solve in practice for inputs of even modest size. Fortunately, not long before I encountered this problem, so had two talented mathematics, David Aldous and Persi Diaconis. Better yet, they had published their findings in the *Bulletin of the American Mathematical Society* in 1999: "Longest increasing subsequences: from patience sorting to the Baik-Deift-Johansson theorem." Aldous and Diaconis described an $O(n \log n)$ algorithm to solve the problem.

Algorithms with $\Theta(n \log n)$ complexity are practical to use, but it helps if they are also simple to implement. This one turns out to be.

Finding the Length of the Longest Increasing Subsequence

Let $X = (x_1, x_2, ..., x_n)$ be a sequence of n real numbers. The length of the longest increasing subsequence of X is the length of the list L generated by the following procedure.

1. Let $k = 1$, and let L be an empty list of numbers.

2. While $k \leq n$:

3. Inspect L for numbers greater than or equal to a_k. If one exists, replace the first (and smallest) of them with a_k. Otherwise (when a_k is greater than every number in L), insert a_k into the list L. Increase k by 1.

Solving the Longest Increasing Subsequence Length Problem in T-SQL

Execute the code in Listing 5-1 to create the tables Locations and Readings and fill them with sample data.

LISTING 5-1 Creating and populating the Locations and Readings tables

```
USE tempdb;
GO
IF OBJECT_ID('dbo.Locations') IS NOT NULL
  DROP TABLE dbo.Locations;

CREATE TABLE dbo.Locations (
  ID INT NOT NULL PRIMARY KEY,
  name VARCHAR(12) NOT NULL
);

INSERT INTO dbo.Locations VALUES (1, 'Uptown'), (2, 'Midtown');

IF OBJECT_ID('dbo.Readings') IS NOT NULL
  DROP TABLE dbo.Readings;

CREATE TABLE dbo.Readings (
  locID INT REFERENCES dbo.Locations(ID),
  readingNum INT,
  ppb DECIMAL(6,3),
  PRIMARY KEY (locID,readingNum)
);

INSERT INTO dbo.Readings VALUES
  (1,1,3.968), (1,2,3.773), (1,3,3.994), (1,4,3.889),
  (1,5,4.015), (1,6,4.002), (1,7,4.043), (1,8,3.932),
  (1,9,4.072), (1,10,4.088), (1,11,3.952), (1,12,3.992),
  (1,13,3.980), (1,14,4.062), (1,15,4.074), (2,1,3.894),
  (2,2,4.184), (2,3,3.939), (2,4,4.050), (2,5,3.940),
  (2,6,4.140), (2,7,3.914), (2,8,4.156), (2,9,4.143),
  (2,10,4.035), (2,11,4.097), (2,12,4.086), (2,13,4.093),
  (2,14,3.932), (2,15,4.046);
GO
```

The pseudocode described how to implement the algorithm for a single sequence X, and the Readings table contains two sequences of readings, one for each of two locations. Therefore, with the code in Listing 5-2, we'll create a user-defined function *dbo.LISL* that returns the longest increasing subsequence length for a single sequence, given a location ID as input.

LISTING 5-2 Code to create the user-defined function *LISL*

```
IF OBJECT_ID('dbo.LISL') IS NOT NULL DROP FUNCTION dbo.LISL;

CREATE FUNCTION dbo.LISL(@locID INT)
RETURNS INT AS BEGIN

  DECLARE @Solitaire TABLE (
    pos int IDENTITY(1,1) PRIMARY KEY,
    ppb decimal(6,3),
    UNIQUE (ppb,pos)
  );
```

```
DECLARE C CURSOR FAST_FORWARD
FOR
  SELECT ppb
  FROM dbo.Readings
  WHERE locID = @locID
  ORDER BY readingNum;

DECLARE @ppb decimal(6,3);

OPEN C;
FETCH NEXT FROM C INTO @ppb;
IF @@fetch_status <> 0 RETURN 0;

INSERT INTO @Solitaire VALUES (@ppb);
WHILE @@fetch_status = 0 BEGIN

  WITH T(pos) AS (
    SELECT MIN(pos)
    FROM @Solitaire
    WHERE ppb >= @ppb
  )
  MERGE INTO @Solitaire AS S
  USING T
  ON T.pos = S.pos
  WHEN MATCHED THEN
    UPDATE SET ppb = @ppb
  WHEN NOT MATCHED BY TARGET THEN
    INSERT (ppb) VALUES (@ppb);

  FETCH NEXT FROM C INTO @ppb;

END;
CLOSE C;
DEALLOCATE C;

RETURN (SELECT COUNT(*) FROM @Solitaire);
END;
GO
```

Listing 5-2 includes a MERGE statement, which is a new feature of SQL Server 2008. You'll learn about MERGE in detail in Chapter 10, "Data Modification." Otherwise, there's not much to explain in the listing, which follows the pseudocode closely. I will point out that I've given the name @*Solitaire* to the table that represents *L* because Diaconis and Aldous describe the algorithm for LISLP in terms of a game of Solitaire (which is known as Patience in some English-speaking countries).

Finally, let's use this function (shown in Listing 5-3) to solve LISLP for our sample data.

LISTING 5-3 Query to find the longest increasing subsequence length

```
SELECT
    name, dbo.LISL(ID) AS LISL
FROM dbo.Locations;
```

This query returns the following results:

```
name          LISL
------------  -----------
Uptown        7
Midtown       6
```

Can you find increasing subsequences of length 7 and 6 for the Uptown and Midtown data, respectively? And can you convince yourself that these are the longest?

Conclusion

This chapter surveyed some key concepts about algorithms and complexity. A close look at complexity dispelled the idea that the answer to every problem is better hardware! After briefly surveying a few algorithms that are particularly important to the SQL Server engine, the chapter ended with a practical example.

Chapter 6
Subqueries, Table Expressions, and Ranking Functions

This chapter covers subqueries, which are queries within queries, and ranking calculations. Subqueries can be scalar, multivalued, or table valued. You can use a *scalar subquery* where a single value is expected. For example, the following query returns the order with the maximum order ID:

```
USE InsideTSQL2008;

SELECT orderid, custid
FROM Sales.Orders
WHERE orderid = (SELECT MAX(orderid) FROM Sales.Orders);
```

The scalar subquery in bold is in charge of returning the maximum order ID. This subquery is self-contained, meaning that it has no dependency on the outer query.

A subquery that has a dependency on the outer query is known as a *correlated subquery*. For example, the following query returns the order with the maximum order ID for each customer:

```
SELECT orderid, custid
FROM Sales.Orders AS O1
WHERE orderid = (SELECT MAX(O2.orderid)
                 FROM Sales.Orders AS O2
                 WHERE O2.custid = O1.custid);
```

The correlated subquery in bold is in charge of returning the maximum order ID for the current customer in the outer table.

You can use a *multivalued subquery* where multiple values are expected. For example, the following query returns customers who placed orders:

```
SELECT custid, companyname
FROM Sales.Customers
WHERE custid IN (SELECT custid FROM Sales.Orders);
```

The multivalued subquery in bold is in charge of returning customer IDs of customers who placed orders. Like scalar subqueries, multivalued subqueries can be correlated.

You can use a *table-valued subquery*, or *table expression*, where a table is expected. For example, the following query returns the maximum order ID for each order year:

```
SELECT orderyear, MAX(orderid) AS max_orderid
FROM (SELECT orderid, YEAR(orderdate) AS orderyear
      FROM Sales.Orders) AS D
GROUP BY orderyear;
```

The table expression D in bold assigns the alias *orderyear* to the expression *YEAR(orderdate)* and returns the order ID and order year for each order.

I'll refer to scalar and multivalued subqueries just as subqueries and to subqueries that are used where a table is expected as table expressions. In this chapter, I'll cover two kinds of table expressions: derived tables and common table expressions (CTE).

In the last part of the chapter, I'll cover ranking functions, including row number, rank, dense rank, and tile.

Because this book is intended for experienced programmers, I assume that you're already familiar with subqueries and table expressions. I'll go over their definitions briefly and focus on their applications and on problem solving.

Subqueries

Subqueries can be characterized in two main ways. One is by the expected number of values (either scalar or multivalued), and another is by the subquery's dependency on the outer query (either self-contained or correlated). Both scalar and multivalued subqueries can be either self-contained or correlated.

Self-Contained Subqueries

As mentioned, a self-contained subquery is a subquery that can be run independently of the outer query. Self-contained subqueries are very convenient to debug, of course, compared to correlated subqueries.

Scalar subqueries can appear anywhere in the query where an expression resulting in a scalar value is expected, while multivalued subqueries can appear anywhere in the query where a collection of multiple values is expected.

A scalar subquery is valid when it returns a single value and also when it returns no values—in which case, the value of the subquery is NULL. However, if a scalar subquery returns more than one value, a run-time error will occur.

For example, run the following code three times: once as shown, a second time with LIKE *N'Kollar'* in place of LIKE *N'Davis'*, and a third time with LIKE *N'D%'*:

```
SELECT orderid FROM Sales.Orders
WHERE empid =
  (SELECT empid FROM HR.Employees
   -- also try with N'Kollar' and N'D%'
   WHERE lastname LIKE N'Davis');
```

With *N'Davis'*, the subquery returns a single value (1) and the outer query returns all orders with employee ID 1.

With *N'Kollar'*, the subquery returns no values and is therefore NULL. The outer query obviously doesn't find any orders for which *empid* = NULL and therefore returns an empty set. Note that the query doesn't break (fail)—it's a valid query.

With *N'D%'*, the subquery returns two values (1, 9), and because the outer query expects a scalar, it breaks at run time and generates the following error:

```
Msg 512, Level 16, State 1, Line 1
Subquery returned more than 1 value. This is not permitted when the subquery follows =,
!=, <, <= , >, >= or when the subquery is used as an expression.
```

Logically, a self-contained subquery can be evaluated just once for the whole outer query. Physically, the optimizer can consider many different ways to achieve the same thing, so you shouldn't think in such strict terms.

Now that we've covered the essentials, let's move on to more sophisticated problems involving self-contained subqueries.

I'll start with a problem belonging to a group of problems called relational division. Relational division problems have many nuances and many practical applications. Logically, it's like dividing one set by another, producing a result set. For example, from the InsideTSQL2008 database, return all customers for whom every employee from the USA has handled at least one order. In this case, you're dividing the set of all orders by the set of all employees from the USA, and you expect the set of matching customers back. Filtering here is not that simple because for each customer you need to inspect multiple rows to figure out whether you have a match.

Here I'll show a technique using GROUP BY and DISTINCT COUNT to solve relational division problems. I'll show you other techniques later in the book.

If you knew ahead of time the list of all employee IDs for USA employees, you could write the following query to solve the problem:

```
SELECT custid
FROM Sales.Orders
WHERE empid IN(1, 2, 3, 4, 8)
GROUP BY custid
HAVING COUNT(DISTINCT empid) = 5;
```

This query generates the following output:

```
custid
-----------
5
9
20
24
34
35
37
38
```

```
39
41
46
47
48
51
55
63
65
71
80
83
84
87
89
```

This query finds all orders with one of the five U.S. employee IDs, groups those orders by *custid*, and returns customer IDs that have (all) five distinct *empid* values in their group of orders.

To make the solution more dynamic and accommodate lists of employee IDs that are unknown ahead of time and also large lists even when known, you can use subqueries instead of literals:

```
SELECT custid
FROM Sales.Orders
WHERE empid IN
  (SELECT empid FROM HR.Employees
   WHERE country = N'USA')
GROUP BY custid
HAVING COUNT(DISTINCT empid) =
  (SELECT COUNT(*) FROM HR.Employees
   WHERE country = N'USA');
```

Another problem involving self-contained subqueries is returning all orders placed on the last actual order date of the month. Note that the last actual order date of the month might be different than the last date of the month—for example, if a company doesn't place orders on weekends. So the last actual order date of the month has to be queried from the data. Here's the solution query:

```
SELECT orderid, custid, empid, orderdate
FROM Sales.Orders
WHERE orderdate IN
  (SELECT MAX(orderdate)
   FROM Sales.Orders
   GROUP BY YEAR(orderdate), MONTH(orderdate));
```

This query produces the following output:

```
orderid      custid       empid        orderdate
-----------  -----------  -----------  -----------------------
10269        89           5            2006-07-31 00:00:00.000
10294        65           4            2006-08-30 00:00:00.000
```

10317	48	6	2006-09-30 00:00:00.000
10343	44	4	2006-10-31 00:00:00.000
10368	20	2	2006-11-29 00:00:00.000
10399	83	8	2006-12-31 00:00:00.000
10432	75	3	2007-01-31 00:00:00.000
10460	24	8	2007-02-28 00:00:00.000
10461	46	1	2007-02-28 00:00:00.000
10490	35	7	2007-03-31 00:00:00.000
10491	28	8	2007-03-31 00:00:00.000
10522	44	4	2007-04-30 00:00:00.000
10553	87	2	2007-05-30 00:00:00.000
10554	56	4	2007-05-30 00:00:00.000
10583	87	2	2007-06-30 00:00:00.000
10584	7	4	2007-06-30 00:00:00.000
10616	32	1	2007-07-31 00:00:00.000
10617	32	4	2007-07-31 00:00:00.000
10650	21	5	2007-08-29 00:00:00.000
10686	59	2	2007-09-30 00:00:00.000
10687	37	9	2007-09-30 00:00:00.000
10725	21	4	2007-10-31 00:00:00.000
10758	68	3	2007-11-28 00:00:00.000
10759	2	3	2007-11-28 00:00:00.000
10806	84	3	2007-12-31 00:00:00.000
10807	27	4	2007-12-31 00:00:00.000
10861	89	4	2008-01-30 00:00:00.000
10862	44	8	2008-01-30 00:00:00.000
10914	62	6	2008-02-27 00:00:00.000
10915	80	2	2008-02-27 00:00:00.000
10916	64	1	2008-02-27 00:00:00.000
10987	19	8	2008-03-31 00:00:00.000
10988	65	3	2008-03-31 00:00:00.000
10989	61	2	2008-03-31 00:00:00.000
11060	27	2	2008-04-30 00:00:00.000
11061	32	4	2008-04-30 00:00:00.000
11062	66	4	2008-04-30 00:00:00.000
11063	37	3	2008-04-30 00:00:00.000
11074	73	7	2008-05-06 00:00:00.000
11075	68	8	2008-05-06 00:00:00.000
11076	9	4	2008-05-06 00:00:00.000
11077	65	1	2008-05-06 00:00:00.000

The self-contained subquery returns the following list of values representing the last actual order date of each month:

```
2007-01-31 00:00:00.000
2008-01-30 00:00:00.000
2007-02-28 00:00:00.000
2008-02-27 00:00:00.000
2007-03-31 00:00:00.000
2008-03-31 00:00:00.000
2007-04-30 00:00:00.000
2008-04-30 00:00:00.000
2007-05-30 00:00:00.000
2008-05-06 00:00:00.000
2007-06-30 00:00:00.000
```

```
2006-07-31 00:00:00.000
2007-07-31 00:00:00.000
2006-08-30 00:00:00.000
2007-08-29 00:00:00.000
2006-09-30 00:00:00.000
2007-09-30 00:00:00.000
2006-10-31 00:00:00.000
2007-10-31 00:00:00.000
2006-11-29 00:00:00.000
2007-11-28 00:00:00.000
2006-12-31 00:00:00.000
2007-12-31 00:00:00.000
```

The subquery achieves this result by grouping the orders by order year and month and returning the *MAX(orderdate)* for each group. The outer query returns all orders with an *orderdate* that appears in the list returned by the subquery.

Correlated Subqueries

Correlated subqueries are subqueries that have references to columns from the outer query. Logically, the subquery is evaluated once for each row of the outer query. Again, physically, it's a much more dynamic process and varies from case to case, with no single physical way to process a correlated subquery.

Isolating One Row Per Group and Applying a Tiebreaker

I'll start dealing with correlated subqueries through a problem that introduces a very important concept in SQL querying—a *tiebreaker*. I'll refer to this concept throughout the book. A tiebreaker is an attribute or attribute list that allows you to uniquely rank elements. For example, suppose you need the most recent order for each employee. You are supposed to return only one order for each employee, but the attributes *empid* and *orderdate* do not necessarily identify a unique order. You need to introduce a tiebreaker to be able to identify a unique most recent order for each employee. For example, out of the multiple orders with the maximum *orderdate* for an employee, you could decide to return the one with the maximum *orderid*. In this case, *MAX(orderid)* is your tiebreaker. Or you could decide to return the row with the maximum *requireddate* and, if you still have multiple rows, return the one with the maximum *orderid*. In this case, your tiebreaker is *MAX(requireddate), MAX(orderid)*. A tiebreaker is not necessarily limited to a single attribute.

Before moving on to the solutions, run the following code to create indexes that support the physical processing of the queries that will follow:

```
CREATE UNIQUE INDEX idx_eid_od_oid
  ON Sales.Orders(empid, orderdate, orderid);
CREATE UNIQUE INDEX idx_eid_od_rd_oid
  ON Sales.Orders(empid, orderdate, requireddate, orderid);
```

I'll explain the indexing guidelines after presenting the solution queries.

Let's start with the basic request to return the orders with the maximum *orderdate* for each employee. Here you can get multiple rows for each employee because an employee can have multiple orders with the same order date.

You might be tempted to use the following solution, which includes a self-contained subquery similar to the one used to return orders on the last actual order date of the month:

```
SELECT orderid, custid, empid, orderdate, requireddate
FROM Sales.Orders
WHERE orderdate IN
  (SELECT MAX(orderdate) FROM Sales.Orders
    GROUP BY empid);
```

However, this solution is incorrect. The result set includes the correct orders (the ones with the maximum *orderdate* for each employee). But you also get any order for employee A with an *orderdate* that happens to be the maximum for employee B, even though it's not also the maximum for employee A. This wasn't an issue with the previous problem because an order date in month A can't be equal to the maximum order date of a different month B.

In our case, the subquery must be correlated to the outer query, matching the inner *empid* to the one in the outer row:

```
SELECT orderid, custid, empid, orderdate, requireddate
FROM Sales.Orders AS O1
WHERE orderdate =
  (SELECT MAX(orderdate)
    FROM Sales.Orders AS O2
    WHERE O2.empid = O1.empid);
```

This query generates the correct results, as the following output shows:

```
orderid     custid      empid     orderdate               requireddate
----------- ----------- --------- ----------------------- -----------------------
11077       65          1         2008-05-06 00:00:00.000 2008-06-03 00:00:00.000
11070       44          2         2008-05-05 00:00:00.000 2008-06-02 00:00:00.000
11073       58          2         2008-05-05 00:00:00.000 2008-06-02 00:00:00.000
11063       37          3         2008-04-30 00:00:00.000 2008-05-28 00:00:00.000
11076       9           4         2008-05-06 00:00:00.000 2008-06-03 00:00:00.000
11043       74          5         2008-04-22 00:00:00.000 2008-05-20 00:00:00.000
11045       10          6         2008-04-23 00:00:00.000 2008-05-21 00:00:00.000
11074       73          7         2008-05-06 00:00:00.000 2008-06-03 00:00:00.000
11075       68          8         2008-05-06 00:00:00.000 2008-06-03 00:00:00.000
11058       6           9         2008-04-29 00:00:00.000 2008-05-27 00:00:00.000
```

The output contains one example of multiple orders for an employee, in the case of employee 2. If you want to return only one row for each employee, you have to introduce a tiebreaker. For example, out of the multiple rows with the maximum *orderdate*, return the one with the maximum *orderid*. You can achieve this by adding another subquery that keeps the order only if *orderid* is equal to the maximum among the orders with the same *empid* and *orderdate* as in the outer row:

```
SELECT orderid, custid, empid, orderdate, requireddate
FROM Sales.Orders AS O1
WHERE orderdate =
  (SELECT MAX(orderdate)
   FROM Sales.Orders AS O2
   WHERE O2.empid = O1.empid)
  AND orderid =
  (SELECT MAX(orderid)
   FROM Sales.Orders AS O2
   WHERE O2.empid = O1.empid
     AND O2.orderdate = O1.orderdate);
```

Of the two orders for employee 2, only the one with the maximum *orderid* remains, as the following output shows:

```
orderid     custid      empid       orderdate               requireddate
----------- ----------- ----------- ----------------------- -----------------------
11077       65          1           2008-05-06 00:00:00.000 2008-06-03 00:00:00.000
11073       58          2           2008-05-05 00:00:00.000 2008-06-02 00:00:00.000
11063       37          3           2008-04-30 00:00:00.000 2008-05-28 00:00:00.000
11076       9           4           2008-05-06 00:00:00.000 2008-06-03 00:00:00.000
11043       74          5           2008-04-22 00:00:00.000 2008-05-20 00:00:00.000
11045       10          6           2008-04-23 00:00:00.000 2008-05-21 00:00:00.000
11074       73          7           2008-05-06 00:00:00.000 2008-06-03 00:00:00.000
11075       68          8           2008-05-06 00:00:00.000 2008-06-03 00:00:00.000
11058       6           9           2008-04-29 00:00:00.000 2008-05-27 00:00:00.000
```

Instead of using two separate subqueries for the sort column (*orderdate*) and the tiebreaker (*orderid*), you can use nested subqueries:

```
SELECT orderid, custid, empid, orderdate, requireddate
FROM Sales.Orders AS O1
WHERE orderid =
  (SELECT MAX(orderid)
   FROM Sales.Orders AS O2
   WHERE O2.empid = O1.empid
     AND O2.orderdate =
       (SELECT MAX(orderdate)
        FROM Sales.Orders AS O3
        WHERE O3.empid = O1.empid));
```

I compared the performance of the two and found it very similar. I find the nested approach more complex, so as long as there's no compelling performance benefit, I'd rather stick to the simpler approach. Simpler is easier to understand and maintain, and therefore less prone to errors.

Going back to the simpler approach, for each tiebreaker attribute you have, you need to add a subquery. Each such subquery must be correlated by the group column, sort column, and all preceding tiebreaker attributes. So, to use *MAX(requireddate), MAX(orderid)* as the tiebreaker, you would write the following query:

```
SELECT orderid, custid, empid, orderdate, requireddate
FROM Sales.Orders AS O1
WHERE orderdate =
  (SELECT MAX(orderdate)
   FROM Sales.Orders AS O2
   WHERE O2.empid = O1.empid)
  AND requireddate =
  (SELECT MAX(requireddate)
   FROM Sales.Orders AS O2
   WHERE O2.empid = O1.empid
     AND O2.orderdate = O1.orderdate)
  AND orderid =
  (SELECT MAX(orderid)
   FROM Sales.Orders AS O2
   WHERE O2.empid = O1.empid
     AND O2.orderdate = O1.orderdate
     AND O2.requireddate = O1.requireddate);
```

The indexing guideline for the preceding tiebreaker queries is to create an index on (*group_cols, sort_cols, tiebreaker_cols*). For example, when the tiebreaker is *MAX(orderid),* you want an index on (*empid, orderdate, orderid*). When the tiebreaker is *MAX(requireddate), MAX(orderid),* you want an index on (*empid, orderdate, requireddate, orderid*). Such an index would allow retrieving the relevant sort value or tiebreaker value for an employee using a seek operation within the index.

When you're done testing the tiebreaker solutions, run the following code to drop the indexes that were created just for these examples:

```
DROP INDEX Sales.Orders.idx_eid_od_oid;
DROP INDEX Sales.Orders.idx_eid_od_rd_oid;
```

I presented here only one approach using ANSI-correlated subqueries to solving the problem of isolating one row per group using a tiebreaker. This approach is neither the most efficient nor the simplest. You will find other solutions to tiebreaker problems in Chapter 8, "Aggregating and Pivoting Data," in the "Tiebreakers" section, and in Chapter 9, "TOP and APPLY," in the "TOP *n* for Each Group" section.

EXISTS

EXISTS is a powerful predicate that allows you to efficiently check whether any rows result from a given query. The input to EXISTS is a subquery, which is typically but not necessarily correlated, and the predicate returns TRUE or FALSE, depending on whether the subquery returns at least one row or none. Unlike other predicates and logical expressions, EXISTS cannot return UNKNOWN. Either the input subquery returns rows or it doesn't. If the subquery's filter returns UNKNOWN for a certain row, the row is not returned. Remember that in a filter, UNKNOWN is treated like FALSE.

In other words, when the input subquery has a filter, EXISTS will return TRUE only if the filter is TRUE for at least one row. The reason I'm stressing this subtle point will become apparent shortly.

First, let's look at an example that will demonstrate the use of EXISTS. The following query returns all customers from Spain who made orders:

```
SELECT custid, companyname
FROM Sales.Customers AS C
WHERE country = N'Spain'
  AND EXISTS
    (SELECT * FROM Sales.Orders AS O
     WHERE O.custid = C.custid);
```

This query generates the following output:

```
custid       companyname
-----------  ---------------------------------------
8            Customer QUHWH
29           Customer MDLWA
30           Customer KSLQF
69           Customer SIUIH
```

The outer query returns customers from Spain for whom the EXISTS predicate finds at least one order row in the Orders table with the same *custid* as in the outer customer row.

Tip The use of the asterisk (*) here is perfectly safe, even though in general it's not a good practice. The optimizer ignores the SELECT list specified in the subquery because EXISTS cares only about the existence of rows and not about any specific attributes. Some resolution overhead may be involved in expanding the * to check column permissions, but this cost is likely so negligible that you will hardly ever notice it.

Examine the execution plan produced for this query, as shown in Figure 6-1.

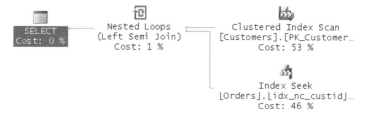

FIGURE 6-1 Execution plan for an EXISTS query

The plan scans the Customers table and filters customers from Spain. For each matching customer, the plan performs a seek within the index on *Orders.custid* to check whether the Orders table contains an order with that customer's *custid*. The index on the filtered column in the subquery (*Orders.custid* in our case) is very helpful here because it provides direct access to the rows of the Orders table with a given *custid* value.

EXISTS vs. IN   Programmers frequently wonder whether a query with the EXISTS predicate is more efficient than a logically equivalent query with the IN predicate. For example, the last query could be written using an IN predicate with a self-contained subquery as follows:

```
SELECT custid, companyname
FROM Sales.Customers AS C
WHERE country = N'Spain'
  AND custid IN(SELECT custid FROM Sales.Orders);
```

The optimizer often generates identical plans for two queries *when they are truly logically equivalent,* and this case qualifies. The plan generated for the last query using IN is identical to the one shown in Figure 6-1, which was generated for the query using EXISTS.

If you're always thinking of the implications of three-valued logic, you might see the difference between IN and EXISTS. Unlike EXISTS, IN can in fact produce an UNKNOWN logical result when the input list contains a NULL. For example, *a IN(b, c, NULL)* is UNKNOWN. However, because UNKNOWN is treated like FALSE in a filter, the result of a query with the IN predicate is the same as with the EXISTS predicate, and the optimizer is aware of that, hence the identical plans.

NOT EXISTS vs. NOT IN   The logical difference between EXISTS and IN does show up if we compare NOT EXISTS and NOT IN, when the input list of NOT IN might contain a NULL.

For example, suppose you need to return customers from Spain who made no orders. Here's the solution using the NOT EXISTS predicate:

```
SELECT custid, companyname
FROM Sales.Customers AS C
WHERE country = N'Spain'
  AND NOT EXISTS
    (SELECT * FROM Sales.Orders AS O
     WHERE O.custid = C.custid);
```

This query generates the following output:

```
custid      companyname
----------- ----------------------------------------
22          Customer DTDMN
```

Even if the Orders table has a NULL *custid,* it is of no concern to us. You get all customers from Spain for which SQL Server cannot find even one row in the Orders table with the same *custid.* The plan generated for this query is shown in Figure 6-2.

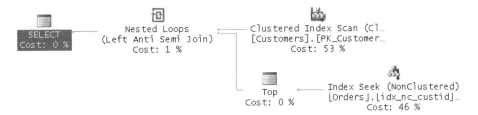

FIGURE 6-2 Execution plan for a NOT EXISTS query

The plan scans the Customers table and filters customers from Spain. For each matching customer, the plan performs a seek within the index on *Orders.custid*. The *Top* operator appears because it's only necessary to see whether you have at least one matching order for the customer—that's the short-circuiting capability of EXISTS in action. This use of *Top* is particularly efficient when the *Orders.custid* column has a high density (that is, a large number of duplicates). The seek takes place only once for each customer, and regardless of the number of orders the customer has, only one row is scanned at the leaf level (the bottom level of the index) to look for a match, as opposed to all matching rows.

In this case, the following solution using the NOT IN predicate does yield the same output. It seems to have the same meaning, but we'll see later that it does not.

```
SELECT custid, companyname
FROM Sales.Customers AS C
WHERE country = N'Spain'
  AND custid NOT IN(SELECT custid FROM Sales.Orders);
```

If you examine the execution plan, shown in Figure 6-3, you will find that it's different from the one generated for the NOT EXISTS query.

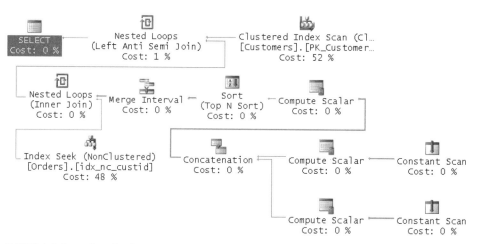

FIGURE 6-3 Execution plan for a NOT IN query

The beginning of this plan has some additional operations compared to the previous plan— steps needed to look for NULL *custid*s. Why is this plan different than the one generated for the NOT EXISTS query? And why would SQL Server care particularly about the existence of NULLs in *Orders.custid*?

The discrepancy between the plans doesn't affect the result because no row in the Orders table has a NULL *custid*. However, because the *custid* column allows NULLs, the optimizer must take this fact into consideration. Let's see what happens if we add a row with a NULL *custid* to the Orders table:

```
INSERT INTO Sales.Orders
  (custid, empid, orderdate, requireddate, shippeddate, shipperid,
   freight, shipname, shipaddress, shipcity, shipregion,
   shippostalcode, shipcountry)
  VALUES(NULL, 1, '20090212', '20090212',
         '20090212', 1, 123.00, N'abc', N'abc', N'abc',
         N'abc', N'abc', N'abc');
```

Now rerun both the NOT EXISTS and NOT IN queries. You will find that the NOT EXISTS query still returns the same output as before, while the NOT IN query now returns an empty set. In fact, when the *Orders.custid* column has a NULL, the NOT IN query always returns an empty set. This is because the predicate *val IN(val1, val2, ..., NULL)* can never return FALSE; rather, it can return only TRUE or UNKNOWN. As a result, *val NOT IN(val1, val2, ..., NULL)* can return only NOT TRUE or NOT UNKNOWN, neither of which is TRUE.

For example, suppose the customer list in this query is *(a, b, NULL)*. Customer *a* appears in the list, and therefore the predicate *a IN(a, b, NULL)* returns TRUE. The predicate *a NOT IN(a, b, NULL)* returns NOT TRUE, or FALSE, and customer *a* is not returned by the query. Customer *c*, on the other hand, does *not* appear in the list *(a, b, NULL)*, but the logical result of *c IN(a, b, NULL)* is UNKNOWN because of the NULL. The predicate *c NOT IN(a, b, NULL)* therefore returns NOT UNKNOWN, which equals UNKNOWN, and customer *c* is not returned by the query, either, even though *c* does not appear in the customer list. Whether or not a customer appears in the customer list, the customer is not returned by the query if the list contains NULL. You realize that when NULLs are potentially involved (such as when the queried column allows NULLs), NOT EXISTS and NOT IN are not logically equivalent. This explains the discrepancy between the plans and the potential difference in results. To make the NOT IN query logically equivalent to the NOT EXISTS query, declare the column as NOT NULL (if appropriate) or add a filter to the subquery to exclude NULLs:

```
SELECT custid, companyname
FROM Sales.Customers AS C
WHERE country = N'Spain'
  AND custid NOT IN(SELECT custid FROM Sales.Orders
                    WHERE custid IS NOT NULL);
```

This query generates the same result as the NOT EXISTS query, as well as the same plan.

When you're done testing the queries, make sure you remove the row with the NULL *custid:*

```
DELETE FROM Sales.Orders WHERE custid IS NULL;
DBCC CHECKIDENT('Sales.Orders', RESEED, 11077);
```

Minimum Missing Value   To put your knowledge of the EXISTS predicate into action, try to solve the following problem. First create and populate the table T1 by running the code in Listing 6-1.

LISTING 6-1 Creating and populating the table T1

```
USE tempdb;
GO
IF OBJECT_ID('dbo.T1') IS NOT NULL
  DROP TABLE dbo.T1;
GO

CREATE TABLE dbo.T1
(
  keycol  INT          NOT NULL PRIMARY KEY CHECK(keycol > 0),
  datacol VARCHAR(10) NOT NULL
);
INSERT INTO dbo.T1(keycol, datacol) VALUES
  (3, 'a'),
  (4, 'b'),
  (6, 'c'),
  (7, 'd');
```

Notice that *keycol* must be positive. Your task is to write a query that returns the lowest missing key, assuming that key values start at 1. For example, the table is currently populated with the keys 3, 4, 6, and 7, so your query should return the value 1. If you insert two more rows, with the keys 1 and 2, your query should return 5.

Here's a suggested CASE expression (incomplete) that I used in my solution:

```
SELECT
  CASE
    WHEN NOT EXISTS(SELECT * FROM dbo.T1 WHERE keycol = 1) THEN 1
    ELSE (...subquery returning minimum missing value...)
  END;
```

If 1 doesn't exist in the table, the CASE expression returns 1; otherwise, it returns the result of a subquery returning the minimum missing value.

Here's the subquery that I used to return the minimum missing value:

```
SELECT MIN(A.keycol) + 1 as missing
FROM dbo.T1 AS A
WHERE NOT EXISTS
  (SELECT * FROM dbo.T1 AS B
   WHERE B.keycol = A.keycol + 1);
```

The NOT EXISTS predicate returns TRUE only for values in T1 that are right before a gap (4 and 7 in our case). A value is right before a gap if the value plus one does not exist in the same table. The outer T1 table has the alias A, and the inner T1 table has the alias B. You could use the expression *B.keycol – 1 = A.keycol* in the subquery's filter, although it might be a bit confusing to use such an expression when looking for a value in B that is greater than the value in A by one. If you think about it, for *B.keycol* to be greater than *A.keycol* by one, *B.keycol* minus one must be equal to *A.keycol*. If this logic confuses you, you can use *B.keycol = A.keycol + 1* instead, as I did. When all points before gaps are isolated, the outer query returns the minimum plus one, which is the first missing value in the first gap. Make a mental note of the technique to identify a point before a gap—it's a very handy fundamental technique.

Now you can incorporate the query returning the minimum missing value in the CASE expression:

```
SELECT
  CASE
    WHEN NOT EXISTS(SELECT * FROM dbo.T1 WHERE keycol = 1) THEN 1
    ELSE (SELECT MIN(A.keycol) + 1
          FROM dbo.T1 AS A
          WHERE NOT EXISTS
            (SELECT * FROM dbo.T1 AS B
             WHERE B.keycol = A.keycol + 1))
  END;
```

If you run this query with the sample data inserted by Listing 6-1, you should get 1 as the result. If you then insert two more rows, with the keys 1 and 2 (as shown in the following code), and rerun the query, you should get 5 as the result.

```
INSERT INTO dbo.T1(keycol, datacol) VALUES(1, 'e'),(2, 'f');
```

Here is an example of how you might use the CASE expression for the minimum missing key in an INSERT ... SELECT statement, perhaps in a scenario where you needed to reuse deleted keys:

```
INSERT INTO dbo.T1(keycol, datacol)
  SELECT
    CASE
      WHEN NOT EXISTS(SELECT * FROM dbo.T1 WHERE keycol = 1) THEN 1
      ELSE (SELECT MIN(A.keycol) + 1
            FROM dbo.T1 AS A
            WHERE NOT EXISTS
              (SELECT * FROM dbo.T1 AS B
               WHERE B.keycol = A.keycol + 1))
    END,
    'g';
```

Query the T1 table after running this INSERT:

```
SELECT * FROM dbo.T1;
```

Notice in the following output that the insert generated the key value 5, which was the minimum missing key:

```
keycol      datacol
----------- ----------
1           e
2           f
3           a
4           b
5           g
6           c
7           d
```

> **Note** Multiple processes running such code simultaneously might get the same key. You can overcome this issue by introducing error-handling code that traps a duplicate key error and then retries. There are other, more efficient techniques to reuse deleted keys, but they are more complex and require you to maintain a table with ranges of missing values. Also note that reusing deleted keys is not often a good idea, for reasons beyond concurrency. Here I just wanted to give you a chance to practice with the EXISTS predicate.

Note that you can merge the two cases where 1 does exist in the table and where 1 doesn't instead of using a CASE expression. The solution requires some tricky logical manipulation:

```
SELECT COALESCE(MIN(A.keycol) + 1, 1)
FROM dbo.T1 AS A
WHERE
  NOT EXISTS(
    SELECT * FROM dbo.T1 AS B
    WHERE B.keycol= A.keycol + 1)
  AND EXISTS(
    SELECT * FROM dbo.T1
    WHERE keycol = 1);
```

The query has both logical expressions from the CASE expression in the WHERE clause. It returns the minimum missing value if 1 does exist in the table (that is, when the second EXISTS predicate is TRUE). If 1 doesn't exist in the table (that is, the second EXISTS predicate is FALSE), the filter generates an empty set, and the expression *MIN(keycol) + 1* yields a NULL. The value of the COALESCE expression is then 1.

Even though this solution achieves the request with a single query, I personally like the original solution better. This solution is a bit tricky and isn't as intuitive as the previous one, and simplicity and readability of code goes a long way.

Reverse Logic Applied to Relational Division Problems   Our minds are usually accustomed to thinking in positive terms. However, positive thinking in some cases can get you only so far. In many fields, including SQL programming, negative thinking or reverse logic can give you new insight or be used as another tool to solve problems. Applying reverse logic can in some cases lead to simpler or more efficient solutions than applying a positive approach. It's another tool in your toolbox.

Euclid, for example, was very fond of applying reverse logic in his mathematical proofs (proof by way of negation). He used reverse logic to prove that there are infinitely many prime numbers. By contradicting a certain assumption and thereby creating a paradox, you prove that the assumption's opposite must be true.

Before I demonstrate an application of reverse logic in SQL, I'd like to deliver the idea through an ancient puzzle. Two guards stand in front of two doors. One door leads to gold and treasures, and the other leads to sudden death, but you don't know which is which. One of the guards always tells the truth and the other always lies, but you don't know which is the liar is and which is sincere (even though the guards do). Obviously, you want to enter the door that leads to the gold and not to sudden death. You have but one opportunity to ask one of the guards a question. What will the question be?

Any question that you ask applying positive thinking will not give you 100 percent assurance of picking the door that leads to the gold. However, applying reverse logic can give you that assurance.

Ask either guard, "If I ask the other guard where the door is that leads to the gold, which door would he point to?"

If you asked the sincere guard, he would point at the door that leads to sudden death, knowing that the other is a liar. If you asked the liar, he'd also point at the door that leads to sudden death, knowing that the other guard is sincere and would point to the door that leads to the gold. All you would have to do is enter the door that was not pointed at.

Reverse logic is sometimes a handy tool in solving problems with SQL. An example of where you can apply reverse logic is in solving relational division problems. At the beginning of the chapter, I discussed the following problem: from the InsideTSQL2008 database, return all customers with orders handled by all employees from the USA. The example I offered for solving the problem used positive thinking. To apply reverse logic, you first need to be able to phrase the request in a negative way. Instead of saying, "Return customers for whom all USA employees handled orders," you can say, "Return customers for whom no USA employee handled no order." Remember that two negatives produce a positive. If for customer A you cannot find even one USA employee who did not handle any orders, all USA employees must have handled orders for customer A.

When you phrase the request in a negative way, the translation to SQL is intuitive using correlated subqueries:

```
USE InsideTSQL2008;

SELECT custid FROM Sales.Customers AS C
WHERE NOT EXISTS
  (SELECT * FROM HR.Employees AS E
   WHERE country = N'USA'
     AND NOT EXISTS
       (SELECT * FROM Sales.Orders AS O
        WHERE O.custid = C.custid
          AND O.empid = E.empid));
```

When you "read" the query, it really sounds like the English phrasing of the request:

```
Return customers
for whom you cannot find
  any employee
  from the USA
  for whom you cannot find
    any order
    placed for the subject customer
    and by the subject employee
```

You get the same 23 customers back as those returned by the query applying the positive approach. Notice, though, that the negative solution gives you access to all the customer attributes, while the positive solution gives you access only to the customer IDs. To access other customer attributes, you need to add a join between the result set and the Customers table.

When comparing the performance of the solutions in this case, the solution applying the positive approach performs better. In other cases, the negative approach might yield better performance. You now have another tool that you can use when solving problems.

Another example where you can apply this kind of reverse logic is in a CHECK constraint that needs to ensure that a character string column (call it *sn* for serial number) allows only digits. Using positive logic, the constraint's predicate can ensure that all characters are digits like so:

```
CHECK (sn LIKE REPLICATE('[0-9]', LEN(sn)))
```

The expression replicates the string '[0-9]' representing a single character that must be a digit as many times as the number of characters in the column *sn*. This means that for a lengthy string in the *sn* column, the pattern will be quite long. A more economical way to express the same idea is to use reverse logic. Another way to say that all characters must be digits is to say that no character can be something that is not a digit. This translates to the following predicate in the constraint:

```
CHECK (sn NOT LIKE '%[^0-9]%')
```

This pattern is much more economical compared with the one that applies positive logic, especially when dealing with long *sn* values.

Note that both CHECK constraints provided here would allow an empty string as a serial number. If you do not want to allow empty strings, you need to add logic to the constraint.

Misbehaving Subqueries

I've occasionally seen a very tricky programming error involving subqueries, and I've even had the misfortune to introduce into production code myself. I'll first describe the bug and then make recommendations for how you can avoid it. To demonstrate the bug, I use a table called Sales.MyShippers that you create and populate in the InsideTSQL2008 database by running the following code:

```
IF OBJECT_ID('Sales.MyShippers', 'U') IS NOT NULL
  DROP TABLE Sales.MyShippers;

CREATE TABLE Sales.MyShippers
(
  shipper_id  INT         NOT NULL,
  companyname NVARCHAR(40) NOT NULL,
  phone       NVARCHAR(24) NOT NULL,
  CONSTRAINT PK_MyShippers PRIMARY KEY(shipper_id)
);
```

```
INSERT INTO Sales.MyShippers(shipper_id, companyname, phone)
  VALUES(1, N'Shipper GVSUA', N'(503) 555-0137'),
        (2, N'Shipper ETYNR', N'(425) 555-0136'),
        (3, N'Shipper ZHISN', N'(415) 555-0138');
```

Suppose that you are asked to return the shippers from the Sales.MyShippers table that did not ship orders (in the Sales.Orders table) to customer 43. Examining the data, shipper 1 (Shipper GVSUA) is the only one that qualifies. The following query is supposed to return the desired result:

```
SELECT shipper_id, companyname
FROM Sales.MyShippers
WHERE shipper_id NOT IN
  (SELECT shipper_id FROM Sales.Orders
   WHERE custid = 43);
```

Surprisingly, this query returns an empty set. Can you tell why? Can you identify the elusive bug in my code?

Well, apparently the column in the Orders table holding the shipper ID is called *shipperid* (no underscore) and not *shipper_id*. The Orders table has no *shipper_id* column. Realizing this, you'd probably expect the query to have failed because of the invalid column name. Sure enough, if you run only the part that was supposed to be a self-contained subquery, it does fail: *Invalid column name 'shipper_id'*. However, in the context of the outer query, apparently the subquery is valid! The name resolution process works from the inner nesting level outward. The query processor first looked for a *shipper_id* column in the Orders table, which is referenced in the current level. Not having found such a column name, it looked for one in the MyShippers table—the outer level—and found it. Unintentionally, the subquery became correlated, as if it were written as the following illustrative code:

```
SELECT shipper_id, companyname
FROM Sales.MyShippers AS S
WHERE shipper_id NOT IN
  (SELECT S.shipper_id FROM Sales.Orders AS O
   WHERE O.custid = 43);
```

Logically, the query doesn't make much sense, of course; nevertheless, it is technically valid.

You can now understand why you got an empty set back. Unless you have no order for customer 43 in the Orders table, shipper *some_val* is obviously always found in the set (*SELECT some_val FROM Sales.Orders WHERE custid = 43*). And the NOT IN predicate always yields FALSE. This buggy query logically became a nonexistence query equivalent to the following illustrative code:

```
SELECT shipper_id, companyname
FROM Sales.MyShippers
WHERE NOT EXISTS
  (SELECT * FROM Sales.Orders
   WHERE custid = 43);
```

To fix the problem, of course, you should use the correct name for the column from Orders that holds the shipper ID—*shippperid*:

```
SELECT shipper_id, companyname
FROM Sales.MyShippers AS S
WHERE shipper_id NOT IN
  (SELECT shipperid FROM Sales.Orders AS O
   WHERE custid = 43);
```

This generates the following expected result:

```
shipper_id  companyname
----------- ----------------------------------------
1           Shipper GVSUA
```

However, to avoid such bugs in the future, it's a good practice to always include the table name or alias for all attributes in a subquery, even when the subquery is self-contained. Had I aliased the *shipper_id* column in the subquery (as shown in the following code), a name resolution error would have been generated, and the bug would have been detected:

```
SELECT shipper_id, companyname
FROM Sales.MyShippers AS S
WHERE shipper_id NOT IN
  (SELECT O.shipper_id FROM Sales.Orders AS O
   WHERE O.custid = 43);
```

```
Msg 207, Level 16, State 1, Line 4
Invalid column name 'shipper_id'.
```

Finally, correcting the bug, here's how the solution query should look:

```
SELECT shipper_id, companyname
FROM Sales.MyShippers AS S
WHERE shipper_id NOT IN
  (SELECT O.shipperid FROM Sales.Orders AS O
   WHERE O.custid = 43);
```

When you're done, run the following code for cleanup:

```
IF OBJECT_ID('Sales.MyShippers', 'U') IS NOT NULL
  DROP TABLE Sales.MyShippers;
```

Uncommon Predicates

In addition to IN and EXISTS, SQL has three more predicates, but they are rarely used: ANY, SOME, and ALL. You can consider them to be generalizations of the IN predicate. (ANY and SOME are synonyms with no logical difference between them.)

An IN predicate is translated to a series of equality predicates separated by OR operators—for example, *v IN(x, y, z)* is translated to *v = x OR v = y OR v = z*. ANY (or SOME) allows you to specify the comparison you want in each predicate, not limiting you to the equality operator. For example, *v < ANY(x, y, z)* is translated to *v < x OR v < y OR v < z*.

ALL is similar, but it's translated to a series of logical expressions separated by AND operators. For example, *v <> ALL(x, y, z)* is translated to *v <> x AND v <> y AND v <> z*.

> **Note** IN allows as input either a list of literals or a subquery returning a single column. ANY/SOME and ALL support only a subquery as input. If you have the need to use these uncommon predicates with a list of literals as input, you must convert the list to a subquery. So, instead of *v <> ANY(x, y, z)*, you would use *v <> ANY(SELECT x UNION ALL SELECT y UNION ALL SELECT z)* or *v <> ANY(SELECT i FROM(VALUES(x),(y),(z)) AS D(i))*.

To demonstrate the use of these uncommon predicates, let's suppose you are asked to return, for each employee, the order with the minimum *orderid*. Here's how you can achieve this with the ANY operator:

```
SELECT orderid, custid, empid, orderdate
FROM Sales.Orders AS O1
WHERE NOT orderid >
  ANY(SELECT orderid
      FROM Sales.Orders AS O2
      WHERE O2.empid = O1.empid);
```

This query generates the following output:

```
orderid      custid       empid        orderdate
-----------  -----------  -----------  ------------------------
10248        85           5            2006-07-04 00:00:00.000
10249        79           6            2006-07-05 00:00:00.000
10250        34           4            2006-07-08 00:00:00.000
10251        84           3            2006-07-08 00:00:00.000
10255        68           9            2006-07-12 00:00:00.000
10258        20           1            2006-07-17 00:00:00.000
10262        65           8            2006-07-22 00:00:00.000
10265        7            2            2006-07-25 00:00:00.000
10289        11           7            2006-08-26 00:00:00.000
```

A row has the minimum *orderid* for an employee if it is not the case that *orderid* is less than or equal to some *orderid* for the same employee.

You can also write a query using ALL to achieve the same thing:

```
SELECT orderid, custid, empid, orderdate
FROM Sales.Orders AS O1
WHERE orderid <=
  ALL(SELECT orderid
      FROM Sales.Orders AS O2
      WHERE O2.empid = O1.empid);
```

A row has the minimum *orderid* for an employee if its *orderid* is less than or equal to all *orderid*s for the same employee.

None of the preceding solutions falls into the category of intuitive solutions, and maybe this explains why these predicates are not commonly used. The natural way to write the solution query would probably be as follows:

```
SELECT orderid, custid, empid, orderdate
FROM Sales.Orders AS O1
WHERE orderid =
  (SELECT MIN(orderid)
   FROM Sales.Orders AS O2
   WHERE O2.empid = O1.empid);
```

Table Expressions

So far, I've covered scalar and multivalued subqueries. This section deals with table subqueries, which are known as table expressions. In this chapter, I'll discuss derived tables and common table expressions (CTE).

> **More Info** For information about the two other types of table expressions—views and inline table-valued functions—please refer to *Inside Microsoft SQL Server 2008: T-SQL Programming* (Microsoft Press, 2009).

Derived Tables

A derived table is a table expression—that is, a virtual result table derived from a query expression. A derived table appears in the FROM clause of a query like any other table. The scope of existence of a derived table is the outer query's scope only.

The general form in which a derived table is used is as follows:

```
FROM (derived_table_query) AS derived_table_alias
```

> **Note** A derived table is completely virtual. It's not physically materialized, nor does the optimizer generate a separate plan for it. The outer query and the inner one are merged, and one plan is generated. You shouldn't have any special concerns regarding performance when using derived tables. Merely using derived tables neither degrades nor improves performance. Their use is more a matter of simplification and clarity of code.

A derived table must be a valid table; therefore, it must follow several rules:

- All columns must have names.
- The column names must be unique.
- ORDER BY is not allowed (unless TOP is also specified).

> **Note** Unlike scalar and multivalued subqueries, derived tables cannot be correlated; they must be self-contained. The exception to this rule occurs when using the APPLY operator, which I'll cover in Chapter 9.

Result Column Aliases

One use of derived tables is to enable the reuse of column aliases when expressions are so long you'd rather not repeat them. For simplicity's sake, I'll demonstrate column alias reuse with short expressions.

Remember from Chapter 1, "Logical Query Processing," that aliases created in the query's SELECT list cannot be used in most of the query elements. This is because the SELECT clause is logically processed almost last, just before the ORDER BY clause. For this reason, the following illustrative query fails:

```
SELECT
  YEAR(orderdate) AS orderyear,
  COUNT(DISTINCT custid) AS numcusts
FROM Sales.Orders
GROUP BY orderyear;
```

The GROUP BY clause is logically processed before the SELECT clause, so at the GROUP BY phase, the *orderyear* alias has not yet been created.

By using a derived table that contains only the SELECT and FROM elements of the original query, you can create aliases and make them available to the outer query in any element.

There are two formats of aliasing the derived table's result columns. One is inline column aliasing:

```
SELECT orderyear, COUNT(DISTINCT custid) AS numcusts
FROM (SELECT YEAR(orderdate) AS orderyear, custid
      FROM Sales.Orders) AS D
GROUP BY orderyear;
```

And the other is external column aliasing following the derived table's alias:

```
SELECT orderyear, COUNT(DISTINCT custid) AS numcusts
FROM (SELECT YEAR(orderdate), custid
      FROM Sales.Orders) AS D(orderyear, custid)
GROUP BY orderyear;
```

I typically use inline column aliasing because I find it more convenient to work with in most cases. You don't have to specify aliases for base columns, and it's more convenient to troubleshoot. When you highlight and run only the derived table query, the result set you get includes all result column names. Also, it's clear which column alias belongs to which expression.

The external column aliasing format lacks all the aforementioned benefits. One case where you may find it convenient to work with is when the query defining the table expression is pretty much a done deal in terms of development, and you want to focus your attention on the name of the table and its attributes.

Using Arguments

Even though a derived table query cannot be correlated (except with APPLY), it can refer to variables defined in the same batch. For example, the following code returns for each year the number of customers handled by employee 3:

```
DECLARE @empid AS INT = 3; -- use separate DECLARE and SET prior to 2008

SELECT orderyear, COUNT(DISTINCT custid) AS numcusts
FROM (SELECT YEAR(orderdate) AS orderyear, custid
      FROM Sales.Orders
      WHERE empid = @empid) AS D
GROUP BY orderyear;
```

 Note SQL Server 2008 introduces the ability to declare and initialize a variable in the same statement. Use separate DECLARE and SET statements prior to SQL Server 2008.

This code generates the following output:

```
orderyear   numcusts
----------- -----------
2006        16
2007        46
2008        30
```

Nesting

One aspect of working with derived tables that I find problematic is the fact that if you want to refer to one derived table in another, they must be nested. This is because the derived table is defined in the FROM clause of the outer query, as opposed to being defined before the outer query. Nesting is a problematic aspect of programming in general, as it tends to complicate the code and make it harder to follow. Logical processing in a case of nested derived tables starts at the innermost level and proceeds outward.

The following query returns the order year and the number of customers for years with more than 70 active customers:

```
SELECT orderyear, numcusts
FROM (SELECT orderyear, COUNT(DISTINCT custid) AS numcusts
      FROM (SELECT YEAR(orderdate) AS orderyear, custid
            FROM Sales.Orders) AS D1
      GROUP BY orderyear) AS D2
WHERE numcusts > 70;
```

This query generates the following output:

```
orderyear    numcusts
-----------  -----------
2007         86
2008         81
```

Although one reason for using table expressions is in an attempt to simplify your code by not repeating expressions, the nesting aspect of derived tables ends up complicating the code.

Multiple References

Out of all the types of table expressions available in T-SQL, derived tables are the only type to suffer from a certain limitation related to multiple references. Because a derived table is defined in the FROM clause of the outer query and not before it, you can't refer to the same derived table multiple times in the same query. For example, suppose you want to compare each year's number of active customers to the previous year's. You want to join two instances of a derived table that contains the yearly aggregates. In such a case, unfortunately, you have to create two derived tables, each repeating the same derived table query:

```sql
SELECT Cur.orderyear,
  Cur.numcusts AS curnumcusts, Prv.numcusts AS prvnumcusts,
  Cur.numcusts - Prv.numcusts AS growth
FROM (SELECT YEAR(orderdate) AS orderyear,
        COUNT(DISTINCT custid) AS numcusts
      FROM Sales.Orders
      GROUP BY YEAR(orderdate)) AS Cur
  LEFT OUTER JOIN
    (SELECT YEAR(orderdate) AS orderyear,
        COUNT(DISTINCT custid) AS numcusts
      FROM Sales.Orders
      GROUP BY YEAR(orderdate)) AS Prv
  ON Cur.orderyear = Prv.orderyear + 1;
```

This query generates the following output:

```
orderyear    curnumcusts prvnumcusts growth
-----------  ----------- ----------- -----------
2006         67          NULL        NULL
2007         86          67          19
2008         81          86          -5
```

Common Table Expressions

A common table expression (CTE) is another type of table expression supported by SQL Server. In many aspects, you will find CTEs very similar to derived tables. However, CTEs have several important advantages, which I'll describe in this section.

Remember that a derived table appears in its entirety in the FROM clause of an outer query. A CTE, however, is defined first using a WITH statement, and then an outer query referring to the CTE's name follows the CTE's definition:

```
WITH cte_name
AS
(
  cte_query
)
outer_query_referring_to_cte_name
```

> **Note** Because the WITH keyword is used in T-SQL for other purposes as well, to avoid ambiguity, the statement preceding the CTE's WITH clause must be terminated with a semicolon. The use of a semicolon to terminate statements is supported by ANSI. It's a good practice, and you should start getting used to it even where T-SQL currently doesn't require it.

A CTE's scope of existence is the outer query's scope. It's not visible to other statements in the same batch.

The same rules I mentioned for the validity of a derived table's query expression apply to the CTE's as well. That is, the query must generate a valid table, so all columns must have names, all column names must be unique, and ORDER BY is not allowed (unless TOP is also specified).

Next, I'll go over aspects of CTEs, demonstrating their syntax and capabilities, and compare them to derived tables.

Result Column Aliases

Just as you can with derived tables, you can provide aliases to result columns either inline in the CTE's query or externally in parentheses following the CTE's name. The following code illustrates the first method:

```
WITH C AS
(
  SELECT YEAR(orderdate) AS orderyear, custid
  FROM Sales.Orders
)
SELECT orderyear, COUNT(DISTINCT custid) AS numcusts
FROM C
GROUP BY orderyear;
```

The next bit of code illustrates how to provide aliases externally in parentheses following the CTE's name:

```
WITH C(orderyear, custid) AS
(
  SELECT YEAR(orderdate), custid
  FROM Sales.Orders
)
```

```
SELECT orderyear, COUNT(DISTINCT custid) AS numcusts
FROM C
GROUP BY orderyear;
```

Using Arguments

Another similarity between CTEs and derived tables is that CTEs can refer to variables declared in the same batch:

```
DECLARE @empid AS INT = 3;

WITH C AS
(
  SELECT YEAR(orderdate) AS orderyear, custid
  FROM Sales.Orders
  WHERE empid = @empid
)
SELECT orderyear, COUNT(DISTINCT custid) AS numcusts
FROM C
GROUP BY orderyear;
```

Multiple CTEs

Unlike derived tables, CTEs cannot be nested directly. That is, you cannot define a CTE within another CTE. However, you can define multiple CTEs using the same WITH statement, each of which can refer to the preceding CTEs. The outer query has access to all the CTEs. Using this capability, you can achieve the same result you would by nesting derived tables, but with CTEs the code won't be as complex as with derived tables—it will be much more modular. For example, the following WITH statement defines two CTEs:

```
WITH C1 AS
(
  SELECT YEAR(orderdate) AS orderyear, custid
  FROM Sales.Orders
),
C2 AS
(
  SELECT orderyear, COUNT(DISTINCT custid) AS numcusts
  FROM C1
  GROUP BY orderyear
)
SELECT orderyear, numcusts
FROM C2
WHERE numcusts > 70;
```

C1 returns order years and customer IDs for each order, generating the *orderyear* alias for the order year. C2 groups the rows returned from C1 by *orderyear* and calculates the count of distinct *custid*s (number of active customers). Finally, the outer query returns only order years with more than 70 active customers.

Multiple References

Besides the fact that CTEs are much more modular than derived tables, they have another advantage over derived tables—you can refer to the same CTE name multiple times in the outer query. You don't need to repeat the same CTE definition like you do with derived tables. For example, the following code demonstrates a CTE solution for the request to compare each year's number of active customers to the previous year's number:

```
WITH YearlyCount AS
(
  SELECT YEAR(orderdate) AS orderyear,
    COUNT(DISTINCT custid) AS numcusts
  FROM Sales.Orders
  GROUP BY YEAR(orderdate)
)
SELECT Cur.orderyear,
  Cur.numcusts AS curnumcusts, Prv.numcusts AS prvnumcusts,
  Cur.numcusts - Prv.numcusts AS growth
FROM YearlyCount AS Cur
  LEFT OUTER JOIN YearlyCount AS Prv
    ON Cur.orderyear = Prv.orderyear + 1;
```

You can see that the outer query refers to the *YearlyCount* CTE twice—once representing the current year (*Cur*) and once representing the previous year (*Prv*).

Note that like derived tables, CTEs are virtual; SQL Server internally rearranges the query so that the underlying objects are accessed directly. The plan that you get for this query is the same as the one you get when using derived tables. Both references to the CTE name will be expanded, meaning that the base table will be accessed twice and aggregated twice. With a large number of rows in the underlying table, you may want to consider using temporary tables or table variables, especially in a case where the result set of the query is so small (a row per year). With a temporary table the base table will be scanned once, and the data will be aggregated once. The join will then take place between two instances of the small temporary table.

Modifying Data

You can modify data through CTEs. To demonstrate this capability, first run the code in Listing 6-2 to create and populate the Sales.CustomersDups table with sample data.

LISTING 6-2 Creating and populating the CustomersDups table

```
IF OBJECT_ID('Sales.CustomersDups') IS NOT NULL
  DROP TABLE Sales.CustomersDups;
GO

SELECT
  custid, companyname, contactname, contacttitle, address,
  city, region, postalcode, country, phone, fax
INTO Sales.CustomersDups
FROM Sales.Customers CROSS JOIN (VALUES(1),(2),(3)) AS Nums(n);
```

The code in Listing 6-2 creates a table of customers with duplicate occurrences of each customer. The following code demonstrates how you can remove duplicate customers using a CTE:

```
WITH CustsDupsRN AS
(
  SELECT *,
    ROW_NUMBER() OVER(PARTITION BY custid ORDER BY (SELECT 0)) AS rn
  FROM Sales.CustomersDups
)
DELETE FROM CustsDupsRN
WHERE rn > 1;
```

The CTE *CustsDupsRN* assigns row numbers (*rn* column) to number the duplicate rows for each customer. I'll provide more details about the ROW_NUMBER function later in the chapter; for now it suffices to say that the duplicate rows for each customer are assigned row numbers beginning with the number 1. The DELETE statement then simply deletes all rows where *rn* is greater than 1. After this code is run, the CustomersDups table contains only unique rows. At this point, you can create a primary key or a unique constraint on the *custid* column to avoid duplicates in the future.

Note that SQL Server also supports modifying data through derived tables. I have to say, though, that I find the syntax to be unintuitive. You need to define the derived table and alias it in a FROM clause, and direct the modification against the derived table alias in a separate clause. For example, the following code uses a derived table to handle the task of deleting duplicates:

```
DELETE FROM CustsDupsRN
FROM ( SELECT *,
         ROW_NUMBER() OVER(PARTITION BY custid ORDER BY (SELECT 0)) AS rn
       FROM Sales.CustomersDups ) AS CustsDupsRN
WHERE rn > 1;
```

CTEs in View and Inline Function Definitions

CTEs can be used in container objects such as views and inline UDFs. Views and inline UDFs provide encapsulation, which is important for modular programming. Also, I mentioned earlier that CTEs cannot be nested directly. However, you can nest CTEs indirectly by encapsulating a CTE in a container object and querying the container object from an outer CTE.

Using CTEs in views or inline UDFs is very trivial. The following example creates a view returning a yearly count of customers:

```
IF OBJECT_ID('dbo.YearCustCount') IS NOT NULL
  DROP VIEW dbo.YearCustCount;
GO
CREATE VIEW dbo.YearCustCount
AS
WITH CYearCustCount AS
(
  SELECT YEAR(orderdate) AS orderyear,
    COUNT(DISTINCT custid) AS numcusts
```

```
  FROM Sales.Orders
  GROUP BY YEAR(orderdate)
)
SELECT * FROM CYearCustCount;
GO
```

Note that in this particular case the CTE is superfluous, and you could define the view based on the underlying query directly. The purpose of this example is only to demonstrate the syntax.

Query the view, as shown in the following code:

```
SELECT * FROM dbo.YearCustCount;
```

You get the following output:

```
orderyear   numcusts
----------- -----------
2006        67
2007        86
2008        81
```

If you want to pass an input argument to the container object—for example, return the yearly count of customers for the given employee—you'd create an inline UDF as follows:

```
IF OBJECT_ID('dbo.EmpYearCustCnt') IS NOT NULL
  DROP FUNCTION dbo.EmpYearCustCnt;
GO
CREATE FUNCTION dbo.EmpYearCustCnt(@empid AS INT) RETURNS TABLE
AS
RETURN
  WITH CEmpYearCustCnt AS
  (
    SELECT YEAR(orderdate) AS orderyear,
      COUNT(DISTINCT custid) AS numcusts
    FROM Sales.Orders
    WHERE empid = @empid
    GROUP BY YEAR(orderdate)
  )
  SELECT * FROM CEmpYearCustCnt;
GO
```

Query the UDF providing employee ID 3 as input:

```
SELECT * FROM dbo.EmpYearCustCnt(3) AS T;
```

You get the following output:

```
orderyear   numcusts
----------- -----------
2006        67
2007        86
2008        81
```

Recursive CTEs

SQL Server supports recursive querying capabilities through CTEs. The types of tasks and activities that can benefit from recursive queries include manipulation of graphs, trees, hierarchies, and many others. Here I'll just introduce you to recursive CTEs. For more information and detailed applications, you can find extensive coverage in Chapter 12, "Graphs, Trees, Hierarchies, and Recursive Queries."

I'll describe a recursive CTE using an example. You're given an input *empid* (for example, employee 5) from the HR.Employees table in the InsideTSQL2008 database. You're supposed to return the input employee and subordinate employees in all levels, based on the hierarchical relationships maintained by the *empid* and *mgrid* attributes. The attributes you need to return for each employee include *empid*, *mgrid*, *firstname*, and *lastname*.

Before I demonstrate and explain the recursive CTE's code, I'll create the following covering index, which is optimal for the task:

```
CREATE UNIQUE INDEX idx_mgr_emp_i_fname_lname
  ON HR.Employees(mgrid, empid)
    INCLUDE(firstname, lastname);
```

This index will allow fetching direct subordinates of each manager by using a single seek plus a partial scan. Note the included columns (*firstname* and *lastname*) that were added for coverage purposes.

Here's the recursive CTE code that will return the desired result:

```
WITH Emps AS
(
  SELECT empid, mgrid, firstname, lastname
  FROM HR.Employees
  WHERE empid = 5

  UNION ALL

  SELECT Emp.empid, Emp.mgrid, Emp.firstname, Emp.lastname
  FROM Emps AS Mgr
    JOIN HR.Employees AS Emp
      ON Emp.mgrid = Mgr.empid
)
SELECT * FROM Emps;
```

This code generates the following output:

```
empid        mgrid        firstname  lastname
-----------  -----------  ---------- --------------------
5            2            Sven       Buck
6            5            Paul       Suurs
7            5            Russell    King
9            5            Zoya       Dolgopyatova
```

A recursive CTE contains a minimum of two queries (also known as *members*). The first query that appears in the preceding CTE's body is known as the *anchor member*. The anchor member is merely a query that returns a valid table and is used as the basis or anchor for the recursion. In our case, the anchor member simply returns the row for the input root employee (employee 5). The second query that appears in the preceding CTE's body is known as the *recursive member*. What makes the query a recursive member is a recursive reference to the CTE's name—Emps. Note that this reference is not the same as the reference to the CTE's name in the outer query. The reference in the outer query gets the final result table returned by the CTE, and it involves no recursion. However, the inner reference is made before the CTE's result table is finalized, and it is the key element that triggers the recursion. This inner reference to the CTE's name stands for "the previous result set," loosely speaking. In the first invocation of the recursive member, the reference to the CTE's name represents the result set returned from the anchor member. In our case, the recursive member returns subordinates of the employees returned in the previous result set—in other words, the next level of employees.

The recursion has no explicit termination check; instead, recursion stops as soon as the recursive member returns an empty set. Because the first invocation of the recursive member yielded a nonempty set (employees 6, 7, and 9), it is invoked again. The second time the recursive member is invoked, the reference to the CTE's name represents the result set returned by the previous invocation of the recursive member (employees 6, 7, and 9). Because these employees have no subordinates, the second invocation of the recursive member yields an empty set, and recursion stops.

The reference to the CTE's name in the outer query stands for the unified (concatenated) results sets of the invocation of the anchor member and all the invocations of the recursive member.

If you run the same code providing employee 2 as input instead of employee 5, you get the following result:

```
empid       mgrid       firstname  lastname
----------- ----------- ---------- --------------------
2           1           Don        Funk
3           2           Judy       Lew
5           2           Sven       Buck
6           5           Paul       Suurs
7           5           Russell    King
9           5           Zoya       Dolgopyatova
4           3           Yael       Peled
8           3           Maria      Cameron
```

Here, the anchor member returns the row for employee 2. The first invocation of the recursive member returns direct subordinates of employee 2: employees 3 and 5. The second invocation of the recursive member returns direct subordinates of employees 3 and 5: employees 4, 8, 6, 7, and 9. The third invocation of the recursive member returns an empty set, and recursion stops. The outer query returns the unified result sets with the rows for employees: 2, 3, 5, 4, 8, 6, 7, and 9.

If you suspect that your data might accidentally contain cycles or that you might have a logical bug in your code, you can specify the MAXRECURSION hint as a safety measure to limit the number of invocations of the recursive member. You specify the hint right after the outer query:

```
WITH cte_name AS (cte_body) outer_query OPTION(MAXRECURSION n);
```

In this line of code, *n* is the limit for the number of recursive iterations. As soon as the limit is exceeded, the query breaks, and an error is generated. Note that MAXRECURSION is set to 100 by default. If you want to remove this limit, specify MAXRECURSION 0. This setting can be specified at the query level only; you can't set a session, database, or server-level option to change the default.

To understand how SQL Server processes the recursive CTE, examine the execution plan in Figure 6-4, which was produced for the earlier query returning subordinates of employee 5.

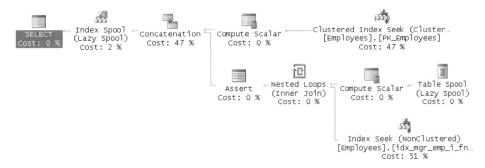

FIGURE 6-4 Execution plan for recursive CTE

As you can see in the plan, the result set of the anchor member (the row for employee 5) is retrieved using a clustered index seek operation (on the *empid* column). The Compute Scalar operator calculates an iteration counter, which is set to 0 initially (at the first occurrence of Compute Scalar in the plan) and incremented by one with each iteration of the recursive member (the second occurrence of Compute Scalar in the plan).

The anchor query is executed, and its result set is spooled (Table Spool operator in the plan). Then the recursive query is executed (using the spooled results for the recursive reference to the CTE). Any results are spooled and the recursive query is executed again using the newly spooled results for the recursive reference (and so on).

You'll also notice later in the plan that a temporary index is created (indicated by the Index Spool operator). The index is created on the iteration counter plus the attributes retrieved (*empid, mgrid, firstname, lastname*).

The interim set of each invocation of the recursive member is retrieved using index seek operations in the covering index I created for the query. The Nested Loops operator invokes a seek for each manager returned and spooled in the previous level to fetch its direct subordinates.

The *Assert* operator checks whether the iteration counter exceeds 100 (the default MAXRECURSION limit). This is the operator in charge of breaking the query in case the number of recursive member invocations exceeds the MAXRECURSION limit.

The Concatenation operator concatenates (unifies) all interim result sets.

When you're done testing and experimenting with the recursive CTE, drop the index created for this purpose:

```
DROP INDEX HR.Employees.idx_mgr_emp_i_fname_lname;
```

Analytical Ranking Functions

SQL Server supports four analytical ranking functions: ROW_NUMBER, RANK, DENSE_RANK, and NTILE. These functions provide a simple and highly efficient way to produce ranking calculations. I will also demonstrate alternative solutions to producing ranking values without the built-in ranking functions. Of course, you can feel free to skip the coverage of the alternative solutions, but I'd recommend spending the time to learn those for several reasons. A lot of existing legacy code out there in production systems makes use of those techniques. Also, some of those techniques are quite convoluted, and some have poor performance, so by being familiar with them you gain a greater appreciation for the simplicity and efficiency of the built-in functions. Also, trying to solve these problems without using the built-in ranking functions provides good exercise in querying logic. And finally, you may find the techniques used in those solutions handy for solving other types of querying problems.

ROW_NUMBER is by far my favorite feature in SQL Server. Even though it might not seem that significant on the surface compared to other features, it has an amazing number of practical applications that extend far beyond classic ranking and scoring calculations. I have been able to optimize many solutions by using the ROW_NUMBER function, as I will demonstrate throughout the book.

Even though the other ranking functions are technically calculated similarly to ROW_NUMBER underneath the covers, they have fewer practical applications.

I'll first describe the ROW_NUMBER function and alternative techniques to calculate row numbers. I'll present a benchmark I did comparing the performance of the different techniques. I'll then cover the other ranking calculations.

In my examples, I'll use a Sales table, which you should create and populate by running the following code:

```
SET NOCOUNT ON;
USE tempdb;
GO
IF OBJECT_ID('dbo.Sales') IS NOT NULL
  DROP TABLE dbo.Sales;
GO
```

```
CREATE TABLE dbo.Sales
(
  empid VARCHAR(10) NOT NULL PRIMARY KEY,
  mgrid VARCHAR(10) NOT NULL,
  qty   INT         NOT NULL
);

INSERT INTO dbo.Sales(empid, mgrid, qty) VALUES
  ('A', 'Z', 300),
  ('B', 'X', 100),
  ('C', 'X', 200),
  ('D', 'Y', 200),
  ('E', 'Z', 250),
  ('F', 'Z', 300),
  ('G', 'X', 100),
  ('H', 'Y', 150),
  ('I', 'X', 250),
  ('J', 'Z', 100),
  ('K', 'Y', 200);

CREATE INDEX idx_qty_empid ON dbo.Sales(qty, empid);
CREATE INDEX idx_mgrid_qty_empid ON dbo.Sales(mgrid, qty, empid);
```

Ranking functions can appear only in the SELECT and ORDER BY clauses of a query. The general form of a ranking function is as follows:

```
ranking_function OVER([PARTITION BY col_list] ORDER BY col_list)
```

Ranking functions are calculated in the context of a window of rows that is defined by an OVER clause—hence, these functions are known as window functions. This clause is not specific to ranking calculations—it is applicable to other types of calculations that are based on a window definition as well, such as aggregates. The concept that the OVER clause represents is profound, and in my eyes this clause is the single most powerful feature in the standard SQL language. First, it enables expressions to break the traditional boundaries of being restricted to the "current row" and allows them access to a whole window of rows. Second, it allows the defining of logical ordering in the window for the purposes of the calculation without breaking any aspects of sets. That is, while a set has no order, an operation or calculation on the set can be defined based on logical ordering. The sources for the operation, as well as the result, are still valid sets with no guaranteed order. This is the part that I find most profound—it bridges the gap between cursors and sets. This gap represents one of the toughest problems for database developers—to stop thinking in terms of individual rows and in certain order and start thinking in terms of sets as a whole and in no order.

The optional PARTITION BY clause allows you to request that the ranking values will be calculated for each partition (or group) of rows separately. For example, if you specify *mgrid* in the PARTITION BY clause, the ranking values will be calculated independently for each manager's rows. In the ORDER BY clause you define the logical order for the calculation—that is, the logical order of assignment of the ranking values.

The optimal index for ranking calculations (regardless of the method you use) is one created on *partitioning_columns, sort_columns,* and (as included columns, not key columns) *covered_columns.* I created optimal indexes on the Sales table for several ranking calculation requests.

Row Number

Row numbers are sequential integers assigned to rows of a query's result set based on a specified logical ordering. In the following sections, I'll describe the tools and techniques to calculate row numbers.

The ROW_NUMBER Function

The ROW_NUMBER function assigns sequential integers to rows of a query's result set based on a specified order, optionally within partitions. For example, the following query returns employee sales rows and assigns row numbers in order of *qty*:

```
SELECT empid, qty,
  ROW_NUMBER() OVER(ORDER BY qty) AS rownum
FROM dbo.Sales
ORDER BY qty;
```

This code returns the output shown in Table 6-1.

TABLE 6-1 Row Numbers Based on *qty* Ordering

empid	qty	rownum
B	100	1
G	100	2
J	100	3
H	150	4
C	200	5
D	200	6
K	200	7
E	250	8
I	250	9
A	300	10
F	300	11

To understand the efficiency of the ranking functions, examine the execution plan shown in Figure 6-5, which was generated for this query.

FIGURE 6-5 Execution plan for ROW_NUMBER

To calculate ranking values, the optimizer needs the data to be sorted first on the partitioning column or columns and then on the ordering column or columns.

If you have an index that already maintains the data in the required order, the leaf level of the index is simply scanned in an ordered fashion (as in our case). Otherwise, the data will be scanned and then sorted with a sort operator. The Sequence Project operator is the operator in charge of calculating the ranking values. For each input row, it needs two flags:

1. Is the row the first in the partition? If it is, the Sequence Project operator will reset the ranking value.

2. Is the sorting value in this row different from the previous one? If it is, the Sequence Project operator will increment the ranking value as dictated by the specific ranking function.

For all ranking functions, a Segment operator produces the first flag value.

The Segment operator basically determines grouping boundaries. It keeps one row in memory and compares it with the next. If they are different, it emits one value. If they are the same, it emits a different value.

To generate the first flag, which indicates whether the row is the first in the partition, the Segment operator compares the PARTITON BY column values of the current and previous rows. Obviously, it emits "true" for the first row read. From the second row on, its output depends on whether the PARTITION BY column value changed. In our example, I didn't specify a PARTITION BY clause, so the whole table is treated as one partition. In this case, Segment will emit "true" for the first row and "false" for all others.

For the second flag ("Is the value different than the previous value?"), the operator that will calculate it depends on which ranking function you requested. For ROW_NUMBER, the ranking value must be incremented for each row regardless of whether the sort value changes. So in our case, we don't need an additional operator. In other cases (for example, with the RANK and DENSE_RANK functions), another Segment operator is used to tell the Sequence Project operator whether the sort value changed to determine whether to increment the ranking value.

The brilliance of this plan and the techniques the optimizer uses to calculate ranking values might not be apparent yet. For now, suffice to say that the data is scanned only once, and if it's not already sorted within an index, it is also sorted. This is much faster than any other technique to calculate ranking values, as I will demonstrate in detail shortly.

Determinism   As you probably noticed in the output of the previous query, row numbers keep incrementing regardless of whether the sort value changes. Row numbers must be unique within the partition. This means that for a nonunique ORDER BY list, the query is nondeterministic. That is, different result sets are correct, not just one. For example, in Table 6-1 you can see that employees B, G, and J, all having a quantity of 100, got the row numbers 1, 2, and 3, respectively. However, the result would also be valid if these three employees received the row numbers 1, 2, and 3 in a different order.

For some applications determinism is mandatory. To guarantee determinism, you simply need to add a tiebreaker that makes the values of *partitioning column(s) + ordering column(s)* unique.

For example, the following query demonstrates both a nondeterministic row number based on the *qty* column alone and also a deterministic one based on the order of *qty, empid*:

```
SELECT empid, qty,
  ROW_NUMBER() OVER(ORDER BY qty)        AS nd_rownum,
  ROW_NUMBER() OVER(ORDER BY qty, empid) AS d_rownum
FROM dbo.Sales
ORDER BY qty, empid;
```

This query generates the following output:

empid	qty	nd_rownum	d_rownum
B	100	1	1
G	100	2	2
J	100	3	3
H	150	4	4
C	200	5	5
D	200	6	6
K	200	7	7
E	250	8	8
I	250	9	9
A	300	10	10
F	300	11	11

> **Tip** The ORDER BY clause is mandatory in ranking functions. Sometimes, though, you may need to apply a ranking calculation in no particular order and would like to avoid the cost associated with scanning an index in order or sorting the data. Unfortunately, you cannot specify ORDER BY <const>. However, apparently SQL Server does allow specifying ORDER BY (SELECT <const>)—for example, ROW_NUMBER() OVER(ORDER BY (SELECT 0)). The optimizer is smart enough in this case to realize that order doesn't matter. As an alternative, you can also order by a previously declared variable: OVER(ORDER BY @v). Here as well, the optimizer recognizes that order doesn't matter.

Partitioning   As I mentioned earlier, you can also calculate ranking values within partitions (groups of rows). The following example calculates row numbers based on the order of *qty* and *empid* for each manager separately:

```
SELECT mgrid, empid, qty,
  ROW_NUMBER() OVER(PARTITION BY mgrid ORDER BY qty, empid) AS rownum
FROM dbo.Sales
ORDER BY mgrid, qty, empid;
```

This query generates the following output:

mgrid	empid	qty	rownum
X	B	100	1
X	G	100	2
X	C	200	3
X	I	250	4

Y	H	150	1
Y	D	200	2
Y	K	200	3
Z	J	100	1
Z	E	250	2
Z	A	300	3
Z	F	300	4

Using Subqueries to Calculate Row Numbers

Several alternative techniques for calculating ranking values without ranking functions are available, and all of them suffer from some limitation. Keep in mind that you can also calculate ranking values at the client. Whatever way you choose, your client will iterate through the records in the record set returned from SQL Server. The client can simply request the rows sorted and, in a loop, increment a counter. Of course, if you need the ranking values for further server-side manipulation before results are sent to the client, client-side ranking is not an option.

I'll start with a technique that is based on subqueries. Unfortunately, it is usually the slowest of all.

Unique Sort Column   Calculating row numbers using a subquery is reasonably simple, given a unique *partitioning + sort column(s)* combination. As I will describe later, solutions without this unique combination also exist, but they are substantially more complex.

All ranking value calculations can be achieved by counting rows. To calculate row numbers, you can employ the following fundamental technique. You simply use a subquery to count the number of rows with a smaller or equal sort value. This count corresponds to the desired row number. For example, the following query produces row numbers based on *empid* ordering:

```
SELECT empid,
  (SELECT COUNT(*)
   FROM dbo.Sales AS S2
   WHERE S2.empid <= S1.empid) AS rownum
FROM dbo.Sales AS S1
ORDER BY empid;
```

This query generates the following output:

```
empid      rownum
---------- -----------
A          1
B          2
C          3
D          4
E          5
F          6
G          7
H          8
I          9
J          10
K          11
```

> **Note** The solutions presented in this chapter for calculating ranking values using subqueries assume that the columns involved are defined as NOT NULL, as is the case with the Sales table used in my examples. Note that in cases where the columns allow NULLs, the solutions based on subqueries won't return the same results as the built-in ranking functions. For ordering purposes ranking functions will consider NULL to be ranked first (lowest). If you count lower-ranking rows with the predicate S2.ranking_column < S1.ranking_column, you'll miss the NULLs. In a similar manner you will find differences between the way ranking functions and subqueries treat NULLs for partitioning and for other purposes as well. Of course, when NULLs can appear in the data, you can add logic to your solutions so that the treatment of NULLs will be the same as with the ranking functions if that's what you need.

This technique to calculate row numbers, though fairly simple, is extremely slow. To understand why, examine the execution plan shown in Figure 6-6 created for the query.

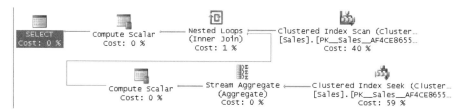

FIGURE 6-6 Execution plan for query calculating row numbers using a subquery

An index on the sort column (*empid*) happens to be the Sales table's clustered index. The table is first fully scanned (as indicated by the Clustered Index Scan operator) to return all rows. For each row returned from the initial full scan, the Nested Loops operator invokes the activity that generates the row number by counting rows. Each row number calculation involves a seek operation within the clustered index, followed by a partial scan operation (from the head of the leaf level's linked list to the last point where *S2.empid* is smaller than or equal to *S1.empid*).

Note that two different operators use the clustered index—first, a full scan to return all rows; second, a seek followed by a partial scan for each outer row to achieve the count.

Remember that the primary factor affecting the performance of queries that do data manipulation is usually I/O. An estimate of the number of rows accessed here will show how inefficient this execution plan is. To calculate *rownum* for the first row of the table, SQL Server needs to scan 1 row in the index. For the second row, it needs to scan 2 rows. For the third row, it needs to scan 3 rows, and so on, and for the *n*th row of the table, it needs to scan *n* rows. For a table with *n* rows, having an index based on the sort column in place, the total number of rows scanned (besides the initial scan of the data) is $1 + 2 + 3 + \ldots + n$. You may not grasp immediately the large number of rows that are going to be scanned. To give you a sense, for a table with 100,000 rows, you're looking at 100,000 + 5,000,050,000 rows that are going to be scanned in total.

As an aside, a story is told about the mathematician Gauss. When he was a child, he and his classmates got an assignment from their teacher to find the sum of all the integers from 1 through 100. Gauss gave the answer almost instantly. When the teacher asked him how he came up with the answer so fast, he said that he added the first and the last values (1 + 100 = 101) and then multiplied that total by half the number of integers (50), which is the number of pairs. Sure enough, the result of *first_val* + *last_val* is equal to the *second_val* + *next_to_last val* and so on. In short, the formula for the sum of the first *n* positive integers is $(n + n^2) / 2$. That's the number of rows that need to be scanned in total to calculate row numbers using this technique when an index is based on the sort column. You're looking at an n^2 graph of I/O cost and run time based on the number of rows in the table. You can play with the numbers in the formula and see that the cost gets humongous pretty quickly.

If you think about it, this technique calculates a running count aggregate, which happens to also have a special meaning for us—a row number. You can use the same technique to calculate other running aggregates, like running totals and running averages, by simply using other aggregate functions operating on the applicable attribute. Therefore, using this technique to calculate running aggregates has n^2 complexity. Unfortunately, unlike in the row number's case—for which we have a much faster built-in function—SQL Server 2008 doesn't support certain elements of the standard OVER clause that would allow faster calculation of running aggregates.

Nonunique Sort Column and Tiebreaker   When the sort column is not unique, you can make it unique by introducing a tiebreaker to allow a solution that keeps a reasonable level of simplicity. Let *sortcol* be the sort column and let *tiebreaker* be the tiebreaker column. To count rows with the same or smaller values of the sort list (*sortcol, tiebreaker*), use the following expression in the subquery:

```
inner_sortcol < outer_sortcol
OR ( inner_sortcol = outer_sortcol
     AND inner_tiebreaker <= outer_tiebreaker )
```

Note that operator precedence dictates that AND will be evaluated prior to OR, so if you omit the parentheses here, you get a logically equivalent expression. But I recommend using parentheses for clarity, manageability, and readability.

The following query produces row numbers based on *qty* and *empid* ordering:

```
SELECT empid, qty,
  (SELECT COUNT(*)
   FROM dbo.Sales AS S2
   WHERE S2.qty < S1.qty
      OR (S2.qty = S1.qty AND S2.empid <= S1.empid)) AS rownum
FROM dbo.Sales AS S1
ORDER BY qty, empid;
```

This query generates the following output:

```
empid       qty           rownum
----------  ------------  -----------
B           100           1
G           100           2
J           100           3
H           150           4
C           200           5
D           200           6
K           200           7
E           250           8
I           250           9
A           300           10
F           300           11
```

Nonunique Sort Column Without a Tiebreaker   The problem becomes substantially more complex when you want to calculate row numbers with subqueries according to a nonunique sort column and using no tiebreaker. This is an excellent challenge if you want to test your T-SQL querying skills. For example, given the table T2, which you create and populate by running the following code, let's say you are supposed to produce row numbers based on *col1* ordering:

```
IF OBJECT_ID('dbo.T2') IS NOT NULL
  DROP TABLE dbo.T2;
GO
CREATE TABLE dbo.T2(col1 VARCHAR(5));
INSERT INTO dbo.T2(col1) VALUES
  ('A'),('A'),('A'),('B'),('B'),('C'),('C'),('C'),('C'),('C');
```

In the solution for this problem, I'll make first use of a very important fundamental technique—generating copies of rows using an auxiliary table of numbers.

I'll explain the concept of the auxiliary table of numbers and how to create one later in the chapter in the section "Auxiliary Table of Numbers." For now, simply run the code from that section in Listing 6-3, which creates the Nums table and populates it with the 1,000,000 integers in the range $1 \le n \le 1,000,000$.

As mentioned, in the solution to our challenge I'm going to use a fundamental technique to generate copies of rows. For example, given a table T2, say you want to generate five copies of each row. To achieve this, you can use the Nums table as follows:

```
SELECT ... FROM dbo.T2 CROSS JOIN dbo.Nums WHERE n <= 5;
```

I will provide more details on the technique to generate copies and its uses in Chapter 7.

Going back to our original problem, you're supposed to generate row numbers for the rows of T2, based on *col1* order. The first step in the solution is "collapsing" the rows by grouping them by *col1*. For each group, you return the number of occurrences (a count of rows in the group). You also return, using a subquery, the number of rows in the base table that have a smaller sort value. Here's the query that accomplishes the first step:

```
SELECT col1, COUNT(*) AS cnt,
  (SELECT COUNT(*) FROM dbo.T2 AS B
   WHERE B.col1 < A.col1) AS smaller
FROM dbo.T2 AS A
GROUP BY col1;
```

This query returns the following output:

```
col1  cnt         smaller
-----  -----------  -----------
A      3            0
B      2            3
C      5            5
```

For example, A appears three times, and 0 rows have a *col1* value smaller than A. B appears two times, and three rows have a *col1* value smaller than B. And so on.

The next step is to expand the number of rows or create sequentially numbered copies of each row. You achieve this by creating a table expression out of the previous query and joining it to the Nums table as follows, based on *n <= cnt*:

```
WITH C AS
(
  SELECT col1, COUNT(*) AS cnt,
    (SELECT COUNT(*) FROM dbo.T2 AS B
     WHERE B.col1 < A.col1) AS smaller
  FROM dbo.T2 AS A
  GROUP BY col1
)
SELECT col1, cnt, smaller, n
FROM C CROSS JOIN Nums
WHERE n <= cnt;
```

This query generates the following output:

```
col1  dups        smaller     n
-----  -----------  -----------  -----------
A      3            0            1
A      3            0            2
A      3            0            3
B      2            3            1
B      2            3            2
C      5            5            1
C      5            5            2
C      5            5            3
C      5            5            4
C      5            5            5
```

Now look carefully at the output and see whether you can figure out how to produce the row numbers.

The row number can be expressed as the number of rows with a smaller sort value, plus the row number within the same sort value group—in other words, *n + smaller*. The following query is the final solution:

```
WITH C AS
(
  SELECT col1, COUNT(*) AS cnt,
    (SELECT COUNT(*) FROM dbo.T2 AS B
     WHERE B.col1 < A.col1) AS smaller
  FROM dbo.T2 AS A
  GROUP BY col1
)
SELECT n + smaller AS rownum, col1
FROM C
  CROSS JOIN Nums
WHERE n <= cnt;
```

This query generates the following output:

```
rownum       col1
-----------  -----
4            B
5            B
6            C
7            C
8            C
9            C
10           C
1            A
2            A
3            A
```

Note that this technique won't generalize in the case T2 has additional columns. This is yet another example of how powerful the ranking functions are.

Partitioning Partitioning is achieved by simply adding a correlation in the subquery based on a match between the partitioning column or columns in the inner and outer tables. For example, the following query against the Sales table calculates row numbers that are partitioned by *mgrid*, ordered by *qty*, and use *empid* as a tiebreaker:

```
SELECT mgrid, empid, qty,
  (SELECT COUNT(*)
   FROM dbo.Sales AS S2
   WHERE S2.mgrid = S1.mgrid
     AND (S2.qty < S1.qty
          OR (S2.qty = S1.qty AND S2.empid <= S1.empid))) AS rownum
FROM dbo.Sales AS S1
ORDER BY mgrid, qty, empid;
```

This query generates the following output:

mgrid	empid	qty	rownum
X	B	100	1
X	G	100	2
X	C	200	3
X	I	250	4
Y	H	150	1
Y	D	200	2
Y	K	200	3
Z	J	100	1
Z	E	250	2
Z	A	300	3
Z	F	300	4

> **Note** As I mentioned earlier, the technique using subqueries to calculate row numbers has n^2 complexity. However, for a fairly small number of rows (in the area of dozens), it's pretty fast. The performance problem has more to do with the partition size than with the table's size. If you create the recommended index based on *partitioning_cols, sort_cols, tiebreaker_cols*, the number of rows scanned within the index is equivalent to the row number generated. The row number is reset (starts from 1) with every new partition. So even for very large tables, when the partition size is fairly small and you have a proper index in place, the solution is pretty fast. If you have *p* partitions and *r* rows in each partition, the number of rows scanned in total is $p * r + p * (r + r^2) / 2$. For example, if you have 100,000 partitions and 10 rows in each partition, you get 6,500,000 rows scanned in total. Though this number might seem large, it's nowhere near the number you get without partitioning. And as long as the partition size remains constant, the graph of query cost compared with the number of rows in the table is linear.

Cursor-Based Solution

You can use a cursor to calculate row numbers. A cursor-based solution for any of the aforementioned variations is pretty straightforward. You create a fast-forward (read-only, forward-only) cursor based on a query that orders the data by *partitioning_cols, sort_cols, tiebreaker_cols*. As you fetch rows from the cursor, you simply increment a counter, resetting it every time a new partition is detected. You can store the result rows along with the row numbers in a temporary table or a table variable.

For example, the following code uses a cursor to calculate row numbers based on the order of *qty* and *empid*:

```
DECLARE @SalesRN TABLE(empid VARCHAR(5), qty INT, rn INT);
DECLARE @empid AS VARCHAR(5), @qty AS INT, @rn AS INT;

BEGIN TRAN

DECLARE rncursor CURSOR FAST_FORWARD FOR
  SELECT empid, qty FROM dbo.Sales ORDER BY qty, empid;
OPEN rncursor;
```

```
SET @rn = 0;

FETCH NEXT FROM rncursor INTO @empid, @qty;
WHILE @@FETCH_STATUS = 0
BEGIN
  SET @rn = @rn + 1;
  INSERT INTO @SalesRN(empid, qty, rn) VALUES(@empid, @qty, @rn);
  FETCH NEXT FROM rncursor INTO @empid, @qty;
END

CLOSE rncursor;
DEALLOCATE rncursor;

COMMIT TRAN

SELECT empid, qty, rn FROM @SalesRN;
```

This code generates the following output:

```
empid qty         rn
----- ----------- -----------
B     100         1
G     100         2
J     100         3
H     150         4
C     200         5
D     200         6
K     200         7
E     250         8
I     250         9
A     300         10
F     300         11
```

Generally, you should avoid working with cursors because they have a lot of overhead that is a drag on performance. However, in this case, unless the partition size is really tiny, the cursor-based solution performs much better than the subquery-based solution because it scans the data only once. This means that as the table grows larger, the cursor-based solution has a linear performance degradation, as opposed to the n^2 one that the subquery-based solution has. Still, the cursor-based solution is significantly slower than using the ROW_NUMBER function.

IDENTITY-Based Solution

Another solution to calculating row numbers is to rely on the IDENTITY function or IDENTITY column property. Before you proceed, though, you should be aware that when you use the IDENTITY function, you cannot guarantee the order of assignment of IDENTITY values. You can, however, guarantee the order of assignment by using an IDENTITY column instead of the IDENTITY function: first create a table with an IDENTITY column and then load the data using an INSERT SELECT statement with an ORDER BY clause.

> **More Info**   You can find a detailed discussion of IDENTITY and ORDER BY in Knowledge
> Base article 273586 (*http://support.microsoft.com/default.aspx?scid=kb;en-us;273586*), which
> I recommend that you read. You can also find information on the subject in the following blog
> entry by Conor Cunningham: *http://blogs.msdn.com/sqltips/archive/2005/07/20/441053.aspx*.

Nonpartitioned   Using the IDENTITY function in a SELECT INTO statement is by far the fastest
way to calculate row numbers without the ROW_NUMBER function. The first reason for this is
that you scan the data only once, without the overhead involved with cursor manipulation. The
second reason is that SELECT INTO is a minimally logged operation when the database recovery
model is not FULL. However, keep in mind that you can trust it only when you don't care about
the order of assignment of the row numbers. Note that SQL Server 2008 can also perform
minimally logged INSERT SELECT statements provided that certain requirements are met. I will
elaborate on this in Chapter 10, "Data Modification."

As an example, the following code demonstrates how to use the *IDENTITY* function to create
and populate a temporary table with row numbers, in no particular order:

```
SELECT empid, qty, IDENTITY(int, 1, 1) AS rn
INTO #SalesRN FROM dbo.Sales;

SELECT * FROM #SalesRN;

DROP TABLE #SalesRN;
```

This technique is handy when you need to generate integer identifiers to distinguish rows for
some processing need.

Don't let the fact that you can technically specify an ORDER BY clause in the SELECT INTO
query mislead you. There's no guarantee that in the execution plan the assignment of
IDENTITY values will take place after the sort.

As mentioned earlier, when you do care about the order of assignment of the IDENTITY values—
in other words, when the row numbers should be based on a given order—first create the table
and then load the data. Prior to SQL Server 2008 this technique was not as fast as the SELECT
INTO approach because INSERT SELECT was always fully logged; however, it was still much faster
than the other techniques that did not utilize the ROW_NUMBER function.

Here's an example for calculating row numbers based on the order of *qty* and *empid*:

```
CREATE TABLE #SalesRN(empid VARCHAR(5), qty INT, rn INT IDENTITY);

INSERT INTO #SalesRN(empid, qty)
  SELECT empid, qty FROM dbo.Sales ORDER BY qty, empid;

SELECT * FROM #SalesRN;

DROP TABLE #SalesRN;
```

Partitioned   Using the IDENTITY approach to create partitioned row numbers requires an additional step. As with the nonpartitioned solution, you insert the data into a table with an IDENTITY column, only this time it is sorted by *partitioning_cols, sort_cols, tiebreaker_cols*.

The additional step is a query that calculates the row number within the partition using the following formula: *general_row_number – min_row_number_within_partition + 1*. The minimum row number within the partition can be obtained by either a correlated subquery or a join.

For example, the following code generates row numbers partitioned by *mgrid*, sorted by *qty* and *empid*. The code presents both the subquery approach and the join approach to obtaining the minimum row number within the partition:

```
CREATE TABLE #SalesRN
  (mgrid VARCHAR(5), empid VARCHAR(5), qty INT, rn INT IDENTITY);
CREATE UNIQUE CLUSTERED INDEX idx_mgrid_rn ON #SalesRN(mgrid, rn);

INSERT INTO #SalesRN(mgrid, empid, qty)
  SELECT mgrid, empid, qty FROM dbo.Sales ORDER BY mgrid, qty, empid;

-- Option 1 - using a subquery
SELECT mgrid, empid, qty,
  rn - (SELECT MIN(rn) FROM #SalesRN AS S2
        WHERE S2.mgrid = S1.mgrid) + 1 AS rn
FROM #SalesRN AS S1;

-- Option 2 - using a join
SELECT S.mgrid, empid, qty, rn - minrn + 1 AS rn
FROM #SalesRN AS S
  JOIN (SELECT mgrid, MIN(rn) AS minrn
        FROM #SalesRN
        GROUP BY mgrid) AS M
    ON S.mgrid = M.mgrid;

DROP TABLE #SalesRN;
```

Performance Comparisons

I presented four different techniques to calculate row numbers server-side. The first uses the ROW_NUMBER function, the second is based on Subqueries, the third is based on Cursors, and the fourth is based on IDENTITY.

I ran a benchmark on my laptop to compare the performance of the different techniques. Even though my laptop is not exactly the best model for a production server, you can get a good sense of the performance differences between the techniques. The benchmark populates a table with increasing numbers of rows, starting with 10,000 and progressing up to 100,000 in steps of 10,000 rows. The benchmark calculates row numbers using all four techniques, with the Discard Results option turned on in SQL Server Management Studio (SSMS) to remove the effect of printing the output. The benchmark records the run times in microseconds in the RNBenchmark table:

```
-- Change Tools|Options setting to Discard Query Results
SET NOCOUNT ON;
USE tempdb;
GO
IF OBJECT_ID('dbo.RNBenchmark') IS NOT NULL
  DROP TABLE dbo.RNBenchmark;
GO
IF OBJECT_ID('dbo.RNTechniques') IS NOT NULL
  DROP TABLE dbo.RNTechniques;
GO
IF OBJECT_ID('dbo.SalesBM') IS NOT NULL
  DROP TABLE dbo.SalesBM;
GO
IF OBJECT_ID('dbo.SalesBMIdentity') IS NOT NULL
  DROP TABLE dbo.SalesBMIdentity;
GO
IF OBJECT_ID('dbo.SalesBMCursor') IS NOT NULL
  DROP TABLE dbo.SalesBMCursor;
GO

CREATE TABLE dbo.RNTechniques
(
  tid INT NOT NULL PRIMARY KEY,
  technique VARCHAR(25) NOT NULL
);
INSERT INTO RNTechniques(tid, technique) VALUES
  (1, 'Subquery'),(2, 'IDENTITY'),(3, 'Cursor'),(4, 'ROW_NUMBER');
GO

CREATE TABLE dbo.RNBenchmark
(
  tid        INT    NOT NULL REFERENCES dbo.RNTechniques(tid),
  numrows    INT    NOT NULL,
  runtimemcs BIGINT NOT NULL,
  PRIMARY KEY(tid, numrows)
);
GO

CREATE TABLE dbo.SalesBM
(
  empid INT NOT NULL IDENTITY PRIMARY KEY,
  qty   INT NOT NULL
);
CREATE INDEX idx_qty_empid ON dbo.SalesBM(qty, empid);
GO
CREATE TABLE dbo.SalesBMIdentity(empid INT, qty INT, rn INT IDENTITY);
GO
CREATE TABLE dbo.SalesBMCursor(empid INT, qty INT, rn INT);
GO

DECLARE
  @maxnumrows    AS INT,
  @steprows      AS INT,
  @curnumrows    AS INT,
  @dt            AS DATETIME2; -- use DATETIME prior to 2008
```

```
SET @maxnumrows    = 100000;
SET @steprows      = 10000;
SET @curnumrows    = 10000;

WHILE @curnumrows <= @maxnumrows
BEGIN

  TRUNCATE TABLE dbo.SalesBM;
  INSERT INTO dbo.SalesBM(qty)
    SELECT CAST(1+999.9999999999*RAND(CHECKSUM(NEWID())) AS INT)
    FROM dbo.Nums
    WHERE n <= @curnumrows;

  -- 'Subquery'

  DBCC FREEPROCCACHE WITH NO_INFOMSGS;
  DBCC DROPCLEANBUFFERS WITH NO_INFOMSGS;

  SET @dt = SYSDATETIME(); -- use GETDATE() prior to 2008

  SELECT empid, qty,
    (SELECT COUNT(*)
     FROM dbo.SalesBM AS S2
     WHERE S2.qty < S1.qty
        OR (S2.qty = S1.qty AND S2.empid <= S1.empid)) AS rn
  FROM dbo.SalesBM AS S1
  ORDER BY qty, empid;

  INSERT INTO dbo.RNBenchmark(tid, numrows, runtimemcs)
    VALUES(1, @curnumrows, DATEDIFF(mcs, @dt, SYSDATETIME()));
                                -- Use ms prior to 2008

  -- 'IDENTITY'

  TRUNCATE TABLE dbo.SalesBMIdentity;

  DBCC FREEPROCCACHE WITH NO_INFOMSGS;
  DBCC DROPCLEANBUFFERS WITH NO_INFOMSGS;

  SET @dt = SYSDATETIME();

  INSERT INTO dbo.SalesBMIdentity(empid, qty)
    SELECT empid, qty FROM dbo.SalesBM ORDER BY qty, empid;

  SELECT empid, qty, rn FROM dbo.SalesBMIdentity;

  INSERT INTO dbo.RNBenchmark(tid, numrows, runtimemcs)
    VALUES(2, @curnumrows, DATEDIFF(mcs, @dt, SYSDATETIME()));

  -- 'Cursor'

  TRUNCATE TABLE dbo.SalesBMCursor;

  DBCC FREEPROCCACHE WITH NO_INFOMSGS;
  DBCC DROPCLEANBUFFERS WITH NO_INFOMSGS;

  SET @dt = SYSDATETIME();
```

```
DECLARE @empid AS INT, @qty AS INT, @rn AS INT;

BEGIN TRAN

DECLARE rncursor CURSOR FAST_FORWARD FOR
  SELECT empid, qty FROM dbo.SalesBM ORDER BY qty, empid;
OPEN rncursor;

SET @rn = 0;

FETCH NEXT FROM rncursor INTO @empid, @qty;
WHILE @@fetch_status = 0
BEGIN
  SET @rn = @rn + 1;
  INSERT INTO dbo.SalesBMCursor(empid, qty, rn)
    VALUES(@empid, @qty, @rn);
  FETCH NEXT FROM rncursor INTO @empid, @qty;
END

CLOSE rncursor;
DEALLOCATE rncursor;

COMMIT TRAN

SELECT empid, qty, rn FROM dbo.SalesBMCursor;

INSERT INTO dbo.RNBenchmark(tid, numrows, runtimemcs)
  VALUES(3, @curnumrows, DATEDIFF(mcs, @dt, SYSDATETIME()));

-- 'ROW_NUMBER'

DBCC FREEPROCCACHE WITH NO_INFOMSGS;
DBCC DROPCLEANBUFFERS WITH NO_INFOMSGS;

SET @dt = SYSDATETIME();

SELECT empid, qty, ROW_NUMBER() OVER(ORDER BY qty, empid) AS rn
FROM dbo.SalesBM;

INSERT INTO dbo.RNBenchmark(tid, numrows, runtimemcs)
  VALUES(4, @curnumrows, DATEDIFF(mcs, @dt, SYSDATETIME()));

SET @curnumrows = @curnumrows + @steprows;

END
```

The following query returns the benchmark's results in a conveniently readable format:

```
SELECT numrows,
  [Subquery], [IDENTITY], [Cursor], [ROW_NUMBER]
FROM (SELECT technique, numrows, runtimems
      FROM dbo.RNBenchmark AS B
        JOIN dbo.RNTechniques AS T
          ON B.tid = T.tid) AS D
PIVOT(MAX(runtimems) FOR technique IN(
  [Subquery], [IDENTITY], [Cursor], [ROW_NUMBER])) AS P
ORDER BY numrows;
```

> **Note** This code uses several features that are new in SQL Server 2008: the DATETIME2 data type, the mcs (microsecond) date part, and the SYSDATETIME function. Inline comments in the code in the first occurrence of each new feature indicate the alternatives that you should use prior to SQL Server 2008.

This query returned the following benchmark results on my system:

```
numrows   Subquery    IDENTITY   Cursor   ROW_NUMBER
--------  ---------   ---------  -------  -----------
10000     8590000     110000     420000   7000
20000     30336000    203000     766000   29000
30000     69403000    250000     1196000  43000
40000     118593000   483000     1596000  29000
50000     184886000   466000     1970000  72000
60000     267536000   686000     2510000  43000
70000     359833000   703000     2723000  49000
80000     475443000   1150000    3410000  57000
90000     612066000   1120000    3613000  66000
100000    770236000   1146000    3956000  71000
```

The query uses a pivoting technique that I'll describe in Chapter 8, so don't try to squeeze your brains if you're not familiar with it. For our discussion, the important thing is the benchmark's results. You can immediately see that the subquery-based technique is dramatically slower than all the rest, and I explained why earlier. You will also notice that the ROW_NUMBER function is dramatically faster than all the rest. I wanted to present a graph with all results, but the run times when the subquery-based technique was used were so great that the lines for the other solutions were simply flat. So I decided to present two separate graphs. Figure 6-7 shows the graph of run times for the IDENTITY-based, cursor-based, and ROW_NUMBER function–based techniques. Figure 6-8 shows the graph for the subquery-based technique.

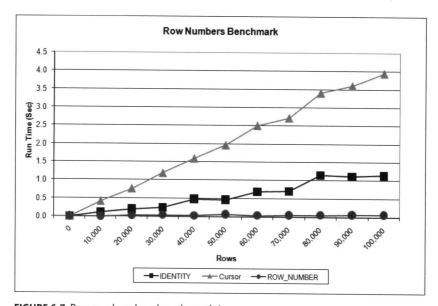

FIGURE 6-7 Row numbers benchmark graph I

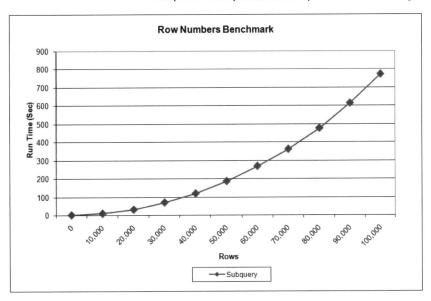

FIGURE 6-8 Row numbers benchmark graph II

You can see in Figure 6-7 that all three techniques have a fairly linear performance graph, while Figure 6-8 shows a beautifully curved n^2 graph.

> **Note** In part, the ROW_NUMBER function is so fast because it doesn't return the results anywhere. The cursor and identity solutions leave the results in a table for use; therefore, they generate considerable I/O. Of course, if you need to materialize the result set even when using the ROW_NUMBER function, you need to consider the added I/O cost. As an exercise, you can run an altered benchmark where you materialize the result set with the row numbers in all tests.

The obvious conclusion is that you should always use the built-in ROW_NUMBER function, and, similarly, you should use the other ranking functions if you need the other types of ranking calculations. And if you have legacy code that uses the alternative techniques, by revising it to use the built-in functions, you can gain dramatic performance improvements, not to mention making the code significantly simpler.

Paging

As I mentioned earlier, row numbers have many practical applications that I'll demonstrate throughout the book. Here I'd like to show one example where I use row numbers to achieve paging—accessing rows of a result set in chunks. Paging is a common need in applications, allowing the user to navigate through chunks or portions of a result set. Paging with row numbers is also a handy technique. This example will also allow me to demonstrate additional optimization techniques that the optimizer applies when using the ROW_NUMBER function.

Ad Hoc Paging   Ad hoc paging is a request for a single page, where the input is the page number and page size (the number of rows in a page). When the user needs a particular single page and won't request additional pages, you implement a different solution than the one you would for multiple page requests. First you have to realize that you cannot access page *n* without physically accessing pages 1 through *n*–1. Bearing this in mind, the following code returns a page of rows from the Sales table ordered by *qty* and *empid*, given the page size and page number as inputs:

```
DECLARE @pagesize AS INT, @pagenum AS INT;
SET @pagesize = 5;
SET @pagenum = 2;

WITH SalesRN AS
(
  SELECT ROW_NUMBER() OVER(ORDER BY qty, empid) AS rownum,
    empid, mgrid, qty
  FROM dbo.Sales
)
SELECT rownum, empid, mgrid, qty
FROM SalesRN
WHERE rownum > @pagesize * (@pagenum-1)
  AND rownum <= @pagesize * @pagenum
ORDER BY rownum;
```

This code generates the following output:

```
rownum                empid      mgrid      qty
--------------------  ---------- ---------- -----------
6                     D          Y          200
7                     K          Y          200
8                     E          Z          250
9                     I          X          250
10                    A          Z          300
```

The CTE called SalesRN assigns row numbers to the sales rows based on the order of *qty* and *empid*. The outer query filters only the target page's rows using a formula based on the input page size and page number.

You might be concerned that the query appears to calculate row numbers for all rows and then filter only the requested page's rows. This might seem to require a full table scan. With very large tables this, of course, would be a serious performance issue. However, before getting concerned, examine the execution plan for this query, which is shown in Figure 6-9.

FIGURE 6-9 Execution plan for the ad hoc paging solution

The figure shows only the left part of the plan starting with the Sequence Project, which assigns the row numbers. If you look at the properties of the Top operator, you can see that the plan scans only the first 10 rows of the table. Because the code requests the second page of five rows, only the first two pages are scanned. Then the Filter operator filters only the second page (rows 6 through 10).

Another way to demonstrate that the whole table is not scanned is by populating the table with a large number of rows and running the query with the SET STATISTICS IO option turned on. You will notice by the number of reads reported that when you request page *n*, regardless of the size of the table, only the first *n* pages of rows are scanned.

This solution can perform well even when you have multiple page requests that usually "move forward"—that is, page 1 is requested, then page 2, then page 3, and so on, as long as a small number of pages is requested and you have an index to support the requests. When the first page of rows is requested, the relevant data/index pages are physically scanned and loaded into cache (if they're not there already). When the second page of rows is requested, the data pages for the first request already reside in cache, and only the data pages for the second page of rows need to be physically scanned. This requires mostly logical reads (reads from cache), and physical reads are needed only for the requested page. Logical reads are much faster than physical reads, but keep in mind that they also have a cost that accumulates.

Multipage Access   Another solution for paging typically performs better overall than the previous solution when you have multiple page requests that do not move forward, if the result set is not very large. First, materialize all pages in a table along with row numbers and create a clustered index on the row number column:

```
SELECT ROW_NUMBER() OVER(ORDER BY qty, empid) AS rownum,
  empid, mgrid, qty
INTO #SalesRN
FROM dbo.Sales;

CREATE UNIQUE CLUSTERED INDEX idx_rn ON #SalesRN(rownum);
```

Now you can satisfy any page request with a query like the following:

```
DECLARE @pagesize AS INT, @pagenum AS INT;
SET @pagesize = 5;
SET @pagenum = 2;

SELECT rownum, empid, mgrid, qty
FROM #SalesRN
WHERE rownum BETWEEN @pagesize * (@pagenum-1) + 1
                 AND @pagesize * @pagenum
ORDER BY rownum;
```

The execution plan for this query is shown in Figure 6-10 (abbreviated by removing the operators that calculate boundaries up to the Merge Interval operator to focus on the actual data access).

FIGURE 6-10 Execution plan for multipaging solution

This is a very efficient plan that performs a seek within the index to reach the low boundary row (row number 6 in this case), followed by a partial scan (not visible in the plan), until it reaches the high boundary row (row number 10). Only the rows of the requested page of results are scanned within the index.

If your application design is such that it disconnects after each request, obviously the temporary table will be gone as soon as the creating session disconnects. In such a case, you might want to create a permanent table that is logically temporary. You can achieve this by naming the table *some_name<some_identifier>*—for example, T<guid> (Global Unique Identifier).

You also need to develop a garbage-collection (cleanup) process that gets rid of tables that the application didn't have a chance to drop explicitly in cases where it terminated in a disorderly way.

In cases where you need to support large result sets or a high level of concurrency, you will have scalability issues related to tempdb resources. You can develop a partitioned solution that materializes only a certain number of pages and not all of them—for example, 1,000 rows at a time. Typically, users don't request more than the first few pages anyway. If a user ends up requesting pages beyond the first batch, you can materialize the next partition (that is, the next 1,000 rows).

When you don't care about materializing the result set in a temporary table for multipage access, you might want to consider using a table variable to hold the first batch of pages (for example, 1,000 rows). Table variables don't involve recompilations, and they suffer less from logging and locking issues. The optimizer doesn't maintain distribution statistics for table variables, so you should be very cautious and selective in choosing the cases to use them for. But when all you need to do is store a small result set and scan it entirely anyway, this technique is fine.

Once you're done using this table, you can drop it:

```
DROP TABLE #SalesRN;
```

Rank and Dense Rank

Rank and dense rank are calculations similar to row number. But unlike row number, which has a large variety of practical applications, rank and dense rank are typically used for ranking and scoring applications.

RANK and DENSE_RANK Functions

SQL Server provides you with built-in RANK and DENSE_RANK functions that are similar to the ROW_NUMBER function. The difference between these functions and ROW_NUMBER is that, as I described earlier, ROW_NUMBER is not deterministic when the ORDER BY list is not unique. RANK and DENSE_RANK are always deterministic—that is, the same ranking values are assigned to rows with the same sort values. The difference between RANK and DENSE_RANK is that RANK might have gaps in the ranking values but allows you to know how many rows have lower sort values. DENSE_RANK values have no gaps.

For example, the following query returns both rank and dense rank values for the sales rows based on an ordering by quantity:

```
SELECT empid, qty,
  RANK() OVER(ORDER BY qty) AS rnk,
  DENSE_RANK() OVER(ORDER BY qty) AS drnk
FROM dbo.Sales
ORDER BY qty;
```

This query generates the following output:

```
empid       qty          rnk                   drnk
----------  -----------  --------------------  --------------------
B           100          1                     1
G           100          1                     1
J           100          1                     1
H           150          4                     2
C           200          5                     3
D           200          5                     3
K           200          5                     3
E           250          8                     4
I           250          8                     4
A           300          10                    5
F           300          10                    5
```

Here's a short quiz: what's the difference between the results of ROW_NUMBER, RANK, and DENSE_RANK given a unique ORDER BY list?

For the answer, run the following code:

```
SELECT REVERSE('!ecnereffid oN');
```

Solutions Based on Subqueries

Subquery-based solutions to rank and dense rank calculations are very similar to subquery-based solutions to row number calculations. To calculate rank, use a subquery that counts the number of rows with a smaller sort value and add one. To calculate dense rank, use a subquery that counts the distinct number of smaller sort values and add one:

```
SELECT empid, qty,
  (SELECT COUNT(*) FROM dbo.Sales AS S2
  WHERE S2.qty < S1.qty) + 1 AS rnk,
```

```
  (SELECT COUNT(DISTINCT qty) FROM dbo.Sales AS S2
   WHERE S2.qty < S1.qty) + 1 AS drnk
FROM dbo.Sales AS S1
ORDER BY qty;
```

Of course, you can add a correlation to return partitioned calculations just like you did with row numbers.

Tile Number

With tile numbers you can distribute rows into a specified number of tiles (or groups). The tiles are numbered 1 and on. Each row is assigned with the tile number to which it belongs. Tile number is based on row number calculation—namely, it is based on a requested order and can optionally be partitioned. Based on the number of rows in the table (or partition), the number of requested tiles, and the row number, you can determine the tile number for each row. For example, given a table with 10 rows, supposed you request to calculate tile numbers for the rows, arranging the rows in two tiles, based on the order of column c. The value of the tile number would be 1 for the first 5 rows in column c order and 2 for the 6th through 10th rows.

Typically, tile number calculations are used for analytical purposes that require you to arrange items in equally sized groups. Don't confuse tiling with paging. With paging, the page size is known, and the number of pages is the result of dividing the number of rows in the set by the page size. With tiling, the number of tiles is known, and the tile size is the result of dividing the number of rows in the set by the requested number of tiles.

The task of tiling has more than one solution, and the SQL Server built-in NTILE function implements a specific solution. I will describe the built-in NTILE function and then cover other solutions.

The Built-in NTILE Function

SQL Server supports a built-in function called NTILE to calculate tile numbers for rows in a result set of a query. Unlike the other ranking functions, the NTILE function accepts an input—the requested number of tiles. Because tile number calculations are based on row numbers, NTILE has exactly the same issues regarding determinism that I described in the row numbers section.

For example, the following query calculates tile numbers for the rows from the Sales table, producing three tiles, based on the order of *qty* and *empid*:

```
SELECT empid, qty,
  NTILE(3) OVER(ORDER BY qty, empid) AS tile
FROM dbo.Sales
ORDER BY qty, empid;
```

This query generates the following output:

```
empid       qty          tile
----------  -----------  --------------------
B           100          1
G           100          1
J           100          1
H           150          1
C           200          2
D           200          2
K           200          2
E           250          2
I           250          3
A           300          3
F           300          3
```

Note that when the number of tiles (*num_tiles*) does not evenly divide the count of rows in the table (*cnt*), the first *r* tiles (where *r* is *cnt % num_tiles*) get one more row than the others. In other words, the remainder is assigned to the first tiles first. In our example, the table has 11 rows, and 3 tiles were requested. The base tile size is 11 / 3 = 3 (integer division). The remainder is 11 % 3 = 2. The % (modulo) operator provides the integer remainder after dividing the first integer by the second one. So the first 2 tiles get an additional row beyond the base tile size and end up with 4 rows.

As a more meaningful example, suppose you need to split the sales rows into three categories based on quantities: low, medium, and high. You want each category to have about the same number of rows. You can calculate *NTILE(3)* values based on *qty* order (using *empid* as a tiebreaker just to ensure deterministic and reproducible results) and use a CASE expression to convert the tile numbers to more meaningful descriptions:

```
SELECT empid, qty,
  CASE NTILE(3) OVER(ORDER BY qty, empid)
    WHEN 1 THEN 'low'
    WHEN 2 THEN 'medium'
    WHEN 3 THEN 'high'
  END AS lvl
FROM dbo.Sales
ORDER BY qty, empid;
```

This query generates the following output:

```
empid       qty          lvl
----------  -----------  ------
B           100          low
G           100          low
J           100          low
H           150          low
C           200          medium
D           200          medium
K           200          medium
E           250          medium
I           250          high
A           300          high
F           300          high
```

To calculate the range of quantities corresponding to each category, simply group the data by the tile number, returning the minimum and maximum sort values for each group:

```
WITH Tiles AS
(
  SELECT empid, qty,
    NTILE(3) OVER(ORDER BY qty, empid) AS tile
  FROM dbo.Sales
)
SELECT tile, MIN(qty) AS lb, MAX(qty) AS hb
FROM Tiles
GROUP BY tile
ORDER BY tile;
```

You get the following output:

```
tile                 lb          hb
-------------------- ----------- -----------
1                    100         150
2                    200         250
3                    250         300
```

Other Solutions to Tile Number

The formula you use to calculate tile number depends on what exactly you want to do with the remainder in case the number of rows in the table doesn't divide evenly by the number of tiles. You might want to use the built-in NTILE function's approach: Just assign the remainder to the first tiles, one to each until it's all consumed. Another approach, which is probably more correct statistically, is to more evenly distribute the remainder among the tiles instead of putting them into the initial tiles only. When you need the former approach, you can simply use the built-in NTILE function. For the sake of completeness, I'll also provide a solution based on subqueries. If you need the latter approach, you have to develop your own solution because this case has no built-in function.

I'll start with the second approach, calculating tile numbers with even distribution. You need two inputs to calculate the tile number for a row: the row number and the tile size. You already know how to calculate row numbers. To calculate the tile size, you divide the number of rows in the table by the requested number of tiles. The formula that calculates the target tile number is

```
(row_number - 1) / tile_size + 1
```

The trick that allows you to distribute the remainder evenly is to use a decimal calculation when calculating the *tile_size* value instead of an integer one. That is, instead of using an integer calculation of the tile size (*num_rows/num_tiles*), which truncates the fraction, use *1.*numrows/numtiles*, which returns a more accurate decimal result. Finally, to get rid of the fraction in the tile number, convert the result back to an integer value.

Here's the complete query that produces tile numbers using the even-distribution approach:

```
DECLARE @numtiles AS INT;
SET @numtiles = 3;

WITH D1 AS
(
  SELECT empid, qty,
    ROW_NUMBER() OVER(ORDER BY qty, empid) AS rn,
    (SELECT COUNT(*) FROM dbo.Sales) AS numrows
  FROM dbo.Sales AS S1
),
D2 AS
(
  SELECT empid, qty, rn,
    1.*numrows/@numtiles AS tilesize
  FROM D1
)
SELECT empid, qty,
  CAST((rn - 1) / tilesize + 1 AS INT) AS tile
FROM D2
ORDER BY qty, empid;
```

This query generates the following output:

```
empid      qty          tile
---------- ------------ -----------
B          100          1
G          100          1
J          100          1
H          150          1
C          200          2
D          200          2
K          200          2
E          250          2
I          250          3
A          300          3
F          300          3
```

With three tiles, you can't see the even distribution of the remaining rows. If you run this code using nine tiles as input, you get the following output, where the even distribution is clearer:

```
empid      qty          tile
---------- ------------ -----------
B          100          1
G          100          1
J          100          2
H          150          3
C          200          4
D          200          5
K          200          5
E          250          6
I          250          7
A          300          8
F          300          9
```

You can see in the result that the first tile contains two rows, the next three tiles contain one row each, the next tile contains two rows, and the last four tiles contain one row each. You can experiment with the input number of tiles to get a clearer picture of the even-distribution algorithm.

For a challenge, see if you can come up with a solution to calculating tile numbers implementing the same logic as the built-in NTILE function without using ranking functions.

To get the same result as the built-in NTILE function, where the remainder is distributed to the lowest-numbered tiles, you need a formula different from the one used with even distribution of remaining rows. First, the calculations involve only integers. The inputs you need for the formula in this case include the row number, tile size, and remainder (*number of rows in the table % number of requested tiles*). These inputs are used in calculating tile number with non-even distribution.

The formula for the target tile number is as follows:

```
if row_number <= (tilesize + 1) * remainder then
  tile_number = (row_number - 1) / (tile_size + 1) + 1
else
  tile_number = (row_number - remainder - 1) / tile_size + 1
```

Translated to T-SQL, the query looks like this:

```
DECLARE @numtiles AS INT;
SET @numtiles = 9;

WITH D1 AS
(
  SELECT empid, qty,
    (SELECT COUNT(*) FROM dbo.Sales AS S2
      WHERE S2.qty < S1.qty
        OR S2.qty = S1.qty
              AND S2.empid <= S1.empid) AS rn,
    (SELECT COUNT(*) FROM dbo.Sales) AS numrows
  FROM dbo.Sales AS S1
),
D2 AS
(
  SELECT empid, qty, rn,
    numrows/@numtiles AS tilesize,
    numrows%@numtiles AS remainder
  FROM D1
)
SELECT empid, qty,
  CASE
    WHEN rn <= (tilesize+1) * remainder
      THEN (rn-1) / (tilesize+1) + 1
    ELSE (rn - remainder - 1) / tilesize + 1
  END AS tile
FROM D2
ORDER BY qty, empid;
```

This query generates the following output:

```
empid      qty          tile
--------   -----------  -----------
B          100          1
G          100          1
J          100          2
H          150          2
C          200          3
D          200          4
K          200          5
E          250          6
I          250          7
A          300          8
F          300          9
```

The output is the same as the one you would get using the built-in NTILE function; the first tiles get an additional row until the remainder is consumed.

Auxiliary Table of Numbers

An auxiliary table of numbers is a very powerful tool that I often use in my solutions. So I decided to dedicate a section in this chapter to it. In this section, I'll simply describe the concept and the methods used to generate such a table. I'll refer to this auxiliary table throughout the book and demonstrate many of its applications.

An auxiliary table of numbers (call it Nums) is simply a table that contains the integers between 1 and *n* for some (typically large) value of *n*. I recommend that you create a permanent Nums table and populate it with as many values as you might need for your solutions.

The code in Listing 6-3 demonstrates how to create such a table containing 1,000,000 rows. Of course, you might want a different number of rows, depending on your needs.

LISTING 6-3 Creating and populating auxiliary table of numbers

```
SET NOCOUNT ON;
USE InsideTSQL2008;

IF OBJECT_ID('dbo.Nums') IS NOT NULL DROP TABLE dbo.Nums;
CREATE TABLE dbo.Nums(n INT NOT NULL PRIMARY KEY);

DECLARE @max AS INT, @rc AS INT;
SET @max = 1000000;
SET @rc = 1;

INSERT INTO Nums VALUES(1);
WHILE @rc * 2 <= @max
```

```
BEGIN
  INSERT INTO dbo.Nums SELECT n + @rc FROM dbo.Nums;
  SET @rc = @rc * 2;
END

INSERT INTO dbo.Nums
  SELECT n + @rc FROM dbo.Nums WHERE n + @rc <= @max;
```

> **Tip** Because a Nums table has so many practical uses, you'll probably end up needing to access it from various databases. To avoid the need to refer to it using the fully qualified name InsideTSQL2008.dbo.Nums, you can create a synonym in the model database pointing to Nums in InsideTSQL2008 like this:
>
> ```
> USE model;
> CREATE SYNONYM dbo.Nums FOR InsideTSQL2008.dbo.Nums;
> ```
>
> Creating the synonym in *model* makes it available in all newly created databases from that point on, including tempdb after SQL Server is restarted. For existing databases, you just need to explicitly run the CREATE SYNONYM command once.

In practice, it doesn't really matter how you populate the Nums table because you run this process only once. Nevertheless, I used an optimized process that populates the table in a very fast manner. The process demonstrates the technique of creating Nums with a multiplying INSERT loop.

The code keeps track of the number of rows already inserted into the table in a variable called @rc. It first inserts into Nums the row where *n = 1*. It then enters a loop while @rc * 2 <= @max (@max is the desired number of rows). In each iteration, the process inserts into Nums the result of a query that selects all rows from Nums after adding @rc to each *n* value. This technique doubles the number of rows in Nums in each iteration—that is, first {1} is inserted, then {2}, then {3, 4}, then {5, 6, 7, 8}, then {9, 10, 11, 12, 13, 14, 15, 16}, and so on.

As soon as the table is populated with more than half the target number of rows, the loop ends. Another INSERT statement after the loop inserts the remaining rows using the same INSERT statement as within the loop, but this time with a filter to ensure that only values <= @max will be inserted.

The main reason that this process runs fast is that it minimizes writes to the transaction log compared to other available solutions. This is achieved by minimizing the number of INSERT statements (the number of INSERT statements is *CEILING(LOG2(@max)) + 1*). This code populated the Nums table with 1,000,000 rows in 11 seconds on my laptop. As an exercise, you can try populating the Nums table using a simple loop of individual inserts and see how long it takes.

Whenever you need the first @n numbers from Nums, simply query it, specifying *WHERE n <= @n* as the filter. An index on the *n* column ensures that the query scans only the required rows and no others.

If you're not allowed to add permanent tables in the database, you can create a table-valued UDF with a parameter for the number of rows needed. You use the same logic as used in the preceding example to generate the required number of values.

You can use CTEs and the ROW_NUMBER function to create extremely efficient solutions that generate a table of numbers on the fly.

I'll start with a naive solution that is fairly slow (about 22 seconds, with results discarded). The following solution uses a simple recursive CTE, where the anchor member generates a row with *n = 1*, and the recursive member adds a row in each iteration with *n = prev n + 1*:

```
DECLARE @n AS BIGINT;
SET @n = 1000000;

WITH Nums AS
(
  SELECT 1 AS n
  UNION ALL
  SELECT n + 1 FROM Nums WHERE n < @n
)
SELECT n FROM Nums
OPTION(MAXRECURSION 0);
```

> **Note** If you're running the code to test it, remember to turn on the Discard Results After Execution option in SSMS; otherwise, you will get an output with a million rows.

You have to use a hint that removes the default recursion limit of 100. This solution runs for about 22 seconds.

You can optimize the solution significantly by using a CTE (call it *Base*) that generates as many rows as the square root of the target number of rows. Take the cross join of two instances of *Base* to get the target number of rows and, finally, generate row numbers for the result to serve as the sequence of numbers.

Here's the code that implements this approach:

```
DECLARE @n AS BIGINT = 1000000;

WITH Base AS
(
  SELECT 1 AS n
  UNION ALL
  SELECT n + 1 FROM Base WHERE n < CEILING(SQRT(@n))
),
Nums AS
(
  SELECT ROW_NUMBER() OVER(ORDER BY (SELECT 0)) AS n
  FROM Base AS B1
    CROSS JOIN Base AS B2
)
SELECT n FROM Nums WHERE n <= @n
OPTION(MAXRECURSION 0);
```

This solution runs for only 0.9 seconds (results discarded).

Next, I'll describe the third approach to generate Nums. You start with a CTE that has only two rows and multiply the number of rows with each following CTE by cross-joining two instances of the previous CTE. With *n* levels of CTEs (0-based), you reach POWER(2, POWER(2, n)) rows (read as "2 in the power of (2 in the power of n)"). For example, with 5 levels, you get 4,294,967,296 rows.

Another CTE generates row numbers, and finally the outer query filters the desired number of values (where *row number column* <= *input*). Remember that when you filter a *row number* <= *some* value, SQL Server doesn't bother to generate row numbers beyond that point. So you shouldn't be concerned about performance. It's not the case that your code will really generate more than four billion rows every time and then filter.

Here's code that implements this approach:

```
DECLARE @n AS BIGINT = 1000000;

WITH
L0   AS(SELECT 1 AS c UNION ALL SELECT 1),
L1   AS(SELECT 1 AS c FROM L0 AS A CROSS JOIN L0 AS B),
L2   AS(SELECT 1 AS c FROM L1 AS A CROSS JOIN L1 AS B),
L3   AS(SELECT 1 AS c FROM L2 AS A CROSS JOIN L2 AS B),
L4   AS(SELECT 1 AS c FROM L3 AS A CROSS JOIN L3 AS B),
L5   AS(SELECT 1 AS c FROM L4 AS A CROSS JOIN L4 AS B),
Nums AS(SELECT ROW_NUMBER() OVER(ORDER BY (SELECT 0)) AS n FROM L5)
SELECT n FROM Nums WHERE n <= @n;
```

It runs for about 0.6 seconds to generate a sequence of 1,000,000 numbers.

As I mentioned earlier, you can wrap the logic in a UDF. The value of this solution is that it does not use recursion, and therefore does not need to explicitly increase the MAXRECURSION limit with a hint. Such a hint cannot be specified in a UDF definition, but this is of no concern in our case. The following code encapsulates the last solution's logic in a UDF:

```
IF OBJECT_ID('dbo.GetNums') IS NOT NULL
  DROP FUNCTION dbo.GetNums;
GO
CREATE FUNCTION dbo.GetNums(@n AS BIGINT) RETURNS TABLE
AS
RETURN
  WITH
  L0   AS(SELECT 1 AS c UNION ALL SELECT 1),
  L1   AS(SELECT 1 AS c FROM L0 AS A, L0 AS B),
  L2   AS(SELECT 1 AS c FROM L1 AS A, L1 AS B),
  L3   AS(SELECT 1 AS c FROM L2 AS A, L2 AS B),
  L4   AS(SELECT 1 AS c FROM L3 AS A, L3 AS B),
  L5   AS(SELECT 1 AS c FROM L4 AS A, L4 AS B),
  Nums AS(SELECT ROW_NUMBER() OVER(ORDER BY (SELECT 0)) AS n FROM L5)
  SELECT n FROM Nums WHERE n <= @n;
GO
```

To test the function, run the following code, which returns an auxiliary table with 10 numbers:

```
SELECT * FROM dbo.GetNums(10) AS Nums;
```

Missing and Existing Ranges (Also Known as Gaps and Islands)

To put your knowledge of subqueries, table expressions, and ranking calculations into action, I'll provide a couple of problems that have many applications in production environments. I'll present a generic form of the problem, though, so you can focus on the techniques and not the data.

The problems at hand deal with a sequence of values that has gaps within it. The sequence can be numeric (for example, keys such as order IDs) or temporal (for example, order dates). Also, the sequence can have unique values (for example, keys), or it can have duplicate values (for example, order dates). The first challenge is to identify the ranges of missing values in the sequence (gaps), and the second challenge is to identify ranges of existing values (islands). These problems manifest in production systems in many forms—for example, availability or nonavailability reports, periods of activity or inactivity, identifying ranges of missing or existing keys, and others.

Use the following code to create and populate a table named NumSeq representing a numeric sequence with unique values:

```
SET NOCOUNT ON;
USE tempdb;

-- dbo.NumSeq (numeric sequence with unique values, interval: 1)
IF OBJECT_ID('dbo.NumSeq', 'U') IS NOT NULL DROP TABLE dbo.NumSeq;

CREATE TABLE dbo.NumSeq
(
  seqval INT NOT NULL
    CONSTRAINT PK_NumSeq PRIMARY KEY
);

INSERT INTO dbo.NumSeq(seqval) VALUES
  (2),(3),(11),(12),(13),(27),(33),(34),(35),(42);
```

Table 6-2 shows the gaps in the sequence in NumSeq, and Table 6-3 shows the islands.

TABLE 6-2 Gaps in NumSeq

start_range	end_range
4	10
14	26
28	32
36	41

TABLE 6-3 Islands in NumSeq

start_range	end_range
2	3
11	13
27	27
33	35
42	42

You can use the small NumSeq table to ensure that you get the correct results when working on the logical aspects of your solutions. To test the performance aspects, you need a bigger sequence. Use the following code to create and populate a table called BigNumSeq that has a big numeric sequence with unique values:

```
-- dbo.BigNumSeq (big numeric sequence with unique values, interval: 1)
IF OBJECT_ID('dbo.BigNumSeq', 'U') IS NOT NULL DROP TABLE dbo.BigNumSeq;

CREATE TABLE dbo.BigNumSeq
(
  seqval INT NOT NULL
    CONSTRAINT PK_BigNumSeq PRIMARY KEY
);
```

```
-- Populate table with values in the range 1 through to 10,000,000
-- with a gap every 1000 (total 9,999 gaps, 10,000 islands)
WITH
L0   AS(SELECT 1 AS c UNION ALL SELECT 1),
L1   AS(SELECT 1 AS c FROM L0 AS A, L0 AS B),
L2   AS(SELECT 1 AS c FROM L1 AS A, L1 AS B),
L3   AS(SELECT 1 AS c FROM L2 AS A, L2 AS B),
L4   AS(SELECT 1 AS c FROM L3 AS A, L3 AS B),
L5   AS(SELECT 1 AS c FROM L4 AS A, L4 AS B),
Nums AS(SELECT ROW_NUMBER() OVER(ORDER BY (SELECT 0)) AS n FROM L5)
INSERT INTO dbo.BigNumSeq WITH(TABLOCK) (seqval)
  SELECT n
  FROM Nums
  WHERE n <= 10000000
    AND n % 1000 <> 0;
```

The *seqval* column in the BigNumSeq table is populated with integer values in the range 1 through to 10,000,000, with 9,999 gaps, 10,000 islands.

Your solutions will likely need certain revisions if you want to apply them to temporal sequences. Use the following code to create and populate a table called TempSeq that represents a temporal sequence with unique values, with a fixed interval of four hours:

```
-- dbo.TempSeq (temporal sequence with unique values, interval: 4 hours)
IF OBJECT_ID('dbo.TempSeq', 'U') IS NOT NULL DROP TABLE dbo.TempSeq;

CREATE TABLE dbo.TempSeq
(
  seqval DATETIME NOT NULL
    CONSTRAINT PK_TempSeq PRIMARY KEY
);
```

```
INSERT INTO dbo.TempSeq(seqval) VALUES
  ('20090212 00:00'),
  ('20090212 04:00'),
  ('20090212 12:00'),
  ('20090212 16:00'),
  ('20090212 20:00'),
  ('20090213 08:00'),
  ('20090213 20:00'),
  ('20090214 00:00'),
  ('20090214 04:00'),
  ('20090214 12:00');
```

The sequence values could represent, for example, a timestamp recorded by a process every fixed interval of time reporting that it's online. And then the gaps information would represent nonavailability of the process, while the islands info would represent availability of the process.

Table 6-4 shows the gaps in TempSeq, and Table 6-5 shows the islands.

TABLE 6-4 **Gaps in TempSeq**

start_range	end_range
2009-02-12 08:00:00.000	2009-02-12 08:00:00.000
2009-02-13 00:00:00.000	2009-02-13 04:00:00.000
2009-02-13 12:00:00.000	2009-02-13 16:00:00.000
2009-02-14 08:00:00.000	2009-02-14 08:00:00.000

TABLE 6-5 **Islands in TempSeq**

start_range	end_range
2009-02-12 00:00:00.000	2009-02-12 04:00:00.000
2009-02-12 12:00:00.000	2009-02-12 20:00:00.000
2009-02-13 08:00:00.000	2009-02-13 08:00:00.000
2009-02-13 20:00:00.000	2009-02-14 04:00:00.000
2009-02-14 12:00:00.000	2009-02-14 12:00:00.000

You may also need to handle sequences that contain duplicate values. Run the following code to create and populate a table called NumSeqDups that represents a numeric sequence with duplicate values:

```
-- dbo.NumSeqDups (numeric sequence with duplicates, interval: 1)
IF OBJECT_ID('dbo.NumSeqDups', 'U') IS NOT NULL DROP TABLE dbo.NumSeqDups;

CREATE TABLE dbo.NumSeqDups
(
  seqval INT NOT NULL
);
CREATE CLUSTERED INDEX idx_seqval ON dbo.NumSeqDups(seqval);

INSERT INTO dbo.NumSeqDups(seqval) VALUES
  (2),(2),(2),(3),(11),(12),(12),(13),(27),(27),(27),(27),
  (33),(34),(34),(35),(35),(35),(42),(42);
```

Missing Ranges (Gaps)

You can take several approaches to solve the gaps problem. I will present four different solutions and discuss both their logical and their performance aspects. I'll always start by presenting a solution for a unique numeric sequence and then explain how to handle the other variations. So unless I explicitly say otherwise, the discussion is about the unique numeric sequence stored in the NumSeq table.

Gaps, Solution 1: Using Subqueries

One approach to solving the gaps problem can be described by the following steps:

1. Find the points before the gaps and add one interval to each.

2. For each starting point of a gap, find the next existing value in the sequence and subtract one interval.

Having the logical aspects of the steps resolved, you can start coding. You will find in the preceding logical steps that the chapter covered all the fundamental techniques that are mentioned—namely, finding points before gaps and finding the next existing value.

The following query returns the points before the gaps (in the sequence stored in NumSeq):

```
SELECT seqval
FROM dbo.NumSeq AS A
WHERE NOT EXISTS(SELECT *
                 FROM dbo.NumSeq AS B
                 WHERE B.seqval = A.seqval + 1);
```

This query generated the following output:

```
seqval
-----------
3
13
27
35
42
```

Remember that a point before a gap is a value after which the next consecutive value doesn't exist.

Notice in the output that the last row is of no interest to us because the gap it precedes is the gap to infinity. The following query returns the starting points of the gaps. It achieves this by adding one to the points before the gaps to get the first values in the gaps, filtering out the point before infinity.

```
SELECT
  seqval + 1 AS start_range
FROM dbo.NumSeq AS A
WHERE NOT EXISTS(SELECT *
                FROM dbo.NumSeq AS B
                WHERE B.seqval = A.seqval + 1)
  AND seqval < (SELECT MAX(seqval) FROM dbo.NumSeq);
```

This query generates the following output:

```
start_range
-----------
4
14
28
36
```

Finally, for each starting point in the gap, you use a subquery to return the next value in the sequence minus 1—in other words, the end of the gap:

```
SELECT
  seqval + 1 AS start_range,
  (SELECT MIN(B.seqval)
   FROM dbo.NumSeq AS B
   WHERE B.seqval > A.seqval) - 1 AS end_range
FROM dbo.NumSeq AS A
WHERE NOT EXISTS(SELECT *
                FROM dbo.NumSeq AS B
                WHERE B.seqval = A.seqval + 1)
  AND seqval < (SELECT MAX(seqval) FROM dbo.NumSeq);
```

To test the performance of this solution, run it against the BigNumSeq table:

```
SELECT
  seqval + 1 AS start_range,
  (SELECT MIN(B.seqval)
   FROM dbo.BigNumSeq AS B
   WHERE B.seqval > A.seqval) - 1 AS end_range
FROM dbo.BigNumSeq AS A
WHERE NOT EXISTS(SELECT *
                FROM dbo.BigNumSeq AS B
                WHERE B.seqval = A.seqval + 1)
  AND seqval < (SELECT MAX(seqval) FROM dbo.BigNumSeq);
```

On my system, this solution ran for 8 seconds and incurred 62,262 logical reads. This is the fastest of all solutions I tested for the gaps problem. To understand why it performs so well (compared to others), examine this query's execution plan, which is shown in Figure 6-11.

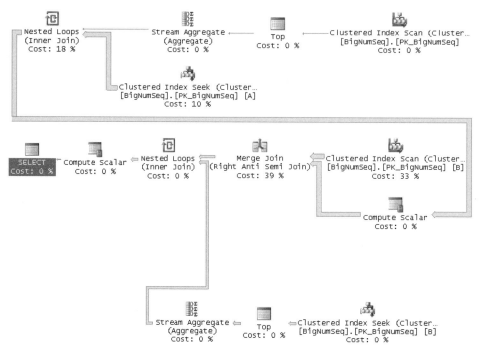

FIGURE 6-11 Query plan for gaps, solution 1

The key to the good performance of this solution is the way the optimizer decided to handle the "point before a gap" part represented in our query by the NOT EXISTS predicate. The optimizer identified this part logically as an anti-semi join and processed it with a merge join operator between two ordered scans of the index on *seqval* (one complete and another almost complete). These two scans incurred a little more than 32,000 reads, with the physical part probably being sequential. For almost 10,000,000 rows, this is far more efficient than doing a seek operation per each row. Next, only for the filtered points identified as points before gaps, the optimizer uses an index seek operation to fetch the next sequence value. Because our sequence has close to 10,000 such points and 3 levels in the index, this activity amounts to about 30,000 reads, with the physical part being random. All in all, the number of logical reads is a little more than 62,000 reads. Note that the number of seek operations depends on the number of gaps in the sequence. Therefore, the performance of this solution varies based on the number of gaps.

To apply this solution to a temporal sequence, instead of using + 1 or −1, simply use the DATEADD function with the appropriate interval, like so:

```
SELECT
  DATEADD(hour, 4, seqval) AS start_range,
  DATEADD(hour, -4,
    (SELECT MIN(B.seqval)
     FROM dbo.TempSeq AS B
     WHERE B.seqval > A.seqval)) AS end_range
```

```
FROM dbo.TempSeq AS A
WHERE NOT EXISTS(SELECT *
                FROM dbo.TempSeq AS B
                WHERE B.seqval = DATEADD(hour, 4, A.seqval))
  AND seqval < (SELECT MAX(seqval) FROM dbo.TempSeq);
```

You have a couple of options for dealing with a nonunique sequence. One is to replace the reference in the outer query to the original table with a reference to a derived table that has only distinct values, like so:

```
SELECT
  seqval + 1 AS start_range,
  (SELECT MIN(B.seqval)
   FROM dbo.NumSeqDups AS B
   WHERE B.seqval > A.seqval) - 1 AS end_range
FROM (SELECT DISTINCT seqval FROM dbo.NumSeqDups) AS A
WHERE NOT EXISTS(SELECT *
                FROM dbo.NumSeqDups AS B
                WHERE B.seqval = A.seqval + 1)
  AND seqval < (SELECT MAX(seqval) FROM dbo.NumSeqDups);
```

Another is to simply use a DISTINCT clause in the SELECT list:

```
SELECT DISTINCT
  seqval + 1 AS start_range,
  (SELECT MIN(B.seqval)
   FROM dbo.NumSeqDups AS B
   WHERE B.seqval > A.seqval) - 1 AS end_range
FROM dbo.NumSeqDups AS A
WHERE NOT EXISTS(SELECT *
                FROM dbo.NumSeqDups AS B
                WHERE B.seqval = A.seqval + 1)
  AND seqval < (SELECT MAX(seqval) FROM dbo.NumSeqDups);
```

Gaps, Solution 2: Using Subqueries

The second approach to solving the gaps problem is one I find to be simpler and more intuitive than the previous. It implements the following steps:

1. To each existing value, match the next existing value, generating current, next pairs.

2. Keep only pairs where next minus current is greater than one interval.

3. With the remaining pairs, add one interval to the current and subtract one interval from the next.

This approach relies on the fact that adjacent values with a difference greater than one interval represent the boundaries of a gap. Identifying a gap based on identification of the next existing value is another useful fundamental technique.

To translate the preceding steps to T-SQL, the following query simply returns the next value for each current value:

```
SELECT
    seqval AS cur,
    (SELECT MIN(B.seqval)
     FROM dbo.NumSeq AS B
     WHERE B.seqval > A.seqval) AS nxt
FROM dbo.NumSeq AS A;
```

This query generates the following output:

```
cur          nxt
-----------  -----------
2            3
3            11
11           12
12           13
13           27
27           33
33           34
34           35
35           42
42           NULL
```

Finally, you create a derived table out of the previous step's query, and you keep only pairs where *nxt – cur* is greater than one. You add one to *cur* to get the actual start of the gap and subtract one from *nxt* to get the actual end of the gap:

```
SELECT cur + 1 AS start_range, nxt - 1 AS end_range
FROM (SELECT
          seqval AS cur,
          (SELECT MIN(B.seqval)
           FROM dbo.NumSeq AS B
           WHERE B.seqval > A.seqval) AS nxt
      FROM dbo.NumSeq AS A) AS D
WHERE nxt - cur > 1;
```

Note that this solution got rid of the point before infinity with no special treatment because the *nxt* value for it was NULL.

Run this solution against BigNumSeq to test its performance:

```
SELECT cur + 1 AS start_range, nxt - 1 AS end_range
FROM (SELECT
          seqval AS cur,
          (SELECT MIN(B.seqval)
           FROM dbo.BigNumSeq AS B
           WHERE B.seqval > A.seqval) AS nxt
      FROM dbo.BigNumSeq AS A) AS D
WHERE nxt - cur > 1;
```

The plan for this query is shown in Figure 6-12.

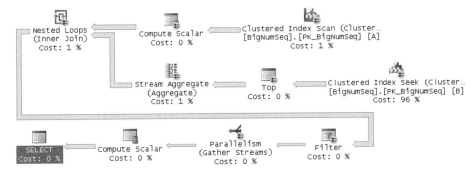

FIGURE 6-12 Query plan for gaps, solution 2

This solution is significantly slower than the previous one. It ran on my system for 48 seconds and incurred 31,875,478 logical reads. The reason for the large number of reads becomes apparent when you examine the plan. The plan shows a full scan of the index to retrieve all sequence values (close to 10,000,000 of them), and per each row, an index seek operation is used to return the next value. With a cost of 3 reads per seek (for the 3 levels of the index), you get about 30,000,000 reads for all seeks.

To apply the solution to a temporal sequence, use the DATEADD function to add or subtract an interval, and the DATEDIFF function to calculate the difference between *cur* and *nxt*:

```
SELECT
  DATEADD(hour, 4, cur) AS start_range,
  DATEADD(hour, -4, nxt) AS end_range
FROM (SELECT
        seqval AS cur,
        (SELECT MIN(B.seqval)
          FROM dbo.TempSeq AS B
          WHERE B.seqval > A.seqval) AS nxt
      FROM dbo.TempSeq AS A) AS D
WHERE DATEDIFF(hour, cur, nxt) > 4;
```

For a sequence with duplicates, again, one approach is to query a derived table that has only distinct values, like so:

```
SELECT cur + 1 AS start_range, nxt - 1 AS end_range
FROM (SELECT
        seqval AS cur,
        (SELECT MIN(B.seqval)
          FROM dbo.NumSeqDups AS B
          WHERE B.seqval > A.seqval) AS nxt
      FROM (SELECT DISTINCT seqval FROM dbo.NumSeqDups) AS A) AS D
WHERE nxt - cur > 1;
```

Or simply add a DISTINCT clause to the SELECT list:

```
SELECT DISTINCT cur + 1 AS start_range, nxt - 1 AS end_range
FROM (SELECT
        seqval AS cur,
        (SELECT MIN(B.seqval)
```

```
        FROM dbo.NumSeqDups AS B
          WHERE B.seqval > A.seqval) AS nxt
      FROM dbo.NumSeqDups AS A) AS D
WHERE nxt - cur > 1;
```

Gaps, Solution 3: Using Ranking Functions

The third solution is similar to the second, but it uses a different method to pair current and next values. It defines a CTE that assigns row numbers to rows based on *seqval* ordering. The outer query then joins two instances, matching current and next values based on an offset of 1 between their row numbers. Here's the complete solution:

```
WITH C AS
(
  SELECT seqval, ROW_NUMBER() OVER(ORDER BY seqval) AS rownum
    FROM dbo.NumSeq
)
SELECT Cur.seqval + 1 AS start_range, Nxt.seqval - 1 AS end_range
FROM C AS Cur
  JOIN C AS Nxt
    ON Nxt.rownum = Cur.rownum + 1
WHERE Nxt.seqval - Cur.seqval > 1;
```

Run the solution against the big sequence to test its performance:

```
WITH C AS
(
  SELECT seqval, ROW_NUMBER() OVER(ORDER BY seqval) AS rownum
    FROM dbo.BigNumSeq
)
SELECT Cur.seqval + 1 AS start_range, Nxt.seqval - 1 AS end_range
FROM C AS Cur
  JOIN C AS Nxt
    ON Nxt.rownum = Cur.rownum + 1
WHERE Nxt.seqval - Cur.seqval > 1;
```

The plan for this query is shown in Figure 6-13.

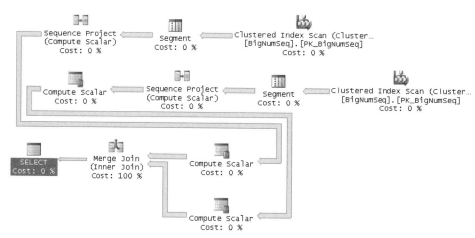

FIGURE 6-13 Query plan for gaps, solution 3

This solution performs better than the previous. It ran on my system for 24 seconds and incurred 32,246 logical reads. It performs two ordered scans of the index on *seqval*, to return the current and next values and their row numbers, and then uses a merge join operator to match current with next values. The merge operator turns out to be quite expensive here. It is handled as a many-to-many join, even though you and I know that in practice it's a one-to-one join.

As in the previous solution, to apply this solution to a temporal sequence, use the DATEADD function to add or subtract an interval and use the DATEDIFF function to calculate the difference between *cur* and *nxt*:

```
WITH C AS
(
  SELECT seqval, ROW_NUMBER() OVER(ORDER BY seqval) AS rownum
  FROM dbo.TempSeq
)
SELECT
  DATEADD(hour, 4, Cur.seqval) AS start_range,
  DATEADD(hour, -4, Nxt.Seqval) AS end_range
FROM C AS Cur
  JOIN C AS Nxt
    ON Nxt.rownum = Cur.rownum + 1
WHERE DATEDIFF(hour, Cur.seqval, Nxt.seqval) > 4;
```

For a sequence with duplicates, one option is as usual to use a derived table with the distinct sequence values, like so:

```
WITH C AS
(
  SELECT seqval, ROW_NUMBER() OVER(ORDER BY seqval) AS rownum
  FROM (SELECT DISTINCT seqval FROM dbo.NumSeqDups) AS D
)
SELECT Cur.seqval + 1 AS start_range, Nxt.seqval - 1 AS end_range
FROM C AS Cur
  JOIN C AS Nxt
    ON Nxt.rownum = Cur.rownum + 1
WHERE Nxt.seqval - Cur.seqval > 1;
```

Another option is to use row numbers to number the occurrences of each unique value and filter only occurrences with the row number 1. The rest is the same as in the original solution. Here's the complete solution query:

```
WITH C1 AS
(
  SELECT seqval, ROW_NUMBER() OVER(PARTITION BY seqval
                                   ORDER BY (SELECT 0)) AS dupnum
  FROM dbo.NumSeqDups
),
C2 AS
(
  SELECT seqval, ROW_NUMBER() OVER(ORDER BY seqval) AS rownum
  FROM C1
  WHERE dupnum = 1
)
```

```
SELECT Cur.seqval + 1 AS start_range, Nxt.seqval - 1 AS end_range
FROM C2 AS Cur
  JOIN C2 AS Nxt
    ON Nxt.rownum = Cur.rownum + 1
WHERE Nxt.seqval - Cur.seqval > 1;
```

Gaps, Solution 4: Using Cursors

I also wrote a solution based on cursors because I was curious about its performance. On the one hand, the cursor can achieve the task using a single ordered scan of the index; on the other hand, a lot of overhead is associated with the record-by-record manipulation of the cursor. You pay overhead per each row that is processed with the cursor that you don't normally pay for set-based manipulation.

The cursor solution is quite straightforward: The cursor scans the sequence values once in order and compares each current value with the previous. If the difference between them is greater than one interval, the pair represents a gap. Here's the complete solution's code:

```
SET NOCOUNT ON;

DECLARE @seqval AS INT, @prvseqval AS INT;
DECLARE @Gaps TABLE(start_range INT, end_range INT);

DECLARE C CURSOR FAST_FORWARD FOR
  SELECT seqval FROM dbo.BigNumSeq ORDER BY seqval;

OPEN C;

FETCH NEXT FROM C INTO @prvseqval;
IF @@FETCH_STATUS = 0 FETCH NEXT FROM C INTO @seqval;

WHILE @@FETCH_STATUS = 0
BEGIN
  IF @seqval - @prvseqval > 1
    INSERT INTO @Gaps(start_range, end_range)
      VALUES(@prvseqval + 1, @seqval - 1);

  SET @prvseqval = @seqval;
  FETCH NEXT FROM C INTO @seqval;
END

CLOSE C;

DEALLOCATE C;

SELECT start_range, end_range FROM @Gaps;
```

As expected, the cursor solution was very slow. It ran for 250 seconds on my system even though it incurred only 16,123 logical reads.

Returning Individual Missing Values

Before I move on to covering the solutions to the islands problem, I want to address a special case of the missing values problem. If you need to return the list of individual missing values as opposed to missing ranges, using the Nums table the task is very simple:

```
SELECT n FROM dbo.Nums
WHERE n BETWEEN (SELECT MIN(seqval) FROM dbo.NumSeq)
           AND (SELECT MAX(seqval) FROM dbo.NumSeq)
  AND n NOT IN(SELECT seqval FROM dbo.NumSeq);
```

Existing Ranges (Islands)

As with the gaps problem, you can take several approaches to solve the islands problem. I'll describe four solutions here.

Islands, Solution 1: Using Subqueries and Ranking Calculations

The first solution to the islands problem is quite straightforward. It involves the following steps:

1. Identify points after gaps and assign them row numbers—these points are starting points of islands.

2. Identify points before gaps and assign with row numbers—these points are ending points of islands.

3. Match starting and ending points of islands based on equality between their row numbers.

Here's the solution code for the unique numeric sequence:

```
WITH StartingPoints AS
(
  SELECT seqval, ROW_NUMBER() OVER(ORDER BY seqval) AS rownum
  FROM dbo.NumSeq AS A
  WHERE NOT EXISTS
    (SELECT *
     FROM dbo.NumSeq AS B
     WHERE B.seqval = A.seqval - 1)
),
EndingPoints AS
(
  SELECT seqval, ROW_NUMBER() OVER(ORDER BY seqval) AS rownum
  FROM dbo.NumSeq AS A
  WHERE NOT EXISTS
    (SELECT *
     FROM dbo.NumSeq AS B
     WHERE B.seqval = A.seqval + 1)
)
SELECT S.seqval AS start_range, E.seqval AS end_range
FROM StartingPoints AS S
  JOIN EndingPoints AS E
    ON E.rownum = S.rownum;
```

To test the performance of this solution, run the code against the BigNumSeq table:

```
WITH StartingPoints AS
(
  SELECT seqval, ROW_NUMBER() OVER(ORDER BY seqval) AS rownum
  FROM dbo.BigNumSeq AS A
  WHERE NOT EXISTS
    (SELECT *
     FROM dbo.BigNumSeq AS B
     WHERE B.seqval = A.seqval - 1)
),
EndingPoints AS
(
  SELECT seqval, ROW_NUMBER() OVER(ORDER BY seqval) AS rownum
  FROM dbo.BigNumSeq AS A
  WHERE NOT EXISTS
    (SELECT *
     FROM dbo.BigNumSeq AS B
     WHERE B.seqval = A.seqval + 1)
)
SELECT S.seqval AS start_range, E.seqval AS end_range
FROM StartingPoints AS S
  JOIN EndingPoints AS E
    ON E.rownum = S.rownum;
```

The plan for this query is shown in Figure 6-14.

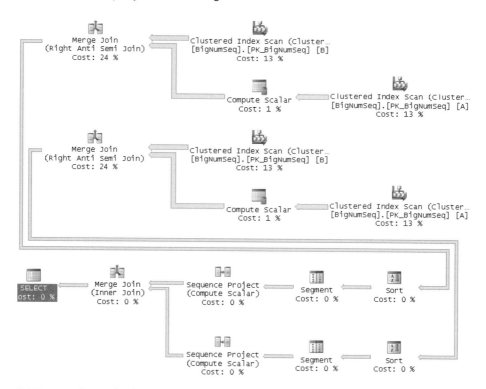

FIGURE 6-14 Query plan for islands, solution 1

The plan shows two merge joins, each between the results of two ordered scans of the index on *seqval*. Each such merge join is used to process a logical anti-semi join that filters points before or after gaps. Each such merge join filters as many rows as the number of islands (10,000 in our case). Finally, another merge join is used to pair starting and ending points. Even though the last merge is many-to-many and can potentially be slow, it's pretty fast because it handles only a small number of islands in our case. This solution ran on my system for 17 seconds and incurred 64,492 logical reads.

To apply the solution to a temporal sequence, simply use the *DATEADD* function as usual to add an interval to the sequence value:

```
WITH StartingPoints AS
(
  SELECT seqval, ROW_NUMBER() OVER(ORDER BY seqval) AS rownum
  FROM dbo.TempSeq AS A
  WHERE NOT EXISTS
    (SELECT *
     FROM dbo.TempSeq AS B
     WHERE B.seqval = DATEADD(hour, -4, A.seqval))
),
EndingPoints AS
(
  SELECT seqval, ROW_NUMBER() OVER(ORDER BY seqval) AS rownum
  FROM dbo.TempSeq AS A
  WHERE NOT EXISTS
    (SELECT *
     FROM dbo.TempSeq AS B
     WHERE B.seqval = DATEADD(hour, 4, A.seqval))
)
SELECT S.seqval AS start_range, E.seqval AS end_range
FROM StartingPoints AS S
  JOIN EndingPoints AS E
    ON E.rownum = S.rownum;
```

To apply the solution to a sequence with duplicates, query a derived table with the distinct values:

```
WITH StartingPoints AS
(
  SELECT seqval, ROW_NUMBER() OVER(ORDER BY seqval) AS rownum
  FROM (SELECT DISTINCT seqval FROM dbo.NumSeqDups) AS A
  WHERE NOT EXISTS
    (SELECT *
     FROM dbo.NumSeqDups AS B
     WHERE B.seqval = A.seqval - 1)
),
EndingPoints AS
(
  SELECT seqval, ROW_NUMBER() OVER(ORDER BY seqval) AS rownum
  FROM (SELECT DISTINCT seqval FROM dbo.NumSeqDups) AS A
  WHERE NOT EXISTS
    (SELECT *
     FROM dbo.NumSeqDups AS B
     WHERE B.seqval = A.seqval + 1)
)
```

```
SELECT S.seqval AS start_range, E.seqval AS end_range
FROM StartingPoints AS S
  JOIN EndingPoints AS E
    ON E.rownum = S.rownum;
```

Islands, Solution 2: Using Group Identifier Based on Subqueries

The second solution to the islands problem involves a concept I haven't discussed yet—a grouping factor, or group identifier. You basically need to group data by a factor that does not exist in the data as a base attribute. In our case, you need to calculate some x value for all members of the first subset of consecutive values {2, 3}, some y value for the second {11, 12, 13}, some z value for the third {27}, and so on. When you have this grouping factor available, you can group the data by this factor and return the minimum and maximum *col1* values in each group.

One approach to calculating this grouping factor brings me to another technique: calculating the *min* or *max* value of a group of consecutive values. Take the group {11, 12, 13} as an example. If you can manage to calculate for each of the members the *max* value in the group (13), you can use it as your grouping factor.

The logic behind the technique to calculating the maximum within a group of consecutive values is: return the minimum value that is greater than or equal to the current, after which there's a gap. Here's the translation to T-SQL:

```
SELECT seqval,
  (SELECT MIN(B.seqval)
   FROM dbo.NumSeq AS B
   WHERE B.seqval >= A.seqval
     AND NOT EXISTS
       (SELECT *
        FROM dbo.NumSeq AS C
        WHERE C.seqval = B.seqval + 1)) AS grp
FROM dbo.NumSeq AS A;
```

This code generates the following output:

```
seqval      grp
----------- -----------
2           3
3           3
11          13
12          13
13          13
27          27
33          35
34          35
35          35
42          42
```

The rest is really easy: create a CTE table out of the previous step's query, group the data by the grouping factor, and return the minimum and maximum values for each group:

```
WITH D AS
(
  SELECT seqval,
    (SELECT MIN(B.seqval)
     FROM dbo.NumSeq AS B
     WHERE B.seqval >= A.seqval
       AND NOT EXISTS
         (SELECT *
          FROM dbo.NumSeq AS C
          WHERE C.seqval = B.seqval + 1)) AS grp
  FROM dbo.NumSeq AS A
)
SELECT MIN(seqval) AS start_range, MAX(seqval) AS end_range
FROM D
GROUP BY grp;
```

This solution solves the problem, but I'm not sure I'd qualify it as a very simple and intuitive solution with satisfactory performance. To test its performance, you can run it against the BigNumSeq table:

```
WITH D AS
(
  SELECT seqval,
    (SELECT MIN(B.seqval)
     FROM dbo.BigNumSeq AS B
     WHERE B.seqval >= A.seqval
       AND NOT EXISTS
         (SELECT *
          FROM dbo.BigNumSeq AS C
          WHERE C.seqval = B.seqval + 1)) AS grp
  FROM dbo.BigNumSeq AS A
)
SELECT MIN(seqval) AS start_range, MAX(seqval) AS end_range
FROM D
GROUP BY grp;
```

The execution plan for this query is shown in Figure 6-15.

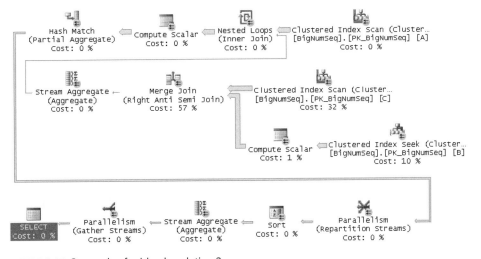

FIGURE 6-15 Query plan for islands, solution 2

This solution is so slow that after 10 minutes I simply canceled it. The cause for the poor performance can be identified in the query's execution plan. The index on *seqval* is fully scanned to retrieve all rows from the instance of the table named A. Recall that the table has almost 10,000,000 rows. For each of those rows a nested loops operator invokes quite expensive activity—a merge join implementing a logical anti-semi join to identify all points before a gap. This merge join happens between the results of a full and a partial scan of the index on *seqval*. Then the minimum of those points is returned.

To apply this solution to a temporal sequence, use the *DATEADD* function to add an interval to the sequence value:

```
WITH D AS
(
  SELECT seqval,
    (SELECT MIN(B.seqval)
     FROM dbo.TempSeq AS B
     WHERE B.seqval >= A.seqval
       AND NOT EXISTS
         (SELECT *
          FROM dbo.TempSeq AS C
          WHERE C.seqval = DATEADD(hour, 4, B.seqval))) AS grp
  FROM dbo.TempSeq AS A
)
SELECT MIN(seqval) AS start_range, MAX(seqval) AS end_range
FROM D
GROUP BY grp;
```

For a sequence with duplicates, the solution actually works as is because the GROUP BY operation eliminates the duplicates:

```
WITH D AS
(
  SELECT seqval,
    (SELECT MIN(B.seqval)
     FROM dbo.NumSeqDups AS B
     WHERE B.seqval >= A.seqval
       AND NOT EXISTS
         (SELECT *
          FROM dbo.NumSeqDups AS C
          WHERE C.seqval = B.seqval + 1)) AS grp
  FROM dbo.NumSeqDups AS A
)
SELECT MIN(seqval) AS start_range, MAX(seqval) AS end_range
FROM D
GROUP BY grp;
```

Islands, Solution 3: Using Group Identifier Based on Ranking Calculations

The third solution to the islands problem is also based on the concept of a group identifier, but it calculates it using a dramatically simpler and faster technique. The solution is based on a certain relationship that can be identified between the sequence with the gaps and a sequence of row numbers. To explain the technique, first run the following query calculating row numbers based on *seqval* order:

```
SELECT seqval, ROW_NUMBER() OVER(ORDER BY seqval) AS rownum
FROM dbo.NumSeq;
```

This query generates the following output:

```
seqval       rownum
-----------  --------------------
2            1
3            2
11           3
12           4
13           5
27           6
33           7
34           8
35           9
42           10
```

See if you can identify a relationship between the way the *seqval* values increment and the way row numbers do.

Because both sequences keep incrementing by the same interval within an island, their difference remains constant within an island. As soon as you get to a new island, the difference between them increases because *seqval* increments by more than 1, while the row number increments by 1. Run the following query to produce this difference:

```
SELECT seqval, seqval - ROW_NUMBER() OVER(ORDER BY seqval) AS diff
FROM dbo.NumSeq;
```

You get the following output:

```
seqval       diff
-----------  --------------------
2            1
3            1
11           8
12           8
13           8
27           21
33           26
34           26
35           26
42           32
```

As you can see, this difference is the same for all members of the same island and different for other islands. Now, simply replace in the previous solution the CTE table query with the preceding query to get the desired result:

```
WITH D AS
(
  SELECT seqval, seqval - ROW_NUMBER() OVER(ORDER BY seqval) AS grp
  FROM dbo.NumSeq
)
```

```
SELECT MIN(seqval) AS start_range, MAX(seqval) AS end_range
FROM D
GROUP BY grp;
```

The performance of this solution is very good. Run it against the BigNumSeq table:

```
WITH D AS
(
  SELECT seqval, seqval - ROW_NUMBER() OVER(ORDER BY seqval) AS grp
  FROM dbo.BigNumSeq
)
SELECT MIN(seqval) AS start_range, MAX(seqval) AS end_range
FROM D
GROUP BY grp;
```

The execution plan for this query is shown in Figure 6-16.

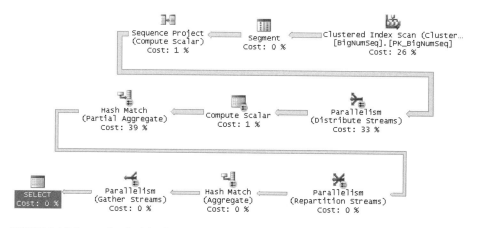

FIGURE 6-16 Query plan for islands, solution 3

The execution plan explains the efficiency of this solution. The index is scanned only once to retrieve the sequence values and also to calculate the row numbers. The rows are then grouped by the difference between the two, and the minimum and maximum *seqval* values are calculated for each group. This code ran for about 10 seconds on my system and incurred 16,123 logical reads. This is the fastest solution to the islands problem out of the ones I present here.

Applying the solution to a temporal sequence is not as trivial as in the previous cases. Here, the temporal sequence and the row numbers sequence have different data types and also different intervals. The trick to applying the efficient technique in this case is to realize that instead of calculating the difference between the two sequences, you can subtract from each of the temporal sequence values as many temporal intervals as the row number. As a result, all members of the same island get a constant date and time value, which is different than it is for other islands. The sequence in the TempSeq table has an interval of four hours;

therefore, to produce the group identifier in this case, you need to subtract from *seqval* row number times four hours, like so:

```
WITH D AS
(
  SELECT seqval, DATEADD(hour, -4 * ROW_NUMBER() OVER(ORDER BY seqval), seqval) AS grp
  FROM dbo.TempSeq
)
SELECT MIN(seqval) AS start_range, MAX(seqval) AS end_range
FROM D
GROUP BY grp;
```

For a sequence with duplicates, the trick is simply not to increment the ranking value for duplicate values. To achieve this, use the DENSE_RANK function instead of ROW_NUMBER, like so:

```
WITH D AS
(
  SELECT seqval, seqval - DENSE_RANK() OVER(ORDER BY seqval) AS grp
  FROM dbo.NumSeqDups
)
SELECT MIN(seqval) AS start_range, MAX(seqval) AS end_range
FROM D
GROUP BY grp;
```

Islands, Solution 4: Using Cursors

Of course, coverage of solutions to the islands problem cannot be considered complete without a cursor-based solution. The logic of the solution is straightforward: scan the sequence values in order, and as soon as the current value is greater than the previous by more than one interval, you know that the previous value closes the last island, and the new value opens a new one. Here's the code implementing this logic:

```
SET NOCOUNT ON;

DECLARE @seqval AS INT, @prvseqval AS INT, @first AS INT;
DECLARE @Islands TABLE(start_range INT, end_range INT);

DECLARE C CURSOR FAST_FORWARD FOR
  SELECT seqval FROM dbo.BigNumSeq ORDER BY seqval;

OPEN C;

FETCH NEXT FROM C INTO @seqval;
SET @first = @seqval;
SET @prvseqval = @seqval;

WHILE @@FETCH_STATUS = 0
BEGIN
  IF @seqval - @prvseqval > 1
  BEGIN
    INSERT INTO @Islands(start_range, end_range)
```

```
        VALUES(@first, @prvseqval);
    SET @first = @seqval;
  END

  SET @prvseqval = @seqval;
  FETCH NEXT FROM C INTO @seqval;
END

IF @first IS NOT NULL
  INSERT INTO @Islands(start_range, end_range)
    VALUES(@first, @prvseqval);

CLOSE C;

DEALLOCATE C;

SELECT start_range, end_range FROM @Islands;
```

Because of the high overhead of the record-by-record manipulation of the cursor, it ran for about 217 seconds against BigNumSeq on my system even though it incurred only 16,123 logical reads.

A Variation of the Islands Problem

In this section I'll describe a variation of the islands problem and a solution based on the group identifier concept.

The problem at hand involves a table (call it T3) with two columns of interest—one column represents a sequence of keys (call it *id*), and another column represents a status value (call it *val*). Run the following code to create a table called T3 and populate it with sample data:

```
USE tempdb;
IF OBJECT_ID('dbo.T3') IS NOT NULL DROP TABLE dbo.T3;
CREATE TABLE dbo.T3
(
  id  INT         NOT NULL PRIMARY KEY,
  val VARCHAR(10) NOT NULL
);
GO

INSERT INTO dbo.T3(id, val) VALUES
  (2,  'a'),
  (3,  'a'),
  (5,  'a'),
  (7,  'b'),
  (11, 'b'),
  (13, 'a'),
  (17, 'a'),
  (19, 'a'),
  (23, 'c'),
  (29, 'c'),
  (31, 'a'),
  (37, 'a'),
```

```
(41, 'a'),
(43, 'a'),
(47, 'c'),
(53, 'c'),
(59, 'c');
```

This kind of data can represent, for example, the status of a product in various stations in an assembly line.

The challenge is to identify the ranges of IDs for each contiguous segment with the same status value. With the given sample data your solution should produce the output shown in Table 6-6.

TABLE 6-6 Desired Result of Solution to a Variation of the Islands Problem

mn	mx	val
2	5	a
7	11	b
13	19	a
23	29	c
31	43	a
47	59	c

The key to solving the problem is to calculate two row numbers—one based on *id* ordering and the other based on *val, id* ordering, like so:

```
SELECT id, val,
  ROW_NUMBER() OVER(ORDER BY id) AS rn_id,
  ROW_NUMBER() OVER(ORDER BY val, id) AS rn_val_id
FROM dbo.T3
ORDER BY id;
```

This query generates the following output:

```
id          val        rn_id                 rn_val_id
----------- ---------- --------------------- --------------------
2           a          1                     1
3           a          2                     2
5           a          3                     3
7           b          4                     11
11          b          5                     12
13          a          6                     4
17          a          7                     5
19          a          8                     6
23          c          9                     13
29          c          10                    14
31          a          11                    7
37          a          12                    8
41          a          13                    9
43          a          14                    10
47          c          15                    15
53          c          16                    16
59          c          17                    17
```

Naturally, both types of row numbers increment the same way within a contiguous segment of a status value. When jumping to the next segment with the same status, the row number based on *val, id* ordering increases by 1, while the row number based on only *id* ordering increases by more than 1. This means that the difference between the two row numbers is constant in a segment and different from those in other segments of the same status value. Run the following query to obtain this difference:

```
SELECT id, val,
  ROW_NUMBER() OVER(ORDER BY id)
    - ROW_NUMBER() OVER(ORDER BY val, id) AS diff
FROM dbo.T3
ORDER BY id;
```

Notice in the output that the combination of *val* and *diff* is unique per segment:

```
id           val          diff
-----------  -----------  --------------------
2            a            0
3            a            0
5            a            0
7            b            -7
11           b            -7
13           a            2
17           a            2
19           a            2
23           c            -4
29           c            -4
31           a            4
37           a            4
41           a            4
43           a            4
47           c            0
53           c            0
59           c            0
```

What's left is simply to group the data by the status value and the difference between the row numbers and return for each group the minimum and maximum ids, and the status value, as the following query shows:

```
WITH C AS
(
  SELECT id, val,
    ROW_NUMBER() OVER(ORDER BY id)
      - ROW_NUMBER() OVER(ORDER BY val, id) AS grp
  FROM dbo.T3
)
SELECT MIN(id) AS mn, MAX(id) AS mx, val
FROM C
GROUP BY val, grp
ORDER BY mn;
```

Conclusion

This chapter covered many subjects, all related to subqueries. I discussed scalar and list subqueries, self-contained and correlated subqueries, table expressions, and ranking calculations.

It's important to make mental notes of the fundamental techniques that I point out here and throughout the book, such as generating copies using an auxiliary table of numbers, introducing a tiebreaker, finding points before gaps, returning the next or previous value, calculating a grouping factor, and so on. This builds your T-SQL vocabulary and enhances your skills. As you progress with this approach, you'll see that it becomes easier and easier to identify fundamental elements in a problem. Having already resolved and polished key techniques separately in a focused manner, you will use them naturally to solve problems.

Chapter 7
Joins and Set Operations

This chapter covers joins and set operations—their logical aspects as well as their physical performance aspects. I'll demonstrate practical applications for each type of join and set operation. I have used the ANSI SQL terminology to categorize the elements of the language that I'll cover here. *Joins* (CROSS, INNER, OUTER) refer to *horizontal* operations (loosely speaking) between tables, while *set operations* (UNION, EXCEPT, INTERSECT) refer to *vertical* operations between tables.

Joins

Joins are operations that allow you to match rows between tables. I informally call these operations horizontal because the virtual table resulting from a join operation between two tables contains all columns from both tables.

I'll first describe the different syntaxes for joins supported by the standard, and I'll also briefly mention legacy proprietary elements in T-SQL. I'll then describe the fundamental join types and their applications followed by further examples of joins. I'll also include a focused discussion on the internal processing of joins—namely, join algorithms.

You'll have a couple of chances to practice what you've learned by trying to solve a problem that encompasses previously discussed aspects of joins.

Old Style vs. New Style

T-SQL supports two different syntaxes for joins. A lot of confusion surrounds the two. When do you use each? Which performs better? Which is standard, and which is proprietary? Will the older syntax be deprecated soon? And so on. I hope this chapter will clear the fog.

I'll start by saying that the ANSI standard supports two different syntaxes for joins, and neither syntax is in the process of deprecation yet. The join elements of the older standard are a complete part of the newer. This means that you can use either one without worrying that it will not be supported by Microsoft SQL Server sometime soon. SQL Server will not remove support for implemented features that were not deprecated by the standard.

The older of the two syntaxes was introduced in ANSI SQL-89. What distinguishes it from the newer syntax is the use of commas to separate table names that appear in the FROM clause and the absence of the JOIN keyword and the ON clause:

```
FROM T1, T2
WHERE where_predicate
```

The ANSI SQL-89 syntax had support only for cross and inner join types. It did not have support for outer joins.

The newer syntax was introduced in ANSI SQL-92, and what distinguishes it from the older syntax is the removal of the commas and the introduction of the JOIN keyword and the ON clause:

```
FROM T1 <join_type> JOIN T2 ON <on_predicate>
WHERE where_predicate
```

ANSI SQL-92 introduced support for outer joins, and this drove the need for a separation of filters—the ON filter and the WHERE filter. I'll explain this in detail in the outer joins section.

Some people think that the comma-based syntax for joins in general is not standard, which is not true. Part of the confusion has to do with the fact that in the past, T-SQL supported a proprietary syntax for outer joins that was based on commas before SQL Server added support for the ANSI SQL-92 syntax. In particular, I'm talking about the old-style proprietary outer join syntax, using *= and =* for left outer and right outer joins, respectively. In addition to not being standard, this syntax was problematic in the sense that in some cases the meaning of the query was ambiguous. SQL Server deprecated this syntax, and it is supported only under a backward-compatibility flag. In short, with cross and inner joins both the comma-based and JOIN keyword-based syntaxes are standard, while with outer joins only the JOIN keyword–based syntax is standard.

In the following section, I'll discuss both syntaxes and explain why I recommend that you stick to the ANSI SQL-92 join syntax even though the old-style syntax for cross and inner joins is standard.

Fundamental Join Types

As I describe the different fundamental join types—cross, inner, and outer—keep in mind the phases in logical query processing that I described in detail in Chapter 1, "Logical Query Processing." In particular, keep in mind the logical phases involved in join processing.

Each fundamental join type takes place only between two tables. Even if you have more than two tables in the FROM clause, the three logical query processing subphases of joins take place between two tables at a time. Each join results in a virtual table, which in turn is joined with the next table in the FROM clause. This process continues until all table operators in the FROM clause are processed.

The fundamental join types differ in the logical subphases that they apply. Cross join applies only the first (Cartesian product), inner join applies the first and the second (Cartesian product and ON filter), and outer join applies all three (Cartesian product, ON filter, add outer rows).

CROSS

A cross join performs a Cartesian product between two tables. In other words, it returns a row for each possible combination of a row from the left table and a row from the right table. If the left table has *n* rows and the right table has *m* rows, a cross join returns a table with *n* × *m* rows.

Before I demonstrate practical applications of cross joins, I'll start with a very simple example—a plain cross.

The following query produces all possible pairs of employees from the Employees table in the InsideTSQL2008 database:

```
USE InsideTSQL2008;

SELECT E1.firstname, E1.lastname AS emp1,
  E2.firstname, E2.lastname AS emp2
FROM HR.Employees AS E1
  CROSS JOIN HR.Employees AS E2;
```

Because the Employees table contains nine rows, the result set contains 81 rows.

Here's the ANSI SQL-89 syntax you would use for the same task:

```
SELECT E1.firstname, E1.lastname AS emp1,
  E2.firstname, E2.lastname AS emp2
FROM HR.Employees AS E1, HR.Employees AS E2;
```

The optimizer produces the same plan for both the ANSI SQL-92 and the ANSI SQL-89 syntaxes, so you shouldn't have any concerns about performance. For reasons that I will explain later in the chapter, I recommend that you stick to the ANSI SQL-92 syntax. Now let's look at more sophisticated uses of cross joins.

In Chapter 6, "Subqueries, Table Expressions, and Ranking Functions," I presented a fundamental technique to generate copies of rows. Recall that I used an auxiliary table of numbers (Nums) as follows to generate the requested number of copies of each row:

```
SELECT ...
FROM T1 CROSS JOIN Nums
WHERE n <= <num_of_copies>
```

The preceding technique generates in the result set as many copies of each row in T1 as *num_of_copies*. As a practical example, suppose you need to fill an Orders table with sample data for testing. You have a Customers table with sample customer information and an Employees table with sample employee information. You want to generate, for each combination of a customer and an employee, an order for each day in January 2009.

I will demonstrate this technique in the InsideTSQL2008 database. The Customers table contains 91 rows, the Employees table contains 9 rows, and for each customer-employee combination, you need an order for each day in January 2009—that is, for 31 days. The result set should contain 25,389 rows (*91 × 9 × 31 = 25,389*). Naturally, you want to store the result set in a target table and generate an order ID for each order.

You already have tables with customers and employees, but a table is missing—you need a table to represent the days. You probably guessed already that the Nums table will assume the role of the missing table:

```
SELECT custid, empid,
  DATEADD(day, n-1, '20090101') AS orderdate
FROM Sales.Customers
  CROSS JOIN HR.Employees
  CROSS JOIN dbo.Nums
WHERE n <= 31;
```

You cross Customers, Employees, and Nums, filtering the first 31 values of *n* from the Nums table for the 31 days of the month. In the SELECT list, you calculate the specific target dates by adding $n - 1$ days to the first date of the month, January 1, 2009.

The last missing element is the order ID. But you can easily generate it using the ROW_NUMBER function.

In practice, you'd probably want to encapsulate this logic in a stored procedure that accepts the date range as input. Instead of using a literal for the number of days in the filter, you use the following expression:

```
DATEDIFF(day, @fromdate, @todate) + 1
```

Similarly, the DATEADD function in the SELECT list will refer to @*fromdate* instead of a literal base date:

```
DATEADD(day, n-1, @fromdate) AS orderdate
```

Here's the code that you need to generate the test data and populate a target table:

```
IF OBJECT_ID('dbo.MyOrders') IS NOT NULL  DROP TABLE dbo.MyOrders;
GO

DECLARE
  @fromdate AS DATE = '20090101',
  @todate   AS DATE = '20090131';

WITH Orders
AS
(
  SELECT custid, empid,
    DATEADD(day, n-1, @fromdate) AS orderdate
  FROM Sales.Customers
    CROSS JOIN HR.Employees
    CROSS JOIN dbo.Nums
  WHERE n <= DATEDIFF(day, @fromdate, @todate) + 1
)
SELECT ROW_NUMBER() OVER(ORDER BY (SELECT 0)) AS orderid,
  custid, empid, orderdate
INTO dbo.MyOrders
FROM Orders;
```

Note the use of the expression *(SELECT 0)* in the ORDER BY clause of the ROW_NUMBER function indicating that the order of assignment of row numbers doesn't matter. If order matters, specify the appropriate attributes that you need—for example, *orderdate*—in case you want the row numbers to be assigned based on order date ordering.

When you're done experimenting with this code, don't forget to drop the MyOrders table:

```
DROP TABLE dbo.MyOrders;
```

Another application of cross joins allows you to improve performance of queries that apply calculations between row attributes and aggregates over rows. To demonstrate this fundamental technique, I'll use a table called MyOrderValues that you create and populate by running the following code in the InsideTSQL2008 database:

```
IF OBJECT_ID('dbo.MyOrderValues', 'U') IS NOT NULL  DROP TABLE dbo.MyOrderValues;
GO

SELECT *
INTO dbo.MyOrderValues
FROM Sales.OrderValues;

ALTER TABLE dbo.MyOrderValues
  ADD CONSTRAINT PK_MyOrderValues PRIMARY KEY(orderid);

CREATE INDEX idx_val ON dbo.MyOrderValues(val);
```

The task at hand is to calculate for each order that order's percentage of total value and the difference between the order value and the average value for all orders. The intuitive way for programmers to write calculations between row attributes and aggregates over rows is to use subqueries. The query in Listing 7-1 demonstrates the subquery approach.

LISTING 7-1 Query obtaining aggregates with subqueries

```
SELECT orderid, custid, val,
  CAST(val / (SELECT SUM(val) FROM dbo.MyOrderValues) * 100.
      AS NUMERIC(5, 2)) AS pct,
  CAST(val - (SELECT AVG(val) FROM dbo.MyOrderValues)
      AS NUMERIC(12, 2)) AS diff
FROM dbo.MyOrderValues;
```

This query generates the following output:

```
orderid      custid      val         pct        diff
-----------  ----------  ----------  ---------  -------------
10248        85          440.00      0.03       -1085.05
10249        79          1863.40     0.15       338.35
10250        34          1552.60     0.12       27.55
10251        84          654.06      0.05       -870.99
```

10252	76	3597.90	0.28	2072.85
10253	34	1444.80	0.11	-80.25
10254	14	556.62	0.04	-968.43
10255	68	2490.50	0.20	965.45
10256	88	517.80	0.04	-1007.25
10257	35	1119.90	0.09	-405.15

. . .

```
(830 row(s) affected)
```

Examine this query's execution plan, which is shown in Figure 7-1.

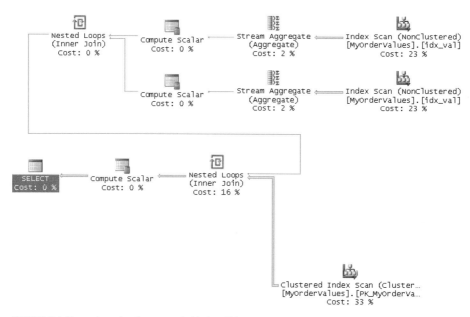

FIGURE 7-1 Execution plan for query in Listing 7-1

Notice that the index I created on the *val* column is scanned twice—once to calculate the sum and once to calculate the average. In other words, provided that you have an index on the aggregated column, the index is scanned once for each subquery that returns an aggregate. If you don't have an index containing the aggregated column, matters are even worse: you'll get a table scan for each subquery.

This query can be optimized using a cross join. You can calculate all needed aggregates in one query that requires only a single index or table scan. Such a query produces a single result row with all aggregates. You create a CTE defined by this query and cross it with the base table. Now you have access to both attributes and aggregates. The solution query is shown in Listing 7-2, and it produces the more optimal plan shown in Figure 7-2.

LISTING 7-2 Query obtaining aggregates with a cross join

```
WITH Aggs AS
(
  SELECT SUM(val) AS sumval, AVG(val) AS avgval
  FROM dbo.MyOrderValues
)
SELECT orderid, custid, val,
  CAST(val / sumval * 100. AS NUMERIC(5, 2)) AS pct,
  CAST(val - avgval AS NUMERIC(12, 2)) AS diff
FROM dbo.MyOrderValues
  CROSS JOIN Aggs;
```

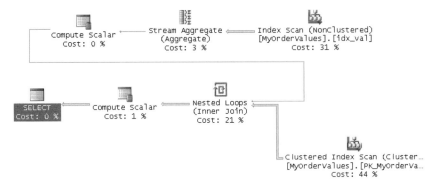

FIGURE 7-2 Execution plan for the query in Listing 7-2

As you can see in the plan, the index on the *val* column is scanned only once, and both aggregates are calculated with the same scan.

In Chapter 8, "Aggregating and Pivoting Data," I'll demonstrate how to use the new OVER clause to tackle similar problems.

When you're done experimenting with this technique, run the following code for cleanup:

```
IF OBJECT_ID('dbo.MyOrderValues', 'U') IS NOT NULL  DROP TABLE dbo.MyOrderValues;
```

INNER

Inner joins are used to match rows between two tables based on some criterion. Out of the first three logical query processing phases, inner joins apply the first two—namely, Cartesian product and ON filter. Neither phase adds outer rows. Consequently, if an INNER JOIN query contains both an ON clause and a WHERE clause, logically they are applied one after the other. With one exception, there's no difference between specifying a logical expression in the ON clause or in the WHERE clause of an INNER JOIN because no intermediate step adds outer rows between the two.

The one exception is when you specify GROUP BY ALL. Remember that GROUP BY ALL adds back groups that were filtered out by the WHERE clause, but it does not add back groups that were filtered out by the ON clause. Remember also that this is a nonstandard legacy feature that you should avoid using.

For performance, when not using the GROUP BY ALL option, you typically get the same plan regardless of where you place the filter expression. That's because the optimizer is aware that there's no difference. I'm always cautious when saying such things related to optimization choices because the process is so dynamic.

For the two supported join syntaxes, using the ANSI SQL-92 syntax, you have more flexibility in choosing which clause you will use to specify a filter expression. Because logically it makes no difference where you place your filters, and typically there's also no performance difference, your guideline should be natural and intuitive writing. Write in a way that feels more natural to you and to the programmers who need to maintain your code. For example, to me a filter that matches attributes between the tables should appear in the ON clause, while a filter on an attribute from only one table should appear in the WHERE clause. I'll use the following query to return orders placed by U.S. customers:

```
SELECT C.custid, companyname, orderid
FROM Sales.Customers AS C
  JOIN Sales.Orders AS O
    ON C.custid = O.custid
WHERE country = N'USA';
```

Using the ANSI SQL-89 syntax, you have no choice but to specify all filter expressions in the WHERE clause:

```
SELECT C.custid, companyname, orderid
FROM Sales.Customers AS C, Sales.Orders AS O
WHERE C.custid = O.custid
  AND country = N'USA';
```

Remember that the discussion here is about inner joins; with outer joins, there are logical differences between specifying a filter expression in the ON clause and specifying it in the WHERE clause.

Note the risk in using the ANSI SQL-89 syntax for inner joins: If you forget to specify the join condition, unintentionally you get a cross join, as demonstrated in the following code:

```
SELECT C.custid, companyname, orderid
FROM Sales.Customers AS C, Sales.Orders AS O;
```

In SQL Server Management Studio (SSMS), the query plan for a cross join includes a join operator marked with a yellow warning symbol, and the pop-up details will say "No Join Predicate" in the Warnings section. This warning is designed to alert you that you might have forgotten to specify a join predicate.

However, if you explicitly specify INNER JOIN when you write an inner join query, an ON clause is required. If you forget to specify any join condition, the parser traps the error, and the query is not run:

```
SELECT C.custid, companyname, orderid
FROM Sales.Customers AS C JOIN Sales.Orders AS O;

Msg 102, Level 15, State 1, Line 2
Incorrect syntax near ';'.
```

The parser finds a semicolon after Sales.Orders AS O, even though it expects something else (an ON clause or other options), so it generates an error saying that there's incorrect syntax near ';'.

> **Note** If you have a composite join (a join based on multiple attributes), and you specify at least one expression but forget the others, neither syntax will trap the error. Similarly, other logical errors won't be trapped—for example, if you mistakenly type **ON C.orderid = C.orderid**.

The ANSI SQL-89 syntax is more prone to mistakes such as forgetting to specify a join condition. You list all table names in the FROM clause separated by commas, and you AND all join predicates in the WHERE clause—for example, FROM T1, T2, T3, T4 WHERE <predicate1> AND <predicate2> AND <predicate3>. Therefore, it's easier not to notice that you forgot one of them. With the ANSI SQL-92 syntax it's harder not to notice that you missed something even before the parser catches the error. That's because you normally express each join predicate immediately after the right table in the join—for example, T1 JOIN T2 ON <predicate1> JOIN T3 ON <predicate2> JOIN T4 ON <predicate3>.

Let's go back to cross joins. You might think that when you intend to write a cross join, using the comma syntax is perfectly fine. However, I'd recommend sticking to the ANSI SQL-92 syntax for several reasons. One reason is for the sake of consistency. Things can especially get awkward when you start mixings different syntaxes in the same query. Another reason is that when other programmers (or even you!) review your code after a while, how will they be able to tell whether you intended to write a cross join or intended to write an inner join and forgot the join predicate? In short, it's a best practice to use the ANSI SQL-92 syntax with all types of joins.

OUTER

Outer joins are used to return matching rows from both tables based on some criterion, together with unmatched rows from the "preserved" table or tables.

You identify preserved tables with the LEFT, RIGHT, or FULL keywords. LEFT marks the left table as preserved, RIGHT marks the right table, and FULL marks both.

Outer joins apply all three logical query processing phases—namely, Cartesian product, ON filter, and adding outer rows. Outer rows added for rows from the preserved table with no match have NULLs for the attributes of the nonpreserved table.

The following query returns customers with their order IDs (just as an inner join with the same ON clause would), but it also returns a row for each customer with no orders because the keyword LEFT identifies the Customers table as preserved:

```
SELECT C.custid, companyname, orderid
FROM Sales.Customers AS C
  LEFT OUTER JOIN Sales.Orders AS O
    ON C.custid = O.custid;
```

The keyword OUTER is optional because the mention of any of the keywords LEFT, RIGHT, or FULL implies an outer join. However, unlike inner joins, where most programmers typically don't specify the optional INNER keyword, most programmers (including me) typically do specify the OUTER keyword. I guess it feels more natural.

As I mentioned earlier, SQL Server 2008 supports the nonstandard proprietary syntax for outer joins only under a backward-compatibility flag. If you still have legacy code with the proprietary outer join syntax, it's important to change it to use the standard syntax. Besides the fact that the old syntax is nonstandard, it's also ambiguous in some cases, as I will demonstrate shortly. Also, starting with SQL Server 2008, only two backward-compatibility modes are supported. To work with the proprietary outer join syntax you need to set the database compatibility mode to 80 (SQL Server 2000). SQL Server 2008 is the last version that still supports this mode. The next major release of SQL Server will support only modes 100 (SQL Server 2008) and 90 (SQL Server 2005). This means that as of the next version of SQL Server, you won't be able to run such legacy code—not even under a backward-compatibility flag.

To demonstrate code with the proprietary outer join syntax, change the InsideTSQL2008 database's compatibility mode to 80 (SQL Server 2000):

```
ALTER DATABASE InsideTSQL2008 SET COMPATIBILITY_LEVEL = 80;
```

> **Note** Changing the compatibility mode of a database to an earlier version will prevent you from using some of the newer language elements (for example, PIVOT, UNPIVOT, and so on). I'm just changing the compatibility mode to demonstrate the code. Once I'm done, I'll instruct you to turn it back to 100 (SQL Server 2008).

The old-style outer join was indicated in the WHERE clause, not the FROM clause. Instead of =, it used *= to represent a left outer join and =* to represent a right outer join. There was no support for a full outer join. For example, the following query returns customers with their order IDs and customers with no orders:

```
SELECT C.custid, companyname, orderid
FROM Sales.Customers AS C, Sales.Orders AS O
WHERE C.custid *= O.custid;
```

This syntax is very problematic because of the lack of separation between an ON filter and a WHERE filter. For example, if you want to return only customers with no orders, using ANSI syntax it's very simple:

```
SELECT C.custid, companyname, orderid
FROM Sales.Customers AS C
  LEFT OUTER JOIN Sales.Orders AS O
    ON C.custid = O.custid
WHERE O.custid IS NULL;
```

You get customers 22 and 57 back. The query initially applies the first three steps in logical query processing, yielding an intermediate virtual table containing customers with their orders (inner rows) and also customers with no orders (outer rows). For the outer rows, the attributes from the Orders table are NULL. The WHERE filter is subsequently applied to this intermediate result. Only the rows with a NULL in the join column from the nonpreserved side, which represent the customers with no orders, satisfy the condition in the WHERE clause.

If you attempt to write the query using the old-style syntax, you get surprising results:

```
SELECT C.custid, companyname, orderid
FROM Sales.Customers AS C, Sales.Orders AS O
WHERE C.custid *= O.custid
  AND O.custid IS NULL;
```

The query returns all 91 customers. Because there's no distinction between an ON clause and a WHERE clause, I specified both expressions in the WHERE clause separated by the logical operator AND. You have no control over which part of the filter takes place before adding the outer rows and which part takes place afterwards. That's at the sole discretion of SQL Server. By looking at the result, you can guess what SQL Server did. Logically, it applied the whole expression before adding outer rows. Obviously, there's no row in the Cartesian product for which both the predicate *C.custid = O.custid* and the predicate *O.custid IS NULL* are TRUE. So the second phase in logical query processing yields an empty set. The third phase adds outer rows for rows from the preserved table (Customers) with no match. Because none of the rows matched the join condition, all customers are added back as outer rows. That's why this query returned all 91 customers.

> **Important** Keep in mind that I demonstrated the older proprietary syntax just to make you aware of its issues in case you still have legacy code using it. It is of course strongly recommended that you refrain from using it and revise all code that does use it to the ANSI syntax. In short, don't try this at home!

When you're done experimenting with the old-style syntax, change the database's compatibility level back to 100 (SQL Server 2008):

```
ALTER DATABASE InsideTSQL2008 SET COMPATIBILITY_LEVEL = 100;
```

In the previous chapter, I provided a solution using subqueries for the minimum missing value problem. As a reminder, you begin with the table T1, which you create and populate by running the following code:

```
USE tempdb;
IF OBJECT_ID('dbo.T1', 'U') IS NOT NULL DROP TABLE dbo.T1;

CREATE TABLE dbo.T1
(
  keycol  INT         NOT NULL PRIMARY KEY,
  datacol VARCHAR(10) NOT NULL
);
GO

INSERT INTO dbo.T1(keycol, datacol) VALUES
  (1, 'e'),
  (2, 'f'),
  (3, 'a'),
  (4, 'b'),
  (6, 'c'),
  (7, 'd');
```

Your task is to find the minimum missing key (in this case, 5) assuming the key starts at 1. I provided the following solution based on subqueries:

```
SELECT MIN(A.keycol) + 1
FROM dbo.T1 AS A
WHERE NOT EXISTS
  (SELECT * FROM dbo.T1 AS B
   WHERE B.keycol = A.keycol + 1);
```

Remember that I provided a CASE expression that returns the value 1 if it is missing; otherwise, it returns the result of the preceding query. You can solve the same problem—returning the minimum missing key when 1 exists in the table—by using the following outer join query between two instances of T1:

```
SELECT MIN(A.keycol) + 1
FROM dbo.T1 AS A
  LEFT OUTER JOIN dbo.T1 AS B
    ON B.keycol = A.keycol + 1
WHERE B.keycol IS NULL;
```

The first step in the solution is applying the left outer join between two instances of T1, called A and B, based on the join condition *B.keycol = A.keycol + 1*. This step involves the first three logical query processing phases I described in Chapter 1 (Cartesian product, ON filter, and adding outer rows). For now, ignore the WHERE filter and the SELECT clause. The join condition matches each row in A with a row from B whose key value is 1 greater than A's key value. Because it's an outer join, rows from A that have no match in B are added as outer rows, producing the virtual table shown in Table 7-1.

Note that the outer rows represent the points before the gaps because the next key value is missing. The second step in the solution is to isolate only the points before the gaps; the WHERE clause filters only rows where *B.keycol* is NULL, producing the virtual table shown in Table 7-2.

TABLE 7-1 Output of Step 1 in Minimum Missing Value Solution

A.keycol	A.datacol	B.keycol	B.datacol
1	e	2	f
2	f	3	a
3	a	4	b
4	b	NULL	NULL
6	c	7	d
7	d	NULL	NULL

TABLE 7-2 Output of Step 2 in Minimum Missing Value Solution

A.keycol	A.datacol	B.keycol	B.datacol
4	b	NULL	NULL
7	d	NULL	NULL

Finally, the last step in the solution isolates the minimum *A.keycol* value, which is the minimum key value before a gap, and adds 1. The result is the requested minimum missing value.

The optimizer generates very similar plans for both queries, with identical costs. So you can use the solution that you feel more comfortable with. Some people feel more comfortable with joins, while others are more comfortable with subqueries, very much like some people feel more comfortable with 1-based offsets, while others are more comfortable with 0-based offsets. Some people are subquery-type people, and some are join-type people, and I guess I qualify as a subquery type. To me, the solution based on subqueries seems more intuitive.

Nonsupported Join Types

ANSI SQL supports a couple of join types that are not supported by T-SQL—natural join and union join. I haven't found practical applications for a union join, so I won't bother to describe or demonstrate it in this book.

A natural join is an inner join where the join condition is implicitly based on equating columns that share the same names in both tables. The syntax for a natural join, not surprisingly, is NATURAL JOIN. For example, the following two queries are logically equivalent, but only the second is recognized by SQL Server:

```
SELECT C.custid, companyname, orderid
FROM Sales.Customers AS C NATURAL JOIN Sales.Orders AS O;
```

and

```
USE InsideTSQL2008;

SELECT C.custid, companyname, orderid
FROM Sales.Customers AS C
  JOIN Sales.Orders AS O
    ON O.custid = O.custid;
```

Further Examples of Joins

So far, I have demonstrated fundamental join types. You can categorize joins in ways other than by their fundamental type. In this section, I'll describe self joins, non-equi-joins, queries with multiple joins, and semi joins.

Self Joins

A self join is simply a join between two instances of the same table. I've already shown examples of self joins without classifying them explicitly as such.

Here's a simple example of a self join between two instances of the Employees table, one representing employees (E) and the other representing managers (M):

```
SELECT E.firstname, E.lastname AS emp,
  M.firstname, M.lastname AS mgr
FROM HR.Employees AS E
  LEFT OUTER JOIN HR.Employees AS M
    ON E.mgrid = M.empid;
```

The query produces the following output, where the employees' names are returned along with their managers' names:

```
firstname    emp                   firstname    mgr
-----------  --------------------  -----------  --------------------
Sara         Davis                 NULL         NULL
Don          Funk                  Sara         Davis
Judy         Lew                   Don          Funk
Yael         Peled                 Judy         Lew
Sven         Buck                  Don          Funk
Paul         Suurs                 Sven         Buck
Russell      King                  Sven         Buck
Maria        Cameron               Judy         Lew
Zoya         Dolgopyatova          Sven         Buck
```

I used a left outer join to include Sara—the CEO—in the result. She has a NULL in the *mgrid* column because she has no manager.

> **Note** When joining two instances of the same table, you must alias at least one of the tables. This provides a unique name or alias to each instance to prevent ambiguity in the result column names and in the column names in the intermediate virtual tables.

Equi-joins are joins with a join condition based on an equality operator. Non-equi-joins have operators other than equality in their join condition.

For example, suppose that you need to generate all pairs of two different employees from an Employees table. Assume that currently the table contains employee IDs A, B, and C. A cross join would generate the following nine pairs:

A, A

A, B

A, C

B, A

B, B

B, C

C, A

C, B

C, C

Obviously, a "self" pair (x, x) that has the same employee ID twice is not a pair of two different employees. Also, for each pair (x, y), you will find its "mirror" pair (y, x) in the result. You need to return only one of the two. To take care of both issues, you can specify a join condition that filters pairs where the key from the left table is smaller than the key from the right table. Pairs where the same employee appears twice are removed. Also, one of the mirror pairs (x, y) and (y, x) is removed because only one has a left key smaller than the right key.

The following query returns the required result, without mirror pairs and without self pairs:

```
SELECT E1.empid, E1.lastname, E1.firstname,
   E2.empid, E2.lastname, E2.firstname
FROM HR.Employees AS E1
   JOIN HR.Employees AS E2
     ON E1.empid < E2.empid;
```

If you need to produce unique triples, simply join to a third instance of the table and have the join predicate verify that the key of the second instance is smaller than the key of the third instance. In a similar manner you can add a fourth instance, a fifth instance, and so on.

You can also calculate row numbers using a non-equi-join. Of course, when you need to calculate row numbers, the most efficient way to do it is with the ROW_NUMBER function. I'll explain how to calculate row numbers with a non-equi-join for illustration purposes and also because the fundamental technique that I will use is applicable to other types of calculations—for example, running aggregates, which have no built-in functions. For example, the following query calculates row numbers for orders from the Orders table, based on increasing *orderid*:

```
SELECT O1.orderid, O1.custid, O1.empid, COUNT(*) AS rn
FROM Sales.Orders AS O1
   JOIN Sales.Orders AS O2
     ON O2.orderid <= O1.orderid
GROUP BY O1.orderid, O1.custid, O1.empid;
```

You can find similarities between this solution and the solution I showed in the previous chapter using subqueries. The join condition here contains the same logical expression I used in a subquery before. After applying the first two phases in logical query processing

(Cartesian product and ON filter), each order from O1 is matched with all orders from O2 that have a smaller or equal *orderid*. This means that a row from O1 with a target row number *n* is matched with *n* rows from O2. Each row from O1 is duplicated in the result of the join *n* times. If this is confusing, bear with me as I try to demonstrate this logic with an example. Say you have orders with the following IDs (in order): x, y, and z. The result of the join is the following:

x, x

y, x

y, y

z, x

z, y

z, z

The join created duplicates out of each row from O1—as many as the target row number. The next step is to collapse each group of rows back to one row, returning the count of rows as the row number:

x, 1

y, 2

z, 3

Note that you must include in the GROUP BY clause all attributes from O1 that you want to return. Remember that in an aggregate query, an attribute that you want to return in the SELECT list must appear in the GROUP BY clause. This query suffers from the same N^2 performance issues I described with the subquery solution. This query also demonstrates an *expand-collapse* technique, where the join achieves the expansion of the number of rows by generating copies, and the grouping achieves the collapsing of the rows allowing you to calculate aggregates.

Being a subquery-type person, I find the subquery technique more appealing because it's so much more intuitive to me. I find the expand-collapse technique to be artificial and nonintuitive.

Remember that in both solutions to generating row numbers you used an aggregate function—a count of rows. You can use very similar logic to calculate other aggregates, either with a subquery or with a join (the expand-collapse technique). I will elaborate on this technique in Chapter 8 in the "Running Aggregations" section, where I'll also describe scenarios in which I'd still consider using the expand-collapse technique even though I find it less intuitive than the subquery technique.

Multiple Joins

A query with multiple joins involves three or more tables. In this section, I'll describe both physical and logical aspects of multi-join queries.

Controlling the Physical Join Evaluation Order   In a multi-join query with no outer joins, you can rearrange the order in which the tables are specified without affecting the result. The optimizer is aware of that and determines the order in which it accesses the tables based on cost estimates. In the query's execution plan, you might find that the optimizer chose to access the tables in a different order than the one you specified in the query.

For example, the query in Listing 7-3 returns customer company name and supplier company name where the supplier supplied products to the customer:

LISTING 7-3 Multi-join query

```
SELECT DISTINCT C.companyname AS customer, S.companyname AS supplier
FROM Sales.Customers AS C
  JOIN Sales.Orders AS O
    ON O.custid = C.custid
  JOIN Sales.OrderDetails AS OD
    ON OD.orderid = O.orderid
  JOIN Production.Products AS P
    ON P.productid = OD.productid
  JOIN Production.Suppliers AS S
    ON S.supplierid = P.supplierid;
```

Examine the execution plan shown in Figure 7-3, and you will find that the tables are accessed physically in a different order than the logical order specified in the query.

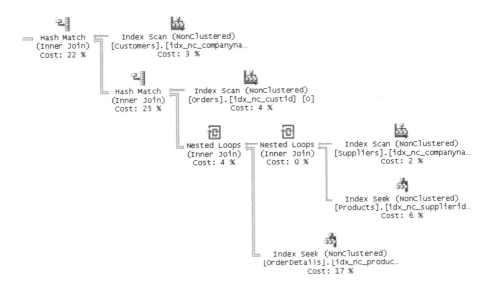

FIGURE 7-3 Execution plan for the query in Listing 7-3

If you suspect that a plan that accesses the tables in a different order than the one chosen by the optimizer will be more efficient, you can force the order of join processing by using one of two options. You can use the FORCE ORDER hint as shown in Listing 7-4, forcing the optimizer to process the joins physically in the same order as the logical one:

LISTING 7-4 Multi-join query with the FORCE ORDER hint

```
SELECT DISTINCT C.companyname AS customer, S.companyname AS supplier
FROM Sales.Customers AS C
  JOIN Sales.Orders AS O
    ON O.custid = C.custid
  JOIN Sales.OrderDetails AS OD
    ON OD.orderid = O.orderid
  JOIN Production.Products AS P
    ON P.productid = OD.productid
  JOIN Production.Suppliers AS S
    ON S.supplierid = P.supplierid
OPTION (FORCE ORDER);
```

This query generates the execution plan shown in Figure 7-4, where you can see that tables are accessed in the order they appear in the query.

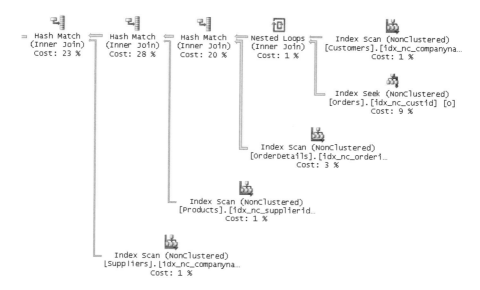

FIGURE 7-4 Execution plan for the query in Listing 7-4

Another option to force the order of join processing is to execute the statement SET FORCEPLAN ON. This will affect all queries in the session.

Hints

Note that in general, using hints to override the optimizer's choice of plan should be the last resort when dealing with performance issues. A hint is not a kind gesture: you're forcing the optimizer to use a particular route in optimization. If you introduce a hint in production code, that aspect of the plan becomes static (for example, the join ordering, the use of a particular index, or the use of a certain join algorithm). Hints prevent the optimizer from making dynamic choices to accommodate changes in data volume and distribution.

There are, nonetheless, several reasons the optimizer might not produce an optimal plan, and when this occurs, a hint can improve performance.

First, the optimizer doesn't necessarily generate all possible execution plans for a query. If it did, the optimization phase could simply take too long. The optimizer calculates a threshold for optimization based on the input table sizes, and it stops optimizing when that threshold is reached, yielding the plan with the lowest cost among the ones it did generate. This means that you won't necessarily get the optimal plan.

Second, optimization in many cases is based on data selectivity and density information, especially with regard to the choice of indexes and access methods. If statistics are not up to date or aren't based on a sufficient sample size, the optimizer might make inaccurate estimates.

Third, the key distribution histograms that SQL Server maintains for indexed columns (and, in some cases, nonindexed ones as well) have at most 200 steps. With many join conditions and filters, the difference between the selectivity or density information that the optimizer estimates and the actual information can be substantial in some cases, leading to inefficient plans. Each selectivity or join density estimate has some level of inaccuracy; the more tables you have in the query and the more join conditions and filters, the more inaccurate the estimates are likely to become. And inaccurate estimates can lead to suboptimal choices. One way to check whether the estimates are inaccurate is to compare the estimated and the actual number of rows coming out of the various operators in the execution plan.

Keep in mind, though, that while you're never guaranteed to get the optimal plan, the optimizer generally does well, and you should do everything in your power to help it succeed. To do this and avoid hints in production code, for example, make sure that statistics are up to date, increase the sampling rate if needed, and in some cases revise the query to help the optimizer make better choices. Use a hint only as a last resort if all other means fail. And if you do end up using a hint, revisit the code from time to time after doing more research or opening a support case with Microsoft.

Controlling the Logical Join Evaluation Order   In some cases you might want to be able to control the logical order of join processing beyond the observable order in which the tables are specified in the FROM clause. For example, consider the previous request to return all pairs of customer company name and supplier company name, where the supplier supplied products to the customer. Suppose you were also asked to return customers that made no orders. By intuition, you'd probably make the following attempt, using a left outer join between Customers and Orders:

```
SELECT DISTINCT C.companyname AS customer, S.companyname AS supplier
FROM Sales.Customers AS C
  LEFT OUTER JOIN Sales.Orders AS O
    ON O.custid = C.custid
  JOIN Sales.OrderDetails AS OD
    ON OD.orderid = O.orderid
  JOIN Production.Products AS P
    ON P.productid = OD.productid
  JOIN Production.Suppliers AS S
    ON S.supplierid = P.supplierid;
```

The previous query returned 1,236 pairs of customer-supplier, and you expected this query to return 1,238 rows (because two customers made no orders). However, this query returns the same result set as the previous one without the outer customers. Remember that the first join takes place only between the first two tables (Customers and Orders), applying the first three phases of logical query processing, and results in a virtual table. The resulting virtual table is then joined with the third table (OrderDetails) and so on.

The first join did, at the logical level, generate outer rows for customers with no orders, but the *orderid* in those outer rows was NULL, of course. The second join—between the result virtual table and OrderDetails—removed those outer rows because an equi-join will never find a match based on a comparison to a NULL. In fact, in terms of physical processing, the optimizer realizes that the second join nullifies the outer part of the outer joins, and therefore it doesn't even bother to process it as an outer join. If you look at the plan for this query, you can see that the plan processed this join as an inner join. In general, when a left outer join is followed by an inner join or a right outer join and the join predicate compares attributes from the nonpreserved part of the join with attributes from the right table, the left outer join gets nullified.

You have several ways to make sure that those outer customers will not disappear. One technique is to use a left outer join in all joins, even though logically you want inner joins between Orders, OrderDetails, Products, and Suppliers:

```
SELECT DISTINCT C.companyname AS customer, S.companyname AS supplier
FROM Sales.Customers AS C
  LEFT OUTER JOIN Sales.Orders AS O
    ON O.custid = C.custid
  LEFT OUTER JOIN Sales.OrderDetails AS OD
    ON OD.orderid = O.orderid
```

```
LEFT OUTER JOIN Production.Products AS P
  ON P.productid = OD.productid
LEFT OUTER JOIN Production.Suppliers AS S
  ON S.supplierid = P.supplierid;
```

The left outer joins keep the outer customers in the intermediate virtual tables. This query correctly produces 1,238 rows, including the two customers that made no orders. However, if you had orders with no related order details, order details with no related products, or products with no related suppliers, this query would have produced incorrect results. That is, you would have received result rows that were unmatched by several join conditions when you wanted only the unmatched rows from the first join condition. Also, remember that the optimizer cannot apply join ordering optimization with outer joins—those have to be processed in specified order, so this technique might hurt optimization.

Another option is to make sure the join with the Customers table is logically last. This can be achieved by using inner joins between all other tables and finally a right outer join with Customers:

```
SELECT DISTINCT C.companyname AS customer, S.companyname AS supplier
FROM Sales.Orders AS O
  JOIN Sales.OrderDetails AS OD
    ON OD.orderid = O.orderid
  JOIN Production.Products AS P
    ON P.productid = OD.productid
  JOIN Production.Suppliers AS S
    ON S.supplierid = P.supplierid
  RIGHT OUTER JOIN Sales.Customers AS C
    ON O.custid = C.custid;
```

This scenario was fairly simple, but in cases where you mix different types of joins—not to mention other table operators (APPLY, PIVOT, UNPIVOT)—it might not be that simple. Furthermore, using left outer joins all along the way is very artificial. It's more intuitive to think of the query as a single left outer join, where the left table is the Customers table and the right table is the result of inner joins between all the other tables. Both ANSI SQL and T-SQL allow you to control the logical order of join processing:

```
SELECT DISTINCT C.companyname AS customer, S.companyname AS supplier
FROM Sales.Customers AS C
  LEFT OUTER JOIN
    (      Sales.Orders AS O
      JOIN Sales.OrderDetails AS OD
        ON OD.orderid = O.orderid
      JOIN Production.Products AS P
        ON P.productid = OD.productid
      JOIN Production.Suppliers AS S
        ON S.supplierid = P.supplierid)
    ON O.custid = C.custid;
```

Technically, the parentheses are ignored here, but I recommend you use them because they will help you write the query correctly. Using parentheses caused you to change another aspect of the query, which is the one that the language really uses to determine the logical order of processing. If you haven't guessed yet, it's the ON clause order. Specifying the ON clause *ON O.custid = C.custid* last causes the other joins to be logically processed first; the left outer join occurs logically between Customers and the inner join of the rest of the tables. You could write the query without parentheses, and it would mean the same thing:

```
SELECT DISTINCT C.companyname AS customer, S.companyname AS supplier
FROM Sales.Customers AS C
  LEFT OUTER JOIN
          Sales.Orders AS O
    JOIN Sales.OrderDetails AS OD
      ON OD.orderid = O.orderid
    JOIN Production.Products AS P
      ON P.productid = OD.productid
    JOIN Production.Suppliers AS S
      ON S.supplierid = P.supplierid
   ON O.custid = C.custid;
```

Other variations that specify the ON clause that refers to *C.custid* last include the following two:

```
SELECT DISTINCT C.companyname AS customer, S.companyname AS supplier
FROM Sales.Customers AS C
  LEFT OUTER JOIN Sales.Orders AS O
  JOIN Production.Products AS P
  JOIN Sales.OrderDetails AS OD
    ON P.productid = OD.productid
    ON OD.orderid = O.orderid
  JOIN Production.Suppliers AS S
    ON S.supplierid = P.supplierid
    ON O.custid = C.custid;

SELECT DISTINCT C.companyname AS customer, S.companyname AS supplier
FROM Sales.Customers AS C
  LEFT OUTER JOIN Sales.Orders AS O
  JOIN Sales.OrderDetails AS OD
  JOIN Production.Products AS P
  JOIN Production.Suppliers AS S
    ON S.supplierid = P.supplierid
    ON P.productid = OD.productid
    ON OD.orderid = O.orderid
    ON O.custid = C.custid;
```

The obvious disadvantage to not using parentheses is a decrease in the readability and clarity of code. Without parentheses, the queries are far from intuitive. But we have another issue, too.

It's important to note that you cannot play with the ON clause's order any way you'd like. There's a certain relationship that must be maintained between the order of the specified tables and the order of the specified ON clauses for the query to be valid. The relationship is called a *chiastic* relationship. A chiastic relationship is neither unique to SQL nor unique to computer science; rather, it appears in many fields, including poetry, linguistics, mathematics, and others. In an ordered series of items, this relationship correlates the first item with the last, the second with the next to last, and so on. For example, palindromes such as "never odd or even" have a chiastic relationship between the letters. As an example of a chiastic relationship in mathematics, recall the arithmetic sequence I described in the last chapter: 1, 2, 3, ..., n. To calculate the sum of the elements, you make n/2 pairs based on a chiastic relationship (1 + n, 2 + n − 1, 3 + n − 2, and so on). The sum of each pair is always 1 + n; therefore, the total sum of the arithmetic sequence is $(1 + n) * n / 2 = (n + n^2) / 2$.

Similarly, the relationship between the tables specified in the FROM clause and the ON clauses must be chiastic for the query to be valid. That is, the first ON clause can refer only to the two tables immediately above it. The second ON clause can refer to the previously referenced tables and to an additional one right above them and so on. Figure 7-5 illustrates the chiastic relationship maintained in the last query. The code in the figure was slightly rearranged for readability.

```
SELECT DISTINCT
       C.companyname AS customer,
       S.companyname AS supplier
FROM
```

Sales.Customers	AS C LEFT OUTER	JOIN
Sales.Orders	AS O	JOIN
Sales.OrderDetails	AS OD	JOIN
Production.Products	AS P	JOIN
Production.Suppliers	AS S	JOIN
ON S.supplierid	= P.supplierid	
ON P.productid	= OD.productid	
ON OD.OrderID	= O.orderid	
ON O.custid	= C.custid;	

FIGURE 7-5 Chiastic relationship in a multi-join query

Without using parentheses, the queries are not very readable, and you need to be aware of the chiastic relationship in order to write a valid query. Conversely, if you do use parentheses, the queries are more readable and intuitive, and you don't need to concern yourself with chiastic relationships because parentheses force you to write correctly.

Bushy Plans   Besides impacting logical join ordering, the ability to change the order of the ON clauses reliably affects optimization in ways that the optimizer alone does not consider. To demonstrate this capability, first run the following code to create the tables T1, T2, T3, and T4:

```
USE tempdb;
IF OBJECT_ID('dbo.T1', 'U') IS NOT NULL DROP TABLE dbo.T1;
IF OBJECT_ID('dbo.T2', 'U') IS NOT NULL DROP TABLE dbo.T2;
IF OBJECT_ID('dbo.T3', 'U') IS NOT NULL DROP TABLE dbo.T3;
IF OBJECT_ID('dbo.T4', 'U') IS NOT NULL DROP TABLE dbo.T4;
GO
```

```
CREATE TABLE dbo.T1(a INT, b INT, c INT, v1 INT);
CREATE TABLE dbo.T2(b INT, v2 INT);
CREATE TABLE dbo.T3(c INT, v3 INT);
CREATE TABLE dbo.T4(d INT, c INT, v4 INT);
GO
```

When you write joins in a traditional manner—namely, each joined table is immediately followed by the join predicate (for example, T1 JOIN T2 ON <predicate1> JOIN T3 ON <predicate2> JOIN T4 ON <predicate3>)—the optimizer considers only certain plan tree layouts. The normal layout is always going to have a join between two base inputs (*base* meaning not a result of a join), then a join between the result of a previous join and another base input, and so on. The optimizer can rearrange the order in which the tables are accessed and can determine whether the base input will be the outer or the inner input of the join, but the optimizer will always consider this kind of tree layout. For example, consider the following query and examine its execution plan, shown in Figure 7-6:

```
SELECT *
FROM dbo.T1
  JOIN dbo.T2
    ON T2.b = T1.b
  JOIN dbo.T3
    ON T3.c = T1.c
  JOIN dbo.T4
    ON T4.c = T3.c;
```

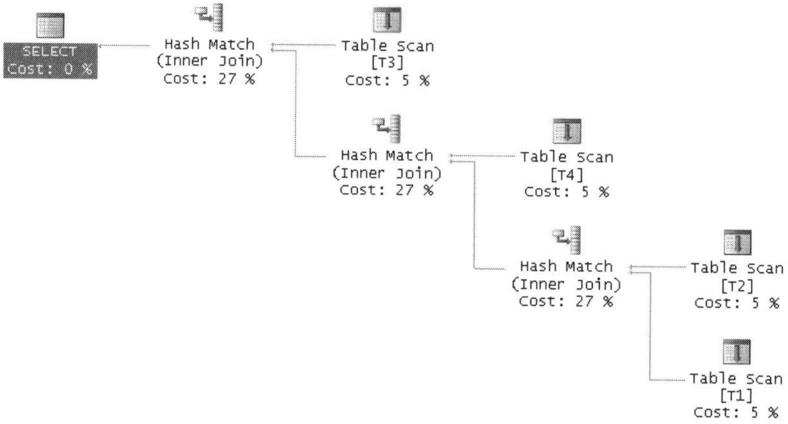

FIGURE 7-6 Query plan for four-table join

This particular tree layout is known as a *right deep tree*, where the result of each join is used as the inner input to the next join. A left deep tree would be one where the result of each join is used as the outer input to the next join. Notice that besides one join that naturally has to take place between two base inputs, all other joins take place between a base input and a result of a join. None of the joins takes place between two results of joins. Unless explicitly instructed, the optimizer does not consider what the members of the SQL Server engine team refer to as a *bushy tree layout*. A bushy plan is one where a join operates on two results of joins as opposed to always having at least one base input. Because the optimizer normally does not consider such plans unless instructed, in some cases you might be able to gain performance improvements by forcing a bushy plan. One example that comes to mind is when each of two different joins can gain significant filtering because of the join itself, and it would make sense to perform each of those joins first and then join their results.

To force a bushy plan you need to rearrange the ON clauses and use the FORCE ORDER hint. For example, the following query forces a join between T1 and T2 and between T3 and T4 and then a join between their results:

```
SELECT *
FROM dbo.T1
  JOIN dbo.T2
    ON T2.b = T1.b
  JOIN dbo.T3
  JOIN dbo.T4
    ON T4.c = T3.c
    ON T3.c = T1.c
OPTION(FORCE ORDER);
```

You might find this query a bit hard to follow. As I mentioned earlier, you can improve the clarity of the code by using parentheses and indentation as the following query shows:

```
SELECT *
FROM   (dbo.T1 JOIN dbo.T2 ON T2.b = T1.b)
  JOIN (dbo.T3 JOIN dbo.T4 ON T4.c = T3.c)
    ON T3.c = T1.c
OPTION(FORCE ORDER);
```

Now it's much easier to see the "bushy" layout that is forced. Figure 7-7 shows the graphical execution plan for this query.

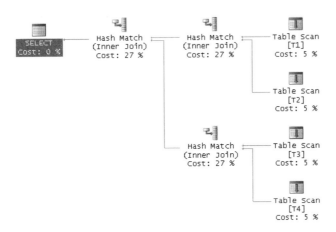

FIGURE 7-7 Bushy plan

Another way to get bushy plans is to use table expressions like so:

```
WITH J1 AS
(
  SELECT T1.a AS T1a, T1.b AS T1b, T1.c, T1.v1, T2.b AS T2b, T2.v2
  FROM dbo.T1 JOIN dbo.T2
    ON T2.b = T1.b
),
J2 AS
(
  SELECT T3.c AS T3c, T3.v3, T4.d, T4.c AS T4c, T4.v4
  FROM dbo.T3 JOIN dbo.T4
    ON T4.c = T3.c
)
SELECT *
FROM J1 JOIN J2
  ON J2.T3c = J1.c
OPTION(FORCE ORDER);
```

Compared to the previous options, this technique requires more code because you need to express the SELECT lists of the queries defining the table expressions.

This optimization technique is interesting to experiment with because the optimizer doesn't consider it normally.

When you're done, run the following code for cleanup:

```
USE tempdb;
IF OBJECT_ID('dbo.T1', 'U') IS NOT NULL DROP TABLE dbo.T1;
IF OBJECT_ID('dbo.T2', 'U') IS NOT NULL DROP TABLE dbo.T2;
IF OBJECT_ID('dbo.T3', 'U') IS NOT NULL DROP TABLE dbo.T3;
IF OBJECT_ID('dbo.T4', 'U') IS NOT NULL DROP TABLE dbo.T4;
```

Semi Joins

Semi joins are joins that return rows from one table based on the existence of related rows in the other table. If you return attributes from the left table, the join is called a left semi join. If you return attributes from the right table, it's called a right semi join.

You can achieve a semi join in several ways: using inner joins, the EXISTS or IN predicate with subqueries, and the INTERSECT set operation (which I'll demonstrate later in the chapter). Using an inner join, you select attributes from only one of the tables. If that table is in the one side of a one-to-many join, you also apply DISTINCT. For example, the following query returns customers from Spain that made orders:

```
USE InsideTSQL2008;

SELECT DISTINCT C.custid, C.companyname
FROM Sales.Customers AS C
```

```
JOIN Sales.Orders AS O
    ON O.custid = C.custid
WHERE country = N'Spain';
```

You can also use the EXISTS predicate as follows:

```
SELECT custid, companyname
FROM Sales.Customers AS C
WHERE country = N'Spain'
  AND EXISTS
    (SELECT * FROM Sales.Orders AS O
     WHERE O.custid = C.custid);
```

If you're wondering about the performance difference between the two, in this case the optimizer generates an identical plan for both. This plan is shown in Figure 7-8.

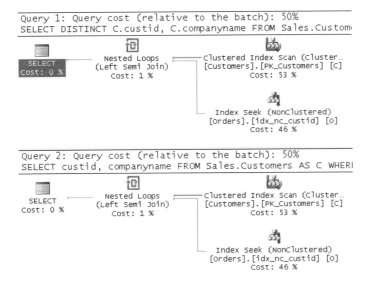

FIGURE 7-8 Execution plan for a left semi join

When the optimizer identifies the join as a semi join, this is typically a good sign. The optimizer knows that per each row from one side, it needs to check only whether at least one matching row exists in the other side as opposed to actually processing all matching rows.

The inverse of a semi join is an anti-semi join, where you're looking for rows in one table based on their nonexistence in the other. You can achieve an anti-semi join (left or right) using an outer join, filtering only outer rows, using the NOT EXISTS or NOT IN predicates with subqueries, and with the EXCEPT set operation. For example, the following query returns customers from Spain that made no orders. The anti-semi join is achieved using an outer join:

```
SELECT C.custid, C.companyname
FROM Sales.Customers AS C
```

```
   LEFT OUTER JOIN Sales.Orders AS O
     ON O.custid = C.custid
 WHERE country = N'Spain'
   AND O.custid IS NULL;
```

You can also use the NOT EXISTS predicate as follows:

```
SELECT custid, companyname
FROM Sales.Customers AS C
WHERE country = N'Spain'
  AND NOT EXISTS
    (SELECT * FROM Sales.Orders AS O
     WHERE O.custid = C.custid);
```

As you can see in the execution plans shown in Figure 7-9 for the two query variations, the solution using the NOT EXISTS predicate is estimated to perform better.

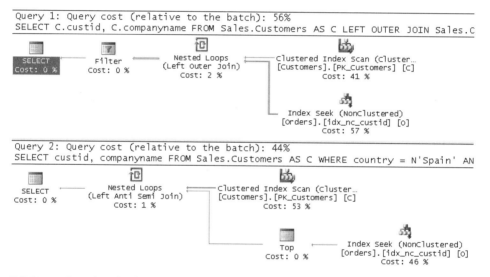

FIGURE 7-9 Execution plan for a left anti-semi join

The plan for the outer join solution shows that all orders for customers from Spain were actually processed. Let *c* equal the number of customers from Spain and *o* equal the average number of orders per customer. You get *c* × *o* orders accessed. Then only the outer rows are filtered.

The plan for the NOT EXISTS solution is more efficient. Like the plan for the LEFT OUTER JOIN solution, this plan performs a seek within the index on *Orders.custid* for each customer. However, the NOT EXISTS plan checks only whether a row with that customer ID was found (shown by the TOP operator), while the plan for the outer join actually scans all index rows for each customer. Note that the tables in our sample database are very small. With more realistic table sizes the optimizer may come up with different plans, so make sure you don't draw any conclusions from this example alone.

Sliding Total of Previous Year

The following exercise demonstrates a mix of several join types and categories: inner and outer joins, self joins, and non-equi-join joins. First create and populate the MonthlyOrders table by running the following code:

```
IF OBJECT_ID('dbo.MonthlyOrders') IS NOT NULL
  DROP TABLE dbo.MonthlyOrders;
GO

SELECT
  DATEADD(month, DATEDIFF(month, '19000101', orderdate), '19000101')
    AS ordermonth,
  SUM(val) AS val
INTO dbo.MonthlyOrders
FROM Sales.OrderValues
GROUP BY DATEADD(month, DATEDIFF(month, '19000101', orderdate), '19000101');

CREATE UNIQUE CLUSTERED INDEX idx_ordermonth ON dbo.MonthlyOrders(ordermonth);

SELECT * FROM dbo.MonthlyOrders ORDER BY ordermonth;
```

The SELECT statement at the end of the script produces the following output:

```
ordermonth                val
------------------------  ---------
2006-07-01 00:00:00.000   27861.90
2006-08-01 00:00:00.000   25485.28
2006-09-01 00:00:00.000   26381.40
2006-10-01 00:00:00.000   37515.73
2006-11-01 00:00:00.000   45600.05
2006-12-01 00:00:00.000   45239.63
2007-01-01 00:00:00.000   61258.08
2007-02-01 00:00:00.000   38483.64
2007-03-01 00:00:00.000   38547.23
2007-04-01 00:00:00.000   53032.95
2007-05-01 00:00:00.000   53781.30
2007-06-01 00:00:00.000   36362.82
2007-07-01 00:00:00.000   51020.86
2007-08-01 00:00:00.000   47287.68
2007-09-01 00:00:00.000   55629.27
2007-10-01 00:00:00.000   66749.23
2007-11-01 00:00:00.000   43533.80
2007-12-01 00:00:00.000   71398.44
2008-01-01 00:00:00.000   94222.12
2008-02-01 00:00:00.000   99415.29
2008-03-01 00:00:00.000   104854.18
2008-04-01 00:00:00.000   123798.70
2008-05-01 00:00:00.000   18333.64
```

Notice that I used the DATETIME data type for the *ordermonth* column. A valid date must include a day portion, so I just used the first of the month. When I need to present data, I'll get rid of the day portion. Storing the order month in a DATETIME data type allows more flexible manipulations using date-and-time-related functions.

The request is to return, for each month, a sliding total of the previous year. In other words, for each month *n*, return the total number of orders from month *n* minus 11 through month *n*.

First I'll demonstrate a solution that assumes that the sequence of months has no gaps. Later I'll provide a solution that works correctly even when some months are missing. Here I won't address performance aspects of the solution; instead, I'll focus on its logical aspects. The purpose of this exercise is to practice with different join types and techniques shown in this chapter. In Chapter 8, you will find a focused discussion on running aggregates, including performance issues.

The following query returns the sliding total of the previous year for each month:

```
SELECT
  CONVERT(CHAR(6), DATEADD(month, -11, O1.ordermonth), 112) AS frommonth,
  CONVERT(CHAR(6), O1.ordermonth, 112) AS tomonth,
  SUM(O2.val) AS totalval,
  COUNT(*) AS nummonths
FROM dbo.MonthlyOrders AS O1
  JOIN dbo.MonthlyOrders AS O2
    ON O2.ordermonth BETWEEN DATEADD(month, -11, O1.ordermonth)
                        AND O1.ordermonth
GROUP BY O1.ordermonth
ORDER BY O1.ordermonth;
```

This query generates the following output:

```
frommonth   tomonth   totalval        nummonths
---------   -------   -------------   -----------
200508      200607    27861.90        1
200509      200608    53347.18        2
200510      200609    79728.58        3
200511      200610    117244.31       4
200512      200611    162844.36       5
200601      200612    208083.99       6
200602      200701    269342.07       7
200603      200702    307825.71       8
200604      200703    346372.94       9
200605      200704    399405.89       10
200606      200705    453187.19       11
200607      200706    489550.01       12
200608      200707    512708.97       12
200609      200708    534511.37       12
200610      200709    563759.24       12
200611      200710    592992.74       12
200612      200711    590926.49       12
200701      200712    617085.30       12
200702      200801    650049.34       12
200703      200802    710980.99       12
200704      200803    777287.94       12
200705      200804    848053.69       12
200706      200805    812606.03       12
```

The query joins two instances of MonthlyOrders: O1 and O2. The left instance (O1) represents the upper boundary point of the month range, and the right instance (O2) represents all months in the range *tomonth – 11* through to *tomonth*. This means that each row in O1 finds up to 12 matches, one for each month. The logic here is similar to the expand technique I mentioned earlier. Now that each upper boundary point has been duplicated up to 12 times, once for each qualifying month from O2, you want to collapse the group back to a single row, returning the total value of orders for each group.

To note that some ranges do not cover a whole year, the query returns also the count of months involved in the aggregation. If you want to return only groups representing complete years, you can simply add a filter in the HAVING clause, ensuring that the number of rows (months) in the group is equal to 12, like so:

```
SELECT
  CONVERT(CHAR(6), DATEADD(month, -11, O1.ordermonth), 112) AS frommonth,
  CONVERT(CHAR(6), O1.ordermonth, 112) AS tomonth,
  SUM(O2.val) AS totalval
FROM dbo.MonthlyOrders AS O1
  JOIN dbo.MonthlyOrders AS O2
    ON O2.ordermonth BETWEEN DATEADD(month, -11, O1.ordermonth)
                         AND O1.ordermonth
GROUP BY O1.ordermonth
HAVING COUNT(*) = 12
ORDER BY O1.ordermonth;
```

This query generates the following output:

```
frommonth    tomonth    totalval
-----------  ---------  -------------
200607       200706     489550.01
200608       200707     512708.97
200609       200708     534511.37
200610       200709     563759.24
200611       200710     592992.74
200612       200711     590926.49
200701       200712     617085.30
200702       200801     650049.34
200703       200802     710980.99
200704       200803     777287.94
200705       200804     848053.69
200706       200805     812606.03
```

This solution assumes that the sequence of months has no gaps. If you don't have such assurance, you can use an auxiliary table that contains all month ranges that you need to cover and perform an outer join between the auxiliary table and MonthlyOrders. You can use the Nums table to produce the month ranges. Here's the complete solution code demonstrating the technique applied for a given *tomonth* range and number of months trailing:

```
DECLARE
  @firsttomonth    AS DATE = '20061201',
  @lasttomonth     AS DATE = '20081201',
  @monthstrailing AS INT  = 11;
```

```
WITH Months AS
(
  SELECT
    DATEADD(month, n-1-@monthstrailing, @firsttomonth) AS frommonth,
    DATEADD(month, n-1, @firsttomonth)                 AS tomonth
  FROM dbo.Nums
  WHERE n <= DATEDIFF(month, @firsttomonth, @lasttomonth) + 1
)
SELECT
  CONVERT(CHAR(6), frommonth, 112) AS frommonth,
  CONVERT(CHAR(6), tomonth, 112) AS tomonth,
  COUNT(O.ordermonth) AS nummonths,
  SUM(O.val) AS totalval
FROM Months M
  LEFT OUTER JOIN
    dbo.MonthlyOrders AS O
      ON O.ordermonth BETWEEN M.frommonth AND M.tomonth
GROUP BY frommonth, tomonth
ORDER BY frommonth;
```

This query generates the following output:

```
frommonth    tomonth    nummonths    totalval
-----------  ---------  -----------  -------------
200601       200612     6            208083.99
200602       200701     7            269342.07
200603       200702     8            307825.71
200604       200703     9            346372.94
200605       200704     10           399405.89
200606       200705     11           453187.19
200607       200706     12           489550.01
200608       200707     12           512708.97
200609       200708     12           534511.37
200610       200709     12           563759.24
200611       200710     12           592992.74
200612       200711     12           590926.49
200701       200712     12           617085.30
200702       200801     12           650049.34
200703       200802     12           710980.99
200704       200803     12           777287.94
200705       200804     12           848053.69
200706       200805     12           812606.03
200707       200806     11           776243.21
200708       200807     10           725222.35
200709       200808     9            677934.67
200710       200809     8            622305.40
200711       200810     7            555556.17
200712       200811     6            512022.37
200801       200812     5            440623.93
```

To clean up, drop the MonthlyOrders table:

```
DROP TABLE dbo.MonthlyOrders;
```

Join Algorithms

Join algorithms are the physical strategies SQL Server can use to process joins. SQL Server supports three join algorithms: nested loops, merge, and hash. In the query execution plan, the join algorithm appears under the join operator's *Physical Operation* property and the logical join type under *Logical Operation*.

The following sections describe the different join algorithms. In my examples I will use the Performance database that was used in Chapter 4, "Query Tuning." The code to create and populate this sample database is provided in Chapter 4, Listing 4-1. In addition, run the following code to create a couple of indexes used in the plans for the queries that I'll demonstrate:

```
USE Performance;

CREATE INDEX idx_nc_cn_i_cid
  ON dbo.Customers(custname) INCLUDE(custid);

CREATE INDEX idx_nc_cid_od_i_oid_eid_sid
  ON dbo.Orders(custid, orderdate)
  INCLUDE(orderid, empid, shipperid);
```

Nested Loops

A nested loops join operator receives one set of rows from its outer input (the upper input in the graphical query plan). These outer input rows are typically the rows of one of the joined tables, after some sorting or filtering, if the optimizer decides such processing is possible and efficient when done before joining the tables and matching rows. Then for each such row of the outer input, using a loop, this operator applies some access method to obtain the matching rows from the inner input of the join (the lower input in the plan).

A nested loops join algorithm can be used with both equi-joins and non-equi-joins, while the other algorithms require at least one equi-join predicate. For logical join types, a nested loops join can be used with cross, inner, left outer, left semi and anti-semi joins, and cross and outer apply. A nested loops join algorithm cannot be used with full and right outer joins and right semi and anti-semi joins. Nested loops usually works best with small inputs (not necessarily small tables).

For each row of the outer input, matching rows are sought from the inner input. Ideally, these matching rows will be found in a small number of efficient searches. The number of searches is smallest when the smaller input is the outer one, and the searches are most efficient when the join condition is selective and there's a useful index on the inner input's join column. With this in mind, the following scale describes the optimization you will get for different indexing options on the inner table's join column, from worst to best. The access method in parentheses occurs once for each row in the join's outer input; this access finds matching rows in the join's inner input:

- No index (table scan)

- Nonclustered noncovering index (when selective enough, seek + partial ordered scan + lookups)

- Clustered index (seek + partial scan)

- Nonclustered covering (seek + partial scan)

The following query, which produces the plan shown in Figure 7-10, is an example of a query for which the optimizer chooses the nested loops operator:

```
SELECT C.custid, C.custname, O.orderid, O.empid, O.shipperid, O.orderdate
FROM dbo.Customers AS C
  JOIN dbo.Orders AS O
    ON O.custid = C.custid
WHERE C.custname LIKE 'Cust[_]1000%'
  AND O.orderdate >= '20080101'
  AND O.orderdate < '20080401';
```

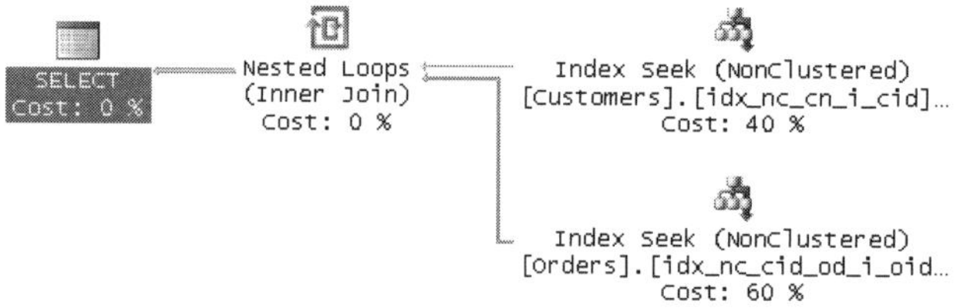

```
           ┌──────┐          ┌─────────────┐           ┌───────────────────────────────┐
           │      │          │             │           │  Index Seek (NonClustered)    │
           │SELECT├──────────┤Nested Loops ├───────────┤ [Customers].[idx_nc_cn_i_cid]…│
           │Cost: 0 %│       │(Inner Join) │           │         Cost: 40 %            │
           └──────┘          │  Cost: 0 %  │           └───────────────────────────────┘
                             └──────┬──────┘
                                    │           ┌───────────────────────────────┐
                                    │           │  Index Seek (NonClustered)    │
                                    └───────────┤ [Orders].[idx_nc_cid_od_i_oid…│
                                                │         Cost: 60 %            │
                                                └───────────────────────────────┘
```

FIGURE 7-10 Execution plan that includes a nested loops operator

Regarding the smaller side of the join, which is usually used as the outer input (Customers in our case), an index to support its filter is not that crucial, but it can prevent the need for a full table scan. So I created a covering index with the key being the filtered column (*custname*) and the *custid* as an included column for coverage purposes.

For the bigger side of the join, which is usually chosen as the inner input of a nested loops join (Orders in our case), you can sometimes arrange one index that supports both the join and additional filters against that table. For example, in our case the join column is *custid*, and there's an additional range filter on *orderdate*. In this case the optimal index is one defined on the keylist (*custid, orderdate*) with the rest of the columns from the table defined as included columns (*orderid, empid, shipperid*).

The plan performs a seek and partial scan in the covering index on the Customers table to retrieve the qualifying customers. For each one of those customers, the plan performs a seek and partial scan in the covering index on the Orders side. The seek predicate contains both the equality condition between the inner and outer tables' *custid* columns as well as the range filter on *orderdate*. With a nested loops join, what you see in this plan is pretty much as good as it can get.

> **Important** With regard to joins and indexing, remember that joins are often based on foreign key/primary key relationships. Although an index (to enforce uniqueness) is automatically created when a primary key is declared, a foreign key declaration doesn't automatically create an index. Remember that for nested loops, typically an index on the join column in the larger table is preferable. So it's your responsibility to create that index explicitly.

Merge

A merge join is a join algorithm that requires both inputs to be sorted based on the join column(s). If an input is already sorted in an index (for example, a clustered index or, even better, a covering nonclustered index), the plan can perform an index order scan. In such a case, the merge join can be pretty efficient even with large table sizes. If an input is not already sorted, the optimizer may decide to apply a sort operation. This typically happens when the input is small because sorting a large number of rows can be quite expensive.

A merge join can be applied either as a one-to-many join or as a many-to-many join. When the optimizer can be certain of the uniqueness of the join column(s) in one of the sides, it can utilize a one-to-many merge join. With a one-to-many join, SQL Server scans both sides only once in an ordered fashion and merges the rows while scanning both inputs. It scans the first row from both sides. As long as the end of the inputs is not reached, it checks whether the rows match. If they do, it returns a result row and reads another row in the many side. If they don't, it reads the next row from the side with the lower value. For example, in a join between T1 that has the values x, y, z in the join column and T2 with the values x, x, y, y, y, y, z, z, z, the merge join reads T1(x), T2(x, x, y), T1(y), T2(y, y, y, z), T1(z), T2(z, z, <end>), T1(<end>).

Things become more complicated and expensive when you have a many-to-many join, where the optimizer might still use a merge join operator with rewind logic. In that case, it needs to use a worktable to save rows from one input aside to be able to reuse them when duplicate matching rows exist in the other side.

A merge join requires at least one of the join predicates to be an equi-join predicate (with the exception of a full outer join). As for logical join types, a merge join algorithm cannot be used with a cross join. It can be used with inner, outer, and semi joins. Cross joins have an exception in which a merge join can be used when it's an inner join disguised as a cross join (for example, T1 CROSS JOIN T2 ON T1.keycol = T2.keycol). Merge can work well with medium- to large-sized inputs provided that they are presorted.

For example, the following query joins Customers and Orders on equal *custid* values:

```
SELECT C.custid, C.custname, O.orderid, O.empid, O.shipperid, O.orderdate
FROM dbo.Customers AS C
  JOIN dbo.Orders AS O
    ON O.custid = C.custid;
```

Both tables have covering indexes on *custid* (clustered index on Customers and covering non-clustered index on Orders), so it's quite a natural choice for the optimizer to go for a merge join in this case. The plan for this query is shown in Figure 7-11.

FIGURE 7-11 Execution plan for a merge join

As mentioned, in some cases the optimizer might decide to use a merge join even when one of the inputs is not presorted by an index, especially if that input is fairly small. In such a case, you will see that the unsorted input is scanned and then sorted, as in the execution plan shown in Figure 7-12 for the following query:

```
SELECT C.custid, C.custname, O.orderid, O.empid, O.shipperid, O.orderdate
FROM dbo.Customers AS C
  JOIN dbo.Orders AS O
    ON O.custid = C.custid
WHERE O.orderdate >= '20080101'
  AND O.orderdate < '20080102';
```

![Execution plan showing SELECT Cost: 0%, Merge Join (Inner Join) Cost: 24%, Clustered Index Scan (Cluster... [Customers].[PK_Customers] [C] Cost: 51%, Sort Cost: 14%, Clustered Index Seek (Cluster... [orders].[idx_cl_od] [o]]

Actual Number of Rows	685
Estimated Number of Rows	1047.62
Estimated Row Size	40 B
Estimated Data Size	41 KB

FIGURE 7-12 Execution plan for a merge join with sort

The rows in the Customers table are already sorted based on the join column (*custid*) in the table's clustered index. As for the Orders table, even if you have a covering index on *custid*, fully scanning it would mean scanning about 1,000,000 rows. The optimizer estimates the selectivity of the filter on the *orderdate* column and realizes that the filter is highly selective. Therefore it decides to use the clustered index on *orderdate* to scan the applicable orders (estimated about 1,000 rows) and sort by *custid* to enable the merge join.

A word of caution here: If the optimizer makes a bad selectivity estimate—especially when the estimate is for a small number of rows (for example, 1,000 rows)—but in practice you get a very large number of rows (for example, 2,000,000 rows), the sort operation ends up being very expensive. You can identify the problem by inspecting the actual execution plan: compare the Estimated and Actual numbers of rows in the arrow going into the sort operator. In such a case you should try to determine the cause of the inaccurate selectivity estimate and fix it, if possible.

Hash

The hash join algorithm is efficient mainly in processing queries that involve medium to large input sizes, especially in data warehouses. A hash join algorithm builds and uses a searching structure called a hash table, which is an alternative searching structure to a balanced tree. SQL Server does not allow us to explicitly create hash indexes, only B-trees, but it does use hash tables internally as part of processing of joins, aggregates, and so on.

The optimizer usually uses the smaller input of the two as the input for building the hash table; hence, this input is known as the *build input*. The reasoning behind using the smaller input as the build input is that the hash table is created in memory (unless there's not enough memory and it spills to disk). It distributes the rows (relevant attributes for query) from the build input into buckets, based on a hash function applied to the join column values. The hash function is chosen to create a predetermined number of buckets of fairly equal size. Once the optimizer finishes building the hash table based on the build input, it scans, or probes, the other input (known as the *probe input*); applies the hash function to the join column value; and, based on the result, knows which bucket in the hash table to scan to look for matches.

As an analogy, say you have a garage with a large number of tools and items. If you don't organize them in a particular manner, every time you look for an item you need to scan all of them. This is similar to a table scan. Of course, you want to organize the items in groups and shelves by some criteria—for example, by functionality, size, color, and so on. You'd probably choose a criterion that would result in fairly equal-sized, manageable groups.

The criterion you would use is analogous to the hash function, and a shelf or group of items is analogous to the hash bucket. Once the items in the garage are organized, every time you need to look for one, apply the same criterion you used to organize the items, go directly to the relevant shelf, and scan that shelf.

A hash join requires at least one of the join predicates to be an equi-join predicate. As for logical join types, a hash join algorithm does not support cross joins. It does support inner, outer, and semi joins of all types. Regarding cross joins, like with the merge join algorithm there's an exception in which a hash join algorithm can be used: when it's an inner join disguised as a cross join (for example, T1 CROSS JOIN T2 ON T1.keycol = T2.keycol).

Note that while in certain scenarios hash joins are the preferable option, sometimes— usually in OLTP type scenarios—SQL Server uses hash joins for lack of existing indexes to support other join algorithms that would have been more efficient. Occasionally, you do see execution plans where the optimizer decides that it's worthwhile to create a temporary index (an Index Spool operator). But in many cases, when no B-tree is in place, it's more expensive to create a temporary index as part of the plan, use it, and drop it than it is to create a hash table and use it. What I'm trying to say is that in some cases, the use of a hash join algorithm is due to lack of existing indexes. But as I said, hash joins can be the optimal option, especially in data warehouse types of scenarios.

To demonstrate a hash join, first run the following code to drop the two indexes created earlier on the Customers and Orders tables:

```
DROP INDEX dbo.Customers.idx_nc_cn_i_cid;
DROP INDEX dbo.Orders.idx_nc_cid_od_i_oid_eid_sid;
```

Next, run the following query:

```
SELECT C.custid, C.custname, O.orderid, O.empid, O.shipperid, O.orderdate
FROM dbo.Customers AS C
  JOIN dbo.Orders AS O
    ON O.custid = C.custid
WHERE C.custname LIKE 'Cust[_]1000%'
  AND O.orderdate >= '20080101'
  AND O.orderdate < '20080401';
```

You will see the Hash Match operator in the execution plan generated for the query, as shown in Figure 7-13:

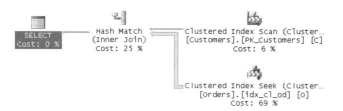

FIGURE 7-13 Execution plan for a hash join

As you can see, the smaller side (Customers) was chosen as the build input (upper input in the plan). The Customers table was fully scanned because no index supported the query's filter on the attribute *custname*. The bigger side (Orders) was chosen as the probe input. Because the filtered column *orderdate* is the clustered index key for Orders, a seek followed by a range scan in the leaf of the index can obtain the qualifying orders. Those qualifying rows are used as the probe input for the hash join.

Bitmap Filters in Star Schema Joins　Bitmap filters are used in parallel query plans to filter data based on a bitmap created by the Bitmap operator. A bitmap is an in-memory compact representation of a set of values. A bitmap filter can use a bitmap representing a set of values obtained by one operator in the plan tree to filter rows as part of another operator in the tree. Using a bitmap filter is efficient when the set of values represented by the bitmap is small.

Bitmap filters were supported prior to SQL Server 2008. However, SQL Server 2008 introduces *optimized bitmap filters*. While regular bitmap filters can be introduced in the query plan only after optimization, optimized bitmap filters can be introduced dynamically by the optimizer during optimization. Optimized bitmap filters can be especially efficient in optimizing data warehouse types of queries, such as star schema joins. The bitmaps in this case would be compact representations of applicable join keys obtained from dimension tables. With regular bitmap filters, all rows from the fact table are processed before the joins with the dimension tables eliminate the non-qualifying rows. With optimized bitmap filters, the non-qualifying rows from the fact table are eliminated immediately as part of the table/index scan operator. If applicable, more than one bitmap filter can be applied.

The query optimizer can use regular bitmap filters in both merge and hash joins. Optimized bitmap filters can be used in hash joins only. The bitmaps are created on the build input (the dimension tables) and applied to the probe input (the fact table). If the join column is an integer, the filtering of the rows from the fact table can be done in-row while scanning the data. Otherwise, the filtering is done by a parallelism operator.

The following query demonstrates using hash joins and bitmap filtering:

```
SELECT C.custname, E.lastname, E.firstname,
  O.orderid, O.orderdate, O.custid, O.empid, O.shipperid
FROM dbo.Orders AS O
  JOIN dbo.Customers AS C
    ON O.custid = C.custid
  JOIN dbo.Employees AS E
    ON O.empid = E.empid
WHERE C.custname LIKE 'Cust[_]100%'
  AND E.lastname LIKE 'Lname[_]100%';
```

The execution plan produced for this query is shown in Figure 7-14.

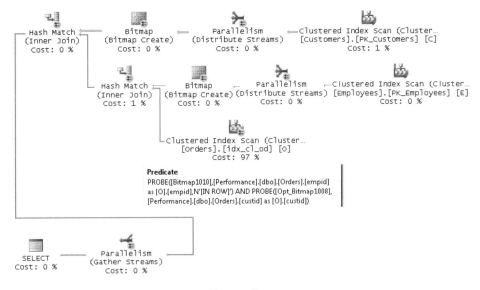

FIGURE 7-14 Execution plan with optimized bitmap filters

Each Bitmap operator creates a bitmap from the dimension table rows returned by a filter. The bitmap represents the set of join keys for these rows. Then when the fact table (Orders in our case) is scanned, rows that don't satisfy the dimension table filter condition can be identified and excluded based on their join key. You can tell that a filter is an optimized bitmap filter when its name starts with *Opt_*, as in *Opt_Bitmap1008*.

If you're trying to reproduce a plan with bitmap filters and can't manage to do so, consider the following. Bitmap filters are used only in parallel execution plans. Parallel plans are considered only if you have more than one processor and the execution plan cost is greater than 5.

> **Tip** If you want to be able to produce plans with bitmap filters on a computer with a single processor for practice purposes, you can start the SQL Server service with the undocumented *−P* switch. Using this switch you can specify how many user mode schedulers (UMSs) you want SQL Server to start with. Normally it starts with one UMS per CPU.

Forcing a Join Strategy

You can force the optimizer to use a particular join algorithm, provided that it's technically supported for the given query. You do so by specifying a hint between the keyword or keywords representing the join type (for example, INNER, LEFT OUTER) and the JOIN keyword. For example, the following query forces a nested loops join:

```
SELECT C.custid, C.custname, O.orderid, O.empid, O.shipperid, O.orderdate
FROM dbo.Customers AS C
  INNER LOOP JOIN dbo.Orders AS O
    ON O.custid = C.custid;
```

> **Note** With inner joins, when forcing a join algorithm, the keyword INNER is not optional. With outer joins, the OUTER keyword is still optional. For example, you can use LEFT LOOP JOIN or LEFT OUTER LOOP JOIN.

In some cases you may want to prevent the optimizer from using a certain join algorithm rather than forcing it to use a specific one. Unfortunately, you cannot do this at the individual join level, but you can do it at the whole query level using a table hint where you specify the algorithms you allow. As long as only one join is in the query, the hint impacts only that join. However, bear in mind that when the query has multiple joins, the hint impacts all of the joins. For example, the following query restricts the optimizer to use either nested loops or hash join algorithms, preventing it from using merge:

```
SELECT C.custid, C.custname, O.orderid, O.empid, O.shipperid, O.orderdate
FROM dbo.Customers AS C
  JOIN dbo.Orders AS O
    ON O.custid = C.custid
OPTION(LOOP JOIN, HASH JOIN);
```

Note Keep in mind the discussion earlier in the chapter regarding using hints to override the optimizer's choices. Limit the use of hints and try to exhaust all other means before you introduce such a hint in production code.

For more information about join algorithms, please refer to Craig Freedman's excellent blog entries on the subject. You can find Craig's blog at *http://blogs.msdn.com/craigfr/*.

Separating Elements

At this point, you have a chance to put your knowledge of joins and the key techniques you learned so far into action. Here I'll present a generic form of a problem that has many practical applications in production. Create and populate a table called Arrays by running the following code:

```
USE tempdb;

IF OBJECT_ID('dbo.Arrays') IS NOT NULL  DROP TABLE dbo.Arrays;

CREATE TABLE dbo.Arrays
(
  arrid VARCHAR(10)    NOT NULL PRIMARY KEY,
  array VARCHAR(8000) NOT NULL
)
GO

INSERT INTO Arrays(arrid, array) VALUES
  ('A', '20,223,2544,25567,14'),
  ('B', '30,-23433,28'),
  ('C', '12,10,8099,12,1200,13,12,14,10,9'),
  ('D', '-4,-6,-45678,-2');
```

The table contains arrays of elements separated by commas. Your task is to write a query that generates the result shown in Table 7-3.

TABLE 7-3 Arrays Split to Elements

arid	pos	element
A	1	20
A	2	223
A	3	2544
A	4	25567
A	5	14
B	1	30
B	2	-23433

TABLE 7-3 **Arrays Split to Elements**

arid	pos	element
B	3	28
C	1	12
C	2	10
C	3	8099
C	4	12
C	5	1200
C	6	13
C	7	12
C	8	14
C	9	10
C	10	9
D	1	-4
D	2	-6
D	3	-45678
D	4	-2

The request is to split the arrays. The result set should have a row for each array element, including the array ID, the element's position within the array, and the element value. The solution is presented in the following paragraphs.

Before you even start coding, it's always a good idea to identify the steps in the solution and resolve them logically. It's often a good starting point to think in terms of the number of rows in the target and consider how that is related to the number of rows in the source. Obviously, here you need to generate multiple rows in the result from each row in Arrays. In other words, as the first step, you need to generate copies.

You already know that to generate copies, you can join the Arrays table with an auxiliary table of numbers. Here the join is not a simple cross join and a filter on a fixed number of rows. The number of copies here should equal the number of elements in the array. Each element is identified by a preceding comma (except for the first element, which we must not forget). So the join condition can be based on the existence of a comma in the nth character position in the array, where n comes from the Nums table.

Obviously, you wouldn't want to check characters beyond the length of the array, so you can limit n to the array's length. The following query implements the first step of the solution:

```
SELECT arrid, array, n
FROM dbo.Arrays
  JOIN dbo.Nums
    ON n <= DATALENGTH(array)
    AND SUBSTRING(array, n, 1) = ',';
```

> **Note** The *array* column is of a regular character type in our case. When working with a Unicode type, make sure that you divide the result of the DATALENGTH function by 2.

This query generates the following output:

```
arrid      array                              n
---------- -------------------------------- -----------
A          20,223,2544,25567,14             3
A          20,223,2544,25567,14             7
A          20,223,2544,25567,14             12
A          20,223,2544,25567,14             18
B          30,-23433,28                     3
B          30,-23433,28                     10
C          12,10,8099,12,1200,13,12,14,10,9 3
C          12,10,8099,12,1200,13,12,14,10,9 6
C          12,10,8099,12,1200,13,12,14,10,9 11
C          12,10,8099,12,1200,13,12,14,10,9 14
C          12,10,8099,12,1200,13,12,14,10,9 19
C          12,10,8099,12,1200,13,12,14,10,9 22
C          12,10,8099,12,1200,13,12,14,10,9 25
C          12,10,8099,12,1200,13,12,14,10,9 28
C          12,10,8099,12,1200,13,12,14,10,9 31
D          -4,-6,-45678,-2                  3
D          -4,-6,-45678,-2                  6
D          -4,-6,-45678,-2                  13
```

You have almost generated the correct number of duplicates for each array, along with the *n* value representing the matching comma's position. You have one fewer copy than the desired number of copies for each array. For example, array A has five elements, but you have only four rows. The reason that a row is missing for each array is that no comma precedes the first element in the array. To fix this small problem, concatenate a comma with the array to specify the first input of the SUBSTRING function:

```
SELECT arrid, array, n
FROM dbo.Arrays
  JOIN dbo.Nums
    ON n <= DATALENGTH(array) + 1
    AND SUBSTRING(',' + array, n, 1) = ',';
```

Note that because you added a comma in front of the original string, the string is now one character longer. Therefore, the filter in the ON clause needs to filter *n* values from Nums that are smaller than or equal to the length of the original array plus one. As you can see in the following output, each array now produces an additional row in the result with *n* = *1*:

```
arrid      array                              n
---------- -------------------------------- -----------
A          20,223,2544,25567,14             1
A          20,223,2544,25567,14             4
A          20,223,2544,25567,14             8
A          20,223,2544,25567,14             13
A          20,223,2544,25567,14             19
```

B	30,-23433,28	1
B	30,-23433,28	4
B	30,-23433,28	11
C	12,10,8099,12,1200,13,12,14,10,9	1
C	12,10,8099,12,1200,13,12,14,10,9	4
C	12,10,8099,12,1200,13,12,14,10,9	7
C	12,10,8099,12,1200,13,12,14,10,9	12
C	12,10,8099,12,1200,13,12,14,10,9	15
C	12,10,8099,12,1200,13,12,14,10,9	20
C	12,10,8099,12,1200,13,12,14,10,9	23
C	12,10,8099,12,1200,13,12,14,10,9	26
C	12,10,8099,12,1200,13,12,14,10,9	29
C	12,10,8099,12,1200,13,12,14,10,9	32
D	-4,-6,-45678,-2	1
D	-4,-6,-45678,-2	4
D	-4,-6,-45678,-2	7
D	-4,-6,-45678,-2	14

Also, because all characters in ',' + *array* appear one character further to the right than they do in the original array, all n values are greater than before by one. That's actually even better for us because now n represents the starting position of the corresponding element within the original array.

The third step is to extract from each row the element starting at the nth character. You know where the element starts—at the nth character—but you need to figure out its length. The length of the element is the position of the next comma minus the element's starting position (n). You can use the CHARINDEX function to find the position of the next comma. You will need to provide the function with the value n as the third argument to tell it to start looking for the comma at or after the nth character and not from the beginning of the string. Just keep in mind that you'll face a very similar problem here to the one that caused you to get one fewer copy than the number of elements. Here, there's no comma after the last element. Just as you added a comma before the first element earlier, you can now add one at the end. The following query shows the third step in the solution:

```
SELECT arrid,
  SUBSTRING(array, n, CHARINDEX(',', array + ',', n) - n) AS element
FROM dbo.Arrays
  JOIN dbo.Nums
    ON n <= DATALENGTH(array) + 1
    AND SUBSTRING(',' + array, n, 1) = ',';
```

This query generates the following output:

arrid	element
A	20
A	223
A	2544
A	25567
A	14
B	30
B	-23433
B	28

C	12
C	10
C	8099
C	12
C	1200
C	13
C	12
C	14
C	10
C	9
D	-4
D	-6
D	-45678
D	-2

Note that the element result column is currently a character string. You might want to convert it to a more appropriate data type (for example, an integer in this case).

Finally, the last step in the solution is to calculate the position of each element within the array. A simple way to achieve this is to use the ROW_NUMBER function, partitioned by *arrid*, ordered by *n*, like so:

```
SELECT arrid,
  ROW_NUMBER() OVER(PARTITION BY arrid ORDER BY n) AS pos,
  CAST(SUBSTRING(array, n, CHARINDEX(',', array + ',', n) - n)
       AS INT) AS element
FROM dbo.Arrays
  JOIN dbo.Nums
    ON n <= DATALENGTH(array) + 1
    AND SUBSTRING(',' + array, n, 1) = ',';
```

But if you feel that this is too easy and you were shortchanged of a challenge, you can try and calculate the position without the ROW_NUMBER function. With this restriction, this step is very tricky. You first need to figure out what determines the position of an element within an array. The position is the number of commas in the original array before the *n*th character (in the first $n - 1$ characters), plus one. Once you figure this out, you need to come up with an expression that will calculate this. You want to avoid writing a T-SQL user-defined function, which would slow the query down. If you come up with an inline expression that uses only built-in functions, you will get a very fast solution. To phrase the problem more technically, you need to take the first $n - 1$ characters (*LEFT(array, n – 1)*) and count the number of commas within that substring. The problem is that most string functions have no notion of repetitions or multiple occurrences of a substring within a string. There is one built-in function, though, that does—REPLACE. This function replaces each occurrence of a certain substring (call it *oldsubstr*) within a string (call it *str*) with another substring (call it *newsubstr*). You invoke the function with the aforementioned arguments in the following order: *REPLACE(str, oldsubstr, newsubstr)*. Here's an interesting way we can use the REPLACE function: *REPLACE(LEFT(array, n – 1), ',', '')*. Here *str* is the first $n - 1$ characters within the array (*LEFT(array, n – 1)*), *oldsubstr* is a comma, and *newsubstr* is an empty string. We replace each occurrence of a comma within the substring with an empty string. Now, what can you say about the difference in length between the original substring ($n - 1$) and the new one?

The new one will obviously be *(n – 1) – num_commas*, where *num_commas* is the number of commas in *str*. In other words, *(n – 1) – ((n – 1) – num_commas)* will give you the number of commas. Add one, and you have the position of the element within the array. Use the DATALENGTH function to return the number of characters in *str* after removing the commas. Here's the complete expression that calculates *pos*:

```
(n - 1) - DATALENGTH(REPLACE(LEFT(array, n - 1), ',', '')) + 1 AS pos
```

Using the REPLACE function to count occurrences of a string within a string is a trick that can come in handy.

The following query shows the final solution to the problem, including the position calculation:

```
SELECT arrid,
  (n - 1) - DATALENGTH(REPLACE(LEFT(array, n - 1), ',', '')) + 1 AS pos,
  CAST(SUBSTRING(array, n, CHARINDEX(',', array + ',', n) - n)
     AS INT) AS element
FROM dbo.Arrays
  JOIN dbo.Nums
    ON n <= DATALENGTH(array) + 1
    AND SUBSTRING(',' + array, n, 1) = ',';
```

Another solution to the problem involves using a recursive CTE to separate elements. It's not as efficient as the previous one, but it does not require an auxiliary table of numbers. Here's the solution's code:

```
WITH Split AS
(
  SELECT arrid, 1 AS pos, 1 AS startpos,
    CHARINDEX(',', array + ',') - 1 AS endpos
  FROM dbo.Arrays
  WHERE DATALENGTH(array) > 0

  UNION ALL

  SELECT Prv.arrid, Prv.pos + 1, Prv.endpos + 2,
    CHARINDEX(',', Cur.array + ',', Prv.endpos + 2) - 1
  FROM Split AS Prv
    JOIN dbo.Arrays AS Cur
      ON Cur.arrid = Prv.arrid
      AND CHARINDEX(',', Cur.array + ',', Prv.endpos + 2) > 0
)
SELECT A.arrid, pos,
  CAST(SUBSTRING(array, startpos, endpos-startpos+1) AS INT) AS element
FROM dbo.Arrays AS A
  JOIN Split AS S
    ON S.arrid = A.arrid
ORDER BY arrid, pos;
```

The CTE calculates the start and end position of each element. The anchor member calculates the values for the first element within each array. The recursive member calculates the values of the next elements, terminating when no "next" elements are found. The *pos* column is initialized with the constant 1 and incremented by 1 in each iteration. The outer query joins the Arrays table with the CTE, and it extracts the individual elements of the arrays based on the start and end positions calculated by the CTE. As mentioned, this solution is slower than the previous one, but it has the advantage of not requiring an auxiliary table of numbers.

I once posted this puzzle in a private SQL trainer's forum. One of the trainers posted the following very witty solution that one of his colleagues came up with:

```
SELECT CAST(arrid AS VARCHAR(10)) AS arrid,
    REPLACE(array, ',',
        CHAR(13)+CHAR(10) + CAST(arrid AS VARCHAR(10))+SPACE(10)) AS value
FROM dbo.Arrays;
```

First examine the solution to see whether you can figure it out and then run it with Results to Text output mode. You will get the following output, which *seems* correct:

```
arrid       value
----------  -------------
A           20
A           223
A           2544
A           25567
A           14
B           30
B           -23433
B           28
C           12
C           10
C           8099
C           12
C           1200
C           13
C           12
C           14
C           10
C           9
D           -4
D           -6
D           -45678
D           -2
```

This solution replaces each comma with a new line *(CHAR(13)+CHAR(10))* + *array id* + *10* spaces. It seems correct when you run it in text mode, but it isn't. If you run it in grid output mode, you will see that the output really contains only one row for each array.

Set Operations

You can think of joins as *horizontal* operations between tables, generating a virtual table that contains columns from both tables. This section covers *vertical* operations between tables, including UNION, EXCEPT, and INTERSECT. Any mention of *set operations* in this section refers to these vertical operations.

A set operation operates on two input tables, each resulting from a query specification. For simplicity's sake, I'll just use the term *inputs* in this section to describe the input tables of the set operations.

UNION returns the unified set of rows from both inputs, EXCEPT returns the rows that appear in the first input but not the second, and INTERSECT returns rows that are common to both inputs.

ANSI SQL:1999 defines native operators for all three set operations, each with two nuances: one optionally followed by DISTINCT (the default) and one followed by ALL. SQL Server supports two nuances of the UNION set operation (UNION and UNION ALL) and only one nuance of the EXCEPT and INTERSECT set operations. Currently, SQL Server does not support the optional use of DISTINCT for set operations. This is not a functional limitation because DISTINCT is implied when you don't specify ALL. I will provide alternative techniques to achieve the set operations that are missing in the product.

Like joins, these set operations always operate on only two inputs, generating a virtual table as the result. You might feel comfortable calling the input tables *left* and *right,* as with joins, or you might feel more comfortable referring to them as the *first* and *second* input tables.

Before I describe each set operation in detail, let's deal with a few technicalities regarding how set operations work.

The two inputs must have the same number of columns, and corresponding columns must have the same data type or at least be implicitly convertible. The column names of the result are determined by the first input.

An ORDER BY clause is not allowed in the individual table expressions. All other logical processing phases (joins, filtering, grouping, and so on) are supported on the individual queries.

Conversely, ORDER BY is the only logical processing phase supported directly on the final result of a set operation. If you specify an ORDER BY clause at the end of the query, it is applied to the final result set. None of the other logical processing phases is allowed directly on the result of a set operation. I will provide alternatives later in the chapter.

Set operations work on complete rows from the two input tables. Note that when comparing rows between the inputs, set operations treat NULLs as equal, just like identical known values. In this regard, set operations are not like query filters (ON, WHERE, HAVING), which as you recall do not treat NULLs as equal.

UNION

UNION generates a result set combining the rows from both inputs. The following sections describe the differences between UNION (implicit DISTINCT) and UNION ALL.

UNION DISTINCT

Specifying UNION without the ALL option combines the rows from both inputs and applies a DISTINCT on top (in other words, removes duplicate rows).

For example, the following query returns all occurrences of *country, region, city* that appear in either the Employees table or the Customers table, with duplicate rows removed:

```
USE InsideTSQL2008;

SELECT country, region, city FROM HR.Employees
UNION
SELECT country, region, city FROM Sales.Customers;
```

The query returns 71 unique rows.

UNION ALL

You can think of UNION ALL as UNION without duplicate removal. That is, you get one result set containing all rows from both inputs, including duplicates. For example, the following query returns all occurrences of *country, region, city* from both tables:

```
SELECT country, region, city FROM HR.Employees
UNION ALL
SELECT country, region, city FROM Sales.Customers;
```

Because the Employees table has 9 rows and the Customers table has 91 rows, you get a result set with 100 rows.

EXCEPT

EXCEPT allows you to identify rows that appear in the first input but not in the second.

EXCEPT DISTINCT

EXCEPT DISTINCT returns distinct rows that appear in the first input but not in the second input. To achieve EXCEPT, programmers sometimes use the NOT EXISTS predicate, or an outer join filtering only outer rows, as I demonstrated earlier in the "Semi Joins" section. However, those solutions treat two NULLs as different from each other. For example, (UK, NULL, London) will not be considered equal to (UK, NULL, London). If both tables contain such a row, *input1 EXCEPT input2* is not supposed to return it, yet the NOT EXISTS and outer join solutions will as typically written, unless you add logic that treats two NULLs as equal. As mentioned, the built-in set operations treat NULLs as equal. The following code uses the built-in EXCEPT set operation to return distinct cities that appear in Employees but not in Customers:

```
SELECT country, region, city FROM HR.Employees
EXCEPT
SELECT country, region, city FROM Sales.Customers;
```

Note that of the three set operations, only EXCEPT is asymmetrical. That is, *input1 EXCEPT input2* is not the same as *input2 EXCEPT input1*.

For example, the query just shown returned the two cities that appear in Employees but not in Customers. The following query returns 66 cities that appear in Customers but not in Employees:

```
SELECT country, region, city FROM Sales.Customers
EXCEPT
SELECT country, region, city FROM HR.Employees;
```

EXCEPT ALL

EXCEPT ALL is trickier than EXCEPT DISTINCT and has not yet been implemented in SQL Server. Besides caring about the existence of a row, it also cares about the number of occurrences of each row. Say you request the result of *input1 EXCEPT ALL input2*. If a row appears n times in *input1* and m times in *input2* (both n and m will be >= 0), it will appear $MAX(0, n - m)$ times in the output. That is, if n is greater than m, the row will appear $n - m$ times in the result; otherwise, it won't appear in the result at all.

Even though you don't have a native operator for EXCEPT ALL in SQL Server 2008, you can easily generate the logical equivalent using EXCEPT and the ROW_NUMBER function. Here's the solution:

```
WITH EXCEPT_ALL
AS
(
  SELECT
    ROW_NUMBER()
      OVER(PARTITION BY country, region, city
           ORDER     BY (SELECT 0) As rn,
    country, region, city
    FROM HR.Employees

  EXCEPT

  SELECT
    ROW_NUMBER()
      OVER(PARTITION BY country, region, city
           ORDER     BY (SELECT 0) As rn,
    country, region, city
  FROM Sales.Customers
)
SELECT country, region, city
FROM EXCEPT_ALL;
```

To understand the solution, I suggest that you first highlight sections (queries) within it and run them separately. This allows you to examine the intermediate result sets and get a better idea of what the following paragraph tries to explain.

The code first assigns row numbers to the rows of each of the inputs, partitioned by the whole attribute list. The row numbers will number the duplicate rows within the input. For example, a row that appears five times in Employees and three times in Customers will get row numbers 1 through 5 in the first input, and row numbers 1 through 3 in the second input. You then apply *input1 EXCEPT input2* and get rows (including the *rn* attribute) that appear in *input1* but not in *input2*. If row R appears five times in *input1* and three times in *input2*, you get the following result:

{(R, 1), (R, 2), (R, 3), (R, 4), (R, 5)}

EXCEPT

{(R, 1), (R, 2), (R, 3)}

And this produces the following result:

{(R, 4), (R, 5)}

In other words, R appears in the result exactly the number of times mandated by EXCEPT ALL. I encapsulated this logic in a CTE to return only the original attribute list without the row number, which is what EXCEPT ALL would do.

INTERSECT

INTERSECT returns rows that appear in both inputs.

To achieve INTERSECT, programmers sometimes use the EXISTS predicate or an inner join, as I demonstrated earlier in the "Semi Joins" section. However, as I explained earlier, those solutions as typically written treat two NULLs as different from each other, and set operations are supposed to treat them as equal. You need to add logic to those solutions to treat two NULLs as equal.

SQL Server provides a built-in INTERSECT operator, but only the nuance with the implicit DISTINCT.

INTERSECT DISTINCT

The INTERSECT DISTINCT set operation returns only distinct rows that appear in both inputs. For example, the following query returns cities that appear in both Employees and Customers:

```
SELECT country, region, city FROM HR.Employees
INTERSECT
SELECT country, region, city FROM Sales.Customers;
```

INTERSECT ALL

Like EXCEPT ALL, INTERSECT ALL also considers multiple occurrences of rows. If a row R appears *n* times in one input table and *m* times in the other, it should appear *MIN(n, m)* times in the result.

The solution to INTERSECT ALL in SQL Server 2008 is similar to the one for EXCEPT ALL except for one obvious difference—the use of the INTERSECT operator instead of EXCEPT:

```
WITH INTERSECT_ALL
AS
(
  SELECT
    ROW_NUMBER()
      OVER(PARTITION BY country, region, city
           ORDER      BY (SELECT 0) AS rn,
    country, region, city
  FROM HR.Employees

  INTERSECT

  SELECT
    ROW_NUMBER()
      OVER(PARTITION BY country, region, city
           ORDER      BY (SELECT 0) AS rn,
    country, region, city
    FROM Sales.Customers
)
SELECT country, region, city
FROM INTERSECT_ALL;
```

Precedence of Set Operations

The INTERSECT set operation has a higher precedence than the others. In a query that mixes multiple set operations, INTERSECT is evaluated first. Other than that, set operations are evaluated from left to right. The exception is that parentheses are always first in precedence, so by using parentheses you have full control of the logical order of evaluation of set operations.

For example, in the following query INTERSECT is evaluated first even though it appears second:

```
SELECT country, region, city FROM Production.Suppliers
EXCEPT
SELECT country, region, city FROM HR.Employees
INTERSECT
SELECT country, region, city FROM Sales.Customers;
```

The meaning of the query is: return supplier cities that do not appear in the intersection of employee cities and customer cities.

However, if you use parentheses, you can change the evaluation order:

```
(SELECT country, region, city FROM Production.Suppliers
 EXCEPT
 SELECT country, region, city FROM HR.Employees)
INTERSECT
SELECT country, region, city FROM Sales.Customers;
```

This query means: return supplier cities that are not employee cities and are also customer cities.

Using INTO with Set Operations

If you want to write a SELECT INTO statement where you use set operations, specify the INTO clause just before the FROM clause of the first input. For example, here's how you populate a temporary table #T with the result of one of the previous queries:

```
SELECT country, region, city INTO #T FROM Production.Suppliers
EXCEPT
SELECT country, region, city FROM HR.Employees
INTERSECT
SELECT country, region, city FROM Sales.Customers;
```

Circumventing Unsupported Logical Phases

As I mentioned earlier, logical processing phases other than sorting (joins, filtering, grouping, TOP, and so on) are not allowed directly on the result of a set operation. This limitation can easily be circumvented by using a derived table or a CTE like so:

```
SELECT DISTINCT TOP ...
FROM (<set operation query>) AS D
  JOIN | PIVOT | UNPIVOT | APPLY ...
WHERE ...
GROUP BY ...
HAVING ...
ORDER BY ...
```

For example, the following query tells you how many cities in each country are covered by customers or employees:

```
SELECT country, COUNT(*) AS numcities
FROM (SELECT country, region, city FROM HR.Employees
      UNION
      SELECT country, region, city FROM Sales.Customers) AS U
GROUP BY country;
```

This query generates the following output:

```
country          numcities
---------------  -----------
Argentina        1
Austria          2
Belgium          2
Brazil           4
Canada           3
Denmark          2
Finland          2
France           9
Germany          11
Ireland          1
Italy            3
Mexico           1
```

Norway	1
Poland	1
Portugal	1
Spain	3
Sweden	2
Switzerland	2
UK	2
USA	14
Venezuela	4

In a similar manner, you can circumvent the limitations on the individual queries used as inputs to the set operation. Each input can be written as a simple SELECT query from a derived table or a CTE, where you use the disallowed elements in the derived table or CTE expression.

For example, the following query returns the two most recent orders for employees 3 and 5:

```
SELECT empid, orderid, orderdate
FROM (SELECT TOP (2) empid, orderid, orderdate
      FROM Sales.Orders
      WHERE empid = 3
      ORDER BY orderdate DESC, orderid DESC) AS D1

UNION ALL

SELECT empid, orderid, orderdate
FROM (SELECT TOP (2) empid, orderid, orderdate
      FROM Sales.Orders
      WHERE empid = 5
      ORDER BY orderdate DESC, orderid DESC) AS D2;
```

This query generates the following output:

```
empid       orderid     orderdate
----------- ----------- -----------------------
3           11063       2008-04-30 00:00:00.000
3           11057       2008-04-29 00:00:00.000
5           11043       2008-04-22 00:00:00.000
5           10954       2008-03-17 00:00:00.000
```

As for the limitation on sorting the individual inputs, suppose you need to sort each input independently. For example, you want to return orders placed by customer 1 and also orders handled by employee 3. As for sorting the rows in the output, you want customer 1's orders to appear first, sorted by *orderid* descending, and then orders handled by employee 3, sorted by *orderdate* ascending. To achieve this, you create a column (*sortcol*) with the constant 1 for the first input (customer 1) and 2 for the second (employee 3). Create a derived table (call it U) out of the UNION ALL between the two. In the outer query, first sort by *sortcol,* and then by a CASE expression for each set. The CASE expression will return the relevant value based on the source set; otherwise, it returns a NULL, which won't affect sorting. Here's the solution query followed by its output (abbreviated):

```
SELECT empid, custid, orderid, orderdate
FROM (SELECT 1 AS sortcol, custid, empid, orderid, orderdate
```

```
        FROM Sales.Orders
        WHERE custid = 1

        UNION ALL

        SELECT 2 AS sortcol, custid, empid, orderid, orderdate
        FROM Sales.Orders
        WHERE empid = 3) AS U
ORDER BY sortcol,
  CASE WHEN sortcol = 1 THEN orderid END,
  CASE WHEN sortcol = 2 THEN orderdate END DESC;
```

```
empid        custid       orderid      orderdate
-----------  -----------  -----------  -----------------------
6            1            10643        2007-08-25 00:00:00.000
4            1            10692        2007-10-03 00:00:00.000
4            1            10702        2007-10-13 00:00:00.000
1            1            10835        2008-01-15 00:00:00.000
1            1            10952        2008-03-16 00:00:00.000
3            1            11011        2008-04-09 00:00:00.000
3            37           11063        2008-04-30 00:00:00.000
3            53           11057        2008-04-29 00:00:00.000
3            34           11052        2008-04-27 00:00:00.000
3            31           11049        2008-04-24 00:00:00.000
3            14           11041        2008-04-22 00:00:00.000
3            63           11021        2008-04-14 00:00:00.000
. . .
```

Conclusion

I covered many aspects of joins and set operations and demonstrated new querying techniques that you might find handy.

Remember that the comma-based syntax for cross and inner joins is part of standard SQL and is fully supported by SQL Server. However, when you intend to write an inner join but you forget to specify the join predicate in the WHERE clause, you get a Cartesian product. For this reason and for consistency's sake, I recommended that you stick to the ANSI SQL-92 join syntax with the JOIN keyword.

SQL Server has native operators for the UNION, UNION ALL, EXCEPT, and INTERSECT set operations. It also provides other tools that allow simple solutions for achieving EXCEPT ALL and INTERSECT ALL.

Chapter 8
Aggregating and Pivoting Data

This chapter covers various data-aggregation techniques, including using the OVER clause with aggregate functions, tiebreakers, running aggregates, pivoting, unpivoting, custom aggregations, histograms, grouping factors, and grouping sets.

In my solutions in this chapter, I'll reuse techniques that I introduced earlier. I'll also introduce new techniques for you to familiarize yourself with.

Logic will naturally be an integral element in the solutions. Remember that at the heart of every querying problem lies a logical puzzle.

OVER Clause

The OVER clause allows you to request window-based calculations—that is, calculations performed over a whole window of rows. In Chapter 6, "Subqueries, Table Expressions, and Ranking Functions," I described in detail how you use the OVER clause with analytical ranking functions. Microsoft SQL Server also supports the OVER clause with scalar aggregate functions; however, currently you can provide only the PARTITION BY clause. Future versions of SQL Server will most likely also support the other ANSI elements of aggregate window functions, including the ORDER BY and ROWS clauses.

The purpose of using the OVER clause with scalar aggregates is to calculate, for each row, an aggregate based on a window of values that extends beyond that row—and to do all this without using a GROUP BY clause in the query. In other words, the OVER clause allows you to add aggregate calculations to the results of an ungrouped query. This capability provides an alternative to requesting aggregates with subqueries in case you need to include both base row attributes and aggregates in your results.

Remember that in Chapter 7, "Joins and Set Operations," I presented a problem in which you were required to calculate two aggregates for each order row: the percentage the row contributed to the total value of all orders and the difference between the row's order value and the average value over all orders. In my examples I used a table called MyOrderValues that you create and populate by running the following code:

```
SET NOCOUNT ON;
USE InsideTSQL2008;

IF OBJECT_ID('dbo.MyOrderValues', 'U') IS NOT NULL
  DROP TABLE dbo.MyOrderValues;
GO
```

```
SELECT *
INTO dbo.MyOrderValues
FROM Sales.OrderValues;

ALTER TABLE dbo.MyOrderValues
  ADD CONSTRAINT PK_MyOrderValues PRIMARY KEY(orderid);

CREATE INDEX idx_val ON dbo.MyOrderValues(val);
```

I showed the following optimized query in which I used a cross join between the base table and a derived table of aggregates instead of using multiple subqueries:

```
SELECT orderid, custid, val,
  CAST(val / sumval * 100. AS NUMERIC(5, 2)) AS pct,
  CAST(val - avgval AS NUMERIC(12, 2)) AS diff
FROM dbo.MyOrderValues
  CROSS JOIN (SELECT SUM(val) AS sumval, AVG(val) AS avgval
              FROM dbo.MyOrderValues) AS Aggs;
```

This query produces the following output:

```
orderid  custid  val        pct    diff
-------- ------- ---------- ----- -------------
10248    85      440.00     0.03  -1085.05
10249    79      1863.40    0.15  338.35
10250    34      1552.60    0.12  27.55
10251    84      654.06     0.05  -870.99
10252    76      3597.90    0.28  2072.85
10253    34      1444.80    0.11  -80.25
10254    14      556.62     0.04  -968.43
10255    68      2490.50    0.20  965.45
10256    88      517.80     0.04  -1007.25
...
```

The motivation for calculating the two aggregates in a single derived table instead of as two separate subqueries stemmed from the fact that each subquery accessed the base table separately, while the derived table calculated the aggregates using a single scan of the data. SQL Server's query optimizer didn't use the fact that the two subqueries aggregated the same data into the same groups.

When you specify multiple aggregates with identical OVER clauses in the same SELECT list, however, the aggregates refer to the same window, as with a derived table, and SQL Server's query optimizer evaluates them all with one scan of the source data. Here's how you use the OVER clause to answer the same request:

```
SELECT orderid, custid, val,
  CAST(val / SUM(val) OVER() * 100. AS NUMERIC(5, 2)) AS pct,
  CAST(val - AVG(val) OVER() AS NUMERIC(12, 2)) AS diff
FROM dbo.MyOrderValues;
```

> **Note** In Chapter 6, I described the PARTITION BY clause, which is used with window functions, including aggregate window functions. This clause is optional. When not specified, the aggregate is based on the whole input rather than being calculated per partition.

Here, because I didn't specify a PARTITION BY clause, the aggregates were calculated based on the whole input. Logically, *SUM(val) OVER()* is equivalent here to the subquery *(SELECT SUM(val) FROM dbo.MyOrderValues)*. Physically, it's a different story. As an exercise, you can compare the execution plans of the following two queries, each requesting a different number of aggregates using the same OVER clause:

```
SELECT orderid, custid, val,
  SUM(val) OVER() AS sumval
FROM dbo.MyOrderValues;

SELECT orderid, custid, val,
  SUM(val)   OVER() AS sumval,
  COUNT(val) OVER() AS cntval,
  AVG(val)   OVER() AS avgval,
  MIN(val)   OVER() AS minval,
  MAX(val)   OVER() AS maxval
FROM dbo.MyOrderValues;
```

You'll find the two plans nearly identical, with the only difference being that the single Stream Aggregate operator calculates a different number of aggregates. The query costs are identical. On the other hand, compare the execution plans of the following two queries, each requesting a different number of aggregates using subqueries:

```
SELECT orderid, custid, val,
  (SELECT SUM(val) FROM dbo.MyOrderValues) AS sumval
FROM dbo.MyOrderValues;

SELECT orderid, custid, val,
  (SELECT SUM(val)   FROM dbo.MyOrderValues) AS sumval,
  (SELECT COUNT(val) FROM dbo.MyOrderValues) AS cntval,
  (SELECT AVG(val)   FROM dbo.MyOrderValues) AS avgval,
  (SELECT MIN(val)   FROM dbo.MyOrderValues) AS minval,
  (SELECT MAX(val)   FROM dbo.MyOrderValues) AS maxval
FROM dbo.MyOrderValues;
```

You'll find that they have different plans, with the latter being more expensive because it rescans the source data for each aggregate.

Another benefit of the OVER clause is that it allows for shorter and simpler code. This is especially apparent when you need to calculate partitioned aggregates. Using OVER, you simply specify a PARTITION BY clause. Using subqueries, you have to correlate the inner query to the outer, making the query longer and more complex.

As an example of using the PARTITION BY clause, the following query calculates the percentage of the order value out of the customer total and the difference from the customer average:

```
SELECT orderid, custid, val,
  CAST(val / SUM(val) OVER(PARTITION BY custid) * 100.
    AS NUMERIC(5, 2)) AS pct,
  CAST(val - AVG(val) OVER(PARTITION BY custid) AS NUMERIC(12, 2)) AS diff
FROM dbo.MyOrderValues
ORDER BY custid;
```

This query generates the following output:

```
orderid  custid  val     pct     diff
-------- ------- ------- ------ ------------
10643    1       814.50  19.06  102.33
10692    1       878.00  20.55  165.83
10702    1       330.00  7.72   -382.17
10835    1       845.80  19.79  133.63
10952    1       471.20  11.03  -240.97
11011    1       933.50  21.85  221.33
10926    2       514.40  36.67  163.66
10759    2       320.00  22.81  -30.74
10625    2       479.75  34.20  129.01
10308    2       88.80   6.33   -261.94
...
```

In short, the OVER clause allows for more concise and faster-running queries.

When you're done, run the following code for cleanup:

```
IF OBJECT_ID('dbo.MyOrderValues', 'U') IS NOT NULL
  DROP TABLE dbo.MyOrderValues;
```

Tiebreakers

In this section, I want to introduce a new technique based on aggregates to solve tiebreaker problems, which I started discussing in Chapter 6. I'll use the same example as I used there—returning the most recent order for each employee—using different combinations of tiebreaker attributes that uniquely identify an order for each employee. Keep in mind that the performance of the solutions that use subqueries depends very strongly on indexing. That is, you need an index on the partitioning column, sort column, and tiebreaker attributes. But in practice, you don't always have the option of adding as many indexes as you like. The subquery-based solutions will greatly suffer in performance from a lack of appropriate indexes. Using aggregation techniques, you'll see that the solution yields reasonable performance even when an optimal index is not in place—in fact, even when no good index is in place.

Let's start by using *MAX(orderid)* as the tiebreaker. To recap, you're after the most recent order for each employee, and if there's a tie for most recent, choose the order with the largest ID. For each employee's most recent order, you're supposed to return the columns *empid, orderdate, orderid, custid,* and *requireddate.*

The aggregate technique to solve the problem applies the following logical idea, given here in pseudocode:

```
SELECT empid, MAX(orderdate, orderid, custid, requireddate)
FROM Sales.Orders
GROUP BY empid;
```

This idea can't be expressed directly in T-SQL, so don't try to run this query. The idea here is to select for each *empid*, the row with largest *orderdate* (most recent), then largest *orderid*—the tiebreaker—among orders with the most recent *orderdate*. Because the combination *empid*, *orderdate*, *orderid* is already unique, there will be no further ties to break, and the other attributes (*custid* and *requireddate*) are simply returned from the selected row. Because a MAX of more than one attribute does not exist in T-SQL, you must mimic it somehow. One way is by merging the attributes into a single input to the MAX function, then extracting back the individual elements in an outer query.

The question is this: What technique should you use to merge the attributes? The trick is to convert each attribute to a fixed-width string and concatenate the strings. You must convert the attributes to strings in a way that doesn't change the sorting order. When dealing exclusively with nonnegative numbers, you can get by with an arithmetic calculation instead of concatenation. For example, say you have the numbers *m* and *n*, each with a valid range of 1 through 999. To merge *m* and *n*, use the following formula: *m*1000 + n AS r*. You can easily extract the individual pieces later: *r* divided by 1000 is *m*, and *r* modulo 1000 is *n*. However, in many cases you may have nonnumeric data to concatenate, so arithmetic wouldn't be possible. You might want to consider converting all values to fixed-width character strings (*CHAR(n)* or *NCHAR(n)*) or to fixed-width binary strings (*BINARY(n)*).

Here's an example of returning the most recent order for each employee, where *MAX(orderid)* is the tiebreaker, using binary concatenation:

```
SELECT empid,
  CAST(SUBSTRING(binstr, 1,  8) AS DATETIME) AS orderdate,
  CAST(SUBSTRING(binstr, 9,  4) AS INT)      AS orderid,
  CAST(SUBSTRING(binstr, 13, 4) AS INT)      AS custid,
  CAST(SUBSTRING(binstr, 17, 8) AS DATETIME) AS requireddate
FROM (SELECT empid,
        MAX(CAST(orderdate     AS BINARY(8))
          + CAST(orderid       AS BINARY(4))
          + CAST(custid        AS BINARY(4))
          + CAST(requireddate  AS BINARY(8))) AS binstr
      FROM Sales.Orders
      GROUP BY empid) AS D;
```

The derived table D contains the maximum concatenated string for each employee. Notice that each value was converted to the appropriate fixed-size string before concatenation based on its data type (DATETIME—8 bytes, INT—4 bytes, and so on).

> **Note** When you convert numbers to binary strings, only nonnegative values preserve their original sort order. As for DATETIME values, as long as they are not earlier than the base date January 1st, 1900, when converted to binary, the values preserve the original sort behavior. Values of the new DATE data type, however, do not preserve their sort behavior when converted to binary. As for character strings, converting them to binary values changes their sort order to one like a binary collation would define. Also note that preserving the original sort order is required only up to the point where uniqueness of a row per group is guaranteed (*orderdate + orderid* in our case).

The outer query uses *SUBSTRING* to extract the individual elements, and it converts them back to their original data types.

The real benefit in this solution is that it scans the data only once regardless of whether you have a good index. If you do, you'll probably get an ordered scan of the index and a sort-based aggregate (a stream aggregate). If you don't have a good index—as is the case here—you'll probably get a hash-based aggregate, as you can see in Figure 8-1.

FIGURE 8-1 Execution plan for a tiebreaker query

Things get trickier when the sort columns and tiebreaker attributes have different sort directions within them. For example, suppose the tiebreaker was *MIN(orderid)*. In that case, you would need to apply *MAX* to *orderdate* and *MIN* to *orderid*. There is a logical solution when the attribute with the opposite direction is numeric. Say you need to calculate the *MIN* value of a nonnegative integer column *n*, using only *MAX*, and you need to use binary concatenation. You can get the minimum by using *<maxint> - MAX(<maxint> - n)*.

The following query incorporates this logical technique:

```
SELECT empid,
  CAST(SUBSTRING(binstr, 1, 8) AS DATETIME)        AS orderdate,
  2147483647 - CAST(SUBSTRING(binstr, 9, 4) AS INT) AS orderid,
  CAST(SUBSTRING(binstr, 13, 4) AS INT)            AS custid,
  CAST(SUBSTRING(binstr, 17, 8) AS DATETIME)       AS requireddate
FROM (SELECT empid,
        MAX(CAST(orderdate          AS BINARY(8))
            + CAST(2147483647 - orderid AS BINARY(4))
            + CAST(custid           AS BINARY(4))
            + CAST(requireddate     AS BINARY(8))) AS binstr
      FROM Sales.Orders
      GROUP BY empid) AS D;
```

Another technique to calculate the minimum by using the MAX function is based on bitwise manipulation and works with nonnegative integers. The minimum value of a column *n* is equal to *~MAX(~n)*, where ~ is the bitwise NOT operator.

The following query incorporates this technique:

```
SELECT empid,
  CAST(SUBSTRING(binstr, 1, 8) AS DATETIME)  AS orderdate,
  ~CAST(SUBSTRING(binstr, 9, 4) AS INT)       AS orderid,
  CAST(SUBSTRING(binstr, 13, 4) AS INT)       AS custid,
  CAST(SUBSTRING(binstr, 17, 8) AS DATETIME) AS requireddate
FROM (SELECT empid,
        MAX(CAST(orderdate      AS BINARY(8))
            + CAST(~orderid     AS BINARY(4))
            + CAST(custid       AS BINARY(4))
            + CAST(requireddate AS BINARY(8))) AS binstr
     FROM Sales.Orders
     GROUP BY empid) AS D;
```

Of course, you can play with the tiebreakers you're using in any way you like. For example, the following query returns the most recent order for each employee, using *MAX(requireddate)*, *MAX(orderid)* as the tiebreaker:

```
SELECT empid,
  CAST(SUBSTRING(binstr, 1, 8)   AS DATETIME) AS orderdate,
  CAST(SUBSTRING(binstr, 9, 8)   AS DATETIME) AS requireddate,
  CAST(SUBSTRING(binstr, 17, 4)  AS INT)       AS orderid,
  CAST(SUBSTRING(binstr, 21, 4)  AS INT)       AS custid
FROM (SELECT empid,
        MAX(CAST(orderdate      AS BINARY(8))
            + CAST(requireddate AS BINARY(8))
            + CAST(orderid      AS BINARY(4))
            + CAST(custid       AS BINARY(4))
            ) AS binstr
     FROM Sales.Orders
     GROUP BY empid) AS D;
```

Running Aggregations

Running aggregations are aggregations of data over a sequence (typically temporal). Running aggregate problems have many variations, and I'll describe several important ones here.

In my examples, I'll use a summary table called EmpOrders that contains one row for each employee and month, with the total quantity of orders made by that employee in that month. Run the following code to create the EmpOrders table and populate it with sample data:

```
USE tempdb;

IF OBJECT_ID('dbo.EmpOrders') IS NOT NULL DROP TABLE dbo.EmpOrders;

CREATE TABLE dbo.EmpOrders
(
  empid    INT  NOT NULL,
  ordmonth DATE NOT NULL,
```

```
  qty        INT  NOT NULL,
  PRIMARY KEY(empid, ordmonth)
);
GO

INSERT INTO dbo.EmpOrders(empid, ordmonth, qty)
  SELECT O.empid,
    DATEADD(month, DATEDIFF(month, 0, O.orderdate), 0) AS ordmonth,
    SUM(qty) AS qty
  FROM InsideTSQL2008.Sales.Orders AS O
    JOIN InsideTSQL2008.Sales.OrderDetails AS OD
      ON O.orderid = OD.orderid
  GROUP BY empid,
    DATEADD(month, DATEDIFF(month, 0, O.orderdate), 0);
```

Tip I will represent each month by its start date stored as a DATE. This allows flexible manipulation of the data using date-related functions. Of course, I'll ignore the day part of the value in my calculations.

Run the following query to get the contents of the EmpOrders table:

```
SELECT empid, CONVERT(VARCHAR(7), ordmonth, 121) AS ordmonth, qty
FROM dbo.EmpOrders
ORDER BY empid, ordmonth;
```

This query generates the following output, shown here in abbreviated form:

```
empid       ordmonth qty
----------- -------- -----------
1           2006-07  121
1           2006-08  247
1           2006-09  255
1           2006-10  143
1           2006-11  318
1           2006-12  536
1           2007-01  304
1           2007-02  168
1           2007-03  275
1           2007-04  20
...
2           2006-07  50
2           2006-08  94
2           2006-09  137
2           2006-10  248
2           2006-11  237
2           2006-12  319
2           2007-01  230
2           2007-02  36
2           2007-03  151
2           2007-04  468
...
```

I'll discuss three types of running aggregation problems: cumulative, sliding, and year-to-date (YTD).

Cumulative Aggregations

Cumulative aggregations accumulate data from the first element within the sequence up to the current point. For example, imagine the following request: for each employee and month, return the total quantity and average monthly quantity from the beginning of the employee's activity through the month in question.

Recall the techniques for calculating row numbers without using the built-in ROW_NUMBER function; using these techniques, you scan the same rows we need here to calculate the total quantities. The difference is that for row numbers you used the aggregate COUNT, and here you'll use the aggregates SUM and AVG. I demonstrated two set-based solutions to calculate row numbers without the ROW_NUMBER function—one using subqueries and one using joins. In the solution using joins, I applied what I called an *expand-collapse technique*. To me, the subquery solution is much more intuitive than the join solution, with its artificial expand-collapse technique. So, when there's no performance difference, I'd rather use subqueries. Typically, you won't see a performance difference when only one aggregate is involved because the plans would be similar. However, when you request multiple aggregates, the subquery solution might result in a plan that scans the data separately for each aggregate. Compare this to the plan for the join solution, which typically calculates all aggregates during a single scan of the source data.

So my choice is usually simple—use a subquery for one aggregate and use a join for multiple aggregates. The following query applies the expand-collapse approach to produce the desired result:

```
SELECT O1.empid, CONVERT(VARCHAR(7), O1.ordmonth, 121) AS ordmonth,
  O1.qty AS qtythismonth, SUM(O2.qty) AS totalqty,
  CAST(AVG(1.*O2.qty) AS NUMERIC(12, 2)) AS avgqty
FROM dbo.EmpOrders AS O1
  JOIN dbo.EmpOrders AS O2
    ON O2.empid = O1.empid
    AND O2.ordmonth <= O1.ordmonth
GROUP BY O1.empid, O1.ordmonth, O1.qty
ORDER BY O1.empid, O1.ordmonth;
```

This query generates the following output, shown here in abbreviated form:

```
empid       ordmonth qtythismonth totalqty    avgqty
----------- -------- ------------ ----------- ----------
1           2006-07  121          121         121.00
1           2006-08  247          368         184.00
1           2006-09  255          623         207.67
1           2006-10  143          766         191.50
1           2006-11  318          1084        216.80
1           2006-12  536          1620        270.00
1           2007-01  304          1924        274.86
1           2007-02  168          2092        261.50
1           2007-03  275          2367        263.00
1           2007-04  20           2387        238.70
...
```

2	2006-07	50	50	50.00
2	2006-08	94	144	72.00
2	2006-09	137	281	93.67
2	2006-10	248	529	132.25
2	2006-11	237	766	153.20
2	2006-12	319	1085	180.83
2	2007-01	230	1315	187.86
2	2007-02	36	1351	168.88
2	2007-03	151	1502	166.89
2	2007-04	468	1970	197.00

...

Now let's say that you are asked to return only one aggregate (say, total quantity). You can safely use the subquery approach:

```
SELECT O1.empid, CONVERT(VARCHAR(7), O1.ordmonth, 121) AS ordmonth,
  O1.qty AS qtythismonth,
  (SELECT SUM(O2.qty)
   FROM dbo.EmpOrders AS O2
   WHERE O2.empid = O1.empid
     AND O2.ordmonth <= O1.ordmonth) AS totalqty
FROM dbo.EmpOrders AS O1
GROUP BY O1.empid, O1.ordmonth, O1.qty;
```

As was the case for calculating row numbers based on subqueries or joins, when calculating running aggregates based on similar techniques, the N^2 performance issues I discussed before apply once again. Because running aggregates typically are calculated on a fairly small number of rows per group, you won't be adversely affected by performance issues, assuming you have appropriate indexes (keyed on grouping columns, then sort columns, and including covering columns).

Let p be the number of partitions involved (employees in our case), let n be the average number of rows per partition (months in our case), and let a be the number of aggregates involved. The total number of rows scanned using the join approach can be expressed as $pn + p(n+n^2)/2$ and as $pn + ap(n+n^2)/2$ using the subquery approach because with subqueries the optimizer uses a separate scan per subquery. It's important to note that the N^2 complexity is relevant to the partition size and not the table size. If the number of rows in the table grows by a factor of f but the partition size doesn't change, the run time increases by a factor of f as well. If, on the other hand, the average partition size grows by a factor of f, the run time increases by a factor of f^2. With small partitions (say, up to several dozen rows), this set-based solution provides reasonable performance. With large partitions, a cursor solution would be faster despite the overhead associated with row-by-row manipulation because a cursor scans the rows only once, and the per-row overhead is constant.

Note ANSI SQL provides support for running aggregates by means of aggregate window functions. SQL Server 2005 introduced the OVER clause for aggregate functions only with the PARTITION BY clause, and unfortunately SQL Server 2008 didn't enhance the OVER clause further. Further enhancements are currently planned for the next major release of SQL Server—SQL

Server 11. Per ANSI SQL—and I hope in future versions of SQL Server—you could provide a solution relying exclusively on window functions, like so:

```
SELECT empid, CONVERT(VARCHAR(7), ordmonth, 121) AS ordmonth, qty,
    SUM(O2.qty) OVER(PARTITION BY empid
                     ORDER BY ordmonth
                     ROWS BETWEEN UNBOUNDED PRECEDING
                                  AND CURRENT ROW) AS totalqty,
    CAST(AVG(1.*O2.qty) OVER(PARTITION BY empid
                             ORDER BY ordmonth
                             ROWS BETWEEN UNBOUNDED PRECEDING
                                          AND CURRENT ROW)
    AS NUMERIC(12, 2)) AS avgqty
FROM dbo.EmpOrders;
```

When this code is finally supported in SQL Server, you can expect dramatic performance improvements and obviously much simpler queries. Being familiar with the way ranking calculations based on the OVER clause are currently optimized, you should expect running aggregates based on the OVER clause to be optimized similarly. That is, given a good index to support the request, you should expect the plan to involve a single ordered scan of the data. Then the total number of rows scanned would simply be the number of rows in the table (*pn*).

You might also be requested to filter the data—for example, return monthly aggregates for each employee only for months before the employee reached a certain target. Typically, you'll have a target for each employee stored in a Targets table that you'll need to join to. To make this example simple, I'll assume that all employees have the same target total quantity—1,000. In practice, you'll use the target attribute from the Targets table. Because you need to filter an aggregate, not an attribute, you must specify the filter expression (in this case, *SUM(O2.qty) < 1000*) in the HAVING clause, not the WHERE clause. The solution is as follows:

```
SELECT O1.empid, CONVERT(VARCHAR(7), O1.ordmonth, 121) AS ordmonth,
    O1.qty AS qtythismonth, SUM(O2.qty) AS totalqty,
    CAST(AVG(1.*O2.qty) AS NUMERIC(12, 2)) AS avgqty
FROM dbo.EmpOrders AS O1
    JOIN dbo.EmpOrders AS O2
        ON O2.empid = O1.empid
        AND O2.ordmonth <= O1.ordmonth
GROUP BY O1.empid, O1.ordmonth, O1.qty
HAVING SUM(O2.qty) < 1000
ORDER BY O1.empid, O1.ordmonth;
```

This query generates the following output, shown here in abbreviated form:

```
empid       ordmonth qtythismonth totalqty    avgqty
----------- -------- ------------ ----------- ----------
1           2006-07  121          121         121.00
1           2006-08  247          368         184.00
1           2006-09  255          623         207.67
1           2006-10  143          766         191.50
2           2006-07  50           50          50.00
2           2006-08  94           144         72.00
2           2006-09  137          281         93.67
2           2006-10  248          529         132.25
```

2	2006-11	237	766	153.20
3	2006-07	182	182	182.00
3	2006-08	228	410	205.00
3	2006-09	75	485	161.67
3	2006-10	151	636	159.00
3	2006-11	204	840	168.00
3	2006-12	100	940	156.67
...				

Things get a bit tricky if you also need to include the rows for those months in which the employees reached their target. If you specify *SUM(O2.qty) <= 1000* (that is, write <= instead of <), you still won't get the row in which the employee reached the target unless the total through that month is exactly 1,000. But remember that you have access to both the cumulative total and the current month's quantity, and using these two values together, you can solve this problem. If you change the HAVING filter to *SUM(O2.qty) – O1.qty < 1000*, you get the months in which the employee's total quantity, *excluding the current month's orders*, had not reached the target. In particular, the first month in which an employee reached or exceeded the target satisfies this new criterion, and that month will appear in the results. The complete solution follows:

```
SELECT O1.empid, CONVERT(VARCHAR(7), O1.ordmonth, 121) AS ordmonth,
  O1.qty AS qtythismonth, SUM(O2.qty) AS totalqty,
  CAST(AVG(1.*O2.qty) AS NUMERIC(12, 2)) AS avgqty
FROM dbo.EmpOrders AS O1
  JOIN dbo.EmpOrders AS O2
    ON O2.empid = O1.empid
    AND O2.ordmonth <= O1.ordmonth
GROUP BY O1.empid, O1.ordmonth, O1.qty
HAVING SUM(O2.qty) - O1.qty < 1000
ORDER BY O1.empid, O1.ordmonth;
```

This query generates the following output, shown here in abbreviated form:

empid	ordmonth	qtythismonth	totalqty	avgqty
1	2006-07	121	121	121.00
1	2006-08	247	368	184.00
1	2006-09	255	623	207.67
1	2006-10	143	766	191.50
1	2006-11	318	1084	216.80
2	2006-07	50	50	50.00
2	2006-08	94	144	72.00
2	2006-09	137	281	93.67
2	2006-10	248	529	132.25
2	2006-11	237	766	153.20
2	2006-12	319	1085	180.83
3	2006-07	182	182	182.00
3	2006-08	228	410	205.00
3	2006-09	75	485	161.67
3	2006-10	151	636	159.00
3	2006-11	204	840	168.00
3	2006-12	100	940	156.67
3	2007-01	364	1304	186.29
...				

Note You might have another solution in mind that seems like a plausible and simpler alternative—to leave the SUM condition alone but change the join condition to *O2.ordmonth < O1.ordmonth*. This way, the query would select rows where the total through the previous month did not meet the target. However, in the end, this solution is not any easier (the AVG is hard to generate, for example); what's worse is that you might come up with a solution that does not work for employees who reach the target in their first month.

Tip If you want to return no fewer than a certain number of rows per partition, simply add the criterion *OR COUNT(*) <= <min_num_of_rows>* to the HAVING clause. This technique works well in our case since the base table contains one row per result row/group.

Suppose you're interested in seeing results only for the specific month in which the employee reached the target of 1,000, without seeing results for preceding months. What's true for only those rows in the output of the last query? You're looking for rows where the total quantity is greater than or equal to 1,000. Simply add this criterion to the HAVING filter. Here's the query followed by its output:

```
SELECT O1.empid, CONVERT(VARCHAR(7), O1.ordmonth, 121) AS ordmonth,
  O1.qty AS qtythismonth, SUM(O2.qty) AS totalqty,
  CAST(AVG(1.*O2.qty) AS NUMERIC(12, 2)) AS avgqty
FROM dbo.EmpOrders AS O1
  JOIN dbo.EmpOrders AS O2
    ON O2.empid = O1.empid
    AND O2.ordmonth <= O1.ordmonth
GROUP BY O1.empid, O1.ordmonth, O1.qty
HAVING SUM(O2.qty) - O1.qty < 1000
  AND SUM(O2.qty) >= 1000
ORDER BY O1.empid, O1.ordmonth;
```

```
empid       ordmonth qtythismonth totalqty     avgqty
----------- -------- ------------ -----------  ----------
1           2006-11  318          1084         216.80
2           2006-12  319          1085         180.83
3           2007-01  364          1304         186.29
4           2006-10  613          1439         359.75
5           2007-05  247          1213         173.29
6           2007-01  64           1027         171.17
7           2007-03  191          1069         152.71
8           2007-01  305          1228         175.43
9           2007-06  161          1007         125.88
```

Sliding Aggregations

Sliding aggregates are calculated over a sliding window in a sequence (again, typically temporal), as opposed to being calculated from the beginning of the sequence until the current point. A *moving average*—such as the employee's average quantity over the last three months—is one example of a sliding aggregate.

> **Note** Without clarification, expressions such as "last three months" are ambiguous. The last three months could mean the previous three months (*not including this month*), or it could mean the previous two months *along with this month*. When you get a problem like this, be sure you know precisely what window of time you are using for aggregation—for a particular row, exactly when does the window begin and end?
>
> In our example, the window of time is this: greater than the point in time starting three months ago and smaller than or equal to the current point in time. Note that this definition works well even in cases where you track finer time granularities than a month (including day, hour, minute, second, millisecond, microsecond, and nanosecond). This definition also addresses implicit conversion issues resulting from the accuracy level supported by SQL Server for the *DATETIME* data type—3.33 milliseconds. To avoid implicit conversion issues, it's wiser to use > and <= predicates than the BETWEEN predicate.

The main difference between the solution for cumulative aggregates and the solution for sliding aggregates is in the join condition (or in the subquery's filter in the case of the alternate solution using subqueries). Instead of using *O2.ordmonth <= O1.current_month*, you use *O2.ordmonth > three_months_before_current AND O2.ordmonth <= O1.current_month*. In T-SQL, this translates to the following query:

```
SELECT O1.empid,
    CONVERT(VARCHAR(7), O1.ordmonth, 121) AS tomonth,
    O1.qty AS qtythismonth,
    SUM(O2.qty) AS totalqty,
    CAST(AVG(1.*O2.qty) AS NUMERIC(12, 2)) AS avgqty
FROM dbo.EmpOrders AS O1
    JOIN dbo.EmpOrders AS O2
        ON O2.empid = O1.empid
        AND (O2.ordmonth > DATEADD(month, -3, O1.ordmonth)
            AND O2.ordmonth <= O1.ordmonth)
GROUP BY O1.empid, O1.ordmonth, O1.qty
ORDER BY O1.empid, O1.ordmonth;
```

This query generates the following output, shown here in abbreviated form:

```
empid       tomonth qtythismonth totalqty    avgqty
----------- ------- ------------ ----------- ----------
1           2006-07 121          121         121.00
1           2006-08 247          368         184.00
1           2006-09 255          623         207.67
1           2006-10 143          645         215.00
1           2006-11 318          716         238.67
1           2006-12 536          997         332.33
1           2007-01 304          1158        386.00
1           2007-02 168          1008        336.00
1           2007-03 275          747         249.00
1           2007-04 20           463         154.33
...
2           2006-07 50           50          50.00
2           2006-08 94           144         72.00
2           2006-09 137          281         93.67
2           2006-10 248          479         159.67
2           2006-11 237          622         207.33
```

2	2006-12 319	804	268.00
2	2007-01 230	786	262.00
2	2007-02 36	585	195.00
2	2007-03 151	417	139.00
2	2007-04 468	655	218.33

. . .

Note that this solution includes aggregates for three-month periods that don't include three months of actual data. If you want to return only periods with three full months accumulated, without the first two periods that do not cover three months, you can add the criterion *MIN(O2.ordmonth) = DATEADD(month, –2, O1.ordmonth)* to the HAVING filter.

> **Note** Per ANSI SQL, you can use the ORDER BY and ROWS subclauses of the OVER clause—which are currently missing in SQL Server—to address sliding aggregates. You would use the following query to return the desired result for the last sliding aggregates request (assuming the data has exactly one row per month):
>
> ```
> SELECT empid, CONVERT(VARCHAR(7), ordmonth, 121) AS ordmonth,
>    qty AS qtythismonth,
>    SUM(O2.qty) OVER(PARTITION BY empid
>                     ORDER BY ordmonth
>                     ROWS BETWEEN 2 PRECEDING
>                               AND CURRENT ROW) AS totalqty,
>    CAST(AVG(1.*O2.qty) OVER(PARTITION BY empid
>                     ORDER BY ordmonth
>                     ROWS BETWEEN 2 PRECEDING
>                               AND CURRENT ROW)
>       AS NUMERIC(12, 2)) AS avgqty
> FROM dbo.EmpOrders;
> ```

Year-to-Date (YTD)

YTD aggregates accumulate values from the beginning of a period based on some date and time unit (say, a year) until the current point. The calculation is very similar to the sliding aggregates solution. The only difference is the lower bound provided in the query's filter, which is the calculation of the beginning of the year. For example, the following query returns YTD aggregates for each employee and month:

```
SELECT O1.empid,
   CONVERT(VARCHAR(7), O1.ordmonth, 121) AS ordmonth,
   O1.qty AS qtythismonth,
   SUM(O2.qty) AS totalqty,
   CAST(AVG(1.*O2.qty) AS NUMERIC(12, 2)) AS avgqty
FROM dbo.EmpOrders AS O1
  JOIN dbo.EmpOrders AS O2
    ON O2.empid = O1.empid
    AND (O2.ordmonth >= CAST(CAST(YEAR(O1.ordmonth) AS CHAR(4))
                         + '0101' AS DATETIME)
         AND O2.ordmonth <= O1.ordmonth)
GROUP BY O1.empid, O1.ordmonth, O1.qty
ORDER BY O1.empid, O1.ordmonth;
```

This query generates the following output, shown here in abbreviated form:

```
empid        ordmonth qtythismonth totalqty     avgqty
-----------  -------- ------------ -----------  ----------
1            2006-07  121          121          121.00
1            2006-08  247          368          184.00
1            2006-09  255          623          207.67
1            2006-10  143          766          191.50
1            2006-11  318          1084         216.80
1            2006-12  536          1620         270.00
1            2007-01  304          304          304.00
1            2007-02  168          472          236.00
1            2007-03  275          747          249.00
1            2007-04  20           767          191.75
...
2            2006-07  50           50           50.00
2            2006-08  94           144          72.00
2            2006-09  137          281          93.67
2            2006-10  248          529          132.25
2            2006-11  237          766          153.20
2            2006-12  319          1085         180.83
2            2007-01  230          230          230.00
2            2007-02  36           266          133.00
2            2007-03  151          417          139.00
2            2007-04  468          885          221.25
...
```

Pivoting

Pivoting is a technique that allows you to rotate rows to columns, possibly performing aggregations along the way. The number of applications for pivoting is simply astounding. In this section, I'll present a few, including pivoting attributes in an open schema environment, solving relational division problems, and formatting aggregated data. Later in the chapter and also in later chapters in the book, I'll show additional applications.

Pivoting Attributes

I'll use *open schema* as the scenario for pivoting attributes. Open schema is a design problem describing an environment that needs to deal with frequent schema changes. The relational model and SQL were conceived to handle frequent changes and requests for data via SQL's data manipulation language (DML). However, SQL's data definition language (DDL) was not conceived to support frequent schema changes. Whenever you need to add new entities, you must create new tables; whenever existing entities change their structures, you must add, alter, or drop columns. Such changes usually require downtime of the affected objects, and they also bring about substantial revisions to the application.

You can choose from several ways to model an open schema environment, each of which has advantages and disadvantages. One of those models is known as Entity Attribute

Value (EAV) and also as the *narrow* representation of data. In this model, you store all data in a single table, where each attribute value resides in its own row along with the entity or object ID and the attribute name or ID. You represent the attribute values using the data type SQL_VARIANT to accommodate multiple attribute types in a single column.

In my examples, I'll use the OpenSchema table, which you can create and populate by running the following code:

```
USE tempdb;

IF OBJECT_ID('dbo.OpenSchema') IS NOT NULL DROP TABLE dbo.OpenSchema;

CREATE TABLE dbo.OpenSchema
(
  objectid  INT          NOT NULL,
  attribute NVARCHAR(30) NOT NULL,
  value     SQL_VARIANT  NOT NULL,
  PRIMARY KEY (objectid, attribute)
);
GO

INSERT INTO dbo.OpenSchema(objectid, attribute, value) VALUES
  (1, N'attr1', CAST(CAST('ABC'      AS VARCHAR(10))   AS SQL_VARIANT)),
  (1, N'attr2', CAST(CAST(10         AS INT)           AS SQL_VARIANT)),
  (1, N'attr3', CAST(CAST('20070101' AS SMALLDATETIME) AS SQL_VARIANT)),
  (2, N'attr2', CAST(CAST(12         AS INT)           AS SQL_VARIANT)),
  (2, N'attr3', CAST(CAST('20090101' AS SMALLDATETIME) AS SQL_VARIANT)),
  (2, N'attr4', CAST(CAST('Y'        AS CHAR(1))       AS SQL_VARIANT)),
  (2, N'attr5', CAST(CAST(13.7       AS NUMERIC(9,3))  AS SQL_VARIANT)),
  (3, N'attr1', CAST(CAST('XYZ'      AS VARCHAR(10))   AS SQL_VARIANT)),
  (3, N'attr2', CAST(CAST(20         AS INT)           AS SQL_VARIANT)),
  (3, N'attr3', CAST(CAST('20080101' AS SMALLDATETIME) AS SQL_VARIANT));

-- show the contents of the table
SELECT * FROM dbo.OpenSchema;
```

This generates the following output:

```
objectid    attribute  value
----------- ---------- ------------------------
1           attr1      ABC
1           attr2      10
1           attr3      2007-01-01 00:00:00.000
2           attr2      12
2           attr3      2009-01-01 00:00:00.000
2           attr4      Y
2           attr5      13.700
3           attr1      XYZ
3           attr2      20
3           attr3      2008-01-01 00:00:00.000
```

Representing data this way allows logical schema changes to be implemented without adding, altering, or dropping tables and columns—you use DML INSERTs, UPDATEs, and DELETEs instead.

Of course, other aspects of working with the data (such as enforcing integrity, tuning, and querying) become more complex and expensive with such a representation. As mentioned, there are other approaches to dealing with open schema environments—for example, storing the data in XML format, using a *wide* representation of data, using CLR types, and others. However, when you weigh the advantages and disadvantages of each representation, you might find the EAV approach demonstrated here more favorable in some scenarios.

Keep in mind that this representation of the data requires very complex queries even for simple requests because different attributes of the same entity instance are spread over multiple rows. Before you query such data, you might want to rotate it to a traditional form with one column for each attribute—perhaps store the result in a temporary table, index it, query it, and then get rid of the temporary table. To rotate the data from its open schema form into a traditional form, you need to use a pivoting technique.

In the following section, I'll describe the steps involved in solving pivoting problems. I'd like to point out that to understand the steps of the solution, it can be very helpful if you think about query logical processing phases, which I described in detail in Chapter 1, "Logical Query Processing." I discussed the query processing phases involved with the native PIVOT table operator, but those phases apply just as well to the standard solution that does not use this proprietary operator. Moreover, in the standard solution the phases are more apparent in the code, while using the PIVOT operator they are implicit.

The first step you might want to try when solving pivoting problems is to figure out how the number of rows in the result correlates to the number of rows in the source data. Here, you need to create a single result row out of the multiple base rows for each object. In SQL, this translates to grouping rows. So our first logical processing phase in pivoting is a *grouping* phase, and the associated element (the element you need to group by) is the *objectid* column.

As the next step in a pivoting problem, you can think in terms of the result columns. You need a result column for each unique attribute. Because the data contains five unique attributes (*attr1*, *attr2*, *attr3*, *attr4*, and *attr5*), you need five expressions in the SELECT list. Each expression is supposed to extract, out of the rows belonging to the grouped object, the value corresponding to a specific attribute. You can think of this logical phase as a *spreading* phase—you need to spread the values, or shift them, from the source column (value in our case) to the corresponding target column. As for the element that dictates where to spread the values, or the *spread by* element, in our case it is the attribute column. This spreading activity can be done with the following CASE expression, which in this example is applied to the attribute *attr2*:

```
CASE WHEN attribute = 'attr2' THEN value END
```

Remember that with no ELSE clause, CASE assumes an implicit ELSE NULL. The CASE expression just shown yields NULL for rows where *attribute* does not equal *attr2* and yields *value* when *attribute* does equal *attr2*. This means that among the rows with a given value of *objectid* (say, 1), the CASE expression would yield several NULLs and, at most, one known value

(10 in our example), which represents the value of the target attribute (*attr2* in our example) for the given *objectid*.

The third phase in pivoting attributes is to extract the known value (if it exists) out of the set of NULLs and the known value. You have to use an aggregate for this purpose because, as you'll recall, the query involves grouping. The trick to extracting the one known value is to use *MAX* or *MIN*. Both ignore NULLs and will return the one non-NULL value present because both the minimum and the maximum of a set containing one value is that value. So our third logical processing phase in pivoting is an *aggregation* phase. The aggregation element is the value column, and the aggregate function is *MAX*. Using the previous expression implementing the second phase with *attr2*, here's the revised expression including the aggregation as well:

```
MAX(CASE WHEN attribute = 'attr2' THEN value END) AS attr2
```

Here's the complete query that pivots the attributes from OpenSchema:

```
SELECT objectid,
  MAX(CASE WHEN attribute = 'attr1' THEN value END) AS attr1,
  MAX(CASE WHEN attribute = 'attr2' THEN value END) AS attr2,
  MAX(CASE WHEN attribute = 'attr3' THEN value END) AS attr3,
  MAX(CASE WHEN attribute = 'attr4' THEN value END) AS attr4,
  MAX(CASE WHEN attribute = 'attr5' THEN value END) AS attr5
FROM dbo.OpenSchema
GROUP BY objectid;
```

This query generates the following output:

```
objectid    attr1       attr2       attr3                    attr4       attr5
-----------  ----------  ----------  -----------------------  ----------  ----------
1            ABC         10          2007-01-01 00:00:00.000  NULL        NULL
2            NULL        12          2009-01-01 00:00:00.000  Y           13.700
3            XYZ         20          2008-01-01 00:00:00.000  NULL        NULL
```

Note To write this query, you have to know the names of the attributes. If you don't, you'll need to construct the query string dynamically. I'll provide an example later in the chapter.

This technique for pivoting data is very efficient because it scans the base table only once.

SQL Server supports a native specialized table operator for pivoting called PIVOT. This operator does not provide any special advantages over the technique I just showed, except that it allows for shorter code. It doesn't support dynamic pivoting, and underneath the covers, it applies very similar logic to the one I presented in the last solution. So you probably won't even find noticeable performance differences. At any rate, here's how you would pivot the OpenSchema data using the PIVOT operator:

```
SELECT objectid, attr1, attr2, attr3, attr4, attr5
FROM dbo.OpenSchema
  PIVOT(MAX(value) FOR attribute
    IN([attr1],[attr2],[attr3],[attr4],[attr5])) AS P;
```

Within this solution, you can identify all the elements I used in the previous solution. The inputs to the PIVOT operator are as follows:

- The aggregate function applied to the aggregation element. In our case, it's *MAX(value)*, which extracts the single non-NULL value corresponding to the target attribute. In other cases, you might have more than one non-NULL value per group and want a different aggregate (for example, SUM or AVG).

- Following the FOR keyword, the name of the *spread by* element (*attribute*, in our case). This is the source column holding the values that become the target column names.

- The list of actual target column names in parentheses following the keyword IN.

As you can see, in the parentheses of the PIVOT operator, you specify the aggregate function and aggregation element and the *spread by* element and spreading values but not the *group by* elements. This is a problematic aspect of the syntax of the PIVOT operator—the grouping elements are implicitly derived from what was not specified. The grouping elements are the list of all columns from the input table to the PIVOT operator that were not mentioned as either the aggregation or the spreading elements. In our case, *objectid* is the only column left. If you unintentionally query the base table directly, you might end up with undesired grouping. If new columns will be added to the table in the future, those columns will be implicitly added to PIVOT's grouping list. Therefore, it is strongly recommended that you apply the PIVOT operator not to the base table directly but rather to a table expression (derived table or CTE) that includes only the elements relevant to the pivoting activity. This way, you can control exactly which columns remain besides the aggregation and spreading elements. Future column additions to the table won't have any impact on what PIVOT ends up operating on. The following query demonstrates applying this approach to our previous query, using a derived table:

```
SELECT objectid, attr1, attr2, attr3, attr4, attr5
FROM (SELECT objectid, attribute, value FROM dbo.OpenSchema) AS D
  PIVOT(MAX(value) FOR attribute
    IN([attr1],[attr2],[attr3],[attr4],[attr5])) AS P;
```

Tip The input to the aggregate function must be a base column from the PIVOT operator's input table with no manipulation—it cannot be an expression (for example: *SUM(qty * price)*). If you want to provide the aggregate function with an expression as input, have the PIVOT operator operate on a derived table or CTE (as suggested for other reasons as well), and in the derived table query assign the expression with a column alias (*qty * price AS value*). Then, as far as the PIVOT operator is concerned, that alias is the name of a base column in its input table, so it is valid to use that column name as input to PIVOT's aggregate function (*SUM(value)*).

Also, you cannot spread attributes from more than one column (the column that appears after the FOR keyword). If you need to pivot more than one column's attributes (say, *empid* and *YEAR(orderdate)*), you can use a similar approach to the previous suggestion: in the derived table or CTE used as the input to the PIVOT operator, concatenate the values from all columns you want to use as the spreading elements and assign the expression with a column alias (*CAST(empid AS VARCHAR(10)) + '_' + CAST(YEAR(orderdate) AS CHAR(4)) AS emp_year*). Then, in the outer query, specify that column after PIVOT's FOR keyword (*FOR emp_year IN([1_2007], [1_2008], [1_2009], [2_2007], ...]*).

Relational Division

You can also use pivoting to solve relational division problems when the number of elements in the divisor set is fairly small. In my examples, I'll use the OrderDetails table, which you create and populate by running the following code:

```
USE tempdb;

IF OBJECT_ID('dbo.OrderDetails') IS NOT NULL
  DROP TABLE dbo.OrderDetails;

CREATE TABLE dbo.OrderDetails
(
  orderid   VARCHAR(10) NOT NULL,
  productid INT         NOT NULL,
  PRIMARY KEY(orderid, productid)
  /* other colums */
);
GO

INSERT INTO dbo.OrderDetails(orderid, productid) VALUES
  ('A', 1),
  ('A', 2),
  ('A', 3),
  ('A', 4),
  ('B', 2),
  ('B', 3),
  ('B', 4),
  ('C', 3),
  ('C', 4),
  ('D', 4);
```

A classic relational division problem is to return orders that contain a certain basket of products—say, products 2, 3, and 4. You use a pivoting technique to rotate only the relevant products into separate columns for each order. Instead of returning an actual attribute value, you produce a 1 if the product exists in the order and a 0 otherwise. Create a derived table out of the pivot query, and in the outer query filter only orders that contain a 1 in all product columns. Here's the full query, which correctly returns orders A and B:

```
SELECT orderid
FROM (SELECT
        orderid,
        MAX(CASE WHEN productid = 2 THEN 1 END) AS P2,
        MAX(CASE WHEN productid = 3 THEN 1 END) AS P3,
        MAX(CASE WHEN productid = 4 THEN 1 END) AS P4
      FROM dbo.OrderDetails
      GROUP BY orderid) AS P
WHERE P2 = 1 AND P3 = 1 AND P4 = 1;
```

If you run only the derived table query, you get the following output with the pivoted products for each order:

```
orderid    P2          P3          P4
---------- ----------- ----------- -----------
A          1           1           1
B          1           1           1
C          NULL        1           1
D          NULL        NULL        1
```

To answer the request at hand using the new PIVOT operator, use the following query:

```
SELECT orderid
FROM (SELECT orderid, productid FROM dbo.OrderDetails) AS D
  PIVOT(MAX(productid) FOR productid IN([2],[3],[4])) AS P
WHERE [2] = 2 AND [3] = 3 AND [4] = 4;
```

The aggregate function must accept a column as input, so I provided the *productid* itself. This means that if the product exists within an order, the corresponding value will contain the actual *productid* and not 1. That's why the filter looks a bit different here.

Note that you can make both queries more intuitive and similar to each other in their logic by using the *COUNT* aggregate instead of *MAX*. This way, both queries would produce a 1 where the product exists and a 0 where it doesn't (instead of NULL). Here's what the query that does not use the PIVOT operator looks like:

```
SELECT orderid
FROM (SELECT
        orderid,
        COUNT(CASE WHEN productid = 2 THEN productid END) AS P2,
        COUNT(CASE WHEN productid = 3 THEN productid END) AS P3,
        COUNT(CASE WHEN productid = 4 THEN productid END) AS P4
     FROM dbo.OrderDetails
     GROUP BY orderid) AS P
WHERE P2 = 1 AND P3 = 1 AND P4 = 1;
```

And here's the query you would use based on the PIVOT operator:

```
SELECT orderid
FROM (SELECT orderid, productid FROM dbo.OrderDetails) AS D
  PIVOT(COUNT(productid) FOR productid IN([2],[3],[4])) AS P
WHERE [2] = 1 AND [3] = 1 AND [4] = 1;
```

Aggregating Data

You can also use a pivoting technique to format aggregated data, typically for reporting purposes. In my examples, I'll use the Orders table, which you create and populate by running the code in Listing 8-1.

LISTING 8-1 Creating and populating the Orders table

```
SET NOCOUNT ON;
USE tempdb;

IF OBJECT_ID('dbo.Orders', 'U') IS NOT NULL DROP TABLE dbo.Orders;

CREATE TABLE dbo.Orders
(
  orderid   INT        NOT NULL,
  orderdate DATETIME   NOT NULL,
  empid     INT        NOT NULL,
  custid    VARCHAR(5) NOT NULL,
  qty       INT        NOT NULL,
  CONSTRAINT PK_Orders PRIMARY KEY(orderid)
);
GO

INSERT INTO dbo.Orders
  (orderid, orderdate, empid, custid, qty)
VALUES
  (30001, '20060802', 3, 'A', 10),
  (10001, '20061224', 1, 'A', 12),
  (10005, '20061224', 1, 'B', 20),
  (40001, '20070109', 4, 'A', 40),
  (10006, '20070118', 1, 'C', 14),
  (20001, '20070212', 2, 'B', 12),
  (40005, '20080212', 4, 'A', 10),
  (20002, '20080216', 2, 'C', 20),
  (30003, '20080418', 3, 'B', 15),
  (30004, '20060418', 3, 'C', 22),
  (30007, '20060907', 3, 'D', 30);

-- show the contents of the table
SELECT * FROM dbo.Orders;
```

This generates the following output:

orderid	orderdate	empid	custid	qty
10001	2006-12-24 00:00:00.000	1	A	12
10005	2006-12-24 00:00:00.000	1	B	20
10006	2007-01-18 00:00:00.000	1	C	14
20001	2007-02-12 00:00:00.000	2	B	12
20002	2008-02-16 00:00:00.000	2	C	20
30001	2006-08-02 00:00:00.000	3	A	10
30003	2008-04-18 00:00:00.000	3	B	15
30004	2006-04-18 00:00:00.000	3	C	22
30007	2006-09-07 00:00:00.000	3	D	30
40001	2007-01-09 00:00:00.000	4	A	40
40005	2008-02-12 00:00:00.000	4	A	10

Suppose you want to return a row for each customer, with the total yearly quantities in a different column for each year. As with all pivoting problems, it boils down to identifying the grouping, spreading, and aggregation elements. In this case, the grouping element is the *custid* column, the spreading element is the expression *YEAR(orderdate),* and the aggregate function and element is *SUM(qty).* What remains is simply to use the solution templates I provided previously. Here's the solution that does not use the PIVOT operator, followed by its output:

```
SELECT custid,
  SUM(CASE WHEN orderyear = 2006 THEN qty END) AS [2006],
  SUM(CASE WHEN orderyear = 2007 THEN qty END) AS [2007],
  SUM(CASE WHEN orderyear = 2008 THEN qty END) AS [2008]
FROM (SELECT custid, YEAR(orderdate) AS orderyear, qty
      FROM dbo.Orders) AS D
GROUP BY custid;
```

```
custid 2006        2007        2008
------ ----------- ----------- -----------
A      22          40          10
B      20          12          15
C      22          14          20
D      30          NULL        NULL
```

Here you can see the use of a derived table to isolate only the relevant elements for the pivoting activity (*custid, orderyear, qty*).

One of the main issues with this pivoting solution is that you might end up with lengthy query strings when the number of elements you need to rotate is large. It's not a problem in this case because we are dealing with order years, and there usually aren't that many, but it could be a problem in other cases when the spreading column has a large number of values. In an effort to shorten the query string, you can use a matrix table that contains a column and a row for each attribute that you need to rotate (*orderyear,* in this case). Only column values in the intersections of corresponding rows and columns contain the value 1, and the other column values are populated with a NULL or a 0, depending on your needs. Run the following code to create and populate the Matrix table:

```
USE tempdb;
GO

IF OBJECTPROPERTY(OBJECT_ID('dbo.Matrix'), 'IsUserTable') = 1
  DROP TABLE dbo.Matrix;
GO

CREATE TABLE dbo.Matrix
(
  orderyear INT NOT NULL PRIMARY KEY,
  y2006 INT NULL,
  y2007 INT NULL,
  y2008 INT NULL
);

INSERT INTO dbo.Matrix(orderyear, y2006) VALUES(2006, 1);
INSERT INTO dbo.Matrix(orderyear, y2007) VALUES(2007, 1);
INSERT INTO dbo.Matrix(orderyear, y2008) VALUES(2008, 1);
```

```
-- show the contents of the table
SELECT * FROM dbo.Matrix;
```

This generates the following output:

```
orderyear   y2006        y2007        y2008
----------- ------------ ------------ -----------
2006        1            NULL         NULL
2007        NULL         1            NULL
2008        NULL         NULL         1
```

You join the base table (or table expression) with the Matrix table based on a match in *orderyear*. This means that each row from the base table will be matched with one row from Matrix—the one with the same *orderyear*. In that row, only the corresponding *orderyear*'s column value will contain a 1. So you can substitute the expression

```
SUM(CASE WHEN orderyear = <some_year> THEN qty END) AS [<some_year>]
```

with the logically equivalent expression

```
SUM(qty*y<some_year>) AS [<some_year>]
```

Here's what the full query looks like:

```
SELECT custid,
  SUM(qty*y2006) AS [2006],
  SUM(qty*y2007) AS [2007],
  SUM(qty*y2008) AS [2008]
FROM (SELECT custid, YEAR(orderdate) AS orderyear, qty
      FROM dbo.Orders) AS D
  JOIN dbo.Matrix AS M ON D.orderyear = M.orderyear
GROUP BY custid;
```

If you need the number of orders instead of the sum of *qty*, in the original solution you produce a 1 instead of the *qty* column for each order and use the COUNT aggregate function, like so:

```
SELECT custid,
  COUNT(CASE WHEN orderyear = 2006 THEN 1 END) AS [2006],
  COUNT(CASE WHEN orderyear = 2007 THEN 1 END) AS [2007],
  COUNT(CASE WHEN orderyear = 2008 THEN 1 END) AS [2008]
FROM (SELECT custid, YEAR(orderdate) AS orderyear
      FROM dbo.Orders) AS D
GROUP BY custid;
```

This code generates the following output:

```
custid 2006         2007         2008
------ ------------ ------------ -----------
A      2            1            1
B      1            1            1
C      1            1            1
D      1            0            0
```

With the Matrix table, simply specify the column corresponding to the target year:

```
SELECT custid,
  COUNT(y2006) AS [2006],
  COUNT(y2007) AS [2007],
  COUNT(y2008) AS [2008]
FROM (SELECT custid, YEAR(orderdate) AS orderyear
      FROM dbo.Orders) AS D
  JOIN dbo.Matrix AS M ON D.orderyear = M.orderyear
GROUP BY custid;
```

Of course, using the PIVOT operator, the query strings are pretty much as short as they can get. You don't explicitly specify the CASE expressions: those are constructed behind the scenes for you (you can actually see them by looking at the properties of the aggregate operator in the plan). In short, you don't need to use the Matrix table approach with the PIVOT operator. Here's the query using the PIVOT operator to calculate total yearly quantities per customer:

```
SELECT *
FROM (SELECT custid, YEAR(orderdate) AS orderyear, qty
      FROM dbo.Orders) AS D
  PIVOT(SUM(qty) FOR orderyear IN([2006],[2007],[2008])) AS P;
```

And here's a query that counts the orders:

```
SELECT *
FROM (SELECT custid, YEAR(orderdate) AS orderyear
      FROM dbo.Orders) AS D
  PIVOT(COUNT(orderyear) FOR orderyear IN([2006],[2007],[2008])) AS P;
```

Remember that static queries performing pivoting require you to know ahead of time the list of attributes you're going to rotate. For dynamic pivoting, you need to construct the query string dynamically.

Unpivoting

Unpivoting is the opposite of pivoting—namely, rotating columns to rows. Unpivoting is usually used to normalize data, but it has other applications as well.

> **Note** Unpivoting is not an exact inverse of pivoting—it won't necessarily allow you to regenerate source rows that were pivoted. However, for the sake of simplicity, think of it as the opposite of pivoting.

In my examples, I'll use the PvtCustOrders table, which you create and populate by running the following code:

```
USE tempdb;

IF OBJECT_ID('dbo.PvtCustOrders') IS NOT NULL
  DROP TABLE dbo.PvtCustOrders;
GO
```

```
SELECT custid,
  COALESCE([2006], 0) AS [2006],
  COALESCE([2007], 0) AS [2007],
  COALESCE([2008], 0) AS [2008]
INTO dbo.PvtCustOrders
FROM (SELECT custid, YEAR(orderdate) AS orderyear, qty
      FROM dbo.Orders) AS D
  PIVOT(SUM(qty) FOR orderyear IN([2006],[2007],[2008])) AS P;

UPDATE dbo.PvtCustOrders
  SET [2007] = NULL, [2008] = NULL
WHERE custid = 'D';

-- Show the contents of the table
SELECT * FROM dbo.PvtCustOrders;
```

This generates the following output:

```
custid 2006         2007         2008
------ -----------  -----------  -----------
A      22           40           10
B      20           12           15
C      22           14           20
D      30           NULL         NULL
```

The goal in this case is to generate a result row for each customer and year, containing the customer ID (*custid*), order year (*orderyear*), and quantity (*qty*).

I'll start with a solution that does not use the native UNPIVOT operator. Here as well, try to think in terms of logical query processing as described in Chapter 1.

The first step in the solution is to generate three copies of each base row—one for each year. You can achieve this by performing a cross join between the base table and a virtual auxiliary table that has one row per year. The SELECT list can then return *custid* and *orderyear* and also calculate the target year's *qty* with the following CASE expression:

```
CASE orderyear
  WHEN 2006 THEN [2006]
  WHEN 2007 THEN [2007]
  WHEN 2008 THEN [2008]
END AS qty
```

You achieve unpivoting this way, but you also get rows corresponding to NULL values in the source table (for example, for customer D in years 2007 and 2008). To eliminate those rows, create a derived table out of the solution query and, in the outer query, eliminate the rows with the NULL in the *qty* column.

Note In practice, you'd typically store a 0 and not a NULL as the quantity for a customer with no orders in a certain year; the order quantity is known to be zero and not unknown. However, I used NULLs here to demonstrate the treatment of NULLs, which is a very common need in unpivoting problems.

Here's the complete solution, followed by its output:

```
SELECT custid, orderyear, qty
FROM (SELECT custid, orderyear,
          CASE orderyear
            WHEN 2006 THEN [2006]
            WHEN 2007 THEN [2007]
            WHEN 2008 THEN [2008]
          END AS qty
        FROM dbo.PvtCustOrders
        CROSS JOIN
          (SELECT 2006 AS orderyear
           UNION ALL SELECT 2007
           UNION ALL SELECT 2008) AS OrderYears) AS D
WHERE qty IS NOT NULL;
```

custid	orderyear	qty
A	2006	22
A	2007	40
A	2008	10
B	2006	20
B	2007	12
B	2008	15
C	2006	22
C	2007	14
C	2008	20
D	2006	30
D	2007	0
D	2008	0

As of SQL Server 2008, you can replace the current definition of the derived table D with a table value constructor based on the VALUES clause, like so:

```
SELECT custid, orderyear, qty
FROM (SELECT custid, orderyear,
          CASE orderyear
            WHEN 2006 THEN [2006]
            WHEN 2007 THEN [2007]
            WHEN 2008 THEN [2008]
          END AS qty
        FROM dbo.PvtCustOrders
        CROSS JOIN
          (VALUES(2006),(2007),(2008)) AS OrderYears(orderyear)) AS D
WHERE qty IS NOT NULL;
```

Either way, using the native proprietary UNPIVOT table operator is dramatically simpler, as the following query shows:

```
SELECT custid, orderyear, qty
FROM dbo.PvtCustOrders
  UNPIVOT(qty FOR orderyear IN([2006],[2007],[2008])) AS U;
```

Unlike the PIVOT operator, I find the UNPIVOT operator simple and intuitive, and obviously it requires significantly less code than the alternative solutions. UNPIVOT's first input is the target column name to hold the source column values (*qty*). Then, following the FOR keyword, you specify the target column name to hold the source column names (*orderyear*). Finally, in the parentheses of the IN clause, you specify the source column names that you want to unpivot ([2006],[2007],[2008]).

> **Tip** All source attributes that are unpivoted must share the same data type. If you want to unpivot attributes defined with different data types, create a derived table or CTE where you first convert all those attributes to SQL_VARIANT. The target column that will hold unpivoted values will also be defined as SQL_VARIANT, and within that column, the values will preserve their original types.

> **Note** Like PIVOT, UNPIVOT requires a static list of column names to be rotated. Also, the UNPIVOT operator applies a logical phase that removes NULL rows. However, unlike in the other solutions where the removal of NULL rows is an optional phase, with the UNPIVOT operator it is not optional.

Custom Aggregations

Custom aggregations are aggregations that are not provided as built-in aggregate functions—for example, concatenating strings, calculating products, performing bitwise manipulations, calculating medians, and others. In this section, I'll provide solutions to several custom aggregate requests. Some techniques that I'll cover are generic, in the sense that you can use similar logic for other aggregate requests; other techniques are specific to one kind of aggregate request.

> **More Info** One of the generic custom aggregate techniques uses cursors. For details about cursors, including handling of custom aggregates with cursors, please refer to *Inside Microsoft SQL Server 2008: T-SQL Programming* (Microsoft Press, 2009).

In my examples, I'll use the generic Groups table, which you create and populate by running the following code:

```
USE tempdb;

IF OBJECT_ID('dbo.Groups') IS NOT NULL DROP TABLE dbo.Groups;

CREATE TABLE dbo.Groups
(
  groupid  VARCHAR(10) NOT NULL,
  memberid INT         NOT NULL,
  string   VARCHAR(10) NOT NULL,
  val      INT         NOT NULL,
  PRIMARY KEY (groupid, memberid)
);
GO
```

```
INSERT INTO dbo.Groups(groupid, memberid, string, val) VALUES
  ('a', 3, 'stra1', 6),
  ('a', 9, 'stra2', 7),
  ('b', 2, 'strb1', 3),
  ('b', 4, 'strb2', 7),
  ('b', 5, 'strb3', 3),
  ('b', 9, 'strb4', 11),
  ('c', 3, 'strc1', 8),
  ('c', 7, 'strc2', 10),
  ('c', 9, 'strc3', 12);

-- Show the contents of the table
SELECT * FROM dbo.Groups;
```

This generates the following output:

```
groupid    memberid    string    val
----------  ----------  ----------  ----------
a           3           stra1     6
a           9           stra2     7
b           2           strb1     3
b           4           strb2     7
b           5           strb3     3
b           9           strb4     11
c           3           strc1     8
c           7           strc2     10
c           9           strc3     12
```

The Groups table has a column representing the group (*groupid*), a column representing a unique identifier within the group (*memberid*), and some value columns (*string* and *val*) that need to be aggregated. I like to use such a generic form of data because it allows you to focus on the techniques and not on the data. Note that this is merely a generic form of a table containing data that you want to aggregate. For example, it could represent a Sales table where *groupid* stands for *empid*, *val* stands for *qty*, and so on.

Custom Aggregations Using Pivoting

One technique for solving custom aggregate problems is pivoting. You pivot the values that need to participate in the aggregate calculation; when they all appear in the same result row, you perform the calculation as a linear one across the columns. With a large number of elements you'll end up with very lengthy query strings; therefore, this pivoting technique is limited to situations where each group has a small number of elements. Note that unless you have a sequencing column within the group, you need to calculate row numbers that will be used to identify the position of elements within the group. For example, if you need to concatenate all values from the string column per group, what do you specify as the pivoted attribute list (the spreading values)? The values in the *memberid* column are not known ahead of time, plus they differ in each group. Row numbers representing positions within the group solve this problem.

String Concatenation Using Pivoting

As the first example, the following query calculates an aggregate string concatenation over the column string for each group with a pivoting technique:

```
SELECT groupid,
    [1]
  + COALESCE(',' + [2], '')
  + COALESCE(',' + [3], '')
  + COALESCE(',' + [4], '') AS string
FROM (SELECT groupid, string,
        ROW_NUMBER() OVER(PARTITION BY groupid ORDER BY memberid) AS rn
      FROM dbo.Groups AS A) AS D
  PIVOT(MAX(string) FOR rn IN([1],[2],[3],[4])) AS P;
```

This query generates the following output:

```
groupid   string
--------- -------------------------
a         stra1,stra2
b         strb1,strb2,strb3,strb4
c         strc1,strc2,strc3
```

The query that generates the derived table D calculates a row number within the group based on *memberid* order. The outer query pivots the values based on the row numbers, and it performs linear concatenation. I'm assuming here that each group has at most four rows, so I specified four row numbers. You need as many row numbers as the maximum number of elements you anticipate.

The COALESCE function is used to replace a NULL representing a nonexistent element with an empty string so as not to cause the result to become NULL. You don't need the COALESCE function with the first element (*[1]*) because at least one element must exist in the group; otherwise, the group won't appear in the table.

Aggregate Product Using Pivoting

In a similar manner, you can calculate the product of the values in the *val* column for each group:

```
SELECT groupid,
    [1]
  * COALESCE([2], 1)
  * COALESCE([3], 1)
  * COALESCE([4], 1) AS product
FROM (SELECT groupid, val,
        ROW_NUMBER() OVER(PARTITION BY groupid ORDER BY memberid) AS rn
      FROM dbo.Groups AS A) AS D
  PIVOT(MAX(val) FOR rn IN([1],[2],[3],[4])) AS P;
```

This query generates the following output:

```
groupid   product
--------- -----------
a         42
b         693
c         960
```

The need for an aggregate product is common in financial applications—for example, to calculate compound interest rates.

User Defined Aggregates (UDA)

SQL Server allows you to create your own user-defined aggregates (UDAs). You write UDAs in a .NET language of your choice (for example, C# or Visual Basic), and you use them in T-SQL. This book is dedicated to T-SQL and not to the common language runtime (CLR), so I won't explain CLR UDAs at great length. Rather, I'll provide you with a couple of examples with step-by-step instructions and, of course, the T-SQL interfaces involved. Examples are provided in both C# and Visual Basic.

CLR Code in a Database

This section discusses .NET common language runtime (CLR) integration in SQL Server; therefore, it's appropriate to spend a couple of words explaining the reasoning behind CLR integration in a database. It is also important to identify the scenarios where using CLR objects is more appropriate than using T-SQL.

Developing in .NET languages such as C# and Visual Basic gives you an incredibly rich programming model. The .NET Framework includes literally thousands of prepared classes, and it is up to you to make astute use of them. .NET languages are not just data oriented like SQL, so you are not as limited. For example, regular expressions are extremely useful for validating data, and they are fully supported in .NET. SQL languages are set oriented and slow to perform row-oriented (row-by-row or one-row-at-a-time) operations. Sometimes you need row-oriented operations inside the database; moving away from cursors to CLR code should improve the performance. Another benefit of CLR code is that it can be much faster than T-SQL code for operations such as string manipulation and iterations and in computationally intensive calculations.

SQL Server 2005 introduced CLR integration, and SQL Server 2008 enhances this integration in a number of ways. Later in this section I'll describe the enhancements that are applicable to UDAs. Although SQL Server supported programmatic extensions even before CLR integration was introduced, CLR integration in .NET code is superior in a number of ways.

For example, you could add functionality to earlier versions of SQL Server (before 2005) using extended stored procedures. However, such procedures can compromise the integrity of SQL Server processes because their memory and thread management is not integrated well enough with SQL Server's resource management. .NET code is managed by the CLR inside SQL Server, and because the CLR itself is managed by SQL Server, it is much safer to use than extended procedure code.

T-SQL—a set-oriented language—was designed to deal mainly with data and is optimized for data manipulation. You should not rush to translate all your T-SQL code to CLR code. T-SQL is still SQL Server's primary language. Data access can be achieved through T-SQL only. If an operation can be expressed as a set-oriented one, you should program it in T-SQL.

You need to make another important decision before you start using CLR code inside SQL Server. You need to decide where your CLR code is going to run—at the server or at the client. CLR code is typically faster and more flexible than T-SQL for computations, and thus it extends the opportunities for server-side computations. However, the server side is typically a single working box, and load balancing at the data tier is still in its infancy. Therefore, you should consider whether it would be more sensible to process those computations at the client side.

With CLR code, you can write stored procedures, triggers, user-defined functions, user-defined types, and user-defined aggregate functions. The last two objects can't be written with declarative T-SQL; rather, they can be written only with CLR code. A user-defined type (UDT) is the most complex CLR object type and demands extensive coverage.

More Info For details about programming CLR UDTs, as well as programming CLR routines, please refer to *Inside Microsoft SQL Server 2008: T-SQL Programming*.

Let's start with a concrete implementation of two UDAs. The steps involved in creating a CLR-based UDA are as follows:

1. Define the UDA as a class in a .NET language.

2. Compile the class you defined to build a CLR assembly.

3. Register the assembly in SQL Server using the CREATE ASSEMBLY command in T-SQL.

4. Use the CREATE AGGREGATE command in T-SQL to create the UDA that references the registered assembly.

Note You can register an assembly and create a CLR object from Microsoft Visual Studio 2008 directly, using the project deployment option (from the Build menu item, choose the Deploy option). Direct deployment from Visual Studio is supported only with the Professional edition or higher; if you're using the Standard edition, your only option is explicit deployment in SQL Server.

This section will provide examples for creating aggregate string concatenation and aggregate product functions in both C# and Visual Basic. You can find the code for the C# classes in Listing 8-2 and the code for the Visual Basic classes in Listing 8-3. You'll be provided with the requirements for a CLR UDA alongside the development of a UDA.

LISTING 8-2 C# code for UDAs

```csharp
using System;
using System.Data;
using Microsoft.SqlServer.Server;
using System.Data.SqlTypes;
using System.IO;
using System.Text;
using System.Runtime.InteropServices;

[Serializable]
[SqlUserDefinedAggregate(
    Format.UserDefined,                 // use user defined serialization
    IsInvariantToNulls = true,          // NULLs don't matter
    IsInvariantToDuplicates = false,    // duplicates matter
    IsInvariantToOrder = false,         // order matters
    IsNullIfEmpty = false,              // do not yield a NULL for a set of zero strings
    MaxByteSize = -1)                   // max size unlimited
]
public struct StringConcat : IBinarySerialize
{
    private StringBuilder sb;

    public void Init()
    {
        this.sb = new StringBuilder();
    }

    //two arguments
    public void Accumulate(SqlString v, SqlString separator)
    {
        if (v.IsNull)
        {
            return; // ignore NULLs approach
        }

        this.sb.Append(v.Value).Append(separator.Value);
    }

    public void Merge(StringConcat other)
    {
        this.sb.Append(other.sb);
    }

    public SqlString Terminate()
    {
        string output = string.Empty;
        if (this.sb != null && this.sb.Length > 0)
        {
            // remove last separator
            output = this.sb.ToString(0, this.sb.Length - 1);
        }

        return new SqlString(output);
    }
}
```

```
  public void Read(BinaryReader r)
  {
    sb = new StringBuilder(r.ReadString());
  }

  public void Write(BinaryWriter w)
  {
    w.Write(this.sb.ToString());
  }
} // end StringConcat

[Serializable]
[StructLayout(LayoutKind.Sequential)]
[SqlUserDefinedAggregate(
    Format.Native,                   // use native serialization
    IsInvariantToNulls = true,       // NULLs don't matter
    IsInvariantToDuplicates = false, // duplicates matter
    IsInvariantToOrder = false)]     // order matters
public class Product
{
  private SqlInt64 si;

  public void Init()
  {
    si = 1;
  }

  public void Accumulate(SqlInt64 v)
  {
    if (v.IsNull || si.IsNull)  // NULL input = NULL output approach
    {
      si = SqlInt64.Null;
      return;
    }
    if (v == 0 || si == 0)        // to prevent an exception in next if
    {
      si = 0;
      return;
    }
    // stop before we reach max v
    if (Math.Abs(v.Value) <= SqlInt64.MaxValue / Math.Abs(si.Value))
    {
      si = si * v;
    }
    else
    {
      si = 0;                    // if we reach too big v, return 0
    }

  }

  public void Merge(Product Group)
  {
    Accumulate(Group.Terminate());
  }
```

```
  public SqlInt64 Terminate()
  {
    return (si);
  }

} // end Product
```

LISTING 8-3 Visual Basic code for UDAs

```
Imports System
Imports System.Data
Imports System.Data.SqlTypes
Imports Microsoft.SqlServer.Server
Imports System.Text
Imports System.IO
Imports System.Runtime.InteropServices

<Serializable(), _
 SqlUserDefinedAggregate( _
              Format.UserDefined, _
              IsInvariantToDuplicates:=False, _
              IsInvariantToNulls:=True, _
              IsInvariantToOrder:=False, _
              IsNullIfEmpty:=False, _
              MaxByteSize:=-1)> _
Public Structure StringConcat
  Implements IBinarySerialize

  Private sb As StringBuilder

  Public Sub Init()
    Me.sb = New StringBuilder()
  End Sub

  Public Sub Accumulate(ByVal v As SqlString, ByVal separator As SqlString)
    If v.IsNull Then
      Return
    End If

    Me.sb.Append(v.Value).Append(separator.Value)
  End Sub

  Public Sub Merge(ByVal other As StringConcat)
    Me.sb.Append(other.sb)
  End Sub

  Public Function Terminate() As SqlString
    Dim output As String = String.Empty

    If Not (Me.sb Is Nothing) AndAlso Me.sb.Length > 0 Then
      output = Me.sb.ToString(0, Me.sb.Length - 1)
    End If

    Return New SqlString(output)
  End Function
```

```vbnet
  Public Sub Read(ByVal r As BinaryReader) _
    Implements IBinarySerialize.Read
    sb = New StringBuilder(r.ReadString())
  End Sub

  Public Sub Write(ByVal w As BinaryWriter) _
    Implements IBinarySerialize.Write
    w.Write(Me.sb.ToString())
  End Sub

End Structure

<Serializable(), _
 StructLayout(LayoutKind.Sequential), _
 SqlUserDefinedAggregate( _
              Format.Native, _
              IsInvariantToOrder:=False, _
              IsInvariantToNulls:=True, _
              IsInvariantToDuplicates:=False)> _
Public Class Product

  Private si As SqlInt64

  Public Sub Init()
    si = 1
  End Sub

  Public Sub Accumulate(ByVal v As SqlInt64)
    If v.IsNull = True Or si.IsNull = True Then
      si = SqlInt64.Null
      Return
    End If
    If v = 0 Or si = 0 Then
      si = 0
      Return
    End If
    If (Math.Abs(v.Value) <= SqlInt64.MaxValue / Math.Abs(si.Value)) _
      Then
      si = si * v
    Else
      si = 0
    End If
  End Sub

  Public Sub Merge(ByVal Group As Product)
    Accumulate(Group.Terminate())
  End Sub

  Public Function Terminate() As SqlInt64
    If si.IsNull = True Then
      Return SqlInt64.Null
    Else
      Return si
    End If
  End Function

End Class
```

Use the following step-by-step instructions to create and deploy the assemblies in Visual Studio 2008.

Creating and Deploying an Assembly in Visual Studio 2008

1. In Visual Studio 2008, create a new C# or Visual Basic project based on your language preference. Use the Database folder and the SQL Server Project template.

> **Note** This template is not available in Visual Studio 2008, Standard edition. If you're working with the Standard edition, use the Class Library template and manually write all the code.

2. In the New Project dialog box, specify the following information:

   ❏ Name   UDAs

   ❏ Location   C:\

   ❏ Solution Name   UDAs

   When you're done entering the information, confirm that it is correct.

3. At this point, you'll be requested to specify a database reference. Create a new database reference to the tempdb database in the SQL Server instance you're working with and choose it. The database reference you choose tells Visual Studio where to deploy the UDAs that you develop.

4. After confirming the choice of database reference, in the Solution Explorer window, right-click the UDAs project, select the menu items Add and Aggregate, and then choose the Aggregate template. If you're using C#, rename the class Aggregate1.cs to **UDAClasses.cs**. If you're using Visual Basic, rename Aggregate1.vb to **UDAClasses.vb**. Confirm.

5. Examine the code of the template. You'll find that a UDA is implemented as a structure (*struct* in C#, *Structure* in Visual Basic). It can be implemented as a class as well. The first block of code in the template includes namespaces that are used in the assembly (lines of code starting with *using* in C# and with *Imports* in Visual Basic). Add three more statements to include the following namespaces: *System.Text*, *System.IO*, and *System.Runtime.InteropServices*. (You can copy those from Listing 8-2 or Listing 8-3.) You'll use the *StringBuilder* class from the *System.Text* namespace, the *BinaryReader* and *BinaryWriter* classes from the *System.IO* namespace, and the *StructLayout* attribute from the *System.Runtime.InteropServices* namespace (in the second UDA).

6. Rename the default name of the UDA—which is currently the same name as the name of the class (*UDAClasses*)—to **StringConcat**.

7. You'll find four methods that are already provided by the template. These are the methods that every UDA must implement. However, if you use the Class Library template for your

project, you have to write them manually. Using the Aggregate template, all you have to do is fill them with your code. Following is a description of the four methods:

- ❏ *Init*   This method is used to initialize the computation. It is invoked once for each group that the query processor is aggregating.

- ❏ *Accumulate*   The name of the method gives you a hint at its purpose— accumulating the aggregate values, of course. This method is invoked once for each value (that is, for every single row) in the group that is being aggregated. It uses input parameters, and the parameters have to be of the data types corresponding to the native SQL Server data types of the columns you are going to aggregate. The data type of the input can also be a CLR UDT. In SQL Server 2005, UDAs supported no more than one input parameter. In SQL Server 2008, UDAs support multiple input parameters.

- ❏ *Merge*   Notice that this method uses an input parameter with the type that is the aggregate class. The method is used to merge multiple partial computations of an aggregation.

- ❏ *Terminate*   This method finishes the aggregation and returns the result.

8. Add an internal (private) variable—*sb*—to the class just before the *Init* method. You can do so by simply copying the code that declares it from Listing 8-2 or Listing 8-3, depending on your choice of language. The variable *sb* is of type *StringBuilder* and will hold the intermediate aggregate value.

9. Override the current code for the four methods with the code implementing them from Listing 8-2 or Listing 8-3. Keep in mind the following points for each method:

- ❏ In the *Init* method, you initialize *sb* with an empty string.

- ❏ The *Accumulate* method accepts two input parameters (new in SQL Server 2008)—*v* and *separator*. The parameter *v* represents the value to be concatenated, and the parameter *separator* is obviously the separator. If *v* is NULL, it is simply ignored, similar to the way built-in aggregates handle NULLs. If *v* is not NULL, the value in *v* and a separator are appended to *sb*.

- ❏ In the *Merge* method, you are simply adding a partial aggregation to the current one. You do so by calling the *Accumulate* method of the current aggregation and adding the termination (final value) of the other partial aggregation. The input of the Merge function refers to the class name, which you revised earlier to *StringConcat*.

- ❏ The *Terminate* method is very simple as well; it just returns the string representation of the aggregated value minus the superfluous separator at the end.

10. Delete the last two rows of the code in the class from the template; these are a placeholder for a member field. You already defined the member field you need at the beginning of the UDA.

11. Next, go back to the top of the UDA, right after the inclusion of the namespaces. You'll find attribute names that you want to include. Attributes help Visual Studio in deployment, and they help SQL Server to optimize the usage of the UDA. UDAs have to include the *Serializable* attribute. Serialization in .NET means saving the values of the fields of a class persistently. UDAs need serialization for intermediate results. The format of the serialization can be native, meaning they are left to SQL Server or defined by the user. Serialization can be native if you use only .NET value types; it has to be user defined if you use .NET reference types. Unfortunately, the *string* type is a reference type in .NET. Therefore, you have to prepare your own serialization. You have to implement the *IBinarySerialize* interface, which defines just two methods: *Read* and *Write*. The implementation of these methods in our UDA is very simple. The *Read* method uses the *ReadString* method of the *StringBuilder* class. The *Write* method uses the default *ToString* method. The *ToString* method is inherited by all .NET classes from the topmost class, called *System.Object*.

Continue implementing the UDA by following these steps:

11.1. Specify that you are going to implement the *IBinarySerialize* interface in the structure. If you're using C#, you do so by adding a colon and the name of the interface right after the name of the structure (the UDA name). If you're using Visual Basic, you do so by adding *Implements IBinarySerialize* after the name of the structure.

11.2. Copy the *Read* and *Write* methods from Listing 8-2 or Listing 8-3 to the end of your UDA.

11.3. Change the *Format.Native* property of the *SqlUserDefinedAggregate* attribute to **Format.UserDefined**. In SQL Server 2005, with user-defined serialization, your aggregate was limited to 8,000 bytes only. You had to specify how many bytes your UDA could return at maximum with the *MaxByteSize* property of the *SqlUserDefinedAggregate* attribute. SQL Server 2008 lifts this restriction and supports unlimited size (or more accurately, the maximum size supported by large object types like VARCHAR(MAX), which is currently 2 GB). A value of –1 in the *MaxByteSize* property indicates unlimited size.

12. You'll find some other interesting properties of the *SqlUserDefinedAggregate* attribute in Listings 8-2 and 8-3. Let's explore them:

❑ *IsInvariantToDuplicates*   This is an optional property. For example, the *MAX* aggregate is invariant to duplicates, while *SUM* is not.

❑ *IsInvariantToNulls*   This is another optional property. It specifies whether the aggregate is invariant to NULLs.

❑ *IsInvariantToOrder*   This property is reserved for future use. It is currently ignored by the query processor. Therefore, order is currently not guaranteed. If you want to concatenate elements in a certain order, you have to implement your own sorting logic either in the *Accumulate* or the *Terminate* methods. This naturally incurs extra cost and unfortunately cannot benefit from index ordering.

❏ *IsNullIfEmpty*   This property indicates whether the aggregate returns a NULL if no values have been accumulated.

13. Add the aforementioned properties to your UDA by copying them from Listing 8-2 or Listing 8-3. Your first UDA is now complete!

14. Listings 8-2 and 8-3 also have the code to implement a product UDA (*Product*). Copy the complete code implementing *Product* to your script. Note that this UDA involves handling of big integers only. Because the UDA internally deals only with value types, it can use native serialization. Native serialization requires that the *StructLayoutAttribute* be specified as *StructLayout.LayoutKind.Sequential* if the UDA is defined in a class and not a structure. Otherwise, the UDA implements the same four methods as your previous UDA. An additional check in the *Accumulate* method prevents out-of-range values.

15. Save all files by choosing the File menu item and then choosing Save All.

16. Create the assembly file in the project folder by building the solution. You do this by choosing the Build menu item and then choosing Build Solution.

17. Deploy the assembly in SQL Server.

> **Note** To automatically deploy the solution in SQL Server, you normally choose the Build menu item and then choose Deploy Solution. However, at the time of this writing, automatic deployment in Visual Studio 2008 with Service Pack 1 fails if you use any of the new UDA features in SQL Server 2008 (multiple input parameters or the unlimited maximum size). Therefore, I'll provide instructions here to do explicit deployment.

18. Explicit deployment of the UDAs in SQL Server involves running the CREATE ASSEMBLY command to import the intermediate language code from the assembly file into the target database (tempdb in our case) and the CREATE AGGREGATE command to register each aggregate. If you used C# to define the UDAs, run the following code while connected to the tempdb database:

```
CREATE ASSEMBLY UDAs
   FROM 'C:\UDAs\UDAs\bin\Debug\UDAs.dll';

CREATE AGGREGATE dbo.StringConcat
(
   @value     AS NVARCHAR(MAX),
   @separator AS NCHAR(1)
)
RETURNS NVARCHAR(MAX)
EXTERNAL NAME UDAs.StringConcat;

CREATE AGGREGATE dbo.Product
(
   @value     AS BIGINT
)
RETURNS BIGINT
EXTERNAL NAME UDAs.Product;
```

If you used Visual Basic, run the following code:

```
CREATE ASSEMBLY UDAs
  FROM 'C:\UDAs\UDAs\bin\UDAs.dll';

CREATE AGGREGATE dbo.StringConcat
(
  @value     AS NVARCHAR(MAX),
  @separator AS NCHAR(1)
)
RETURNS NVARCHAR(MAX)
EXTERNAL NAME UDAs.[UDAs.StringConcat];

CREATE AGGREGATE dbo.Product
(
  @value     AS BIGINT
)
RETURNS BIGINT
EXTERNAL NAME UDAs.[UDAs.Product];
```

The assembly should be cataloged at this point, and both UDAs should be created.

You can check whether the deployment was successful by browsing the *sys.assemblies* and *sys.assembly_modules* catalog views, which are in the tempdb database in our case. Run the following code to query those views:

```
SELECT * FROM sys.assemblies;
SELECT * FROM sys.assembly_modules;
```

Note that to run user-defined assemblies in SQL Server, you need to enable the server configuration option *'clr enabled'* (which is disabled by default). You do so by running the following code:

```
EXEC sp_configure 'clr enabled', 1;
RECONFIGURE WITH OVERRIDE;
```

This requirement is applicable only if you want to run user-defined assemblies; this option is not required to be turned on if you want to run system-supplied assemblies.

That's basically it. You use UDAs just like you use any built-in aggregate function—and that's one of their great advantages compared to other solutions to custom aggregates. To test the new functions, run the following code, and you'll get the same results returned by the other solutions to custom aggregates I presented earlier:

```
SELECT groupid, dbo.StringConcat(string, N',') AS string
FROM dbo.Groups
GROUP BY groupid;

SELECT groupid, dbo.Product(val) AS product
FROM dbo.Groups
GROUP BY groupid;
```

Note that the *StringConcat* function expects a non-NULL separator as input and will fail if provided with a NULL. Of course, you can add logic to the function's definition to use some default separator when a NULL is specified.

Specialized Solutions

Another type of solution for custom aggregates is developing a specialized, optimized solution for each aggregate. The advantage is usually the improved performance of the solution. The disadvantage is that you probably won't be able to use similar logic for other aggregate calculations.

Specialized Solution for Aggregate String Concatenation

A specialized solution for aggregate string concatenation uses the PATH mode of the FOR XML query option. This beautiful (and extremely fast) technique was devised by Michael Rys, a program manager with the Microsoft SQL Server development team, and Eugene Kogan, a technical lead on the Microsoft SQL Server Engine team. The PATH mode provides an easier way to mix elements and attributes than the EXPLICIT directive. Here's the specialized solution for aggregate string concatenation:

```
SELECT groupid,
   STUFF((SELECT ',' + string AS [text()]
          FROM dbo.Groups AS G2
          WHERE G2.groupid = G1.groupid
          ORDER BY memberid
          FOR XML PATH('')), 1, 1, '') AS string
FROM dbo.Groups AS G1
GROUP BY groupid;
```

The subquery basically returns an ordered path of all strings within the current group. Because an empty string is provided to the PATH clause as input, a wrapper element is not generated. An expression with no alias (for example, *','* + *string*) or one aliased as *[text()]* is inlined, and its contents are inserted as a text node. The purpose of the STUFF function is simply to remove the first comma (by substituting it with an empty string).

Dynamic Pivoting   Now that you are familiar with a fast, specialized solution to string concatenation, you can put it to use to achieve dynamic pivoting. Recall from the "Pivoting" section that the static solutions for pivoting in SQL Server require you to explicitly list the spreading values (the values in the spreading element). Consider the following static query, which I covered earlier in the "Pivoting" section:

```
SELECT *
FROM (SELECT custid, YEAR(orderdate) AS orderyear, qty
      FROM dbo.Orders) AS D
  PIVOT(SUM(qty) FOR orderyear IN([2006],[2007],[2008])) AS P;
```

Note that this query is against the dbo.Orders table that you created and populated earlier by running the code in Listing 8-1. Here you have to explicitly list the order years in the IN clause. If you want to make this solution more dynamic, query the distinct order years from the table and use the FOR XML PATH technique to construct the comma-separated list of years. You can use the QUOTENAME function to convert the integer years to Unicode character strings and add brackets around them. Also, using QUOTENAME is critical to prevent SQL Injection if this technique is used for a nonnumeric spreading column. The query that produces the comma-separated list of years looks like this:

```
SELECT
  STUFF(
    (SELECT N',' + QUOTENAME(orderyear) AS [text()]
     FROM (SELECT DISTINCT YEAR(orderdate) AS orderyear
           FROM dbo.Orders) AS Years
     ORDER BY orderyear
     FOR XML PATH('')), 1, 1, '');
```

Note that this useful technique has some limitations, though not serious ones, because it's XML based. For example, characters that have special meaning in XML, like '<', will be converted to codes (like <), yielding the wrong pivot statement.

What's left is to construct the whole query string, store it in a variable and use the *sp_executesql* stored procedure to execute it dynamically, like so:

```
DECLARE @sql AS NVARCHAR(1000);

SET @sql = N'SELECT *
FROM (SELECT custid, YEAR(orderdate) AS orderyear, qty
      FROM dbo.Orders) AS D
  PIVOT(SUM(qty) FOR orderyear IN(' +

STUFF(
  (SELECT N',' + QUOTENAME(orderyear) AS [text()]
   FROM (SELECT DISTINCT YEAR(orderdate) AS orderyear
         FROM dbo.Orders) AS Years
   ORDER BY orderyear
   FOR XML PATH('')), 1, 1, '') + N')) AS P;';

EXEC sp_executesql @stmt = @sql;
```

Specialized Solution for Aggregate Product

Keep in mind that to calculate an aggregate product, you have to scan all values in the group. So the performance potential your solution can reach is to achieve the calculation by scanning the data only once, using a set-based query. In the case of an aggregate product, this can be achieved using mathematical manipulation based on logarithms. I'll rely on the following logarithmic equations:

Equation 1: $\log_a(b) = x$ if and only if $a^x = b$

Equation 2: $log_a(v1 * v2 * \ldots * vn) = log_a(v1) + log_a(v2) + \ldots + log_a(vn)$

Basically, what you're going to do here is a transformation of calculations. You have support in T-SQL for the LOG, POWER, and SUM functions. Using those, you can generate the missing product. Group the data by the *groupid* column, as you would with any built-in aggregate. The expression *SUM(LOG10(val))* corresponds to the right side of Equation 2, where the base *a* is equal to 10 in our case, because you used the LOG10 function. To get the product of the elements, all you have left to do is raise the base (10) to the power of the right side of the equation. In other words, the expression *POWER(10., SUM(LOG10(val)))* gives you the product of elements within the group. Here's what the full query looks like:

```
SELECT groupid, POWER(10., SUM(LOG10(val))) AS product
FROM dbo.Groups
GROUP BY groupid;
```

This is the final solution if you're dealing only with positive values. However, the logarithm function is undefined for zero and negative numbers. You can use pivoting techniques to identify and deal with zeros and negatives as follows:

```
SELECT groupid,
   CASE
     WHEN MAX(CASE WHEN val = 0 THEN 1 END) = 1 THEN 0
     ELSE
       CASE WHEN COUNT(CASE WHEN val < 0 THEN 1 END) % 2 = 0
         THEN 1 ELSE -1
       END * POWER(10., SUM(LOG10(NULLIF(ABS(val), 0))))
   END AS product
FROM dbo.Groups
GROUP BY groupid;
```

The outer CASE expression first uses a pivoting technique to check whether a 0 value appears in the group, in which case it returns a 0 as the result. The ELSE clause invokes another CASE expression, which also uses a pivoting technique to count the number of negative values in the group. If that number is even, it produces a +1; if it's odd, it produces a –1. The purpose of this calculation is to determine the numerical sign of the result. The sign (–1 or +1) is then multiplied by the product of the absolute values of the numbers in the group to give the desired product.

Note that NULLIF is used here to substitute zeros with NULLs. You might expect this part of the expression not to be evaluated at all if a zero is found. But remember that the optimizer can consider many different physical plans to execute your query. As a result, you can't be certain of the actual order in which parts of an expression will be evaluated. By substituting zeros with NULLs, you ensure that you'll never get a domain error if the LOG10 function ends up being invoked with a zero as an input. This use of NULLIF, together with the use of ABS, allows this solution to accommodate inputs of any sign (negative, zero, and positive).

You could also use a pure mathematical approach to handle zeros and negative values using the following query:

```
SELECT groupid,
  CAST(ROUND(EXP(SUM(LOG(ABS(NULLIF(val,0)))))*
    (1-SUM(1-SIGN(val))%4)*(1-SUM(1-SQUARE(SIGN(val)))),0) AS INT)
 AS product
FROM dbo.Groups
GROUP BY groupid;
```

This example shows that you should never lose hope when searching for an efficient solution. If you invest the time and think outside the box, in most cases you'll find a solution.

Specialized Solutions for Aggregate Bitwise Operations

In this section, I'll introduce specialized solutions for aggregating the T-SQL bitwise operations—bitwise OR (|), bitwise AND (&), and bitwise XOR (^). I'll assume that you're familiar with the basics of bitwise operators and their uses and provide only a brief overview. If you're not, please refer first to the section "Bitwise Operators" in SQL Server Books Online.

Bitwise operations are operations performed on the individual bits of integer data. Each bit has two possible values, 1 and 0. Integers can be used to store *bitmaps,* or strings of bits, and in fact they are used internally by SQL Server to store metadata information—for example, properties of indexes (clustered, unique, and so on) and properties of databases (readonly, restrict access, autoshrink, and so on). You might also choose to store bitmaps yourself to represent sets of binary attributes—for example, a set of permissions where each bit represents a different permission.

Some experts advise against using such a design because it violates 1NF (first normal form, which requires attributes to be atomic). You might well prefer to design your data in a more normalized form, where attributes like this are stored in separate columns. I don't want to get into a debate about which design is better. Here I'll assume a given design that does store bitmaps with sets of flags, and I'll assume that you need to perform aggregate bitwise activities on these bitmaps. I just want to introduce the techniques for cases where you do find the need to use them.

Bitwise OR (|) is usually used to construct bitmaps or to generate a result bitmap that accumulates all bits that are turned on. In the result of bitwise OR, bits are turned on (that is, have value 1) if they are turned on in at least one of the separate bitmaps.

Bitwise AND (&) is usually used to check whether a certain bit (or a set of bits) is turned on by ANDing the source bitmap and a mask. It's also used to accumulate only bits that are turned on in all bitmaps. It generates a result bit that is turned on if that bit is turned on in all the individual bitmaps.

Bitwise XOR (^) is usually used to calculate parity or as part of a scheme to encrypt data. For each bit position, the result bit is turned on if it is on in an odd number of the individual bitmaps.

Note Bitwise XOR is the only bitwise operator that is reversible. That's why it's used for parity calculations and encryption.

Aggregate versions of the bitwise operators are not provided in SQL Server, and I'll provide solutions here to perform aggregate bitwise operations. I'll use the same Groups table that I used in my other custom aggregate examples. Assume that the integer column *val* represents a bitmap. To see the bit representation of each integer, first create the function *DecToBase* by running the following code:

```
IF OBJECT_ID('dbo.DecToBase') IS NOT NULL
  DROP FUNCTION dbo.DecToBase;
GO
CREATE FUNCTION dbo.DecToBase(@val AS BIGINT, @base AS INT)
  RETURNS VARCHAR(63)
AS
BEGIN
  DECLARE @r AS VARCHAR(63), @alldigits AS VARCHAR(36);

  SET @alldigits = '0123456789ABCDEFGHIJKLMNOPQRSTUVWXYZ';

  SET @r = '';
  WHILE @val > 0
  BEGIN
    SET @r = SUBSTRING(@alldigits, @val % @base + 1, 1) + @r;
    SET @val = @val / @base;
  END

  RETURN @r;
END
GO
```

The function accepts two inputs: a 64-bit integer holding the source bitmap and a base in which you want to represent the data. Use the following query to return the bit representation of the integers in the *val* column of Groups:

```
SELECT groupid, val,
  RIGHT(REPLICATE('0', 32) + CAST(dbo.DecToBase(val, 2) AS VARCHAR(64)),
        32) AS binval
FROM dbo.Groups;
```

This code generates the following output (only the 10 rightmost digits of *binval* are shown):

```
groupid    val          binval
---------- ------------ ---------
a          6            00000110
a          7            00000111
b          3            00000011
b          7            00000111
b          3            00000011
b          11           00001011
c          8            00001000
c          10           00001010
c          12           00001100
```

The *binval* column shows the *val* column in base 2 representation, with leading zeros to create a string with a fixed number of digits. Of course, you can adjust the number of leading zeros according to your needs, which I did to produce the outputs I'll show. To avoid distracting you from the techniques I want to focus on, however, the code for that adjustment is not in my code samples.

Aggregate Bitwise OR   Without further ado, let's start with calculating an aggregate bitwise OR. To give tangible context to the problem, imagine that you're maintaining application security in the database. The *groupid* column represents a user, and the *val* column represents a bitmap with permission states (either 1 for granted or 0 for not granted) of a role the user is a member of. You're after the effective permissions bitmap for each user (group), which should be calculated as the aggregate bitwise OR between all bitmaps of roles the user is a member of.

The main aspect of a bitwise OR operation that I'll rely on in my solutions is the fact that it's equivalent to the arithmetic sum of the values represented by each distinct bit value that is turned on in the individual bitmaps. Within an integer, a bit represents the value $2^{(bit\_pos-1)}$. For example, the bit value of the third bit is $2^2 = 4$. Take, for example, the bitmaps for user c: 8 (1000), 10 (1010), and 12 (1100). The bitmap 8 has only one bit turned on—the bit value representing 8; 10 has the bits representing 8 and 2 turned on; and 12 has the 8 and 4 bits turned on. The distinct bits turned on in any of the integers 8, 10, and 12 are the 2, 4, and 8 bits, so the aggregate bitwise OR of 8, 10, and 12 is equal to $2 + 4 + 8 = 14$ *(1110)*.

The following solution relies on the aforementioned logic by extracting the individual bit values that are turned on in any of the participating bitmaps. The extraction is achieved using the expression *MAX(val & <bitval>)*. The query then performs an arithmetic sum of the individual bit values:

```
SELECT groupid,
      MAX(val & 1)
   + MAX(val & 2)
   + MAX(val & 4)
   + MAX(val & 8)
-- ...
   + MAX(val & 1073741824) AS agg_or
FROM dbo.Groups
GROUP BY groupid;
```

This query generates the following output:

```
groupid     agg_or      binval
---------- ----------- --------
a           7           00000111
b           15          00001111
c           14          00001110
```

Note that I added a third column (*binval*) to the output showing the 10 rightmost digits of the binary representation of the result value. I'll continue to do so with the rest of the queries that apply aggregate bitwise operations.

Similarly, you can use *SUM(DISTINCT val & <bitval>)* instead of *MAX(val & <bitval>)* because the only possible results are *<bitval>* and *0*:

```
SELECT groupid,
    SUM(DISTINCT val & 1)
  + SUM(DISTINCT val & 2)
  + SUM(DISTINCT val & 4)
  + SUM(DISTINCT val & 8)
-- ...
  + SUM(DISTINCT val & 1073741824) AS agg_or
FROM dbo.Groups
GROUP BY groupid;
```

Both solutions suffer from the same limitation—lengthy query strings—because of the need for a different expression for each bit value. In an effort to shorten the query strings, you can use an auxiliary table. You join the Groups table with an auxiliary table that contains all relevant bit values, using *val & bitval = bitval* as the join condition. The result of the join will include all bit values that are turned on in any of the bitmaps. You can then find *SUM(DISTINCT <bitval>)* for each group. You can easily generate the auxiliary table of bit values from the Nums table used earlier. Filter as many numbers as the bits that you might need and raise 2 to the power *n–1*. Here's the complete solution:

```
SELECT groupid, SUM(DISTINCT bitval) AS agg_or
FROM dbo.Groups
   JOIN (SELECT POWER(2, n-1) AS bitval
         FROM dbo.Nums
         WHERE n <= 31) AS Bits
     ON val & bitval = bitval
GROUP BY groupid;
```

Aggregate Bitwise AND   In a similar manner, you can calculate an aggregate bitwise AND. In the permissions scenario, an aggregate bitwise AND represents the most restrictive permission set. Just keep in mind that a bit value should be added to the arithmetic sum only if it's turned on in all bitmaps. So first group the data by *groupid* and *bitval* and filter only the groups where *MIN(val & bitval) > 0*, meaning that the bit value was turned on in all bitmaps. In an outer query, group the data by *groupid* and perform the arithmetic sum of the bit values from the inner query:

```
SELECT groupid, SUM(bitval) AS agg_and
FROM (SELECT groupid, bitval
      FROM dbo.Groups,
         (SELECT POWER(2, n-1) AS bitval
          FROM dbo.Nums
          WHERE n <= 31) AS Bits
      GROUP BY groupid, bitval
      HAVING MIN(val & bitval) > 0) AS D
GROUP BY groupid;
```

This query generates the following output:

```
groupid    agg_and     binval
---------- ----------- --------
a          6           00000110
b          3           00000011
c          8           00001000
```

Aggregate Bitwise XOR   To calculate an aggregate bitwise XOR operation, filter only the *groupid, bitval* groups that have an odd number of bits turned on, as shown in the following code, which illustrates an aggregate bitwise XOR using Nums:

```
SELECT groupid, SUM(bitval) AS agg_xor
FROM (SELECT groupid, bitval
      FROM dbo.Groups,
        (SELECT POWER(2, n-1) AS bitval
         FROM dbo.Nums
         WHERE n <= 31) AS Bits
      GROUP BY groupid, bitval
      HAVING SUM(SIGN(val & bitval)) % 2 = 1) AS D
GROUP BY groupid;
```

This query produces the following output:

```
groupid    agg_xor     binval
---------- ----------- --------
a          1           00000001
b          12          00001100
c          14          00001110
```

Median

As another example of a specialized custom aggregate solution, I'll use the statistical median calculation. Suppose that you need to calculate the median of the *val* column for each group. There are two different definitions of median. Here we will return the middle value in case we have an odd number of elements and the average of the two middle values in case we have an even number of elements.

The following code shows a technique for calculating the median:

```
WITH Tiles AS
(
  SELECT groupid, val,
    NTILE(2) OVER(PARTITION BY groupid ORDER BY val) AS tile
  FROM dbo.Groups
),
GroupedTiles AS
(
  SELECT groupid, tile, COUNT(*) AS cnt,
    CASE WHEN tile = 1 THEN MAX(val) ELSE MIN(val) END AS val
  FROM Tiles
  GROUP BY groupid, tile
)
```

```
SELECT groupid,
  CASE WHEN MIN(cnt) = MAX(cnt) THEN AVG(1.*val)
       ELSE MIN(val) END AS median
FROM GroupedTiles
GROUP BY groupid;
```

This code generates the following output:

```
groupid    median
---------- ----------
a          6.500000
b          5.000000
c          10.000000
```

The Tiles CTE calculates the *NTILE(2)* value within the group, based on *val* order. When you have an even number of elements, the first half of the values gets tile number 1, and the second half gets tile number 2. In an even case, the median is supposed to be the average of the highest value within the first tile and the lowest in the second. When you have an odd number of elements, remember that an additional row is added to the first group. This means that the highest value in the first tile is the median.

The second CTE (GroupedTiles) groups the data by group and tile number, returning the row count for each group and tile as well as the *val* column, which for the first tile is the maximum value within the tile and for the second tile is the minimum value within the tile.

The outer query groups the two rows in each group (one representing each tile). A CASE expression in the SELECT list determines what to return based on the parity of the group's row count. When the group has an even number of rows (that is, the group's two tiles have the same row count), you get the average of the maximum in the first tile and the minimum in the second. When the group has an odd number of elements (that is, the group's two tiles have different row counts), you get the minimum of the two values, which happens to be the maximum within the first tile, which, in turn, happens to be the median.

Using the ROW_NUMBER function, you can come up with additional solutions to finding the median that are more elegant and somewhat simpler. Here's the first example:

```
WITH RN AS
(
  SELECT groupid, val,
    ROW_NUMBER()
      OVER(PARTITION BY groupid ORDER BY val, memberid) AS rna,
    ROW_NUMBER()
      OVER(PARTITION BY groupid ORDER BY val DESC, memberid DESC) AS rnd
  FROM dbo.Groups
)
SELECT groupid, AVG(1.*val) AS median
FROM RN
WHERE ABS(rna - rnd) <= 1
GROUP BY groupid;
```

The idea is to calculate two row numbers for each row: one based on *val, memberid* (the tiebreaker) in ascending order (*rna*) and the other based on the same attributes in descending order (*rnd*). Two sequences sorted in opposite directions have an interesting mathematical relationship that you can use to your advantage. The absolute difference between the two is smaller than or equal to 1 only for the elements that need to participate in the median calculation. Take, for example, a group with an odd number of elements; *ABS(rna – rnd)* is equal to 0 only for the middle row. For all other rows, it is greater than 1. Given an even number of elements, the difference is 1 for the two middle rows and greater than 1 for all others.

The reason for using *memberid* as a tiebreaker is to guarantee determinism of the row number calculations. Because you're calculating two different row numbers, you want to make sure that a value that appears at the *n*th position from the beginning in ascending order appears at the *n*th position from the end in descending order.

Once the values that need to participate in the median calculation are isolated, you just need to group them by *groupid* and calculate the average per group.

You can avoid the need to calculate two separate row numbers by deriving the second from the first. The descending row numbers can be calculated by subtracting the ascending row numbers from the count of rows in the group and adding one. For example, in a group of four elements, the row that got an ascending row number 1 would get the descending row number *4–1+1 = 4*. Ascending row number 2 would get the descending row number *4–2+1 = 3* and so on. Deriving the descending row number from the ascending one eliminates the need for a tiebreaker. You're not dealing with two separate calculations; therefore, nondeterminism is not an issue anymore.

So the calculation *rna – rnd* becomes the following: *rn – (cnt-rn+1) = 2*rn – cnt – 1*. Here's a query that implements this logic:

```
WITH RN AS
(
  SELECT groupid, val,
    ROW_NUMBER() OVER(PARTITION BY groupid ORDER BY val) AS rn,
    COUNT(*) OVER(PARTITION BY groupid) AS cnt
  FROM dbo.Groups
)
SELECT groupid, AVG(1.*val) AS median
FROM RN
WHERE ABS(2*rn - cnt - 1) <= 1
GROUP BY groupid;
```

Here's another way to figure out which rows participate in the median calculation based on the row number and the count of rows in the group: *rn IN((cnt+1)/2, (cnt+2)/2)*. For an odd number of elements, both expressions yield the middle row number. For example, if you have 7 rows, both *(7+1)/2* and *(7+2)/2* equal 4. For an even number of elements, the first expression yields the row number just before the middle point, and the second yields the row number just after it. If you have 8 rows, *(8+1)/2* yields 4, and *(8+2)/2* yields 5. Here's the query that implements this logic:

```
WITH RN AS
(
  SELECT groupid, val,
    ROW_NUMBER() OVER(PARTITION BY groupid ORDER BY val) AS rn,
    COUNT(*) OVER(PARTITION BY groupid) AS cnt
  FROM dbo.Groups
)
SELECT groupid, AVG(1.*val) AS median
FROM RN
WHERE rn IN((cnt+1)/2, (cnt+2)/2)
GROUP BY groupid;
```

Mode

The last specialized solution of a custom aggregate that I'll cover is for the mode of a distribution. The mode is the most frequently occurring value. As an example of mode calculation, consider a request to return for each customer the ID of the employee who handled the most orders for that customer, according to the Sales.Orders table in the InsideTSQL2008 database. In case of ties, you need to determine what you want to do. One option is to return all tied employees; another option is to use a tiebreaker to determine which to return—for example, the one with the higher employee ID.

The first solution that I'll present is based on ranking calculations. I'll first describe a solution that applies a tiebreaker, and then I'll explain the required revisions for the solution to return all ties.

You group the rows by customer ID and employee ID. You calculate a count of orders per group, plus a row number partitioned by customer ID, based on the order of count descending and employee ID descending. The rows with the employee ID that is the mode—with the higher employee ID used as a tiebreaker—have row number 1. What's left is to define a table expression based on the query and in the outer query filter only the rows where the row number is equal to 1, like so:

```
USE InsideTSQL2008;

WITH C AS
(
  SELECT custid, empid, COUNT(*) AS cnt,
    ROW_NUMBER() OVER(PARTITION BY custid
                      ORDER BY COUNT(*) DESC, empid DESC) AS rn
  FROM Sales.Orders
  GROUP BY custid, empid
)
SELECT custid, empid, cnt
FROM C
WHERE rn = 1;
```

This query generates the following output, shown here in abbreviated form:

```
custid      empid       cnt
----------- ----------- -----------
1           4           2
2           3           2
3           3           3
4           4           4
5           3           6
6           9           3
7           4           3
8           4           2
9           4           4
10          3           4
11          6           2
12          8           2
...
```

If you want to return all ties, simply use the RANK function instead of ROW_NUMBER and calculate it based on count ordering alone (without the employee ID tiebreaker), like so:

```
WITH C AS
(
  SELECT custid, empid, COUNT(*) AS cnt,
    RANK() OVER(PARTITION BY custid
                 ORDER BY COUNT(*) DESC) AS rn
  FROM Sales.Orders
  GROUP BY custid, empid
)
SELECT custid, empid, cnt
FROM C
WHERE rn = 1;
```

This time, as you can see in the following output, ties are returned:

```
custid      empid       cnt
----------- ----------- -----------
1           1           2
1           4           2
2           3           2
3           3           3
4           4           4
5           3           6
6           9           3
7           4           3
8           4           2
9           4           4
10          3           4
11          6           2
11          4           2
11          3           2
12          8           2
...
```

In case you do want to apply a tiebreaker, you can use another solution that is very efficient. It is based on the concatenation technique that I presented earlier in the chapter. Write a query that groups the data by customer ID and employee ID, and for each group, concatenate the count of rows and the employee ID to a single value (call it *binval*). Define a table expression based on this query. Have the outer query group the data by customer ID and calculate for each customer the maximum *binval*. This maximum value contains the max count and within it the maximum employee ID. What's left is to extract the count and employee ID from the binary value by using the SUBSTRING function and convert the values to the original types. Here's the complete solution query:

```
SELECT custid,
  CAST(SUBSTRING(MAX(binval), 5, 4) AS INT) AS empid,
  CAST(SUBSTRING(MAX(binval), 1, 4) AS INT) AS cnt
FROM (SELECT custid,
        CAST(COUNT(*) AS BINARY(4)) + CAST(empid AS BINARY(4)) AS binval
      FROM Sales.Orders
      GROUP BY custid, empid) AS D
GROUP BY custid;
```

As an exercise, you can test the solutions against a table with a large number of rows. You will see that this solution is very fast.

Histograms

Histograms are powerful analytical tools that express the distribution of items. For example, suppose you need to figure out from the order information in the Sales.OrderValues view how many small, medium, and large orders you have, based on the order values. In other words, you need a histogram with three steps. The extreme values (the minimum and maximum values) are what defines values as small, medium, or large. Suppose for the sake of simplicity that the minimum order value is 10 and the maximum is 40. Take the difference between the two extremes ($40 - 10 = 30$) and divide it by the number of steps (3) to get the step size. In this case, it's 30 divided by 3, which is 10. So the boundaries of step 1 (small) would be 10 and 20; for step 2 (medium), they would be 20 and 30; and for step 3 (large), they would be 30 and 40.

To generalize this, let $mn = MIN(val)$ and $mx = MAX(val)$ and let $stepsize = (mx - mn) / @numsteps$. Given a step number n, the lower bound of the step (*lb*) is $mn + (n - 1) * stepsize$ and the higher bound (*hb*) is $mn + n * stepsize$. Something is tricky here. What predicate do you use to bracket the elements that belong in a specific step? You can't use *val* BETWEEN *lb and hb* because a value that is equal to *hb* appears in this step and also in the next step, where it equals the lower bound. Remember that the same calculation yielded the higher bound of one step and the lower bound of the next step. One approach to deal with this problem is to increase each of the lower bounds besides the first by one so that they exceed the previous step's higher bounds. With integers, this is a fine solution, but with another data type (such as NUMERIC in our case) it doesn't work because there are potential values between adjacent steps but not within either one—between the cracks, so to speak.

What I like to do to solve the problem is keep the same value in both bounds, and instead of using BETWEEN, I use *val* >= *lb* and *val* < *hb*. This technique has its own issues, but I find it easier to deal with than the previous technique. The issue here is that the item with the highest quantity (40, in our simplified example) is left out of the histogram. To solve this, I add a very small number to the maximum value before calculating the step size: *stepsize = ((1E0*mx + 0.0000000001) – mn) / @numsteps*. This technique allows the item with the highest value to be included, and the effect on the histogram is otherwise negligible. I multiplied *mx* by the float value *1E0* to protect against the loss of the upper data point when *val* is typed as MONEY or SMALLMONEY.

So you need the following ingredients to generate the lower and higher bounds of the histogram's steps: *@numsteps* (given as input), step number (the *n* column from the Nums auxiliary table), *mn*, and *stepsize*, which I described earlier.

Here's the T-SQL code required to produce the step number, lower bound, and higher bound for each step of the histogram:

```
USE InsideTSQL2008;

DECLARE @numsteps AS INT;
SET @numsteps = 3;

SELECT n AS step,
   mn + (n - 1) * stepsize AS lb,
   mn + n * stepsize AS hb
FROM dbo.Nums
   CROSS JOIN
     (SELECT MIN(val) AS mn,
        ((1E0*MAX(val) + 0.0000000001) - MIN(val))
        / @numsteps AS stepsize
      FROM Sales.OrderValues) AS D
WHERE n < = @numsteps;
```

This code generates the following output:

step	lb	hb
1	12.5	5470.83333333337
2	5470.83333333337	10929.1666666667
3	10929.1666666667	16387.5000000001

You might want to encapsulate this code in a user-defined function to simplify the queries that return the actual histograms, like so:

```
IF OBJECT_ID('dbo.HistSteps') IS NOT NULL
  DROP FUNCTION dbo.HistSteps;
GO
CREATE FUNCTION dbo.HistSteps(@numsteps AS INT) RETURNS TABLE
AS
RETURN
  SELECT n AS step,
    mn + (n - 1) * stepsize AS lb,
    mn + n * stepsize AS hb
```

```
    FROM dbo.Nums
      CROSS JOIN
        (SELECT MIN(val) AS mn,
           ((1E0*MAX(val) + 0.0000000001) - MIN(val))
           / @numsteps AS stepsize
        FROM Sales.OrderValues) AS D
  WHERE n < = @numsteps;
GO
```

To test the function, run the following query, which will give you a three-row histogram steps table:

```
SELECT * FROM dbo.HistSteps(3) AS S;
```

To return the actual histogram, simply join the steps table and the OrderValues view on the predicate I described earlier (*val >= lb AND val < hb*), group the data by step number, and return the step number and row count:

```
SELECT step, COUNT(*) AS numorders
FROM dbo.HistSteps(3) AS S
  JOIN Sales.OrderValues AS O
    ON val >= lb AND val < hb
GROUP BY step;
```

This query generates the following histogram:

```
step        numorders
----------- -----------
1           803
2           21
3           6
```

You can see that there are 803 small orders, 21 medium orders, and 6 large order. To return a histogram with 10 steps, simply provide 10 as the input to the *HistSteps* function:

```
SELECT step, COUNT(*) AS numorders
FROM dbo.HistSteps(10) AS S
  JOIN Sales.OrderValues AS O
    ON val >= lb AND val < hb
GROUP BY step;
```

This query generates the following output:

```
step        numorders
----------- -----------
1           578
2           172
3           46
4           14
5           3
6           6
7           8
8           1
10          2
```

Note that because you're using an inner join, empty steps are not returned like in the case of step 9. To return empty steps also, you can use the following outer join query:

```
SELECT step, COUNT(val) AS numorders
FROM dbo.HistSteps(10) AS S
  LEFT OUTER JOIN Sales.OrderValues AS O
    ON val >= lb AND val < hb
GROUP BY step;
```

As you can see in the output of this query, empty steps are included this time:

```
step         numorders
-----------  -----------
1            578
2            172
3            46
4            14
5            3
6            6
7            8
8            1
9            0
10           2
```

> **Note** Notice that COUNT(*val*) is used here and not COUNT(***). COUNT(***) would incorrectly return 1 for empty steps because the group has an outer row. You have to provide the COUNT function an attribute from the nonpreserved side (*Orders*) to get the correct count.

There's another alternative to taking care of the issue with the step boundaries and the predicate used to identify a match. You can simply check whether the step number is 1, in which case you subtract 1 from the lower bound. Then, in the query generating the actual histogram, you use the predicate *val > lb AND val <= hb*.

Another approach is to check whether the step is the last, and if it is, add 1 to the higher bound. Then use the predicate *val >= lb AND val < hb*.

Here's the revised function implementing the latter approach:

```
ALTER FUNCTION dbo.HistSteps(@numsteps AS INT) RETURNS TABLE
AS
RETURN
  SELECT n AS step,
    mn + (n - 1) * stepsize AS lb,
    mn + n * stepsize + CASE WHEN n = @numsteps THEN 1 ELSE 0 END AS hb
  FROM dbo.Nums
    CROSS JOIN
      (SELECT MIN(val) AS mn,
        (1E0*MAX(val) - MIN(val)) / @numsteps AS stepsize
    FROM Sales.OrderValues) AS D
  WHERE n < = @numsteps;
GO
```

And the following query generates the actual histogram:

```
SELECT step, COUNT(val) AS numorders
FROM dbo.HistSteps(3) AS S
  LEFT OUTER JOIN Sales.OrderValues AS O
    ON val >= lb AND val < hb
GROUP BY step;
```

Grouping Factor

In earlier chapters, Chapter 6 in particular, I described a concept called a *grouping factor*. I used it in a problem to isolate islands, or ranges of consecutive elements in a sequence. Recall that the grouping factor is the factor you end up using in your GROUP BY clause to identify the group. In the earlier problem, I demonstrated two techniques to calculate the grouping factor. One method was calculating the maximum value within the group (specifically, the smallest value that is both greater than or equal to the current value and followed by a gap). The other method used row numbers.

Because this chapter covers aggregates, it is appropriate to revisit this very practical problem. In my examples here, I'll use the Stocks table, which you create and populate by running the following code:

```
USE tempdb;

IF OBJECT_ID('Stocks') IS NOT NULL DROP TABLE Stocks;

CREATE TABLE dbo.Stocks
(
  dt    DATE NOT NULL PRIMARY KEY,
  price INT  NOT NULL
);
GO

INSERT INTO dbo.Stocks(dt, price) VALUES
  ('20090801', 13),
  ('20090802', 14),
  ('20090803', 17),
  ('20090804', 40),
  ('20090805', 40),
  ('20090806', 52),
  ('20090807', 56),
  ('20090808', 60),
  ('20090809', 70),
  ('20090810', 30),
  ('20090811', 29),
  ('20090812', 29),
  ('20090813', 40),
  ('20090814', 45),
  ('20090815', 60),
  ('20090816', 60),
```

```
('20090817', 55),
('20090818', 60),
('20090819', 60),
('20090820', 15),
('20090821', 20),
('20090822', 30),
('20090823', 40),
('20090824', 20),
('20090825', 60),
('20090826', 60),
('20090827', 70),
('20090828', 70),
('20090829', 40),
('20090830', 30),
('20090831', 10);
```

```
CREATE UNIQUE INDEX idx_price_dt ON Stocks(price, dt);
```

The Stocks table contains daily stock prices.

 Note Stock prices are rarely restricted to integers, and there is usually more than one stock, but I'll use integers and a single stock for simplification purposes. Also, stock markets usually don't have activity on Saturdays; because I want to demonstrate a technique over a sequence with no gaps, I introduced rows for Saturdays as well, with the same value that was stored in the preceding Friday.

The request is to isolate consecutive periods where the stock price was greater than or equal to 50. Figure 8-2 has a graphical depiction of the stock prices over time, and the arrows represent the periods you're supposed to return.

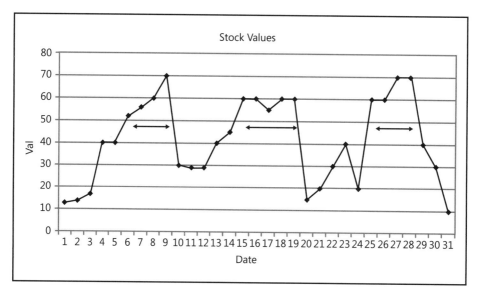

FIGURE 8-2 Periods in which stock values were greater than or equal to 50

For each such period, you need to return the starting date, ending date, duration in days, and the peak (maximum) price.

Let's start with a solution that does not use row numbers. The first step here is to filter only the rows where the price is greater than or equal to 50. Unlike the traditional problem where you really have gaps in the data, here the gaps appear only after filtering. The whole sequence still appears in the Stocks table. You can use this fact to your advantage. Of course, you could take the long route of calculating the maximum date within the group (the first date that is both later than or equal to the current date and followed by a gap). However, a much simpler and faster technique to calculate the grouping factor would be to return the first date that is greater than the current, on which the stock's price is less than 50. Here, you still get the same grouping factor for all elements of the same target group, yet you need only one nesting level of subqueries instead of two.

Here's the query:

```
SELECT MIN(dt) AS startrange, MAX(dt) AS endrange,
  DATEDIFF(day, MIN(dt), MAX(dt)) + 1 AS numdays,
  MAX(price) AS maxprice
FROM (SELECT dt, price,
        (SELECT MIN(dt)
          FROM dbo.Stocks AS S2
          WHERE S2.dt > S1.dt
            AND price < 50) AS grp
      FROM dbo.Stocks AS S1
      WHERE price >= 50) AS D
GROUP BY grp;
```

This query generates the following output, which is the desired result:

```
startrange endrange   numdays      maxprice
---------- ---------- ------------ -----------
2009-08-06 2009-08-09 4            70
2009-08-15 2009-08-19 5            60
2009-08-25 2009-08-28 4            70
```

Of course, post filtering, you could consider the problem as a classic islands problem in a temporal sequence scenario and address it with the very efficient technique that uses the ROW_NUMBER function, as I described in Chapter 6:

```
SELECT MIN(dt) AS startrange, MAX(dt) AS endrange,
  DATEDIFF(day, MIN(dt), MAX(dt)) + 1 AS numdays,
  MAX(price) AS maxprice
FROM (SELECT dt, price,
        DATEADD(day, -1 * ROW_NUMBER() OVER(ORDER BY dt), dt) AS grp
      FROM dbo.Stocks AS S1
      WHERE price >= 50) AS D
GROUP BY grp;
```

Grouping Sets

A grouping set is simply a set of attributes that you group by, such as in a query that has the following GROUP BY clause:

```
GROUP BY custid, empid, YEAR(orderdate)
```

You define a single grouping set—*(custid, empid, YEAR(orderdate))*. Traditionally, aggregate queries define a single grouping set, as demonstrated in the previous example. SQL Server supports features that allow you to define multiple grouping sets in the same query and return a single result set with aggregates calculated for the different grouping sets. The ability to define multiple grouping sets in the same query was available prior to SQL Server 2008 in the form of options called WITH CUBE and WITH ROLLUP and a helper function called GROUPING. However, those options were neither standard nor flexible enough. SQL Server 2008 introduces several new features that allow you to define multiple grouping sets in the same query. The new features include the GROUPING SETS, CUBE, and ROLLUP subclauses of the GROUP BY clause (not to be confused with the older WITH CUBE and WITH ROLLUP options) and the helper function GROUPING_ID. These new features are ISO compliant and substantially more flexible than the older, nonstandard ones.

Before I provide the technicalities of the grouping sets–related features, I'd like to explain the motivation for using those and the kind of problems that they solve. If you're interested only in the technicalities, feel free to skip this section.

Consider a data warehouse with a large volume of sales data. Users of this data warehouse frequently need to analyze aggregated views of the data by various dimensions, such as customer, employee, product, time, and so on. When a user such as a sales manager starts the analysis process, the user asks for some initial aggregated view of the data—for example, the total quantities for each customer and year. This request translates in more technical terms to a request to aggregate data for the grouping set *(custid, YEAR(orderdate))*. The user then analyzes the data, and based on the findings the user makes the next request—say, to return total quantities for each year and month. This is a request to aggregate data for a new grouping set—*(YEAR(orderdate), MONTH(orderdate))*. In this manner the user keeps asking for different aggregated views of the data—in other words, to aggregate data for different grouping sets.

To address such analysis needs of your system's users, you could develop an application that generates a different GROUP BY query for each user request. Each query would need to scan all applicable base data and process the aggregates. With large volumes of data, this approach is very inefficient, and the response time will probably be unreasonable.

To provide fast response time, you need to preprocess aggregates for all grouping sets that users might ask for and store those in the data warehouse. For example, you could do this every night. When the user requests aggregates for a certain grouping set, the aggregates will be readily available. The problem is that given n dimensions, 2^n possible grouping sets can be constructed from those dimensions. For example, with 10 dimensions you get 1,024 grouping sets. If you actually run a separate GROUP BY query for each, it will take a very long time to process all aggregates, and you might not have a sufficient processing window for this.

This is where the new grouping features come into the picture. They allow you to calculate aggregates for multiple grouping sets without rescanning the base data separately for each. Instead, SQL Server scans the data the minimum number of times that the optimizer figures is optimal, calculates the base aggregates, and on top of the base aggregates calculates the super aggregates (aggregates of aggregates).

Note that the product Microsoft SQL Server Analysis Services (SSAS, or just AS) specializes in preprocessing aggregates for multiple grouping sets and storing them in a specialized multidimensional database. It provides very fast response time to user requests, which are made with a language called Multidimensional Expressions (MDX). The recommended approach to handling needs for dynamic analysis of aggregated data is to implement an Analysis Services solution. However, some organizations don't need the scale and sophistication levels provided by Analysis Services and would rather get the most they can from their relational data warehouse with T-SQL. For those organizations, the new grouping features provided by SQL Server can come in very handy.

The following sections describe the technicalities of the grouping sets–related features supported by SQL Server 2008.

Sample Data

In my examples I will use the Orders table that you create and populate in tempdb by running the code provided earlier in Listing 8-1. This code is provided here again for your convenience:

```
SET NOCOUNT ON;
USE tempdb;

IF OBJECT_ID('dbo.Orders', 'U') IS NOT NULL DROP TABLE dbo.Orders;
GO

CREATE TABLE dbo.Orders
(
  orderid   INT        NOT NULL,
  orderdate DATETIME   NOT NULL,
  empid     INT        NOT NULL,
  custid    VARCHAR(5) NOT NULL,
  qty       INT        NOT NULL,
  CONSTRAINT PK_Orders PRIMARY KEY(orderid)
);
GO

INSERT INTO dbo.Orders
  (orderid, orderdate, empid, custid, qty)
VALUES
  (30001, '20060802', 3, 'A', 10),
  (10001, '20061224', 1, 'A', 12),
  (10005, '20061224', 1, 'B', 20),
  (40001, '20070109', 4, 'A', 40),
  (10006, '20070118', 1, 'C', 14),
```

```
(20001, '20070212', 2, 'B', 12),
(40005, '20080212', 4, 'A', 10),
(20002, '20080216', 2, 'C', 20),
(30003, '20080418', 3, 'B', 15),
(30004, '20060418', 3, 'C', 22),
(30007, '20060907', 3, 'D', 30);
```

The GROUPING SETS Subclause

SQL Server 2008 allows you to define multiple grouping sets in the same query by using the new GROUPING SETS subclause of the GROUP BY clause. Within the outermost pair of parentheses, you specify a list of grouping sets separated by commas. Each grouping set is expressed by a pair of parentheses containing the set's elements separated by commas. For example, the following query defines four grouping sets:

```
SELECT custid, empid, YEAR(orderdate) AS orderyear, SUM(qty) AS qty
FROM dbo.Orders
GROUP BY GROUPING SETS
(
  ( custid, empid, YEAR(orderdate) ),
  ( custid, YEAR(orderdate)        ),
  ( empid, YEAR(orderdate)         ),
  ()
);
```

The first grouping set is *(custid, empid, YEAR(orderdate))*, the second is *(custid, YEAR(orderdate))*, the third is *(empid, YEAR(orderdate))*, and the fourth is the empty grouping set *()*, which is used to calculate grand totals. This query generates the following output:

```
custid empid        orderyear    qty
------ -----------  -----------  -----------
A      1            2006         12
B      1            2006         20
NULL   1            2006         32
C      1            2007         14
NULL   1            2007         14
B      2            2007         12
NULL   2            2007         12
C      2            2008         20
NULL   2            2008         20
A      3            2006         10
C      3            2006         22
D      3            2006         30
NULL   3            2006         62
B      3            2008         15
NULL   3            2008         15
A      4            2007         40
NULL   4            2007         40
A      4            2008         10
NULL   4            2008         10
NULL   NULL         NULL         205
A      NULL         2006         22
B      NULL         2006         20
```

C	NULL	2006	22
D	NULL	2006	30
A	NULL	2007	40
B	NULL	2007	12
C	NULL	2007	14
A	NULL	2008	10
B	NULL	2008	15
C	NULL	2008	20

Note To specify a single-element grouping set, the parentheses are optional. (A one-element grouping set means the same as a simple group by item.) If you simply list elements directly within the outer pair of parentheses of the GROUPING SETS clause itself, as opposed to listing them within an inner pair of parentheses, you get a separate grouping set made of each element. For example, *GROUPING SETS(a, b, c)* defines three grouping sets: one with the element *a*, one with *b* and one with *c*. *GROUPING SETS((a, b, c))* defines a single grouping set made of the elements *a, b, c*.

As you can see in the output of the query, NULLs are used as placeholders in inapplicable attributes. You could also think of these NULLs as indicating that the row represents an aggregate over all values of that column. This way, SQL Server can combine rows associated with different grouping sets to one result set. So, for example, in rows associated with the grouping set *(custid, YEAR(orderdate))*, the *empid* column is NULL. In rows associated with the empty grouping set, the columns *empid, custid,* and *orderyear* are NULLs and so on.

Compared to a query that unifies the result sets of four GROUP BY queries, our query that uses the GROUPING SETS subclause requires much less code. It has a performance advantage as well. Examine the execution plan of this query shown in Figure 8-3.

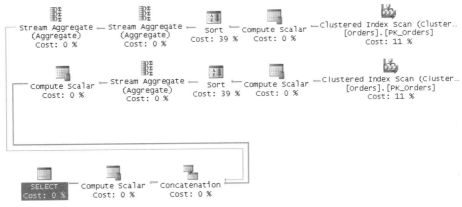

FIGURE 8-3 Execution plan of query with GROUPING SETS subclause

Observe that even though the query defines four grouping sets, the execution plan shows only two scans of the data. In particular, observe that the first branch of the plan shows two Stream Aggregate operators. The Sort operator sorts the data by *empid, YEAR(orderdate), custid*. Based on this sorting, the first Stream Aggregate operator calculates the aggregates for the grouping set *(custid, empid, YEAR(orderdate))*; the second Stream Aggregate operates on the results of the first and calculates the aggregates for the grouping set *(empid, YEAR(orderdate))* and the empty grouping set. The second branch of the plan sorts the data by *YEAR(orderdate), custid,* to allow the Stream Aggregate operator that follows to calculate aggregates for the grouping set *(custid, YEAR(orderdate))*.

Following is a query that is logically equivalent to the previous one, except that this one actually invokes four GROUP BY queries—one for each grouping set—and unifies their result sets:

```
SELECT custid, empid, YEAR(orderdate) AS orderyear, SUM(qty) AS qty
FROM dbo.Orders
GROUP BY custid, empid, YEAR(orderdate)

UNION ALL

SELECT custid, NULL AS empid, YEAR(orderdate) AS orderyear, SUM(qty) AS qty
FROM dbo.Orders
GROUP BY custid, YEAR(orderdate)

UNION ALL

SELECT NULL AS custid, empid, YEAR(orderdate) AS orderyear, SUM(qty) AS qty
FROM dbo.Orders
GROUP BY empid, YEAR(orderdate)

UNION ALL

SELECT NULL AS custid, NULL AS empid, NULL AS orderyear, SUM(qty) AS qty
FROM dbo.Orders;
```

The execution plan for this query is shown in Figure 8-4. You can see that the data is scanned four times.

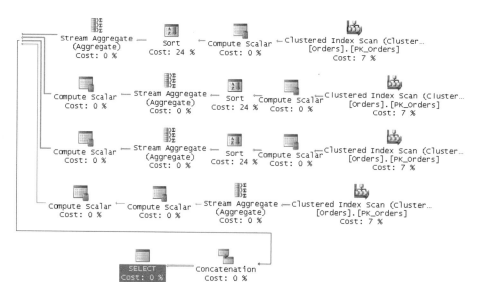

FIGURE 8-4 Execution plan of code unifying four GROUP BY queries

SQL Server 2008 allows you to define up to 4,096 grouping sets in a single query.

The CUBE Subclause

SQL Server 2008 also introduces the CUBE subclause of the GROUP BY clause (not to be confused with the older WITH CUBE option). The CUBE subclause is merely an abbreviated way to express a large number of grouping sets without actually listing them in a GROUPING SETS subclause. CUBE accepts a list of elements as input and defines all possible grouping sets out of those, including the empty grouping set. In set theory, this is called the *power set* of a set. The power set of a set V is the set of all subsets of V. Given *n* elements, CUBE produces 2^n grouping sets. For example, *CUBE(a, b, c)* is equivalent to *GROUPING SETS((a, b, c), (a, b), (a, c), (b, c), (a), (b), (c), ())*.

The following query uses the CUBE option to define all four grouping sets that can be made of the elements *custid* and *empid*:

```
SELECT custid, empid, SUM(qty) AS qty
FROM dbo.Orders
GROUP BY CUBE(custid, empid);
```

This query generates the following output:

custid	empid	qty
A	1	12
B	1	20
C	1	14
NULL	1	46
B	2	12
C	2	20
NULL	2	32
A	3	10
B	3	15
C	3	22
D	3	30
NULL	3	77
A	4	50
NULL	4	50
NULL	NULL	205
A	NULL	72
B	NULL	47
C	NULL	56
D	NULL	30

The following query using the GROUPING SETS subclause is equivalent to the previous query:

```
SELECT custid, empid, SUM(qty) AS qty
FROM dbo.Orders
GROUP BY GROUPING SETS
  (
    ( custid, empid ),
    ( custid        ),
    ( empid         ),
    ()
  );
```

Note that each of the elements in the list you provide to CUBE as input can be made of either a single attribute or multiple attributes. The previous CUBE expression used two single-attribute elements. To define a multi-attribute element, simply list the element's attributes in parentheses. As an example, the expression CUBE(*x, y, z*) has three single-attribute elements and defines eight grouping sets: *(x, y, z), (x, y), (x, z), (y, z), (x), (y), (z), ()*. The expression CUBE(*(x, y), z*) has one two-attribute element and one single-attribute element and defines four grouping sets: *(x, y, z), (x, y), (z), ()*.

Prior to SQL Server 2008, you could achieve something similar to what the CUBE subclause gives you by using a WITH CUBE option that you specified after the GROUP BY clause, like so:

```
SELECT custid, empid, SUM(qty) AS qty
FROM dbo.Orders
GROUP BY custid, empid
WITH CUBE;
```

This is an equivalent to our previous CUBE query, but it has two drawbacks. First, it's not standard, while the new CUBE subclause is. Second, when you specify the WITH CUBE option, you cannot define additional grouping sets beyond the ones defined by CUBE, while you can with the new CUBE subclause.

The ROLLUP Subclause

The new ROLLUP subclause of the GROUP BY clause is similar to the CUBE subclause. It also allows defining multiple grouping sets in an abbreviated way. However, while CUBE defines all possible grouping sets that can be made of the input elements (the power set), ROLLUP defines only a subset of those. ROLLUP assumes a hierarchy between the input elements. For example, *ROLLUP(a, b, c)* assumes a hierarchy between the elements a, b, and c. When there is a hierarchy, not all possible grouping sets that can be made of the input elements make sense in terms of having business value. Consider, for example, the hierarchy country, region, city. You can see the business value in the grouping sets *(country, region, city), (country, region), (country)*, and *()*. But as grouping sets, *(city), (region), (region, city)* and *(country, city)* have no business value. For example, the grouping set *(city)* has no business value because different cities can have the same name, and a business typically needs totals by city, not by city name. When the input elements represent a hierarchy, ROLLUP produces only the grouping sets that make business sense for the hierarchy. Given *n* elements, ROLLUP will produce *n + 1* grouping sets.

The following query shows an example of using the ROLLUP subclause:

```
SELECT
  YEAR(orderdate) AS orderyear,
  MONTH(orderdate) AS ordermonth,
  DAY(orderdate) AS orderday,
  SUM(qty) AS qty
FROM dbo.Orders
GROUP BY
  ROLLUP(YEAR(orderdate), MONTH(orderdate), DAY(orderdate));
```

Out of the three input elements, ROLLUP defines four (3 + 1) grouping sets—*(YEAR(orderdate), MONTH(orderdate), DAY(orderdate)), (YEAR(orderdate), MONTH(orderdate)), (YEAR(orderdate)),* and *()*. This query generates the following output:

```
orderyear   ordermonth   orderday    qty
----------- ------------ ----------- -----------
2006        4            18          22
2006        4            NULL        22
2006        8            2           10
2006        8            NULL        10
2006        9            7           30
2006        9            NULL        30
2006        12           24          32
2006        12           NULL        32
2006        NULL         NULL        94
2007        1            9           40
2007        1            18          14
2007        1            NULL        54
2007        2            12          12
2007        2            NULL        12
2007        NULL         NULL        66
2008        2            12          10
2008        2            16          20
2008        2            NULL        30
2008        4            18          15
2008        4            NULL        15
2008        NULL         NULL        45
NULL        NULL         NULL        205
```

This query is equivalent to the following query that uses the GROUPING SETS subclause to define the aforementioned grouping sets explicitly:

```
SELECT
  YEAR(orderdate) AS orderyear,
  MONTH(orderdate) AS ordermonth,
  DAY(orderdate) AS orderday,
  SUM(qty) AS qty
FROM dbo.Orders
GROUP BY
  GROUPING SETS
  (
    ( YEAR(orderdate), MONTH(orderdate), DAY(orderdate) ),
    ( YEAR(orderdate), MONTH(orderdate)                 ),
    ( YEAR(orderdate)                                   ),
    ()
  );
```

Like with CUBE, each of the elements in the list you provide to ROLLUP as input can be made of either a single attribute or multiple attributes. As an example, the expression *ROLLUP(x, y, z)* defines four grouping sets: *(x, y, z), (x, y), (x), ()*. The expression *ROLLUP((x, y), z)* defines three grouping sets: *(x, y, z), (x, y), ()*.

Similar to the WITH CUBE option that I described earlier, previous versions of SQL Server prior to SQL Server 2008 supported a WITH ROLLUP option. Following is a query that is equivalent to the previous ROLLUP query, except that it uses the older WITH ROLLUP option:

```
SELECT
  YEAR(orderdate) AS orderyear,
  MONTH(orderdate) AS ordermonth,
  DAY(orderdate) AS orderday,
  SUM(qty) AS qty
FROM dbo.Orders
GROUP BY YEAR(orderdate), MONTH(orderdate), DAY(orderdate)
WITH ROLLUP;
```

Like the WITH CUBE option, the WITH ROLLUP option is nonstandard and doesn't allow you to define further grouping sets in the same query.

Grouping Sets Algebra

One beautiful thing about the design of the grouping sets–related features implemented in SQL Server 2008 is that they support a whole algebra of operations that can help you define a large number of grouping sets using minimal coding. You have support for operations that you can think of as multiplication, division, and addition.

Multiplication

Multiplication means producing a Cartesian product of grouping sets. You perform multiplication by separating GROUPING SETS subclauses (or the abbreviated CUBE and ROLLUP subclauses) by commas. For example, if A represents a set of attributes $a1, a2, \ldots, an$, and B represents a set of attributes $b1, b2, \ldots, bn$, and so on, the product GROUPING SETS((A), (B), (C)), GROUPING SETS((D), (E)) is equal to GROUPING SETS ((A, D), (A, E), (B, D), (B, E), (C, D), (C, E)).

Consider the following query and try to figure out which grouping sets it defines:

```
SELECT custid, empid,
  YEAR(orderdate) AS orderyear,
  MONTH(orderdate) AS ordermonth,
  DAY(orderdate) AS orderday,
  SUM(qty) AS qty
FROM dbo.Orders
GROUP BY
  CUBE(custid, empid),
  ROLLUP(YEAR(orderdate), MONTH(orderdate), DAY(orderdate));
```

First, expand the CUBE and ROLLUP subclauses to the corresponding GROUPING SETS subclauses, and you get the following query:

```
SELECT custid, empid,
  YEAR(orderdate) AS orderyear,
  MONTH(orderdate) AS ordermonth,
  SUM(qty) AS qty
```

```
FROM dbo.Orders
GROUP BY
  GROUPING SETS
  (
    ( custid, empid ),
    ( custid        ),
    ( empid         ),
    ()
  ),
  GROUPING SETS
  (
    ( YEAR(orderdate), MONTH(orderdate), DAY(orderdate) ),
    ( YEAR(orderdate), MONTH(orderdate)                 ),
    ( YEAR(orderdate)                                   ),
    ()
  );
```

Now apply the multiplication between the GROUPING SETS subclauses, and you get the following query:

```
SELECT custid, empid,
  YEAR(orderdate) AS orderyear,
  MONTH(orderdate) AS ordermonth,
  SUM(qty) AS qty
FROM dbo.Orders
GROUP BY
  GROUPING SETS
  (
    ( custid, empid, YEAR(orderdate), MONTH(orderdate), DAY(orderdate) ),
    ( custid, empid, YEAR(orderdate), MONTH(orderdate)                 ),
    ( custid, empid, YEAR(orderdate)                                   ),
    ( custid, empid                                                    ),
    ( custid, YEAR(orderdate), MONTH(orderdate), DAY(orderdate)        ),
    ( custid, YEAR(orderdate), MONTH(orderdate)                        ),
    ( custid, YEAR(orderdate)                                          ),
    ( custid                                                           ),
    ( empid, YEAR(orderdate), MONTH(orderdate), DAY(orderdate)         ),
    ( empid, YEAR(orderdate), MONTH(orderdate)                         ),
    ( empid, YEAR(orderdate)                                           ),
    ( empid                                                            ),
    ( YEAR(orderdate), MONTH(orderdate), DAY(orderdate)                ),
    ( YEAR(orderdate), MONTH(orderdate)                                ),
    ( YEAR(orderdate)                                                  ),
    ()
  );
```

Division

When multiple grouping sets in an existing GROUPING SETS subclause share common elements, you can separate the common elements to another GROUPING SETS subclause and multiply the two. The concept is similar to arithmetic division, where you divide operands of an expression by a common element and pull it outside the parentheses. For example, (5×3 + 5×7) can be expressed as (5)×(3 + 7). Based on this logic, you can sometimes reduce the amount of code needed to define multiple grouping sets. For example, see if you can reduce the code in the following query while preserving the same grouping sets:

```
SELECT
  custid,
  empid,
  YEAR(orderdate) AS orderyear,
  MONTH(orderdate) AS ordermonth,
  SUM(qty) AS qty
FROM dbo.Orders
GROUP BY
  GROUPING SETS
  (
    ( custid, empid, YEAR(orderdate), MONTH(orderdate) ),
    ( custid, empid, YEAR(orderdate)                    ),
    ( custid,        YEAR(orderdate), MONTH(orderdate) ),
    ( custid,        YEAR(orderdate)                    ),
    ( empid,         YEAR(orderdate), MONTH(orderdate) ),
    ( empid,         YEAR(orderdate)                    )
  );
```

Because *YEAR(orderdate)* is a common element to all grouping sets, you can move it to another GROUPING SETS subclause and multiply the two, like so:

```
SELECT
  custid,
  empid,
  YEAR(orderdate) AS orderyear,
  MONTH(orderdate) AS ordermonth,
  SUM(qty) AS qty
FROM dbo.Orders
GROUP BY
  GROUPING SETS
  (
    ( YEAR(orderdate)                )
  ),
  GROUPING SETS
  (
    ( custid, empid, MONTH(orderdate) ),
    ( custid, empid                   ),
    ( custid,        MONTH(orderdate) ),
    ( custid                          ),
    ( empid,         MONTH(orderdate) ),
    ( empid                           )
  );
```

Note that when a GROUPING SETS subclause contains only one grouping set, it is equivalent to listing the grouping set's elements directly in the GROUP BY clause. Hence, the previous query is logically equivalent to the following:

```
SELECT
  custid,
  empid,
  YEAR(orderdate) AS orderyear,
```

```
  MONTH(orderdate) AS ordermonth,
  SUM(qty) AS qty
FROM dbo.Orders
GROUP BY
  YEAR(orderdate),
  GROUPING SETS
  (
    ( custid, empid, MONTH(orderdate) ),
    ( custid, empid                   ),
    ( custid,        MONTH(orderdate) ),
    ( custid                          ),
    ( empid,         MONTH(orderdate) ),
    ( empid                           )
  );
```

You can reduce this form even further. Notice in the remaining GROUPING SETS subclause that three subsets of elements appear once with *MONTH(orderdate)* and once without. Hence, you can reduce this form to a multiplication between a GROUPING SETS subclause containing those three and another containing two grouping sets, *(MONTH(orderdate))* and the empty grouping set, like so:

```
SELECT
  custid,
  empid,
  YEAR(orderdate) AS orderyear,
  MONTH(orderdate) AS ordermonth,
  SUM(qty) AS qty
FROM dbo.Orders
GROUP BY
  YEAR(orderdate),
  GROUPING SETS
  (
    ( custid, empid ),
    ( custid        ),
    ( empid         )
  ),
  GROUPING SETS
  (
    ( MONTH(orderdate) ),
    ()
  );
```

Addition

Recall that when you separate GROUPING SETS, CUBE, and ROLLUP subclauses by commas, you get a Cartesian product between the sets of grouping sets that each represents. But what if you have an existing GROUPING SETS subclause and you just want to add—not multiply—the grouping sets that are defined by a CUBE or ROLLUP subclause? This can be achieved by specifying the CUBE or ROLLUP subclause (or multiple ones) within the parentheses of the GROUPING SETS subclause.

For example, the following query demonstrates adding the grouping sets defined by a
ROLLUP subclause to the grouping sets defined by the hosting GROUPING SETS subclause:

```
SELECT
  custid,
  empid,
  YEAR(orderdate) AS orderyear,
  MONTH(orderdate) AS ordermonth,
  SUM(qty) AS qty
FROM dbo.Orders
GROUP BY
  GROUPING SETS
  (
    ( custid, empid ),
    ( custid        ),
    ( empid         ),
    ROLLUP(YEAR(orderdate), MONTH(orderdate), DAY(orderdate))
  );
```

This query is a logical equivalent of the following query:

```
SELECT
  custid,
  empid,
  YEAR(orderdate) AS orderyear,
  MONTH(orderdate) AS ordermonth,
  SUM(qty) AS qty
FROM dbo.Orders
GROUP BY
  GROUPING SETS
  (
    ( custid, empid ),
    ( custid        ),
    ( empid         ),
    ( YEAR(orderdate), MONTH(orderdate), DAY(orderdate) ),
    ( YEAR(orderdate), MONTH(orderdate)                 ),
    ( YEAR(orderdate)                                   ),
    ()
  );
```

Unfortunately, there is no built-in option to do subtraction. For example, you can't somehow
express the idea of CUBE(a, b, c, d) minus GROUPING SETS ((a, c), (b, d), ()). Of course, you can
achieve this with the EXCEPT set operation and other techniques but not as a direct algebraic
operation on grouping sets–related subclauses.

The GROUPING_ID Function

In your applications you may need to be able to identify the grouping set with which each result
row of your query is associated. Relying on the NULL placeholders may lead to convoluted
code, not to mention the fact that if a column is defined in the table as allowing NULLs, a NULL
in the result will be ambiguous. SQL Server 2008 introduces a very convenient tool for this

purpose in the form of a function called GROUPING_ID. This function accepts a list of attributes as input and constructs an integer bitmap where each bit represents the corresponding attribute (the rightmost bit represents the rightmost input attribute). The bit is 0 when the corresponding attribute is a member of the grouping set and 1 otherwise.

You provide the function with all attributes that participate in any grouping set as input, and you will get a unique integer representing each grouping set. So, for example, the expression GROUPING_ID(a, b, c, d) would return 0 (0×8 + 0×4 + 0×2 + 0×1) for rows associated with the grouping set (a, b, c, d), 1 (0×8 + 0×4 + 0×2 + 1×1) for the grouping set (a, b, c), 2 (0×8 + 0×4 + 1×2 + 0×1) for the grouping set (a, b, d), 3 (0×8 + 0×4 + 1×2 + 1×1) for the grouping set (a, b), and so on.

The following query demonstrate the use of the GROUPING_ID function:

```
SELECT
  GROUPING_ID(
    custid, empid,
    YEAR(orderdate), MONTH(orderdate), DAY(orderdate) ) AS grp_id,
  custid, empid,
  YEAR(orderdate) AS orderyear,
  MONTH(orderdate) AS ordermonth,
  DAY(orderdate) AS orderday,
  SUM(qty) AS qty
FROM dbo.Orders
GROUP BY
  CUBE(custid, empid),
  ROLLUP(YEAR(orderdate), MONTH(orderdate), DAY(orderdate));
```

This query generates the following output:

grp_id	custid	empid	orderyear	ordermonth	orderday	qty
0	C	3	2006	4	18	22
16	NULL	3	2006	4	18	22
0	A	3	2006	8	2	10
24	NULL	NULL	2006	4	18	22
25	NULL	NULL	2006	4	NULL	22
16	NULL	3	2006	8	2	10
24	NULL	NULL	2006	8	2	10
25	NULL	NULL	2006	8	NULL	10
0	D	3	2006	9	7	30
16	NULL	3	2006	9	7	30
...						

For example, the *grp_id* value 25 represents the grouping set (*YEAR(orderdate)*, *MONTH(orderdate)*). These attributes are represented by the second (value 2) and third (value 4) bits. However, remember that the bits representing members that participate in the grouping set are turned off. The bits representing the members that do not participate in the grouping set are turned on. In our case, those are the first (1), fourth (8), and fifth (16) bits representing the attributes *DAY(orderdate)*, *empid* and *custid*, respectively. The sum of the values of the bits that are turned on is 1 + 8 + 16 = 25.

The following query helps you see which bits are turned on or off in each integer bitmap generated by the GROUPING_ID function with five input elements:

```
SELECT
  GROUPING_ID(e, d, c, b, a) as n,
  COALESCE(e, 1) as [16],
  COALESCE(d, 1) as [8],
  COALESCE(c, 1) as [4],
  COALESCE(b, 1) as [2],
  COALESCE(a, 1) as [1]
FROM (VALUES(0, 0, 0, 0, 0)) AS D(a, b, c, d, e)
GROUP BY CUBE (a, b, c, d, e)
ORDER BY n;
```

This query generates the following output:

n	16	8	4	2	1
0	0	0	0	0	0
1	0	0	0	0	1
2	0	0	0	1	0
3	0	0	0	1	1
4	0	0	1	0	0
5	0	0	1	0	1
6	0	0	1	1	0
7	0	0	1	1	1
8	0	1	0	0	0
9	0	1	0	0	1
10	0	1	0	1	0
11	0	1	0	1	1
12	0	1	1	0	0
13	0	1	1	0	1
14	0	1	1	1	0
15	0	1	1	1	1
16	1	0	0	0	0
17	1	0	0	0	1
18	1	0	0	1	0
19	1	0	0	1	1
20	1	0	1	0	0
21	1	0	1	0	1
22	1	0	1	1	0
23	1	0	1	1	1
24	1	1	0	0	0
25	1	1	0	0	1
26	1	1	0	1	0
27	1	1	0	1	1
28	1	1	1	0	0
29	1	1	1	0	1
30	1	1	1	1	0
31	1	1	1	1	1

Remember—when the bit is off, the corresponding member *is* part of the grouping set.

As mentioned, the GROUPING_ID function was introduced in SQL Server 2008. You could produce a similar integer bitmap prior to SQL Server 2008, but it involved more work. You could use a function called GROUPING that accepts a single attribute as input and returns 0 if the attribute is a member of the grouping set and 1 otherwise. You could construct the integer bitmap by multiplying the GROUPING value of each attribute by a different power of 2 and summing all values. Here's an example of implementing this logic in a query that uses the older WITH CUBE option:

```
SELECT
  GROUPING(custid)          * 4 +
  GROUPING(empid)           * 2 +
  GROUPING(YEAR(orderdate)) * 1 AS grp_id,
  custid, empid, YEAR(orderdate) AS orderyear,
  SUM(qty) AS totalqty
FROM dbo.Orders
GROUP BY custid, empid, YEAR(orderdate)
WITH CUBE;
```

This query generates the following output:

```
grp_id      custid empid       orderyear   totalqty
----------- ------ ----------- ----------- -----------
0           A      1           2006        12
0           B      1           2006        20
4           NULL   1           2006        32
0           A      3           2006        10
0           C      3           2006        22
0           D      3           2006        30
4           NULL   3           2006        62
6           NULL   NULL        2006        94
0           C      1           2007        14
4           NULL   1           2007        14
...
```

Materialize Grouping Sets

Recall that before I started describing the technicalities of the grouping sets–related features, I explained that one of their uses is to preprocess aggregates for multiple grouping sets and store those in the data warehouse for fast retrieval. The following code demonstrates materializing aggregates for multiple grouping sets, including an integer identifier of the grouping set calculated with the GROUPING_ID function in a table called MyGroupingSets:

```
USE tempdb;
IF OBJECT_ID('dbo.MyGroupingSets', 'U') IS NOT NULL  DROP TABLE dbo.MyGroupingSets;
GO

SELECT
  GROUPING_ID(
    custid, empid,
    YEAR(orderdate), MONTH(orderdate), DAY(orderdate) ) AS grp_id,
  custid, empid,
  YEAR(orderdate) AS orderyear,
  MONTH(orderdate) AS ordermonth,
  DAY(orderdate) AS orderday,
  SUM(qty) AS qty
INTO dbo.MyGroupingSets
```

```
FROM dbo.Orders
GROUP BY
  CUBE(custid, empid),
  ROLLUP(YEAR(orderdate), MONTH(orderdate), DAY(orderdate));

CREATE UNIQUE CLUSTERED INDEX idx_cl_grp_id_grp_attributes
  ON dbo.MyGroupingSets(grp_id, custid, empid, orderyear, ordermonth, orderday);
```

The index created on the table MyGroupingSets is defined on the *grp_id* column as the first key to allow efficient retrieval of all rows associated with a single grouping set. For example, consider the following query, which asks for all rows associated with the grouping set (*custid, YEAR(orderdate), MONTH(orderdate)*):

```
SELECT *
FROM dbo.MyGroupingSets
WHERE grp_id = 9;
```

This query generates the following output:

grp_id	custid	empid	orderyear	ordermonth	orderday	qty
9	A	NULL	2006	8	NULL	10
9	A	NULL	2006	12	NULL	12
9	A	NULL	2007	1	NULL	40
9	A	NULL	2008	2	NULL	10
9	B	NULL	2006	12	NULL	20
9	B	NULL	2007	2	NULL	12
9	B	NULL	2008	4	NULL	15
9	C	NULL	2006	4	NULL	22
9	C	NULL	2007	1	NULL	14
9	C	NULL	2008	2	NULL	20
9	D	NULL	2006	9	NULL	30

Figure 8-5 shows the plan for this query.

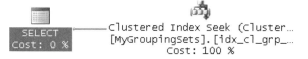

```
SELECT          Clustered Index Seek (Cluster...
Cost: 0 %        [MyGroupingSets].[idx_cl_grp_...
                      Cost: 100 %
```

FIGURE 8-5 Execution plan of query that filters a single grouping set

This plan is very efficient. It scans only the rows that are associated with the requested grouping set because they reside in a consecutive section in the leaf of the clustered index.

Provided that you are using aggregates that are additive measures, like SUM, COUNT, and AVG, you can apply incremental updates to the stored aggregates with only the delta of additions since you last processed those aggregates. You can achieve this by using the new MERGE statement that was introduced in SQL Server 2008. Here I'm just going to show the code to demonstrate how this is done. For details about the MERGE statement, please refer to Chapter 10, "Data Modification."

Run the following code to simulate another day's worth of order activity (April 19, 2008):

```
INSERT INTO dbo.Orders
  (orderid, orderdate, empid, custid, qty)
VALUES
  (50001, '20080419', 1, 'A', 10),
  (50002, '20080419', 1, 'B', 30),
  (50003, '20080419', 2, 'A', 20),
  (50004, '20080419', 2, 'B',  5),
  (50005, '20080419', 3, 'A', 15)
```

Then run the following code to incrementally update the stored aggregates with the new day's worth of data:

```
WITH LastDay AS
(
  SELECT
    GROUPING_ID(
      custid, empid,
      YEAR(orderdate), MONTH(orderdate), DAY(orderdate) ) AS grp_id,
    custid, empid,
    YEAR(orderdate) AS orderyear,
    MONTH(orderdate) AS ordermonth,
    DAY(orderdate) AS orderday,
    SUM(qty) AS qty
  FROM dbo.Orders
  WHERE orderdate = '20080419'
  GROUP BY
    CUBE(custid, empid),
    ROLLUP(YEAR(orderdate), MONTH(orderdate), DAY(orderdate))
)
MERGE INTO dbo.MyGroupingSets AS TGT
USING LastDay AS SRC
  ON     (TGT.grp_id    = SRC.grp_id)
     AND (TGT.orderyear = SRC.orderyear
          OR (TGT.orderyear IS NULL AND SRC.orderyear IS NULL))
     AND (TGT.ordermonth = SRC.ordermonth
          OR (TGT.ordermonth IS NULL AND SRC.ordermonth IS NULL))
     AND (TGT.orderday   = SRC.orderday
          OR (TGT.orderday IS NULL AND SRC.orderday IS NULL))
     AND (TGT.custid   = SRC.custid
          OR (TGT.custid IS NULL AND SRC.custid IS NULL))
     AND (TGT.empid    = SRC.empid
          OR (TGT.empid IS NULL AND SRC.empid IS NULL))
WHEN MATCHED THEN
  UPDATE SET
    TGT.qty += SRC.qty
WHEN NOT MATCHED THEN
  INSERT (grp_id, custid, empid, orderyear, ordermonth, orderday)
  VALUES (SRC.grp_id, SRC.custid, SRC.empid, SRC.orderyear, SRC.ordermonth, SRC.orderday);
```

The code in the CTE LastDay calculates aggregates for the same grouping sets as in the original query but filters only the last day's worth of data. The MERGE statement then increments the quantities of groups that already exist in the target by adding the new quantities and inserts the groups that don't exist in the target.

Sorting

Consider a request to calculate the total quantity aggregate for all grouping sets in the hierarchy order year > order month > order day. You can achieve this, of course, by simply using the ROLLUP subclause. However, a tricky part of the request is that you need to sort the rows in the output in a hierarchical manner, that is, days of a month, followed by the month total, months of a year followed by the yearly total, and finally the grand total. This can be achieved with the help of the GROUPING function as follows:

```
SELECT
  YEAR(orderdate)  AS orderyear,
  MONTH(orderdate) AS ordermonth,
  DAY(orderdate)   AS orderday,
  SUM(qty)         AS totalqty
FROM dbo.Orders
GROUP BY
  ROLLUP(YEAR(orderdate), MONTH(orderdate), DAY(orderdate))
ORDER BY
  GROUPING(YEAR(orderdate))  , YEAR(orderdate),
  GROUPING(MONTH(orderdate)), MONTH(orderdate),
  GROUPING(DAY(orderdate))   , DAY(orderdate);
```

Remember that the GROUPING function returns 0 when the element is a member of a grouping set (representing detail) and 1 when the element isn't (representing an aggregate). Because we want to present detail before aggregates, the GROUPING function is very convenient. We want to first see the detail of years and at the end the grand total. Within the detail of years, we want to sort by year. Within each year, we want to first see the detail of months and then the year total. Within the detail of months, we want to sort by month. Within the month we want to sort by the detail of days and then month total. Within the detail of days, we want to sort by day.

This query generates the following output:

```
orderyear   ordermonth  orderday    totalqty
----------- ----------- ----------- -----------
2006        4           18          22
2006        4           NULL        22
2006        8           2           10
2006        8           NULL        10
2006        9           7           30
2006        9           NULL        30
2006        12          24          32
2006        12          NULL        32
2006        NULL        NULL        94
2007        1           9           40
2007        1           18          14
2007        1           NULL        54
2007        2           12          12
2007        2           NULL        12
2007        NULL        NULL        66
```

2008	2	12	10
2008	2	16	20
2008	2	NULL	30
2008	4	18	15
2008	4	19	80
2008	4	NULL	95
2008	NULL	NULL	125
NULL	NULL	NULL	285

Conclusion

This chapter covered various solutions to data-aggregation problems that reused fundamental querying techniques I introduced earlier in the book. It also introduced new techniques, such as dealing with tiebreakers by using concatenation, calculating a minimum using the MAX function, pivoting, unpivoting, calculating custom aggregates by using specialized techniques, and more. This chapter also covered the new grouping sets features in SQL Server 2008 and showed how you can use those to efficiently address the need for dynamic analysis of aggregates.

As you probably noticed, data-aggregation techniques involve a lot of logical manipulation. If you're looking for ways to improve your logic, you can practice pure logical puzzles, which have a lot in common with querying problems in terms of the thought processes involved. You can find pure logic puzzles in Appendix A.

Chapter 9
TOP and APPLY

This chapter covers two query elements that might seem unrelated. One element is the TOP option, which allows you to limit the number of rows affected by a query. The other is the APPLY table operator, which allows you to apply a table expression to each row of another table expression—basically creating a correlated join. I decided to cover both elements in the same chapter because I find that quite often you can use them together to solve querying problems.

I'll first describe the fundamentals of TOP and APPLY and then follow with solutions to common problems using these elements.

SELECT TOP

In a SELECT query or table expression, TOP is used with an ORDER BY clause to limit the result to rows that come first in the ORDER BY ordering. You can specify the quantity of rows you want in one of two ways: as an exact number of rows, from TOP (0) to TOP (9223372036854775807) (the largest BIGINT value), or as a percentage of rows, from TOP (0E0) PERCENT to TOP (100E0) PERCENT, using a FLOAT value. SQL Server supports any self-contained expression, not just constants, with TOP.

To make it clear which rows are the "top" rows affected by a TOP query, you must indicate an ordering of the rows. Just as you can't tell top from bottom unless you know which way is up, you won't know which rows TOP affects unless you specify an ORDER BY clause. You should think of TOP and ORDER BY together as a logical filter rather than a sorting mechanism. That's why a query with both a TOP clause and an ORDER BY clause is allowed to define a table expression. Recall from Chapter 1, "Logical Query Processing," that when a TOP query is the outermost query, the ORDER BY clause serves two purposes—to define logical ordering for TOP and to define presentation ordering in the result cursor. However, when a TOP query is used to define a table expression, the ORDER BY clause serves only one purpose—to define logical ordering for TOP. Hence, the result can qualify as a relational table. The existing design of the TOP option can be quite confusing. Later in this chapter I'll describe a design that I think wouldn't have been confusing, and I'll show how you can provide an alternative that isn't confusing.

 Note Interestingly, you can specify the TOP option in a query without an ORDER BY clause, but the logical meaning of TOP in such a query is not completely defined. I'll explain this aspect of TOP shortly.

Let's start with a basic example. The following query returns the three most recent orders:

```
USE InsideTSQL2008;

SELECT TOP (3) orderid, custid, orderdate
FROM Sales.Orders
ORDER BY orderdate DESC, orderid DESC;
```

This query generates the following output:

```
orderid      custid      orderdate
-----------  ----------- -----------------------
11077        65          2008-05-06 00:00:00.000
11076        9           2008-05-06 00:00:00.000
11075        68          2008-05-06 00:00:00.000
```

Sorting first by *orderdate* DESC guarantees that you get the most recent orders. Because *orderdate* is not unique, I added *orderid* DESC to the ORDER BY list as a tiebreaker. Among orders with the same *orderdate*, the tiebreaker gives precedence to orders with higher *orderid* values.

> **Note** Notice the usage of parentheses here for the input expression to the TOP option. Because SQL Server supports any self-contained expression as input, the expression must reside within parentheses. For purposes of backward compatibility, SQL Server still supports SELECT TOP queries that use a constant without parentheses. However, it's good practice to put TOP constants in parentheses to conform to the current requirements.

As an example of the PERCENT option, the following query returns the most recent 1 percent of orders:

```
SELECT TOP (1) PERCENT orderid, custid, orderdate
FROM Sales.Orders
ORDER BY orderdate DESC, orderid DESC;
```

This query generates the following output:

```
orderid      custid      orderdate
-----------  ----------- -----------------------
11077        65          2008-05-06 00:00:00.000
11076        9           2008-05-06 00:00:00.000
11075        68          2008-05-06 00:00:00.000
11074        73          2008-05-06 00:00:00.000
11073        58          2008-05-05 00:00:00.000
11072        20          2008-05-05 00:00:00.000
11071        46          2008-05-05 00:00:00.000
11070        44          2008-05-05 00:00:00.000
11069        80          2008-05-04 00:00:00.000
```

The Orders table has 830 rows, and 1 percent of 830 is 8.3. Because only whole rows can be returned and 8.3 were requested, the actual number of rows returned is 9. When TOP ... PERCENT is used and the specified percent includes a fractional row, the exact number of rows requested is rounded up.

TOP and Determinism

As I mentioned earlier, a TOP query doesn't require an ORDER BY clause. However, such a query is nondeterministic. That is, running the same query twice against the same data might yield different result sets, and both would be correct. The following query returns three orders, with no rule governing which three are returned:

```
SELECT TOP (3) orderid, custid, orderdate
FROM Sales.Orders;
```

When I ran this query, I got the following output:

```
orderid     custid      orderdate
----------- ----------- -----------------------
10248       85          2006-07-04 00:00:00.000
10249       79          2006-07-05 00:00:00.000
10250       34          2006-07-08 00:00:00.000
```

But you might get a different output. SQL Server will return the first three rows it happened to access first.

> **Note** I can think of very few reasons to use SELECT TOP without ORDER BY, and I don't recommend it. One reason is to serve as a quick reminder of the structure or column names of a table or to find out if the table contains any data at all. Another reason is to create an empty table with the same structure as another table or query. In this case, you can use SELECT TOP *(0)* *<column list>* INTO *<table name>* FROM .... Obviously, you don't need an ORDER BY clause to indicate "which zero rows" you want to select!

A TOP query can be nondeterministic even when an ORDER BY clause is specified if the ORDER BY list is nonunique. For example, the following query returns the first three orders in order of increasing *custid*:

```
SELECT TOP (3) orderid, custid, orderdate
FROM Sales.Orders
ORDER BY custid;
```

This query generates the following output:

```
orderid     custid      orderdate
----------- ----------- -----------------------
10643       1           2007-08-25 00:00:00.000
10692       1           2007-10-03 00:00:00.000
10702       1           2007-10-13 00:00:00.000
```

You are guaranteed to get the orders with the lowest *custid* values. However, because the *custid* column is not unique, you cannot guarantee which rows among the ones with the same custid values will be returned in case of ties. Again, you will get the ones that SQL

Server happens to access first. One way to guarantee determinism is to add a tiebreaker that makes the ORDER BY list unique—for example, the primary key:

```
SELECT TOP (3) orderid, custid, orderdate
FROM Sales.Orders
ORDER BY custid, orderid;
```

Another way to guarantee determinism is to use the WITH TIES option. When you use WITH TIES, the query generates a result set including any additional rows that have the same values in the sort column or columns as the last row returned. For example, consider the following query:

```
SELECT TOP (3) WITH TIES orderid, custid, orderdate
FROM Sales.Orders
ORDER BY custid;
```

This query specifies TOP (3), yet it returns the following six rows:

```
orderid      custid      orderdate
-----------  ----------- -----------------------
10643        1           2007-08-25 00:00:00.000
10692        1           2007-10-03 00:00:00.000
10702        1           2007-10-13 00:00:00.000
10835        1           2008-01-15 00:00:00.000
10952        1           2008-03-16 00:00:00.000
11011        1           2008-04-09 00:00:00.000
```

Three additional orders are returned because they have the same *custid* value (1) as the third row.

> **Note** Some applications must guarantee determinism. For example, if you're using the TOP option to implement paging, you don't want the same row to end up on two successive pages just because the query was nondeterministic. Remember that you can always add the primary key as a tiebreaker to guarantee determinism in case the ORDER BY list is not unique.

TOP and Input Expressions

As the input to TOP, SQL Server supports any self-contained expression yielding a scalar result. An expression that is independent of the outer query can be used—a variable or parameter, an arithmetic expression, or even the result of a subquery. For example, the following query returns the *@n* most recent orders, where *@n* is a variable:

```
DECLARE @n AS INT = 2;

SELECT TOP (@n) orderid, orderdate, custid, empid
FROM Sales.Orders
ORDER BY orderdate DESC, orderid DESC;
```

The following query shows the use of a subquery as the input to TOP. As always, the input to TOP specifies the number of rows the query returns—for this example, the number of rows returned is the monthly average number of orders. The ORDER BY clause in this example specifies that the rows returned are the most recent ones, where *orderid* is the tiebreaker (higher ID wins):

```
SELECT TOP (SELECT COUNT(*)/(DATEDIFF(month,
              MIN(orderdate), MAX(orderdate))+1)
           FROM Sales.Orders)
  orderid, orderdate, custid, empid
FROM Sales.Orders
ORDER BY orderdate DESC, orderid DESC;
```

The average number of monthly orders is the count of orders divided by one more than the difference in months between the maximum and minimum order dates. Because 830 orders in the table were placed during a period of 23 months, the output has the most recent 36 orders.

TOP and Modifications

SQL Server provides a TOP option for data modification statements (INSERT, UPDATE, and DELETE).

> **Note** Before SQL Server 2005, the SET ROWCOUNT option provided the same capability as some of TOP's newer features. SET ROWCOUNT accepted a variable as input, and it affected both data modification statements and SELECT statements. Microsoft no longer recommends SET ROWCOUNT as a way to affect INSERT, UPDATE, and DELETE statements—in fact, SET ROWCOUNT enters a deprecation process, and in the next planned release of SQL Server (SQL Server 11), it will not affect data modification statements at all. Use TOP to limit the number of rows affected by data modification statements.

SQL Server supports the TOP option with modification statements, allowing you to limit the number or percentage of affected rows. A TOP specification can follow the keyword DELETE, UPDATE, or INSERT.

An ORDER BY clause is not supported with modification statements, even when using TOP, so none of them can rely on logical ordering. SQL Server simply affects the specified number of rows that it happens to access first.

In the following statement, SQL Server does not guarantee which rows will be inserted from the source table:

```
INSERT TOP (10) INTO target_table
  SELECT col1, col2, col3
  FROM source_table;
```

Note Although you cannot use ORDER BY with INSERT TOP, you can guarantee which rows will be inserted if you specify TOP and ORDER BY in the SELECT statement, like so:

```
INSERT INTO target_table
  SELECT TOP (10) col1, col2, col3
  FROM source_table
  ORDER BY col1;
```

An INSERT TOP is handy when you want to load a subset of rows from a large table or result set into a target table and you don't care which subset will be chosen; instead, you care only about the number of rows.

 Note Although ORDER BY cannot be used with UPDATE TOP and DELETE TOP, you can overcome the limitation by creating a CTE from a SELECT TOP query that has an ORDER BY clause and then issue your UPDATE or DELETE against the CTE:

```
WITH CTE_DEL AS
(
  SELECT TOP (10) * FROM some_table ORDER BY col1
)
DELETE FROM CTE_DEL;

WITH CTE_UPD AS
(
  SELECT TOP (10) * FROM some_table ORDER BY col1
)
UPDATE CTE_UPD SET col2 += 1;
```

One such situation is when you need to insert or modify large volumes of data and, for practical reasons, you split it into batches, modifying one subset of the data at a time. For example, purging historic data might involve deleting millions of rows of data. Unless the target table is partitioned and you can simply drop a partition, the purging process requires a DELETE statement. Deleting such a large set of rows in a single transaction has several drawbacks. A DELETE statement is fully logged, and it will require enough space in the transaction log to accommodate the whole transaction. During the delete operation (which can take a long time), no part of the log from the oldest open transaction up to the current point can be overwritten. Furthermore, if the transaction breaks in the middle for some reason, all the activity that took place to that point will be rolled back, and this will take a while. Finally, when many rows are deleted at once, SQL Server might escalate the individual locks held on the deleted rows to an exclusive table lock, preventing both read and write access to the target table until the DELETE is completed.

It makes sense to break the single large DELETE transaction into several smaller ones— small enough to avoid lock escalation (typically, a few thousand rows per transaction) and to allow recycling of the transaction log. You can easily verify that the number you chose doesn't cause lock escalation by testing a DELETE with the TOP option while monitoring Lock

Escalation events with Profiler. Splitting the large DELETE also allows overwriting the inactive section of the log.

To demonstrate purging data in multiple transactions, run the following code, which creates the LargeOrders table and populates it with sample data:

```
IF OBJECT_ID('dbo.LargeOrders') IS NOT NULL
  DROP TABLE dbo.LargeOrders;
GO
SELECT ROW_NUMBER() OVER(ORDER BY (SELECT 0)) AS orderid,
  O1.custid, O1.empid, O1.orderdate, O1.requireddate,
  O1.shippeddate, O1.shipperid, O1.freight, O1.shipname, O1.shipaddress,
  O1.shipcity, O1.shipregion, O1.shippostalcode, O1.shipcountry
INTO dbo.LargeOrders
FROM Sales.Orders AS O1
  CROSS JOIN Sales.Orders AS O2;

CREATE UNIQUE CLUSTERED INDEX idx_od_oid
  ON dbo.LargeOrders(orderdate, orderid);
```

To split a large DELETE, use the following solution:

```
WHILE 1 = 1
BEGIN
  DELETE TOP (5000) FROM dbo.LargeOrders
  WHERE orderdate < '20070101';

  IF @@rowcount < 5000 BREAK;
END
```

The code sets the TOP option to 5,000, limiting the number of rows affected by the statement to 5,000. An endless loop attempts to delete 5,000 rows in each iteration, where each 5,000-row deletion resides in a separate transaction. The loop breaks as soon as the last batch is handled (that is, when the number of affected rows is less than 5,000).

In a similar manner, you can split large updates into batches, as long as the attribute that you are changing is also the attribute that you filter by. For example, say you need to change the value of *custid* from 55 to 123 wherever it appears in the LargeOrders table. Here's the solution you would use with UPDATE TOP:

```
WHILE 1 = 1
BEGIN
  UPDATE TOP (5000) dbo.LargeOrders
    SET custid = 123
  WHERE custid = 55;

  IF @@rowcount < 5000 BREAK;
END
```

If, however, you need to filter one attribute and modify another, you won't be able to use this solution. Rather, you will need to implement paging logic, which I'll describe later in this chapter.

TOP on Steroids

Earlier I talked about TOP's confusing design. This confusion stems from the fact that the same ORDER BY clause that was traditionally designed for presentation purposes also serves the logical filtering purpose for TOP. What I believe would have been a simpler design would have been to designate the TOP option with its own ORDER BY clause, unrelated to the traditional presentation ORDER BY clause. This way, there would be no confusion as to whether the query returns a relational table result because this aspect depends solely on whether a presentation ORDER BY clause was specified. Also, such a design would have allowed defining logical ordering for TOP that is different than presentation ordering. The OVER clause that is used for other purposes in SQL (for example, ranking calculations) fits TOP's needs like a glove. In fact, it would have also allowed accommodating a concept of partitioned TOP (applying TOP per partition). Had such a design been implemented, you would have been able to express a request for the three most recent orders for each employee, like so:

```
SELECT
  TOP (3) OVER(PARTITION BY empid
              ORDER BY orderdate DESC, orderid DESC)
    empid, orderid, orderdate, custid
FROM Sales.Orders;
```

Alas, SQL Server doesn't support such syntax. However, you can get quite close by defining a row number based on the same OVER clause specification and then filtering any number of rows that you want per partition based on the row number, like so:

```
WITH C AS
(
  SELECT
    ROW_NUMBER() OVER(PARTITION BY empid
                      ORDER BY orderdate DESC, orderid DESC) AS rownum,
    empid, orderid, orderdate, custid
  FROM Sales.Orders
)
SELECT *
FROM C
WHERE rownum <= 3;
```

And in fact, as I mentioned earlier, modifications with TOP don't allow you to control logical ordering. Because you can modify data through table expressions, you can control which rows will be modified by using row numbers. For example, the following code deletes the 1,000 least recent orders for each employee:

```
WITH C AS
(
  SELECT
    ROW_NUMBER() OVER(PARTITION BY empid
                      ORDER BY orderdate, orderid) AS rownum,
    empid, orderid, orderdate, custid
  FROM dbo.LargeOrders
)
DELETE FROM C
WHERE rownum <= 1000;
```

When you're done experimenting with the batch modifications, drop the LargeOrders table:

```
IF OBJECT_ID('dbo.LargeOrders', 'U') IS NOT NULL
  DROP TABLE dbo.LargeOrders;
```

APPLY

The APPLY table operator applies the right-hand table expression to every row of the left-hand table expression. Unlike a join, where the order in which each of the table expressions is evaluated is unimportant, APPLY must logically evaluate the left table expression first. This logical evaluation order of the inputs allows the right table expression to be correlated with the left one. The concept can probably be made clearer with an example.

Run the following code to create an inline table-valued function called *GetTopProducts*:

```
IF OBJECT_ID('dbo.GetTopProducts') IS NOT NULL
  DROP FUNCTION dbo.GetTopProducts;
GO
CREATE FUNCTION dbo.GetTopProducts
  (@supid AS INT, @catid INT, @n AS INT)
  RETURNS TABLE
AS
RETURN
  SELECT TOP (@n) WITH TIES productid, productname, unitprice
  FROM Production.Products
  WHERE supplierid = @supid
    AND categoryid = @catid
  ORDER BY unitprice DESC;
GO
```

The function accepts three inputs: a supplier ID (*@supid*), a category ID (*@catid*), and a requested number of products (*@n*). The function returns the requested number of products of the given category, supplied by the given supplier, with the highest unit prices. The query uses the TOP option WITH TIES to ensure a deterministic result set by including all products that have the same unit price as the least expensive product returned.

The following query uses the APPLY operator in conjunction with *GetTopProducts* to return, for each supplier, the two most expensive beverages. The category ID for beverages is 1, so 1 is supplied for the parameter *@catid*:

```
SELECT S.supplierid, S.companyname, P.productid, P.productname, P.unitprice
FROM Production.Suppliers AS S
  CROSS APPLY dbo.GetTopProducts(S.supplierid, 1, 2) AS P;
```

This query generates the following output:

supplierid	companyname	productid	productname	unitprice
20	Supplier CIYNM	43	Product ZZZHR	46.00
23	Supplier ELCRN	76	Product JYGFE	18.00
7	Supplier GQRCV	70	Product TOONT	15.00
18	Supplier LVJUA	38	Product QDOMO	263.50

18	Supplier LVJUA	39	Product LSOFL	18.00
12	Supplier AARON	75	Product BWRLG	7.75
1	Supplier SWRXU	2	Product RECZE	19.00
1	Supplier SWRXU	1	Product HHYDP	18.00
16	Supplier UHZRG	35	Product NEVTJ	18.00
16	Supplier UHZRG	67	Product XLXQF	14.00
16	Supplier UHZRG	34	Product SWNJY	14.00
10	Supplier UNAHG	24	Product QOGNU	4.50

There are two forms of the APPLY operator: CROSS APPLY and OUTER APPLY. The operators CROSS APPLY and OUTER APPLY behave like correlated versions of INNER JOIN and LEFT OUTER JOIN, respectively. Recall that rows from an inner join's left input table won't automatically appear in the result set; the join condition might never be true for a particular left input row. Similarly, rows from a CROSS APPLY's left input table won't automatically appear in the result set; the right table expression could be empty for a particular (left input) row. Such is the case here, for example, for suppliers that don't supply beverages. To include results for those suppliers as well, use the OUTER APPLY operator instead of CROSS APPLY, as the following query shows:

```
SELECT S.supplierid, S.companyname, P.productid, P.productname, P.unitprice
FROM Production.Suppliers AS S
  OUTER APPLY dbo.GetTopProducts(S.supplierid, 1, 2) AS P;
```

This query returns 33 rows. The result set with OUTER APPLY includes left rows for which the right table expression yielded an empty set, and for these rows the right table expression's attributes are NULL.

A nice side effect resulted from the technology added to SQL Server's engine to support the APPLY operator. You are now allowed to pass a column reference parameter from an outer query to a table-valued function. As an example of this capability, the following query returns, for each supplier, the lower of the two most expensive beverage prices (assuming there are at least two):

```
SELECT supplierid, companyname,
  (SELECT MIN(P.unitprice)
    FROM dbo.GetTopProducts(S.supplierid, 1, 2) AS P) AS price
FROM Production.Suppliers AS S;
```

This query generates the following output:

```
supplierid  companyname      price
----------- ---------------- -------
8           Supplier BWGYE   NULL
20          Supplier CIYNM   46.00
23          Supplier ELCRN   18.00
5           Supplier EQPNC   NULL
25          Supplier ERVYZ   NULL
22          Supplier FNUXM   NULL
7           Supplier GQRCV   15.00
19          Supplier JDNUG   NULL
24          Supplier JNNES   NULL
14          Supplier KEREV   NULL
18          Supplier LVJUA   18.00
```

```
15          Supplier NZLIF  NULL
28          Supplier OAVQT  NULL
29          Supplier OGLRK  NULL
4           Supplier QOVFD  NULL
9           Supplier QQYEU  NULL
6           Supplier QWUSF  NULL
17          Supplier QZGUF  NULL
3           Supplier STUAZ  NULL
12          Supplier AARON  7.75
1           Supplier SWRXU  18.00
13          Supplier TEGSC  NULL
16          Supplier UHZRG  14.00
10          Supplier UNAHG  4.50
2           Supplier VHQZD  NULL
21          Supplier XOXZA  NULL
11          Supplier ZPYVS  NULL
27          Supplier ZRYDZ  NULL
26          Supplier ZWZDM  NULL
```

Solutions to Common Problems Using TOP and APPLY

Now that I've covered the fundamentals of TOP and APPLY, I'll present common problems and solutions that use TOP and APPLY.

TOP *n* for Each Group

In Chapter 6, "Subqueries, Table Expressions, and Ranking Functions," and Chapter 8, "Aggregating and Pivoting Data," I discussed a problem involving tiebreakers in which you were asked to return the most recent order for each employee. This problem is actually a special case of a more generic problem in which you are after the top *n* rows for each group—for example, returning the three most recent orders for each employee. Again, orders with higher *orderdate* values have precedence, but you need to introduce a tiebreaker to determine precedence in case of ties. Here I'll use the maximum *orderid* as the tiebreaker. I'll present solutions to this class of problems using TOP and APPLY. You will find that these solutions are dramatically simpler than the ones I presented previously, and in some cases they are substantially faster. Indexing guidelines, though, remain the same. That is, you want an index with the key list being the partitioning columns (*empid*), sort columns (*orderdate*), tiebreaker columns (*orderid*), and, for covering purposes, the other columns mentioned in the query as the included column list (*custid* and *requireddate*).

Before going over the different solutions, run the following code to create the desired indexes on the Orders and OrderDetails tables that participate in my examples:

```
CREATE UNIQUE INDEX idx_eid_od_oid_i_cid_rd
  ON Sales.Orders(empid, orderdate, orderid)
    INCLUDE(custid, requireddate);

CREATE UNIQUE INDEX idx_oid_qtyd_pid
  ON Sales.OrderDetails(orderid, qty DESC, productid);
```

The first solution that I'll present will find the most recent order for each employee. The solution queries the Orders table, filtering only orders that have an *orderid* value equal to the result of a subquery. The subquery returns the *orderid* value of the most recent order for the current employee by using a simple TOP (1) logic. Listing 9-1 contains the solution query.

LISTING 9-1 Solution 1 to the Single Most Recent Order for Each Employee problem

```
SELECT empid, orderid, custid, orderdate, requireddate
FROM Sales.Orders AS O1
WHERE orderid =
  (SELECT TOP (1) orderid
   FROM Sales.Orders AS O2
   WHERE O2.empid = O1.empid
   ORDER BY orderdate DESC, orderid DESC);
```

The query in Listing 9-1 generates the following output:

```
empid   orderid  custid  orderdate               requireddate
------  -------  ------  ----------------------  -----------------------
5       11043    74      2008-04-22 00:00:00.000 2008-05-20 00:00:00.000
6       11045    10      2008-04-23 00:00:00.000 2008-05-21 00:00:00.000
9       11058    6       2008-04-29 00:00:00.000 2008-05-27 00:00:00.000
3       11063    37      2008-04-30 00:00:00.000 2008-05-28 00:00:00.000
2       11073    58      2008-05-05 00:00:00.000 2008-06-02 00:00:00.000
7       11074    73      2008-05-06 00:00:00.000 2008-06-03 00:00:00.000
8       11075    68      2008-05-06 00:00:00.000 2008-06-03 00:00:00.000
4       11076    9       2008-05-06 00:00:00.000 2008-06-03 00:00:00.000
1       11077    65      2008-05-06 00:00:00.000 2008-06-03 00:00:00.000
```

Figure 9-1 shows the execution plan for the query in Listing 9-1.

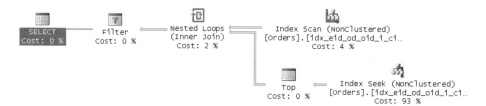

FIGURE 9-1 Execution plan for the query in Listing 9-1

This solution has several advantages over the solutions I presented earlier in the book. Compared to the ANSI subqueries solution I presented in Chapter 6, this one is much simpler, especially when you have multiple sort/tiebreaker columns: You simply extend the ORDER BY list in the subquery to include the additional columns. Compared to the solution based on aggregations I presented in Chapter 8, this solution may be slower, but it is substantially simpler.

Examine the query's execution plan in Figure 9-1. The Index Scan operator shows that the covering index *idx_eid_od_oid_i_cid_rd* is scanned once. The bottom branch of the Nested Loops operator represents the work done for each row of the Index Scan. Here you see that for each row of the Index Scan, an Index Seek and a Top operation take place to find the given employee's most recent order. Remember that the index leaf level holds the data sorted by *empid, orderdate, orderid,* in that order; this means that the last row within each group of rows per employee represents the sought row. The Index Seek operation reaches the end of the group of rows for the current employee, and the Top operator goes one step backward to return the key of the most recent order. A filter operator then keeps only orders where the outer *orderid* value matches the one returned by the subquery.

The I/O cost of this query is 1,786 logical reads, and this number breaks down as follows: The full scan of the covering index requires six logical reads because the index spans six data pages, each of the 830 index seeks requires at least two logical reads because the index has two levels, and some of the index seeks require three logical reads in all because the seek might lead to the beginning of one data page and the most recent *orderid* might be at the end of the preceding page.

Realizing that a separate seek operation within the index was invoked for each outer order, you can figure out that you have room for optimization here. The performance potential is to invoke only a single seek per employee, not per order, because ultimately you are after the most recent order for each employee. I'll describe how to achieve such optimization shortly. But before that, I'd like to point out another advantage of this solution over the ones I presented earlier in the book. Previous solutions were limited to returning only a single order per employee. This solution, however, can be easily extended to support any number of orders per employee by converting the equality operator to an IN predicate. The solution query is shown in Listing 9-2.

LISTING 9-2 Solution 1 to the Three Most Recent Orders for Each Employee problem

```
SELECT empid, orderid, custid, orderdate, requireddate
FROM Sales.Orders AS O1
WHERE orderid IN
  (SELECT TOP (3) orderid
   FROM Sales.Orders AS O2
   WHERE O2.empid = O1.empid
   ORDER BY orderdate DESC, orderid DESC);
```

Now let's go to the optimization technique. Remember that you are attempting to give the optimizer a hint that you want one index seek operation per employee, not one per order. You can achieve this by querying the Employees table and retrieving the most recent *orderid* for each employee. Create a derived table out of this query against Employees and join the derived table to the Orders table on matching *orderid* values. Listing 9-3 has the solution query, generating the execution plan shown in Figure 9-2.

LISTING 9-3 Solution 2 to the Single Most Recent Order for Each Employee problem

```
SELECT O.empid, O.orderid, custid, O.orderdate, O.requireddate
FROM (SELECT E.empid,
         (SELECT TOP (1) orderid
          FROM Sales.Orders AS O2
          WHERE O2.empid = E.empid
          ORDER BY orderdate DESC, orderid DESC) AS toporder
      FROM HR.Employees AS E) AS EO
  JOIN Sales.Orders AS O
    ON O.orderid = EO.toporder;
```

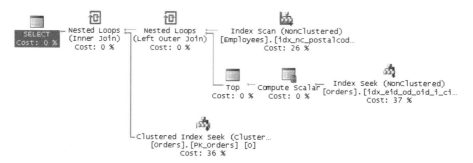

FIGURE 9-2 Execution plan for the query in Listing 9-3

You can see in the plan that one of the indexes on the Employees table is scanned to access the *empids*. The next operator that appears in the plan (Nested Loops) drives a seek in the index on Orders to retrieve the ID of the employee's most recent order. With nine employees, only nine seek operations will be performed, compared to the previous 830 that were driven by the number of orders. Finally, another Nested Loops operator drives one seek per employee in the clustered index on *Orders.orderid* to look up the attributes of the order based on the *orderid* value. If the index on *orderid* wasn't clustered, you would have seen an additional lookup to access the full data row. The I/O cost of this query is only 36 logical reads against the Orders table and two reads against the Employees table.

An attempt to regenerate the same success when you're after more than one order per employee is disappointing. Because you cannot return more than one key in the SELECT list using a subquery, you might attempt to do something similar in a join condition between Employees and Orders. The solution query is shown in Listing 9-4.

LISTING 9-4 Solution 2 to the Three Most Recent Orders for Each Employee problem

```
SELECT O1.empid, O1.orderid, O1.custid, O1.orderdate, O1.requireddate
FROM HR.Employees AS E
  JOIN Sales.Orders AS O1
    ON orderid IN
      (SELECT TOP (3) orderid
       FROM Sales.Orders AS O2
       WHERE O2.empid = E.empid
       ORDER BY orderdate DESC, orderid DESC);
```

However, this solution yields the poor plan shown in Figure 9-3, generating 15,944 logical reads against the Orders table and two logical reads against the Employees table. In this case, you're better off using the solution I showed earlier that supports returning multiple orders per employee.

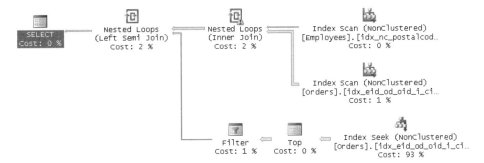

FIGURE 9-3 Execution plan for the query in Listing 9-4

Another solution to the problem involves using the APPLY operator. This solution outperforms all others thus far, and it also supports returning multiple orders per employee. You apply to the Employees table a table expression that returns, for a given row of the Employees table, the *n* most recent orders for the employee in that row. Listing 9-5 has the solution query, generating the execution plan shown in Figure 9-4.

LISTING 9-5 Solution 3 to the Three Most Recent Orders for Each Employee problem

```
SELECT E.empid, A.orderid, A.custid, A.orderdate, A.requireddate
FROM HR.Employees AS E
  CROSS APPLY
    (SELECT TOP (3) orderid, custid, orderdate, requireddate
     FROM Sales.Orders AS O
     WHERE O.empid = E.empid
     ORDER BY orderdate DESC, orderid DESC) AS A;
```

FIGURE 9-4 Execution plan for the query in Listing 9-5

The plan scans an index on the Employees table for the *empid* values. Each *empid* value drives a single seek within the covering index on Orders to return the requested most recent three orders for that employee. The interesting part here is that you don't get only the keys of the rows found; rather, this plan allows for returning multiple attributes. So you don't need any additional activities to return the nonkey attributes. The I/O cost of this query is only 18 logical reads against the Orders table and two reads against the Employees table.

Surprisingly, one solution can be even faster than the one using the APPLY operator in certain circumstances, which I'll describe shortly. The solution uses the ROW_NUMBER function. You calculate the row number of each order, partitioned by *empid* and based on *orderdate* DESC, *orderid* DESC order. Then, in an outer query, you filter only results with a row number less than or equal to 3. The optimal index for this solution is similar to the covering index created earlier, but with the *orderdate* and *orderid* columns defined in descending order:

```
CREATE UNIQUE INDEX idx_eid_odD_oidD_i_cid_rd
  ON Sales.Orders(empid, orderdate DESC, orderid DESC)
    INCLUDE(custid, requireddate);
```

Listing 9-6 has the solution query, generating the execution plan shown in Figure 9-5.

LISTING 9-6 Solution 4 to the Three Most Recent Orders for Each Employee problem

```
SELECT orderid, custid, orderdate, requireddate
FROM (SELECT orderid, custid, orderdate, requireddate,
        ROW_NUMBER() OVER(PARTITION BY empid
                        ORDER BY orderdate DESC, orderid DESC) AS rownum
      FROM Sales.Orders) AS D
WHERE rownum <= 3;
```

FIGURE 9-5 Execution plan for the query in Listing 9-6

I already described the execution plans generated for ranking functions in Chapter 6, and this plan is very similar. The I/O cost here is only six logical reads caused by the single full scan of the covering index. Note that to calculate the row numbers here, the index must be fully scanned. With large tables, when you're seeking a small percentage of rows per group, the APPLY operator will be faster because the total cost of the multiple seek operations—one per group—is lower than a full scan of the covering index.

The last two solutions that use the APPLY operator and the ROW_NUMBER function have an important advantage over the other solutions that I've shown. The other solutions are supported only when the table at hand has a single column key because they rely on a subquery returning a scalar. The last two solutions, on the other hand, are just as applicable with composite keys. For example, say you were after the top three order details for each order, with precedence determined by *qty* DESC and where *productid* ASC is used as the tiebreaker ordering. The OrderDetails table has a composite primary key, *(orderid, productid)*, so you can't return a key for this table from a subquery. On the other hand, the APPLY operator doesn't rely on having a single-column key. It cares only about the correlation of the inner OrderDetails table to the outer Orders table based on *orderid* match and on a sort based on *qty* DESC and *productid* ASC:

```
SELECT D.orderid, D.productid, D.qty
FROM Sales.Orders AS O
  CROSS APPLY
    (SELECT TOP (3) OD.orderid, OD.productid, OD.qty
     FROM Sales.OrderDetails AS OD
     WHERE OD.orderid = O.orderid
     ORDER BY qty DESC, productid) AS D;
```

Similarly, the ROW_NUMBER–based solution doesn't rely on having a single-column key. It simply calculates row numbers partitioned by *orderid*, sorted by *qty* DESC and *productid* ASC:

```
SELECT orderid, productid, qty
FROM (SELECT ROW_NUMBER() OVER(PARTITION BY orderid
                               ORDER BY qty DESC, productid) AS rownum,
        orderid, productid, qty
      FROM Sales.OrderDetails) AS D
WHERE rownum <= 3;
```

Matching Current and Previous Occurrences

Matching current and previous occurrences is yet another problem for which you can use the TOP option. The problem is matching to each "current" row, a row from the same table that is considered the "previous" row based on some ordering criteria—typically, time-based criteria. Such a request serves the need to make calculations involving measurements from both a "current" row and a "previous" row. Examples for such requests are calculating trends, differences, ratios, and so on. When you need to include only one value from the previous row for your calculation, use a simple TOP (1) subquery to get that value. But when you need multiple measurements from the previous row, it makes more sense in terms of performance to use a join rather than multiple subqueries.

Suppose you need to match each employee's order with her previous order, using *orderdate* to determine the previous order and using *orderid* as a tiebreaker. Once the employee's orders are matched, you can request calculations involving attributes from both sides—for example, calculating differences between the current and previous order dates, required dates, and so on. For brevity's sake, I won't show the actual calculations of differences; rather, I'll just focus on the matching techniques. One solution is to join two instances of the Orders table: one representing the current rows (C) and the other representing the previous row (P). The join condition will match *P.orderid* with the *orderid* representing the previous order, which you return from a TOP (1) subquery. You use a LEFT OUTER join to keep the "first" order for each employee. An inner join would eliminate such orders because a match would not be found for them. Listing 9-7 has the solution query to the matching problem.

LISTING 9-7 Query Solution 1 to the Matching Current and Previous Occurrences problem

```
SELECT C.empid,
    C.orderid AS curorderid, P.orderid AS prvorderid,
    C.orderdate AS curorderdate, P.orderdate AS prvorderdate,
    C.requireddate AS curreqdate, P.requireddate AS prvreqdate
FROM Sales.Orders AS C
  LEFT OUTER JOIN Sales.Orders AS P
    ON P.orderid =
        (SELECT TOP (1) orderid
         FROM Sales.Orders AS O
         WHERE O.empid = C.empid
           AND (O.orderdate < C.orderdate
               OR (O.orderdate = C.orderdate
                   AND O.orderid < C.orderid))
         ORDER BY orderdate DESC, orderid DESC)
ORDER BY C.empid, C.orderdate, C.orderid;
```

The subquery's filter is a bit tricky because precedence is determined by two attributes: *orderdate* (ordering column) and *orderid* (tiebreaker). Had the request been for precedence based on a single column—say, *orderid* alone—the filter would have been much simpler— *O.orderid < C.orderid*. Because two attributes are involved, "previous" rows are identified with a logical expression that says *inner_sort_col < outer_sort_col or (inner_sort_col = outer_sort_col and inner_tiebreaker < outer_tiebreaker)*.

This query generates the execution plan shown in Figure 9-6, with an I/O cost of 4,844 logical reads.

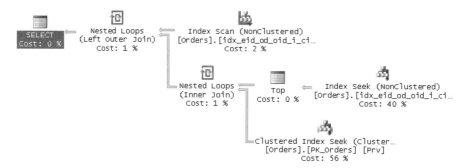

FIGURE 9-6 Execution plan for the query in Listing 9-7

The plan first scans the covering index I created earlier on the key list (*empid, orderdate, orderid*), with the covered columns (*custid, requireddate*) specified as included columns. This scan's purpose is to return the "current" rows. For each current row, a Nested Loops operator initiates an Index Seek operation in the same index, driven by the subquery to fetch the key (*orderid*) of the "previous" row. For each returned previous *orderid*, another Nested Loops operator retrieves the requested list of attributes of the previous row. You realize that one of the two seek operations is superfluous and that there's potential for a revised query that would issue only one seek per current order.

You can try various query revisions that might improve performance. Listing 9-8 has an example of a query revision that generates the plan shown in Figure 9-7.

LISTING 9-8 Query Solution 2 to the Matching Current and Previous Occurrences problem

```
SELECT C.empid,
  C.orderid AS curorderid, P.orderid AS prvorderid,
  C.orderdate AS curorderdate, P.orderdate AS prvorderdate,
  C.requireddate AS curreqdate, P.requireddate AS prvreqdate
FROM (SELECT empid, orderid, orderdate, requireddate,
        (SELECT TOP (1) orderid
          FROM Sales.Orders AS O2
          WHERE O2.empid = O1.empid
            AND (O2.orderdate < O1.orderdate
              OR O2.orderdate = O1.orderdate
                AND O2.orderid < O1.orderid)
          ORDER BY orderdate DESC, orderid DESC) AS prvorderid
      FROM Sales.Orders AS O1) AS C
  LEFT OUTER JOIN Sales.Orders AS P
    ON C.prvorderid = P.orderid
ORDER BY C.empid, C.orderdate, C.orderid;
```

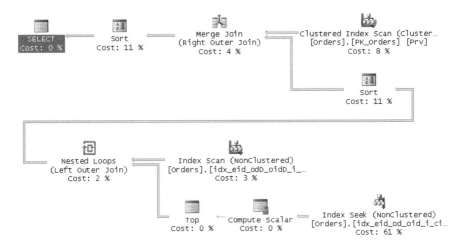

FIGURE 9-7 Execution plan for the query in Listing 9-8

This plan incurs an I/O cost of 3,223 logical reads, but it also involves a sort operation. The solution creates a derived table called C that contains current orders, with an additional column (*prvorderid*) holding the *orderid* of the previous order as obtained by a correlated subquery. The outer query then joins C with another instance of Orders, aliased as P, which supplies the full list of attributes from the previous order. The lower I/O cost is mainly the result of the Merge join algorithm that the plan uses. In the graphical query plan, the upper input to the Merge Join operator is the result of an ordered scan of the clustered index on *orderid*, representing the "previous" orders, and this is the nonpreserved side of the outer join. The lower input is the result of scanning the covering index and fetching each previous *orderid* with a seek operation followed by a Top 1.

A merge join turned out to be cost effective here because the rows of the Orders table were presorted on the clustered index key column *orderid* and it was not too much work to sort the other input in preparation for the merge. In larger production systems, circumstances will most likely be different. With a much larger number of rows and a different clustered index—on a column that frequently appears in range queries, perhaps—you shouldn't expect to see the same query plan.

This is where the APPLY operator comes in handy. It often leads to simple and efficient plans that perform well even with large volumes of data. Using the APPLY operator in this case leads to a plan that scans the data once to get the current orders and performs a single index seek for each current order to fetch from the covering index all the attributes of the previous order at once.

Listing 9-9 has the solution query, which generates the plan shown in Figure 9-8, with an I/O cost of 3,202 logical reads and no sorting involved.

LISTING 9-9 Query Solution 3 to the Matching Current and Previous Occurrences problem

```
SELECT C.empid,
  C.orderid AS curorderid, P.orderid AS prvorderid,
  C.orderdate AS curorderdate, P.orderdate AS prvorderdate,
  C.requireddate AS curreqdate, P.requireddate AS prvreqdate
FROM Sales.Orders AS C
  OUTER APPLY
    (SELECT TOP (1) orderid, orderdate, requireddate
     FROM Sales.Orders AS O
     WHERE O.empid = C.empid
       AND (O.orderdate < C.orderdate
            OR (O.orderdate = C.orderdate
                AND O.orderid < C.orderid))
     ORDER BY orderdate DESC, orderid DESC) AS P
ORDER BY C.empid, C.orderdate, C.orderid;
```

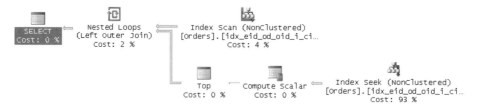

FIGURE 9-8 Execution plan for the query in Listing 9-9

But a more efficient solution is based on the ROW_NUMBER function. You can create a CTE that calculates row numbers for orders partitioned by *empid* and based on *orderdate*, *orderid* ordering. Join two instances of the CTE, one representing the current orders and the other representing the previous orders. The join condition will be based on matching *empid* values and row numbers that differ by one. Listing 9-10 has the solution query, generating the execution plan shown in Figure 9-9.

LISTING 9-10 Query Solution 4 to the Matching Current and Previous Occurrences problem

```
WITH OrdersRN AS
(
  SELECT empid, orderid, orderdate, requireddate,
    ROW_NUMBER() OVER(PARTITION BY empid
                      ORDER BY orderdate, orderid) AS rn
  FROM Sales.Orders
)
SELECT C.empid,
  C.orderid AS curorderid, P.orderid AS prvorderid,
  C.orderdate AS curorderdate, P.orderdate AS prvorderdate,
  C.requireddate AS curreqdate, P.requireddate AS prvreqdate
FROM OrdersRN AS C
  LEFT OUTER JOIN OrdersRN AS P
  ON C.empid = P.empid
  AND C.rn = P.rn + 1
ORDER BY C.empid, C.orderdate, C.orderid;
```

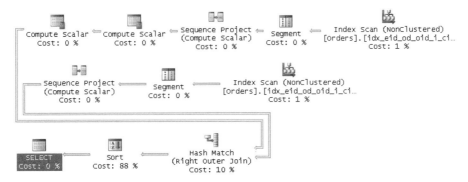

FIGURE 9-9 Execution plan for the query in Listing 9-10

Because the plan scans the covering index only twice to access the order attributes and calculate the row numbers, it incurs a total I/O cost of 12 logical reads, leaving all other solutions lagging far behind in terms of I/O cost.

To clean up, run the following code, which drops indexes used for the solutions presented here:

```
DROP INDEX Sales.Orders.idx_eid_od_oid_i_cid_rd;
DROP INDEX Sales.Orders.idx_eid_odD_oidD_i_cid_rd;
DROP INDEX Sales.OrderDetails.idx_oid_qtyd_pid;
```

Paging

I started talking about paging in Chapter 6, where I presented solutions based on row numbers. As a reminder, you're looking to return rows from the result set of a query in pages or chunks, allowing the user to navigate through the pages. In my examples, I used the Orders table in the InsideTSQL2008 database.

In production environments, paging typically involves dynamic filters and sorting based on user requests. To focus on the paging techniques, I'll assume no filters here and a desired order of *orderdate* with *orderid* as a tiebreaker.

The optimal index for the paging solutions that I'll present follows similar guidelines to other TOP solutions I presented—that is, an index on the sort column or columns and the tiebreaker column or columns. If you can afford to, make the index a covering index, either by making it the table's clustered index or, if it is nonclustered, by including the other columns mentioned in the query. Remember from Chapter 4, "Query Tuning," that an index can contain nonkey columns, which are specified in the INCLUDE clause of the CREATE INDEX command. The nonkey columns of an index appear only in the leaf level of the index. If you cannot afford a covering index, at least make sure that you create one on the *sort+tiebreaker* columns. The plans will be less efficient than with a covering one because lookups will be involved to obtain the data row, but at least you won't get a table scan for each page request.

For sorting by *orderdate* and *orderid* and to cover the columns *custid* and *empid*, create the following index:

```
CREATE INDEX idx_od_oid_i_cid_eid
  ON Sales.Orders(orderdate, orderid) INCLUDE(custid, empid);
```

The solution I'll present here supports paging through consecutive pages. That is, you request the first page and then proceed to the next. You might also want to provide the option to request a previous page. It is strongly recommended to implement the first, next, and previous page requests as stored procedures for both performance and encapsulation reasons. This way you can get efficient plan reuse, and you can always alter the implementation of the stored procedures if you find more efficient techniques, without affecting the users of the stored procedures.

First Page

Implementing the stored procedure that returns the first page is really simple because you don't need an anchor to mark the starting point. You simply return the number of rows requested from the top, like so:

```
CREATE PROC dbo.GetFirstPage
  @n AS INT = 10
AS
SELECT TOP (@n) orderid, orderdate, custid, empid
FROM Sales.Orders
ORDER BY orderdate, orderid;
GO
```

Note In this example, ORDER BY has two purposes: to specify which rows TOP should filter and to control the order of rows in the result set for presentation purposes.

Having an index on the sort columns, especially if it's a covering one like I created for this purpose, allows for an optimal plan where only the relevant page of rows is scanned within the index in order. You can see this by running the following stored procedure and examining the plan shown in Figure 9-10:

```
EXEC dbo.GetFirstPage;
```

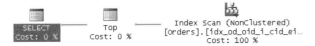

FIGURE 9-10 Execution plan for stored procedure *dbo.GetFirstPage*

Rows are scanned within the index, starting with the head of the linked list and moving forward in an ordered fashion. The Top operator stops the scan as soon as the requested number of rows is accessed.

Next Page

The request for a "next" page has to rely on some anchor row that marks where the page should start. This anchor should be provided to the stored procedure as input. The anchor could be the sort column values of the last row on the previous page because, as you might remember, for determinism purposes the sort values must be unique. In the client application, you already retrieved the previous page. So you can simply set aside the sort column values from the last row in the previous page. When you get a request for the next page, you can provide those as an input to the stored procedure.

Bearing in mind that, in practice, filters and sorting are usually dynamic, you can't rely on any particular number or type of columns as input parameters. So a smarter design, which would accommodate later enhancement of the procedure to support dynamic execution, would be to provide the primary key as input and not the sort column values. The client application would set aside the primary key value from the last row it retrieved and use it as input to the next invocation of the stored procedure.

Here's the implementation of the *GetNextPage* stored procedure:

```
CREATE PROC dbo.GetNextPage
  @anchor AS INT, -- key of last row in prev page
  @n AS INT = 10
AS
SELECT TOP (@n) O.orderid, O.orderdate, O.custid, O.empid
FROM Sales.Orders AS O
  JOIN Sales.Orders AS A
    ON A.orderid = @anchor
    AND (O.orderdate > A.orderdate
        OR (O.orderdate = A.orderdate
            AND O.orderid > A.orderid))
ORDER BY O.orderdate, O.orderid;
GO
```

The procedure joins the two instances of the orders table: one called O, representing the next page, and one called A, representing the anchor. The join condition first filters the anchor instance with the input key, and then it filters the instance representing the next page so that only rows following the anchor will be returned. The columns *orderdate* and *orderid* determine precedence both in terms of the logical expression in the ON clause that filters rows following the anchor and in terms of the ORDER BY clause that TOP relies on. To test the stored procedure, first execute it with the *orderid* from the last row returned from the first page (10257) as the anchor. Then execute it again with the *orderid* of the last row in the second page (10267) as the anchor:

```
EXEC dbo.GetNextPage @anchor = 10257;
EXEC dbo.GetNextPage @anchor = 10267;
```

Remember that the client application iterates through the rows it got back from SQL Server, so naturally it can pick up the key from the last row and use it as input to the next invocation of the stored procedure.

Both procedure calls yield the same execution plan, which is shown in Figure 9-11.

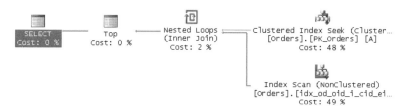

FIGURE 9-11 Execution plan for the stored procedure *GetNextPage*

You will see a single seek operation within the clustered index to fetch the anchor row, followed by an ordered scan within the covering index to fetch the next page of rows. That's not a very efficient plan. Ideally, the optimizer would have performed a seek within the covering index to the first row from the desired page of orders, then it would have followed with a partial ordered scan to grab the rest of the rows in the desired page of orders, physically accessing only the relevant rows. The reason for getting an inefficient plan is because the filter has an OR operator between the expression *O.orderdate > A.orderdate* and the expression *O.orderdate = A.orderdate AND O.orderid > A.orderid*. SQL Server's optimizer tends to produce better plans for predicates that use AND logic instead of OR logic for reasons that I'll describe later in the chapter under the section "Logical Transformations." For our *GetNextPage* procedure, here's the optimized implementation that transforms the OR logic to AND logic:

```
ALTER PROC dbo.GetNextPage
  @anchor AS INT, -- key of last row in prev page
  @n AS INT = 10
AS
SELECT TOP (@n) O.orderid, O.orderdate, O.custid, O.empid
```

```
FROM Sales.Orders AS O
  JOIN Sales.Orders AS A
    ON A.orderid = @anchor
    AND (O.orderdate >= A.orderdate
         AND (O.orderdate > A.orderdate
              OR O.orderid > A.orderid))
ORDER BY O.orderdate, O.orderid;
GO
```

Notice that the AND expression within the parentheses is logically equivalent to the previous OR expression. (I just implemented the techniques described in the section "Logical Transformations" later in the chapter.) To show that the AND implementation is really optimized better, run the following code and examine the execution plan shown in Figure 9-12:

```
EXEC dbo.GetNextPage @anchor = 10257;
```

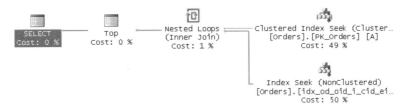

FIGURE 9-12 Execution plan for the stored procedure *GetNextPage*—second version

Now you get the desired plan. You see a single seek operation within the clustered index to fetch the anchor row, followed by a seek within the covering index and a partial ordered scan, physically accessing only the relevant rows in the desired page of orders.

Previous Page

You can use two approaches to dealing with requests for previous pages. One is to locally cache pages already retrieved to the client. This means that you need to develop a caching mechanism in the client. A simpler approach is to implement another stored procedure that works like the *GetNextPage* procedure in reverse. The anchor parameter will be the key of the first row after the page you want. The comparisons within the procedure will use < instead of >, and the TOP clause will use an ORDER BY list that defines the opposite sorting direction. If these were the only changes, you would get the correct page but in reverse order from normal. To fix the ordering of the result set, encapsulate the query as a derived table and apply SELECT … ORDER BY to this derived table, with the desired ordering.

Here's the implementation of the *GetPrevPage* procedure:

```
CREATE PROC dbo.GetPrevPage
  @anchor AS INT, -- key of first row in next page
  @n AS INT = 10
AS
SELECT orderid, orderdate, custid, empid
```

```
FROM (SELECT TOP (@n) O.orderid, O.orderdate, O.custid, O.empid
      FROM Sales.Orders AS O
        JOIN Sales.Orders AS A
          ON A.orderid = @anchor
          AND (O.orderdate <= A.orderdate
               AND (O.orderdate < A.orderdate
                    OR O.orderid < A.orderid))
      ORDER BY O.orderdate DESC, O.orderid DESC) AS D
ORDER BY orderdate, orderid;
GO
```

To test the procedure, run it with *orderid* values from the first rows on the pages you already got:

```
EXEC dbo.GetPrevPage @anchor = 10268;
EXEC dbo.GetPrevPage @anchor = 10258;
```

Examine the execution plan shown in Figure 9-13, produced for the execution of the *GetPrevPage* procedure.

FIGURE 9-13 Execution plan for the previous page

You will find an almost identical plan to the one produced for the *GetNextPage* procedure, with an additional Sort operator, which is a result of the extra ORDER BY clause in the *GetPrevPage* procedure.

When you're finished, drop the covered index created for the paging solutions:

```
DROP INDEX Sales.Orders.idx_od_oid_i_cid_eid;
```

Random Rows

This section covers another class of problems that you can solve with the TOP option—returning rows in a random fashion. Dealing with randomness in T-SQL is quite tricky. Typical requests for randomness involve returning a random row from a table, sorting rows in random order, and the like. The first attempt you might make when asked to return a random row might be to use the RAND function as follows:

```
SELECT TOP (1) orderid, orderdate, custid, empid
FROM Sales.Orders
ORDER BY RAND();
```

However, if you try running this query several times, you will probably be disappointed to find that you're not really getting a random row. RAND as well as most other nondeterministic functions (for example, GETDATE) are invoked once per query, not once per row. So you end up getting the same value of RAND for every row, and the ORDER BY clause does not affect the ordering of the query's result set.

> **Tip** You might be surprised to find that the RAND function—when given an integer seed as input—is not really nondeterministic; rather, it's sort of a hash function. Given the same seed, *RAND(<seed>)* always yields the same result. For example, run the following code multiple times:
>
> ```
> SELECT RAND (5);
> ```
>
> You will always get back 0.713666525097956. And if that's not enough, when you don't specify a seed, SQL Server doesn't really choose a random seed. Rather, the new seed is based on the previous invocation of RAND. Hence, running the following code multiple times will always yield the same two results (0.713666525097956 and 0.454560299686459):
>
> ```
> SELECT RAND(5);
> SELECT RAND();
> ```
>
> The most important use of *RAND(<seed>)* is probably to create reproducible sample data because you can seed it once and then call it repeatedly without a seed to get a well-distributed sequence of values.

If you're seeking a random value, you will have much better success with the following expression:

```
SELECT CHECKSUM(NEWID());
```

And for a random value in the range 1 through @n, use this:

```
SELECT ABS(CHECKSUM(NEWID())) % @n + 1;
```

> **Note** The NEWID function appears to have good distribution properties; however, I haven't yet found any documentation from Microsoft that specifies that this is guaranteed or supported.

An interesting behavior of the NEWID function is that unlike other nondeterministic functions, NEWID is evaluated separately for each row if you invoke it in a query. Bearing this in mind, you can get a random row by using the preceding expression in the ORDER BY clause as follows:

```
SELECT TOP (1) orderid, orderdate, custid, empid
FROM Sales.Orders
ORDER BY CHECKSUM(NEWID());
```

This gives me an opportunity to present another example for using the new functionality of TOP, which allows you to specify a self-contained expression as an input. The following query also returns a random row:

```
SELECT TOP (1) orderid, orderdate, custid, empid
FROM (SELECT TOP (100e0*(CHECKSUM(NEWID()) + 2147483649)/4294967296e0) PERCENT
        orderid, orderdate, custid, empid
```

```
      FROM Sales.Orders
      ORDER BY orderid) AS D
ORDER BY orderid DESC;
```

CHECKSUM returns an integer between –2147483648 and 2147483647. Adding 2147483649 and then dividing by the float value 4294967296e0 yields a random number in the range 0 through 1 (excluding 0). Multiplying this random number by 100 returns a random float value greater than 0 and less than or equal to 100. Remember that the TOP PERCENT option accepts a float percentage in the range 0 through 100, and it rounds up the number of returned rows. A percentage greater than 0 guarantees that at least one row will be returned. The query creating the derived table D thus returns a random number of rows from the table based on *orderid* (primary key) sort. The outer query then simply returns the last row from the derived table—that is, the one with the greatest *orderid* values. This solution is not necessarily more efficient than the previous one I presented, but it was a good opportunity to show how you can use TOP's ability to accept an expression as input.

With the new APPLY operator, you can now answer other randomness requests easily and efficiently, without the need to explicitly apply iterative logic. For example, the following query returns three random orders for each employee:

```
SELECT orderid, custid, empid, orderdate, requireddate
FROM HR.Employees AS E
  CROSS APPLY
    (SELECT TOP (3) orderid, custid, orderdate, requireddate
     FROM Sales.Orders AS O
     WHERE O.empid = E.empid
     ORDER BY CHECKSUM(NEWID())) AS A;
```

Median

In the "Custom Aggregations" section in Chapter 8, I discussed techniques to calculate the median value for each group based on ranking calculations. Here, for the sake of the exercise, I'll present techniques relying on TOP. First run the following code to create the Groups table that I used in my previous solutions to obtain a median:

```
USE tempdb;

IF OBJECT_ID('dbo.Groups') IS NOT NULL DROP TABLE dbo.Groups;

CREATE TABLE dbo.Groups
(
  groupid  VARCHAR(10) NOT NULL,
  memberid INT         NOT NULL,
  string   VARCHAR(10) NOT NULL,
  val      INT         NOT NULL,
  PRIMARY KEY (groupid, memberid)
);
GO
```

```
INSERT INTO dbo.Groups(groupid, memberid, string, val) VALUES
  ('a', 3, 'stra1', 6),
  ('a', 9, 'stra2', 7),
  ('b', 2, 'strb1', 3),
  ('b', 4, 'strb2', 7),
  ('b', 5, 'strb3', 3),
  ('b', 9, 'strb4', 11),
  ('c', 3, 'strc1', 8),
  ('c', 7, 'strc2', 10),
  ('c', 9, 'strc3', 12);
```

Remember that median is the middle value (assuming a sorted list) when the group has an odd number of elements, and it's the average of the two middle values when it has an even number.

It's always a good idea to handle each case separately and then try to figure out whether the solutions can be merged. So first assume an odd number of elements. You can use a TOP (50) PERCENT query to access the first half of the elements, including the middle one. Remember that the PERCENT option rounds up. Then simply query the maximum value from the returned result set.

Now handle the even case. The same query you use to get the middle value from an odd number of rows will produce the largest value of the first half of an even number of rows. You can then write a similar query to return the smallest value of the second half. Sum the two values, divide by two, and you have the median in the even case.

Now try to figure out whether the two solutions can be merged. Interestingly, running the solution for the even case against an odd number of elements yields the correct result because both subqueries used in the even case solution end up returning the same row when you have an odd number of rows. The average of two values that are equal is obviously the same value.

Here's what the solution looks like when you want to return the median of the *val* column for the whole table:

```
SELECT
  ((SELECT MAX(val)
    FROM (SELECT TOP (50) PERCENT val
          FROM dbo.Groups
          ORDER BY val) AS M1)
   +
   (SELECT MIN(val)
    FROM (SELECT TOP (50) PERCENT val
          FROM dbo.Groups
          ORDER BY val DESC) AS M2))
  /2. AS median;
```

To return the median for each group, you need to apply the preceding logic in a correlated subquery against a table that holds one row per group. In our example we don't have such a table, so you can create a virtual one by selecting the distinct *groupid* values from the existing table, like so:

```
SELECT groupid,
  ((SELECT MAX(val)
    FROM (SELECT TOP (50) PERCENT val
          FROM dbo.Groups AS H1
          WHERE H1.groupid = G.groupid
          ORDER BY val) AS M1)
   +
   (SELECT MIN(val)
    FROM (SELECT TOP (50) PERCENT val
          FROM dbo.Groups AS H2
          WHERE H2.groupid = G.groupid
          ORDER BY val DESC) AS M2))
  /2. AS median
FROM (SELECT DISTINCT groupid FROM dbo.Groups) AS G;
```

Logical Transformations

In several solutions I've presented, I used logical expressions with an OR operator to deal with precedence based on multiple attributes. Such was the case in the recent solutions for paging, matching current and previous occurrences, and other problems. I used OR logic because this is how human minds are accustomed to thinking. The logical expressions using OR logic are fairly intuitive for the purpose of determining precedence and identifying rows that follow a certain anchor.

However, because of the way SQL Server's optimizer works, OR logic is problematic in terms of performance, especially when some of the filtered columns are not indexed. For example, consider a filter such as *col1* = 5 OR *col2* = 10. If you have individual indexes on *col1* and *col2*, the optimizer can filter the rows in each index and then perform an index intersection between the two. However, if you have an index on only one of the columns, even when the filter is very selective, the index is useless. SQL Server would still need to scan the whole table to see whether rows that didn't match the first filter qualify for the second condition.

On the other hand, AND logic has much better performance potential. With each expression, you narrow down the result set. Rows filtered by one index are already a superset of the rows you'll end up returning. So potentially you can use an index on any of the filtered columns to your advantage. Whether it is worthwhile to use the existing index is a matter of selectivity, but the potential is there. For example, consider the filter *col1* = 5 AND *col2* = 10. The optimal index here is a composite one created on both columns. However, if you have an index on only one of them and it's selective enough, that's sufficient already. SQL Server can filter the data through that index and then look up the rows and examine whether they also meet the second condition.

In this chapter, the logical expressions I used in my solutions used OR logic to identify rows following a given anchor. For example, say you're looking at the row with an *orderid* of 11075 and you're supposed to identify the rows that follow, where precedence is based on *orderdate* and *orderid* is the tiebreaker. The *orderdate* of the anchor is '20080506'. A query returning the rows that come after this anchor row is very selective. I used the following logic to filter these rows:

```
orderdate > '20080506' OR (orderdate = '20080506' AND orderid > 11075)
```

Say that you could afford creating only one index, on *orderdate*. Such an index is not sufficient in the eyes of the optimizer to filter the relevant rows because the logical expression referring to *orderdate* is followed by an OR operator, with the right side of the operator referring to other columns (*orderid*, in this case). Such a filter would yield a table scan. You can perform a logical transformation here and end up with an equivalent expression that uses AND logic. Here's the transformed expression:

```
orderdate >= '20080506' AND (orderdate > '20080506' OR orderid > 11075)
```

Instead of specifying *orderdate > '20080506'*, you specify *orderdate >= '20080506'*. Now you can use an AND operator and request either rows where the *orderdate* is greater than the anchor's *orderdate* (meaning the *orderdate* is not equal to the anchor's *orderdate*, in which case you don't care about the value of *orderid*) or rows where the *orderid* is greater than the anchor's *orderid* (meaning the *orderdate* is equal to the anchor's *orderdate*). The logical expressions are equivalent. However, the transformed one has the form *orderdate_comparison* AND *other_logical_expression*—meaning that now an index on *orderdate* alone can be considered. To put these words into action, first create a table called MyOrders containing the same data as the Orders table and an index only on *orderdate*:

```
IF OBJECT_ID('dbo.MyOrders') IS NOT NULL
  DROP TABLE dbo.MyOrders;
GO
SELECT * INTO dbo.MyOrders FROM Sales.Orders
CREATE INDEX idx_dt ON dbo.MyOrders(orderdate);
```

Next, run the query in Listing 9-11, which uses OR logic, and examine the plan shown in Figure 9-14.

LISTING 9-11 Query using OR logic

```
SELECT orderid, orderdate, custid, empid
FROM dbo.MyOrders
WHERE orderdate > '20080506'
   OR (orderdate = '20080506' AND orderid > 11075);
```

FIGURE 9-14 Execution plan for the query in Listing 9-11

You will see a table scan, which in the case of this table costs 20 logical reads. Of course, with more realistic table sizes you will see substantially more I/O.

Next, run the query in Listing 9-12, which uses AND logic, and examine the plan shown in Figure 9-15.

LISTING 9-12 Query using AND logic

```
SELECT orderid, orderdate, custid, empid
FROM dbo.MyOrders
WHERE orderdate >= '20080506'
  AND (orderdate > '20080506' OR orderid > 11075);
```

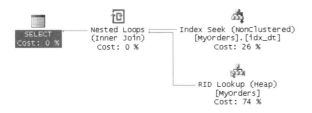

FIGURE 9-15 Execution plan for the query in Listing 9-12

You will see that the index on *orderdate* is used. The I/O cost of this query is six logical reads. Creating an index on both columns (*orderdate, orderid*) is even better:

```
CREATE INDEX idx_dt_oid ON dbo.MyOrders(orderdate, orderid);
```

Run the query in Listing 9-11, which uses the OR logic. You will see in the plan, shown in Figure 9-16, that the new index is used. The I/O cost for this plan is six logical reads.

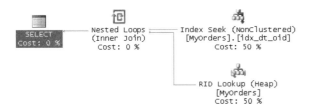

FIGURE 9-16 Execution plan for the query in Listing 9-11, with the new index in place

Run the query in Listing 9-12, which uses the AND logic. You will see the plan shown in Figure 9-17, which might seem similar, but it yields even a lower I/O cost of only four logical reads.

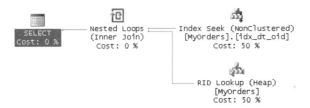

FIGURE 9-17 Execution plan for the query in Listing 9-12, with the new index in place

The conclusion is, of course, that SQL Server can optimize AND logic better than OR logic. All the solutions I presented in this chapter would be better off in terms of performance if you transformed their OR logic to AND logic. Similarly, you might be able to achieve such transformations with other logical expressions.

Another conclusion is that it's better to have an index on all columns determining precedence. The problem is that in production environments you can't always afford it.

> **Note** When discussing subjects that involve logic, I like to use small tables such as those in InsideTSQL2008, with simple and recognizable data. With such tables, the differences in logical reads that you see when testing your solutions are small. In real performance tests and benchmarks, you should use more realistic table sizes as your test data, such as the test data I used in Chapter 4. For example, if you use the *GetNextPage* procedure, which returns the next page of orders, you see very small I/O differences between OR logic and the AND logic, as I'll present shortly. But when I tested the solution against an Orders table with about a million rows, the OR implementation costs more than 1,000 logical reads, while the AND implementation costs only 11 logical reads, physically accessing only the relevant page of orders.

When you're done, don't forget to get rid of the MyOrders table created for these examples:

```
IF OBJECT_ID('dbo.MyOrders') IS NOT NULL
  DROP TABLE dbo.MyOrders;
```

Conclusion

As you probably realized from this chapter, TOP and APPLY are two features that complement each other in many ways. Remember that the SET ROWCOUNT option is a legacy feature and is supported in SQL Server only for purposes of backward compatibility. It is a good idea to replace all references to SET ROWCOUNT with the TOP option. Compared to the alternatives, the APPLY operator allows for very simple and fast queries whenever you need to apply a table expression to each row of an outer query.

Chapter 10
Data Modification

This chapter covers different facets of data modification. I'll discuss aspects of inserting, deleting, updating, and merging data, as well as the OUTPUT clause for data modification statements. I'll also cover new features related to data modification in Microsoft SQL Server 2008, which include an enhanced VALUES clause, minimally logged inserts, the MERGE statement, and a new feature I call composable DML.

Inserting Data

In this section, I'll cover several subjects related to inserting data, including the enhanced VALUES clause, the SELECT INTO statement, the BULK rowset provider, minimally logged inserts, the INSERT EXEC statement, and sequence mechanisms.

Enhanced VALUES Clause

Traditionally the VALUES clause was used in SQL Server to insert a single row into a table. SQL Server 2008 enhances the VALUES clause in two ways—you can now use the VALUES clause in an INSERT statement to insert multiple rows into a table, and you can also use the VALUES clause to define a virtual derived table. Because the VALUES clause can be used to construct a virtual table, it is also known as a *table value constructor*. Each row specification within the clause is called a *row value constructor*.

To demonstrate using the enhanced VALUES clause, first create the Customers table in the tempdb database by running the following code:

```
SET NOCOUNT ON;
USE tempdb;

IF OBJECT_ID('dbo.Customers', 'U') IS NOT NULL DROP TABLE dbo.Customers;

CREATE TABLE dbo.Customers
(
  custid      INT         NOT NULL,
  companyname VARCHAR(25) NOT NULL,
  phone       VARCHAR(20) NOT NULL,
  address     VARCHAR(50) NOT NULL,
  CONSTRAINT PK_Customers PRIMARY KEY(custid)
);
```

Run the following code to insert five rows into the Customers table:

```
INSERT INTO dbo.Customers(custid, companyname, phone, address)
  VALUES
    (1, 'cust 1', '(111) 111-1111', 'address 1'),
    (2, 'cust 2', '(222) 222-2222', 'address 2'),
    (3, 'cust 3', '(333) 333-3333', 'address 3'),
    (4, 'cust 4', '(444) 444-4444', 'address 4'),
    (5, 'cust 5', '(555) 555-5555', 'address 5');
```

As you can see, each pair of parentheses encloses a single row. The individual rows are separated by commas.

Compared to writing a separate INSERT VALUES statement per row, the enhanced INSERT VALUES statement for multiple rows has an obvious advantage in terms of the brevity of code. Also, such a statement is executed as an atomic operation, and therefore if any row fails to enter the target table, the whole operation fails. However, for now the INSERT VALUES clause is internally algebrized like an INSERT SELECT statement that unifies individual rows using the UNION ALL set operation. For example, the previous INSERT VALUES statement is processed like this statement:

```
INSERT INTO dbo.Customers(custid, companyname, phone, address)
            SELECT 1, 'cust 1', '(111) 111-1111', 'address 1'
  UNION ALL SELECT 2, 'cust 2', '(222) 222-2222', 'address 2'
  UNION ALL SELECT 3, 'cust 3', '(333) 333-3333', 'address 3'
  UNION ALL SELECT 4, 'cust 4', '(444) 444-4444', 'address 4'
  UNION ALL SELECT 5, 'cust 5', '(555) 555-5555', 'address 5';
```

Therefore, you shouldn't expect the INSERT VALUES statement to give you any performance benefits compared to the alternative method. If you care about conforming to the ANSI SQL standard, though, you should use the INSERT VALUES clause, which is standard. The alternative—using UNION ALL—relies on a proprietary aspect of T-SQL that allows a SELECT statement without a FROM clause.

You can also use the VALUES clause to define a derived table, as the following query shows:

```
SELECT *
FROM
  (VALUES
    (1, 'cust 1', '(111) 111-1111', 'address 1'),
    (2, 'cust 2', '(222) 222-2222', 'address 2'),
    (3, 'cust 3', '(333) 333-3333', 'address 3'),
    (4, 'cust 4', '(444) 444-4444', 'address 4'),
    (5, 'cust 5', '(555) 555-5555', 'address 5')
  ) AS C(custid, companyname, phone, address);
```

This query generates the following output:

```
custid       companyname phone           address
-----------  ----------- --------------- ---------
1            cust 1      (111) 111-1111  address 1
2            cust 2      (222) 222-2222  address 2
```

```
3          cust 3      (333) 333-3333 address 3
4          cust 4      (444) 444-4444 address 4
5          cust 5      (555) 555-5555 address 5
```

Unfortunately, SQL Server 2008 does not support defining a CTE by a VALUES clause.

SELECT INTO

The SELECT INTO statement creates a new table from the result set of a query. For example, the following statement creates the temporary table #MyShippers and populates it with all rows from the Sales.Shippers table in the InsideTSQL2008 database:

```
SET NOCOUNT ON;
USE tempdb;

IF OBJECT_ID('tempdb..#MyShippers') IS NOT NULL DROP TABLE #MyShippers;

SELECT shipperid, companyname, phone
INTO #MyShippers
FROM InsideTSQL2008.Sales.Shippers;
```

The columns of the new table inherit their names, data types, nullability, and IDENTITY property from the query's result set. SELECT INTO doesn't copy constraints, indexes, or triggers from the query's source. If you need the results in a table with the same indexes, constraints, and triggers as the source, you have to add them afterward.

SELECT INTO is a bulk operation. (See the "Minimally Logged Operations" section later in the chapter for details.) If the recovery model of the destination database is not FULL, the SELECT INTO is done with minimal logging, which can be substantially faster than full logging.

Unlike some other database platforms, in SQL Server both DDL and DML are transactional. Remember that the SELECT INTO statement both creates the target table (DDL) and populates it with the result set produced by the query (DML). It is quite obvious that the data that is inserted into the target table is exclusively locked until the SELECT INTO transaction finishes; however, you need to keep in mind that metadata describing the definition of the table and its columns in system tables is also exclusively locked for the duration of the transaction. If the SELECT INTO statement deals with a large result set, it may take it some time to finish; during that time both the data and the metadata are exclusively locked. If, from another transaction, you try to obtain conflicting locks on the metadata that is exclusively locked by the SELECT INTO transaction, even unintentionally (for example, a full scan of sys.objects or sys.columns), your transaction will be blocked. To avoid such blocking, you may want to consider creating the target table in one transaction and inserting the data into the table using an INSERT SELECT statement in another transaction. Prior to SQL Server 2008, an INSERT SELECT statement was always fully logged and therefore slower than a minimally logged SELECT INTO statement. However, SQL Server 2008 introduces support for minimally logged INSERT SELECT statements. I'll provide more details about minimally logged operations later in the chapter.

If you need a quick and dirty empty copy of some table, SELECT INTO allows you to obtain such a copy very simply. You don't have to script the CREATE TABLE statement and change the table's name—you just need to issue the following statement:

```
SELECT * INTO target_table FROM source_table WHERE 1 = 2;
```

The optimizer is smart enough to realize that no source row will satisfy the filter *1 = 2.* Therefore, SQL Server doesn't bother to physically access the source data; rather, it creates the target table based on the schema of the source. Here's an example that creates a table called MyOrders in tempdb, based on the schema of the Sales.Orders table in InsideTSQL2008:

```
IF OBJECT_ID('dbo.MyOrders') IS NOT NULL DROP TABLE dbo.MyOrders;

SELECT *
INTO dbo.MyOrders
FROM InsideTSQL2008.Sales.Orders
WHERE 1 = 2;
```

Keep in mind that if a source column has the IDENTITY property, the target has it as well. For example, the *orderid* column in the Orders table has the IDENTITY property. If you don't want the IDENTITY property to be copied to the target column, simply apply any type of manipulation to the source column. For example, you can use the expression *orderid + 0 AS orderid* as follows:

```
IF OBJECT_ID('dbo.MyOrders') IS NOT NULL DROP TABLE dbo.MyOrders;

SELECT orderid+0 AS orderid, custid, empid, orderdate,
   requireddate, shippeddate, shipperid, freight, shipname,
   shipaddress, shipcity, shipregion, shippostalcode, shipcountry
INTO dbo.MyOrders
FROM InsideTSQL2008.Sales.Orders
WHERE 1 = 2;
```

In this case, the *orderid* column in the target MyOrders table doesn't have the IDENTITY property.

> **Tip** Suppose you want to insert the result set of a stored procedure or a dynamic batch into a new table, but you don't know what table structure you need to create. You can use a SELECT INTO statement, specifying OPENQUERY in the FROM clause, referring to your own server as if it were a linked server:
>
> ```
> EXEC sp_serveroption <your_server>, 'data access', true;
>   SELECT * INTO <target_table>
>   FROM OPENQUERY(<your_server>,
>     'EXEC {<proc_name> | (<dynamic_batch>)}') AS O;
> ```

BULK Rowset Provider

SQL Server supports the BULK rowset provider, which allows you to use the BULK engine to load file data as a rowset or as a single large object (LOB) value. You specify BULK as the provider in the OPENROWSET function, along with other options that are relevant to your request.

For example, the following code returns the data from a file called shippers.txt as a row set, based on the format file shippers.fmt:

```
SELECT shipperid, companyname, phone
FROM OPENROWSET(BULK 'c:\temp\shippers.txt',
                FORMATFILE = 'c:\temp\shippers.fmt') AS S;
```

This code generates the following output:

```
shipperid  companyname     phone
---------- --------------- ---------------
1          Shipper GVSUA   (503) 555-0137
2          Shipper ETYNR   (425) 555-0136
3          Shipper ZHISN   (415) 555-0138
```

> **More Info** You can download the files used in this section's examples from
> *http://www.insidetsql.com* as part of the book's source code download. For more information,
> see the Introduction.

The format file is the same format file you're familiar with when working with bcp.exe or BULK INSERT. In fact, you can generate it either manually or by using bcp.exe as you have used it thus far. Besides FORMATFILE, you can also specify other read-related bulk options: CODEPAGE, ERRORFILE, FIRSTROW, LASTROW, MAXERRORS, and ROWS_PER_BATCH.

You can also use the BULK provider to specify a file source for an INSERT statement. This way, you can efficiently utilize the BULK engine. In such an INSERT statement, you can control insert options using table hints, including KEEPIDENTITY, KEEPDEFAULTS, IGNORE_ CONSTRAINTS, IGNORE_TRIGGERS, and TABLOCK. To demonstrate inserting a rowset into a table using the BULK provider, first run the following code, which creates the Shippers table in the tempdb database:

```
USE tempdb;

IF OBJECT_ID('dbo.Shippers') IS NOT NULL DROP TABLE dbo.Shippers;

CREATE TABLE dbo.Shippers
(
  shipperid    INT          NOT NULL PRIMARY KEY,
  companyname  NVARCHAR(40) NOT NULL,
  phone        NVARCHAR(24) NOT NULL
);
```

The following code is an example of inserting the contents of a file called shippers.txt into the target table Shippers, using shippers.fmt as the format file:

```
INSERT INTO dbo.Shippers WITH (TABLOCK) (shipperid, companyname, phone)
  SELECT shipperid, companyname, phone
  FROM OPENROWSET(BULK 'c:\temp\shippers.txt',
                  FORMATFILE = 'c:\temp\shippers.fmt') AS S;
```

The hint TABLOCK tells SQL Server to take a table lock during the insert operation, minimizing lock overhead. In the case of an INSERT SELECT FROM OPENROWSET(BULK ...) statement, the TABLOCK hint has special meaning. It tells SQL Server to obtain a bulk update table-level lock that will allow an optimized BULK operation while also allowing other sessions to obtain a bulk update table-level lock as well. This way multiple processes can run such optimized bulk inserts in parallel.

If you're asking yourself why use the INSERT SELECT FROM OPENROWSET(BULK ...) statement rather than the BULK INSERT statement or the bcp.exe tool, the first statement has an advantage. Unlike the BULK INSERT command or the bcp.exe tool, the INSERT SELECT FROM OPENROWSET(BULK ...) statement allows you to apply usual query manipulation on the source. This means that you can use table operators like joins, APPLY, PIVOT, UNPIVOT, filter data with the WHERE clause, group data with the GROUP BY clause, and so on.

The BULK rowset provider can also be used to insert the content of a file as a scalar LOB value in an INSERT, UPDATE, or MERGE statement. You use the OPENROWSET function and specify the BULK option, the source filename, and one of three options for the type of data: SINGLE_CLOB for regular character data, SINGLE_NCLOB for Unicode data, and SINGLE_BLOB for binary data.

> **Note** When you want to load XML data from a file, you use either SINGLE_CLOB or SINGLE_NCLOB, depending on whether the XML file contains regular character data or Unicode data.

To demonstrate using the BULK rowset provider to insert file content as a scalar LOB value, first create the CustomerData table by running the code in Listing 10-1.

LISTING 10-1 Creating the CustomerData table

```
IF OBJECT_ID('dbo.CustomerData') IS NOT NULL DROP TABLE dbo.CustomerData;

CREATE TABLE dbo.CustomerData
(
  custid      INT          NOT NULL PRIMARY KEY,
  txt_data    VARCHAR(MAX)  NULL,
  ntxt_data   NVARCHAR(MAX) NULL,
  binary_data VARBINARY(MAX) NULL,
  xml_data    XML          NULL
);
```

As an example, the following INSERT statement inserts a new customer into the CustomerData table, with *custid* 101, and an XML value read from the file xmlfile101.xml into the xml_data column:

```
INSERT INTO dbo.CustomerData(custid, xml_data)
  VALUES(
    101,
    (SELECT xml_data FROM OPENROWSET(
      BULK 'c:\temp\xmlfile101.xml', SINGLE_CLOB) AS F(xml_data)));
```

Similarly, the following UPDATE statement reads the three files textfile101.txt, unicodefile101.txt, and binaryfile101.jpg and updates customer 101's columns: *txt_data, ntxt_data,* and *binary_data*, respectively:

```
UPDATE dbo.CustomerData
  SET txt_data  = (SELECT txt_data FROM OPENROWSET(
    BULK 'c:\temp\textfile101.txt', SINGLE_CLOB) AS F(txt_data)),
  ntxt_data  = (SELECT ntxt_data FROM OPENROWSET(
    BULK 'c:\temp\unicodefile101.txt', SINGLE_NCLOB) AS F(ntxt_data)),
  binary_data  = (SELECT binary_data FROM OPENROWSET(
    BULK 'c:\temp\binaryfile101.jpg', SINGLE_BLOB) AS F(binary_data))
WHERE custid = 101;
```

Run the following code to examine the row in CustomerData for customer 101:

```
SELECT * FROM dbo.CustomerData WHERE custid = 101;
```

You get the following output, shown here in abbreviated form and in three parts because of the length of the output row:

```
custid  txt_data
-------  -------------------------------------------------
101     This file contains character data for customer 101

custid  ntxt_data
-------  ------------------------------------------------
101     This file contains Unicode data for customer 101

custid  binary_data            xml_data
-------  ---------------------  ---------------
101     0xFFD8FFE000104A46...  <ShowPlanXML...
```

Minimally Logged Operations

SQL Server can perform minimal logging with certain kinds of operations. An operation done with minimal logging can run substantially faster than when done with full logging. One reason for the big difference is that writes to the transaction log are done sequentially, so in many cases writes to the log become the bottleneck of the operation. The following operations can benefit from minimal logging: SELECT INTO, index operations, operations on large object values, BULK INSERT, bcp.exe, INSERT SELECT FROM OPENROWSET(BULK ...), and, new to SQL Server 2008, regular INSERT SELECT.

> **More Info** For more information on Bulk Import/Export, see Sunil Agarwal's blog posts on the subject: *http://blogs.msdn.com/sqlserverstorageengine/archive/tags/Bulk+Import_2F00_Export/ default.aspx*.

SQL Server has certain requirements for minimal logging. First of all, the recovery model of the target database cannot be FULL; rather, minimal logging is possible only if the recovery model is SIMPLE or BULK_LOGGED. As far as SELECT INTO is concerned, that's the only requirement. All other insert methods (BULK INSERT, bcp.exe, INSERT SELECT FROM OPENROWSET(BULK . . .), and INSERT SELECT) have additional requirements. Besides the requirement that the target database have a non-FULL recovery model, there are two requirements on the target table: it must not be marked for replication, and one of the following must be true:

The target is a heap, and you specify TABLOCK. The target can be empty or nonempty, and no trace flag is required.

The target is an empty B-tree, and you specify TABLOCK. No trace flag is required.

The target is an empty B-tree, and trace flag 610 is on. The TABLOCK option is not required. This case is new in SQL Server 2008.

The target is a nonempty B-tree, and trace flag 610 is on—minimal logging will apply to new key ranges that allocate and populate new pages. The TABLOCK option is not required. This case is also new in SQL Server 2008.

Note that while a database backup is running, minimal logging is disabled temporarily. The backup does not prevent the operation from running—it just causes it to perform full logging.

For now this list of requirements might be a bit overwhelming. I provide it here for reference purposes. I'll provide more details and examples shortly and also show you how to analyze the logging behavior yourself.

As mentioned, regular INSERT SELECT statements in SQL Server 2008 can also benefit from minimal logging. Note, however, that some aspects of optimized bulk imports do not apply to INSERT SELECT but do apply to the other bulk import methods (BULK INSERT, bcp.exe, and INSERT SELECT FROM OPENROWSET(BULK . . .)). I'll collectively call the last three methods the other methods. The other methods support a table-level bulk update lock that reduces lock overhead while still allowing parallel bulk imports from multiple processes. The INSERT SELECT statement supports the TABLOCK option, but it results in an exclusive table lock that only one process can hold at a time. The other methods also support defining a batch size that indicates after every how many rows to commit, while INSERT SELECT doesn't support this option. You will find other such differences between the other methods and INSERT SELECT; for details please consult SQL Server Books Online.

Analyzing Logging Behavior

This section describes tools and techniques that you can use to analyze logging behavior. You can use these tools to do your own research and figure out how SQL Server handles certain insert scenarios when those scenarios are not documented or when you are in doubt.

One of the main tools I use to analyze logging behavior is the undocumented *fn_dblog* function. This function accepts two inputs indicating the from log sequence number and the to log sequence number, and it returns all log records in the requested range from the transaction log of the database where the function is queried. To get all records from the transaction log, specify NULL in both inputs.

To check how much logging was involved in processing an insert operation against a certain table, you can aggregate measures from the function's result set before and after the operation and calculate the difference between the before and after values. The general form of the code may look like this:

```
CHECKPOINT;
GO

DECLARE @numrecords AS INT, @size AS BIGINT, @dt AS DATETIME;

SELECT
  @numrecords = COUNT(*),
  @size       = COALESCE(SUM([Log Record Length]), 0),
  @dt         = CURRENT_TIMESTAMP
FROM fn_dblog(NULL, NULL) AS D
WHERE AllocUnitName = '<table_name>' OR AllocUnitName LIKE '<table_name>.%';

-- <operation>

SELECT
  COUNT(*) - @numrecords AS numrecords,
  CAST((COALESCE(SUM([Log Record Length]), 0) - @size)
    / 1024. / 1024. AS NUMERIC(12, 2)) AS size_mb,
  CAST(DATEDIFF(millisecond, @dt, CURRENT_TIMESTAMP)/1000. AS DECIMAL(12,3))
    AS duration_sec
FROM fn_dblog(NULL, NULL) AS D
WHERE AllocUnitName = '<table_name>' OR AllocUnitName LIKE '<table_name>.%';
```

The code first applies a checkpoint to flush dirty pages from cache to disk, allowing truncation of the inactive portion of the log. The code then aggregates measures of the log records associated with the table of interest before the insert operation. The code then applies the insert operation. Finally, the code calculates the difference between the before and after values.

You may also be interested in the distribution of log records based on their lengths. To achieve this you can produce a histogram with as many steps as you would like to analyze. The following code demonstrates how to produce a histogram with 10 steps:

```
DECLARE @numsteps AS INT = 10;
DECLARE @log AS TABLE(id INT IDENTITY, size INT, PRIMARY KEY(size, id));
```

```
INSERT INTO @log(size)
  SELECT [Log Record Length]
  FROM fn_dblog(null, null) AS D
  WHERE AllocUnitName = '<table_name>' OR AllocUnitName LIKE '<table_name>.%';

WITH Args AS
(
  SELECT MIN(size) AS mn, MAX(size) AS mx,
    1E0*(MAX(size) - MIN(size)) / @numsteps AS stepsize
  FROM @log
),
Steps AS
(
  SELECT n,
    mn + (n-1)*stepsize - CASE WHEN n = 1 THEN 1 ELSE 0 END AS lb,
    mn + n*stepsize AS hb
  FROM Nums
    CROSS JOIN Args
  WHERE n <= @numsteps
)
SELECT n, lb, hb, COUNT(size) AS numrecords
FROM Steps
  LEFT OUTER JOIN @log
    ON size > lb AND size <= hb
GROUP BY n, lb, hb
ORDER BY n;
```

I also find it very useful to analyze the actual log records involved in logging the operation to figure out what was logged and not just how much logging was done. The following query gives you aggregated information with a breakdown by average log record length in units of 100 bytes, log operation, and log context:

```
SELECT Operation, Context,
  AVG([Log Record Length]) AS AvgLen, COUNT(*) AS Cnt
FROM fn_dblog(null, null) AS D
WHERE AllocUnitName = '<table_name>' OR AllocUnitName LIKE '<table_name>.%'
GROUP BY Operation, Context, ROUND([Log Record Length], -2)
ORDER BY AvgLen, Operation, Context;
```

The rounding of log record lengths to units of 100 bytes is achieved by specifying −2 as the second argument to the ROUND function. If you need to round to units of 1,000, specify −3. As an alternative, you may prefer to get a logarithmic breakdown (10s, 100s, 1,000s). To achieve this, use the length of the string holding the log record length as the grouped expression, like so:

```
SELECT Operation, Context,
  '1'+REPLICATE('0',-1+LEN([Log Record Length]))+'s' AS [Log Entry Sizes],
  AVG([Log Record Length]) AS AvgLen, COUNT(*) AS Cnt
FROM fn_dblog(null, null) AS D
WHERE AllocUnitName = '<table_name>' OR AllocUnitName LIKE '<table_name>.%'
GROUP BY Operation, Context, LEN([Log Record Length])
ORDER BY AvgLen, Operation, Context;
```

Testing Insert Scenarios

This section demonstrates tests of different insert scenarios and the logging behavior involved. I will demonstrate some scenarios using the SELECT INTO and INSERT SELECT statements, but of course you can apply similar analysis with other scenarios that you're interested in.

All tests will be run in a sample database called testdb that you create and use by running the following code:

```
USE master;
IF DB_ID('testdb') IS NULL CREATE DATABASE testdb;
GO
USE testdb;
```

Scenario 1: SELECT INTO, FULL Recovery   The first scenario demonstrates using the SELECT INTO statement in a database set to the FULL recovery model. Run the following code to set the recovery model of the testdb database to FULL and back up the database to get out of log truncate mode:

```
ALTER DATABASE testdb SET RECOVERY FULL;
BACKUP DATABASE testdb TO DISK = 'c:\temp\testdb.bak' WITH INIT;
```

Next, run the code in Listing 10-2 to use the SELECT INTO statement to create a table called T1 and populate it with 100,000 rows, each of which is more than 2,000 bytes long (~200 MB total).

LISTING 10-2 Script with SELECT INTO

```
USE testdb;

-- Preparation
-- Replace this code with your preparation code
IF OBJECT_ID('dbo.T1', 'U') IS NOT NULL DROP TABLE dbo.T1;
CHECKPOINT;
GO

-- Collect values prior to operation
DECLARE @numrecords AS INT, @size AS BIGINT, @dt AS DATETIME;

SELECT
  @numrecords = COUNT(*),
  @size       = COALESCE(SUM([Log Record Length]), 0),
  @dt         = CURRENT_TIMESTAMP
FROM fn_dblog(NULL, NULL) AS D
WHERE AllocUnitName = 'dbo.T1' OR AllocUnitName LIKE 'dbo.T1.%';

-- Operation
-- Replace this code with your operation code
SELECT n, CAST('a' AS CHAR(2000)) AS filler
INTO dbo.T1
FROM dbo.Nums
WHERE n <= 100000;
```

```
-- Calculate delta of values for operation
SELECT
  COUNT(*) - @numrecords AS numrecords,
  CAST((COALESCE(SUM([Log Record Length]), 0) - @size)
    / 1024. / 1024. AS NUMERIC(12, 2)) AS size_mb,
  CAST(DATEDIFF(millisecond, @dt, CURRENT_TIMESTAMP)/1000. AS DECIMAL(12,3))
    AS duration_sec
FROM fn_dblog(NULL, NULL) AS D
WHERE AllocUnitName = 'dbo.T1' OR AllocUnitName LIKE 'dbo.T1.%';

-- Generate histogram
DECLARE @numsteps AS INT = 10;
DECLARE @log AS TABLE(id INT IDENTITY, size INT, PRIMARY KEY(size, id));

INSERT INTO @log(size)
  SELECT [Log Record Length]
  FROM fn_dblog(null, null) AS D
  WHERE AllocUnitName = 'dbo.T1' OR AllocUnitName LIKE 'dbo.T1.%';

WITH Args AS
(
  SELECT MIN(size) AS mn, MAX(size) AS mx,
    1E0*(MAX(size) - MIN(size)) / @numsteps AS stepsize
  FROM @log
),
Steps AS
(
  SELECT n,
    mn + (n-1)*stepsize - CASE WHEN n = 1 THEN 1 ELSE 0 END AS lb,
    mn + n*stepsize AS hb
  FROM Nums
    CROSS JOIN Args
  WHERE n <= @numsteps
)
SELECT n, lb, hb, COUNT(size) AS numrecords
FROM Steps
  LEFT OUTER JOIN @log
    ON size > lb AND size <= hb
GROUP BY n, lb, hb
ORDER BY n;

-- Get breakdown of log record types
SELECT Operation, Context,
  AVG([Log Record Length]) AS AvgLen, COUNT(*) AS Cnt
FROM fn_dblog(null, null) AS D
WHERE AllocUnitName = 'dbo.T1' OR AllocUnitName LIKE 'dbo.T1.%'
GROUP BY Operation, Context, ROUND([Log Record Length], -2)
ORDER BY AvgLen, Operation, Context;
```

The code in Listing 10-2 uses as its source table the Nums table described in Chapter 6, "Subqueries, Table Expressions, and Ranking Functions," under the section "Auxiliary Table of Numbers." The code uses the tools described earlier to calculate how much logging was involved, to produce a histogram showing the distribution of the log record lengths, and to show a breakdown of the log records by length, operation, and context. You can use the code in Listing 10-2 as a template to investigate the logging behavior of other kinds of activities. Simply replace the sections marked with the comments -- *Preparation* and -- *Operation* with the applicable preparation and operation code that you want to test.

The code in Listing 10-2 produced the following results on my system:

```
numrecords  size_mb  duration_sec
----------- -------- ------------
34522       197.95   24.000

n           lb                       hb                       numrecords
----------- ------------------------ ------------------------ -----------
1           59                       881.6                    9522
2           881.6                    1703.2                   0
3           1703.2                   2524.8                   0
4           2524.8                   3346.4                   0
5           3346.4                   4168                     0
6           4168                     4989.6                   0
7           4989.6                   5811.2                   0
8           5811.2                   6632.8                   0
9           6632.8                   7454.4                   0
10          7454.4                   8276                     25000

Operation         Context   AvgLen      Cnt
----------------- --------- ----------- -----------
LOP_SET_BITS      LCX_GAM   60          3147
LOP_SET_BITS      LCX_IAM   60          3147
LOP_FORMAT_PAGE   LCX_HEAP  84          1
LOP_FORMAT_PAGE   LCX_IAM   84          1
LOP_MODIFY_ROW    LCX_IAM   88          1
LOP_MODIFY_ROW    LCX_PFS   88          3225
LOP_FORMAT_PAGE   LCX_HEAP  8276        25000
```

From these outputs you can learn that SQL Server applied full logging, amounting in total to about 200 MB. The histogram shows the distribution of the log records based on their size in 10 steps. Each row in the histogram has the step number (n), low boundary point of the step (lb), high boundary point of step (hb), and number of log records matching this step. You can learn from this histogram that there were 9,522 log records with lengths in the range 59 bytes to 881.6 bytes and 25,000 records in the range 7,454.4 bytes to 8,276 bytes.

The breakdown of the log operations shows 25,000 log records with the log operation (LOP) LOP_FORMAT_PAGE and log context (LCX) LCX_HEAP, meaning that 25,000 heap pages were allocated and populated during the SELECT INTO operation and that the data populated in those pages was fully logged. From the log operation LOP_SET_BITS with the contexts LCX_GAM and LCX_IAM and the operation LOP_MODIFY_ROW with the context LCK_PFS, you learn that some logging is also taking place for modifications of GAM, IAM, and PFS pages (allocation bitmaps and page free space bitmaps).

From this test you learn that a SELECT INTO statement running in a database that is set to the FULL recovery model is fully logged. In fact, when the recovery model of the database is set to FULL, all insert methods perform full logging.

In the following scenarios, I will show the results from Listing 10-2 under a variety of different circumstances: with a different database recovery model in place, with a trace flag turned on, or with changes to the sections of the code identified with the comments -- *Preparation* and -- *Operation*. The parts of Listing 10-2 that produce the logging information will stay the same, so in those scenarios where I change the code, I won't provide the entire listing—I'll just provide the new Preparation and Operation code. When I do, I will assume that you are still running the full Listing 10-2 with replacement versions of these two sections.

Scenario 2: SELECT INTO, Non-FULL Recovery   To test the SELECT INTO statement in a database with a non-FULL recovery model, first change the recovery model to SIMPLE by running the following code:

```
ALTER DATABASE testdb SET RECOVERY SIMPLE;
```

Next, run the code in Listing 10-2 again. I got the following outputs when running the code on my system:

```
numrecords  size_mb  duration_sec
----------- -------- ------------
9521        0.63     10.000
```

n	lb	hb	numrecords
1	59	63.2	6272
2	63.2	66.4	0
3	66.4	69.6	0
4	69.6	72.8	22
5	72.8	76	0
6	76	79.2	0
7	79.2	82.4	1
8	82.4	85.6	1
9	85.6	88.8	3137
10	88.8	92	88

Operation	Context	AvgLen	Cnt
LOP_SET_BITS	LCX_GAM	60	3147
LOP_SET_BITS	LCX_IAM	60	3147
LOP_FORMAT_PAGE	LCX_IAM	84	1
LOP_MODIFY_ROW	LCX_IAM	88	1
LOP_MODIFY_ROW	LCX_PFS	88	3225

As you can see, this time the actual contents of the inserted data were not logged. Instead, there was only minimal logging of changes to GAM, IAM, and PFS pages (allocation bitmaps and page free space bitmaps). In total, the logging amounted to less than 1 MB.

From this test you learn that a SELECT INTO statement running in a database that is set to a non-FULL recovery model is minimally logged.

As mentioned, when the database recovery model is set to FULL, you get full logging regardless of the insert method. For the subsequent scenarios, the testdb database will remain in SIMPLE recovery model.

Scenario 3: INSERT SELECT, Empty Heap, TABLOCK   This scenario involves an INSERT SELECT statement against an empty heap using the TABLOCK table hint. Recall that prior to SQL Server 2008, regular INSERT SELECT statements always performed full logging, but in SQL Server 2008, they can be done with minimal logging, similar to other bulk import methods.

In order to test this scenario, replace the Preparation and Operation sections of Listing 10-2 with this code:

```
-- Preparation
IF OBJECT_ID('dbo.T1', 'U') IS NOT NULL DROP TABLE dbo.T1;

CREATE TABLE dbo.T1
(
  n INT NOT NULL,
  filler CHAR(2000) NOT NULL
);

CHECKPOINT;
GO

-- Operation
INSERT INTO dbo.T1 WITH (TABLOCK) (n, filler)
  SELECT n, CAST('a' AS CHAR(2000)) AS filler
  FROM dbo.Nums
  WHERE n <= 100000;
```

I got the following results on my system from this test:

numrecords	size_mb	duration_sec
9521	0.63	9.000

n	lb	hb	numrecords
1	59	63.2	6272
2	63.2	66.4	0
3	66.4	69.6	0
4	69.6	72.8	22
5	72.8	76	0
6	76	79.2	0
7	79.2	82.4	1
8	82.4	85.6	1
9	85.6	88.8	3137
10	88.8	92	88

Operation	Context	AvgLen	Cnt
LOP_SET_BITS	LCX_GAM	60	3147
LOP_SET_BITS	LCX_IAM	60	3147
LOP_FORMAT_PAGE	LCX_IAM	84	1
LOP_MODIFY_ROW	LCX_IAM	88	1
LOP_MODIFY_ROW	LCX_PFS	88	3225

As you can learn from these results, you also get minimal logging in this scenario.

Scenario 4: INSERT SELECT, Nonempty Heap, TABLOCK   This scenario is similar to Scenario 3, except that this time the target heap is not empty. Use the following code for the Preparation and Operation sections this time:

```
-- Preparation
CHECKPOINT;
GO

-- Operation
INSERT INTO dbo.T1 WITH (TABLOCK) (n, filler)
  SELECT n, CAST('a' AS CHAR(2000)) AS filler
  FROM dbo.Nums
  WHERE n BETWEEN 100001 AND 200000;
```

I got the following logging results for this test on my system:

numrecords	size_mb	duration_sec
9518	0.63	8.000

n	lb	hb	numrecords
1	59	63.2	6272
2	63.2	66.4	0
3	66.4	69.6	0
4	69.6	72.8	22
5	72.8	76	0
6	76	79.2	0
7	79.2	82.4	0
8	82.4	85.6	0
9	85.6	88.8	3136
10	88.8	92	88

Operation	Context	AvgLen	Cnt
LOP_SET_BITS	LCX_GAM	60	3147
LOP_SET_BITS	LCX_IAM	60	3147
LOP_MODIFY_ROW	LCX_PFS	88	3224

As you can see, even when the target heap is nonempty, you still get minimal logging.

Scenario 5: INSERT SELECT, Empty Heap, Without TABLOCK   This scenario is similar to Scenario 3, except that in this case you do not specify the TABLOCK table hint. The following code provides the Preparation and Operation parts of this test:

```
-- Preparation
IF OBJECT_ID('dbo.T1', 'U') IS NOT NULL DROP TABLE dbo.T1;

CREATE TABLE dbo.T1
(
  n INT NOT NULL,
  filler CHAR(2000) NOT NULL
);

CHECKPOINT;
GO


-- Operation
INSERT INTO dbo.T1 (n, filler)
  SELECT n, CAST('a' AS CHAR(2000)) AS filler
  FROM dbo.Nums
  WHERE n <= 100000;
```

This test generates the following results on my system:

```
numrecords  size_mb  duration_sec
----------- -------- ------------
159384      204.46   12.000
```

n	lb	hb	numrecords
1	59	264.4	59384
2	264.4	468.8	0
3	468.8	673.2	0
4	673.2	877.6	0
5	877.6	1082	0
6	1082	1286.4	0
7	1286.4	1490.8	0
8	1490.8	1695.2	0
9	1695.2	1899.6	0
10	1899.6	2104	100000

Operation	Context	AvgLen	Cnt
LOP_SET_BITS	LCX_GAM	60	3125
LOP_SET_BITS	LCX_IAM	60	3125
LOP_MODIFY_ROW	LCX_PFS	80	28125
LOP_FORMAT_PAGE	LCX_HEAP	84	25000
LOP_FORMAT_PAGE	LCX_IAM	84	1
LOP_MODIFY_ROW	LCX_IAM	88	8
LOP_INSERT_ROWS	LCX_HEAP	2096	100000

The simple fact that this time you didn't specify the TABLOCK hint caused the operation to be fully logged. The 100,000 INSERT statements, each of which inserted a row of over

2,000 bytes, were logged individually. Further logging was due to the page allocations that took place (25,000 of those) and to the updates of the GAM, IAM, and PFS pages.

As you can guess, when the target heap is not empty, you also get full logging when not specifying TABLOCK.

Scenario 6: INSERT SELECT, Empty B-Tree, TABLOCK   This scenario involves an INSERT SELECT statement against an empty B-tree (as opposed to a heap) using the TABLOCK hint. The following code shows the Preparation and Operation parts of this test:

```
-- Preparation
IF OBJECT_ID('dbo.T1', 'U') IS NOT NULL DROP TABLE dbo.T1;

CREATE TABLE dbo.T1
(
  n INT NOT NULL,
  filler CHAR(2000) NOT NULL
);

CREATE UNIQUE CLUSTERED INDEX idx_n ON dbo.T1(n);

CHECKPOINT;
GO

-- Operation
INSERT INTO dbo.T1 WITH (TABLOCK) (n, filler)
  SELECT n, CAST('a' AS CHAR(2000)) AS filler
  FROM dbo.Nums
  WHERE n <= 200000
    AND n % 2 = 0
  ORDER BY n;
```

The INSERT SELECT statement filters the 100,000 rows with even values of *n* smaller than or equal to 200,000 from the Nums table. Later I'll insert odd numbers to show what happens when you insert rows into existing pages as opposed to allocating new ones. Also notice that the INSERT SELECT statement has an ORDER BY clause that ensures that the data is inserted in the target B-tree order. Note that in this particular example the ORDER BY clause might not have mattered in terms of optimization because the Nums table has a clustered index on the column *n*; however, in other cases where the source data is not preordered, specifying an ORDER BY clause could help optimizing the operation.

I got the following results on my system for this test:

numrecords	size_mb	duration_sec
9868	0.66	8.000

n	lb	hb	numrecords
1	59	63.2	6394
2	63.2	66.4	0
3	66.4	69.6	0

4	69.6	72.8	6
5	72.8	76	0
6	76	79.2	0
7	79.2	82.4	264
8	82.4	85.6	1
9	85.6	88.8	3173
10	88.8	92	30

Operation	Context	AvgLen	Cnt
LOP_SET_BITS	LCX_GAM	60	3200
LOP_SET_BITS	LCX_IAM	60	3200
LOP_FORMAT_PAGE	LCX_IAM	84	1
LOP_MODIFY_ROW	LCX_PFS	87	3459
LOP_MODIFY_ROW	LCX_IAM	88	8

As you can see, an INSERT SELECT against an empty B-tree using the TABLOCK option performs minimal logging.

In the next few scenarios, we will learn how trace flag 610 affects logging, and in what follows, we'll use the abbreviation TF-610 for this trace flag.

Scenario 7: INSERT SELECT, Nonempty B-Tree, TABLOCK, TF-610 Off, New Key Range   This scenario is similar to Scenario 6, except that the target B-tree already contains data. TF-610 is off. The following code contains the Preparation and Operation sections for this test:

```
-- Preparation
CHECKPOINT;
GO

-- Operation
INSERT INTO dbo.T1 WITH (TABLOCK) (n, filler)
  SELECT n, CAST('a' AS CHAR(2000)) AS filler
  FROM dbo.Nums
  WHERE n BETWEEN 200001 AND 300000
  ORDER BY n;
```

Notice that the key range for the inserted rows is new (between 200,001 and 300,000). In other words, the inserted rows do not enter existing pages; instead, they populate newly allocated pages. The following output shows the logging information that I got on my system for this test:

numrecords	size_mb	duration_sec
209969	208.91	11.000

n	lb	hb	numrecords
1	59	555.2	109876
2	555.2	1050.4	0
3	1050.4	1545.6	0
4	1545.6	2040.8	0
5	2040.8	2536	100000
6	2536	3031.2	0

7	3031.2	3526.4	0
8	3526.4	4021.6	0
9	4021.6	4516.8	1
10	4516.8	5012	92

Operation	Context	AvgLen	Cnt
LOP_DELETE_SPLIT	LCX_CLUSTERED	60	1
LOP_DELETE_SPLIT	LCX_INDEX_INTERIOR	60	92
LOP_SET_BITS	LCX_GAM	60	3137
LOP_SET_BITS	LCX_IAM	60	3137
LOP_MODIFY_ROW	LCX_PFS	80	28230
LOP_FORMAT_PAGE	LCX_HEAP	84	25001
LOP_FORMAT_PAGE	LCX_INDEX_INTERIOR	84	92
LOP_INSERT_ROWS	LCX_INDEX_INTERIOR	84	25093
LOP_MODIFY_HEADER	LCX_HEAP	84	25001
LOP_MODIFY_HEADER	LCX_INDEX_INTERIOR	84	92
LOP_INSERT_ROWS	LCX_CLUSTERED	2096	100000
LOP_INSERT_ROWS	LCX_CLUSTERED	4096	1
LOP_INSERT_ROWS	LCX_INDEX_INTERIOR	5012	92

As you can see, in this scenario the operation was fully logged. In addition to the log records for each INSERT statement, there are log records for page allocations (including leaf and nonleaf pages), log records for each insertion into a nonleaf page, and log records for the updates of the GAM, IAM, and PFS bitmaps.

Scenario 8: INSERT SELECT, Nonempty B-Tree, TABLOCK, TF-610 On, New Key Range This scenario is similar to Scenario 7, except that this time you turn on TF-610. This trace flag is available in SQL Server 2008 to enable minimal logging against a B-tree even when not using the TABLOCK hint and for new key ranges that allocate and populate new pages even when the target is nonempty.

Turn this trace flag on for your SQL Server 2008 instance by running the following code:

```
DBCC TRACEON(610, -1);
DBCC TRACESTATUS;
```

You can also turn this trace flag on whenever SQL Server starts by specifying -T610 as a the service startup parameter.

Now, with the trace flag turned on, the following code provides the Preparation and Operation parts of this test:

```
-- Preparation
IF OBJECT_ID('dbo.T1', 'U') IS NOT NULL DROP TABLE dbo.T1;

CREATE TABLE dbo.T1
(
  n INT NOT NULL,
  filler CHAR(2000) NOT NULL
);

CREATE UNIQUE CLUSTERED INDEX idx_n ON dbo.T1(n);
```

```
INSERT INTO dbo.T1 WITH (TABLOCK) (n, filler)
  SELECT n, CAST('a' AS CHAR(2000)) AS filler
  FROM dbo.Nums
  WHERE n <= 200000
    AND n % 2 = 0
  ORDER BY n;

CHECKPOINT;
GO

-- Operation
INSERT INTO dbo.T1 WITH (TABLOCK) (n, filler)
  SELECT n, CAST('a' AS CHAR(2000)) AS filler
  FROM dbo.Nums
  WHERE n BETWEEN 200001 AND 300000
  ORDER BY n;
```

I got the following logging information on my system for this test:

numrecords	size_mb	duration_sec
135131	10.94	15.000

n	lb	hb	numrecords
1	59	555.2	135036
2	555.2	1050.4	0
3	1050.4	1545.6	0
4	1545.6	2040.8	0
5	2040.8	2536	2
6	2536	3031.2	0
7	3031.2	3526.4	0
8	3526.4	4021.6	0
9	4021.6	4516.8	1
10	4516.8	5012	92

Operation	Context	AvgLen	Cnt
LOP_DELETE_SPLIT	LCX_CLUSTERED	60	1
LOP_DELETE_SPLIT	LCX_INDEX_INTERIOR	60	92
LOP_SET_BITS	LCX_GAM	60	3142
LOP_SET_BITS	LCX_IAM	60	3142
LOP_MODIFY_HEADER	LCX_BULK_OPERATION_PAGE	76	25093
LOP_FORMAT_PAGE	LCX_BULK_OPERATION_PAGE	84	25120
LOP_FORMAT_PAGE	LCX_INDEX_INTERIOR	84	92
LOP_INSERT_ROWS	LCX_INDEX_INTERIOR	84	25093
LOP_MODIFY_HEADER	LCX_HEAP	84	50002
LOP_MODIFY_HEADER	LCX_INDEX_INTERIOR	84	92
LOP_MODIFY_ROW	LCX_PFS	88	3167
LOP_INSERT_ROWS	LCX_CLUSTERED	2096	2
LOP_INSERT_ROWS	LCX_CLUSTERED	4096	1
LOP_INSERT_ROWS	LCX_INDEX_INTERIOR	5012	92

As you can see, this scenario produced minimal logging. A bit more logging is involved here (~10 MB) compared to what was needed for an empty B-tree (~1 MB) because more changes are required to balance the tree.

When you want to turn trace flag 610 off, run the following code:

```
DBCC TRACEOFF(610, -1);
DBCC TRACESTATUS;
```

Scenario 9: INSERT SELECT, Nonempty B-Tree, TABLOCK, Merged Key Range   This
scenario is similar to Scenario 7, except that here the new keys are such that the new rows are
merged into existing pages. In this scenario, regardless of whether TF-610 is on or off, rows
inserted into existing pages will be fully logged.

The following code provides the Preparation and Operation sections you need to demonstrate
the full logging involved with inserts into existing pages:

```
-- Preparation
IF OBJECT_ID('dbo.T1', 'U') IS NOT NULL DROP TABLE dbo.T1;

CREATE TABLE dbo.T1
(
  n INT NOT NULL,
  filler CHAR(2000) NOT NULL
);

CREATE UNIQUE CLUSTERED INDEX idx_n ON dbo.T1(n);

INSERT INTO dbo.T1 WITH (TABLOCK) (n, filler)
  SELECT n, CAST('a' AS CHAR(2000)) AS filler
  FROM dbo.Nums
  WHERE n <= 200000
    AND n % 2 = 0
  ORDER BY n;

CHECKPOINT;
GO

-- Operation
INSERT INTO dbo.T1 WITH (TABLOCK) (n, filler)
  SELECT n, CAST('a' AS CHAR(2000)) AS filler
  FROM dbo.Nums
  WHERE n <= 200000
    AND n % 2 = 1
  ORDER BY n;
```

Before the INSERT SELECT statement in the Operation section is executed, there are already
100,000 rows in table T1, and the primary key values in those rows are the even numbers up
to 200,000. The INSERT SELECT statement inserts 100,000 new rows using as primary keys
the odd numbers from dbo.Nums that are smaller than 200,000. I got the following logging
information on my system for this test both when TF-610 was turned off and when it was
turned on:

```
numrecords  size_mb  duration_sec
----------- -------- ------------
284972       309.94   24.000
```

n	lb	hb	numrecords
1	59	555.2	159891
2	555.2	1050.4	0
3	1050.4	1545.6	0
4	1545.6	2040.8	0
5	2040.8	2536	100000
6	2536	3031.2	0
7	3031.2	3526.4	0
8	3526.4	4021.6	0
9	4021.6	4516.8	25001
10	4516.8	5012	80

Operation	Context	AvgLen	Cnt
LOP_DELETE_SPLIT	LCX_CLUSTERED	60	25001
LOP_DELETE_SPLIT	LCX_INDEX_INTERIOR	60	80
LOP_SET_BITS	LCX_GAM	60	3136
LOP_SET_BITS	LCX_IAM	60	3136
LOP_MODIFY_ROW	LCX_PFS	80	28217
LOP_FORMAT_PAGE	LCX_HEAP	84	25001
LOP_FORMAT_PAGE	LCX_INDEX_INTERIOR	84	80
LOP_INSERT_ROWS	LCX_INDEX_INTERIOR	84	25081
LOP_MODIFY_HEADER	LCX_HEAP	84	50002
LOP_MODIFY_HEADER	LCX_INDEX_INTERIOR	84	160
LOP_INSERT_ROWS	LCX_CLUSTERED	2096	100000
LOP_INSERT_ROWS	LCX_CLUSTERED	4096	25001
LOP_INSERT_ROWS	LCX_INDEX_INTERIOR	5012	80

You can see that in addition to the full logging of the 100,000 inserted rows (each with ~2,000 bytes), significant logging also occurred because of page splits that caused rows to move (25,001 times ~4,000 bytes). The total amount of logging was more than 300 MB.

Remember that only new key ranges that allocate and populate new pages will be minimally logged when TF-610 is on. Of course the rows you insert could cover both existing and new key ranges. When that's the case, rows destined for existing pages will be fully logged and rows destined for new pages minimally logged when trace flag 610 is on.

Scenario 10: INSERT SELECT, Empty B-Tree, Without TABLOCK, TF-610 Off   This scenario is similar to Scenario 6 except that here you do not specify the TABLOCK option. Remember that in this scenario TF-610 is off. Use the following Preparation and Operation parts for this test:

```
-- Preparation
DBCC TRACEOFF(610, -1);

IF OBJECT_ID('dbo.T1', 'U') IS NOT NULL DROP TABLE dbo.T1;

CREATE TABLE dbo.T1
(
  n INT NOT NULL,
  filler CHAR(2000) NOT NULL
);

CREATE UNIQUE CLUSTERED INDEX idx_n ON dbo.T1(n);
```

```
CHECKPOINT;
GO

-- Operation
INSERT INTO dbo.T1 (n, filler)
  SELECT n, CAST('a' AS CHAR(2000)) AS filler
  FROM dbo.Nums
  WHERE n <= 200000
    AND n % 2 = 0
  ORDER BY n;
```

I got the following logging information on my system for this test:

```
numrecords  size_mb  duration_sec
----------- -------- ------------
209967      209.20   11.000
```

n	lb	hb	numrecords
1	59	555.2	109876
2	555.2	1050.4	0
3	1050.4	1545.6	0
4	1545.6	2040.8	0
5	2040.8	2536	100000
6	2536	3031.2	0
7	3031.2	3526.4	0
8	3526.4	4021.6	0
9	4021.6	4516.8	0
10	4516.8	5012	91

Operation	Context	AvgLen	Cnt
LOP_DELETE_SPLIT	LCX_INDEX_INTERIOR	60	91
LOP_SET_BITS	LCX_GAM	60	3136
LOP_SET_BITS	LCX_IAM	60	3136
LOP_MODIFY_ROW	LCX_PFS	80	28229
LOP_FORMAT_PAGE	LCX_HEAP	84	25000
LOP_FORMAT_PAGE	LCX_IAM	84	1
LOP_FORMAT_PAGE	LCX_INDEX_INTERIOR	84	93
LOP_INSERT_ROWS	LCX_INDEX_INTERIOR	84	25092
LOP_MODIFY_HEADER	LCX_HEAP	84	24999
LOP_MODIFY_HEADER	LCX_INDEX_INTERIOR	84	91
LOP_MODIFY_ROW	LCX_IAM	88	8
LOP_INSERT_ROWS	LCX_CLUSTERED	2099	100000
LOP_INSERT_ROWS	LCX_INDEX_INTERIOR	5012	91

As you can see, this scenario involves full logging because the TABLOCK option wasn't used and trace flag 610 was off.

Scenario 11: INSERT SELECT, Empty B-Tree, Without TABLOCK, TF-610 On   This scenario is similar to Scenario 10 except that here you run it when TF-610 is on. The following code contains the Preparation and Operation Parts for this test:

```
-- Preparation
DBCC TRACEON(610, -1);
```

```
IF OBJECT_ID('dbo.T1', 'U') IS NOT NULL DROP TABLE dbo.T1;

CREATE TABLE dbo.T1
(
  n INT NOT NULL,
  filler CHAR(2000) NOT NULL
);

CREATE UNIQUE CLUSTERED INDEX idx_n ON dbo.T1(n);

CHECKPOINT;
GO

-- Operation
INSERT INTO dbo.T1 (n, filler)
  SELECT n, CAST('a' AS CHAR(2000)) AS filler
  FROM dbo.Nums
  WHERE n <= 200000
    AND n % 2 = 0
  ORDER BY n;
```

I got the following logging information on my system for this test:

numrecords	size_mb	duration_sec
135160	10.94	18.000

n	lb	hb	numrecords
1	59	555.2	135065
2	555.2	1050.4	0
3	1050.4	1545.6	0
4	1545.6	2040.8	0
5	2040.8	2536	4
6	2536	3031.2	0
7	3031.2	3526.4	0
8	3526.4	4021.6	0
9	4021.6	4516.8	0
10	4516.8	5012	91

Operation	Context	AvgLen	Cnt
LOP_DELETE_SPLIT	LCX_INDEX_INTERIOR	60	91
LOP_SET_BITS	LCX_GAM	60	3144
LOP_SET_BITS	LCX_IAM	60	3144
LOP_MODIFY_HEADER	LCX_BULK_OPERATION_PAGE	76	25092
LOP_FORMAT_PAGE	LCX_BULK_OPERATION_PAGE	84	25127
LOP_FORMAT_PAGE	LCX_HEAP	84	1
LOP_FORMAT_PAGE	LCX_IAM	84	1
LOP_FORMAT_PAGE	LCX_INDEX_INTERIOR	84	93
LOP_INSERT_ROWS	LCX_INDEX_INTERIOR	84	25092
LOP_MODIFY_HEADER	LCX_HEAP	84	49998
LOP_MODIFY_HEADER	LCX_INDEX_INTERIOR	84	91
LOP_MODIFY_ROW	LCX_IAM	88	8
LOP_MODIFY_ROW	LCX_PFS	88	3183
LOP_INSERT_ROWS	LCX_CLUSTERED	2112	4
LOP_INSERT_ROWS	LCX_INDEX_INTERIOR	5012	91

As you can see, this time there was minimal logging; compared to the previous scenario, you only had to turn on TF-610 to allow minimal logging.

Scenario 12: INSERT SELECT, Nonempty B-Tree, without TABLOCK, TF-610 Off, New Key Range   This scenario is similar to Scenario 7 except that here you don't specify the TABLOCK hint. Note that when TF-610 is not turned on and the TABLOCK hint isn't specified, you get full logging regardless of whether the target table is empty. Use the following Preparation and Operation parts to test this scenario:

```
-- Preparation
DBCC TRACEOFF(610, -1);

IF OBJECT_ID('dbo.T1', 'U') IS NOT NULL DROP TABLE dbo.T1;

CREATE TABLE dbo.T1
(
  n INT NOT NULL,
  filler CHAR(2000) NOT NULL
);

CREATE UNIQUE CLUSTERED INDEX idx_n ON dbo.T1(n);

INSERT INTO dbo.T1 WITH (TABLOCK) (n, filler)
  SELECT n, CAST('a' AS CHAR(2000)) AS filler
  FROM dbo.Nums
  WHERE n <= 200000
    AND n % 2 = 0
  ORDER BY n;

CHECKPOINT;
GO

-- Operation
INSERT INTO dbo.T1 (n, filler)
  SELECT n, CAST('a' AS CHAR(2000)) AS filler
  FROM dbo.Nums
  WHERE n BETWEEN 200001 AND 300000
  ORDER BY n;
```

Here's the logging information I got for this test on my system:

```
numrecords  size_mb  duration_sec
----------- -------- ------------
209969      209.21   9.000
```

n	lb	hb	numrecords
1	59	555.2	109876
2	555.2	1050.4	0
3	1050.4	1545.6	0
4	1545.6	2040.8	0
5	2040.8	2536	100000
6	2536	3031.2	0
7	3031.2	3526.4	0

8	3526.4	4021.6	0
9	4021.6	4516.8	0
10	4516.8	5012	93

Operation	Context	AvgLen	Cnt
LOP_DELETE_SPLIT	LCX_INDEX_INTERIOR	60	93
LOP_SET_BITS	LCX_GAM	60	3137
LOP_SET_BITS	LCX_IAM	60	3137
LOP_MODIFY_ROW	LCX_PFS	80	28230
LOP_FORMAT_PAGE	LCX_HEAP	84	25000
LOP_FORMAT_PAGE	LCX_INDEX_INTERIOR	84	93
LOP_INSERT_ROWS	LCX_INDEX_INTERIOR	84	25093
LOP_MODIFY_HEADER	LCX_HEAP	84	25000
LOP_MODIFY_HEADER	LCX_INDEX_INTERIOR	84	93
LOP_INSERT_ROWS	LCX_CLUSTERED	2099	100000
LOP_INSERT_ROWS	LCX_INDEX_INTERIOR	5012	93

As you can see, full logging took place.

Scenario 13: INSERT SELECT, Nonempty B-Tree, without TABLOCK, TF-610 On, New Key Range   This scenario is identical to Scenario 12 except that this time TF-610 is on. It is also the same as Scenario 8 without the TABLOCK option. Use the following Preparation and Operation parts to test this scenario:

```
-- Preparation
DBCC TRACEON(610, -1);

IF OBJECT_ID('dbo.T1', 'U') IS NOT NULL DROP TABLE dbo.T1;

CREATE TABLE dbo.T1
(
  n INT NOT NULL,
  filler CHAR(2000) NOT NULL
);

CREATE UNIQUE CLUSTERED INDEX idx_n ON dbo.T1(n);

INSERT INTO dbo.T1 WITH (TABLOCK) (n, filler)
  SELECT n, CAST('a' AS CHAR(2000)) AS filler
  FROM dbo.Nums
  WHERE n <= 200000
    AND n % 2 = 0
  ORDER BY n;

CHECKPOINT;
GO

-- Operation
INSERT INTO dbo.T1(n, filler)
  SELECT n, CAST('a' AS CHAR(2000)) AS filler
  FROM dbo.Nums
  WHERE n BETWEEN 200001 AND 300000
  ORDER BY n;
```

I got the following logging information for this test on my system:

```
numrecords  size_mb  duration_sec
----------- -------- ------------
135131      10.94    16.000
```

```
n           lb                      hb                      numrecords
----------- ----------------------- ----------------------- -----------
1           59                      555.2                   135038
2           555.2                   1050.4                  0
3           1050.4                  1545.6                  0
4           1545.6                  2040.8                  0
5           2040.8                  2536                    0
6           2536                    3031.2                  0
7           3031.2                  3526.4                  0
8           3526.4                  4021.6                  0
9           4021.6                  4516.8                  0
10          4516.8                  5012                    93
```

```
Operation          Context                  AvgLen      Cnt
------------------ ------------------------ ----------- -----------
LOP_DELETE_SPLIT   LCX_INDEX_INTERIOR       60          93
LOP_SET_BITS       LCX_GAM                  60          3143
LOP_SET_BITS       LCX_IAM                  60          3143
LOP_MODIFY_HEADER  LCX_BULK_OPERATION_PAGE  76          25093
LOP_FORMAT_PAGE    LCX_BULK_OPERATION_PAGE  84          25120
LOP_FORMAT_PAGE    LCX_INDEX_INTERIOR       84          93
LOP_INSERT_ROWS    LCX_INDEX_INTERIOR       84          25093
LOP_MODIFY_HEADER  LCX_HEAP                 84          50000
LOP_MODIFY_HEADER  LCX_INDEX_INTERIOR       84          93
LOP_MODIFY_ROW     LCX_PFS                  88          3167
LOP_INSERT_ROWS    LCX_INDEX_INTERIOR       5012        93
```

As you can see, this time the test generated minimal logging. So even when the TABLOCK hint isn't specified, turning TF-610 on will provide minimal logging of rows inserted into new key ranges.

Scenario 14: INSERT SELECT, Nonempty B-Tree, without TABLOCK, Merged Key Range   The last scenario is similar to Scenario 9 but without the TABLOCK option. Whenever you insert rows into existing pages of a B-tree, you get full logging—regardless of whether you use TABLOCK and regardless of whether TF-610 is on or off. To test this scenario, use the following Preparation and Operation parts:

```
-- Preparation
IF OBJECT_ID('dbo.T1', 'U') IS NOT NULL DROP TABLE dbo.T1;

CREATE TABLE dbo.T1
(
  n INT NOT NULL,
  filler CHAR(2000) NOT NULL
);

CREATE UNIQUE CLUSTERED INDEX idx_n ON dbo.T1(n);
```

```
INSERT INTO dbo.T1 WITH (TABLOCK) (n, filler)
  SELECT n, CAST('a' AS CHAR(2000)) AS filler
  FROM dbo.Nums
  WHERE n <= 200000
    AND n % 2 = 0
  ORDER BY n;

CHECKPOINT;
GO

-- Operation
INSERT INTO dbo.T1(n, filler)
  SELECT n, CAST('a' AS CHAR(2000)) AS filler
  FROM dbo.Nums
  WHERE n <= 200000
    AND n % 2 = 1
```

Both when TF-610 was on and when it was off, I got the following logging information indicating full logging:

```
numrecords  size_mb  duration_sec
----------- -------- ------------
284385      309.67   12.000
```

n	lb	hb	numrecords
1	59	463.6	159384
2	463.6	867.2	0
3	867.2	1270.8	0
4	1270.8	1674.4	0
5	1674.4	2078	0
6	2078	2481.6	100000
7	2481.6	2885.2	0
8	2885.2	3288.8	0
9	3288.8	3692.4	0
10	3692.4	4096	25001

Operation	Context	AvgLen	Cnt
LOP_DELETE_SPLIT	LCX_CLUSTERED	60	25001
LOP_SET_BITS	LCX_GAM	60	3126
LOP_SET_BITS	LCX_IAM	60	3126
LOP_MODIFY_ROW	LCX_PFS	80	28127
LOP_FORMAT_PAGE	LCX_HEAP	84	25001
LOP_INSERT_ROWS	LCX_INDEX_INTERIOR	84	25001
LOP_MODIFY_HEADER	LCX_HEAP	84	50002
LOP_INSERT_ROWS	LCX_CLUSTERED	2097	100000
LOP_INSERT_ROWS	LCX_CLUSTERED	4096	25001

Remember that you can have a mixed case with some key ranges that are new and with some rows destined for existing pages. For rows with key ranges that are new, you get minimal logging when TF-610 is on regardless of whether the TABLOCK hint is used. For rows inserted into existing pages, you always get full logging.

Summary of Minimal Logging

This section summarizes the requirements for minimal logging.

The SELECT INTO statement has one requirement to be processed with minimal logging—the database recovery model should be set to a non-FULL recovery model (SIMPLE or BULK_LOGGED). Note that if you're populating a temporary table, what matters is tempdb's recovery model, which is SIMPLE and can't be changed.

You can summarize the requirements for minimal logging for the other insert methods (BULK INSERT, bcp.exe, INSERT SELECT FROM OPENROWSET(BULK . . .), and regular INSERT SELECT) with the following logical expression:

```
    non-FULL recovery model
AND not replicated
AND (
        (Heap AND TABLOCK)
    OR (B-tree AND empty AND TABLOCK)
    OR (B-tree AND empty AND TF-610)
    OR (B-tree AND nonempty AND TF-610 AND new key-range)
    )
```

SQL Server 2008 introduces support for minimal logging with the regular INSERT SELECT statement. The INSERT SELECT method is sometimes preferable to SELECT INTO because it does not involve locks on metadata, and it gives you control over the schema of the target table that you create.

SQL Server 2008 also introduces support for minimal logging when inserting data into a nonempty B-tree (clustered or nonclustered index). Minimal logging is used when inserting new key ranges that allocate and populate new pages while TF-610 is on regardless of whether the TABLOCK hint is specified. For those new key ranges, SQL Server internally takes key-range locks to ensure that other processes don't run conflicting activities.

I demonstrated only a sample of the possible insert scenarios just to give you a sense of how you can do your own research. Using the tools I provided here, you can figure out for yourself what kind of logging you get for the scenarios that are of interest to you.

Unfortunately, the INSERT EXEC and MERGE statements currently do not support minimal logging.

INSERT EXEC

The INSERT EXEC statement allows you to direct a table result set returned from a stored procedure or dynamic batch to an existing table:

```
INSERT INTO <target_table> EXEC {<proc_name> | (<dynamic_batch>)};
```

This statement is very handy when you need to set aside the result set of a stored procedure or dynamic batch for further processing at the server, as opposed to just returning the result set back to the client.

I'll demonstrate practical uses of the INSERT EXEC statement through an example. Recall the discussion about paging techniques in Chapter 9, "TOP and APPLY." I provided a stored procedure called *GetFirstPage*, which returns the first page of orders based on *orderdate*, *orderid* ordering. I also provided a stored procedure called *GetNextPage*, which returns the next page of orders based on an input key (*@anchor*) representing the last row in the previous page. In this section, I will use slightly revised forms of the stored procedures, which I'll call *GetFirstRows* and *GetNextRows*. Run the following code to create both procedures:

```
USE InsideTSQL2008;
GO

-- Index for paging problem
IF INDEXPROPERTY(OBJECT_ID('Sales.Orders'),
      'idx_od_oid_i_cid_eid', 'IndexID') IS NOT NULL
  DROP INDEX Sales.Orders.idx_od_oid_i_cid_eid;
GO
CREATE INDEX idx_od_oid_i_cid_eid
  ON Sales.Orders(orderdate, orderid, custid, empid);
GO

-- First Rows
IF OBJECT_ID('dbo.GetFirstRows') IS NOT NULL
  DROP PROC dbo.GetFirstRows;
GO
CREATE PROC dbo.GetFirstRows
  @n AS INT = 10 -- num rows
AS
SELECT TOP(@n) ROW_NUMBER() OVER(ORDER BY orderdate, orderid) AS rownum,
  orderid, orderdate, custid, empid
FROM Sales.Orders
ORDER BY orderdate, orderid;
GO

-- Next Rows
IF OBJECT_ID('dbo.GetNextRows') IS NOT NULL
  DROP PROC dbo.GetNextRows;
GO
CREATE PROC dbo.GetNextRows
  @anchor_rownum  AS INT = 0, -- row number of last row in prev page
  @anchor_key     AS INT,     -- key of last row in prev page,
  @n              AS INT = 10 -- num rows
AS
SELECT TOP(@n)
  @anchor_rownum
    + ROW_NUMBER() OVER(ORDER BY O.orderdate, O.orderid) AS rownum,
  O.orderid, O.orderdate, O.custid, O.empid
FROM Sales.Orders AS O
  JOIN Sales.Orders AS A
```

```
      ON A.orderid = @anchor_key
      AND (O.orderdate >= A.orderdate
            AND (O.orderdate > A.orderdate
                  OR O.orderid > A.orderid))
ORDER BY O.orderdate, O.orderid;
GO
```

The stored procedure *GetFirstRows* returns the first *@n* rows of Orders, based on *orderdate* and *orderid* ordering. In addition to the columns that *GetFirstPage* returned, *GetFirstRows* (as well as *GetNextRows*) also returns *rownum*, a column representing the global logical position of the row in the full Orders table under the aforementioned ordering. Because *GetFirstRows* returns the first page of rows, *rownum* is just the row number within the result set.

The stored procedure *GetNextRows* returns the *@n* rows following an anchor row, whose key is provided as input (*@anchor_key*). For a row in the result set of *GetNextRows*, *rownum* equals the anchor's global row number (*@anchor_rownum*) plus the result row's logical position within the qualifying set. If you don't want the stored procedure to return a global row number—rather, just the row number within the qualifying set—don't specify a value in the input parameter. In such a case, the default 0 is used as the anchor row number, and the minimum row number assigned is 1.

Suppose you want to allow the user to request any range of rows without limiting the solution to forward-only paging. You also want to avoid rescanning large portions of data from the Orders table. You need to develop some caching mechanism where you set aside a copy of the rows you already scanned, along with row numbers representing their global logical position throughout the pages. Upon a request for a range of rows (a page), you first check whether rows are missing from the cache. In such a case, you insert the missing rows into the cache. You then query the cache to return the requested page. Here's an example of how you can implement a server-side solution of such a mechanism.

Run the following code to create the #CachedPages temporary table:

```
IF OBJECT_ID('tempdb..#CachedPages') IS NOT NULL
  DROP TABLE #CachedPages;
GO
CREATE TABLE #CachedPages
(
  rownum      INT       NOT NULL PRIMARY KEY,
  orderid     INT       NOT NULL UNIQUE,
  orderdate   DATETIME  NOT NULL,
  custid      INT       NOT NULL,
  empid       INT       NOT NULL
);
```

The caching logic is encapsulated in the stored procedure *GetPage*, which you create by running the following code:

```
IF OBJECT_ID('dbo.GetPage') IS NOT NULL
  DROP PROC dbo.GetPage;
GO
```

```
CREATE PROC dbo.GetPage
  @from_rownum AS INT,        -- row number of first row in requested page
  @to_rownum   AS INT,        -- row number of last row in requested page
  @rc          AS INT OUTPUT -- number of rows returned
AS

SET NOCOUNT ON;

DECLARE
  @last_key    AS INT, -- key of last row in #CachedPages
  @last_rownum AS INT, -- row number of last row in #CachedPages
  @numrows     AS INT; -- number of missing rows in #CachedPages

-- Get anchor values from last cached row
SELECT @last_rownum = rownum, @last_key = orderid
FROM (SELECT TOP(1) rownum, orderid
      FROM #CachedPages ORDER BY rownum DESC) AS D;

-- If temporary table is empty insert first rows to #CachedPages
IF @last_rownum IS NULL
  INSERT INTO #CachedPages
    EXEC dbo.GetFirstRows
      @n = @to_rownum;
ELSE
BEGIN
  SET @numrows = @to_rownum - @last_rownum;
  IF @numrows > 0
    INSERT INTO #CachedPages
      EXEC dbo.GetNextRows
        @anchor_rownum = @last_rownum,
        @anchor_key    = @last_key,
        @n             = @numrows;
END

-- Return requested page
SELECT *
FROM #CachedPages
WHERE rownum BETWEEN @from_rownum AND @to_rownum
ORDER BY rownum;

SET @rc = @@rowcount;
GO
```

The stored procedure accepts the row numbers representing the first row in the requested page (*@from_rownum*) and the last (*@to_rownum*) as inputs. Besides returning the requested page of rows, the stored procedure also returns an output parameter holding the number of rows returned (*@rc*). You can inspect the output parameter to determine whether you've reached the last page.

The stored procedure's code first queries the #CachedPages temporary table to store in the local variables *@last_rownum* and *@last_key* the row number and key of the last cached row, respectively. If the temporary table is empty (*@last_rownum IS NULL*), the code invokes the *GetFirstRows* procedure with an INSERT EXEC statement to populate #CachedPages with the first rows up to the requested high boundary row number. If the temporary table already contains rows, the code checks whether rows from the requested page are missing from it (@to_rownum - @last_rownum > 0). In such a case, the code invokes the *GetNextRows* procedure to insert all missing rows up to the requested high boundary row number to the temporary table.

Finally, the code queries the #CachedPages temporary table to return the requested range of rows, and it stores the number of returned rows in the output parameter *@rc*.

To get the first page of rows, assuming a page size of 10, run the following code:

```
DECLARE @rc AS INT;

EXEC dbo.GetPage
  @from_rownum = 1,
  @to_rownum   = 10,
  @rc          = @rc OUTPUT;

IF @rc = 0
  PRINT 'No more pages.'
ELSE IF @rc < 10
  PRINT 'Reached last page.';
```

You get back the first 10 rows based on *orderdate* and *orderid* ordering. Notice in the code that you can inspect the output parameter to determine whether there are no more pages (*@rc = 0*) or whether you've reached the last page (*@rc < 10*).

Query the #CachedPages temporary table, and you can see that 10 rows were cached:

```
SELECT * FROM #CachedPages;
```

Further requests for rows that were already cached will be satisfied from #CachedPages without the need to access the Orders table. Querying #CachedPages is very efficient because the table contains a clustered index on the *rownum* column. Only the requested rows are physically accessed.

If you now run the preceding code specifying row numbers 21 to 30 as inputs, the *GetPage* procedure adds rows 11 through 30 to the temporary table and returns rows 21 through 30. Subsequent requests for rows up to row 30 will be satisfied solely from the temporary table.

Once you're done experimenting with this paging technique, run the following code for cleanup:

```
IF OBJECT_ID('tempdb..#CachedPages') IS NOT NULL
  DROP TABLE #CachedPages;
GO
IF INDEXPROPERTY(OBJECT_ID('Sales.Orders'),
     'idx_od_oid_i_cid_eid', 'IndexID') IS NOT NULL
  DROP INDEX Sales.Orders.idx_od_oid_i_cid_eid;
GO
```

```
IF OBJECT_ID('dbo.GetFirstRows') IS NOT NULL
  DROP PROC dbo.GetFirstRows;
GO
IF OBJECT_ID('dbo.GetNextRows') IS NOT NULL
  DROP PROC dbo.GetNextRows;
GO
IF OBJECT_ID('dbo.GetPage') IS NOT NULL
  DROP PROC dbo.GetPage;
GO
```

Sequence Mechanisms

Sequence mechanisms produce numbers that you usually use as keys. SQL Server provides a sequencing mechanism via the IDENTITY column property. The IDENTITY property has several characteristics that might cause you to look for an alternative sequencing mechanism. In this section, I'll describe some of these characteristics and alternative mechanisms to generate keys—some that use built-in features, such as globally unique identifiers (GUIDs), and some that you can develop yourself.

Identity Columns

The IDENTITY property can be convenient when you want SQL Server to generate single column keys in a table. To guarantee uniqueness, create a PRIMARY KEY or UNIQUE constraint on the identity column. Upon INSERT, SQL Server increments the table's identity value and stores it in the new row.

However, several aspects of the IDENTITY property might make it an impractical sequencing mechanism for some applications.

One aspect is that the IDENTITY property is table dependent. It's not an independent sequencing mechanism that assigns new values that you can then use in any manner you like. Imagine that you need to generate sequence values that will be used as keys that cannot conflict across tables.

Another aspect is that an identity value is generated when an INSERT statement is issued, not before. In some cases you might need to generate the new sequence value and then use it in an INSERT statement and not the other way around.

Another aspect of the IDENTITY property that can be considered a limitation in some cases is that identity values are assigned in an asynchronous manner. This means that multiple sessions issuing multirow inserts might end up getting nonsequential identity values. Moreover, the assignment of a new identity value is not part of the transaction in which the INSERT was issued. The identity resource is internally locked momentarily when the value is incremented but not for the duration of the transaction. These facts have several implications. SQL Server increments the table's identity value regardless of whether the insert succeeds or fails and whether the transaction hosting the insert succeeds or fails. You might end up with gaps in the sequence that were not generated by deletions. Some systems cannot allow missing values that cannot be accounted for (for example, some invoicing systems). Try telling the Internal Revenue Service that some of the missing invoice IDs in your system are a result of the nonblocking manner in which identity values are managed.

Custom Sequences

I'll suggest a couple of solutions to the problem of maintaining a custom sequencing mechanism. I'll show solutions with both blocking and nonblocking sequence mechanisms. With a blocking sequence mechanism, the sequence resource is locked for the duration of the transaction. This prevents gaps from occurring in the sequence values. With a nonblocking sequence mechanism, the sequence resource is not locked for the duration of the transaction. This mechanism gives better performance than the blocking one, but gaps in the sequence values are possible.

Blocking Sequences   You need a blocking sequence mechanism when you must account for all values in the sequence. The classic scenario for such a sequence is generating invoice numbers. The way to guarantee that no gaps occur is to lock the sequence resource when you need to increment it and release the lock only when the transaction is finished. If you think about it, that's exactly how exclusive locks behave when you modify data in a transaction—that is, a lock is acquired to modify data, and it's released when the transaction is finished (committed or rolled back). To maintain such a sequence, create a table with a single row and a single column holding the last sequence value used. Initially, populate it with a zero if you want the first value in the sequence to be 1:

```
USE tempdb;
IF OBJECT_ID('dbo.Sequence') IS NOT NULL DROP TABLE dbo.Sequence;
CREATE TABLE dbo.Sequence(val INT);
GO
INSERT INTO dbo.Sequence VALUES(0);
```

Now that the sequence table is in place, I'll describe how you get a single sequence value or a block of consecutive sequence values at once.

Single Sequence Value   To get a single sequence value, you increment the sequence value by 1 and return the resulting value. You can achieve this by beginning a transaction, modifying the sequence value, and then retrieving it. Or you can both increment and retrieve the new sequence value in a single atomic operation using a specialized UPDATE syntax. Run the following code to create a stored procedure that uses the specialized T-SQL UPDATE syntax, increments the sequence value, and returns the new value as an output parameter:

```
IF OBJECT_ID('dbo.GetSequence') IS NOT NULL
  DROP PROC dbo.GetSequence;
GO

CREATE PROC dbo.GetSequence
  @val AS INT OUTPUT
AS
```

```
UPDATE dbo.Sequence
  SET @val = val = val + 1;
GO
```

The assignment *SET @val = val = val + 1* is equivalent to *SET val = val + 1, @val = val + 1*.
Note that SQL Server first locks the row exclusively and then increments *val*, retrieves it, and
releases the lock only when the transaction is completed.

Whenever you need a new sequence value, use the following code:

```
DECLARE @key AS INT;
EXEC dbo.GetSequence @val = @key OUTPUT;
SELECT @key;
```

To reset the sequence—for example, when the sequence value is about to overflow—set its
value to zero:

```
UPDATE dbo.Sequence SET val = 0;
```

Block of Sequence Values   If you want a mechanism to allocate a block of sequence values
all at once, you need to slightly alter the stored procedure's implementation as follows:

```
ALTER PROC dbo.GetSequence
  @val AS INT OUTPUT,
  @n   AS INT = 1
AS
UPDATE dbo.Sequence
  SET @val = val = val + @n;

SET @val = @val - @n + 1;
GO
```

In the additional argument (*@n*), you specify the block size (how many sequence values you
need). The stored procedure increments the current sequence value by *@n* and returns the
first value in the block via the *@val* output parameter. This procedure allocates the block
of sequence values from *@val* to *@val + @n – 1*.

The following code provides an example of acquiring and using a whole block of sequence values:

```
DECLARE @firstkey AS INT, @rc AS INT;

IF OBJECT_ID('tempdb..#CustsStage') IS NOT NULL DROP TABLE #CustsStage;

SELECT custid, ROW_NUMBER() OVER(ORDER BY (SELECT 0)) AS rownum
INTO #CustsStage
FROM InsideTSQL2008.Sales.Customers
WHERE country = N'UK';

SET @rc = @@rowcount;
EXEC dbo.GetSequence @val = @firstkey OUTPUT, @n = @rc;

SELECT custid, @firstkey + rownum - 1 AS keycol
FROM #CustsStage;
```

This example generates surrogate keys for UK customers. This code uses a SELECT INTO statement to insert UK customers into a temporary table called #CustsStage, along with row numbers (attribute *rownum*) calculated in no particular order. The code then stores the number of affected rows (*@@rowcount*) in the variable *@rc*. Next, the code invokes the *GetSequence* procedure to request a block of a size *@rc* of new sequence values. The stored procedure stores the first sequence value from the block in the variable *@firstkey* through the output parameter *@val*. Next, the code queries the #CustsStage table and calculates the surrogate customer key using the expression *@firstkey + rownum − 1*.

Nonblocking Sequences   The blocking sequencing mechanism doesn't allow gaps, but it might cause concurrency problems. Remember that you must exclusively lock the sequence to increment it, and then you must maintain the lock until the transaction finishes. The longer the transaction is, the longer you lock the sequence. Obviously, this solution can cause queues of processes waiting for the sequence resource to be released. But there's not much you can do if you want to maintain a blocking sequence.

However, in some cases you might not care about having gaps. For example, suppose that all you need is a key generator that guarantees that you don't generate the same key twice. Say that you need those keys to uniquely identify rows across tables. You don't want the sequence resource to be locked for the duration of the transaction. Rather, you want the sequence to be locked for a fraction of a second while incrementing it, just to prevent multiple processes from getting the same value. In other words, you need a nonblocking sequence, one that works much faster than the blocking one, allowing better concurrency.

One option that would address these requirements is to use built-in functions that SQL Server provides you to generate GUIDs. I'll discuss this option shortly. However, GUIDs are long (16 bytes). You might prefer to use integer sequence values, which are substantially smaller (4 bytes). To achieve such a nonblocking sequencing mechanism, you create a table (Sequence) with an identity column as follows:

```
USE tempdb;
IF OBJECT_ID('dbo.Sequence') IS NOT NULL DROP TABLE dbo.Sequence;
CREATE TABLE dbo.Sequence(val INT IDENTITY);
```

Create the following *GetSequence* procedure to generate a new sequence value and return it through the *@val* output parameter:

```
IF OBJECT_ID('dbo.GetSequence') IS NOT NULL
  DROP PROC dbo.GetSequence;
GO

CREATE PROC dbo.GetSequence
  @val AS INT OUTPUT
AS
BEGIN TRAN
  SAVE TRAN S1;
  INSERT INTO dbo.Sequence DEFAULT VALUES;
```

```
   SET @val = SCOPE_IDENTITY();
   ROLLBACK TRAN S1;
COMMIT TRAN
GO
```

The procedure opens a transaction just for the sake of creating a save point called S1. It inserts a new row to Sequence, which generates a new identity value in the table and stores it in the @val output parameter. The procedure then rolls back the INSERT. But a rollback doesn't undo a variable assignment, nor does it undo incrementing the identity value. Plus, the identity resource is not locked for the duration of an outer transaction; rather, it's locked only for a fraction of a second to increment. This behavior of the IDENTITY property is crucial for maintaining a nonblocking sequence.

> **Note** As of this writing, I haven't found any official documentation from Microsoft that describes this behavior of the IDENTITY property.

Rolling back to a save point ensures that the rollback does not have any effect on an external transaction. The rollback prevents the Sequence table from growing. In fact, it will never contain any committed rows from calls to *GetSequence*.

Whenever you need the next sequence value, run the *GetSequence*, just like you did with the blocking sequence:

```
DECLARE @key AS INT;
EXEC dbo.GetSequence @val = @key OUTPUT;
SELECT @key;
```

This time, however, the sequence does not block if you increment it within an external transaction. One drawback to this sequence solution is that it can generate only one sequence value at a time.

If you want to reset the sequence value, you can truncate the table, which resets the identity value:

```
TRUNCATE TABLE dbo.Sequence;
```

You can further optimize this sequencing mechanism by avoiding the rollback to undo the insertion. The stored procedure simply inserts a new row into the table and returns the newly generated identity value, like so:

```
IF OBJECT_ID('dbo.GetSequence') IS NOT NULL
   DROP PROC dbo.GetSequence;
GO

CREATE PROC dbo.GetSequence
   @val AS INT OUTPUT
AS
```

```
INSERT INTO dbo.Sequence DEFAULT VALUES;
SET @val = SCOPE_IDENTITY();
GO
```

As before, use the stored procedure to get new sequence values:

```
DECLARE @key AS INT;
EXEC dbo.GetSequence @val = @key OUTPUT;
SELECT @key;
```

The only problem is that the Sequence table keeps growing as new sequence values are generated. You need to run a job on scheduled basis that periodically clears the table. Be careful, though, with the technique that you use to clear the table. If you use a DELETE statement, it will take time to finish because it's a fully logged operation, and it might also cause lock escalation. If you use the minimally logged TRUNCATE TABLE statement, it will be fast, but the identity value will be reseeded. To use the fast TRUNCATE TABLE statement while preserving the seed before the emptying of the table, you need to do the following:

1. Open a transaction.

2. Lock the table.

3. Set aside the current identity value plus one.

4. Truncate the table.

5. Reseed the identity value to the value you kept aside.

6. Commit the transaction and release the lock.

Here's how the code might look:

```
BEGIN TRAN
  DECLARE @val AS INT;
  SELECT TOP (1) @val = val FROM dbo.Sequence WITH (TABLOCKX); -- lock table
  SET @val = IDENT_CURRENT('dbo.Sequence') + 1;
  TRUNCATE TABLE dbo.Sequence;
  DBCC CHECKIDENT('dbo.Sequence', RESEED, @val);
COMMIT
```

Run this code in a job on scheduled basis—say once a day—and you will get a faster sequencing mechanism, while the Sequence table won't get too large.

GUIDs

SQL Server provides you with the NEWID function, which generates a new GUID every time it is invoked. The function returns a 16-byte value typed as UNIQUEIDENTIFIER. If you need an automatic mechanism that assigns unique keys in a table or even across different tables, you can create a UNIQUEIDENTIFIER column with the default value NEWID(). The downside of a UNIQUEIDENTIFIER column used as a key is that it's pretty big—16 bytes. This, of course, has an impact on index sizes, join performance, and so on.

Note that the NEWID function does not guarantee that a newly generated GUID will be greater than any previously generated one in the same computer. If you need such a guarantee, use the NEWSEQUENTIALID function. Note that this function guarantees that a new value is greater than any previously generated one only on the same computer, not across computers.

Deleting Data

In this section, I'll cover different aspects of deleting data, including TRUNCATE versus DELETE, removing rows with duplicate data, DELETE using joins, and large DELETEs.

TRUNCATE vs. DELETE

If you need to remove all rows from a table, use TRUNCATE TABLE and not DELETE without a WHERE clause. DELETE is always fully logged, and with large tables it can take a while to complete. TRUNCATE TABLE is always minimally logged regardless of the recovery model of the database, and therefore it is always significantly faster than DELETE. Note, though, that TRUNCATE TABLE does not fire any DELETE triggers on the table. To give you a sense of the difference, using TRUNCATE TABLE to clear a table with millions of rows can take a matter of seconds, while clearing the table with DELETE can take hours.

> **Tip** SQL Server rejects DROP TABLE attempts if a schema-bound object is pointing to the target table. It rejects both DROP TABLE and TRUNCATE TABLE attempts if a foreign key is pointing to the target table. This limitation applies even when the foreign table is empty and even when the foreign key is disabled. If you want to prevent accidental TRUNCATE TABLE and DROP TABLE attempts against sensitive production tables, simply create dummy tables with foreign keys pointing to them and disable the foreign keys.

In addition to the substantial performance difference between TRUNCATE TABLE and DELETE, each also handles the IDENTITY property differently: TRUNCATE TABLE resets the IDENTITY property to its original seed, while DELETE doesn't.

Removing Rows with Duplicate Data

Duplicate data can arise for various reasons. Users might enter duplicate data by mistake, or an import process might be invoked accidentally more than once and so on. If you don't enforce data integrity with constraints such as primary keys and unique constraints or with other mechanisms, you may end up with duplicate data in your database. Of course, the best practice is to enforce uniqueness with constraints where the data is supposed to be unique. But sometimes you don't have control over the system, and sometimes you intentionally don't want to enforce uniqueness in special cases, such as a staging table in a data warehouse. Regardless of how you end up with duplicate data in your table, this section will provide you with a solution to remove rows with duplicate data.

To demonstrate techniques to remove rows with duplicate data, first create and populate the OrdersDups table in the tempdb database by running the following code:

```
USE tempdb;
IF OBJECT_ID('dbo.OrdersDups') IS NOT NULL DROP TABLE dbo.OrdersDups;
GO

SELECT orderid, custid, empid, orderdate
INTO dbo.OrdersDups
FROM InsideTSQL2008.Sales.Orders
  CROSS JOIN dbo.Nums
WHERE n <= 3;
```

OrdersDups contains three copies of each order, and the task at hand is to remove rows with duplicate data, keeping only one occurrence of each unique *orderid* value. I suggest two techniques for handling the task. The factor that determines which technique is most efficient is the percentage of rows that need to be removed out of the total number of rows in the table. With a small percentage, you're better off deleting the relevant rows directly from the table using a fully logged DELETE statement. However, with a large percentage, you might be better off copying the rows you need to keep to another table using a minimally logged operation, dropping the original table, renaming the new one to the original table name, and re-creating all constraints, indexes, and triggers.

Here's the code that implements the solution I recommend when a small percentage of rows needs to be removed:

```
WITH Dups AS
(
  SELECT orderid, custid, empid, orderdate,
    ROW_NUMBER() OVER(PARTITION BY orderid ORDER BY (SELECT 0)) AS rn
  FROM dbo.OrdersDups
)
DELETE FROM Dups
WHERE rn > 1;
```

The query defining the CTE Dups assigns row numbers to the rows from OrdersDups partitioned by *orderid*, in no particular order. Rows with the same *orderid* value are numbered starting at 1. Here I'm making the assumption that you don't care which of the duplicates you wish to keep. Of course, if you do have some preference when the rows are not completely identical copies, you can specify the applicable attributes in the ORDER BY clause of the ROW_NUMBER function. The outer DELETE statement against the CTE deletes all rows with a row number greater than 1, leaving a single row in the table for each unique *orderid* value.

My friend and colleague Javier Loria showed me another cool technique. You calculate both a row number and a rank for each row partitioned by *orderid* and then delete all rows where the two are different. For only one occurrence of each unique *orderid* value will the two be the same. The code looks like this:

```
WITH Dups AS
(
  SELECT orderid, custid, empid, orderdate,
    ROW_NUMBER() OVER(PARTITION BY orderid ORDER BY (SELECT 0)) AS rn,
    RANK() OVER(PARTITION BY orderid ORDER BY (SELECT 0)) AS rnk
  FROM dbo.OrdersDups
)
DELETE FROM Dups
WHERE rn <> rnk;
```

For a scenario with a large percentage of rows that need to be deleted, the solutions that apply a fully logged DELETE statement might end up being very slow. In this case, you might be better off copying the unique rows to a new table using a minimally logged operation, then dropping the original table and renaming the new table. Here's the code implementing this solution:

```
WITH Dups AS
(
  SELECT orderid, custid, empid, orderdate,
    ROW_NUMBER() OVER(PARTITION BY orderid ORDER BY (SELECT 0)) AS rn
  FROM dbo.OrdersDups
)
SELECT orderid, custid, empid, orderdate
INTO dbo.OrdersDupsTmp
FROM Dups
WHERE rn = 1;

DROP TABLE dbo.OrdersDups;

EXEC sp_rename 'dbo.OrdersDupsTmp', 'OrdersDups';
```

Here as before, the solution assigns row numbers to the copies of each unique *orderid* value, except that here the solution filters the rows where the row number is equal to 1, and copies those rows to another table using the minimally logged SELECT INTO statement (assuming the recovery model of the database is not set to FULL). The solution then drops the original table and renames the new table to the original table name. At this point you can re-create any constraints, indexes, and triggers if needed.

DELETE Using Joins

T-SQL supports a proprietary syntax for DELETE and UPDATE based on joins. Here I'll cover DELETEs based on joins. Later, in the UPDATE section, I'll cover UPDATEs based on joins.

 Note This syntax is not standard, and you should avoid it unless it has a compelling benefit over the standard syntax using subqueries.

I'll first describe the syntax and then show examples where it provides functionality not available with subqueries.

You write a DELETE based on a join in a similar manner to writing a SELECT based on a join. You substitute the SELECT clause with a DELETE FROM *<target_table>*, where *<target_table>* is the table from which you want to delete rows. Note that you should specify the table alias if one was provided.

Some people feel more comfortable using joins than using subqueries and hence prefer to also express DELETE statements that require access to other tables with joins rather than subqueries .

As an example of how a SELECT join query and a DELETE join statement are similar, first look at this query, which returns order details for orders placed on or after May 6, 2008:

```
USE InsideTSQL2008;

SELECT OD.*
FROM Sales.OrderDetails AS OD
  JOIN Sales.Orders AS O
    ON OD.orderid = O.orderid
WHERE O.orderdate >= '20080506';
```

If you want to delete order details for orders placed on or after May 6, 2008, simply replace SELECT OD.* in the preceding query with DELETE FROM OD:

```
BEGIN TRAN

DELETE FROM OD
FROM Sales.OrderDetails AS OD
  JOIN Sales.Orders AS O
    ON OD.orderid = O.orderid
WHERE O.orderdate >= '20080506';

ROLLBACK TRAN
```

In some of my examples I use a transaction and roll back the modification so that you can try out the examples without permanently modifying the sample tables. This particular nonstandard DELETE query can be rewritten as a standard one using a subquery:

```
BEGIN TRAN

DELETE FROM Sales.OrderDetails
WHERE EXISTS
  (SELECT *
   FROM Sales.Orders AS O
   WHERE O.orderid = Sales.OrderDetails.orderid
     AND O.orderdate >= '20080506');

ROLLBACK TRAN
```

In this case, the nonstandard DELETE has no advantage over the standard one—either in performance or in simplicity—so I don't see any point in using it. However, you will find cases in which it is hard to get by without using the proprietary syntax. For example, suppose you need to delete from a table variable and you must refer to the table variable from a subquery. T-SQL doesn't support qualifying a column name with a table variable name.

The following code declares a table variable called *@MyOD* and populates it with some order details, identified by (*orderid, productid*). The code then attempts to delete all rows from *@MyOD* with keys that already appear in the OrderDetails table:

```
DECLARE @MyOD TABLE
(
  orderid   INT NOT NULL,
  productid INT NOT NULL,
  PRIMARY KEY(orderid, productid)
);

INSERT INTO @MyOD VALUES(10001, 14);
INSERT INTO @MyOD VALUES(10001, 51);
INSERT INTO @MyOD VALUES(10001, 65);
INSERT INTO @MyOD VALUES(10248, 11);
INSERT INTO @MyOD VALUES(10248, 42);

DELETE FROM @MyOD
WHERE EXISTS
  (SELECT * FROM Sales.OrderDetails AS OD
   WHERE OD.orderid = @MyOD.orderid
     AND OD.productid = @MyOD.productid);
```

This code fails with the following error:

```
Msg 137, Level 15, State 2, Line 17
Must declare the scalar variable "@MyOD".
```

Essentially, the reason for the failure is that T-SQL doesn't support qualifying a column name with a table variable name. Moreover, T-SQL doesn't allow you to alias the target table directly; rather, it requires you to do so via a second FROM clause, like so:

```
DELETE FROM MyOD
FROM @MyOD AS MyOD
WHERE EXISTS
  (SELECT * FROM Sales.OrderDetails AS OD
   WHERE OD.orderid = MyOD.orderid
     AND OD.productid = MyOD.productid);
```

Note If you want to test this code, make sure you run it right after declaring and populating the table variable in the same batch. Otherwise, you will get an error saying that the variable *@MyOD* was not declared. Like any other variable, the scope of a table variable is the local batch.

Another solution is to use a join instead of the subquery, where you can also alias tables:

```
DELETE FROM MyOD
FROM @MyOD AS MyOD
  JOIN Sales.OrderDetails AS OD
    ON OD.orderid = MyOD.orderid
   AND OD.productid = MyOD.productid;
```

You can also use a CTE as an alternative to aliasing the table variable, allowing a simpler solution:

```
WITH MyOD AS (SELECT * FROM @MyOD)
DELETE FROM MyOD
WHERE EXISTS
  (SELECT * FROM Sales.OrderDetails AS OD
   WHERE OD.orderid = MyOD.orderid
     AND OD.productid = MyOD.productid);
```

CTEs are extremely useful in other scenarios where you need to modify data in one table based on data that you inspect in another. It allows you to simplify your code and, in many cases, avoid relying on modification statements that use joins.

In SQL Server 2008 you can also handle such tasks using the new MERGE statement. I'll describe this statement later in the chapter.

Updating Data

This section covers several aspects of updating data, including UPDATEs using joins, updating large values types, and SELECT and UPDATE statements that perform assignments to variables.

UPDATE Using Joins

Earlier in this chapter, I mentioned that T-SQL supports a nonstandard syntax for modifying data based on a join, and I showed DELETE examples. Here I'll cover UPDATEs based on joins, focusing on cases where the nonstandard syntax has advantages over the supported standard syntax using subqueries. I'll also show how you can use CTEs to update data based on joins.

I'll start with one of the cases where an UPDATE based on a join has a performance advantages over an UPDATE using subqueries. Suppose you wanted to update the shipping information for orders placed by USA customers, overwriting the *shipcountry*, *shipregion*, and *shipcity* attributes with the customer's *country*, *region*, and *city* attributes from the Customers table. You could use one subquery for each of the new attribute values plus one in the WHERE clause to filter orders placed by USA customers as follows:

```
USE InsideTSQL2008;

BEGIN TRAN

  UPDATE Sales.Orders
    SET shipcountry = (SELECT C.country FROM Sales.Customers AS C
                       WHERE C.custid = Sales.Orders.custid),
```

```
      shipregion =   (SELECT C.region FROM Sales.Customers AS C
                       WHERE C.custid = Sales.Orders.custid),
      shipcity =     (SELECT C.city FROM Sales.Customers AS C
                       WHERE C.custid = Sales.Orders.custid)
  WHERE custid IN
    (SELECT custid FROM Sales.Customers WHERE country = N'USA');
```

```
ROLLBACK TRAN
```

Again, I'm rolling back the transaction so that the change does not take effect in the InsideTSQL2008 database. Though standard, this technique is very slow. Each such subquery involves separate access to return the requested attribute from the Customers table. I wanted to provide a figure with the graphical execution plan for this UPDATE, but it's just too big! Request a graphical execution plan in SSMS to see for yourself.

You can write an UPDATE based on a join to perform the same task as follows:

```
BEGIN TRAN

  UPDATE O
    SET shipcountry = C.country,
        shipregion = C.region,
        shipcity = C.city
  FROM Sales.Orders AS O
    JOIN Sales.Customers AS C
      ON O.custid = C.custid
  WHERE C.country = N'USA';
```

```
ROLLBACK TRAN
```

This code is shorter and simpler, and the optimizer generates a more efficient plan for it, as you will notice if you request the graphical execution plan in SSMS. You will find in the execution plan that the Customers table is scanned only once, and through that scan, the query processor accesses all the customer attributes it needs. This plan reports half the estimated execution cost of the previous one. In practice, if you compare the two solutions against larger tables, you will find that the performance difference is substantially higher. Alas, the UPDATE with a join technique is nonstandard.

Earlier in the chapter I introduced the enhanced VALUES clause in SQL Server 2008, which implements one aspect of the standard *row value constructors*. Other aspects of the standard row value constructors have not yet been implemented in SQL Server. One of those aspects allows you to simplify queries like the one just shown. This syntax allows you to specify vectors of attributes and expressions and eliminates the need to issue a subquery for each attribute separately. The following example shows this syntax:

```
UPDATE Sales.Orders
  SET (shipcountry, shipregion, shipcity) =
    (SELECT country, region, city
      FROM Sales.Customers AS C
      WHERE C.custid = Sales.Orders.custid)
WHERE custid IN
  (SELECT custid FROM Sales.Customers WHERE country = 'USA');
```

Such support would allow for simple standard solutions and naturally also lend itself to better optimization.

Another option to handle the task at hand is to use a CTE. By using a CTE, you can come up with a simple solution that is easy to troubleshoot and maintain, yielding an efficient plan very similar to the one that uses a join UPDATE. Simply create a CTE out of a join SELECT and then UPDATE the target table through the CTE, like so:

```
BEGIN TRAN;

WITH UPD_CTE AS
(
  SELECT
    O.shipcountry AS set_country, C.country AS get_country,
    O.shipregion  AS set_region,  C.region  AS get_region,
    O.shipcity    AS set_city,    C.city    AS get_city
  FROM Sales.Orders AS O
    JOIN Sales.Customers AS C
      ON O.custid = C.custid
  WHERE C.country = 'USA'
)
UPDATE UPD_CTE
  SET set_country = get_country,
      set_region  = get_region,
      set_city    = get_city;

ROLLBACK TRAN
```

Note Even though CTEs are defined by ANSI SQL, the DELETE and UPDATE syntax against CTEs implemented in SQL Server is not standard.

This UPDATE generates an identical plan to the one generated for the UPDATE based on a join.

In SQL Server 2008 you can handle such tasks using a MERGE statement that you also express using join semantics. I'll discuss MERGE and provide examples later in this chapter.

You should be aware of another issue when using the join-based UPDATE. When you modify the table on the "one" side of a one-to-many join, you might end up with a nondeterministic update. To demonstrate the problem, run the following code, which creates the tables Customers and Orders and populates them with sample data:

```
USE tempdb;
GO
IF OBJECT_ID('dbo.Orders') IS NOT NULL
  DROP TABLE dbo.Orders;
IF OBJECT_ID('dbo.Customers') IS NOT NULL
  DROP TABLE dbo.Customers;
GO
```

```
CREATE TABLE dbo.Customers
(
  custid VARCHAR(5) NOT NULL PRIMARY KEY,
  qty     INT         NULL
);

INSERT INTO dbo.Customers(custid) VALUES('A'),('B');

CREATE TABLE dbo.Orders
(
  orderid INT         NOT NULL PRIMARY KEY,
  custid  VARCHAR(5) NOT NULL REFERENCES dbo.Customers,
  qty     INT         NOT NULL
);

INSERT INTO dbo.Orders(orderid, custid, qty) VALUES
  (1, 'A', 20),
  (2, 'A', 10),
  (3, 'A', 30),
  (4, 'B', 35),
  (5, 'B', 45),
  (6, 'B', 15);
```

Customers and Orders have a one-to-many relationship. Notice that each row in Customers currently has three related rows in Orders. Now, examine the following UPDATE and see if you can guess how Customers would look after the UPDATE:

```
UPDATE C
  SET qty = O.qty
FROM dbo.Customers AS C
  JOIN dbo.Orders AS O
    ON C.custid = O.custid;
```

The truth is that the UPDATE is nondeterministic. You can't guarantee which of the values from the related Orders rows is used to update the *qty* value in Customers. Remember that you cannot assume or rely on any physical order of the data. For example, run the following query against Customers after running the preceding UPDATE:

```
SELECT custid, qty FROM dbo.Customers;
```

You might get the following output:

```
custid qty
------ -----------
A       20
B       35
```

But you might just as easily get the following output:

```
custid qty
------ -----------
A       10
B       45
```

It is interesting to note that if you attempt such an update with the MERGE statement, where the same target row is modified more than once, SQL Server raises an error, and the statement fails to execute. The MERGE statement doesn't allow such a nondeterministic update like the join UPDATE allows.

When you're done experimenting with nondeterministic UPDATEs, run the following code to drop Orders and Customers:

```
IF OBJECT_ID('dbo.Orders') IS NOT NULL
  DROP TABLE dbo.Orders;
IF OBJECT_ID('dbo.Customers') IS NOT NULL
  DROP TABLE dbo.Customers;
```

Updating Large Value Types

This section covers updates of large value types (VARCHAR(MAX), NVARCHAR(MAX), and VARBINARY(MAX)) using the WRITE method. In my examples I'll use the CustomerData table that you create by running the code provided earlier in the chapter in Listing 10-1. Then run the following code to insert a row into the table:

```
INSERT INTO dbo.CustomerData(custid, txt_data)
  VALUES(102, 'Customer 102 text data');
```

To update a column of a large value type, you can use a regular UPDATE statement setting the column to a result of an expression. For example, if you want to modify a certain section within, such as the *txt_data* column value for customer 102, you could set the column to the result of an expression using the STUFF function. However, an update using regular data manipulation would result in overwriting the entire string using full logging, which is inefficient with large values. Instead, the UPDATE statement supports a WRITE method for large value types. The WRITE method allows you to modify only a section within the string and not overwrite the whole thing. Plus, when the database recovery model is not set to FULL, some of the updates using the WRITE method can benefit from minimal logging. Those include inserting or appending new data.

Logically, the WRITE method is similar to the STUFF function. It accepts three arguments: *@expression*, *@offset*, and *@length*. The *@expression* argument replaces *@length* units (characters/bytes) starting from *@offset* position in the target value.

Note The *@offset* argument is zero based.

For example, the following code operates on the *txt_data* column value for customer 102. It replaces the string '102' located at offset 9 (zero based) with the string *'one hundred and two'*, resulting in the string *'Customer one hundred and two text data'*:

```
UPDATE dbo.CustomerData
  SET txt_data.WRITE('one hundred and two', 9, 3)
WHERE custid = 102;
```

Note If the target LOB is NULL, an update that uses *WRITE* will fail.

If *@expression* is NULL, *@length* is ignored, and the value is truncated at the *@offset* position. For example, the following code truncates the string at the 28th position, resulting in the string *'Customer one hundred and two'*:

```
UPDATE dbo.CustomerData
  SET txt_data.WRITE(NULL, 28, 0)
WHERE custid = 102;
```

If *@length* is NULL, the string is truncated at the *@offset* position, and *@expression* is appended at the end. For example, the following code truncates the string at the ninth position and appends *'102'* at the end, resulting in the string *'Customer 102'*:

```
UPDATE dbo.CustomerData
  SET txt_data.WRITE('102', 9, NULL)
WHERE custid = 102;
```

If *@offset* is NULL and *@length* is 0, *@expression* is simply appended at the end. For example, the following code appends the string *' is discontinued'* at the end, resulting in the string *'Customer 102 is discontinued'*:

```
UPDATE dbo.CustomerData
  SET txt_data.WRITE(' is discontinued', NULL, 0)
WHERE custid = 102;
```

If *@expression* is an empty string, no data is inserted; rather, you just remove a substring at the *@offset* position in the size of *@length*. For example, the following code removes four characters at the ninth position:

```
UPDATE dbo.CustomerData
  SET txt_data.WRITE('', 9, 4)
WHERE custid = 102;
```

If you query the data at this point, you get the string *'Customer is discontinued'*:

```
SELECT txt_data FROM dbo.CustomerData WHERE custid = 102;
```

SELECT and UPDATE Statement Assignments

This section covers statements that assign values to variables and that, in the case of UPDATE, can modify data at the same time. Such assignments have some tricky issues that you might want to be aware of. Being familiar with the way assignments work in T-SQL is important for programming correctly—that is, programming what you intended to.

Assignment SELECT

I'll start with assignment SELECT statements. T-SQL supports assigning values to variables using a SELECT statement, but the ANSI form of assignment, which is also supported by T-SQL, is to use a SET statement. So, as a rule, unless you have a compelling reason to do otherwise, it's a good practice to stick to using SET. I'll describe cases where you might want to use SELECT because it has advantages over SET in those cases. However, as I will demonstrate shortly, you should be aware that when using SELECT, your code is more prone to errors.

As an example of the way an assignment SELECT works, suppose you need to assign the employee ID whose last name matches a given pattern (*@pattern*) to the *@empid* variable. You assume that only one employee will match the pattern. The following code, which uses an assignment SELECT, doesn't accomplish the requirement:

```
USE InsideTSQL2008;

DECLARE @empid AS INT, @pattern AS NVARCHAR(100);

SET @pattern = N'Davis'; -- Try also N'Ben-Gan', N'D%';
SET @empid = 999;

SELECT @empid = empid
FROM HR.Employees
WHERE lastname LIKE @pattern;

SELECT @empid;
```

Given *N'Davis'* as the input pattern, you get the employee ID 1 in the *@empid* variable. In this case, only one employee matched the filter. However, if you're given a pattern that does not apply to any existing last name in the Employees table (for example, *N'Ben-Gan'*), the assignment doesn't take place even once. The content of the *@empid* variable remains as it was before the assignment—999. (This value is used for demonstration purposes.) If you're given a pattern that matches more than one last name (for example, *N'D%'*), this code issues multiple assignments, overwriting the previous value in *@empid* with each assignment. The final value of *@empid* is the employee ID from the qualifying row that SQL Server happened to access last.

A much safer way to assign the qualifying employee ID to the *@empid* variable is to use a SET statement as follows:

```
DECLARE @empid AS INT, @pattern AS NVARCHAR(100);

SET @pattern = N'Davis'; -- Try also N'Ben-Gan', N'D%';
SET @empid = 999;

SET @empid = (SELECT empid
              FROM HR.Employees
              WHERE lastname LIKE @pattern);

SELECT @empid;
```

If only one employee qualifies, you get the employee ID in the *@empid* variable. If no employee qualifies, the subquery sets *@empid* to NULL. When you get a NULL, you know that you had no matches. If multiple employees qualify, you get an error saying that the subquery returned more than one value. In such a case, you will realize that something is wrong with your assumptions or with the design of your code. But the problem will surface as opposed to eluding you.

When you understand how an assignment SELECT works, you can use it to your advantage. For example, a SET statement can assign only one variable at a time. An assignment SELECT can assign values to multiple variables within the same statement. With well-designed code, this capability can give you performance benefits. For example, the following code assigns the first name and last name of a given employee to variables:

```
DECLARE @firstname AS NVARCHAR(10), @lastname AS NVARCHAR(20);

SELECT @firstname = NULL, @lastname = NULL;

SELECT @firstname = firstname, @lastname = lastname
FROM HR.Employees
WHERE empid = 3;

SELECT @firstname, @lastname;
```

Notice that this code uses the primary key to filter an employee, meaning that you cannot get more than one row back. The code also initializes the *@firstname* and *@lastname* variables with NULLs. If no employee qualifies, the variables simply retain the NULLs. This type of assignment is especially useful in triggers when you want to read attributes from the special tables inserted and deleted into your own variables, after you verify that only one row was affected.

Technically, you could rely on the fact that an assignment SELECT performs multiple assignments when multiple rows qualify. For example, you could do aggregate calculations, such as concatenating all order IDs for a given customer:

```
DECLARE @Orders AS VARCHAR(8000), @custid AS INT;
SET @custid = 1;
SET @Orders = '';

SELECT @Orders = @Orders + CAST(orderid AS VARCHAR(10)) + ';'
FROM Sales.Orders
WHERE custid = @custid;

SELECT @Orders;
```

However, this code is far from being standard, and the ability to apply such an assignment SELECT with multiple rows is not officially documented. This type of assignment is also often used with an ORDER BY clause, assuming that the order of concatenation is guaranteed, like so:

```
DECLARE @Orders AS VARCHAR(8000), @custid AS INT;
SET @custid = 1;
SET @Orders = '';
```

```
SELECT @Orders = @Orders + CAST(orderid AS VARCHAR(10)) + ';'
FROM Sales.Orders
WHERE custid = @custid
ORDER BY orderdate, orderid;

SELECT @Orders;
```

But again, no official documentation defines the behavior of such multirow assignment SELECT statements, let alone ones that include an ORDER BY clause. I did stumble across the following blog by Microsoft's Conor Cunningham, in which he indicates that this undocumented technique does guarantee concatenation order: *http://blogs.msdn.com/ sqltips/archive/2005/07/20/441053.aspx*.

However, I have to stress that I feel very awkward about this technique, and I'm reluctant to trust it to always work, including in future versions of the product. You have enough supported and guaranteed techniques to choose from for such calculations, many of which I covered in Chapter 8, "Aggregating and Pivoting Data."

Assignment UPDATE

T-SQL also supports a nonstandard UPDATE syntax that can assign values to variables in addition to modifying data. To demonstrate the technique, first run the following code, which creates the table T1 and populates it with sample data:

```
USE tempdb;
IF OBJECT_ID('dbo.T1') IS NOT NULL DROP TABLE dbo.T1;
CREATE TABLE dbo.T1
(
  col1 INT        NOT NULL,
  col2 VARCHAR(5) NOT NULL
);
GO

INSERT INTO dbo.T1(col1, col2) VALUES
  (0, 'A'),
  (0, 'B'),
  (0, 'C'),
  (0, 'C'),
  (0, 'C'),
  (0, 'B'),
  (0, 'A'),
  (0, 'A'),
  (0, 'C'),
  (0, 'C');
```

Currently, the T1 table has no primary key, and there's no way to uniquely identify the rows. Suppose that you wanted to assign unique integers to *col1* and then make it the primary key. You can use the following assignment UPDATE to achieve this task:

```
DECLARE @i AS INT;
SET @i = 0;
UPDATE dbo.T1 SET @i = col1 = @i + 1;

SELECT * FROM dbo.T1;
```

This code declares the variable @*i* and initializes it with 0. The UPDATE statement then scans the data and, for each row, sets the current *col1* value to @*i* + 1 and then sets @*i*'s value to *col1*'s new value. Logically, the SET clause is equivalent to SET *col1* = @*i* + 1, @*i* = @*i* + 1. However, in such an UPDATE statement, you have no way to control the order in which the rows in T1 are scanned and modified. For example, when I queried the table after applying the preceding assignment UPDATE, I got the following output:

```
col1        col2
----------- -----
1           A
2           B
3           C
4           C
5           C
6           B
7           A
8           A
9           C
10          C
```

But keep in mind that the UPDATE statement's assignment of *col1* values might be different. As long as you don't care about the order in which the data is scanned and modified, you might be happy with this technique. It is very fast because it scans the data only once.

SQL Server supports another technique to achieve this task that is much more elegant and that allows you to specify the logical ordering of the resulting row numbers. This technique involves issuing an UPDATE through a CTE that calculates row numbers based on any desired order, like so:

```
WITH T1RN AS
(
  SELECT col1, ROW_NUMBER() OVER(ORDER BY col2) AS rownum
  FROM dbo.T1
)
UPDATE T1RN SET col1 = rownum;

SELECT * FROM dbo.T1;
```

This code generates the following output:

```
col1        col2
----------- -----
1           A
4           B
6           C
7           C
8           C
5           B
2           A
3           A
9           C
10          C
```

Recall that if you want to assign the row numbers in no particular order and would rather not pay for any costs associated with ordering, you can specify ORDER BY (SELECT 0). By now, you have probably figured out why my favorite features in SQL Server are the ROW_NUMBER function and CTEs.

Merging Data

SQL Server 2008 introduces support for the MERGE statement. This statement allows you to identify a source and a target table and modify the target with data from the source, applying different modification actions (INSERT, UPDATE, DELETE) based on conditional logic. SQL Server implements the standard MERGE statement with a couple of extensions that are not part of the standard.

The MERGE statement has many uses both in OLTP and in data warehouse environments. For example, in an OLTP environment you can use it to merge data you get from an external source into an existing target table. In a data warehouse environment you can use it to apply incremental updates to aggregated data, process slowly changing dimensions, and so on.

In the following sections I'll cover the details of the MERGE statement and how to use it. In the examples I provide, I'll use two tables, Customers and CustomersStage, that you will create in tempdb and populate with initial sample data by running the code in Listing 10-3.

LISTING 10-3 Script creating and populating the Customers and CustomersStage tables

```
SET NOCOUNT ON;
USE tempdb;

IF OBJECT_ID('dbo.Customers', 'U') IS NOT NULL
  DROP TABLE dbo.Customers;
GO
CREATE TABLE dbo.Customers
(
  custid       INT         NOT NULL,
  companyname  VARCHAR(25) NOT NULL,
  phone        VARCHAR(20) NOT NULL,
  address      VARCHAR(50) NOT NULL,
  inactive     BIT         NOT NULL DEFAULT (0),
  CONSTRAINT PK_Customers PRIMARY KEY(custid)
);

INSERT INTO dbo.Customers(custid, companyname, phone, address)
  VALUES
  (1, 'cust 1', '(111) 111-1111', 'address 1'),
  (2, 'cust 2', '(222) 222-2222', 'address 2'),
  (3, 'cust 3', '(333) 333-3333', 'address 3'),
  (4, 'cust 4', '(444) 444-4444', 'address 4'),
  (5, 'cust 5', '(555) 555-5555', 'address 5');
```

```
IF OBJECT_ID('dbo.CustomersStage', 'U') IS NOT NULL
  DROP TABLE dbo.CustomersStage;
GO
CREATE TABLE dbo.CustomersStage
(
  custid      INT         NOT NULL,
  companyname VARCHAR(25) NOT NULL,
  phone       VARCHAR(20) NOT NULL,
  address     VARCHAR(50) NOT NULL,
  CONSTRAINT PK_CustomersStage PRIMARY KEY(custid)
);

INSERT INTO dbo.CustomersStage(custid, companyname, phone, address)
  VALUES
  (2, 'AAAAA', '(222) 222-2222', 'address 2'),
  (3, 'cust 3', '(333) 333-3333', 'address 3'),
  (5, 'BBBBB', 'CCCCC', 'DDDDD'),
  (6, 'cust 6 (new)', '(666) 666-6666', 'address 6'),
  (7, 'cust 7 (new)', '(777) 777-7777', 'address 7');
GO

SELECT * FROM dbo.Customers;
SELECT * FROM dbo.CustomersStage;
```

The queries against the Customers and CustomersStage tables generate the following output:

custid	companyname	phone	address	inactive
1	cust 1	(111) 111-1111	address 1	0
2	cust 2	(222) 222-2222	address 2	0
3	cust 3	(333) 333-3333	address 3	0
4	cust 4	(444) 444-4444	address 4	0
5	cust 5	(555) 555-5555	address 5	0

custid	companyname	phone	address
2	AAAAA	(222) 222-2222	address 2
3	cust 3	(333) 333-3333	address 3
5	BBBBB	CCCCC	DDDDD
6	cust 6 (new)	(666) 666-6666	address 6
7	cust 7 (new)	(777) 777-7777	address 7

MERGE Fundamentals

The MERGE statement is expressed using join semantics. Two tables are involved, but in a MERGE statement one table is identified as the target and one as the source. A MERGE predicate determines what it means for a source row to match a target row. You can specify which action to take when a source row matches a target row and which action to take when a source row doesn't match a target row. The T-SQL MERGE statement even allows you to specify which action to take when a target row matches no source row—but I'm getting ahead of myself. I'll start with the basic form of a MERGE statement, and in subsequent sections I'll cover the more advanced options. A basic MERGE statement has the following general form:

```
MERGE [INTO] <target>
USING <source>
  ON <predicate>
WHEN MATCHED THEN <action>
WHEN NOT MATCHED [BY TARGET] THEN <action>;
```

In the MERGE INTO clause you identify the target for the operation. The target can be a table or a view. In the USING clause you identify the source for the operation. Think of the USING clause in similar terms to a FROM clause in a SELECT query. You can specify a table, a table expression (view, derived table, CTE), or a table function (for example, OPENROWSET, OPENXML). You can use table operators such as JOIN, APPLY, PIVOT, and UNPIVOT to specify the source in the USING clause.

In the ON clause you specify the merge predicate that defines matches and nonmatches. In the WHEN MATCHED THEN clause you specify an action to take place when the MERGE predicate is TRUE, that is, when a source row is matched by a target row. The actions that are supported by this clause are UPDATE and DELETE. In the WHEN NOT MATCHED [BY TARGET] THEN clause you specify an action to take place when the MERGE predicate is FALSE or UNKNOWN, that is, when a source row isn't matched by a target row. The only action supported by this clause is INSERT.

If this is the first time that you've seen the MERGE statement, the technical details are probably confusing. An example should make things clearer. The following code demonstrates how to merge the contents of the CustomersStage table into the Customers table, updating existing customers and adding new ones:

```
SET NOCOUNT OFF;

BEGIN TRAN

MERGE INTO dbo.Customers AS TGT
USING dbo.CustomersStage AS SRC
  ON TGT.custid = SRC.custid
WHEN MATCHED THEN
  UPDATE SET
    TGT.companyname = SRC.companyname,
    TGT.phone = SRC.phone,
    TGT.address = SRC.address
WHEN NOT MATCHED THEN
  INSERT (custid, companyname, phone, address)
  VALUES (SRC.custid, SRC.companyname, SRC.phone, SRC.address);

SELECT * FROM dbo.Customers;

ROLLBACK TRAN
```

I run the code within a transaction and then roll the transaction back for test purposes so that after each example the Customers table is returned to its original form. I also run the examples with the NOCOUNT option set to OFF so that you get a message indicating how many rows were affected.

This MERGE statement identifies the Customers table as the target and the CustomersStage table as the source. The MERGE predicate indicates that a source row is matched by a target row if the source *custid* and the target *custid* values are equal.

When a source row is matched by a target row, the nonkey attributes of the target row are overwritten with those from the source row using an UPDATE action. Notice that the syntax of the UPDATE action is very similar to that of a regular UPDATE statement except that you don't need to indicate the name of the target table because you already identified it earlier in the merge statement's INTO clause.

When a source row isn't matched by a target row, a new row is inserted into the target based on the attributes of the source row using an INSERT action. Again, the syntax of the INSERT action is very similar to that of a regular INSERT statement except that you don't need to indicate the name of the target table because you already identified it earlier in the INTO clause.

When the preceding MERGE statement completes, you get a message indicating that five rows were affected, and the query against the Customers table generates the following output:

```
custid  companyname    phone             address     inactive
-------  -------------  ----------------  ----------  ------------
1        cust 1         (111) 111-1111    address 1   0
2        AAAAA          (222) 222-2222    address 2   0
3        cust 3         (333) 333-3333    address 3   0
4        cust 4         (444) 444-4444    address 4   0
5        BBBBB          CCCCC             DDDDD       0
6        cust 6 (new)   (666) 666-6666    address 6   0
7        cust 7 (new)   (777) 777-7777    address 7   0
```

The five affected rows include three rows that were updated (customers 2, 3, and 5) and two that were inserted (customers 6 and 7).

The MERGE statement is similar to a join not only semantically but also in terms of its physical processing. When both the WHEN MATCHED and the WHEN NOT MATCHED clauses appear in the statement, it is processed as a one-sided outer join. For example, Figure 10-1 shows the plan for the preceding MERGE statement, showing that it was processed as a left outer join.

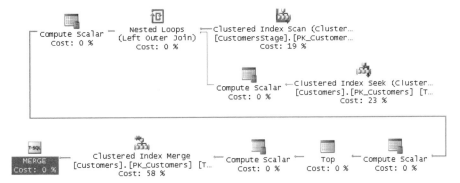

FIGURE 10-1 MERGE processed with left outer join

The MERGE statement doesn't require you to specify both the WHEN MATCHED and the WHEN NOT MATCHED clauses; instead, it supports having only one clause. For example, the following code demonstrates using only the WHEN MATCHED clause to update existing customers without adding new ones:

```
BEGIN TRAN

MERGE INTO dbo.Customers AS TGT
USING dbo.CustomersStage AS SRC
  ON TGT.custid = SRC.custid
WHEN MATCHED THEN
  UPDATE SET
    TGT.companyname = SRC.companyname,
    TGT.phone = SRC.phone,
    TGT.address = SRC.address;

ROLLBACK TRAN
```

Figure 10-2 shows the execution plan SQL Server generated for this statement.

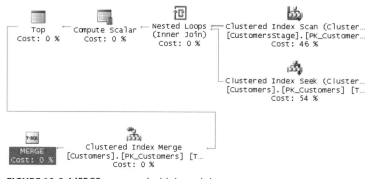

FIGURE 10-2 MERGE processed with inner join

As you can see, the statement was processed using an inner join. Later I will show you cases where a MERGE statement is processed as a full outer join.

Returning to the original task—updating existing customers and adding new ones—the alternative prior to SQL Server 2008 was to issue separate UPDATE and INSERT statements, like so:

```
BEGIN TRAN

UPDATE TGT
  SET TGT.companyname = SRC.companyname,
      TGT.phone = SRC.phone,
      TGT.address = SRC.address
FROM dbo.Customers AS TGT
  JOIN dbo.CustomersStage AS SRC
    ON TGT.custid = SRC.custid;
```

```
INSERT INTO dbo.Customers (custid, companyname, phone, address)
  SELECT custid, companyname, phone, address
  FROM dbo.CustomersStage AS SRC
  WHERE NOT EXISTS
    (SELECT * FROM dbo.Customers AS TGT
     WHERE TGT.custid = SRC.custid);

ROLLBACK TRAN
```

The advantages of using the MERGE statement are that you don't need to access the data twice, plus the MERGE statement is processed as an atomic operation without the need for explicit transactions. Unfortunately though, my tests show that the MERGE statement is processed with full logging. Recall that in SQL Server 2008 the INSERT SELECT statement can be processed with minimal logging in certain cases.

Earlier in the chapter I covered nondeterministic UPDATE statements. A MERGE statement is safer in the sense that if a target row is modified more than once, the statement fails at run time. This usually happens when the target table is the "one" side in a one-to-many relationship.

Adding a Predicate

The various WHEN clauses of the MERGE statement support specifying the AND operator followed by an additional predicate. In the case of the WHEN MATCHED clause, you can specify WHEN MATCHED AND <predicate> THEN <action>. Only when both the original ON predicate and the additional predicate following the AND operator are TRUE does the action following the THEN clause take place.

Here's an example of where this capability might be handy. Consider again the task to update existing customers and add new ones. You want to update a target customer row only if at least one of the nonkey attributes in the source row is different. If the source and target rows are identical, you don't want to apply the update. Avoiding an update in such a case would improve performance and also prevent triggers from including the rows in the inserted and deleted tables.

Following is the revised MERGE statement including the additional predicate that ensures that at least one nonkey attribute is different to apply the UPDATE action:

```
BEGIN TRAN

MERGE dbo.Customers AS TGT
USING dbo.CustomersStage AS SRC
  ON TGT.custid = SRC.custid
WHEN MATCHED AND
        (   TGT.companyname <> SRC.companyname
         OR TGT.phone       <> SRC.phone
         OR TGT.address      <> SRC.address) THEN
  UPDATE SET
    TGT.companyname = SRC.companyname,
```

```
      TGT.phone = SRC.phone,
      TGT.address = SRC.address
WHEN NOT MATCHED THEN
  INSERT (custid, companyname, phone, address)
  VALUES (SRC.custid, SRC.companyname, SRC.phone, SRC.address);

SELECT * FROM dbo.Customers;

ROLLBACK TRAN
```

This time, the Messages pane should indicate that four rows were affected and not five. The row for customer 3 was not updated because the source and the target rows were identical.

The query against the Customers table generates the following output showing the new data for the updated customers 2 and 5 and the new customers 6 and 7:

```
custid  companyname    phone             address     inactive
-------  -------------  ---------------  ----------  ------------
1       cust 1         (111) 111-1111   address 1   0
2       AAAAA          (222) 222-2222   address 2   0
3       cust 3         (333) 333-3333   address 3   0
4       cust 4         (444) 444-4444   address 4   0
5       BBBBB          CCCCC            DDDDD       0
6       cust 6 (new)   (666) 666-6666   address 6   0
7       cust 7 (new)   (777) 777-7777   address 7   0
```

Note that I used the <> operator to check whether the source and target values are different. Remember that according to the three-valued logic in SQL, an expression can return TRUE, FALSE, and UNKNOWN. I didn't worry about the UNKNOWN case because you get it only when one of the values is NULL, and I defined all columns in both cases as NOT NULL. However, if the attributes do allow NULLs, you need to enhance the expressions to check for cases where one is NULL and the other isn't. Your code would look like this:

```
BEGIN TRAN

MERGE dbo.Customers AS TGT
USING dbo.CustomersStage AS SRC
  ON TGT.custid = SRC.custid
WHEN MATCHED AND
    (  (    TGT.companyname <> SRC.companyname
        OR (TGT.companyname IS NOT NULL AND SRC.companyname IS NULL)
        OR (TGT.companyname IS NULL AND SRC.companyname IS NOT NULL) )
    OR (    TGT.phone <> SRC.phone
        OR (TGT.phone IS NOT NULL AND SRC.phone IS NULL)
        OR (TGT.phone IS NULL AND SRC.phone IS NOT NULL) )
    OR (    TGT.address <> SRC.address
        OR (TGT.address IS NOT NULL AND SRC.address IS NULL)
        OR (TGT.address IS NULL AND SRC.address IS NOT NULL) ) )
  THEN UPDATE SET
    TGT.companyname = SRC.companyname,
    TGT.phone = SRC.phone,
    TGT.address = SRC.address
```

```
WHEN NOT MATCHED THEN
  INSERT (custid, companyname, phone, address)
  VALUES (SRC.custid, SRC.companyname, SRC.phone, SRC.address);

SELECT * FROM dbo.Customers;

ROLLBACK TRAN
```

In a similar manner you can specify an additional predicate in the WHEN NOT MATCHED clause. The complete clause would be WHEN NOT MATCHED [BY TARGET] AND <predicate>.

It is interesting to note that ANSI SQL supports operators that apply two-valued logic when comparing values, treating two NULLs as equal to each other and a NULL and non-NULL values as different from one another. Those operators are IS NOT DISTINCT FROM (a two-valued-logic alternative to equality) and IS DISTINCT FROM (a two-valued-logic alternative to inequality). These operators would simplify the WHEN MATCHED clause of the preceding code, but they have not yet been implemented in SQL Server. Steve Kass posted a feature enhancement request to add such support in SQL Server at the following URL: *http://connect.microsoft.com/ SQLServer/feedback/ViewFeedback.aspx?FeedbackID=286422*.

Multiple WHEN Clauses

The MERGE statement supports up to two WHEN MATCHED clauses. When you use two WHEN MATCHED clauses, the first must include an additional predicate, while the second can be specified either with or without an additional predicate. When two clauses are specified, the MERGE statement applies the action in the first only when both the ON predicate is TRUE and the additional predicate in the first clause is TRUE. If the ON predicate is TRUE but the additional predicate in the first clause is FALSE or UNKNOWN, the second clause is evaluated.

As an example where multiple WHEN MATCHED clauses could be useful, consider the following requirement. When the *custid* value in the source exists in the target, you need to update the target row only if at least one of the nonkey attributes changed. But if the source and target rows are identical, that's actually a signal that you need to delete the target row. When the source *custid* value doesn't appear in the target, as before you need to insert the row. You can implement the update or delete part by using two WHEN MATCHED clauses, like so:

```
BEGIN TRAN

MERGE dbo.Customers AS TGT
USING dbo.CustomersStage AS SRC
  ON TGT.custid = SRC.custid
WHEN MATCHED AND
        (   TGT.companyname <> SRC.companyname
         OR TGT.phone       <> SRC.phone
         OR TGT.address      <> SRC.address) THEN
  UPDATE SET
    TGT.companyname = SRC.companyname,
    TGT.phone = SRC.phone,
    TGT.address = SRC.address
```

```
WHEN MATCHED THEN
  DELETE
WHEN NOT MATCHED THEN
  INSERT (custid, companyname, phone, address)
  VALUES (SRC.custid, SRC.companyname, SRC.phone, SRC.address);

SELECT * FROM dbo.Customers;

ROLLBACK TRAN
```

The Messages pane should indicate five affected rows (two updated, one deleted, and two inserted). The query against the Customers table generates the following output:

```
custid  companyname    phone            address     inactive
------- -------------  ---------------  ----------  ------------
1       cust 1         (111) 111-1111   address 1   0
2       AAAAA          (222) 222-2222   address 2   0
4       cust 4         (444) 444-4444   address 4   0
5       BBBBB          CCCCC            DDDDD       0
6       cust 6 (new)   (666) 666-6666   address 6   0
7       cust 7 (new)   (777) 777-7777   address 7   0
```

Customers 2 and 5 were updated, customer 3 was deleted, and customers 6 and 7 were added.

Unlike the WHEN MATCHED clause, the MERGE statement supports only one WHEN NOT MATCHED [BY TARGET] clause.

WHEN NOT MATCHED BY SOURCE

The WHEN MATCHED clause allows you to specify an action to take when a source row is matched by a target row, and the WHEN NOT MATCHED [BY TARGET] clause allows you to specify an action to take when a source row is not matched by a target row. The MERGE statement in T-SQL supports a third clause called WHEN NOT MATCHED BY SOURCE, which allows you to indicate an action to take against a target row that is not matched by any source row.

As an example of using this third clause, let's say that when a target row in our Customers table isn't matched by a source row in our CustomersStage table, you need to set the *inactive* attribute of the target row to 1. Here's the previous MERGE statement with this added logic:

```
BEGIN TRAN

MERGE dbo.Customers AS TGT
USING dbo.CustomersStage AS SRC
  ON TGT.custid = SRC.custid
WHEN MATCHED AND
      (   TGT.companyname <> SRC.companyname
       OR TGT.phone       <> SRC.phone
       OR TGT.address      <> SRC.address) THEN
  UPDATE SET
    TGT.companyname = SRC.companyname,
    TGT.phone = SRC.phone,
    TGT.address = SRC.address
```

```
WHEN MATCHED THEN
  DELETE
WHEN NOT MATCHED THEN
  INSERT (custid, companyname, phone, address)
  VALUES (SRC.custid, SRC.companyname, SRC.phone, SRC.address)
WHEN NOT MATCHED BY SOURCE THEN
  UPDATE SET
    inactive = 1;


SELECT * FROM dbo.Customers;

ROLLBACK TRAN
```

The code updates existing customers that changed, deletes existing customers that did
not change, adds missing customers, and discontinues target customers that are missing in
the source. In total, seven rows were modified this time. Customers 2 and 5 were updated,
customer 3 was deleted, customers 6 and 7 were added, and customers 1 and 4 became
inactive. The query against the Customers table generates the following output:

```
custid  companyname    phone            address     inactive
-------  -------------  ---------------  ----------  -------------
1        cust 1         (111) 111-1111   address 1   1
2        AAAAA          (222) 222-2222   address 2   0
4        cust 4         (444) 444-4444   address 4   1
5        BBBBB          CCCCC            DDDDD        0
6        cust 6 (new)   (666) 666-6666   address 6   0
7        cust 7 (new)   (777) 777-7777   address 7   0
```

Because all three clauses are involved this time, SQL Server processes this MERGE statement
using a full outer join, as you can see in Figure 10-3.

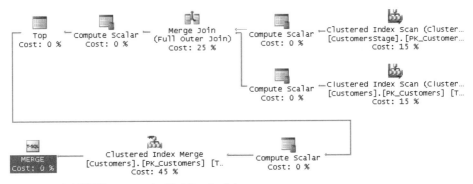

FIGURE 10-3 *MERGE* processed with full outer join

Similarly to the WHEN MATCHED clause, the WHEN NOT MATCHED BY SOURCE clause
supports the DELETE and UPDATE actions. Another similarity is that you can specify up to
two WHEN NOT MATCHED BY SOURCE clauses, following rules similar to those for using two
WHEN MATCHED clauses.

MERGE Values

A common task involving merging data is the need to write a stored procedure that updates or adds a new row (such as a customer). That is, the procedure accepts the attributes of a customer and updates the target row if the customer already exists and inserts a row if the customer doesn't exist. Of course, you may need to apply additional logic such as updating the target customer if it already exists and at least one of the nonkey attributes changed.

Prior to SQL Server 2008 you could handle the task in different ways, but all of them were quite tricky to implement. One way is to use IF EXISTS to determine whether to apply an UPDATE or an INSERT. Another way is apply an UPDATE first and, if the value of the @@*rowcount* function equals 0, issue an INSERT. Either way, there is an opportunity for another transaction to introduce a new row in between the activities (the IF EXISTS and the INSERT or the check of the @@*rowcount* value and the INSERT). To address the problem you may consider performing all activities in one transaction using the serializable isolation level, but this approach can turn out to be very inefficient because it is likely to result in many deadlocks. Other approaches exist, but the point remains that addressing this task is not trivial.

In SQL Server 2008 you can simply use the MERGE statement to implement this task. Recall that the MERGE statement supports specifying a derived table as input. You can define a derived table based on a row value constructor (the enhanced VALUES clause described earlier in the chapter), where the row is made of the procedure's input parameters. Run the following code to implement such a stored procedure called *AddCust*:

```
IF OBJECT_ID('dbo.AddCust', 'P') IS NOT NULL DROP PROC dbo.AddCust;
GO

CREATE PROC dbo.AddCust
  @custid        INT,
  @companyname   VARCHAR(25),
  @phone         VARCHAR(20),
  @address       VARCHAR(50)
AS

MERGE dbo.Customers AS TGT
USING (VALUES(@custid, @companyname, @phone, @address))
      AS SRC(custid, companyname, phone, address)
  ON TGT.custid = SRC.custid
WHEN MATCHED AND
        (   TGT.companyname <> SRC.companyname
         OR TGT.phone       <> SRC.phone
         OR TGT.address      <> SRC.address) THEN
  UPDATE SET
    TGT.companyname = SRC.companyname,
    TGT.phone = SRC.phone,
    TGT.address = SRC.address
WHEN NOT MATCHED THEN
  INSERT (custid, companyname, phone, address)
  VALUES (SRC.custid, SRC.companyname, SRC.phone, SRC.address);
GO
```

Run the following code to test the procedure:

```
BEGIN TRAN

EXEC dbo.AddCust
  @custid       = 8,
  @companyname  = 'cust 8 (new)',
  @phone        = '(888) 888-8888',
  @address      = 'address 8';

SELECT * FROM dbo.Customers;

ROLLBACK TRAN
```

The query against the Customers table generates the following output showing the new customer 8:

```
custid  companyname    phone             address     inactive
-------  -------------  ---------------   ----------  ------------
1        cust 1         (111) 111-1111    address 1   0
2        cust 2         (222) 222-2222    address 2   0
3        cust 3         (333) 333-3333    address 3   0
4        cust 4         (444) 444-4444    address 4   0
5        cust 5         (555) 555-5555    address 5   0
8        cust 8 (new)   (888) 888-8888    address 8   0
```

MERGE and Triggers

SQL Server doesn't support MERGE triggers. However, if INSERT, UPDATE, and DELETE triggers are defined on the target table, the MERGE statement causes those to fire if the corresponding actions take place. You get only one occurrence of each trigger to fire even if the MERGE statement ends up invoking more than one occurrence of the same action. As usual, you can access all rows modified by the triggering actions via the inserted and deleted tables within the trigger.

To demonstrate trigger behavior for a MERGE statement, create INSERT, UPDATE, and DELETE triggers on the Customers table by running the following code:

```
CREATE TRIGGER trg_Customers_INSERT ON dbo.Customers AFTER INSERT
AS
PRINT 'INSERT detected.';
GO
CREATE TRIGGER trg_Customers_UPDATE ON dbo.Customers AFTER UPDATE
AS
PRINT 'UPDATE detected.';
GO
CREATE TRIGGER trg_Customers_DELETE ON dbo.Customers AFTER DELETE
AS
PRINT 'DELETE detected.';
GO
```

The trigger simply prints the action that was detected. Run the following MERGE statement that involves all actions and even an action that appears twice in the statement:

```
BEGIN TRAN

MERGE dbo.Customers AS TGT
USING dbo.CustomersStage AS SRC
  ON TGT.custid = SRC.custid
WHEN MATCHED AND
        (   TGT.companyname <> SRC.companyname
         OR TGT.phone       <> SRC.phone
         OR TGT.address      <> SRC.address) THEN
  UPDATE SET
    TGT.companyname = SRC.companyname,
    TGT.phone = SRC.phone,
    TGT.address = SRC.address
WHEN MATCHED THEN
  DELETE
WHEN NOT MATCHED THEN
  INSERT (custid, companyname, phone, address)
  VALUES (SRC.custid, SRC.companyname, SRC.phone, SRC.address)
WHEN NOT MATCHED BY SOURCE THEN
  UPDATE SET
    inactive = 1;

ROLLBACK TRAN
```

This code generates the following output:

```
INSERT detected.
UPDATE detected.
DELETE detected.

(7 row(s) affected)
```

Notice that even though the UPDATE action was activated by two different clauses, only one occurrence of the UPDATE trigger was invoked for all updated rows. This is in accord with the fact that in SQL Server a trigger fires for each statement.

OUTPUT Clause

SQL Server supports returning output from a data modification statement via the OUTPUT clause. The OUTPUT clause is supported for INSERT, DELETE, UPDATE, and MERGE statements. In the OUTPUT clause, you can refer to the special tables inserted and deleted. These special tables contain the rows affected by the data modification statement—in their new (after-modification) and old (before-modification) versions, respectively. You use the inserted and deleted tables here much like you do in triggers. With INSERTs, you refer to the inserted table to identify attributes from the new rows. With DELETEs, you refer to the deleted table to identify attributes from the old rows. With UPDATEs, you refer to the deleted table to identify the attributes from the updated rows before the change, and you refer to the inserted table to identify the attributes from the updated rows after the change. With the MERGE statement you refer to the relevant tables depending on the actions that you invoke. The output can be directed to the caller (client application), a table, or even both.

The feature is probably best explained through examples. In the following sections I'll give examples for each kind of modification statement. Then I'll cover a new feature in SQL Server 2008 called composable DML that is related to the OUTPUT clause.

INSERT with OUTPUT

An example of an INSERT statement in which the OUTPUT clause can be very handy is when you issue a multirow INSERT into a table with an identity column and want to capture the new identity values. With single-row INSERTs, this isn't a problem: The SCOPE_IDENTITY function provides the last identity value generated by your session in the current scope. But for a multirow INSERT statement, how do you find the new identity values? You use the OUTPUT clause to return the new identity values or insert them into a table.

To demonstrate this technique, first run the following code, which creates the CustomersDim table:

```
USE tempdb;
IF OBJECT_ID('dbo.CustomersDim') IS NOT NULL DROP TABLE dbo.CustomersDim;
CREATE TABLE dbo.CustomersDim
(
  keycol  INT NOT NULL IDENTITY PRIMARY KEY,
  custid  INT NOT NULL,
  companyname NVARCHAR(40) NOT NULL,
  /* ... other columns ... */
);
```

Imagine that this table represents a customer dimension in your data warehouse. You now need to insert into the CustomersDim table the UK customers from the Sales.Customers table in the InsideTSQL2008 database. Notice that the target has an identity column called *keycol* that contains surrogate keys for customers. I won't get into the reasoning behind the common use of surrogate keys in dimension tables in data warehouses (as opposed to relying on natural keys only); that's not the focus of my discussion here. I just want to demonstrate a technique that uses the OUTPUT clause. Suppose that after each insert you need to do some processing of the newly added customers and identify which surrogate key was assigned to each customer.

The following code declares a table variable (*@NewCusts*), issues an INSERT statement inserting UK customers into *CustomersDim* and directing the new *custid* and *keycol* values into *@NewCusts*, and queries the table variable:

```
DECLARE @NewCusts TABLE
(
  custid INT NOT NULL PRIMARY KEY,
  keycol INT NOT NULL UNIQUE
);
```

```
INSERT INTO dbo.CustomersDim(custid, companyname)
    OUTPUT inserted.custid, inserted.keycol
    INTO @NewCusts
    -- OUTPUT inserted.custid, inserted.keycol
  SELECT custid, companyname
  FROM InsideTSQL2008.Sales.Customers
  WHERE country = N'UK';

SELECT custid, keycol FROM @NewCusts;
```

This code generates the following output, where you can see the new identity values in the column *keycol*:

```
custid      keycol
----------- -----------
4           1
11          2
16          3
19          4
38          5
53          6
72          7
```

Notice the commented second OUTPUT clause in the code, which isn't followed by an INTO clause. Uncomment it if you also want to send the output to the caller; you will have two OUTPUT clauses in the INSERT statement.

DELETE with OUTPUT

In Chapter 9, I described a technique to delete large volumes of data from an existing table in batches to avoid log explosion and lock escalation problems. Here I will show how you can use the new OUTPUT clause to archive the data that you purge. To demonstrate the technique, first run the following code, which creates the LargeOrders table and populates it with more than two million orders placed in years 2004 through 2008:

```
USE tempdb;
IF OBJECT_ID('dbo.LargeOrders') IS NOT NULL DROP TABLE dbo.LargeOrders;
CREATE TABLE dbo.LargeOrders
(
  orderid   INT       NOT NULL
    CONSTRAINT PK_LargeOrders PRIMARY KEY NONCLUSTERED,
  custid    INT       NOT NULL,
  empid     INT       NOT NULL,
  orderdate DATE      NOT NULL,
  filler    CHAR(200) NOT NULL DEFAULT ('a')
)
GO

CREATE UNIQUE CLUSTERED INDEX idx_od_oid
  ON dbo.LargeOrders(orderdate, orderid);
GO
```

```
INSERT INTO dbo.LargeOrders WITH (TABLOCK)(orderid, custid, empid, orderdate)
  SELECT ROW_NUMBER() OVER(ORDER BY (SELECT 0)),
    custid, empid, DATEADD(day, n-1, '20040101')
  FROM InsideTSQL2008.Sales.Customers AS C
    CROSS JOIN InsideTSQL2008.HR.Employees AS E
    CROSS JOIN dbo.Nums
  WHERE n <= DATEDIFF(day, '20000401', '20081231') + 1;
```

 Warning It should take the code a few minutes to run, and it will require about a gigabyte of space in your tempdb database. Also, the code refers to the Nums auxiliary table, which I covered in Chapter 6.

Remember, you use the following technique to delete all rows with an *orderdate* older than 2006 in batches of 5,000 rows (but don't run it yet):

```
WHILE 1 = 1
BEGIN
  DELETE TOP (5000) FROM dbo.LargeOrders WHERE orderdate < '20060101';
  IF @@rowcount < 5000 BREAK;
END
```

Suppose you wanted to enhance the solution that purges historic data in batches by also archiving the data that you purge. Run the following code to create the OrdersArchive table, where you will store the archived orders:

```
IF OBJECT_ID('dbo.Archive') IS NOT NULL DROP TABLE dbo.Archive;
CREATE TABLE dbo.Archive
(
  orderid     INT        NOT NULL PRIMARY KEY NONCLUSTERED,
  custid      INT        NOT NULL,
  empid       INT        NOT NULL,
  orderdate   DATE       NOT NULL,
  filler      CHAR(200)  NOT NULL
);
GO
CREATE UNIQUE CLUSTERED INDEX idx_od_oid
  ON dbo.Archive(orderdate, orderid);
```

Using the OUTPUT clause, you can direct the deleted rows from each batch into the OrdersArchive table. Here is the enhanced solution, which purges orders with an *orderdate* before 2006 in batches and also archives them:

```
WHILE 1 = 1
BEGIN
  DELETE TOP(5000) FROM dbo.LargeOrders
    OUTPUT deleted.orderid, deleted.custid, deleted.empid,
           deleted.orderdate, deleted.filler
      INTO dbo.Archive(orderid, custid, empid, orderdate, filler)
  WHERE orderdate < '20060101';

  IF @@rowcount < 5000 BREAK;
END
```

> **Note** It should take this code a few minutes to run.

The OrdersArchive table now holds archived orders placed before 2006.

> **Note** When using the OUTPUT clause to direct the output to a table, the table cannot have enabled triggers or CHECK constraints, nor can it participate on either side of a foreign key constraint. If the target table doesn't meet these requirements, you can direct the output to a staging table and then copy the rows from there to the target table.

Using the OUTPUT clause has important benefits when you want to archive data that you delete. Without the OUTPUT clause, you need to first query the data to archive it and then delete it. This technique is slower and more complex. To guarantee that new rows matching the filter (also known as *phantoms*) are not added between the SELECT and the DELETE, you must lock the data you archive using a serializable isolation level. With the OUTPUT clause, you not only get better performance, but you don't need to worry about phantoms because you are guaranteed to get exactly what you deleted back from the OUTPUT clause.

UPDATE with OUTPUT

As with the INSERT and DELETE statements, UPDATE statements also support an OUTPUT clause, allowing you to return output when you update data. Remember that with an UPDATE statement there are both new and old versions of rows, so you can refer to both the deleted and the inserted tables. UPDATEs with the OUTPUT clause have many interesting applications. I will give an example of managing a simple message or event queue without using Service Broker.

To demonstrate managing a queue, run the following code, which creates the Messages table:

```
USE tempdb;
IF OBJECT_ID('dbo.Messages') IS NOT NULL DROP TABLE dbo.Messages;
CREATE TABLE dbo.Messages
(
  msgid  INT         NOT NULL IDENTITY ,
  msgts  DATETIME    NOT NULL DEFAULT(CURRENT_TIMESTAMP),
  msg    VARCHAR(MAX) NOT NULL,
  status VARCHAR(20)  NOT NULL DEFAULT('new'),
  CONSTRAINT PK_Messages
    PRIMARY KEY NONCLUSTERED(msgid),
  CONSTRAINT UNQ_Messages_status_msgid
    UNIQUE CLUSTERED(status, msgid),
  CONSTRAINT CHK_Messages_status
    CHECK (status IN('new', 'open', 'done'))
);
```

For each message, you store a message ID, an entry date, message text, and a status code indicating whether the message has yet to be processed (*'new'*), is being processed (*'open'*), or has already been processed (*'done'*).

The following code simulates a session that generates messages by using a loop that inserts a message with random text every second for five minutes. The status of newly inserted messages is *'new'* because the status column was assigned with the default value *'new'*. Run this code from multiple sessions at the same time:

```
SET NOCOUNT ON;
USE tempdb;
GO
DECLARE @msg AS VARCHAR(MAX);
DECLARE @now AS DATETIME = CURRENT_TIMESTAMP;
WHILE 1=1 AND DATEDIFF(second,@now,CURRENT_TIMESTAMP) < 300
BEGIN
  SET @msg = 'msg' + RIGHT('000000000'
    + CAST(1 + ABS(CHECKSUM(NEWID())) AS VARCHAR(10)), 10);
  INSERT INTO dbo.Messages(msg) VALUES(@msg);
  WAITFOR DELAY '00:00:01';
END
```

Of course, you can play with the delay period as you wish.

The following code simulates a session that processes messages repeatedly using these steps:

1. Lock @*n* available new messages using an UPDATE TOP (@*n)* statement with the READPAST hint to skip locked rows and change their status to *'open'*. The integer @*n* is a configurable input that determines the maximum number of messages to process in each iteration.

2. Store the attributes of the messages in the @*Msgs* table variable using the OUTPUT clause.

3. Process the messages.

4. Set the status of the messages to *'done'* by joining the Messages table and the @*Msgs* table variable.

5. If no new message was found in the Messages table, wait for one second.

```
SET NOCOUNT ON;
USE tempdb;
GO

DECLARE @Msgs TABLE(msgid INT, msgts DATETIME, msg VARCHAR(MAX));
DECLARE @n AS INT;
SET @n = 3;

WHILE 1 = 1
BEGIN
  UPDATE TOP(@n) dbo.Messages WITH(READPAST) SET status = 'open'
```

```
      OUTPUT inserted.msgid, inserted.msgts, inserted.msg INTO @Msgs
      OUTPUT inserted.msgid, inserted.msgts, inserted.msg
  WHERE status = 'new';

  IF @@rowcount > 0
  BEGIN
    PRINT 'Processing messages...';
    /* ...process messages here... */

    WITH UPD_CTE AS
    (
      SELECT M.status
      FROM dbo.Messages AS M
        JOIN @Msgs AS N
          ON M.msgid = N.msgid
    )
    UPDATE UPD_CTE
      SET status = 'done';

/*
    -- Alternatively you can delete the processed messages:
    DELETE FROM M
    FROM dbo.Messages AS M
     JOIN @Msgs AS N
       ON M.msgid = N.msgid;
*/

    DELETE FROM @Msgs;
  END
  ELSE
  BEGIN
    PRINT 'No messages to process.';
    WAITFOR DELAY '00:00:01';
  END
END
```

You can run this code from multiple sessions at the same time. You can increase the number of sessions that run this code based on the processing throughput that you need to accommodate.

Note that for demonstration purposes only, I included in the first UPDATE statement a second OUTPUT clause, which returns the messages back to the caller.

When you're done, stop the executing code in the various sessions and run the following code for cleanup:

```
IF OBJECT_ID('dbo.Messages') IS NOT NULL DROP TABLE dbo.Messages;
```

MERGE with OUTPUT

The MERGE statement also supports the OUTPUT clause, but with MERGE things are a bit trickier than with the other modification statements. One MERGE statement can involve multiple modification actions. You may need to be able to tell whether an output row was generated by an INSERT, DELETE, or UPDATE action. For this purpose SQL Server provides you with the *$action* function, which returns a character string indicating the action that generated the output row: 'INSERT', 'DELETE', or 'UPDATE'.

To demonstrate using the OUTPUT clause and the *$action* function with the MERGE statement, first create and populate the Customers and CustomersStage tables by running the code provided earlier in Listing 10-3.

The following code demonstrates one of the merge scenarios discussed earlier—update existing customers and add new customers—except that this MERGE statement also contains an OUTPUT clause showing the action and the deleted and inserted values:

```
BEGIN TRAN

MERGE INTO dbo.Customers AS TGT
USING dbo.CustomersStage AS SRC
  ON TGT.custid = SRC.custid
WHEN MATCHED THEN
  UPDATE SET
    TGT.companyname = SRC.companyname,
    TGT.phone = SRC.phone,
    TGT.address = SRC.address
WHEN NOT MATCHED THEN
  INSERT (custid, companyname, phone, address)
  VALUES (SRC.custid, SRC.companyname, SRC.phone, SRC.address)
OUTPUT $action AS action,
  inserted.custid,
  deleted.companyname AS Dcompanyname,
  deleted.phone AS Dphone,
  deleted.address AS Daddress,
  inserted.companyname AS Icompanyname,
  inserted.phone AS Iphone,
  inserted.address AS Iaddress;

ROLLBACK TRAN
```

This code generates the following output, which is shown here in two parts to fit on the page:

```
action  custid  Dcompanyname  Dphone           Daddress
-------  ------  ------------  ---------------  -----------
UPDATE  2       cust 2        (222) 222-2222   address 2
UPDATE  3       cust 3        (333) 333-3333   address 3
UPDATE  5       cust 5        (555) 555-5555   address 5
INSERT  6       NULL          NULL             NULL
INSERT  7       NULL          NULL             NULL

action  custid  Icompanyname  Iphone           Iaddress
-------  ------  ------------  ---------------  ----------
UPDATE  2       AAAAA         (222) 222-2222   address 2
UPDATE  3       cust 3        (333) 333-3333   address 3
UPDATE  5       BBBBB         CCCCC            DDDDD
INSERT  6       cust 6 (new)  (666) 666-6666   address 6
INSERT  7       cust 7 (new)  (777) 777-7777   address 7
```

As you can see, three rows were updated, and for those you get both deleted (old) and inserted (new) values. Two rows were inserted, and for those you get only inserted values; deleted values are NULLs.

Composable DML

Consider situations where you need to modify data, but you need to generate output rows only for a subset of the modified rows. For example, you may need to audit only rows that meet certain criteria.

One way to achieve this is to output all modified rows into a staging table and then copy the relevant subset of rows to the final target table. But of course this approach can be very inefficient, especially when the subset that you actually need to keep is a small percentage of the modified rows.

SQL Server 2008 provides an answer to this need with a feature called *composable DML*. Composable DML allows you to use a data modification statement (INSERT, DELETE, UPDATE, MERGE) as a table expression in the FROM clause of an outer INSERT SELECT statement, so long as the data modification statement contains an OUTPUT clause. The outer INSERT SELECT statement can filter the relevant subset of rows from the output and insert them into a target table. The general form of this feature looks like this:

```
INSERT INTO <target_table>
  SELECT ...
  FROM (<modification_with_output>) AS D
  WHERE <where_predicate>;
```

As an example of using this feature, suppose that in the last shown MERGE statement, which updates existing customers and adds new ones, you need to audit information only for new customers. Run the following code to create the CustomersAudit table:

```
IF OBJECT_ID('dbo.CustomersAudit', 'U') IS NOT NULL
  DROP TABLE dbo.CustomersAudit;

CREATE TABLE dbo.CustomersAudit
(
  audit_lsn   INT NOT NULL IDENTITY,
  login_name  SYSNAME NOT NULL DEFAULT (SUSER_SNAME()),
  post_time   DATETIME NOT NULL DEFAULT (CURRENT_TIMESTAMP),
  custid      INT         NOT NULL,
  companyname VARCHAR(25) NOT NULL,
  phone       VARCHAR(20) NOT NULL,
  address     VARCHAR(50) NOT NULL,
  CONSTRAINT PK_CustomersAudit PRIMARY KEY(audit_lsn)
);
```

The following code demonstrates how to handle this request:

```
BEGIN TRAN

INSERT INTO dbo.CustomersAudit(custid, companyname, phone, address)
  SELECT custid, Icompanyname, Iphone, Iaddress
  FROM (MERGE INTO dbo.Customers AS TGT
        USING dbo.CustomersStage AS SRC
          ON TGT.custid = SRC.custid
        WHEN MATCHED THEN
          UPDATE SET
            TGT.companyname = SRC.companyname,
            TGT.phone = SRC.phone,
            TGT.address = SRC.address
        WHEN NOT MATCHED THEN
          INSERT (custid, companyname, phone, address)
          VALUES (SRC.custid, SRC.companyname, SRC.phone, SRC.address)
        OUTPUT $action AS action,
          inserted.custid,
          inserted.companyname AS Icompanyname,
          inserted.phone AS Iphone,
          inserted.address AS Iaddress) AS D
  WHERE action = 'INSERT';

SELECT * FROM dbo.CustomersAudit;

ROLLBACK TRAN
```

The MERGE statement invokes an UPDATE action to update existing customers and an INSERT action to add new ones. The OUTPUT clause returns the action that generated the output rows and inserted attributes. The outer INSERT SELECT statement filters only output rows where the action is equal to 'INSERT' and stores those in the audit table. The subsequent SELECT statement returns the contents of the audit table, and that statement generates the following output, which is shown here in two parts to fit on the page:

```
audit_lsn login_name     post_time
--------- ------------- -----------------------
1         DOJO\Gandalf  2009-02-12 12:59:17.957
2         DOJO\Gandalf  2009-02-12 12:59:17.957

audit_lsn custid companyname    phone           address
--------- ------ ------------- --------------- ----------
1         6      cust 6 (new)  (666) 666-6666  address 6
2         7      cust 7 (new)  (777) 777-7777  address 7
```

For now, composable DML is implemented in a very basic form. You can use this feature only in an INSERT SELECT statement. You can specify a WHERE filter, but you cannot apply any further manipulations like joins or other table operators, grouping, and so on. I hope that in the future this feature will be enhanced.

Finally, this feature has restrictions very similar to those for the OUTPUT clause. The target table can be a permanent table, temporary table, or table variable. The target cannot do the following:

- Be a table expression, such as a view.

- Have triggers.

- Participate in primary key–foreign key relationships.

- Participate in merge replication or updatable subscriptions for transactional replication.

Conclusion

Data modifications involve many challenges. You need to be familiar with SQL Server's architecture and internals if you want to design systems that can cope with large volumes of data and large-scale modifications. Many challenging logical problems are related to data modifications, such as maintaining your own custom sequence, deleting rows with duplicate data, and assigning unique values to existing rows. In this chapter, I covered performance aspects of data modifications as well as logical ones. I also introduced the new features in SQL Server 2008 including the enhanced VALUES clause, minimal logging enhancements, the MERGE statement, and composable DML.

Chapter 11
Querying Partitioned Tables

The primary reasons to consider table partitioning in SQL Server are manageability and data availability. By splitting a large table into several smaller partitions you can perform some of the most time-consuming and resource-demanding tasks—including backups, consistency checks using DBCC commands, and index maintenance—one partition at a time. Partitioning enables you to move large chunks of data into and out of a partitioned table with minimal impact on concurrent operations on the table, requiring only a very brief period of exclusive table access.

Database architects often carefully design partitioning to achieve manageability and availability goals only to find a negative impact on workload performance that is unacceptable to end users. This chapter explains how partitioning affects query plans and, consequently, query performance. You will learn how to write efficient queries against partitioned objects and how to analyze the query plans and execution information.

For information about creating partitioned tables and indexes, see SQL Server Books Online.

Partitioning in SQL Server

It is hard to say exactly when partitioning was introduced in the SQL Server relational engine for the first time. Clever programmers can create a UNION ALL view over several SELECTs, each from one table. The tables can be, for example, daily customer transactions, and a new table is introduced and included in the view definition every day. Most people believe the first true partitioning was introduced by supporting partitioned tables and indexes without the need to use views in Microsoft SQL Server 2005. This may be true because the keyword PARTITION found its way into T-SQL syntax for the very first time in SQL Server 2005.

Partitioned Views

There are two orthogonal classifications of partitioned views. The first is guided by the physical placement of the component tables: If all tables constituting a partitioned view are located in a single instance of SQL Server, we refer to the view as a local partitioned view. If the tables are located across two or more instances, we call it a distributed partitioned view.

The second classification concerns updatability. A partitioned view (distributed or local) may be updatable or not updatable. An updatable partitioned view has a single column constraint on each participating table that makes it possible to decide for every single row which table it belongs to. This constraint must be contained in a primary key in all tables as well. Please consult the "Create View" section of SQL Server Books Online for detailed conditions for creating partitioned or updatable partitioned views.

In most updatable partitioned views the constraints are defined such that each inserted row satisfies the constraint on one and only one participating table. It is possible to define constraints with "holes" in the domain of the partitioning column when some partitioning column values violate all constraints. If that is the case, you will see following error message if you are inserting a new row or updating an existing one and the resulting partitioning column value violates constraints in all participating tables:

```
Msg 4457, Level 16, State 1, Line 1
```

```
The attempted insert or update of the partitioned view failed because the value of the
partitioning column does not belong to any of the partitions.
```

```
The statement has been terminated.
```

Comparing Partitioned Views and Partitioned Tables

Partitioned views and partitioned tables have several significant differences. Data Definition Language (DDL) differences and the need to manage more objects with partitioned views are obvious—all participating tables must have coordinated constraints and primary keys. Less obvious is the fact that all partitions of a partitioned table must reside in the same database, while in the case of partitioned views the participating tables may reside not only in different databases but also on different servers and on separate machines. Probably the least-known discrepancies are in query compilation, optimization, and execution. During query compilation and optimization, each branch of a partitioned view is processed separately. This is required because the tables may reside in different databases and they may have different statistics and indexes. Therefore, each branch may have a different query plan as well. While this may be advantageous in some cases, in most cases the compilation cost is too high, especially when the number of partitions is large. A partitioned view with dozens of partitions takes significantly longer to compile and optimize compared to similar partitioned tables. When SQL Server is compiling a query with a partitioned table, SQL Server knows the table is partitioned and that each partition has exactly the same attributes, including indexes and statistics, as the rest of the partitions. Therefore, the compilation is performed only once, and the same plan is used for all partitions of the table.

Partitioned tables and indexes are supported only in the SQL Server Enterprise and Developer editions. Partitioned views are available in all editions.

The rest of this chapter concerns partitioned tables and indexes.

Partitioned Tables

We will start with query plans for simple queries to explain how partitioned tables appear in SQL Server 2005 and SQL Server 2008 query plans. Then we will take a look at specifics of statistics on partitioned tables and indexes. Later, we will examine partition elimination. Because partitioned tables are usually introduced in large databases on multi-CPU computers, we will talk about how parallelism and table partitioning work together.

Query Plans for Partitioned Tables

Query plans involving partitioned tables in SQL Server 2005 and in SQL Server 2008 are substantially different. I will use a modification of the TPC-H table LINEITEM to illustrate the differences. TPC-H is a decision support performance benchmark defined by the Transaction Processing Performance Council (TPC). For more information about TPC and its benchmarks, see *www.tpc.org*. I use the following partition function and partition scheme definitions as a basis for a partitioned version of the LINEITEM table:

```
CREATE PARTITION FUNCTION PF2009 (SMALLDATETIME)
AS RANGE RIGHT FOR VALUES ('20090101','20090201','20090301','20090401','20090501','20090601',
 '20090701','20090801','20090901','20091001','20091101','20091201','20100101');

CREATE PARTITION SCHEME PSYEAR AS PARTITION PF2009 ALL TO ([PRIMARY]);
```

Next is the definition of our partitioned version of the LINEITEM table:

```
CREATE TABLE LINEITEMPART
(              L_ORDERKEY        INT              NOT NULL,
               L_PARTKEY         INT              NOT NULL,
               L_SUPPKEY         INT              NOT NULL,
               L_LINENUMBER      INT              NOT NULL,
               L_QUANTITY        MONEY            NOT NULL,
               L_EXTENDEDPRICE   MONEY            NOT NULL,
               L_DISCOUNT        MONEY            NOT NULL,
               L_TAX             MONEY            NOT NULL,
               L_RETURNFLAG      CHAR(1)          NOT NULL,
               L_LINESTATUS      CHAR(1)          NOT NULL,
               L_SHIPDATE        SMALLDATETIME    NOT NULL,
               L_COMMITDATE      SMALLDATETIME    NOT NULL,
               L_RECEIPTDATE     SMALLDATETIME    NOT NULL,
               L_SHIPINSTRUCT    CHAR(25)         NOT NULL,
               L_SHIPMODE        CHAR(10)         NOT NULL,
               L_COMMENT         VARCHAR(44)      NOT NULL)
  ON PSYEAR (L_SHIPDATE);
```

In TPC-H the values in columns L_SHIPDATE, L_COMMITDATE, and L_RECEIPTDATE are spread over seven years, but in the following script, which generates data and populates LINEITEMPART, I have modified the year values so that all dates are within the year 2009.

```
/***
1. Get the TPC-H data generator tool DBGEN from www.tpc.org (warning: the site contains
   only the source and make files; you have to use your own C compiler to build
   the executable dbgen.exe using instructions at http://www.tpc.org/tpch/default.asp

2. Execute dgben with the following parameters to generate the table data:
   dbgen -vf -s 1 -T L
   One of the files generated is lineitem.tbl, and it contains 6+ million rows

3. Create a staging table named LINEITEM in your database, using the same definition
   as LINEITEMPART but without partitioning
```

```
   4. Load the data into the staging table using the following bcp command
      bcp <dbname>..LINEITEM in "lineitem.tbl"  -c -b 1000 -a 65535 -t"|" -r"|\n" -T

   5. Perform the following insert to transform the dates to the year 2009
      and at the same time copy data into your partitioned table

***/

INSERT INTO LINEITEMPART SELECT
     L_ORDERKEY                ,
     L_PARTKEY                 ,
     L_SUPPKEY                 ,
     L_LINENUMBER              ,
     L_QUANTITY                ,
     L_EXTENDEDPRICE           ,
     L_DISCOUNT                ,
     L_TAX                     ,
     L_RETURNFLAG              ,
     L_LINESTATUS              ,
     DATEADD (YY,2009-DATEPART(YY,L_SHIPDATE),L_SHIPDATE),
     DATEADD (YY,2009-DATEPART(YY,L_COMMITDATE),L_COMMITDATE),
     DATEADD (YY,2009-DATEPART(YY,L_RECEIPTDATE),L_RECEIPTDATE),
     L_SHIPINSTRUCT            ,
     L_SHIPMODE                ,
     L_COMMENT FROM LINEITEM
```

Because I ran dbgen.exe with a 1-GB scale factor, the LINEITEMPART table has 6,001,215 rows. Later in the chapter I will introduce a clustered index on the table, but let's work with the heap to explain query plans for the simplest scans in both SQL Server 2005 and SQL Server 2008. Following the best practices for a sliding window scenario, the table has 14 partitions holding 12 months of data with the first and last partitions empty. A partition function with empty first and last partitions makes it efficient to remove the oldest partition and introduce a new one.

> **Tip** If you are using the sliding window type of partitioning (adding a new partition to one end of the partition function intervals and removing one from the opposite end), keep the first and last partitions empty.

Figure 11-1 shows the query plan for SELECT * FROM LINEITEMPART in SQL Server 2005.

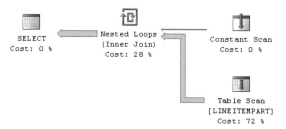

FIGURE 11-1 Execution plan for simple SELECT from partitioned table in SQL Server 2005

If you rest the cursor on the Constant Scan operator, you will see 14 values, as shown in Figure 11-2. The constants enumerate the visited partitions. Each partition is then accessed by Table Scan, as shown in Figure 11-3. The internally generated variable PtnIds1004 is assigned values 1, 2, 3..., 14 in the Constant Scan, and then each value is used as a parameter for the Table Scan operator.

Constant Scan
Scan an internal table of constants.

Physical Operation	Constant Scan
Logical Operation	Constant Scan
Estimated I/O Cost	0
Estimated CPU Cost	0.0000142
Estimated Number of Executions	1
Estimated Operator Cost	0.0000142 (0%)
Estimated Subtree Cost	0.0000142
Estimated Number of Rows	14
Estimated Row Size	11 B
Node ID	1

Values
(Scalar Operator((1))), (Scalar Operator((2))), (Scalar Operator((3))), (Scalar Operator((4))), (Scalar Operator ((5))), (Scalar Operator((6))), (Scalar Operator((7))), (Scalar Operator((8))), (Scalar Operator((9))), (Scalar Operator((10))), (Scalar Operator((11))), (Scalar Operator ((12))), (Scalar Operator((13))), (Scalar Operator((14)))
Output List
PtnIds1004

FIGURE 11-2 Constant Scan enumerating partitions in SQL Server 2005

Table Scan
Scan rows from a table.

Physical Operation	Table Scan
Logical Operation	Table Scan
Estimated I/O Cost	5.44164
Estimated CPU Cost	0.471827
Estimated Number of Executions	14
Estimated Operator Cost	77.3428 (72%)
Estimated Subtree Cost	77.3428
Estimated Number of Rows	428658
Estimated Row Size	131 B
Partition ID	PtnIds1004
Ordered	False
Node ID	16

Object
[TPCD1G2005].[dbo].[LINEITEMPART]

FIGURE 11-3 Table Scan for one partition in SQL Server 2005

The preceding SQL Server showplan of a simple SELECT statement suggests that the lower levels of the engine (Storage Engine) perform scans and seeks knowing nothing about the partitioning above. They access each partition as if it is a new table after the Query Processor has translated a single partitioned table access into a join of a list of enumerated constants and parameterized table scans. Figure 11-4 shows the plan for the same statement against the same database in SQL Server 2008. Compared with the SQL Server 2005 plan in Figure 11-1, this plan is missing the Constant Scan enumerating partitions and the Nested Loops that performs the scan one partition after another.

SELECT
Cost: 0 %

Table Scan
[LINEITEMPART]
Cost: 100 %

FIGURE 11-4 Execution plan for simple SELECT from partitioned table in SQL Server 2008

The Table Scan properties are shown in Figure 11-5. Instead of the Partition ID we have only a True/False value for the *Partitioned* attribute. Observe that from the Estimated Execution Plan in SQL Server 2008, we cannot determine how many partitions the table has.

Table Scan	
Scan rows from a table.	
Physical Operation	Table Scan
Logical Operation	Table Scan
Estimated I/O Cost	76.1823
Estimated CPU Cost	6.60353
Estimated Number of Executions	1
Estimated Operator Cost	82.7858 (100%)
Estimated Subtree Cost	82.7858
Estimated Number of Rows	6001220
Estimated Row Size	131 B
Partitioned	True
Ordered	False
Node ID	0

Object
[TPCD1G2008].[dbo].[LINEITEMPART]

FIGURE 11-5 Table Scan for a partitioned table in SQL Server 2008 in the Estimated Execution Plan

We only know the table is partitioned. The apparent advantage of SQL Server 2005 Estimated Execution Plans disappears as soon as we have to work with hundreds of partitions or access several partitioned tables in a single query. The Actual Execution Plan in SQL Server 2008 does contain an Actual Partition Count attribute for every partitioned table scan and for every partitioned index scan or seek, as you can see in Figure 11-6.

Before we start talking about statistics on partitioned tables and examining various examples of partition elimination, let's create a partitioned clustered index on our LINEITEMPART table:

```
CREATE CLUSTERED INDEX L_IDX_SHIPDATE ON LINEITEMPART (L_SHIPDATE);
```

```
            Clustered Index Scan (Clustered)
 Scanning a clustered index, entirely or only a range.

 Physical Operation               Clustered Index Scan
 Logical Operation                Clustered Index Scan
 Actual Number of Rows                     6001215
 Estimated I/O Cost                        80.0867
 Estimated CPU Cost                        6.60353
 Number of Executions                            1
 Estimated Number of Executions                  1
 Estimated Operator Cost            86.6902 (100%)
 Estimated Subtree Cost                    86.6902
 Estimated Number of Rows                  6001220
 Estimated Row Size                          131 B
 Actual Rebinds                                  0
 Actual Rewinds                                  0
 Partitioned                                  True
 Actual Partition Count                         14
 Ordered                                     False
 Node ID                                         0

 Object
 [tpcd1G].[dbo].[lineitempart].[L_IDX_SHIPDATE]
```

FIGURE 11-6 Table Scan for partitioned table in SQL Server 2008 in Actual Execution Plan

Notice that we didn't indicate the use of a partition key or partition scheme in the CREATE CLUSTERED INDEX statement. The resulting index will still be partitioned using the same partition scheme and partition column as the original table. This behavior is by design. Even before SQL Server introduced partitioning in SQL Server 2005, if no filegroup is specified by the CREATE INDEX statement's ON <filegroup> clause, SQL Server creates the index in the same filegroup where the table resides. The ON <filegroup> clause is generalized for partitioning to allow not only ON <filegroup> but also ON <partition_scheme_name (column_name)> in SQL Server 2005. The concept of inheriting the same physical location is preserved by using the same partitioning scheme and column if none is specified explicitly.

Statistics on Partitioned Tables

In most cases creating and maintaining statistics on partitioned tables is the same as if the tables were not partitioned. All CREATE, UPDATE, and DROP statistics commands can be executed the same way they are executed against nonpartitioned tables. In some sense table and index partitioning is ignored when creating, updating, and using statistics. Rows participate in creating and maintaining statistics regardless of partition boundaries. In two cases the context of statistics on partitioned tables require special attention: the ALTER TABLE SWITCH command and statistics created by the CREATE INDEX statement on an index partitioned on nonleading column.

ALTER TABLE SWITCH is a powerful data manipulation command introduced in SQL Server 2005. It can be used to switch whole partitions of data in or out of a partitioned table. One way to explain the effect of ALTER TABLE SWITCH is to visualize each table as a pointer from its metadata description in the catalog to the physical location where the rows are stored. Similarly, for each index the pointer is to the root of the index tree. For partitioned tables and indexes each partition may reside in a different physical location. Therefore, there is a separate pointer to each table and index partition within the metadata describing the partitioned table and index. ALTER TABLE SWITCH command works with two partitioned or nonpartitioned tables. One table (or partition, if the table is partitioned) is the source, and the other is the target of the operation. The SWITCH command causes the toggling of the pointers between the source and target tables. After the command is complete, the source table and index pointers will point to the original target table and indexes and vice versa. This is shown in Figure 11-7, for the statement ALTER TABLE T SWITCH TO PT PARTITION 2, where T is a nonpartitioned table T with index I, and PT is a partitioned table PT with index PI. No data movement is involved when performing the SWITCH command. Therefore, the execution time is the same (usually milliseconds) regardless of the size of data volume involved. This is the major advantage of the ALTER TABLE SWITCH command.

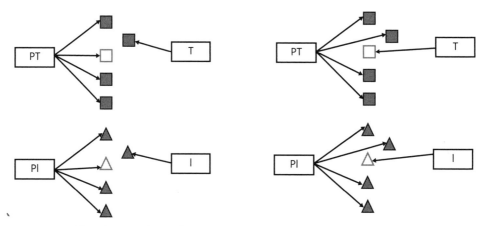

FIGURE 11-7 Changing metadata pointers

SQL Server requires the target partition or nonpartitioned table to be empty before the command is performed. Several more conditions must be met for the SWITCH command to work. For example, all indexes on the table must be aligned—meaning they must be partitioned the same way as the heap or clustered index. And if the target is a partitioned table, there must be an implicit (a partition of a partitioned table) or explicit (column constraint) constraint on the source to ensure that all data in the source correctly belongs to the target partition. You can find a complete list of all SWITCH restrictions in SQL Server Books Online under "Transferring Data Efficiently by Using Partition Switching."

Almost all uses of the SWITCH command fall into one of two categories:

1. The source is a nonpartitioned table containing data that will fill a partition of the partitioned table (the target). This is also known as "switching data into a partitioned table."

2. The source is a partition of a table containing "old" data, and the target is an empty nonpartitioned table. This is the case of "switching data out of a partitioned table."

From the perspective of statistics maintenance, SWITCH IN is equivalent to inserting data (usually a large amount) into the table, and SWITCH OUT is equivalent to deleting data. Therefore, SQL Server treats the statistics the same way as if INSERT or DELETE has been performed on the table. You can investigate the column *rowmodctr* for the heap or clustered index (indid 0 or 1) in the sysindexes system table before and after you perform the switch. You'll notice that the *rowmodctr* increases by the number of rows switched in or out. Consequently, if you have auto-update statistics ON for the table, statistics will be automatically updated when they are needed to generate a plan for a query if any of the following conditions is satisfied:

1. The table size has increased from 0 rows to more than 0 rows.

2. The number of rows in the table when original statistics were gathered was 500 or less, and one or more SWITCH commands cumulatively added or removed more than 500 rows.

3. The table had more than 500 rows when the statistics were originally gathered, and the *rowmodctr* has changed by more than 500 plus 20 percent of the number of rows in the table.

Note You can control this setting in several ways: the ALTER DATABASE option AUTO_UPDATE_STATISTICS, sp_autostats, and the NORECOMPUTE option on CREATE STATISTICS and UPDATE STATISTICS.

If the partitioned table is large, it may take significant time to update the statistics, and the first query that needs the statistics will be affected by this time increase unless you have set your auto-statistics update to be performed asynchronously (the ALTER DATABASE option AUTO_UPDATE_STATISTICS_ASYNC). The SWITCH commands are usually performed in regular intervals, and often it is the only way rows are added and removed from the partitioned table. If SWITCH operations are routine, then it may be better to turn auto-update statistics OFF for the table and run a manual update as an integral part of the process of inserting and deleting large amounts of rows.

Tip If you add or remove large amounts of rows from your table periodically in separate time windows, you should consider updating statistics for the affected table at the end of the data change.

Now let's talk about statistics created by the CREATE INDEX statement on an index partitioned on a column that is not the leading column of the index key. To understand the problem we first need to understand the history of the relationship between indexes and statistics in SQL Server. SQL Server in releases prior to 7.0 created statistics only as a by-product of index creation. When an index is created, SQL Server must read the table, order all index key values, and build the index tree. When statistics with FULLSCAN are created, reading the whole table or index and sorting the columns on which the statistics are built represent the majority of the work. But this all happens when creating an index; therefore, the additional cost to create statistics with FULLSCAN is minimal. Thus when any index or unique constraint is created, SQL Server creates statistics with FULLSCAN for the index or constraint, and this logic still exists in SQL Server 2008. SQL Server 7.0 is the first release introducing CREATE STATISTICS, auto-create, and auto-update statistics commands and options. The CREATE STATISTICS equivalent of the by-product of CREATE INDEX described earlier would require a scan of the whole table or index, perform sort, and build statistics. This could be a very costly operation; therefore, SQL Server by default creates statistics on large tables using sampling. The default may be overwritten in CREATE or UPDATE STATISTICS commands, but it cannot be changed for auto-created and auto-updated statistics.

The problem with statistics on partitioned indexes is specific to a case when the partitioning column is not the leading column of the index key. For example, to efficiently join our table LINEITEMPART with a table of all suppliers, we need to create an index with the leading column L_SUPPKEY on LINEITEMPART. If we need to perform a SWITCH on the table as well, all our indexes must be partitioned on the same column—in our case, L_SHIPDATE. Therefore, the new index satisfying these conditions could be defined as follows:

```
CREATE INDEX L_IDX_SUPPKEY ON LINEITEMPART (L_SUPPKEY) ON PSYEAR (L_SHIPDATE);
```

Because our index is partitioned on L_SHIPDATE, the same value of L_SUPPKEY may appear in more than one partition if the supplier shipped goods we track in different months. SQL Server is creating partitioned indexes on partitioned tables by creating a separate index tree for each of the partitions. Therefore, we will have a completely sorted sequence of L_SUPPKEY in each of the partitions, but the same supplier—and thus the same value of L_SUPPKEY—may appear in more than one partition. In the specific case where an index is partitioned on one column, but another column is the leading key of the index, SQL Server 2005 and SQL Server 2008 cannot create correct histograms during index creation. This may be fixed in the upcoming service packs or releases of SQL Server.

Tip Whenever you build or rebuild a partitioned index that is partitioned on a column that is not the leading column of the index, you should run update statistics on the index immediately after you build or rebuild this index.

The following query against metadata tables identifies all partitioned indexes in a database that are partitioned on a column different from the leading column of the index key.

```
SELECT OBJECT_NAME(IX.object_id) AS table_name, IX.name AS index_name
FROM sys.index_columns AS IC
  JOIN sys.indexes AS IX
    ON IC.object_id = IX.object_id AND IC.index_id = ix.index_id
WHERE IC.partition_ordinal = 1 AND IC.key_ordinal <> 1;
```

Partition Elimination

Partition elimination is a technique to avoid accessing partitions that cannot contain any rows contributing to the result. Most frequently this is accomplished by a WHERE clause using predicates that restrict the values of the partitioning column. Nested Loops joins have a similar effect, with an equality join predicate on the partitioning column. The outer row contains the partitioning column value because we are joining on it. The value determines single partition where we seek for the match for the outer row.

Let's investigate the query plan for the SELECT query in Listing 11-1.

LISTING 11-1 SELECT query with simple predicate on its partitioning column

```
SELECT * FROM LINEITEMPART WHERE L_SHIPDATE = '20090301';
```

Because we specify the value of L_SHIPDATE in an equality predicate in the WHERE clause, and L_SHIPDATE is the partitioning column, we know that all resulting rows reside in a single partition. Figure 11-8 illustrates this query's executionplan, which is the same for both SQL Server 2005 and SQL Server 2008. But the interpretation is very different. Because we don't see the partition enumerating Constant Scan in the SQL Server 2005 plan (as you saw earlier in Figure 11-1), we know we are accessing only a single partition if this is SQL Server 2005 plan. However, in SQL Server 2008, partition-enumerating Constant Scans are not displayed graphically. Therefore, we cannot tell by looking only at Figure 11-8 whether the partition elimination happened. For this we have to investigate the properties of the Clustered Index Seek operator in the SQL Server Management Studio (SSMS) window.

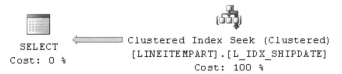

FIGURE 11-8 Query plan for index seek into partitioned table with equal predicate on the partitioning column

If you right-click the Clustered Index Seek icon in the SQL Server 2008 query plan, a dialog box pops up with several actions (for example, Zoom In, Zoom Out); the last action is Properties. Choose Properties, and the properties of the Clustered Index Seek operator are displayed in a separate Properties window in Management Studio. After expanding several levels under the Seek Predicates in the Properties Window, the Properties dialog box shown in Figure 11-9 opens.

FIGURE 11-9 Clustered Index Seek operator properties

> **Tip** You can expand all the nodes below a selected expandable node by typing *.

Figure 11-9 shows two Range Columns ([1] and [2]) and two corresponding Range Expressions. The first Range Column is generated by SQL Server to perform partition elimination. We recognize it by its internally generated PtnId1000 name. The second Range Column is generated for the predicate L_SHIPDATE= '20090301' in the query. The first Range Expression is not shown completely in Figure 11-9, but it can be seen in a separate pop-up window, and its content is shown in Listing 11-2. The second Range Expression is Scalar Operator(CONVERT_IMPLICIT(smalldatetime,[@1],0)) and it represents the value of constant '20090301' converted to the smalldatetime type. Observe that both Range Expressions are referring to [@1] instead of the constant '20090301'. This is because the query was auto-parameterized by SQL Server, and its query plan can be used for any other constant in the place of '20090301'.

Evaluating the first Range Expression for Range Column PtnId1000 generates the correct partition number, and only this partition is accessed by the Clustered Index Seek operator. The second Range Expression is used to seek the partition of the clustered index for all rows with the correct values of L_SHIPDATE. If the query uses a parameter value instead of the constant '20090301', the query plan will be exactly the same, except that instead of [@1], you will see the parameter name.

LISTING 11-2 First Scalar Operator Range Expression from Index Seek in Figure 11-9

```
Scalar Operator(RangePartitionNew(CONVERT_IMPLICIT(smalldatetime,[@1],0),(1),'2009-01-01
00:00:00.000','2009-02-01 00:00:00.000','2009-03-01 00:00:00.000','2009-04-01
00:00:00.000','2009-05-01 00:00:00.000','2009-06-01 00:00:00.000','2009-07-01
00:00:00.000','2009-08-01 00:00:00.000','2009-09-01 00:00:00.000','2009-10-01
00:00:00.000','2009-11-01 00:00:00.000','2009-12-01 00:00:00.000','2010-01-01
00:00:00.000'))
```

Listing 11-3 contains a query in which we use the BETWEEN predicate on the partitioning column.

LISTING 11-3 A SELECT query that uses the BETWEEN predicate

```
SELECT * FROM LINEITEMPART WHERE L_SHIPDATE BETWEEN '20090301' AND '20090531';
```

In this case, the SQL Server 2005 and SQL Server 2008 query plans are different. Let's first look at the SQL Server 2005 plan, shown in Figure 11-10.

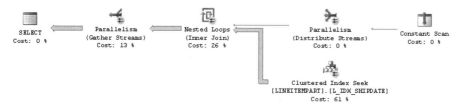

FIGURE 11-10 SQL Server 2005 plan for the query in Listing 11-3

Because this query is accessing more than one partition, we see again the Constant Scan enumerating the accessed partitions in the query plan. Figure 11-11 shows the properties of the Constant Scan operator, which can be displayed by resting the cursor on the operator in SSMS.

Constant Scan
Scan an internal table of constants.

Physical Operation	Constant Scan
Logical Operation	Constant Scan
Estimated I/O Cost	0
Estimated CPU Cost	0.0000032
Estimated Number of Executions	1
Estimated Operator Cost	0.0000032 (0%)
Estimated Subtree Cost	0.0000032
Estimated Number of Rows	3
Estimated Row Size	11 B
Node ID	3

Values
(Scalar Operator((4))), (Scalar Operator((5))), (Scalar
Operator((6)))
Output List
PtnIds1006

FIGURE 11-11 Properties for the Constant Scan operator in Figure 11-10

The Values list shows that partition numbers 4, 5, and 6 are accessed to get the result of the query.

In SQL Server 2008, the plan for the query in Listing 11-3 looks exactly the same as the plan in Figure 11-8. Deeper investigation of the properties of the Clustered Index Seek reveals the difference: For the BETWEEN query we will see two different Range Expressions for Range Column PtnId1000. One is called "Start," and the other is called "End." The Range Expressions are, respectively,

```
Scalar Operator(RangePartitionNew(CONVERT_IMPLICIT(smalldatetime,[@1],0),(1),'2009-01-01
00:00:00.000','2009-02-01 00:00:00.000','2009-03-01 00:00:00.000','2009-04-01
00:00:00.000','2009-05-01 00:00:00.000','2009-06-01 00:00:00.000','2009-07-01
00:00:00.000','2009-08-01 00:00:00.000','2009-09-01 00:00:00.000','2009-10-01
00:00:00.000','2009-11-01 00:00:00.000','2009-12-01 00:00:00.000','2010-01-01
00:00:00.000'))

Scalar Operator(RangePartitionNew(CONVERT_IMPLICIT(smalldatetime,[@2],0),(1),'2009-01-01
00:00:00.000','2009-02-01 00:00:00.000','2009-03-01 00:00:00.000','2009-04-01
00:00:00.000','2009-05-01 00:00:00.000','2009-06-01 00:00:00.000','2009-07-01
00:00:00.000','2009-08-01 00:00:00.000','2009-09-01 00:00:00.000','2009-10-01
00:00:00.000','2009-11-01 00:00:00.000','2009-12-01 00:00:00.000','2010-01-01
00:00:00.000'))
```

As in the case of the equality predicate, the query is auto-parameterized (the auto-generated parameter [@1] replaces the Start constant '20090301' and [@2] replaces the End constant '20090531'). Therefore, the execution plan may be reused for various values of the range constants.

Partitioning and Parallelism

Partitioning is usually introduced for large tables processed on big multi-CPU servers. Therefore, it is important to pay attention to parallelism of queries against partitioned tables. When investigating parallelism, we should first determine whether a parallel query plan is generated at all. Subsequently we can evaluate execution efficiency of the query from the point of view of parallelism.

In this section I will explain how to recognize what parts of a query plan are parallel, what special considerations we should have in the context of partitioning and parallelism, and how to investigate execution efficiency for parallel query plans. I will also give the details of one substantial change in parallel plan processing for partitioned tables between SQL Server 2005 and SQL Server 2008.

Take a look back at the query plan in Figure 11-10 for our BETWEEN query in SQL Server 2005. It has four parallel operators as well as two operators without parallelism (Constant Scan and SELECT). The parallel operators are indicated by a round yellow icon with two arrows at the base of the operator icon. A parallel query plan has at least one Parallelism operator. Figure 11-10 shows two kinds of Parallelism operators: Gather Streams on the left and Distribute Streams after the Constant Scan operator. The Distribute Streams operator creates multiple streams from a single input data stream. The Gather Streams operator merges several input streams into single output. There is one more type of Parallelism operator that does not occur in our example. It is called Redistribute Streams, and it has multiple input and multiple output data streams.

Parallel execution of SQL Server query plan is performed by distributing single stream of rows into several streams, each processed by a separate thread. The distribution can be initiated either by a parallel scan or parallel seek operator, or by the afore mentioned Distribute Streams Parallelism operator. The effectiveness of parallel processing is then determined by how equally the work is distributed into the parallel streams. In some cases, the Gather and Redistribute Streams operators must preserve order, and this may introduce stalling because they can produce a new row only when they have received at least one row or end-of-stream indication from all input streams.

SQL Server considers query parallelism only if there is more than one processor (multiple CPUs, cores, hyperthreading, or any combination of these) available to SQL Server. Query Optimizer then decides for each individual query whether to generate a parallel plan. For low-cost queries, the overhead of parallelism may be bigger than the gain. Therefore, parallelism is not considered for queries with estimated cost less than 5. (You may see parallel query plans with an estimated cost lower than 5 if the parallelism is what caused the plan's cost to drop below 5.)

The degree of parallelism of a query with a parallel plan in SQL Server is the maximum number of active threads executing the query. The number of worker threads required for parallel query is usually much higher because every Parallelism operator creates a thread boundary—each input stream and output stream is assigned a separate worker thread. The degree of parallelism restricts the number of *active* worker threads at any point of single query execution.

The same parallel query plan may be executed with different degrees of parallelism. SQL Server decides at the time of query startup what degree of parallelism to use. This is affected by the available resources at that moment. Therefore, the same query with a single parallel query plan may be executed with different degrees of parallelism at different times. You can use either the Degree of Parallelism Event in the SQL Server's Performance Event profiler category or the Actual Execution Plan captured in SSMS or profiler to monitor the actual degree of parallelism for a particular instance of query execution.

You can use *sp_configure* with the 'max degree or parallelism' option to lower the maximum considered by SQL Server for the whole instance. An individual query can include the clause OPTION (MAXDOP <value>) to change the maximum for its own execution.

The query in Listing 11-4 demonstrates a major discrepancy in parallel query execution for partitioned tables between SQL Server 2005 and SQL Server 2008. As a by-product of the explanation, we will learn how to investigate the efficiency of parallelism.

LISTING 11-4 Query to investigate parallel execution

```
SELECT  COUNT(*) FROM LINEITEMPART WHERE L_SHIPDATE BETWEEN '20090301' AND '20090531';
```

First let's look at the SQL Server 2005 query plan. Because we want to know what was happening *during* the execution, we have to turn on Include Actual Execution Plan in Management Studio and run the query. The result is the plan shown in Figure 11-12. The actual plan looks the same as the estimated plan, but it contains additional information from the execution inside the properties of individual operators and connecting edges.

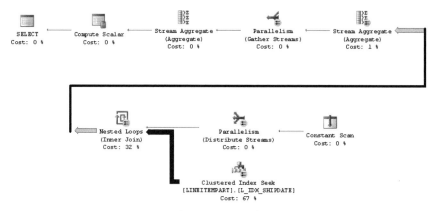

FIGURE 11-12 SQL Server 2005 Actual Execution Plan for the query in Listing 11-4

Let's go over the plan in Figure 11-12 in the order of execution from right to left. By now we know that the Constant Scan enumerates the partitions the query has to access in SQL Server 2005. It produces three constant values—IDs for partitions 4, 5, and 6. We are running the query with degree of parallelism 8; therefore, the Distribute Streams Parallelism operator has threads ready to accept values on the output. But there are only three values on input, and while they end up on three different threads, the remaining five threads are empty. Therefore, the query executes only three (and not eight) concurrent seek loops into the LINITEMPART.L_IDX_SHIPDATE clustered index. The Nested Loops join is ready to be performed concurrently on eight threads, but only three have input values, so the remaining five threads stay idle. Figure 11-13 displays the properties of the edge exiting from the Nested Loops join.

> **Note** The Properties window in Figure 11-13 incorrectly enumerates threads. Thread 0 is not used.

Properties ▾ ◻ ✕	
Edge	▾
□ Misc	
□ Actual Number of Rows	1568280
Thread 0	0
Thread 1	0
Thread 2	512423
Thread 3	0
Thread 4	514501
Thread 5	0
Thread 6	0
Thread 7	541356
Thread 8	0
Estimated Data Size	13 MB
Estimated Number of Rows	1551330
Estimated Row Size	9 B

FIGURE 11-13 SQL Server 2005 Actual Number of Rows generated from the Nested Loops join

Following the Nested Loops join is a parallel Stream Aggregate operator, which we also call Partial Aggregation. Because we are performing COUNT(*), this operator is prepared to count the rows in each of the eight streams. Only three streams have any rows and return a nonzero number. The remaining five will return no rows without doing any work except to check for the end of stream. The next Gather Streams Parallelism operator merges the eight streams, where five are empty and the remaining three have one Partial Aggregate value, into a single stream that flows into another Stream Aggregate operator called Global Aggregation because it is producing a final count from partial counts generated earlier by the Parallel Partial Aggregations.

Let's turn our attention to the SQL Server 2008 plan for the same query in Listing 11-4 against the same table LINEITEMPART. The Actual Execution Plan is shown in Figure 11-14.

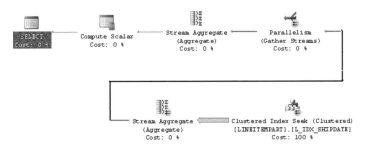

FIGURE 11-14 SQL Server 2008 Actual Execution Plan for the query in Listing 11-4

The plan is similar to the SQL Server 2005 plan shown in Figure 11-12. It performs partial aggregation on eight streams and then performs global aggregation. But if we investigate the properties of the edge exiting the Clustered Index Seek operator, we see a very different row distribution compared to the SQL Server 2005 row distribution. Figure 11-15 shows that each of the eight threads from Thread 1 to Thread 8 has processed some rows. Therefore, the SQL Server 2008 query plan is executing more efficiently.

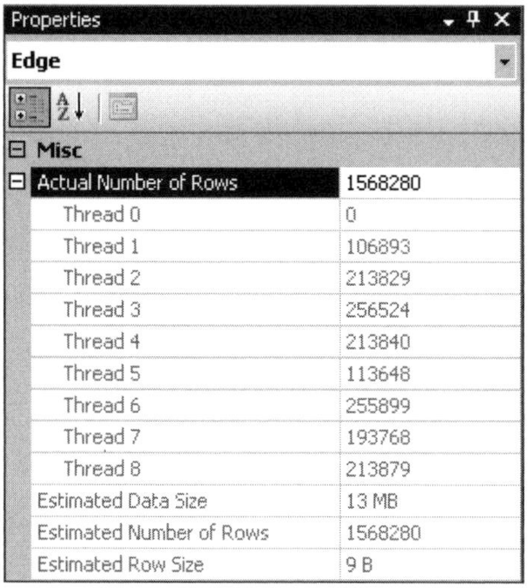

Properties ▾ ⊣ ✕	
Edge	▾
⊟ **Misc**	
⊟ Actual Number of Rows	1568280
Thread 0	0
Thread 1	106893
Thread 2	213829
Thread 3	256524
Thread 4	213840
Thread 5	113648
Thread 6	255899
Thread 7	193768
Thread 8	213879
Estimated Data Size	13 MB
Estimated Number of Rows	1568280
Estimated Row Size	9 B

FIGURE 11-15 SQL Server 2008 Actual Number of Rows generated from the Nested Loops join

Let's summarize and generalize our investigation of parallel plans on partitioned tables in SQL Server 2005 and 2008.

In SQL Server 2005, for queries that access partitioned table or index, the parallelism is driven by the partitions. Each individual table or index partition is processed by a separate single thread. Therefore, if there are fewer partitions than degree of parallelism, some of the parallel threads will end up idle. That was the case with accessing only three partitions on an eight-core machine. On the other hand, if there are more partitions, some will be processed only after one of the previous partitions has been handled. But at most, one thread is always active on one partition at a time. There is a significant exception to this rule: If SQL Server 2005 knows *at compile time* that only a single partition of partitioned table is accessed, a fully parallel plan is considered and potentially generated exactly as if accessing a nonpartitioned table. The *at compile time* exception is important when designing your queries using parameters in SQL Server 2005. For example, if instead of the existing WHERE clause in the query in Listing 11-4

```
WHERE L_SHIPDATE BETWEEN '20090301' AND '20090531'
```

we access only a single month, and therefore a single partition:

```
WHERE L_SHIPDATE BETWEEN '20090301' AND '20090331'
```

the SQL Server 2005 query plan will look exactly like the SQL Server 2008 plan in Figure 11-14, and all threads (eight in our case) will be used during query execution. But if we use parameters instead of the constants

```
WHERE L_SHIPDATE BETWEEN @date1 AND @date2
```

SQL Server has to generate the Constant Scan with Nested Loop plan, because we don't know at compile time whether only one partition or more than one partition is accessed. If, for example, the value '20090301' is then substituted for @date1 and '20090331' is substituted for @date2, the query will still be executed on a single thread instead of eight threads, as were used when the query was written without parameters!

The preceding problems with parallelism on partitioned tables were addressed when developing SQL Server 2008 by implementing a round-robin strategy when assigning threads to partitions. Therefore, the same query plan is used for one or many partitions and the assignment of threads is adjusted at query startup time.

Conclusion

When we write queries accessing partitioned tables, we should first pay attention to all the normal pitfalls surrounding query plan selection. In addition, partitioned tables bring further challenges in the area of partition elimination, statistics, and parallelism. When writing queries against partitioned tables, pay special attention to partition elimination (for example, ask whether your query provides enough information so that only some partitions will be accessed) and how parallelism works across multiple partitions. We have learned that the best way to investigate any issue affecting query execution is to analyze the Actual Execution Plans that contain information about query execution.

Chapter 12
Graphs, Trees, Hierarchies, and Recursive Queries

This chapter covers treatment of specialized data structures called graphs, trees, and hierarchies in Microsoft SQL Server using T-SQL. Of the three, probably the most commonly used among T-SQL programmers is the *hierarchy*, and this term is sometimes used even when the data structure involved is not really a hierarchy. I'll start with a terminology section describing each data structure to clear the confusion.

Treatment (representation, maintenance, and manipulation) of graphs, trees, and hierarchies in an RDBMS is far from trivial. I'll discuss two main approaches, one based on iterative/recursive logic and another based on materializing extra information in the database that describes the data structure.

This chapter also covers the HIERARCHYID data type introduced in SQL Server 2008, which is designed to help in maintaining and querying graphs.

Terminology

 Note The explanations in this section are based on definitions from the National Institute of Standards and Technology (NIST). I made some revisions and added some narrative to the original definitions to make them less formal and keep them relevant to the subject area (T-SQL).

For more complete and formal definitions of graphs, trees, and related terms, please refer to *http://www.nist.gov/dads/.*

Graphs

A graph is a set of items connected by *edges*. Each item is called a *vertex* or *node*. An edge is a connection between two vertices of a graph.

A *graph* is a catchall term for a data structure, and many scenarios can be represented as graphs—for example, employee organizational charts, bills of materials (BOMs), road systems, and so on. To narrow down the type of graph to a more specific case, you need to identify its properties:

Directed/Undirected In a directed graph (also known as a *digraph*), the two vertices of an edge have a direction or order. For example, in a BOM graph for coffee shop products,

Latte contains Milk and not the other way around. The graph has an edge (containment relationship) for the pair of vertices/items (Latte, Milk) but has no edge for the pair (Milk, Latte).

In an undirected graph, each edge simply connects two vertices, with no particular order. For example, a road system graph could have a road between Los Angeles and San Francisco. The edge (road) between the vertices (cities) Los Angeles and San Francisco can be expressed as either of the following: {Los Angeles, San Francisco} or {San Francisco, Los Angeles}.

Acyclic   An acyclic graph is a graph with no cycle—that is, no *path* that starts and ends at the same vertex—for example, employee organizational charts and BOMs. A directed acyclic graph is also known as a *DAG*.

If the graph has paths that start and end at the same vertex—as there usually are in road systems—the graph is not acyclic.

Connected   A connected graph is a graph where there's a path between every pair of vertices—for example, employee organizational charts.

Trees

A *tree* is a special kind of graph—a connected, acyclic graph.

A *rooted tree* is accessed beginning at the *root* node. Each node is either a *leaf* or an *internal node*. An internal node has one or more *child* nodes and is called the *parent* of its child nodes. All children of the same node are *siblings*. Contrary to the appearance in a physical tree, the root is usually depicted at the top of the structure, and the leaves are depicted at the bottom, as illustrated in Figure 12-1.

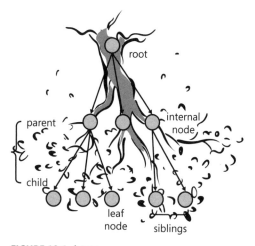

FIGURE 12-1 A tree

A *forest* is a collection of one or more trees—for example, forum discussions can be represented as a forest where each thread is a tree.

Hierarchies

Some scenarios can be described as hierarchies and modeled as directed acyclic graphs—for example, inheritance among types/classes in object-oriented programming and reports-to relationships in an employee organizational chart. In the former, the edges of the graph locate the inheritance. Classes can inherit methods and properties from other classes (and possibly from multiple classes). In the latter, the edges represent the reports-to relationship between employees. Note the acyclic, directed nature of these scenarios. The management chain of responsibility in a company cannot go around in circles, for example.

Scenarios

Throughout the chapter, I will use three scenarios: Employee Organizational Chart (tree, hierarchy); Bill Of Materials, or BOM (DAG); and Road System (undirected cyclic graph). Note what distinguishes a (directed) tree from a DAG. All trees are DAGs, but not all DAGs are trees. In a tree, an item can have at most one parent; in some management hierarchies, an employee can have more than one manager.

Employee Organizational Chart

The employee organizational chart that I will use is depicted graphically in Figure 12-2.

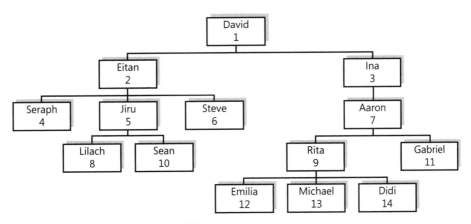

FIGURE 12-2 Employee organizational chart

To create the Employees table and populate it with sample data, run the code in Listing 12-1. The contents of the Employees table are shown in Table 12-1.

LISTING 12-1 Data definition language and sample data for the Employees table

```
SET NOCOUNT ON;
USE tempdb;
GO
IF OBJECT_ID('dbo.Employees') IS NOT NULL
  DROP TABLE dbo.Employees;
GO
CREATE TABLE dbo.Employees
(
  empid    INT        NOT NULL PRIMARY KEY,
  mgrid    INT        NULL      REFERENCES dbo.Employees,
  empname VARCHAR(25) NOT NULL,
  salary  MONEY       NOT NULL,
  CHECK (empid <> mgrid)
);

INSERT INTO dbo.Employees(empid, mgrid, empname, salary) VALUES
  (1,  NULL, 'David'  , $10000.00),
  (2,  1,    'Eitan'  , $7000.00),
  (3,  1,    'Ina'    , $7500.00),
  (4,  2,    'Seraph' , $5000.00),
  (5,  2,    'Jiru'   , $5500.00),
  (6,  2,    'Steve'  , $4500.00),
  (7,  3,    'Aaron'  , $5000.00),
  (8,  5,    'Lilach' , $3500.00),
  (9,  7,    'Rita'   , $3000.00),
  (10, 5,    'Sean'   , $3000.00),
  (11, 7,    'Gabriel', $3000.00),
  (12, 9,    'Emilia' , $2000.00),
  (13, 9,    'Michael', $2000.00),
  (14, 9,    'Didi'   , $1500.00);

CREATE UNIQUE INDEX idx_unc_mgrid_empid ON dbo.Employees(mgrid, empid);
```

TABLE 12-1 Contents of Employees Table

empid	mgrid	empname	salary
1	NULL	David	10000.0000
2	1	Eitan	7000.0000
3	1	Ina	7500.0000
4	2	Seraph	5000.0000
5	2	Jiru	5500.0000
6	2	Steve	4500.0000
7	3	Aaron	5000.0000
8	5	Lilach	3500.0000
9	7	Rita	3000.0000
10	5	Sean	3000.0000

TABLE 12-1 Contents of Employees Table

empid	mgrid	empname	salary
11	7	Gabriel	3000.0000
12	9	Emilia	2000.0000
13	9	Michael	2000.0000
14	9	Didi	1500.0000

The Employees table represents a management hierarchy as an adjacency list, where the manager and employee represent the parent and child nodes, respectively.

Bill of Materials (BOM)

I will use a BOM of coffee shop products, which is depicted graphically in Figure 12-3.

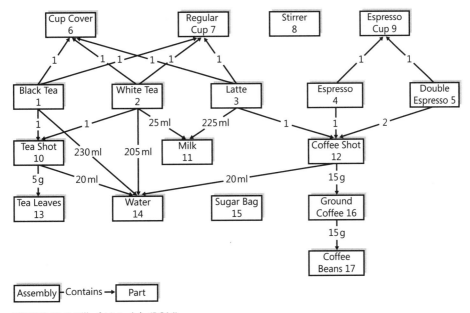

FIGURE 12-3 Bill of Materials (BOM)

To create the Parts and BOM tables and populate them with sample data, run the code in Listing 12-2. The contents of the Parts and BOM tables are shown in Tables 12-2 and 12-3.

Notice that the first scenario (employee organizational chart) requires only one table because it is modeled as a tree; both an edge (manager, employee) and a vertex (employee) can be represented by the same row. The BOM scenario requires two tables because it is modeled as a DAG, where multiple paths can lead to each node; an edge (assembly, part) is represented by a row in the BOM table, and a vertex (part) is represented by a row in the Parts table.

LISTING 12-2 Data definition language and sample data for the Parts and BOM tables

```
SET NOCOUNT ON;
USE tempdb;
GO
IF OBJECT_ID('dbo.BOM') IS NOT NULL
  DROP TABLE dbo.BOM;
GO
IF OBJECT_ID('dbo.Parts') IS NOT NULL
  DROP TABLE dbo.Parts;
GO
CREATE TABLE dbo.Parts
(
  partid   INT        NOT NULL PRIMARY KEY,
  partname VARCHAR(25) NOT NULL
);

INSERT INTO dbo.Parts(partid, partname) VALUES
  ( 1, 'Black Tea'       ),
  ( 2, 'White Tea'       ),
  ( 3, 'Latte'           ),
  ( 4, 'Espresso'        ),
  ( 5, 'Double Espresso'),
  ( 6, 'Cup Cover'       ),
  ( 7, 'Regular Cup'     ),
  ( 8, 'Stirrer'         ),
  ( 9, 'Espresso Cup'    ),
  (10, 'Tea Shot'        ),
  (11, 'Milk'            ),
  (12, 'Coffee Shot'     ),
  (13, 'Tea Leaves'      ),
  (14, 'Water'           ),
  (15, 'Sugar Bag'       ),
  (16, 'Ground Coffee'   ),
  (17, 'Coffee Beans'    );

CREATE TABLE dbo.BOM
(
  partid     INT         NOT NULL REFERENCES dbo.Parts,
  assemblyid INT         NULL     REFERENCES dbo.Parts,
  unit       VARCHAR(3)  NOT NULL,
  qty        DECIMAL(8, 2) NOT NULL,
  UNIQUE(partid, assemblyid),
  CHECK (partid <> assemblyid)
);

INSERT INTO dbo.BOM(partid, assemblyid, unit, qty) VALUES
  ( 1, NULL, 'EA',  1.00),
  ( 2, NULL, 'EA',  1.00),
  ( 3, NULL, 'EA',  1.00),
  ( 4, NULL, 'EA',  1.00),
  ( 5, NULL, 'EA',  1.00),
  ( 6,    1, 'EA',  1.00),
  ( 7,    1, 'EA',  1.00),
```

```
(10,    1, 'EA',    1.00),
(14,    1, 'mL', 230.00),
( 6,    2, 'EA',    1.00),
( 7,    2, 'EA',    1.00),
(10,    2, 'EA',    1.00),
(14,    2, 'mL', 205.00),
(11,    2, 'mL',   25.00),
( 6,    3, 'EA',    1.00),
( 7,    3, 'EA',    1.00),
(11,    3, 'mL', 225.00),
(12,    3, 'EA',    1.00),
( 9,    4, 'EA',    1.00),
(12,    4, 'EA',    1.00),
( 9,    5, 'EA',    1.00),
(12,    5, 'EA',    2.00),
(13,   10, 'g' ,    5.00),
(14,   10, 'mL',   20.00),
(14,   12, 'mL',   20.00),
(16,   12, 'g' ,   15.00),
(17,   16, 'g' ,   15.00);
```

TABLE 12-2 Contents of Parts Table

partid	partname
1	Black Tea
2	White Tea
3	Latte
4	Espresso
5	Double Espresso
6	Cup Cover
7	Regular Cup
8	Stirrer
9	Espresso Cup
10	Tea Shot
11	Milk
12	Coffee Shot
13	Tea Leaves
14	Water
15	Sugar Bag
16	Ground Coffee
17	Coffee Beans

TABLE 12-3 Contents of BOM Table

partid	assemblyid	unit	qty
1	NULL	EA	1.00
2	NULL	EA	1.00
3	NULL	EA	1.00
4	NULL	EA	1.00
5	NULL	EA	1.00
6	1	EA	1.00
7	1	EA	1.00
10	1	EA	1.00
14	1	mL	230.00
6	2	EA	1.00
7	2	EA	1.00
10	2	EA	1.00
14	2	mL	205.00
11	2	mL	25.00
6	3	EA	1.00
7	3	EA	1.00
11	3	mL	225.00
12	3	EA	1.00
9	4	EA	1.00
12	4	EA	1.00
9	5	EA	1.00
12	5	EA	2.00
13	10	g	5.00
14	10	mL	20.00
14	12	mL	20.00
16	12	g	15.00
17	16	g	15.00

BOM represents a directed acyclic graph (DAG). It holds the parent and child node IDs in the *assemblyid* and *partid* attributes, respectively. BOM also represents a *weighted* graph, where a weight/number is associated with each edge. In our case, that weight is the *qty* attribute that holds the quantity of the part within the assembly (assembly of sub parts). The unit attribute holds the unit of the *qty* (EA for each, g for gram, mL for milliliter, and so on).

Road System

The Road System scenario that I will use is that of several major cities in the United States, and it is depicted graphically in Figure 12-4. In this scenario, I've chosen an International Air Transport Association (IATA) code to identify each city.

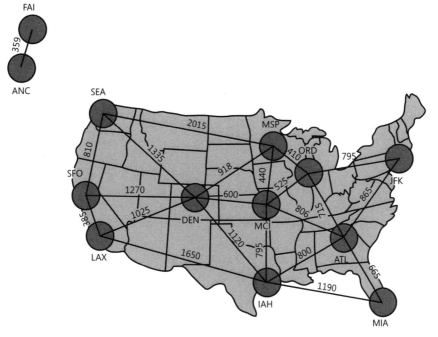

FIGURE 12-4 Road system

To create the Cities and Roads tables and populate them with sample data, run the code in Listing 12-3. The contents of the Cities and Roads tables are shown in Tables 12-4 and 12-5.

LISTING 12-3 Data definition language and sample data for the Cities and Roads tables

```
SET NOCOUNT ON;
USE tempdb;
GO
IF OBJECT_ID('dbo.Roads') IS NOT NULL
  DROP TABLE dbo.Roads;
GO
IF OBJECT_ID('dbo.Cities') IS NOT NULL
  DROP TABLE dbo.Cities;
GO

CREATE TABLE dbo.Cities
(
  cityid  CHAR(3)     NOT NULL PRIMARY KEY,
  city    VARCHAR(30) NOT NULL,
  region  VARCHAR(30) NULL,
  country VARCHAR(30) NOT NULL
);

INSERT INTO dbo.Cities(cityid, city, region, country) VALUES
  ('ATL', 'Atlanta', 'GA', 'USA'),
  ('ORD', 'Chicago', 'IL', 'USA'),
  ('DEN', 'Denver', 'CO', 'USA'),
  ('IAH', 'Houston', 'TX', 'USA'),
  ('MCI', 'Kansas City', 'KS', 'USA'),
```

```
    ('LAX', 'Los Angeles', 'CA', 'USA'),
    ('MIA', 'Miami', 'FL', 'USA'),
    ('MSP', 'Minneapolis', 'MN', 'USA'),
    ('JFK', 'New York', 'NY', 'USA'),
    ('SEA', 'Seattle', 'WA', 'USA'),
    ('SFO', 'San Francisco', 'CA', 'USA'),
    ('ANC', 'Anchorage', 'AK', 'USA'),
    ('FAI', 'Fairbanks', 'AK', 'USA');

CREATE TABLE dbo.Roads
(
    city1     CHAR(3) NOT NULL REFERENCES dbo.Cities,
    city2     CHAR(3) NOT NULL REFERENCES dbo.Cities,
    distance INT     NOT NULL,
    PRIMARY KEY(city1, city2),
    CHECK(city1 < city2),
    CHECK(distance > 0)
);

INSERT INTO dbo.Roads(city1, city2, distance) VALUES
    ('ANC', 'FAI',  359),
    ('ATL', 'ORD',  715),
    ('ATL', 'IAH',  800),
    ('ATL', 'MCI',  805),
    ('ATL', 'MIA',  665),
    ('ATL', 'JFK',  865),
    ('DEN', 'IAH', 1120),
    ('DEN', 'MCI',  600),
    ('DEN', 'LAX', 1025),
    ('DEN', 'MSP',  915),
    ('DEN', 'SEA', 1335),
    ('DEN', 'SFO', 1270),
    ('IAH', 'MCI',  795),
    ('IAH', 'LAX', 1550),
    ('IAH', 'MIA', 1190),
    ('JFK', 'ORD',  795),
    ('LAX', 'SFO',  385),
    ('MCI', 'ORD',  525),
    ('MCI', 'MSP',  440),
    ('MSP', 'ORD',  410),
    ('MSP', 'SEA', 2015),
    ('SEA', 'SFO',  815);
```

TABLE 12-4 Contents of Cities Table

cityid	city	region	country
ANC	Anchorage	AK	USA
ATL	Atlanta	GA	USA
DEN	Denver	CO	USA

TABLE 12-4 Contents of Cities Table

cityid	city	region	country
FAI	Fairbanks	AK	USA
IAH	Houston	TX	USA
JFK	New York	NY	USA
LAX	Los Angeles	CA	USA
MCI	Kansas City	KS	USA
MIA	Miami	FL	USA
MSP	Minneapolis	MN	USA
ORD	Chicago	IL	USA
SEA	Seattle	WA	USA
SFO	San Francisco	CA	USA

TABLE 12-5 Contents of Roads Table

city1	city2	distance
ANC	FAI	359
ATL	IAH	800
ATL	JFK	865
ATL	MCI	805
ATL	MIA	665
ATL	ORD	715
DEN	IAH	1120
DEN	LAX	1025
DEN	MCI	600
DEN	MSP	915
DEN	SEA	1335
DEN	SFO	1270
IAH	LAX	1550
IAH	MCI	795
IAH	MIA	1190
JFK	ORD	795
LAX	SFO	385
MCI	MSP	440
MCI	ORD	525
MSP	ORD	410
MSP	SEA	2015
SEA	SFO	815

The Roads table represents an undirected cyclic weighted graph. Each edge (road) is represented by a row in the table. The attributes *city1 and city2* are two city IDs representing the nodes of the edge. The weight in this case is the distance attribute, which holds the distance between the cities in miles. Note that the Roads table has a CHECK constraint (*city1 < city2*) as part of its schema definition to reject attempts to enter the same edge twice (for example, {SEA, SFO} and {SFO, SEA}).

Having all the scenarios and sample data in place, let's go over the approaches to treatment of graphs, trees, and hierarchies. I'll cover three main approaches: iterative/recursive, materialized path, and nested sets.

Iteration/Recursion

Iterative approaches apply some form of loops or recursion. Many iterative algorithms traverse graphs. Some traverse graphs a node at a time and are usually implemented with cursors, but these are typically very slow. I will focus on algorithms that traverse graphs one level at a time using a combination of iterative or recursive logic and set-based queries. Given a set of nodes *U*, the *next level of subordinates* refers to the set *V*, which consists of the direct subordinates (children) of the nodes in *U*. In my experience, implementations of iterative algorithms that traverse a graph one level at a time perform much better than the ones that traverse a graph one node at a time.

Using iterative solutions has several advantages over the other methods. First, you don't need to materialize any extra information describing the graph to the database besides the node IDs in the edges. In other words, you don't need to redesign your tables. The solutions traverse the graph by relying solely on the stored edge information—for example, (*mgrid, empid*), (*assemblyid, partid*), (*city1, city2*), and so on.

Second, most of the solutions that apply to trees also apply to the more generic digraphs. In other words, most solutions that apply to graphs where only one path can lead to a given node also apply to graphs where multiple paths may lead to a given node.

Finally, most of the solutions that I will describe in this section support a virtually unlimited number of levels.

I will use two main tools to implement solutions in my examples: user-defined functions (UDFs) with loops and recursive common table expressions (CTEs). The core algorithms are similar in both versions.

In my solutions, I focused on UDFs and CTEs, but note that in some cases when performance of a UDF or CTE is not satisfactory, you might get better performance by implementing a solution with a stored procedure. Stored procedures give you more control—for example, you can materialize and index interim sets in temporary tables. However, I used UDFs and CTEs because I wanted to focus on the algorithms and the clarity of the solutions.

Subordinates

Let's start with a classical request to return subordinates; for example, return all subordinates of a given employee. More technically, you're after a subgraph/subtree of a given root in a digraph. The iterative algorithm is very simple:

Input: @root

Algorithm:

- set @lvl = 0; insert into table @Subs row for @root

- while there were rows in the previous level of employees:

- set @lvl = @lvl + 1; insert into table @Subs rows for the next level (mgrid in (empid values in previous level))

- return @Subs

Run the following code to create the *Subordinates1* function, which implements this algorithm as a UDF:

```
------------------------------------------------------------------
-- Function: Subordinates1, Descendants
--
-- Input    : @root INT: Manager id
--
-- Output   : @Subs Table: id and level of subordinates of
--                         input manager (empid = @root) in all levels
--
-- Process : * Insert into @Subs row of input manager
--            * In a loop, while previous insert loaded more than 0 rows
--              insert into @Subs next level of subordinates
------------------------------------------------------------------
USE tempdb;
GO
IF OBJECT_ID('dbo.Subordinates1') IS NOT NULL
  DROP FUNCTION dbo.Subordinates1;
GO
CREATE FUNCTION dbo.Subordinates1(@root AS INT) RETURNS @Subs TABLE
(
  empid INT NOT NULL PRIMARY KEY NONCLUSTERED,
  lvl   INT NOT NULL,
  UNIQUE CLUSTERED(lvl, empid)  -- Index will be used to filter level
)
AS
BEGIN
  DECLARE @lvl AS INT = 0;       -- Initialize level counter with 0

  -- Insert root node into @Subs
  INSERT INTO @Subs(empid, lvl)
    SELECT empid, @lvl FROM dbo.Employees WHERE empid = @root;

  WHILE @@rowcount > 0          -- while previous level had rows
```

```
BEGIN
  SET @lvl = @lvl + 1;           -- Increment level counter

    -- Insert next level of subordinates to @Subs
    INSERT INTO @Subs(empid, lvl)
      SELECT C.empid, @lvl
      FROM @Subs AS P               -- P = Parent
        JOIN dbo.Employees AS C -- C = Child
          ON P.lvl = @lvl - 1   -- Filter parents from previous level
          AND C.mgrid = P.empid;
END

  RETURN;
END
GO
```

The function accepts the *@root* input parameter, which is the ID of the requested subtree's root employee. The function returns the @Subs table variable, with all subordinates of employee with ID = @root in all levels. Besides containing the employee attributes, @Subs also has a column called *lvl* that keeps track of the level in the subtree (0 for the subtree's root and increasing from there by 1 in each iteration).

The function's code keeps track of the current level being handled in the *@lvl* local variable, which is initialized with zero.

The function's code first inserts into @Subs the row from Employees where *empid* = *@root*.

Then in a loop, while the last insert affects more than zero rows, the code increments the *@lvl* variable's value by one and inserts into @Subs the next level of employees—in other words, direct subordinates of the managers inserted in the previous level.

To insert the next level of employees into @Subs, the query in the loop joins @Subs (representing managers) with Employees (representing subordinates).

The *lvl* column is important because it allows you to isolate the managers that were inserted into @Subs in the last iteration. To return only subordinates of the previously inserted managers, the join condition filters from @Subs only rows where the *lvl* column is equal to the previous level (@*lvl* – 1).

To test the function, run the following code, which returns the subordinates of employee 3:

```
SELECT empid, lvl FROM dbo.Subordinates1(3) AS S;
```

This code generates the following output:

```
empid       lvl
----------- -----------
3           0
7           1
9           2
11          2
12          3
13          3
14          3
```

You can verify that the output is correct by examining Figure 12-2 and following the subtree of the root employee (ID = 3).

To get other attributes of the employees besides just the employee ID, you can either rewrite the function and add those attributes to the @Subs table or simply join the function with the Employees table, like so:

```
SELECT E.empid, E.empname, S.lvl
FROM dbo.Subordinates1(3) AS S
  JOIN dbo.Employees AS E
    ON E.empid = S.empid;
```

You get the following output:

```
empid        empname                  lvl
-----------  -----------------------  -----------
3            Ina                      0
7            Aaron                    1
9            Rita                     2
11           Gabriel                  2
12           Emilia                   3
13           Michael                  3
14           Didi                     3
```

To limit the result set to leaf employees under the given root, simply add a filter with a NOT EXISTS predicate to select only employees that are not managers of other employees:

```
SELECT empid
FROM dbo.Subordinates1(3) AS P
WHERE NOT EXISTS
  (SELECT * FROM dbo.Employees AS C
   WHERE c.mgrid = P.empid);
```

This query returns employee IDs 11, 12, 13, and 14.

So far, you've seen a UDF implementation of a subtree under a given root, which contains a WHILE loop. The following code has the CTE solution, which contains no explicit loop:

```
DECLARE @root AS INT = 3;

WITH Subs
AS
(
  -- Anchor member returns root node
  SELECT empid, empname, 0 AS lvl
  FROM dbo.Employees
  WHERE empid = @root

  UNION ALL

  -- Recursive member returns next level of children
  SELECT C.empid, C.empname, P.lvl + 1
  FROM Subs AS P
    JOIN dbo.Employees AS C
      ON C.mgrid = P.empid
)
SELECT * FROM Subs;
```

This code generates the following output:

```
empid         empname                    lvl
-----------   ------------------------   -----------
3             Ina                        0
7             Aaron                      1
9             Rita                       2
11            Gabriel                    2
12            Emilia                     3
13            Michael                    3
14            Didi                       3
```

The solution applies very similar logic to the UDF implementation. It's simpler in the sense that you don't need to explicitly define the returned table or to filter the previous level's managers.

The first query in the CTE's body returns the row from Employees for the given root employee. It also returns zero as the level of the root employee. In a recursive CTE, a query that doesn't have any recursive references is known as an *anchor member.*

The second query in the CTE's body (following the UNION ALL set operation) has a recursive reference to the CTE's name. This makes it a *recursive member,* and it is treated in a special manner. The recursive reference to the CTE's name (Subs) represents the result set returned previously. The recursive member query joins the previous result set, which represents the managers in the previous level, with the Employees table to return the next level of employees. The recursive query also calculates the level value as the employee's manager level plus one. The first time that the recursive member is invoked, Subs stands for the result set returned by the anchor member (root employee). There's no explicit termination check for the recursive member; rather, it is invoked repeatedly until it returns an empty set. Thus, the first time it is invoked, it returns direct subordinates of the subtree's root employee. The second time it is invoked, Subs represents the result set of the first invocation of the recursive member (first level of subordinates), so it returns the second level of subordinates. The recursive member is invoked repeatedly until there are no more subordinates, in which case it returns an empty set and recursion stops.

The reference to the CTE name in the outer query represents the UNION ALL of all the result sets returned by the invocation of the anchor member and all the invocations of the recursive member.

As I mentioned earlier, using iterative logic to return a subgraph of a digraph where multiple paths might exist to a node is similar to returning a subtree. Run the following code to create the *PartsExplosion* function:

```
---------------------------------------------------------------------
-- Function: PartsExplosion, Parts Explosion
--
-- Input    : @root INT: assembly id
--
-- Output   : @PartsExplosion Table:
--                id and level of contained parts of input part
--                in all levels
--
```

```
-- Process : * Insert into @PartsExplosion row of input root part
--           * In a loop, while previous insert loaded more than 0 rows
--             insert into @PartsExplosion next level of parts
---------------------------------------------------------------------
USE tempdb;
GO
IF OBJECT_ID('dbo.PartsExplosion') IS NOT NULL
  DROP FUNCTION dbo.PartsExplosion;
GO
CREATE FUNCTION dbo.PartsExplosion(@root AS INT)
  RETURNS @PartsExplosion Table
(
  partid INT           NOT NULL,
  qty    DECIMAL(8, 2) NOT NULL,
  unit   VARCHAR(3)    NOT NULL,
  lvl    INT           NOT NULL,
  n      INT           NOT NULL IDENTITY, -- surrogate key
  UNIQUE CLUSTERED(lvl, n)  -- Index will be used to filter lvl
)
AS
BEGIN
  DECLARE @lvl AS INT = 0;        -- Initialize level counter with 0

  -- Insert root node to @PartsExplosion
  INSERT INTO @PartsExplosion(partid, qty, unit, lvl)
    SELECT partid, qty, unit, @lvl
    FROM dbo.BOM
    WHERE partid = @root;

  WHILE @@rowcount > 0            -- while previous level had rows
  BEGIN
    SET @lvl = @lvl + 1;          -- Increment level counter

    -- Insert next level of subordinates to @PartsExplosion
    INSERT INTO @PartsExplosion(partid, qty, unit, lvl)
      SELECT C.partid, P.qty * C.qty, C.unit, @lvl
      FROM @PartsExplosion AS P  -- P = Parent
        JOIN dbo.BOM AS C        -- C = Child
          ON P.lvl = @lvl - 1    -- Filter parents from previous level
          AND C.assemblyid = P.partid;
  END

  RETURN;
END
GO
```

The function accepts a part ID representing an assembly in a BOM, and it returns the parts explosion (the direct and indirect subitems) of the assembly. The implementation of the *PartsExplosion* function is similar to the implementation of the function *Subordinates1*. The row for the root part is inserted into the @PartsExplosion table variable (the function's output parameter). And then in a loop, while the previous insert found more than zero rows, the next level parts are inserted into @PartsExplosion. A small addition here is specific to a

BOM: calculating the quantity. The root part's quantity is simply the one stored in the part's row. The contained (child) part's quantity is the quantity of its containing (parent) item multiplied by its own quantity.

Run the following code to test the function, returning the part explosion of *partid* 2 (White Tea):

```
SELECT P.partid, P.partname, PE.qty, PE.unit, PE.lvl
FROM dbo.PartsExplosion(2) AS PE
  JOIN dbo.Parts AS P
    ON P.partid = PE.partid;
```

This code generates the following output:

```
partid  partname      qty     unit lvl
-------  ------------  -------  ----  ----
2        White Tea     1.00    EA   0
6        Cup Cover     1.00    EA   1
7        Regular Cup   1.00    EA   1
10       Tea Shot      1.00    EA   1
14       Water         205.00  mL   1
11       Milk          25.00   mL   1
13       Tea Leaves    5.00    g    2
14       Water         20.00   mL   2
```

You can check the correctness of this output by examining Figure 12-3.

Following is the CTE solution for the parts explosion, which, again, is similar to the subtree solution with the addition of the quantity calculation:

```
DECLARE @root AS INT = 2;

WITH PartsExplosion
AS
(
    -- Anchor member returns root part
    SELECT partid, qty, unit, 0 AS lvl
    FROM dbo.BOM
    WHERE partid = @root

    UNION ALL

    -- Recursive member returns next level of parts
    SELECT C.partid, CAST(P.qty * C.qty AS DECIMAL(8, 2)),
      C.unit, P.lvl + 1
    FROM PartsExplosion AS P
      JOIN dbo.BOM AS C
        ON C.assemblyid = P.partid
)
SELECT P.partid, P.partname, PE.qty, PE.unit, PE.lvl
FROM PartsExplosion AS PE
  JOIN dbo.Parts AS P
    ON P.partid = PE.partid;
```

A parts explosion might contain more than one occurrence of the same part because different parts in the assembly might contain the same subpart. For example, you can notice in the result of the explosion of *partid 2* that water appears twice because white tea contains 205 milliliters of water directly, and it also contains a tea shot, which in turn contains 20 milliliters of water. You might want to aggregate the result set by part and unit as follows:

```
SELECT P.partid, P.partname, PES.qty, PES.unit
FROM (SELECT partid, unit, SUM(qty) AS qty
      FROM dbo.PartsExplosion(2) AS PE
      GROUP BY partid, unit) AS PES
  JOIN dbo.Parts AS P
    ON P.partid = PES.partid;
```

You get the following output:

```
partid  partname      qty      unit
------- ------------- -------  ----
2       White Tea      1.00    EA
6       Cup Cover      1.00    EA
7       Regular Cup    1.00    EA
10      Tea Shot       1.00    EA
13      Tea Leaves     5.00    g
11      Milk          25.00    mL
14      Water        225.00    mL
```

I won't get into issues with grouping of parts that might contain different units of measurements here. Obviously, you'll need to deal with those by applying conversion factors.

As another example, the following code explodes part 5 (Double Espresso):

```
SELECT P.partid, P.partname, PES.qty, PES.unit
FROM (SELECT partid, unit, SUM(qty) AS qty
      FROM dbo.PartsExplosion(5) AS PE
      GROUP BY partid, unit) AS PES
  JOIN dbo.Parts AS P
    ON P.partid = PES.partid;
```

This code generates the following output:

```
partid  partname         qty     unit
------- ---------------- ------- ----
5       Double Espresso   1.00   EA
9       Espresso Cup      1.00   EA
12      Coffee Shot       2.00   EA
16      Ground Coffee    30.00   g
17      Coffee Beans    450.00   g
14      Water            40.00   mL
```

Going back to returning a subtree of a given employee, in some cases you might need to limit the number of returned levels. To achieve this, you need to make a minor addition to the original algorithm:

Input: @root, @maxlevels (besides root)

Algorithm:

- set @lvl = 0; insert into table @Subs row for @root

- while there were rows in the previous level, and @lvl < @maxlevels:

- set @lvl = @lvl + 1; *insert into table* @Subs *rows for the next level (*mgrid *in (*empid *values in previous level))*

- return @Subs

Run the following code to create the *Subordinates2* function, which is a revision of *Subordinates1* that also supports a level limit:

```
--------------------------------------------------------------------
-- Function: Subordinates2,
--           Descendants with optional level limit
--
-- Input   : @root      INT: Manager id
--           @maxlevels INT: Max number of levels to return
--
-- Output  : @Subs TABLE: id and level of subordinates of
--                        input manager in all levels <= @maxlevels
--
-- Process : * Insert into @Subs row of input manager
--           * In a loop, while previous insert loaded more than 0 rows
--             and previous level is smaller than @maxlevels
--             insert into @Subs next level of subordinates
--------------------------------------------------------------------
USE tempdb;
GO
IF OBJECT_ID('dbo.Subordinates2') IS NOT NULL
  DROP FUNCTION dbo.Subordinates2;
GO
CREATE FUNCTION dbo.Subordinates2
  (@root AS INT, @maxlevels AS INT = NULL) RETURNS @Subs TABLE
(
  empid INT NOT NULL PRIMARY KEY NONCLUSTERED,
  lvl   INT NOT NULL,
  UNIQUE CLUSTERED(lvl, empid)  -- Index will be used to filter level
)
AS
BEGIN
  DECLARE @lvl AS INT = 0;      -- Initialize level counter with 0
  -- If input @maxlevels is NULL, set it to maximum integer
  -- to virtually have no limit on levels
  SET @maxlevels = COALESCE(@maxlevels, 2147483647);

  -- Insert root node to @Subs
  INSERT INTO @Subs(empid, lvl)
    SELECT empid, @lvl FROM dbo.Employees WHERE empid = @root;

  WHILE @@rowcount > 0          -- while previous level had rows
    AND @lvl < @maxlevels       -- and previous level < @maxlevels
  BEGIN
    SET @lvl = @lvl + 1;        -- Increment level counter
```

```
        -- Insert next level of subordinates to @Subs
      INSERT INTO @Subs(empid, lvl)
        SELECT C.empid, @lvl
        FROM @Subs AS P              -- P = Parent
          JOIN dbo.Employees AS C -- C = Child
            ON P.lvl = @lvl - 1    -- Filter parents from previous level
            AND C.mgrid = P.empid;
    END

    RETURN;
END
GO
```

In addition to the original input, *Subordinates2* also accepts the @*maxlevels* input that indicates the maximum number of requested levels under @*root* to return. For no limit on levels, a NULL should be specified in @*maxlevels*. Notice that if @*maxlevels* is NULL, the function substitutes the NULL with the maximum possible integer value to practically have no limit.

The loop's condition, besides checking that the previous insert affected more than zero rows, also checks that the @*lvl* variable is smaller than @*maxlevels*. Except for these minor revisions, the function's implementation is the same as *Subordinates1*.

To test the function, run the following code that requests the subordinates of employee 3 in all levels (@*maxlevels* is NULL):

```
SELECT empid, lvl
FROM dbo.Subordinates2(3, NULL) AS S;
```

You get the following output:

```
empid       lvl
----------- -----------
3           0
7           1
9           2
11          2
12          3
13          3
14          3
```

To get only two levels of subordinates under employee 3, run the following code:

```
SELECT empid, lvl
FROM dbo.Subordinates2(3, 2) AS S;
```

This code generates the following output:

```
empid       lvl
----------- -----------
3           0
7           1
9           2
11          2
```

To get only the second-level employees under employee 3, add a filter on the level:

```
SELECT empid
FROM dbo.Subordinates2(3, 2) AS S
WHERE lvl = 2;
```

You get the following output:

```
empid
-----------
9
11
```

Caution To limit levels using a CTE, you might be tempted to use the hint called MAXRECURSION, which raises an error and aborts when the number of invocations of the recursive member exceeds the input. However, MAXRECURSION was designed as a safety measure to avoid infinite recursion in cases of problems in the data or bugs in the code. When not specified, MAXRECURSION defaults to 100. You can specify MAXRECURSION 0 to have no limit, but be aware of the implications.

To test this approach, run the following code:

```
DECLARE @root AS INT = 3;

WITH Subs
AS
(
  SELECT empid, empname, 0 AS lvl
  FROM dbo.Employees
  WHERE empid = @root

  UNION ALL

  SELECT C.empid, C.empname, P.lvl + 1
  FROM Subs AS P
    JOIN dbo.Employees AS C
      ON C.mgrid = P.empid
)
SELECT * FROM Subs
OPTION (MAXRECURSION 2);
```

This is the same subtree CTE shown earlier, with the addition of the MAXRECURSION hint, limiting recursive invocations to 2. This code generates the following output, including an error message:

```
empid       empname                  lvl
----------- ------------------------ -----------
3           Ina                      0
7           Aaron                    1
9           Rita                     2
11          Gabriel                  2
Msg 530, Level 16, State 1, Line 4
The statement terminated. The maximum recursion 2 has been exhausted before
    statement completion.
```

> The code breaks as soon as the recursive member is invoked the third time. There are two reasons not to use the MAXRECURSION hint to logically limit the number of levels. First, an error is generated even though there's no logical error here. Second, SQL Server does not guarantee to return any result set if an error is generated. In this particular case, a result set was returned, but this is not guaranteed to happen in other cases.

To logically limit the number of levels, simply filter the level column in the outer query, as in the following code:

```
DECLARE @root AS INT = 3, @maxlevels AS INT = 2;

WITH Subs
AS
(
  SELECT empid, empname, 0 AS lvl
  FROM dbo.Employees
  WHERE empid = @root

  UNION ALL

  SELECT C.empid, C.empname, P.lvl + 1
  FROM Subs AS P
    JOIN dbo.Employees AS C
      ON C.mgrid = P.empid
)
SELECT * FROM Subs
WHERE lvl <= @maxlevels;
```

It is interesting to note that in terms of optimization, SQL Server expands the definition of the CTE and applies the filter as part of the processing of the inner queries. This means that it doesn't bother to first process all levels and then filter the applicable ones; instead, it processes only the requested number of levels.

Ancestors

Requests for ancestors of a given node are also common—for example, returning the chain of management for a given employee. Not surprisingly, the algorithms for returning ancestors using iterative logic are similar to those for returning subordinates. Simply put, instead of traversing the graph starting with a given node and proceeding "downward" to child nodes, you start with a given node and proceed "upward" to parent nodes.

Run the following code to create the *Managers* function:

```
-------------------------------------------------------------------
-- Function: Managers, Ancestors with optional level limit
--
-- Input     : @empid INT : Employee id
--             @maxlevels : Max number of levels to return
--
```

```
-- Output  : @Mgrs Table: id and level of managers of
--                         input employee in all levels <= @maxlevels
--
-- Process : * In a loop, while current manager is not null
--             and previous level is smaller than @maxlevels
--             insert into @Mgrs current manager,
--             and get next level manager
--------------------------------------------------------------------
USE tempdb;
GO
IF OBJECT_ID('dbo.Managers') IS NOT NULL
  DROP FUNCTION dbo.Managers;
GO
CREATE FUNCTION dbo.Managers
  (@empid AS INT, @maxlevels AS INT = NULL) RETURNS @Mgrs TABLE
(
  empid INT NOT NULL PRIMARY KEY,
  lvl   INT NOT NULL
)
AS
BEGIN
  IF NOT EXISTS(SELECT * FROM dbo.Employees WHERE empid = @empid)
    RETURN;

  DECLARE @lvl AS INT = 0;      -- Initialize level counter with 0
  -- If input @maxlevels is NULL, set it to maximum integer
  -- to virtually have no limit on levels
  SET @maxlevels = COALESCE(@maxlevels, 2147483647);

  WHILE @empid IS NOT NULL      -- while current employee has a manager
    AND @lvl <= @maxlevels      -- and previous level <= @maxlevels
  BEGIN
    -- Insert current manager to @Mgrs
    INSERT INTO @Mgrs(empid, lvl) VALUES(@empid, @lvl);
    SET @lvl = @lvl + 1;        -- Increment level counter
    -- Get next level manager
    SET @empid = (SELECT mgrid FROM dbo.Employees
                    WHERE empid = @empid);
  END

  RETURN;
END
GO
```

The function accepts an input employee ID (*@empid*) and, optionally, a level limit (*@maxlevels*), and it returns managers up to the requested number of levels from the input employee (if a limit was specified). The function first checks whether the input node ID exists and then breaks if it doesn't. It then initializes the *@lvl* counter to zero, and it assigns the maximum possible integer to the *@maxlevels* variable if a NULL was specified in it to practically have no level limit.

The function then enters a loop that iterates as long as *@empid* is not NULL (because NULL represents the root's manager ID) and the current level is smaller than or equal to the requested number of levels. The loop's body inserts the current employee ID along with the level counter into the @Mgrs output table variable, increments the level counter, and assigns the current employee's manager's ID to the *@empid* variable.

I should point out a couple of differences between this function and the subordinates function. This function uses a scalar subquery to get the manager ID in the next level, unlike the subordinates function, which used a join to get the next level of subordinates. The reason for the difference is that a given employee can have only one manager, while a manager can have multiple subordinates. Also, this function uses the expression *@lvl <= @maxlevels* to limit the number of levels, while the subordinates function used the expression *@lvl < @maxlevels*. The reason for the discrepancy is that this function doesn't have a separate INSERT statement to get the root employee and a separate one to get the next level of employees; rather, it has only one INSERT statement in the loop. Consequently, the *@lvl* counter here is incremented after the INSERT, while in the subordinates function it was incremented before the INSERT.

To test the function, run the following code:

```
SELECT empid, lvl
FROM dbo.Managers(8, NULL) AS M;
```

This code returns managers in all levels of employee 8 and generates the following output:

```
empid       lvl
----------- -----------
1           3
2           2
5           1
8           0
```

The CTE solution to returning ancestors is almost identical to the CTE solution returning a subtree. The minor difference is that here the recursive member treats the CTE as the child part of the join and the Employees table as the parent part, while in the subtree solution the roles were opposite. Run the following code to get the management chain of employee 8:

```
DECLARE @empid AS INT = 8;

WITH Mgrs
AS
(
  SELECT empid, mgrid, empname, 0 AS lvl
  FROM dbo.Employees
  WHERE empid = @empid

  UNION ALL

  SELECT P.empid, P.mgrid, P.empname, C.lvl + 1
  FROM Mgrs AS C
    JOIN dbo.Employees AS P
      ON C.mgrid = P.empid
)
SELECT * FROM Mgrs;
```

This code generates the following output:

```
empid  mgrid  empname   lvl
------ ------ --------  ----
8      5      Lilach    0
5      2      Jiru      1
2      1      Eitan     2
1      NULL   David     3
```

To get only two levels of managers of employee 8 using the *Managers* function, run the following code:

```
SELECT empid, lvl
FROM dbo.Managers(8, 2) AS M;
```

You get the following output:

```
empid       lvl
----------- -----------
2           2
5           1
8           0
```

And to return only the second-level manager, simply add a filter in the outer query, returning employee ID 2:

```
SELECT empid
FROM dbo.Managers(8, 2) AS M
WHERE lvl = 2;
```

To return two levels of managers for employee 8 with a CTE, simply add a filter on the *lvl* attribute in the outer query, like so:

```
DECLARE @empid AS INT = 8, @maxlevels AS INT = 2;

WITH Mgrs
AS
(
  SELECT empid, mgrid, empname, 0 AS lvl
  FROM dbo.Employees
  WHERE empid = @empid

  UNION ALL

  SELECT P.empid, P.mgrid, P.empname, C.lvl + 1
  FROM Mgrs AS C
    JOIN dbo.Employees AS P
      ON C.mgrid = P.empid
)
SELECT * FROM Mgrs
WHERE lvl <= @maxlevels;
```

Subgraph/Subtree with Path Enumeration

In the subgraph/subtree solutions, you might also want to generate for each node an enumerated path consisting of all node IDs in the path to that node, using some separator (such as '.'). For example, the enumerated path for employee 8 in the Organization Chart scenario is '.1.2.5.8.' because employee 5 is the manager of employee 8, employee 2 is the manager of 5, employee 1 is the manager of 2, and employee 1 is the root employee.

The enumerated path has many uses—for example, to sort the nodes from the hierarchy in the output, to detect cycles, and other uses that I'll describe later in the "Materialized Path" section. Fortunately, you can make minor additions to the solutions I provided for returning a subgraph/subtree to calculate the enumerated path without any additional I/O.

The algorithm starts with the subtree's root node and in a loop or recursive call returns the next level. For the root node, the path is simply '.' + *node id* + '.'. For successive level nodes, the path is *parent's path* + *node id* + '.'.

Run the following code to create the *Subordinates3* function, which is the same as *Subordinates2* except for the addition of the enumerated path calculation:

```
-------------------------------------------------------------------
-- Function: Subordinates3,
--           Descendants with optional level limit
--           and path enumeration
--
-- Input   : @root      INT: Manager id
--           @maxlevels INT: Max number of levels to return
--
-- Output  : @Subs TABLE: id, level and materialized ancestors path
--                        of subordinates of input manager
--                        in all levels <= @maxlevels
--
-- Process : * Insert into @Subs row of input manager
--           * In a loop, while previous insert loaded more than 0 rows
--             and previous level is smaller than @maxlevels:
--             - insert into @Subs next level of subordinates
--             - calculate a materialized ancestors path for each
--               by concatenating current node id to parent's path
-------------------------------------------------------------------
USE tempdb;
GO
IF OBJECT_ID('dbo.Subordinates3') IS NOT NULL
  DROP FUNCTION dbo.Subordinates3;
GO
CREATE FUNCTION dbo.Subordinates3
  (@root AS INT, @maxlevels AS INT = NULL) RETURNS @Subs TABLE
(
  empid INT         NOT NULL PRIMARY KEY NONCLUSTERED,
  lvl   INT         NOT NULL,
  path  VARCHAR(900) NOT NULL
  UNIQUE CLUSTERED(lvl, empid)  -- Index will be used to filter level
)
```

```
AS
BEGIN
  DECLARE @lvl AS INT = 0;        -- Initialize level counter with 0
  -- If input @maxlevels is NULL, set it to maximum integer
  -- to virtually have no limit on levels
  SET @maxlevels = COALESCE(@maxlevels, 2147483647);

  -- Insert root node to @Subs
  INSERT INTO @Subs(empid, lvl, path)
    SELECT empid, @lvl, '.' + CAST(empid AS VARCHAR(10)) + '.'
    FROM dbo.Employees WHERE empid = @root;

  WHILE @@rowcount > 0            -- while previous level had rows
    AND @lvl < @maxlevels         -- and previous level < @maxlevels
  BEGIN
    SET @lvl = @lvl + 1;          -- Increment level counter

    -- Insert next level of subordinates to @Subs
    INSERT INTO @Subs(empid, lvl, path)
      SELECT C.empid, @lvl,
        P.path + CAST(C.empid AS VARCHAR(10)) + '.'
      FROM @Subs AS P             -- P = Parent
        JOIN dbo.Employees AS C -- C = Child
          ON P.lvl = @lvl - 1   -- Filter parents from previous level
          AND C.mgrid = P.empid;
  END

  RETURN;
END
GO
```

Run the following code to returns all subordinates of employee 1 and their paths:

```
SELECT empid, lvl, path
FROM dbo.Subordinates3(1, NULL) AS S;
```

This code generates the following output:

```
empid       lvl         path
----------- ----------- -------------------
1           0           .1.
2           1           .1.2.
3           1           .1.3.
4           2           .1.2.4.
5           2           .1.2.5.
6           2           .1.2.6.
7           2           .1.3.7.
8           3           .1.2.5.8.
9           3           .1.3.7.9.
10          3           .1.2.5.10.
11          3           .1.3.7.11.
12          4           .1.3.7.9.12.
13          4           .1.3.7.9.13.
14          4           .1.3.7.9.14.
```

With both the *lvl* and *path* values, you can easily return output that graphically shows the hierarchical relationships of the employees in the subtree:

```
SELECT E.empid, REPLICATE(' | ', lvl) + empname AS empname
FROM dbo.Subordinates3(1, NULL) AS S
  JOIN dbo.Employees AS E
    ON E.empid = S.empid
ORDER BY path;
```

The query joins the subtree returned from the *Subordinates3* function with the Employees table based on employee ID match. From the function, you get the *lvl* and *path* values, and from the table, you get other employee attributes of interest, such as the employee name. You generate indentation before the employee name by replicating a string (in this case, ' | ') *lvl* times and concatenating the employee name to it. Sorting the employees by the *path* column produces a correct hierarchical sort, which requires a child node to appear later than its parent node—or, in other words, that a child node will have a higher sort value than its parent node. By definition, a child's path is greater than a parent's path because it is prefixed with the parent's path. Following is the output of this query:

```
empid        empname
-----------  -----------------------
1            David
2            | Eitan
4            | | Seraph
5            | | Jiru
10           | | | Sean
8            | | | Lilach
6            | | Steve
3            | Ina
7            | | Aaron
11           | | | Gabriel
9            | | | Rita
12           | | | | Emilia
13           | | | | Michael
14           | | | | Didi
```

Similarly, you can add path calculation to the subtree CTE, like so:

```
DECLARE @root AS INT = 1;

WITH Subs
AS
(
  SELECT empid, empname, 0 AS lvl,
    -- Path of root = '.' + empid + '.'
    CAST('.' + CAST(empid AS VARCHAR(10)) + '.'
        AS VARCHAR(MAX)) AS path
  FROM dbo.Employees
  WHERE empid = @root

  UNION ALL
```

```
SELECT C.empid, C.empname, P.lvl + 1,
    -- Path of child = parent's path + child empid + '.'
    CAST(P.path + CAST(C.empid AS VARCHAR(10)) + '.'
        AS VARCHAR(MAX))
FROM Subs AS P
    JOIN dbo.Employees AS C
        ON C.mgrid = P.empid
)
SELECT empid, REPLICATE(' | ', lvl) + empname AS empname
FROM Subs
ORDER BY path;
```

> **Note** Corresponding columns between an anchor member and a recursive member of a CTE must match in both data type and size. That's why I converted the path strings in both to the same data type and size: VARCHAR(MAX).

Sorting

Sorting is a presentation request and usually is used by the client rather than the server. This means that you might want the sorting of hierarchies to take place on the client. In this section, however, I'll present server-side sorting techniques with T-SQL that you can use when you prefer to handle sorting on the server.

A *topological sort* of a DAG is defined as one that provides a child with a higher sort value than its parent. Occasionally, I will refer to a topological sort informally as *correct hierarchical sort*. More than one way of ordering the items in a DAG may qualify as correct. You might or might not care about the order among siblings. If the order among siblings doesn't matter to you, you can achieve sorting by constructing an enumerated path for each node, as described in the previous section, and sort the nodes by that path.

Remember that the enumerated path is a character string made of the IDs of the ancestors leading to the node, using some separator. This means that siblings are sorted by their node IDs. Because the path is character based, you get character-based sorting of IDs, which might be different than the integer sorting. For example, employee ID 11 sorts lower than its sibling with ID 9 ('.1.3.7.11.' < '.1.3.7.9.'), even though 9 < 11. You can guarantee that sorting by the enumerated path produces a correct hierarchical sort, but it doesn't guarantee the order of siblings. If you need such a guarantee, you need a different solution.

For optimal sorting flexibility, you might want to guarantee the following:

1. A correct topological sort—that is, a sort in which a child has a higher sort value than its parent's.

2. Siblings are sorted in a requested order (for example, by *empname* or by *salary*).

3. Integer sort values are generated, as opposed to lengthy strings.

In the enumerated path solution, requirement 1 is met. Requirement 2 is not met because the path is made of node IDs and is character based; comparison and sorting among characters is based on collation properties, yielding different comparison and sorting behavior than with integers. Requirement 3 is not met because the solution orders the results by the path, which is lengthy compared to an integer value. To meet all three requirements, we can still make use of a path for each node, but with several differences:

- Instead of node IDs, the path is constructed from values that represent a position (row number) among nodes based on a requested order (for example, *empname* or *salary*).

- Instead of using a character string with varying lengths for each level in the path, use a binary string with a fixed length for each level.

- Once the binary paths are constructed, calculate integer values representing path order (row numbers) and ultimately use those to sort the hierarchy.

The core algorithm to traverse the subtree is maintained, but the paths are constructed differently, based on the binary representation of row numbers. The implementation uses CTEs and the ROW_NUMBER function.

Run the following code to return the subtree of employee 1, with siblings sorted by *empname* with indentation:

```
DECLARE @root AS INT = 1;

WITH Subs
AS
(
  SELECT empid, empname, 0 AS lvl,
    -- Path of root is 1 (binary)
    CAST(1 AS VARBINARY(MAX)) AS sort_path
  FROM dbo.Employees
  WHERE empid = @root

  UNION ALL

  SELECT C.empid, C.empname, P.lvl + 1,
    -- Path of child = parent's path + child row number (binary)
    P.sort_path + CAST(
      ROW_NUMBER() OVER(PARTITION BY C.mgrid
                          ORDER BY C.empname) -- sort col(s)
      AS BINARY(4))
  FROM Subs AS P
    JOIN dbo.Employees AS C
      ON C.mgrid = P.empid
)
SELECT empid, ROW_NUMBER() OVER(ORDER BY sort_path) AS sortval,
  REPLICATE(' | ', lvl) + empname AS empname
FROM Subs
ORDER BY sortval;
```

This code generates the following output:

```
empid  sortval  empname
------ -------- --------------------
1      1        David
2      2        | Eitan
5      3        | | Jiru
8      4        | | | Lilach
10     5        | | | Sean
4      6        | | Seraph
6      7        | | Steve
3      8        | Ina
7      9        | | Aaron
11     10       | | | Gabriel
9      11       | | | Rita
14     12       | | | | Didi
12     13       | | | | Emilia
13     14       | | | | Michael
```

The anchor member query returns the root, with 1 as the binary path. The recursive member query calculates the row number of an employee among siblings based on *empname* ordering and concatenates that row number converted to binary(4) to the parent's path.

The outer query simply calculates row numbers to generate the sort values based on the binary path order, and it sorts the subtree by those sort values, adding indentation based on the calculated level.

If you want siblings sorted in a different way, you need to change only the ORDER BY list of the ROW_NUMBER function in the recursive member query. The following code has the revision that sorts siblings by *salary*:

```
DECLARE @root AS INT = 1;

WITH Subs
AS
(
  SELECT empid, empname, salary, 0 AS lvl,
    -- Path of root = 1 (binary)
    CAST(1 AS VARBINARY(MAX)) AS sort_path
  FROM dbo.Employees
  WHERE empid = @root

  UNION ALL

  SELECT C.empid, C.empname, C.salary, P.lvl + 1,
    -- Path of child = parent's path + child row number (binary)
    P.sort_path + CAST(
      ROW_NUMBER() OVER(PARTITION BY C.mgrid
                        ORDER BY C.salary) -- sort col(s)
      AS BINARY(4))
  FROM Subs AS P
    JOIN dbo.Employees AS C
      ON C.mgrid = P.empid
)
```

```
SELECT empid, salary, ROW_NUMBER() OVER(ORDER BY sort_path) AS sortval,
  REPLICATE(' | ', lvl) + empname AS empname
FROM Subs
ORDER BY sortval;
```

This code generates the following output:

```
empid  salary     sortval  empname
------ ---------- -------- --------------------
1      10000.00   1        David
2      7000.00    2        | Eitan
6      4500.00    3        | | Steve
4      5000.00    4        | | Seraph
5      5500.00    5        | | Jiru
10     3000.00    6        | | | Sean
8      3500.00    7        | | | Lilach
3      7500.00    8        | Ina
7      5000.00    9        | | Aaron
9      3000.00    10       | | | Rita
14     1500.00    11       | | | | Didi
12     2000.00    12       | | | | Emilia
13     2000.00    13       | | | | Michael
11     3000.00    14       | | | Gabriel
```

> **Note** If you need to sort siblings by a single integer sort column (for example, by *empid*),
> you can construct the binary sort path from the sort column values themselves instead of row
> numbers based on that column.

Cycles

Cycles in graphs are paths that begin and end at the same node. In some scenarios, cycles are
natural (for example, road systems). If you have a cycle in what's supposed to be an acyclic
graph, it might indicate a problem in your data. Either way, you need a way to identify them. If a
cycle indicates a problem in the data, you need to identify the problem and fix it. If cycles are
natural, you don't want to endlessly keep returning to the same point while traversing the graph.

Cycle detection with T-SQL can be a very complex and expensive task. However, I'll show
you a fairly simple technique to detect cycles with reasonable performance, relying on path
enumeration, which I discussed earlier. For demonstration purposes, I'll use this technique
to detect cycles in the tree represented by the Employees table, but you can apply this
technique to forests as well and also to more generic graphs, as I will demonstrate later.

Suppose that Didi (*empid* 14) is unhappy with her location in the company's management
hierarchy. Didi also happens to be the database administrator and has full access to the Employees
table. Didi runs the following code, making her the manager of the CEO and introducing a cycle:

```
UPDATE dbo.Employees SET mgrid = 14 WHERE empid = 1;
```

The Employees table currently contains the following cycle of employee IDs:

$1 \rightarrow 3 \rightarrow 7 \rightarrow 9 \rightarrow 14 \rightarrow 1$

As a baseline, I'll use one of the solutions I covered earlier, which constructs an enumerated path. In my examples, I'll use a CTE solution, but of course you can apply the same logic to the UDF solution that uses loops.

Simply put, a cycle is detected when you follow a path leading to a given node if its parent's path already contains the child node ID. You can keep track of cycles by maintaining a *cycle* column, which contain 0 if no cycle is detected and 1 if one is detected. In the anchor member of the solution CTE, the *cycle* column value is simply the constant 0 because obviously the root level has no cycle. In the recursive member's query, use a LIKE predicate to check whether the parent's path contains the child node ID. Return 1 if it does and 0 otherwise. Note the importance of the dots at both the beginning and end of both the path and the pattern—without the dots, you get an unwanted match for employee ID n (for example $n = 3$) if the path contains employee ID nm (for example $m = 15$, $nm = 315$). The following code returns a subtree with an enumerated path calculation and has the addition of the *cycle* column calculation:

```
DECLARE @root AS INT = 1;

WITH Subs
AS
(
  SELECT empid, empname, 0 AS lvl,
    CAST('.' + CAST(empid AS VARCHAR(10)) + '.'
        AS VARCHAR(MAX)) AS path,
    -- Obviously root has no cycle
    0 AS cycle
  FROM dbo.Employees
  WHERE empid = @root

  UNION ALL

  SELECT C.empid, C.empname, P.lvl + 1,
    CAST(P.path + CAST(C.empid AS VARCHAR(10)) + '.'
        AS VARCHAR(MAX)),
    -- Cycle detected if parent's path contains child's id
    CASE WHEN P.path LIKE '%.' + CAST(C.empid AS VARCHAR(10)) + '.%'
      THEN 1 ELSE 0 END
  FROM Subs AS P
    JOIN dbo.Employees AS C
      ON C.mgrid = P.empid
)
SELECT empid, empname, cycle, path
FROM Subs;
```

If you run this code, it always breaks after 100 levels (the default MAXRECURSION value) because cycles are detected but not avoided. You need to avoid cycles—in other words, don't pursue paths for which cycles are detected. To achieve this, simply add a filter to the recursive member that returns a child only if its parent's *cycle* value is 0, like so:

```
DECLARE @root AS INT = 1;

WITH Subs
AS
(
  SELECT empid, empname, 0 AS lvl,
    CAST('.' + CAST(empid AS VARCHAR(10)) + '.'
        AS VARCHAR(MAX)) AS path,
    -- Obviously root has no cycle
    0 AS cycle
  FROM dbo.Employees
  WHERE empid = @root

  UNION ALL

  SELECT C.empid, C.empname, P.lvl + 1,
    CAST(P.path + CAST(C.empid AS VARCHAR(10)) + '.'
        AS VARCHAR(MAX)),
    -- Cycle detected if parent's path contains child's id
    CASE WHEN P.path LIKE '%.' + CAST(C.empid AS VARCHAR(10)) + '.%'
      THEN 1 ELSE 0 END
  FROM Subs AS P
    JOIN dbo.Employees AS C
      ON C.mgrid = P.empid
      AND P.cycle = 0 -- do not pursue branch for parent with cycle
)
SELECT empid, empname, cycle, path
FROM Subs;
```

This code generates the following output:

```
empid   empname   cycle   path
------  --------   ------  ----------------
1       David      0       .1.
2       Eitan      0       .1.2.
3       Ina        0       .1.3.
7       Aaron      0       .1.3.7.
9       Rita       0       .1.3.7.9.
11      Gabriel    0       .1.3.7.11.
12      Emilia     0       .1.3.7.9.12.
13      Michael    0       .1.3.7.9.13.
14      Didi       0       .1.3.7.9.14.
1       David      1       .1.3.7.9.14.1.
4       Seraph     0       .1.2.4.
5       Jiru       0       .1.2.5.
6       Steve      0       .1.2.6.
8       Lilach     0       .1.2.5.8.
10      Sean       0       .1.2.5.10.
```

Notice in the output that the second time employee 1 was reached, a cycle was detected for it, and the path was not pursued any further. In a cyclic graph, that's all the logic you usually need to add. In our case, the cycle indicates a problem with the data that needs to be fixed.

To isolate only the cyclic path (in our case, *.1.3.7.9.14.1.*), simply add the filter *cycle = 1* to the outer query, like so:

```
DECLARE @root AS INT = 1;

WITH Subs
AS
(
  SELECT empid, empname, 0 AS lvl,
    CAST('.' + CAST(empid AS VARCHAR(10)) + '.'
        AS VARCHAR(MAX)) AS path,
    -- Obviously root has no cycle
    0 AS cycle
  FROM dbo.Employees
  WHERE empid = @root

  UNION ALL

  SELECT C.empid, C.empname, P.lvl + 1,
    CAST(P.path + CAST(C.empid AS VARCHAR(10)) + '.'
        AS VARCHAR(MAX)),
    -- Cycle detected if parent's path contains child's id
    CASE WHEN P.path LIKE '%.' + CAST(C.empid AS VARCHAR(10)) + '.%'
      THEN 1 ELSE 0 END
  FROM Subs AS P
    JOIN dbo.Employees AS C
      ON C.mgrid = P.empid
      AND P.cycle = 0
)
SELECT path FROM Subs WHERE cycle = 1;
```

Now that the cyclic path has been identified, you can fix the data by running the following code:

```
UPDATE dbo.Employees SET mgrid = NULL WHERE empid = 1;
```

Didi will probably find herself unemployed.

Materialized Path

So far I presented solutions where paths were computed when the code was executed. In the materialized path solution, the paths are stored so that they need not be computed repeatedly. You basically store an enumerated path and a level for each node of the tree in two additional columns. The solution works optimally with trees and forests.

This approach has two main advantages over the iterative/recursive approach. Queries are simpler and set based (without relying on recursive CTEs). Also, queries typically perform much faster because they can rely on indexing of the path.

However, now that you have two additional attributes in the table, you need to keep them in sync with the tree as it undergoes changes. The cost of modifications determines whether it's reasonable to synchronize the path and level values with every change in the tree. For example, what is the effect of adding a new leaf to the tree? I like to refer to the effect of such a modification informally as the *shake effect*. Fortunately, as I will elaborate on shortly, the shake effect of adding new leaves is minor. Also, the effect of dropping or moving a small subtree is typically not very significant.

The enumerated path can get lengthy when the tree is deep—in other words, when there are many levels of managers. SQL Server limits the size of index keys to 900 bytes. To achieve the performance benefits of an index on the path column, you must limit the size of that column to 900 bytes. Before you become concerned by this fact, try thinking in practical terms: 900 bytes is enough for trees with hundreds of levels. Will your tree ever reach more than hundreds of levels? I'll admit that I never had to model a hierarchy with hundreds of levels. In short, apply common sense and think in practical terms.

Maintaining Data

First run the following code to create the Employees table with the new *lvl* and *path* columns:

```
SET NOCOUNT ON;
USE tempdb;
GO
IF OBJECT_ID('dbo.Employees') IS NOT NULL
  DROP TABLE dbo.Employees;
GO
CREATE TABLE dbo.Employees
(
  empid    INT          NOT NULL PRIMARY KEY NONCLUSTERED,
  mgrid    INT          NULL     REFERENCES dbo.Employees,
  empname  VARCHAR(25)  NOT NULL,
  salary   MONEY        NOT NULL,
  lvl      INT          NOT NULL,
  path     VARCHAR(900) NOT NULL UNIQUE CLUSTERED
);
CREATE UNIQUE INDEX idx_unc_mgrid_empid ON dbo.Employees(mgrid, empid);
GO
```

To handle modifications in a tree, it's recommended that you use stored procedures that also take care of the *lvl* and *path* values. Alternatively, you can use triggers, and their logic will be very similar to that in the following stored procedures.

Adding Employees Who Manage No One (Leaves)

Let's start with handling inserts. The logic of the insert procedure is simple. If the new employee is a root employee (that is, the manager ID is NULL), its level is 0, and its path is '.' + *employee id* + '.'. Otherwise, its level is the parent's level plus 1, and its path is *parent path* + *employee id* + '.'. As you can figure out, the shake effect here is minor. You don't need to make any changes to other employees, and to calculate the new employee's *lvl* and *path* values, you need only to query the employee's parent.

Run the following code to create the *AddEmp* stored procedure and populate the Employees table with sample data:

```
------------------------------------------------------------------------
-- Stored Procedure: AddEmp,
--    Inserts new employee who manages no one into the table
------------------------------------------------------------------------
USE tempdb;
GO
IF OBJECT_ID('dbo.AddEmp') IS NOT NULL
  DROP PROC dbo.AddEmp;
GO
CREATE PROC dbo.AddEmp
  @empid   INT,
  @mgrid   INT,
  @empname VARCHAR(25),
  @salary  MONEY
AS

SET NOCOUNT ON;

-- Handle case where the new employee has no manager (root)
IF @mgrid IS NULL
  INSERT INTO dbo.Employees(empid, mgrid, empname, salary, lvl, path)
    VALUES(@empid, @mgrid, @empname, @salary,
      0, '.' + CAST(@empid AS VARCHAR(10)) + '.');
-- Handle subordinate case (non-root)
ELSE
  INSERT INTO dbo.Employees(empid, mgrid, empname, salary, lvl, path)
    SELECT @empid, @mgrid, @empname, @salary,
      lvl + 1, path + CAST(@empid AS VARCHAR(10)) + '.'
    FROM dbo.Employees
    WHERE empid = @mgrid;
GO

EXEC dbo.AddEmp
  @empid = 1, @mgrid = NULL, @empname = 'David', @salary = $10000.00;
EXEC dbo.AddEmp
  @empid = 2, @mgrid = 1, @empname = 'Eitan', @salary = $7000.00;
EXEC dbo.AddEmp
  @empid = 3, @mgrid = 1, @empname = 'Ina', @salary = $7500.00;
EXEC dbo.AddEmp
  @empid = 4, @mgrid = 2, @empname = 'Seraph', @salary = $5000.00;
EXEC dbo.AddEmp
  @empid = 5, @mgrid = 2, @empname = 'Jiru', @salary = $5500.00;
EXEC dbo.AddEmp
  @empid = 6, @mgrid = 2, @empname = 'Steve', @salary = $4500.00;
EXEC dbo.AddEmp
  @empid = 7, @mgrid = 3, @empname = 'Aaron', @salary = $5000.00;
EXEC dbo.AddEmp
  @empid = 8, @mgrid = 5, @empname = 'Lilach', @salary = $3500.00;
EXEC dbo.AddEmp
  @empid = 9, @mgrid = 7, @empname = 'Rita', @salary = $3000.00;
EXEC dbo.AddEmp
  @empid = 10, @mgrid = 5, @empname = 'Sean', @salary = $3000.00;
```

```
EXEC dbo.AddEmp
  @empid = 11, @mgrid = 7, @empname = 'Gabriel', @salary = $3000.00;
EXEC dbo.AddEmp
  @empid = 12, @mgrid = 9, @empname = 'Emilia', @salary = $2000.00;
EXEC dbo.AddEmp
  @empid = 13, @mgrid = 9, @empname = 'Michael', @salary = $2000.00;
EXEC dbo.AddEmp
  @empid = 14, @mgrid = 9, @empname = 'Didi', @salary = $1500.00;
```

Run the following query to examine the resulting contents of Employees:

```
SELECT empid, mgrid, empname, salary, lvl, path
FROM dbo.Employees
ORDER BY path;
```

You get the following output:

empid	mgrid	empname	salary	lvl	path
1	NULL	David	10000.00	0	.1.
2	1	Eitan	7000.00	1	.1.2.
4	2	Seraph	5000.00	2	.1.2.4.
5	2	Jiru	5500.00	2	.1.2.5.
10	5	Sean	3000.00	3	.1.2.5.10.
8	5	Lilach	3500.00	3	.1.2.5.8.
6	2	Steve	4500.00	2	.1.2.6.
3	1	Ina	7500.00	1	.1.3.
7	3	Aaron	5000.00	2	.1.3.7.
11	7	Gabriel	3000.00	3	.1.3.7.11.
9	7	Rita	3000.00	3	.1.3.7.9.
12	9	Emilia	2000.00	4	.1.3.7.9.12.
13	9	Michael	2000.00	4	.1.3.7.9.13.
14	9	Didi	1500.00	4	.1.3.7.9.14.

Moving a Subtree

Moving a subtree is a bit tricky. A change in someone's manager affects the row for that employee and for all of his or her subordinates. The inputs are the root of the subtree and the new parent (manager) of that root. The level and path values of all employees in the subtree are going to be affected. So you need to be able to isolate that subtree and also figure out how to revise the level and path values of all the subtree's members. To isolate the affected subtree, you join the row for the root (R) with the Employees table (E) based on *E.path LIKE R.path* + '%'. To calculate the revisions in level and path, you need access to the rows of both the old manager of the root (OM) and the new one (NM). The new level value for all nodes is their current level value plus the difference in levels between the new manager's level and the old manager's level. For example, if you move a subtree to a new location so that the difference in levels between the new manager and the old one is 2, you need to add 2 to the level value of all employees in the affected subtree. Similarly, to amend the path value of all nodes in the subtree, you need to remove the prefix containing the root's old manager's path and substitute it with the new manager's path. This can be achieved simply by using the STUFF function.

Run the following code to create the *MoveSubtree* stored procedure, which implements the logic I just described:

```
---------------------------------------------------------------------
-- Stored Procedure: MoveSubtree,
--    Moves a whole subtree of a given root to a new location
--    under a given manager
---------------------------------------------------------------------
USE tempdb;
GO
IF OBJECT_ID('dbo.MoveSubtree') IS NOT NULL
  DROP PROC dbo.MoveSubtree;
GO
CREATE PROC dbo.MoveSubtree
  @root  INT,
  @mgrid INT
AS

SET NOCOUNT ON;

BEGIN TRAN;
  -- Update level and path of all employees in the subtree (E)
  -- Set level =
  --    current level + new manager's level - old manager's level
  -- Set path =
  --    in current path remove old manager's path
  --    and substitute with new manager's path
  UPDATE E
    SET lvl  = E.lvl + NM.lvl - OM.lvl,
        path = STUFF(E.path, 1, LEN(OM.path), NM.path)
  FROM dbo.Employees AS E          -- E = Employees    (subtree)
    JOIN dbo.Employees AS R        -- R = Root          (one row)
      ON R.empid = @root
      AND E.path LIKE R.path + '%'
    JOIN dbo.Employees AS OM       -- OM = Old Manager (one row)
      ON OM.empid = R.mgrid
    JOIN dbo.Employees AS NM       -- NM = New Manager (one row)
      ON NM.empid = @mgrid;

  -- Update root's new manager
  UPDATE dbo.Employees SET mgrid = @mgrid WHERE empid = @root;
COMMIT TRAN;
GO
```

The implementation of this stored procedure is simplistic and is provided for demonstration purposes. Good behavior is not guaranteed for invalid parameter choices. To make this procedure more robust, you should also check the inputs to make sure that attempts to make someone his or her own manager or to generate cycles are rejected. For example, this can be achieved by using an EXISTS predicate with a SELECT statement that first generates a result set with the new paths and making sure that the employees' IDs do not appear in their managers' paths.

To test the procedure, first examine the tree before moving the subtree:

```
SELECT empid, REPLICATE(' | ', lvl) + empname AS empname, lvl, path
FROM dbo.Employees
ORDER BY path;
```

You get the following output:

```
empid       empname               lvl  path
----------- --------------------- ---- -------------
1           David                 0    .1.
2           | Eitan               1    .1.2.
4           | | Seraph            2    .1.2.4.
5           | | Jiru              2    .1.2.5.
10          | | | Sean            3    .1.2.5.10.
8           | | | Lilach          3    .1.2.5.8.
6           | | Steve             2    .1.2.6.
3           | Ina                 1    .1.3.
7           | | Aaron             2    .1.3.7.
11          | | | Gabriel         3    .1.3.7.11.
9           | | | Rita            3    .1.3.7.9.
12          | | | | Emilia        4    .1.3.7.9.12.
13          | | | | Michael       4    .1.3.7.9.13.
14          | | | | Didi          4    .1.3.7.9.14.
```

Then run the following code to move Aaron's subtree under Sean:

```
BEGIN TRAN;

    EXEC dbo.MoveSubtree
    @root  = 7,
    @mgrid = 10;

    -- After moving subtree
    SELECT empid, REPLICATE(' | ', lvl) + empname AS empname, lvl, path
    FROM dbo.Employees
    ORDER BY path;

ROLLBACK TRAN; -- rollback used in order not to apply the change
```

 Note The change is rolled back for demonstration only, so the data is the same at the start of each test script.

Examine the result tree to verify that the subtree moved correctly:

```
empid       empname                   lvl  path
----------- ------------------------- ---- -------------------
1           David                     0    .1.
2           | Eitan                   1    .1.2.
4           | | Seraph                2    .1.2.4.
5           | | Jiru                  2    .1.2.5.
10          | | | Sean                3    .1.2.5.10.
7           | | | | Aaron             4    .1.2.5.10.7.
11          | | | | | Gabriel         5    .1.2.5.10.7.11.
```

9						Rita	5	.1.2.5.10.7.9.
12							Emilia	6	.1.2.5.10.7.9.12.
13							Michael	6	.1.2.5.10.7.9.13.
14							Didi	6	.1.2.5.10.7.9.14.
8				Lilach		3	.1.2.5.8.
6			Steve		2	.1.2.6.
3		Ina		1	.1.3.

Removing a Subtree

Removing a subtree is a simple task. You just delete all employees whose path value has the subtree's root path as a prefix.

To test this solution, first examine the current state of the tree by running the following query:

```
SELECT empid, REPLICATE(' | ', lvl) + empname AS empname, lvl, path
FROM dbo.Employees
ORDER BY path;
```

You get the following output:

empid	empname	lvl	path
1	David	0	.1.
2		Eitan	1	.1.2.
4			Seraph	2	.1.2.4.
5			Jiru	2	.1.2.5.
10				Sean	3	.1.2.5.10.
8				Lilach	3	.1.2.5.8.
6			Steve	2	.1.2.6.
3		Ina	1	.1.3.
7			Aaron	2	.1.3.7.
11				Gabriel	3	.1.3.7.11.
9				Rita	3	.1.3.7.9.
12					Emilia	4	.1.3.7.9.12.
13					Michael	4	.1.3.7.9.13.
14					Didi	4	.1.3.7.9.14.

Issue the following code, which first removes Aaron and his subordinates and then displays the resulting tree:

```
BEGIN TRAN;

  DELETE FROM dbo.Employees
  WHERE path LIKE
    (SELECT M.path + '%'
     FROM dbo.Employees as M
     WHERE M.empid = 7);

  -- After deleting subtree
  SELECT empid, REPLICATE(' | ', lvl) + empname AS empname, lvl, path
  FROM dbo.Employees
  ORDER BY path;

ROLLBACK TRAN; -- rollback used in order not to apply the change
```

You get the following output:

```
empid        empname          lvl   path
-----------  ---------------  ----  -----------
1            David            0     .1.
2            | Eitan          1     .1.2.
4            | | Seraph       2     .1.2.4.
5            | | Jiru         2     .1.2.5.
10           | | | Sean       3     .1.2.5.10.
8            | | | Lilach     3     .1.2.5.8.
6            | | Steve        2     .1.2.6.
3            | Ina            1     .1.3.
```

Querying

Querying data in the materialized path solution is simple and elegant. For subtree-related requests, the optimizer can always use a clustered or covering index that you create on the *path* column. If you create a nonclustered, noncovering index on the *path* column, the optimizer can still use it if the query is selective enough.

Let's review typical requests from a tree. For each request, I'll provide a sample query followed by its output.

Return the subtree with a given root:

```
SELECT REPLICATE(' | ', E.lvl - M.lvl) + E.empname
FROM dbo.Employees AS E
  JOIN dbo.Employees AS M
    ON M.empid = 3 -- root
    AND E.path LIKE M.path + '%'
ORDER BY E.path;
```

```
Ina
| Aaron
| | Gabriel
| | Rita
| | | Emilia
| | | Michael
| | | Didi
```

The query joins two instances of Employees. One represents the managers (*M*) and is filtered by the given root employee. The other represents the employees in the subtree (*E*). The subtree is identified using the following logical expression in the join condition, *E.path LIKE M.path + '%'*, which identifies a subordinate if it contains the root's path as a prefix. Indentation is achieved by replicating a string (*' | '*) as many times as the employee's level within the subtree. The output is sorted by the path of the employee.

This query generates the execution plan shown in Figure 12-5.

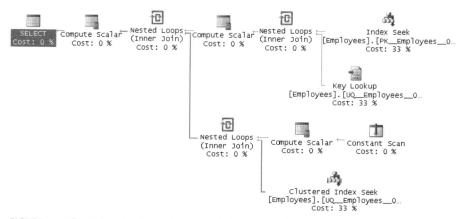

FIGURE 12-5 Execution plan for custom materialized path subtree query

The first Index Seek operator in the plan and the associated Key Lookup are in charge of retrieving the row for the filtered employee (*empid* 3). The second Index Seek operator in the plan performs a range scan in the index on the *path* attribute to retrieve the requested subtree of employees. Because the *path* attribute represents topological sorting, an index on *path* ensures that all members of the same subtree are stored continuously in the leaf level of the index. Therefore, a request for a subtree is processed with a simple range scan in the index, touching only the nodes that are in fact members of the requested subtree.

To exclude the subtree's root (top-level manager) from the output, simply add an underscore before the percent sign in the LIKE pattern:

```
SELECT REPLICATE(' | ', E.lvl - M.lvl - 1) + E.empname
FROM dbo.Employees AS E
  JOIN dbo.Employees AS M
    ON M.empid = 3
    AND E.path LIKE M.path + '_%'
ORDER BY E.path;
```

```
Aaron
 | Gabriel
 | Rita
 | | Emilia
 | | Michael
 | | Didi
```

With the additional underscore in the LIKE condition, an employee is returned only if its path starts with the root's path and has at least one subsequent character.

To return leaf nodes under a given root (including the root itself if it is a leaf), add a NOT EXISTS predicate to identify only employees that are not managers of another employee:

```
SELECT E.empid, E.empname
FROM dbo.Employees AS E
  JOIN dbo.Employees AS M
    ON M.empid = 3
    AND E.path LIKE M.path + '%'
```

```
WHERE NOT EXISTS
  (SELECT *
   FROM dbo.Employees AS E2
   WHERE E2.mgrid = E.empid);
```

```
empid       empname
----------- --------
11          Gabriel
12          Emilia
13          Michael
14          Didi
```

To return a subtree with a given root, limiting the number of levels under the root, add a filter in the join condition that limits the level difference between the employee and the root:

```
SELECT REPLICATE(' | ', E.lvl - M.lvl) + E.empname
FROM dbo.Employees AS E
  JOIN dbo.Employees AS M
    ON M.empid = 3
    AND E.path LIKE M.path + '%'
    AND E.lvl - M.lvl <= 2
ORDER BY E.path;
```

```
Ina
 | Aaron
 | | Gabriel
 | | Rita
```

To return only the nodes exactly *n* levels under a given root, use an equal to operator (=) to identify the specific level difference instead of a less than or equal to (<=) operator:

```
SELECT E.empid, E.empname
FROM dbo.Employees AS E
  JOIN dbo.Employees AS M
    ON M.empid = 3
    AND E.path LIKE M.path + '%'
    AND E.lvl - M.lvl = 2;
```

```
empid       empname
----------- --------
11          Gabriel
9           Rita
```

To return management chain of a given node, you use a query similar to the subtree query, with one small difference: you filter a specific employee ID, as opposed to filtering a specific manager ID:

```
SELECT REPLICATE(' | ', M.lvl) + M.empname
FROM dbo.Employees AS E
  JOIN dbo.Employees AS M
    ON E.empid = 14
    AND E.path LIKE M.path + '%'
ORDER BY E.path;
```

```
David
 | Ina
 | | Aaron
 | | | Rita
 | | | | Didi
```

You get all managers whose paths are a prefix of the given employee's path.

Note that requesting a subtree and requesting the ancestors have an important difference in performance, even though they look very similar. For each query, either *M.path* or *E.path* is a constant. If *M.path* is constant, *E.path LIKE M.path* + '%' uses an index because it asks for all paths with a given prefix. If *E.path* is constant, it does not use an index because it asks for all prefixes of a given path. The subtree query can seek within an index to the first path that meets the filter, and it can scan to the right until it gets to the last path that meets the filter. In other words, only the relevant paths in the index are accessed. While in the ancestors query, ALL paths must be scanned to check whether they match the filter. In large tables, this translates to a slow query. To handle ancestor requests more efficiently, you can create a function that accepts an employee ID as input, splits its path, and returns a table with the path's node IDs in separate rows. You can join this table with the tree and use index seek operations for the specific employee IDs in the path. The split function uses an auxiliary table of numbers, which I covered in Chapter 6, "Subqueries, Table Expressions, and Ranking Functions," under the section "Auxiliary Table of Numbers." If you currently don't have a Nums table in tempdb, first create it by running the following code:

```
SET NOCOUNT ON;
USE tempdb;
GO
IF OBJECT_ID('dbo.Nums') IS NOT NULL
  DROP TABLE dbo.Nums;
GO
CREATE TABLE Nums(n INT NOT NULL PRIMARY KEY);
DECLARE @max AS INT = 1000000, @rc AS INT = 1;

INSERT INTO Nums VALUES(1);
WHILE @rc * 2 <= @max
BEGIN
  INSERT INTO dbo.Nums SELECT n + @rc FROM dbo.Nums;
  SET @rc = @rc * 2;
END

INSERT INTO dbo.Nums
  SELECT n + @rc FROM dbo.Nums WHERE n + @rc <= @max;
```

Run the following code to create the *SplitPath* function:

```
USE tempdb;
GO
IF OBJECT_ID('dbo.SplitPath') IS NOT NULL
  DROP FUNCTION dbo.SplitPath;
GO
CREATE FUNCTION dbo.SplitPath(@empid AS INT) RETURNS TABLE
AS
```

```
RETURN
  SELECT
    ROW_NUMBER() OVER(ORDER BY n) AS pos,
    CAST(SUBSTRING(path, n + 1,
          CHARINDEX('.', path, n + 1) - n - 1) AS INT) AS empid
  FROM dbo.Employees
    JOIN dbo.Nums
      ON empid = @empid
      AND n < LEN(path)
      AND SUBSTRING(path, n, 1) = '.';
GO
```

You can find details on the logic behind the split technique that the function implements in Chapter 6 under the section "Separating Elements."

To test the function, run the following code, which splits employee 14's path:

```
SELECT pos, empid FROM dbo.SplitPath(14);
```

This code generates the following output:

```
pos   empid
----  ------
1     1
2     3
3     7
4     9
5     14
```

To get the management chain of a given employee, simply join the table returned by the function with the Employees table:

```
SELECT REPLICATE(' | ', lvl) + empname
FROM dbo.SplitPath(14) AS SP
  JOIN dbo.Employees AS E
    ON E.empid = SP.empid
ORDER BY path;
```

When presenting information from a tree or a subtree, a common need is to present the nodes in topological sort order (parent before child). Because the *path* column already gives you topological sorting, you can simply sort the rows by *path*. Having an index on the *path* column means that the optimizer can satisfy the request with an index order scan as opposed to needing to apply a sort operation. As shown earlier, indentation of nodes can be achieved by replicating a string *lvl* times. For example, the following query presents the employees in topological sort order:

```
SELECT REPLICATE(' | ', lvl) + empname
FROM dbo.Employees
ORDER BY path;
```

This code generates the following output:

```
David
 | Eitan
 | | Seraph
 | | Jiru
 | | | Sean
 | | | Lilach
 | | Steve
 | Ina
 | | Aaron
 | | | Gabriel
 | | | Rita
 | | | | Emilia
 | | | | Michael
 | | | | Didi
```

The execution plan for this query is shown in Figure 12-6. Notice that the clustered index created on the *path* column is scanned in an ordered fashion.

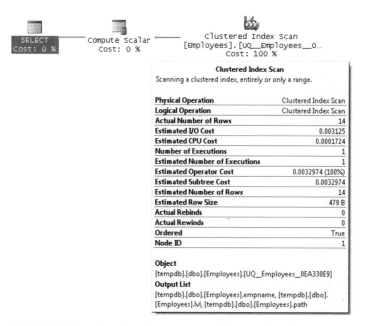

FIGURE 12-6 Execution plan for custom materialized path sorting query

Materialized Path with the HIERARCHYID Data Type

SQL Server 2008 introduces a CLR-based data type called HIERARCHYID that you can use to represent graphs. This type provides a built-in implementation for the materialized path model. Like the custom materialized path model, it works ideally for trees. As with the custom model, the HIERARCHYID values provide topological ordering, positioning a node in a certain place in the tree with respect to other nodes. Besides providing topological sorting, the HIERARCHYID paths position each node under a certain path of ancestors and in a certain place with respect to siblings. The HIERARCHYID paths differ from the custom model's paths in two main ways. First, the custom model's paths are made of the actual node IDs, while the HIERARCHYID paths are made of internally generated values. Second, the custom model's path is character based, while the HIERARCHYID paths are binary. One of the major benefits I've found with the HIERARCHYID type paths is that they tend to be much more economical compared to the custom model's paths. The encoding of the paths in the HIERARCHYID data type cannot exceed 892 bytes, but this limit shouldn't present a problem for most trees. Also, you typically want to index the paths, and index keys are limited to 900 bytes anyway.

The HIERARCHYID type provides the following set of methods and properties that help you maintain and query the tree: *GetLevel, GetRoot, GetAncestor, GetDescendant, GetReparentedValue, IsDescendantOf, ToString, Parse, Read,* and *Write.* I will describe the methods and properties in context of tasks where they need to be used.

> **Note** I should mention several points about working with the HIERARCHYID type in terms of case sensitivity:
>
> ❑ As a T-SQL type identifier, HIERARCHYID is always case insensitive, like any T-SQL keyword.
>
> ❑ The method names associated with this type, like *GetAncestor()*, are always case sensitive, like any CLR identifier, whether they are static methods or not.
>
> ❑ HIERARCHYID/hierarchyid, when used to identify the CLR class of a static method, as in *hierarchyid::GetRoot()*, is case sensitive or case insensitive according to the current database context. When the current database is case sensitive, lowercase must be used to identify the CLR class of a static method.
>
> ❑ I've chosen to write the T-SQL type as HIERARCHYID for typographical reasons, but lowercase hierarchyid is the most portable choice for code.

In my examples I will use an employee organizational chart to demonstrate working with the HIERARCHYID type. Run the following code to create the Employees table, along with a few indexes to support typical queries:

```
SET NOCOUNT ON;
USE tempdb;
GO
IF OBJECT_ID('dbo.Employees') IS NOT NULL
  DROP TABLE dbo.Employees;
GO
CREATE TABLE dbo.Employees
(
  empid   INT NOT NULL,
  hid     HIERARCHYID NOT NULL,
  lvl AS hid.GetLevel() PERSISTED,
  empname VARCHAR(25) NOT NULL,
  salary  MONEY       NOT NULL
);
```

```
CREATE UNIQUE CLUSTERED INDEX idx_depth_first ON dbo.Employees(hid);
CREATE UNIQUE INDEX idx_breadth_first ON dbo.Employees(lvl, hid);
CREATE UNIQUE INDEX idx_empid ON dbo.Employees(empid);
```

In addition to the *hid* column that holds the path, the table has a computed *persisted* column based on the *GetLevel* method applied to the *hid* column. As its name implies, the method returns the level of the node in the tree—in other words, the distance from the root.

Besides the obvious index on the *empid* attribute that supports queries requesting a particular employee, the code creates two other indexes. First, a clustered index is created on the *hid* column. Because HIERARCHYID provides topological sorting, an index on the *hid* column stores all members of the same subtree close to each other. Such an index allows efficient processing of requests that need to traverse the tree in a depth-first manner—for example, a request for a whole subtree of employees. Second, an index is created on *lvl* and *hid*, in that order. This index supports efficient processing of requests that need to traverse the tree in a breadth-first manner—for example, returning a whole level of employees.

Notice that the Employees table does not include an attribute for the manager ID. With the HIERARCHYID type you can easily address requests that would normally require such an attribute.

Maintaining Data

Whenever you need to apply changes to the tree, such as adding new leaf nodes or moving a subtree, you want to make sure that you produce new HIERARCHYID values or adjust existing ones correctly. The HIERARCHYID type's methods and properties can help you in such tasks. Also, it's important to note that the type itself does not enforce the validity of your tree—that's your responsibility. For example, if you do not enforce uniqueness of the HIERARCHYID values with a constraint, the type itself won't reject attempts to insert multiple rows with the same HIERARCHYID value. Also, it is your responsibility to develop a process that prevents concurrent sessions that perform tree maintenance tasks from producing conflicting (the same) HIERARCHYID values for different nodes. I will explain how this can be achieved.

I will demonstrate techniques for adding employees who manage no one (leaf nodes) and for moving a subtree. I'll leave other tasks—such as dropping a subtree and changing a manager—as exercises because those apply similar techniques to the ones I will cover.

Adding Employees

The task of adding a new employee who manages no one requires you to produce a HIERARCHYID value for the new node that positions it correctly within the tree and then insert the new employee row into the table. Run the following code to create a stored procedure called *AddEmp* that implements this task:

```
-----------------------------------------------------------------------
-- Stored Procedure: AddEmp,
--    Inserts new employee who manages no one into the table
-----------------------------------------------------------------------
IF OBJECT_ID('dbo.AddEmp', 'P') IS NOT NULL
  DROP PROC dbo.AddEmp;
GO
CREATE PROC dbo.AddEmp
  @empid   AS INT,
  @mgrid   AS INT,
  @empname AS VARCHAR(25),
  @salary  AS MONEY
AS

DECLARE
  @hid            AS HIERARCHYID,
  @mgr_hid        AS HIERARCHYID,
  @last_child_hid AS HIERARCHYID;

BEGIN TRAN

  IF @mgrid IS NULL
    SET @hid = hierarchyid::GetRoot();
  ELSE
  BEGIN
    SET @mgr_hid = (SELECT hid FROM dbo.Employees WITH (UPDLOCK)
                    WHERE empid = @mgrid);
    SET @last_child_hid =
      (SELECT MAX(hid) FROM dbo.Employees
       WHERE hid.GetAncestor(1) = @mgr_hid);
    SET @hid = @mgr_hid.GetDescendant(@last_child_hid, NULL);
  END

  INSERT INTO dbo.Employees(empid, hid, empname, salary)
    VALUES(@empid, @hid, @empname, @salary);

COMMIT TRAN
GO
```

The procedure accepts as inputs all attributes of the new employee (employee ID, manager ID, employee name, and salary). It then applies logic to generate the HIERARCHYID value of the new employee and store it in the variable *@hid*. Finally, the procedure uses the new HIERARCHYID value, *@hid*, in the new row it inserts into the Employees table.

The procedure's code first checks whether the input employee is the root employee (manager ID is NULL). In such a case, the code calculates the employee's path with the static method *hierarchyid::GetRoot*. As you can imagine, the purpose of this method is to produce the path for the tree's root node. In terms of the binary value that actually represents the path, this method simply returns an empty binary string (0x). You could, if you wanted, replace the static method call with the constant 0x, but with the method call the code is clearer and more self-explanatory.

The next section of the procedure's code (the ELSE block of the IF statement) handles an input employee that is not the root employee. To calculate a path for an employee that is not the root employee, you can invoke the *GetDescendant* method applied to the HIERARCHYID value of the employee's manager. The code retrieves the manager's HIERARCHYID value into the *@mgr_hid* variable and later applies to it the *GetDescendant* method.

The *GetDescendant* method accepts two input HIERARCHYID values and returns a HIERARCHYID value that is positioned under the node it is applied to and between the input left and right nodes. If both inputs are NULL, the method simply generates a value below the parent node. If the left input is not NULL, the method generates a value greater than the left input. If the right input is not NULL, the method generates a value less than the right input. Note that the method has no knowledge of other values in your tree; all it cares about is the value to which it is applied and the two input values. If you call the method twice and in both cases apply it to the same value with the same inputs, you get the same output back. It is your responsibility to prevent such conflicts. A simple technique to achieve this is to run the code in a transaction (as in the *AddEmp* procedure) and specify the UPDLOCK hint in the query that retrieves the manager's path. Remember that an update lock can be held by only one process on the same resource at a time. This hint allows only one session to request a new HIERARCHYID value under the same manager. This simple technique will guarantee that distinct HIERARCHYID values are generated by each process.

You need to be specific about where to position the new node with respect to other siblings under the same manager. For example, the inputs to the stored procedure could be the IDs of two employees between which you want to position the new employee, and the stored procedure could retrieve their HIERARCHYID values and provide those as the left and right values to the *GetDescendant* method. I decided for this implementation that I simply wanted to position the new employee right after the last under the target manager. This strategy, coupled with the use of the UPDLOCK described earlier, is always safe in the sense that HIERARCHYID values of employees will never conflict. If you choose to implement a solution that allows specifying the left and right employees, the responsibility to prevent conflicts is now yours and not the procedure's; that is, you will need to ensure that you never call the procedure more than once with the same left and right employees. To apply my chosen strategy, immediately after a query that retrieves the path of the target manager, another query retrieves the maximum path among the existing subordinates of the manager, and the result is stored in the *@last_child_hid* variable. The method *GetAncestor* helps identify direct subordinates of the target manager. The method is applied to a HIERARCHYID value of a node, and it returns the HIERARCHYID value of an ancestor that is *n* levels up, where *n* is provided as input. For *n=1*, you get the node's parent. So all employees for whom *GetAncestor(1)* returns the path of the manager are direct subordinates of the manager.

Once you have the path of the manager stored in the *@hid* variable and the path of the manager's last direct subordinate is stored in the variable *@last_child_hid*, you can generate the input employee's path with the expression *@hid.GetDescendant(@last_child_hid, NULL)*. Once the path for the input employee is generated, you can insert the employee's row into the Employees table and commit the transaction. Committing the transaction releases the update lock held on the manager's row, allowing those who want to add other subordinates under that manager to generate new HIERARCHYID values.

Run the following code to populate the Employees table with sample data:

```
EXEC dbo.AddEmp @empid =  1, @mgrid = NULL, @empname = 'David'  , @salary = $10000.00;
EXEC dbo.AddEmp @empid =  2, @mgrid =    1, @empname = 'Eitan'  , @salary = $7000.00;
EXEC dbo.AddEmp @empid =  3, @mgrid =    1, @empname = 'Ina'    , @salary = $7500.00;
EXEC dbo.AddEmp @empid =  4, @mgrid =    2, @empname = 'Seraph' , @salary = $5000.00;
EXEC dbo.AddEmp @empid =  5, @mgrid =    2, @empname = 'Jiru'   , @salary = $5500.00;
EXEC dbo.AddEmp @empid =  6, @mgrid =    2, @empname = 'Steve'  , @salary = $4500.00;
EXEC dbo.AddEmp @empid =  7, @mgrid =    3, @empname = 'Aaron'  , @salary = $5000.00;
EXEC dbo.AddEmp @empid =  8, @mgrid =    5, @empname = 'Lilach' , @salary = $3500.00;
EXEC dbo.AddEmp @empid =  9, @mgrid =    7, @empname = 'Rita'   , @salary = $3000.00;
EXEC dbo.AddEmp @empid = 10, @mgrid =    5, @empname = 'Sean'   , @salary = $3000.00;
EXEC dbo.AddEmp @empid = 11, @mgrid =    7, @empname = 'Gabriel', @salary = $3000.00;
EXEC dbo.AddEmp @empid = 12, @mgrid =    9, @empname = 'Emilia' , @salary = $2000.00;
EXEC dbo.AddEmp @empid = 13, @mgrid =    9, @empname = 'Michael', @salary = $2000.00;
EXEC dbo.AddEmp @empid = 14, @mgrid =    9, @empname = 'Didi'   , @salary = $1500.00;
```

Run the following query to present the contents of the Employees table:

```
SELECT hid, hid.ToString() AS path, lvl, empid, empname, salary
FROM dbo.Employees
ORDER BY hid;
```

The *ToString* method returns a canonical representation of the path, using slashes to separate the values at each level. This query generates the following output:

hid	path	lvl	empid	empname	salary
0x	/	0	1	David	10000.00
0x58	/1/	1	2	Eitan	7000.00
0x5AC0	/1/1/	2	4	Seraph	5000.00
0x5B40	/1/2/	2	5	Jiru	5500.00
0x5B56	/1/2/1/	3	8	Lilach	3500.00
0x5B5A	/1/2/2/	3	10	Sean	3000.00
0x5BC0	/1/3/	2	6	Steve	4500.00
0x68	/2/	1	3	Ina	7500.00
0x6AC0	/2/1/	2	7	Aaron	5000.00
0x6AD6	/2/1/1/	3	9	Rita	3000.00
0x6AD6B0	/2/1/1/1/	4	12	Emilia	2000.00
0x6AD6D0	/2/1/1/2/	4	13	Michael	2000.00
0x6AD6F0	/2/1/1/3/	4	14	Didi	1500.00
0x6ADA	/2/1/2/	3	11	Gabriel	3000.00

This output gives you a sense of the logic that the *GetDescendant* method applies to calculate the values. The root (empty binary string) is represented by the canonical path /. The first child under a node obtains its HIERARCHYID from a call to *GetDescendant* with two NULL inputs. The result is the parent's canonical path plus 1/. So the path of the first child of the root becomes /1/.

If you add someone to the right of an existing child and under that child's parent, the new child's *hid* is obtained by a call to *GetDescendant* with the existing child's *hid* as left input and

NULL as right input. The new *path* value is like the existing child's value but with a rightmost number that is greater by one. So, for example, the value under / and to the right of /1/ would be /2/. Similarly, the value under /1/ and to the right of /1/1/ would be /1/2/.

If you add someone under a certain parent and to the left of an existing child, the left input to *GetDescendant* is NULL, and the new *path* value will be like the existing child's but with a rightmost number that is less by one. So, for example, the value under /1/ and to the left of /1/1/ would be /1/0/. Similarly, the value under /1/ and to the left of /1/0/ would be /1/-1/.

If you add someone under a certain parent and provide two of that parent's existing children's *hid* values as inputs to *GetDescendant*, the resulting *path* matches the existing children's paths except for the last number. If the last numbers in the existing children's paths aren't consecutive, the last number of the new child's path will be one greater than that of the left child. For example, when the method is applied to the parent /1/1/ and the input children are /1/1/1/ and /1/1/4/, you get /1/1/2/. If the last path numbers of the input children are consecutive, you get the last number of the left child, followed by .1 (read "dot one"). For example, when the method is applied to the parent /1/1/ and the input children's paths are /1/1/1/ and /1/1/2/, you get /1/1/1.1/. Similarly, when the method is applied to the parent /1/2.1/3/4/5/ and the input children are /1/2.1/3/4/5/2.1.3.4/ and /1/2.1/3/4/5/2.1.3.5/, you get /1/2.1/3/4/5/2.1.3.4.1/. I could go on, but at this point you probably get the general idea and realize that the paths are simpler if you add new nodes either to the right of the last child or to the left of the first child.

Later in the chapter, in the section "Normalizing HIERARCHYID Values," I'll provide details as to how you can normalize paths.

Moving a Subtree

The HIERARCHYID type supports a method called *GetReparentedValue* that helps in calculating new paths when you need to move a whole subtree to a new location in the tree. The method is applied to the HIERARCHYID value of a node that you want to reparent, but it doesn't perform the actual reparenting. It simply returns a new value that you can then use to overwrite the existing path. The method accepts two inputs (call them *@old_root* and *@new_root*) and returns a new value with the target node's path where the *@new_root* prefix replaces the *@old_root* prefix. It's as simple as that.

> **Note** When you call *GetReparentedValue* on a HIERARCHYID *h*, the path of *@old_root* must be a prefix of *h*'s path. If it is not, you'll get an exception of type *HierarchyIdException*.

For example, if you apply the *GetReparentedValue* method to a HIERARCHYID whose canonical path is /1/1/2/3/2/, providing /1/1/ as the old root and /2/1/4/ as the new root, you get a HIERARCHYID whose canonical path is /2/1/4/2/3/2/. By the way, you can cast a canonical path representation to the HIERARCHYID data type by using the CAST function or the static method *hierarchyid::Parse*. With this in mind, you can test the aforementioned example by using the *GetReparentedValue* with constants, like so:

```
SELECT
  CAST('/1/1/2/3/2/' AS HIERARCHYID).GetReparentedValue('/1/1/', '/2/1/4/').ToString();
```

You get the path /2/1/4/2/3/2/ as output.

With this in mind, consider the task to create a stored procedure called *MoveSubtree* that accepts two inputs called *@empid* and *@new_mgrid*. The stored procedure's purpose is to move the subtree of employee *@empid* under *@new_mgrid*. The stored procedure can implement the task in three steps:

1. Store the existing paths of the employees represented by *@new_mgrid* and *@empid* in variables (call them *@new_mgr_hid* and *@old_root*, respectively).

2. Apply the *GetDescendant* method to *@new_mgr_hid*, providing the maximum among the new manager's existing subordinates (or NULL if there are none) as left input, to get a new path under the target manager for employee *@empid*. Store the new path in a variable (call it *@new_root*).

3. Update the *hid* value of all descendants of the employee represented by *@empid* (including itself) to *hid.GetReparentedValue(@old_root, @new_root)*. To identify all descendants of a node you can check the value of the method *IsDescendantOf* on each *hid* in the table. This method returns 1 when the node it is applied to is a descendant of the input node and 0 otherwise.

Run the following code to create the *MoveSubtree* stored procedure, which implements the preceding steps:

```
---------------------------------------------------------------------
-- Stored Procedure: MoveSubtree,
--    Moves a whole subtree of a given root to a new location
--    under a given manager
---------------------------------------------------------------------
IF OBJECT_ID('dbo.MoveSubtree') IS NOT NULL
  DROP PROC dbo.MoveSubtree;
GO
CREATE PROC dbo.MoveSubtree
  @empid     AS INT,
  @new_mgrid AS INT
AS

DECLARE
  @old_root AS HIERARCHYID,
  @new_root AS HIERARCHYID,
  @new_mgr_hid AS HIERARCHYID;

BEGIN TRAN

  SET @new_mgr_hid = (SELECT hid FROM dbo.Employees WITH (UPDLOCK)
                      WHERE empid = @new_mgrid);
  SET @old_root = (SELECT hid FROM dbo.Employees
                   WHERE empid = @empid);
```

```
   -- First, get a new hid for the subtree root employee that moves
   SET @new_root = @new_mgr_hid.GetDescendant
     ((SELECT MAX(hid)
       FROM dbo.Employees
       WHERE hid.GetAncestor(1) = @new_mgr_hid),
      NULL);

   -- Next, reparent all descendants of employee that moves
   UPDATE dbo.Employees
     SET hid = hid.GetReparentedValue(@old_root, @new_root)
   WHERE hid.IsDescendantOf(@old_root) = 1;

COMMIT TRAN
GO
```

Notice that the code uses an explicit transaction, and as the first step when querying the target manager's row, the statement obtains an update lock on that row. Much like in the *AddEmp* procedure discussed earlier, this technique guarantees that only one subtree is moved under a given target manager at a time, which prevents conflicts in the newly generated HIERARCHYID values.

To test the *MoveSubtree* procedure run the following code, moving the subtree of employee 5 (Jiru) under employee 9 (Rita):

```
SELECT empid, REPLICATE(' | ', lvl) + empname AS empname, hid.ToString() AS path
FROM dbo.Employees
ORDER BY hid;

BEGIN TRAN

  EXEC dbo.MoveSubtree
    @empid    = 5,
    @new_mgrid = 9;

  SELECT empid, REPLICATE(' | ', lvl) + empname AS empname, hid.ToString() AS path
  FROM dbo.Employees
  ORDER BY hid;

ROLLBACK TRAN
```

The code presents the before and after states of the data, and because this is just a demonstration, it runs the activity in a transaction so that the changes won't be committed. Following are the outputs of this code showing that the subtree was moved correctly:

```
empid       empname                path
----------- ---------------------- ------------
1           David                  /
2           | Eitan                /1/
4           | | Seraph             /1/1/
5           | | Jiru               /1/2/
8           | | | Lilach           /1/2/1/
10          | | | Sean             /1/2/2/
6           | | Steve              /1/3/
3           | Ina                  /2/
```

```
7          |  |  Aaron             /2/1/
9          |  |  |  Rita           /2/1/1/
12         |  |  |  |  Emilia      /2/1/1/1/
13         |  |  |  |  Michael     /2/1/1/2/
14         |  |  |  |  Didi        /2/1/1/3/
11         |  |  |  Gabriel        /2/1/2/
```

```
empid       empname                path
----------- ---------------------- ------------
1           David                  /
2           |  Eitan               /1/
4           |  |  Seraph           /1/1/
6           |  |  Steve            /1/3/
3           |  Ina                 /2/
7           |  |  Aaron            /2/1/
9           |  |  |  Rita          /2/1/1/
12          |  |  |  |  Emilia     /2/1/1/1/
13          |  |  |  |  Michael    /2/1/1/2/
14          |  |  |  |  Didi       /2/1/1/3/
5           |  |  |  |  Jiru       /2/1/1/4/
8           |  |  |  |  |  Lilach  /2/1/1/4/1/
10          |  |  |  |  |  Sean    /2/1/1/4/2/
11          |  |  |  Gabriel       /2/1/2/
```

Querying

As with the custom materialized path solution, querying data in the built-in materialized path solution that is based on the HIERARCHYID data type is simple and elegant. With the depth-first and breadth-first indexes in place, you can enable SQL Server's optimizer to handle certain types of requests efficiently.

I won't cover all possible requests against the tree here because there are so many. Instead, I'll show a sample of the common ones. As I did before, I'll provide a sample query for each request followed by its output.

Subtree

Return the subtree of employee 3, limiting the number of levels under the input employee to 3:

```
SELECT E.empid, E.empname
FROM dbo.Employees AS M
  JOIN dbo.Employees AS E
    ON M.empid = 3
    AND E.hid.IsDescendantOf(M.hid) = 1
WHERE E.lvl - M.lvl <= 3;
```

The query uses the *IsDescendantOf* method. Recall that this method returns 1 if the node to which it is applied is a descendant of the input node and 0 otherwise. The query joins two instances of the Employees table: one representing the input manager (M) and one representing the subordinates (E). The predicate in the ON clause filters only one row from the instance M—the one for employee 3—and returns all employees from E that are descendants of the employee in M. The predicate in the WHERE clause filters only employees that are up to three levels below the employee in M.

This query generates the following output:

```
empid        empname
-----------  -------------------------
3            Ina
7            Aaron
9            Rita
12           Emilia
13           Michael
14           Didi
11           Gabriel
```

The execution plan of this query is shown in Figure 12-7.

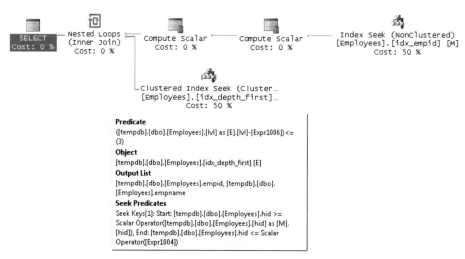

FIGURE 12-7 Execution plan for HIERARCHYID subtree query

The first Index Seek operator in the plan (the top one) is responsible for returning the row for employee 3 from the index on the *empid* column. A Compute Scalar operator (the second one) then calculates the boundary points of the HIERARCHYID values at the edges of the requested subtree. Recall that because the HIERARCHYID values give you topological sorting, an index on the *hid* column arranges all members of the same subtree together. The second Index Seek operator in the plan (the bottom one) performs a range scan between the boundary points in the index on *hid*, which retrieves the members of the requested subtree. This plan is pretty much as good as it can get for this kind of request because SQL Server ends up scanning only the members of the applicable subtree.

Path

Next, I'll explain how to handle a request to return all managers in the path leading to a certain employee. You can implement a solution that is very similar to the one used to handle the subtree request. Instead of filtering the row representing the one manager (from an instance M of Employees) and then returning the attributes of all qualifying subordinates (from an instance E), you filter the row representing the one employee and then return the attributes of all qualifying managers. For example, the following query returns all managers of employee 14, direct or indirect:

```
SELECT M.empid, M.empname
FROM dbo.Employees AS M
  JOIN dbo.Employees AS E
    ON E.empid = 14
    AND E.hid.IsDescendantOf(M.hid) = 1;
```

This query generates the following output:

```
empid       empname
----------- ------------------------
1           David
3           Ina
7           Aaron
9           Rita
14          Didi
```

Although this query is very similar to the one that implemented the subtree request, it cannot be optimized as efficiently. That's because members of the same path do not reside close to each other in the index.

Direct Subordinates

Next, I'll describe how to handle a request to get direct subordinates of an employee. To handle this request you can use a similar join form as in the previous queries. Filter the one row representing the employee whose subordinates you want from an instance (M) of the Employees table and return all employees (from another instance, E) whose parent is the employee filtered from M. A node's parent is its ancestor one level up, and the *GetAncestor* method with input value 1 returns the parent HIERARCHYID. As an example of finding direct subordinates, the following query returns direct subordinates of employee 2:

```
SELECT E.empid, E.empname
FROM dbo.Employees AS M
  JOIN dbo.Employees AS E
    ON M.empid = 2
    AND E.hid.GetAncestor(1) = M.hid;
```

This code generates the following output:

```
empid       empname
----------- ------------------------
4           Seraph
5           Jiru
6           Steve
```

Leaf Nodes

You can also use the *GetAncestor* method with input value 1 to identify leaf nodes. Leaf nodes, or employees who manage no one, are employees that do not appear as the parent of other employees. This logic can be implemented with a NOT EXISTS predicate, like so:

```
SELECT empid, empname
FROM dbo.Employees AS M
WHERE NOT EXISTS
  (SELECT * FROM dbo.Employees AS E
   WHERE E.hid.GetAncestor(1) = M.hid);
```

This code generates the following output:

```
empid       empname
----------- ------------------------
4           Seraph
8           Lilach
10          Sean
6           Steve
12          Emilia
13          Michael
14          Didi
11          Gabriel
```

Presentation

Finally, to present the hierarchy of employees so that a subordinate appears under and to the right of its manager, use the following query:

```
SELECT REPLICATE(' | ', lvl) + empname AS empname, hid.ToString() AS path
FROM dbo.Employees
ORDER BY hid;
```

Recall that the HIERARCHYID data type gives you topological sorting, so all you need to do to get the desired presentation ordering is to order by the *hid* attribute. Indentation is achieved by replicating a string *lvl* times. This query generates the following output:

```
empname               path
--------------------- ----------
David                 /
| Eitan               /1/
| | Seraph            /1/1/
| | Jiru              /1/2/
| | | Lilach          /1/2/1/
| | | Sean            /1/2/2/
| | Steve             /1/3/
| Ina                 /2/
| | Aaron             /2/1/
| | | Rita            /2/1/1/
| | | | Emilia        /2/1/1/1/
| | | | Michael       /2/1/1/2/
| | | | Didi          /2/1/1/3/
| | | Gabriel         /2/1/2/
```

The execution plan of this query is shown in Figure 12-8.

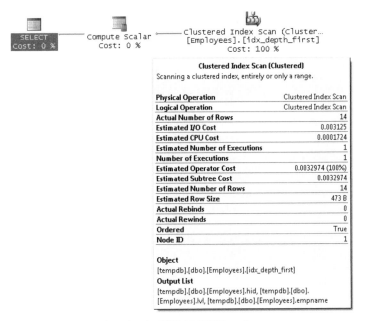

FIGURE 12-8 Execution plan for HIERARCHYID sorting query

You can see that the optimizer efficiently processed the request with an ordered scan of the index on the *hid* column.

Further Aspects of Working with HIERARCHYID

This section covers further aspects of working with the HIERARCHYID data type. I'll explain the circumstances in which paths can get lengthy and provide you with a solution to normalize them. I'll show you how to convert a representation of a tree as an adjacency list to one that is based on the HIERARCHYID data type. Finally, I'll show you how you can use the HIERARCHYID data type to sort separated lists of values.

Normalizing HIERARCHYID Values

When you use the HIERARCHYID data type to represent trees, in certain cases the paths can become long. With very deep trees this is natural because the HIERARCHYID value represents a path of all nodes leading to the current node, starting with the root. However, in certain cases, even when the tree is not very deep, the path can become long. First I'll explain the circumstances in which this can happen, and then I'll provide a solution to normalizing the values, making them shorter. Note that in this section, the word *normalizing* does not refer to database normalization.

HIERARCHYID values can become long when you keep adding new nodes between existing nodes whose canonical paths have consecutive last numbers. For example, say you have nodes with canonical paths /1/ and /2/ and you add a node between them. You get a new value whose canonical path is /1.1/. Now add a value between /1.1/ and /2/, and you get /1.2/. Now add a value between /1.1/ and /1.2/, and you get /1.1.1/. As you see, if you keep adding nodes between existing nodes in this manner, you can get lengthy paths (which represent lengthy HIERARCHYID values) even when the tree is not deep.

If order among siblings is not important, you can always make sure to add new child nodes after the last existing child or before the first one; this way, the paths are more economical. But when order among siblings matters, you can't control this. If you must frequently add new nodes between existing ones, you may end up with very long HIERARCHYID values. In such a case, you can periodically run a procedure, which I will provide here, that normalizes the HIERARCHYID values for the whole graph, making them shorter.

Run the following code to create a new version of the *AddEmp* stored procedure:

```
---------------------------------------------------------------------
-- Stored Procedure: AddEmp,
--     Inserts new employee who manages no one into the table
---------------------------------------------------------------------
IF OBJECT_ID('dbo.AddEmp', 'P') IS NOT NULL
  DROP PROC dbo.AddEmp;
GO
CREATE PROC dbo.AddEmp
  @empid      AS INT,
  @mgrid      AS INT,
  @leftempid  AS INT,
  @rightempid AS INT,
  @empname    AS VARCHAR(25) ,
  @salary     AS MONEY = 1000
AS

DECLARE @hid AS HIERARCHYID;

IF @mgrid IS NULL
  SET @hid = hierarchyid::GetRoot();
ELSE
  SET @hid = (SELECT hid FROM dbo.Employees WHERE empid = @mgrid).GetDescendant
    ( (SELECT hid FROM dbo.Employees WHERE empid = @leftempid),
      (SELECT hid FROM dbo.Employees WHERE empid = @rightempid) );

INSERT INTO dbo.Employees(empid, hid, empname, salary)
  VALUES(@empid, @hid, @empname, @salary);
GO
```

This version accepts the IDs of the two child employees between which you want to add the new one.

Next, run the following code, which truncates the Employees table and populates it with data in such a manner that lengthy paths are produced:

```
TRUNCATE TABLE dbo.Employees;

EXEC dbo.AddEmp @empid =  1, @mgrid = NULL, @leftempid = NULL, @rightempid = NULL,
    @empname = 'A';
EXEC dbo.AddEmp @empid =  2, @mgrid =     1, @leftempid = NULL, @rightempid = NULL,
    @empname = 'B';
EXEC dbo.AddEmp @empid =  3, @mgrid =     1, @leftempid =    2, @rightempid = NULL,
    @empname = 'C';
EXEC dbo.AddEmp @empid =  4, @mgrid =     1, @leftempid =    2, @rightempid =    3,
    @empname = 'D';
EXEC dbo.AddEmp @empid =  5, @mgrid =     1, @leftempid =    4, @rightempid =    3,
    @empname = 'E';
EXEC dbo.AddEmp @empid =  6, @mgrid =     1, @leftempid =    4, @rightempid =    5,
    @empname = 'F';
EXEC dbo.AddEmp @empid =  7, @mgrid =     1, @leftempid =    6, @rightempid =    5,
    @empname = 'G';
EXEC dbo.AddEmp @empid =  8, @mgrid =     1, @leftempid =    6, @rightempid =    7,
    @empname = 'H';
EXEC dbo.AddEmp @empid =  9, @mgrid =     8, @leftempid = NULL, @rightempid = NULL,
    @empname = 'I';
EXEC dbo.AddEmp @empid = 10, @mgrid =     8, @leftempid =    9, @rightempid = NULL,
    @empname = 'J';
EXEC dbo.AddEmp @empid = 11, @mgrid =     8, @leftempid =    9, @rightempid =   10,
    @empname = 'K';
EXEC dbo.AddEmp @empid = 12, @mgrid =     8, @leftempid =   11, @rightempid =   10,
    @empname = 'J';
EXEC dbo.AddEmp @empid = 13, @mgrid =     8, @leftempid =   11, @rightempid =   12,
    @empname = 'L';
EXEC dbo.AddEmp @empid = 14, @mgrid =     8, @leftempid =   13, @rightempid =   12,
    @empname = 'M';
EXEC dbo.AddEmp @empid = 15, @mgrid =     8, @leftempid =   13, @rightempid =   14,
    @empname = 'N';
EXEC dbo.AddEmp @empid = 16, @mgrid =     8, @leftempid =   15, @rightempid =   14,
    @empname = 'O';
EXEC dbo.AddEmp @empid = 17, @mgrid =     8, @leftempid =   15, @rightempid =   16,
    @empname = 'P';
EXEC dbo.AddEmp @empid = 18, @mgrid =     8, @leftempid =   17, @rightempid =   16,
    @empname = 'Q';
EXEC dbo.AddEmp @empid = 19, @mgrid =     8, @leftempid =   17, @rightempid =   18,
    @empname = 'E';
EXEC dbo.AddEmp @empid = 20, @mgrid =     8, @leftempid =   19, @rightempid =   18,
    @empname = 'S';
EXEC dbo.AddEmp @empid = 21, @mgrid =     8, @leftempid =   19, @rightempid =   20,
    @empname = 'T';
```

Then run the following code to show the current HIERARCHYID values and their canonical paths:

```
SELECT
  empid,
  REPLICATE(' | ', lvl) + empname AS emp,
  hid,
  hid.ToString() AS path
FROM dbo.Employees
ORDER BY hid;
```

You get the following output:

```
empid  emp       hid                 path
------ --------  ------------------  -----------------------
1      A         0x                  /
2      | B       0x58                /1/
4      | D       0x62C0              /1.1/
6      | F       0x6316              /1.1.1/
8      | H       0x6318B0            /1.1.1.1/
9      | | I     0x6318B580          /1.1.1.1/1/
11     | | K     0x6318B62C          /1.1.1.1/1.1/
13     | | L     0x6318B63160        /1.1.1.1/1.1.1/
15     | | N     0x6318B6318B        /1.1.1.1/1.1.1.1/
17     | | P     0x6318B6318C58      /1.1.1.1/1.1.1.1.1/
19     | | E     0x6318B6318C62C0    /1.1.1.1/1.1.1.1.1.1/
21     | | T     0x6318B6318C6316    /1.1.1.1/1.1.1.1.1.1.1/
20     | | S     0x6318B6318C6340    /1.1.1.1/1.1.1.1.1.2/
18     | | Q     0x6318B6318C68      /1.1.1.1/1.1.1.2/
16     | | O     0x6318B6318D        /1.1.1.1/1.1.1.2/
14     | | M     0x6318B631A0        /1.1.1.1/1.1.2/
12     | | J     0x6318B634          /1.1.1.1/1.2/
10     | | J     0x6318B680          /1.1.1.1/2/
7      | G       0x631A              /1.1.2/
5      | E       0x6340              /1.2/
3      | C       0x68                /2/
```

As you can see, even though the tree is only three levels deep, some of the HIERARCHYID values became quite long because of the insertion order of children.

The solution that normalizes the values involves the following steps:

1. Define a CTE called EmpsRN that calculates for each node a row number, partitioned by parent and ordered by current *hid* value.

2. Define a recursive CTE called EmpPaths that iterates through the levels of the tree, starting with the root node and proceeding to the next level of children in each iteration. Use this CTE to construct a new canonical path for the nodes. The root should be assigned the path /, and for each node in the next level the path is obtained by concatenating the parent's path, the current node's row number from the previous step, and another / character.

3. Join the Employees table with the EmpPaths CTE and update the existing *hid* values with new ones converted from the canonical paths generated in the previous step.

Here's the code that performs this normalization process:

```
WITH EmpsRN AS
(
  SELECT
    empid,
    hid,
    ROW_NUMBER() OVER(PARTITION BY hid.GetAncestor(1) ORDER BY hid) AS rownum
  FROM dbo.Employees
),
```

```
EmpPaths AS
(
  SELECT empid, hid, CAST('/' AS VARCHAR(900)) AS path
  FROM dbo.Employees
  WHERE hid = hierarchyid::GetRoot()

  UNION ALL

  SELECT C.empid, C.hid,
    CAST(P.path + CAST(C.rownum AS VARCHAR(20)) + '/' AS VARCHAR(900))
  FROM EmpPaths AS P
    JOIN EmpsRN AS C
      ON C.hid.GetAncestor(1) = P.hid
)
UPDATE E
  SET hid = CAST(EP.path AS HIERARCHYID)
FROM dbo.Employees AS E
  JOIN EmpPaths AS EP
    ON E.empid = EP.empid;
```

Now query the data after normalization:

```
SELECT
  empid,
  REPLICATE(' | ', lvl) + empname AS emp,
  hid,
  hid.ToString() AS path
FROM dbo.Employees
ORDER BY hid;
```

As you can see in the output, you get nice compact paths:

```
empid        emp      hid      path
-----------  -------- -------  -------
1            A        0x       /
2             | B     0x58     /1/
4             | D     0x68     /2/
6             | F     0x78     /3/
8             | H     0x84     /4/
9             |  | I  0x8560   /4/1/
11            |  | K  0x85A0   /4/2/
13            |  | L  0x85E0   /4/3/
15            |  | N  0x8610   /4/4/
17            |  | P  0x8630   /4/5/
19            |  | E  0x8650   /4/6/
21            |  | T  0x8670   /4/7/
20            |  | S  0x8688   /4/8/
18            |  | Q  0x8698   /4/9/
16            |  | O  0x86A8   /4/10/
14            |  | M  0x86B8   /4/11/
12            |  | J  0x86C8   /4/12/
10            |  | J  0x86D8   /4/13/
7             | G     0x8C     /5/
5             | E     0x94     /6/
3             | C     0x9C     /7/
```

Convert Parent-Child Representation to HIERARCHYID

This section explains how to convert an existing representation of a tree that is based on an adjacency list (parent-child relationships) to one that is based on the HIERARCHYID data type.

Run the following code to create and populate the EmployeesOld table that implements an adjacency list representation of an employee tree:

```
SET NOCOUNT ON;
USE tempdb;
GO
IF OBJECT_ID('dbo.EmployeesOld') IS NOT NULL
  DROP TABLE dbo.EmployeesOld;
GO
IF OBJECT_ID('dbo.EmployeesNew') IS NOT NULL
  DROP TABLE dbo.EmployeesNew;
GO
CREATE TABLE dbo.EmployeesOld
(
  empid    INT           PRIMARY KEY,
  mgrid    INT           NULL REFERENCES dbo.EmployeesOld,
  empname  VARCHAR(25)   NOT NULL,
  salary   MONEY         NOT NULL
);
CREATE UNIQUE INDEX idx_unc_mgrid_empid ON dbo.EmployeesOld(mgrid, empid);

INSERT INTO dbo.EmployeesOld(empid, mgrid, empname, salary) VALUES
  (1,  NULL, 'David',   $10000.00),
  (2,  1,    'Eitan',   $7000.00),
  (3,  1,    'Ina',     $7500.00),
  (4,  2,    'Seraph',  $5000.00),
  (5,  2,    'Jiru',    $5500.00),
  (6,  2,    'Steve',   $4500.00),
  (7,  3,    'Aaron',   $5000.00),
  (8,  5,    'Lilach',  $3500.00),
  (9,  7,    'Rita',    $3000.00),
  (10, 5,    'Sean',    $3000.00),
  (11, 7,    'Gabriel', $3000.00),
  (12, 9,    'Emilia' , $2000.00),
  (13, 9,    'Michael', $2000.00),
  (14, 9,    'Didi',    $1500.00);
```

Run the following code to create the target EmployeesNew table that will represent the employee tree using HIERARCHYID values:

```
CREATE TABLE dbo.EmployeesNew
(
  empid    INT NOT NULL PRIMARY KEY,
  hid      HIERARCHYID NOT NULL,
  lvl AS hid.GetLevel() PERSISTED,
  empname VARCHAR(25) NOT NULL,
  salary  MONEY       NOT NULL
);
```

The task is now to query the EmployeesOld table that contains the source data, calculate HIERARCHYID values for the employees, and populate the target EmployeesNew table.

This task can be achieved in a similar manner to normalizing existing HIERARCHYID values as described earlier. You apply the following steps:

1. Define a CTE called EmpsRN that calculates for each node a row number partitioned by *mgrid*, ordered by the attributes that you want to dictate order among siblings—for example, *empid*.

2. Define a recursive CTE called EmpPaths that iterates through the levels of the tree, starting with the root node and proceeding to the next level of children in each iteration. Use this CTE to construct a new canonical path for the nodes. The root should be assigned the path /, and for each node in the next level the path is obtained by concatenating the parent's path, the current node's row number from the previous step, and another / character.

3. Insert into the target table EmployeesNew the employee rows along with their newly generated HIERARCHYID values from the EmpPaths CTE.

Here's the code that performs this conversion process:

```
WITH EmpsRN
AS
(
  SELECT empid, mgrid, empname, salary,
    ROW_NUMBER() OVER(PARTITION BY mgrid ORDER BY empid) AS rn
  FROM dbo.EmployeesOld
),
EmpPaths AS
(
  SELECT empid, mgrid, empname, salary,
    CAST('/' AS VARCHAR(900)) AS cpath
  FROM dbo.EmployeesOld
  WHERE mgrid IS NULL

  UNION ALL

  SELECT C.empid, C.mgrid, C.empname, C.salary,
    CAST(cpath + CAST(C.rn AS VARCHAR(20)) + '/' AS VARCHAR(900))
  FROM EmpPaths AS P
    JOIN EmpsRN AS C
      ON C.mgrid = P.empid
)
INSERT INTO dbo.EmployeesNew(empid, empname, salary, hid)
  SELECT empid, empname, salary,
    CAST(cpath AS HIERARCHYID) AS hid
  FROM EmpPaths;
```

Run the following code to present the contents of the EmployeesNew table after the conversion:

```
SELECT REPLICATE(' | ', lvl) + empname AS empname, hid.ToString() AS path
FROM dbo.EmployeesNew
ORDER BY hid;
```

You get the following output:

```
empname                 path
--------------------    ----------
David                   /
 | Eitan                /1/
 | | Seraph             /1/1/
 | | Jiru               /1/2/
 | | | Lilach           /1/2/1/
 | | | Sean             /1/2/2/
 | | Steve              /1/3/
 | Ina                  /2/
 | | Aaron              /2/1/
 | | | Rita             /2/1/1/
 | | | | Emilia         /2/1/1/1/
 | | | | Michael        /2/1/1/2/
 | | | | Didi           /2/1/1/3/
 | | | Gabriel          /2/1/2/
```

Sorting Separated Lists of Values

Some applications store information about arrays and lists of numbers in the form of character strings with separated lists of values. I won't get into a discussion here regarding whether such representation of data is really appropriate. Instead, I'll address a certain need involving such representation. Sometimes you don't have control over the design of certain systems, and you need to provide solutions to requests using the existing design.

The request at hand involves sorting such lists, but based on the numeric values of the elements and not by their character representation. For example, consider the lists '13,41,17' and '13,41,3'. If you sort the lists based on the character representation of the elements, the former would be returned before the latter because the character '1' is considered smaller than the character '3'. You want the second string to sort before the first because the number 3 is smaller than the number 17.

A special case of the problem is sorting IP addresses represented as character strings. In this special case you have an assurance that each string always has exactly four elements, and the length of each element never exceeds three digits. I'll first cover this special case and then discuss the more generic one.

Run the following code to create the IPs table and populate it with some sample IP addresses:

```
USE tempdb;
IF OBJECT_ID('dbo.IPs', 'U') IS NOT NULL DROP TABLE dbo.IPs;

-- Creation script for table IPs
CREATE TABLE dbo.IPs
(
  ip varchar(15) NOT NULL,
  CONSTRAINT PK_IPs PRIMARY KEY(ip),
  -- CHECK constraint that validates IPs
```

```
   CONSTRAINT CHK_IP_valid CHECK
   (
       -- 3 periods and no empty octets
       ip LIKE '_%._%._%._%'
     AND
       -- not 4 periods or more
       ip NOT LIKE '%.%.%.%.%'
     AND
       -- no characters other than digits and periods
       ip NOT LIKE '%[^0-9.]%'
     AND
       -- not more than 3 digits per octet
       ip NOT LIKE '%[0-9][0-9][0-9][0-9]%'
     AND
       -- NOT 300 - 999
       ip NOT LIKE '%[3-9][0-9][0-9]%'
     AND
       -- NOT 260 - 299
       ip NOT LIKE '%2[6-9][0-9]%'
     AND
       -- NOT 256 - 259
       ip NOT LIKE '%25[6-9]%'
   )
);
GO

-- Sample data
INSERT INTO dbo.IPs(ip) VALUES
   ('131.107.2.201'),
   ('131.33.2.201'),
   ('131.33.2.202'),
   ('3.107.2.4'),
   ('3.107.3.169'),
   ('3.107.104.172'),
   ('22.107.202.123'),
   ('22.20.2.77'),
   ('22.156.9.91'),
   ('22.156.89.32');
```

I'll first describe one of the solutions that I had for this need prior to SQL Server 2008.

An IP address must be one of 81 (3^4) possible patterns in terms of the number of digits in each octet (assuming we are talking about IPv4). You can write a query that produces all possible patterns that a LIKE predicate would recognize, representing each digit with an underscore. You can use an auxiliary table of numbers (call it Nums with a column n) that has three numbers for the three possible octet lengths. By joining four instances of the Nums table, you get the 81 possible variations of the four octet sizes. You can then easily construct the LIKE patterns representing the IP addresses and, using the numbers from the Nums table, calculate the starting position and length of each octet.

Run the following code to create and query the view IPPatterns, which implements this logic:

```
IF OBJECT_ID('dbo.IPPatterns') IS NOT NULL DROP VIEW dbo.IPPatterns;
GO
CREATE VIEW dbo.IPPatterns
AS
```

```
SELECT
  REPLICATE('_', N1.n) + '.' + REPLICATE('_', N2.n) + '.'
    + REPLICATE('_', N3.n) + '.' + REPLICATE('_', N4.n) AS pattern,
  N1.n AS l1, N2.n AS l2, N3.n AS l3, N4.n AS l4,
  1 AS s1, N1.n+2 AS s2, N1.n+N2.n+3 AS s3, N1.n+N2.n+N3.n+4 AS s4
FROM dbo.Nums AS N1, dbo.Nums AS N2, dbo.Nums AS N3, dbo.Nums AS N4
WHERE N1.n <= 3 AND N2.n <= 3 AND N3.n <= 3 AND N4.n <= 3;
GO

SELECT * FROM dbo.IPPatterns;
```

When you query the view you get the possible IP patterns and the starting position and
length of each pattern, as shown here in abbreviated form:

```
pattern           l1  l2  l3  l4  s1  s2  s3  s4
---------------   --- --- --- --- --- --- --- ---
_._._._           1   1   1   1   1   3   5   7
_._._.__          1   1   1   2   1   3   5   7
_._._.___         1   1   1   3   1   3   5   7
_._.__._          1   1   2   1   1   3   5   8
_._.__.__         1   1   2   2   1   3   5   8
_._.__.___        1   1   2   3   1   3   5   8
_._.___._         1   1   3   1   1   3   5   9
_._.___.__        1   1   3   2   1   3   5   9
_._.___.___       1   1   3   3   1   3   5   9
_.__._._          1   2   1   1   1   3   6   8
_.__._.__         1   2   1   2   1   3   6   8
_.__._.___        1   2   1   3   1   3   6   8
_.__.__._         1   2   2   1   1   3   6   9
_.__.__.__        1   2   2   2   1   3   6   9
_.__.__.___       1   2   2   3   1   3   6   9
_.__.___._        1   2   3   1   1   3   6   10
_.__.___.__       1   2   3   2   1   3   6   10
_.__.___.___      1   2   3   3   1   3   6   10
_.___._._         1   3   1   1   1   3   7   9
_.___._.__        1   3   1   2   1   3   7   9
...
```

Of course, you can implement similar logic to create the possible patterns for IP addresses of IPv6.

Now you can write a query that joins the IPs table with the IPPatterns view based on a match
between the IP address and the IP pattern. This way you identify the IP pattern for each IP
address, along with the measures indicating the starting position and length of each octet.
You can then specify four expressions in the ORDER BY clause that apply the SUBSTRING
function to extract the octets and cast the character string representation of the octet to a
numeric one. Here's what the query looks like:

```
SELECT ip
FROM dbo.IPs
  JOIN dbo.IPPatterns
    ON ip LIKE pattern
ORDER BY
```

```
CAST(SUBSTRING(ip, s1, 11) AS TINYINT),
CAST(SUBSTRING(ip, s2, 12) AS TINYINT),
CAST(SUBSTRING(ip, s3, 13) AS TINYINT),
CAST(SUBSTRING(ip, s4, 14) AS TINYINT);
```

This query generates the following output:

```
ip
---------------
3.107.2.4
3.107.3.169
3.107.104.172
22.20.2.77
22.107.202.123
22.156.9.91
22.156.89.32
131.33.2.201
131.33.2.202
131.107.2.201
```

The problem with this solution is that it's not very efficient, and it doesn't work in the more generic cases of lists where you have an unknown number of elements.

Interestingly, the canonical representation of HIERARCHYID values in SQL Server 2008 is also a separated list of numbers. Within a level you can have values separated by dots, and between levels the values are separated by slashes. With this in mind, you can handle the task at hand by concatenating a slash before and after the IP address, then sorting the rows after converting the result to the HIERARCHYID data type, like so:

```
SELECT ip
FROM dbo.IPs
ORDER BY CAST('/' + ip + '/' AS HIERARCHYID);
```

This solution works just as well with the more generic case of the problem. To demonstrate this, first create and populate the table T1 by running the following code:

```
SET NOCOUNT ON;
USE tempdb;
IF OBJECT_ID('dbo.T1', 'U') IS NOT NULL DROP TABLE dbo.T1;

CREATE TABLE dbo.T1
(
  id  INT          NOT NULL IDENTITY PRIMARY KEY,
  val VARCHAR(500) NOT NULL
);
GO

INSERT INTO dbo.T1(val) VALUES
  ('100'),
  ('7,4,250'),
  ('22,40,5,60,4,100,300,478,19710212'),
  ('22,40,5,60,4,99,300,478,19710212'),
  ('22,40,5,60,4,99,300,478,9999999'),
  ('10,30,40,50,20,30,40'),
```

```
('7,4,250'),
('-1'),
('-2'),
('-11'),
('-22'),
('-123'),
('-321'),
('22,40,5,60,4,-100,300,478,19710212'),
('22,40,5,60,4,-99,300,478,19710212');
```

As you can see, the lists in the table have varying numbers of elements. Note that because the separator used in these lists is a comma, you need to replace the separators by slashes or dots before converting to the HIERARCHYID data type. Here's the solution query that sorts the lists by the numeric values of the elements:

```
SELECT id, val
FROM dbo.T1
ORDER BY CAST('/' + REPLACE(val, ',', '/') + '/' AS HIERARCHYID);
```

This query generates the following output:

```
id            val
-----------   -----------------------------------
13            -321
12            -123
11            -22
10            -11
9             -2
8             -1
7             7,4,250
2             7,4,250
6             10,30,40,50,20,30,40
14            22,40,5,60,4,-100,300,478,19710212
15            22,40,5,60,4,-99,300,478,19710212
5             22,40,5,60,4,99,300,478,9999999
4             22,40,5,60,4,99,300,478,19710212
3             22,40,5,60,4,100,300,478,19710212
1             100
```

Note that you can create a computed persisted column in the table based on this expression and index that column. Such an index can support a request to sort the data without the need for an explicit sort operation in the query's execution plan.

Nested Sets

The nested sets solution is one of the most beautiful solutions I've seen for modeling trees.

> **More Info** Joe Celko has extensive coverage of the Nested Sets model in his writings. You can find Joe Celko's coverage of nested sets in his book *Joe Celko's Trees and Hierarchies in SQL for Smarties* (Morgan-Kaufmann, 2004).

The main advantages of the nested sets solution are simple and fast queries, which I'll describe later, and no level limit. Unfortunately, however, with large data sets the solution's practicality is usually limited to static trees. For dynamic environments, the solution is limited to small trees (or forests of small trees).

Instead of representing a tree as an adjacency list (parent-child relationship), this solution models the tree relationships as nested sets. A parent is represented in the nested sets model as a containing set, and a child is represented as a contained set. Set containment relationships are represented with two integer values assigned to each set: left and right. For all sets, a set's left value is smaller than all contained sets' left values, and a set's right value is higher than all contained sets' right values. Naturally, this containment relationship is transitive in terms of *n*-level relationships (ancestor/descendant). The queries are based on these nested sets relationships. Logically, it's as if a set spreads two arms around all its contained sets.

Assigning Left and Right Values

Figure 12-9 provides a graphical visualization of the Employees hierarchy with the left and right values assigned to each employee.

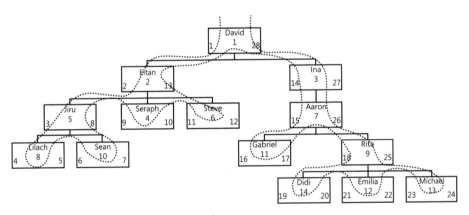

FIGURE 12-9 Employees hierarchy as nested sets

The curved line that walks the tree represents the order of assignment of the left and right values. Note that the model allows you to choose in which order you assign values to siblings. In this particular case, I chose to traverse siblings by employee name order.

You start with the root, traversing the tree counterclockwise. Every time you enter a node, you increment a counter and set it as the node's left value. Every time you leave a node, you increment the counter and set it as the node's right value. This algorithm can be implemented to the letter as an iterative or recursive routine that assigns each node with left and right values. However, such an implementation requires traversing the tree one node at a time, which can be very slow. I'll show an algorithm that traverses the tree one level at a time, which is faster. The core algorithm is based on logic I discussed earlier in the chapter, traversing the tree one level at a time and calculating binary sort paths. To understand this algorithm, examine Figure 12-10.

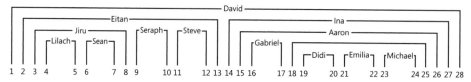

FIGURE 12-10 The nested sets model

The figure illustrates each employee as spreading two arms around its subordinates. Left and right values can now be assigned to the different arms by simply incrementing a counter from left to right. Keep this illustration in mind—it's the key to understanding the solution that I will present.

Again, the baseline is the original algorithm that traverses a subtree one level at a time and constructs a binary sort path based on a desired ordering of siblings (for example, *empname, empid*).

> **Note** For good performance, you should create an index on the parent ID and sort columns—for example, *(mgrid, empname, empid)*.

Instead of generating one row for each node (as was the case in the earlier solutions for generating sort values based on a binary path), you generate two rows by cross-joining each level with an auxiliary table that has two numbers: *n=1* represents the left arm, and *n=2* represents the right arm. The binary paths are still constructed from row numbers, but in this case the arm number is taken into consideration in addition to the other sort elements (for example, *empname, empid, n*). The query that returns the next level of subordinates returns the subordinates of the left arm only—again, cross-joined with two numbers (*n=1, n=2*) to generate two arms for each node.

The following code is the CTE implementation of this algorithm. The purpose of this code is to generate two binary sort paths for each employee that are later used to calculate left and right values. Before you run this code, make sure you have the original Employees table in the tempdb database. If you don't, rerun the code in Listing 12-1 first:

```
USE tempdb;
GO
-- Create index to speed sorting siblings by empname, empid
CREATE UNIQUE INDEX idx_unc_mgrid_empname_empid
  ON dbo.Employees(mgrid, empname, empid);
GO

DECLARE @root AS INT = 1;
```

```
-- CTE with two numbers: 1 and 2
WITH TwoNums
AS
(
  SELECT n FROM(VALUES(1),(2)) AS D(n)
),
-- CTE with two binary sort paths for each node:
--   One smaller than descendants sort paths
--   One greater than descendants sort paths
SortPath
AS
(
  SELECT empid, 0 AS lvl, n,
    CAST(n AS VARBINARY(MAX)) AS sort_path
  FROM dbo.Employees CROSS JOIN TwoNums
  WHERE empid = @root

  UNION ALL

  SELECT C.empid, P.lvl + 1, TN.n,
    P.sort_path + CAST(
      (-1+ROW_NUMBER() OVER(PARTITION BY C.mgrid
                        -- *** determines order of siblings ***
                        ORDER BY C.empname, C.empid))/2*2+TN.n
      AS BINARY(4))
  FROM SortPath AS P
    JOIN dbo.Employees AS C
      ON P.n = 1
      AND C.mgrid = P.empid
    CROSS JOIN TwoNums AS TN
)
SELECT * FROM SortPath
ORDER BY sort_path;
```

This code generates the following output:

```
empid  lvl  n   sort_path
------ ---- --  ------------------------------------------
1      0    1   0x00000001
2      1    1   0x0000000100000001
5      2    1   0x000000010000000100000001
8      3    1   0x00000001000000010000000100000001
8      3    2   0x00000001000000010000000100000002
10     3    1   0x00000001000000010000000100000003
10     3    2   0x00000001000000010000000100000004
5      2    2   0x000000010000000100000002
4      2    1   0x000000010000000100000003
4      2    2   0x000000010000000100000004
6      2    1   0x000000010000000100000005
6      2    2   0x000000010000000100000006
2      1    2   0x0000000100000002
3      1    1   0x0000000100000003
7      2    1   0x000000010000000300000001
11     3    1   0x00000001000000030000000100000001
11     3    2   0x00000001000000030000000100000002
9      3    1   0x00000001000000030000000100000003
```

```
14   4   1   0x000000010000000300000001000000030000001
14   4   2   0x000000010000000300000001000000030000002
12   4   1   0x000000010000000300000001000000030000003
12   4   2   0x000000010000000300000001000000030000004
13   4   1   0x000000010000000300000001000000030000005
13   4   2   0x000000010000000300000001000000030000006
9    3   2   0x0000000100000003000000010000004
7    2   2   0x00000001000000030000002
3    1   2   0x0000000100000004
1    0   2   0x00000002
```

TwoNums is the auxiliary table with two numbers representing the two arms. Of course, if you wanted to, you could use a real Nums table instead of generating a virtual one.

Two sort paths are generated for each node. The left one is represented by $n=1$, and the right one is represented by $n=2$. Notice that for a given node, the left sort path is smaller than all left sort paths of subordinates, and the right sort path is greater than all right sort paths of subordinates. The sort paths are used to generate the left and right values in Figure 12-10. You need to generate left and right integer values to represent the nested sets relationships between the employees. To assign the integer values to the arms (*sortval*), simply use the ROW_NUMBER function based on *sort_path* order. Finally, to return one row for each employee containing the left and right integer values, group the rows by employee and level and return the *MIN(sortval)* as the left value and *MAX(sortval)* as the right value. Here's the complete solution to generate left and right values, followed by its output:

```
DECLARE @root AS INT = 1;

-- CTE with two numbers: 1 and 2
WITH TwoNums
AS
(
  SELECT n FROM(VALUES(1),(2)) AS D(n)
),
-- CTE with two binary sort paths for each node:
--    One smaller than descendants sort paths
--    One greater than descendants sort paths
SortPath
AS
(
  SELECT empid, 0 AS lvl, n,
    CAST(n AS VARBINARY(MAX)) AS sort_path
  FROM dbo.Employees CROSS JOIN TwoNums
  WHERE empid = @root

  UNION ALL

  SELECT C.empid, P.lvl + 1, TN.n,
    P.sort_path + CAST(
      (-1+ROW_NUMBER() OVER(PARTITION BY C.mgrid
                  -- *** determines order of siblings ***
                  ORDER BY C.empname, C.empid))/2*2+TN.n
      AS BINARY(4))
```

```
    FROM SortPath AS P
      JOIN dbo.Employees AS C
        ON P.n = 1
        AND C.mgrid = P.empid
      CROSS JOIN TwoNums AS TN
),
-- CTE with Row Numbers Representing sort_path Order
Sort
AS
(
  SELECT empid, lvl,
    ROW_NUMBER() OVER(ORDER BY sort_path) AS sortval
  FROM SortPath
),
-- CTE with Left and Right Values Representing
-- Nested Sets Relationships
NestedSets
AS
(
  SELECT empid, lvl, MIN(sortval) AS lft, MAX(sortval) AS rgt
  FROM Sort
  GROUP BY empid, lvl
)
SELECT * FROM NestedSets
ORDER BY lft;
```

empid	lvl	lft	rgt
1	0	1	28
2	1	2	13
5	2	3	8
8	3	4	5
10	3	6	7
4	2	9	10
6	2	11	12
3	1	14	27
7	2	15	26
11	3	16	17
9	3	18	25
14	4	19	20
12	4	21	22
13	4	23	24

In the opening paragraph of the "Nested Sets" section, I mentioned that this solution is not adequate for large dynamic trees (trees that incur frequent changes). Suppose you stored left and right values in two additional columns in the Employees table. Note that you won't need the *mgrid* column in the table anymore because the two additional columns with the left and right values are sufficient to answer requests for subordinates, ancestors, and so on. Consider the shake effect of adding a node to the tree. For example, take a look at Figures 12-9 and 12-10 and try to figure out the effect of adding a new subordinate to Steve. Steve has left and right values of 11 and 12, respectively. The new node should get left and right values of 12 and 13, respectively. Steve's right value—and in fact all left and right values in the tree that were greater than or equal to 12—should be increased by two. On average, at least half the nodes in the tree must be updated every time a new node is inserted. As you can see here, the shake effect is very dramatic. That's why the nested sets solution is adequate for a large tree only if it's static or if you need to run queries against a static snapshot of the tree periodically.

Nested sets can provide reasonably good performance with dynamic trees that are small (or forests of small trees)—for example, when maintaining forum discussions where each thread is a small independent tree in a forest. You can implement a solution that synchronizes the left and right values of the tree with every change. You can achieve this by using stored procedures or even triggers, as long as the cost of modification is small enough to be bearable. I won't even get into variations of the nested sets model that maintain gaps between the values (that is, leave room to insert new leaves without as much work) because they are all ultimately limited.

To generate a table of employees (EmployeesNS) with the employee ID, employee name, salary, level, left, and right values, join the outer query of the CTE solution and use a SELECT INTO statement. Run the following code to create this as the EmployeesNS table with siblings ordered by *empname, empid*:

```
SET NOCOUNT ON;
USE tempdb;
GO

DECLARE @root AS INT = 1;

WITH TwoNums
AS
(
  SELECT n FROM(VALUES(1),(2)) AS D(n)
),
SortPath
AS
(
  SELECT empid, 0 AS lvl, n,
    CAST(n AS VARBINARY(MAX)) AS sort_path
  FROM dbo.Employees CROSS JOIN TwoNums
  WHERE empid = @root

  UNION ALL

  SELECT C.empid, P.lvl + 1, TN.n,
    P.sort_path + CAST(
      ROW_NUMBER() OVER(PARTITION BY C.mgrid
                        -- *** determines order of siblings ***
                        ORDER BY C.empname, C.empid, TN.n)
      AS BINARY(4))
  FROM SortPath AS P
    JOIN dbo.Employees AS C
      ON P.n = 1
```

```
      AND C.mgrid = P.empid
    CROSS JOIN TwoNums AS TN
),
Sort
AS
(
  SELECT empid, lvl,
    ROW_NUMBER() OVER(ORDER BY sort_path) AS sortval
  FROM SortPath
),
NestedSets
AS
(
    SELECT empid, lvl, MIN(sortval) AS lft, MAX(sortval) AS rgt
    FROM Sort
    GROUP BY empid, lvl
)
SELECT E.empid, E.empname, E.salary, NS.lvl, NS.lft, NS.rgt
INTO dbo.EmployeesNS
FROM NestedSets AS NS
  JOIN dbo.Employees AS E
    ON E.empid = NS.empid;

ALTER TABLE dbo.EmployeesNS ADD PRIMARY KEY NONCLUSTERED(empid);
CREATE UNIQUE CLUSTERED INDEX idx_unc_lft_rgt ON dbo.EmployeesNS(lft, rgt);
GO
```

Querying

The EmployeesNS table models a tree of employees as nested sets. Querying is simple, elegant, and fast with the index on left and right values.

In the following section, I'll present common requests against a tree and the query solution for each, followed by the output of the query.

Return the subtree of a given root:

```
SELECT C.empid, REPLICATE(' | ', C.lvl - P.lvl) + C.empname AS empname
FROM dbo.EmployeesNS AS P
  JOIN dbo.EmployeesNS AS C
    ON P.empid = 3
    AND C.lft >= P.lft AND C.rgt <= P.rgt
ORDER BY C.lft;
```

```
empid       empname
----------- ------------------
3           Ina
7           | Aaron
11          | | Gabriel
9           | | Rita
14          | | | Didi
12          | | | Emilia
13          | | | Michael
```

The query joins two instances of EmployeesNS. One represents the parent (*P*) and is filtered by the given root. The other represents the child (*C*). The two are joined based on the child's left being greater than or equal to the parent's left and the child's right being smaller than or equal to the parent's right. Indentation of the output is achieved by replicating a string ('| ') child level minus parent level times. The output is sorted by the child's left value, which by definition represents correct hierarchical sorting, and the desired sort of siblings. This subtree query is used as the baseline for most of the following queries.

If you want to exclude the subtree's root node from the output, simply use greater than (>) and less than (<) operators instead of greater than or equal to (>=) and less than or equal to (<=) operators. To the subtree query, add a filter in the join condition that returns only nodes where the child's level minus the parent's level is smaller than or equal to the requested number of levels under the root.

Return the subtree of a given root, limiting two levels of subordinates under the root:

```
SELECT C.empid, REPLICATE(' | ', C.lvl - P.lvl) + C.empname AS empname
FROM dbo.EmployeesNS AS P
  JOIN dbo.EmployeesNS AS C
    ON P.empid = 3
    AND C.lft >= P.lft AND C.rgt <= P.rgt
    AND C.lvl - P.lvl <= 2
ORDER BY C.lft;
```

```
empid       empname
----------- ----------------
3           Ina
7           | Aaron
11          | | Gabriel
9           | | Rita
```

Return leaf nodes under a given root:

```
SELECT C.empid, C.empname
FROM dbo.EmployeesNS AS P
  JOIN dbo.EmployeesNS AS C
    ON P.empid = 3
    AND C.lft >= P.lft AND C.rgt <= P.rgt
WHERE C.rgt - C.lft = 1;
```

```
empid       empname
----------- ---------
11          Gabriel
14          Didi
12          Emilia
13          Michael
```

A leaf node is a node for which the right value is greater than the left value by 1 (no subordinates). Add this filter to the subtree query's WHERE clause. As you can see, the nested sets solution allows for dramatically faster identification of leaf nodes than other solutions using a NOT EXISTS predicate.

Return the count of subordinates of each node:

```
SELECT empid, (rgt - lft - 1) / 2 AS cnt,
  REPLICATE(' | ', lvl) + empname AS empname
FROM dbo.EmployeesNS
ORDER BY lft;
```

```
empid   cnt   empname
------  ----  -------------------
1       13    David
2       5     | Eitan
5       2     | | Jiru
8       0     | | | Lilach
10      0     | | | Sean
4       0     | | Seraph
6       0     | | Steve
3       6     | Ina
7       5     | | Aaron
11      0     | | | Gabriel
9       3     | | | Rita
14      0     | | | | Didi
12      0     | | | | Emilia
13      0     | | | | Michael
```

Because each node accounts for exactly two *lft* and *rgt* values and in our implementation no gaps exist, you can calculate the count of subordinates by accessing the subtree's root alone. The count is *(rgt – lft – 1) / 2*.

Return all ancestors of a given node:

```
SELECT P.empid, P.empname, P.lvl
FROM dbo.EmployeesNS AS P
  JOIN dbo.EmployeesNS AS C
    ON C.empid = 14
    AND C.lft >= P.lft AND C.rgt <= P.rgt;
```

```
empid   empname   lvl
------  --------  ----
1       David     0
3       Ina       1
7       Aaron     2
9       Rita      3
14      Didi      4
```

The ancestors query is almost identical to the subtree query. The nested sets relationships remain the same. The only difference is that here you filter a specific child node ID, while in the subtree query you filtered a specific parent node ID.

When you're done querying the EmployeesNS table, run the following code for cleanup:

```
DROP TABLE dbo.EmployeesNS;
```

Transitive Closure

The transitive closure of a directed graph G is the graph with the same vertices as G and with an edge connecting each pair of nodes that are connected by a path (not necessarily containing just one edge) in G. The transitive closure helps answer a number of questions immediately, without the need to explore paths in the graph. For example, is David a manager of Aaron (directly or indirectly)? If the transitive closure of the Employees graph contains an edge from David to Aaron, he is. Does Double Espresso contain water? Can I drive from Los Angeles to New York? If the input graph contains the edges (a, b) and (b, c), a and c have a transitive relationship. The transitive closure contains the edges (a, b), (b, c), and also (a, c). If David is the direct manager of Ina and Ina is the direct manager of Aaron, David transitively is a manager of Aaron, or Aaron transitively is a subordinate of David.

Problems related to transitive closure deal with specialized cases of transitive relationships. An example is the "shortest path" problem, where you're trying to determine the shortest path between two nodes. For example, what's the shortest path between Los Angeles and New York?

In this section, I will describe iterative/recursive solutions for transitive closure and shortest path problems.

> **Note** The performance of some of the solutions that I will show (specifically those that use recursive CTEs) degrades exponentially as the input graph grows. I'll present them for demonstration purposes because they are fairly simple and natural. They are adequate for fairly small graphs. Some efficient algorithms for transitive closure–related problems (for example, Floyd's and Warshall's algorithms) can be implemented as "level at a time" (breadth-first) iterations. For details on those, please refer to *http://www.nist.gov/dads/.* I'll show efficient solutions provided by Steve Kass that can be applied to larger graphs.

Directed Acyclic Graph

The first problem that I will discuss is generating a transitive closure of a directed acyclic graph (DAG). Later I'll show you how to deal with undirected and cyclic graphs as well. Whether the graph is directed or undirected doesn't really complicate the solution significantly, but dealing with cyclic graphs does. The input DAG that I will use in my example is the BOM I used earlier in the chapter, which you create by running the code in Listing 12-2.

The code that generates the transitive closure of BOM is somewhat similar to solutions for the subgraph problem (that is, the parts explosion). Specifically, you traverse the graph one level at a time (or, more accurately, you are using breadth-first search techniques). However, instead of returning only a root node here, the anchor member returns all first-level relationships in BOM. In most graphs, this simply means all existing source/target pairs. In our case, this means all assembly/part pairs where the assembly is not NULL. The recursive member joins the CTE representing the previous level or parent (*P*) with BOM representing the next level or child (*C*). It returns the original product ID (*P*) as the source and the child product ID (*C*) as the target. The outer query returns the distinct assembly/part pairs. Keep in mind that multiple paths may lead to a part in BOM, but you need to return each unique pair only once.

Run the following code to generate the transitive closure of BOM:

```
WITH BOMTC
AS
(
  -- Return all first-level containment relationships
  SELECT assemblyid, partid
  FROM dbo.BOM
  WHERE assemblyid IS NOT NULL

  UNION ALL

  -- Return next-level containment relationships
  SELECT P.assemblyid, C.partid
  FROM BOMTC AS P
    JOIN dbo.BOM AS C
      ON C.assemblyid = P.partid
)
-- Return distinct pairs that have
-- transitive containment relationships
SELECT DISTINCT assemblyid, partid
FROM BOMTC;
```

This code generates the following output:

```
assemblyid  partid
----------- -----------
1           6
1           7
1           10
1           13
1           14
2           6
2           7
2           10
2           11
2           13
2           14
3           6
3           7
3           11
3           12
3           14
3           16
3           17
4           9
4           12
4           14
4           16
4           17
5           9
5           12
5           14
```

5	16
5	17
10	13
10	14
12	14
12	16
12	17
16	17

This solution eliminates duplicate edges found in the BOMTC by applying a DISTINCT clause in the outer query. A more efficient solution would be to avoid getting duplicates altogether by using a NOT EXISTS predicate in the query that runs repeatedly; such a predicate would filter newly found edges that do not appear in the set of edges that were already found. However, such an implementation can't use a CTE because the recursive member in the CTE has access only to the immediate previous level, as opposed to all previous levels obtained thus far. Instead, you can use a UDF that invokes the query that runs repeatedly in a loop and inserts each obtained level of nodes into a table variable. Run the following code to create the *BOMTC* UDF, which implements this logic:

```
IF OBJECT_ID('dbo.BOMTC') IS NOT NULL
  DROP FUNCTION dbo.BOMTC;
GO

CREATE FUNCTION BOMTC() RETURNS @BOMTC TABLE
(
  assemblyid INT NOT NULL,
  partid     INT NOT NULL,
  PRIMARY KEY (assemblyid, partid)
)
AS
BEGIN
  INSERT INTO @BOMTC(assemblyid, partid)
    SELECT assemblyid, partid
    FROM dbo.BOM
    WHERE assemblyid IS NOT NULL

  WHILE @@rowcount > 0
    INSERT INTO @BOMTC
    SELECT P.assemblyid, C.partid
    FROM @BOMTC AS P
      JOIN dbo.BOM AS C
        ON C.assemblyid = P.partid
    WHERE NOT EXISTS
      (SELECT * FROM @BOMTC AS P2
       WHERE P2.assemblyid = P.assemblyid
       AND P2.partid = C.partid);

  RETURN;
END
GO
```

Query the function to get the transitive closure of BOM:

```
SELECT assemblyid, partid FROM BOMTC();
```

If you want to return all paths in BOM, along with the distance in levels between the parts, you use a similar algorithm with a few additions and revisions. You calculate the distance the same way you calculated the level value in the subgraph/subtree solutions. That is, the anchor assigns a constant distance of 1 for the first level, and the recursive member simply adds one in each iteration. Also, the path calculation is similar to the one used in the subgraph/subtree solutions. The anchor generates a path made of '.' + *source_id* + '.' + *target_id* + '.'. The recursive member generates it as *parent's path* + *target_id* + '.'. Finally, the outer query simply returns all paths (without applying DISTINCT in this case).

Run the following code to generate all possible paths in BOM and their distances:

```
WITH BOMPaths
AS
(
  SELECT assemblyid, partid,
    1 AS distance, -- distance in first level is 1
    -- path in first level is .assemblyid.partid.
    '.' + CAST(assemblyid AS VARCHAR(MAX)) +
    '.' + CAST(partid      AS VARCHAR(MAX)) + '.' AS path
  FROM dbo.BOM
  WHERE assemblyid IS NOT NULL

  UNION ALL

  SELECT P.assemblyid, C.partid,
    -- distance in next level is parent's distance + 1
    P.distance + 1,
    -- path in next level is parent_path.child_partid.
    P.path + CAST(C.partid AS VARCHAR(MAX)) + '.'
  FROM BOMPaths AS P
    JOIN dbo.BOM AS C
      ON C.assemblyid = P.partid
)
-- Return all paths
SELECT * FROM BOMPaths;
```

You get the following output:

```
assemblyid  partid      distance    path
----------- ----------- ----------- ----------------
1           6           1           .1.6.
2           6           1           .2.6.
3           6           1           .3.6.
1           7           1           .1.7.
2           7           1           .2.7.
3           7           1           .3.7.
4           9           1           .4.9.
5           9           1           .5.9.
1           10          1           .1.10.
2           10          1           .2.10.
2           11          1           .2.11.
3           11          1           .3.11.
3           12          1           .3.12.
4           12          1           .4.12.
5           12          1           .5.12.
```

10	13	1	.10.13.
1	14	1	.1.14.
2	14	1	.2.14.
10	14	1	.10.14.
12	14	1	.12.14.
12	16	1	.12.16.
16	17	1	.16.17.
12	17	2	.12.16.17.
5	14	2	.5.12.14.
5	16	2	.5.12.16.
5	17	3	.5.12.16.17.
4	14	2	.4.12.14.
4	16	2	.4.12.16.
4	17	3	.4.12.16.17.
3	14	2	.3.12.14.
3	16	2	.3.12.16.
3	17	3	.3.12.16.17.
2	13	2	.2.10.13.
2	14	2	.2.10.14.
1	13	2	.1.10.13.
1	14	2	.1.10.14.

To isolate only the shortest paths, add a second CTE (BOMMinDist) that groups all paths by assembly and part, returning the minimum distance for each group. In the outer query, join the first CTE (BOMPaths) with BOMMinDist, based on *assembly*, *part*, and *distance* match to return the actual paths.

Run the following code to produce the shortest paths in BOM:

```
WITH BOMPaths -- All paths
AS
(
  SELECT assemblyid, partid,
    1 AS distance,
    '.' + CAST(assemblyid AS VARCHAR(MAX)) +
    '.' + CAST(partid    AS VARCHAR(MAX)) + '.' AS path
  FROM dbo.BOM
  WHERE assemblyid IS NOT NULL

  UNION ALL

  SELECT P.assemblyid, C.partid,
    P.distance + 1,
    P.path + CAST(C.partid AS VARCHAR(MAX)) + '.'
  FROM BOMPaths AS P
    JOIN dbo.BOM AS C
      ON C.assemblyid = P.partid
),
BOMMinDist AS -- Minimum distance for each pair
(
  SELECT assemblyid, partid, MIN(distance) AS mindist
  FROM BOMPaths
  GROUP BY assemblyid, partid
)
```

```
-- Shortest path for each pair
SELECT BP.*
FROM BOMMinDist AS BMD
  JOIN BOMPaths AS BP
    ON BMD.assemblyid = BP.assemblyid
    AND BMD.partid = BP.partid
    AND BMD.mindist = BP.distance;
```

This code generates the following output:

```
assemblyid  partid      distance    path
----------- ----------- ----------- -------------------
1           6           1           .1.6.
2           6           1           .2.6.
3           6           1           .3.6.
1           7           1           .1.7.
2           7           1           .2.7.
3           7           1           .3.7.
4           9           1           .4.9.
5           9           1           .5.9.
1           10          1           .1.10.
2           10          1           .2.10.
2           11          1           .2.11.
3           11          1           .3.11.
3           12          1           .3.12.
4           12          1           .4.12.
5           12          1           .5.12.
10          13          1           .10.13.
1           14          1           .1.14.
2           14          1           .2.14.
10          14          1           .10.14.
12          14          1           .12.14.
12          16          1           .12.16.
16          17          1           .16.17.
12          17          2           .12.16.17.
5           14          2           .5.12.14.
5           16          2           .5.12.16.
5           17          3           .5.12.16.17.
4           14          2           .4.12.14.
4           16          2           .4.12.16.
4           17          3           .4.12.16.17.
3           14          2           .3.12.14.
3           16          2           .3.12.16.
3           17          3           .3.12.16.17.
2           13          2           .2.10.13.
1           13          2           .1.10.13.
```

Undirected Cyclic Graph

Even though transitive closure is defined for a directed graph, you can also define and generate it for undirected graphs where each edge represents a two-way relationship. In my examples, I will use the Roads graph, which you create and populate by running the code in Listing 12-3. To see a visual representation of Roads, examine Figure 12-4. To apply the transitive closure and shortest path solutions to Roads, first convert it to a digraph by generating two directed edges from each existing edge:

```
SELECT city1 AS from_city, city2 AS to_city FROM dbo.Roads
UNION ALL
SELECT city2, city1 FROM dbo.Roads
```

For example, the edge (*JFK, ATL*) in the undirected graph appears as two edges, (*JFK, ATL*) and (*ATL, JFK*), in the digraph. The former represents the road from New York to Atlanta, and the latter represents the road from Atlanta to New York.

Because Roads is a cyclic graph, you also need to use the cycle-detection logic I described earlier in the chapter to avoid traversing cyclic paths. Armed with the techniques to generate a digraph out of an undirected graph and to detect cycles, you have all the tools you need to produce the transitive closure of roads.

Run the following code to generate the transitive closure of Roads:

```
WITH Roads2 -- Two rows for each pair (from-->to, to-->from)
AS
(
  SELECT city1 AS from_city, city2 AS to_city FROM dbo.Roads
  UNION ALL
  SELECT city2, city1 FROM dbo.Roads
),
RoadPaths AS
(
  -- Return all first-level reachability pairs
  SELECT from_city, to_city,
    -- path is needed to identify cycles
    CAST('.' + from_city + '.' + to_city + '.' AS VARCHAR(MAX)) AS path
  FROM Roads2

  UNION ALL

  -- Return next-level reachability pairs
  SELECT F.from_city, T.to_city,
    CAST(F.path + T.to_city + '.' AS VARCHAR(MAX))
  FROM RoadPaths AS F
    JOIN Roads2 AS T
      -- if to_city appears in from_city's path, cycle detected
      ON CASE WHEN F.path LIKE '%.' + T.to_city + '.%'
              THEN 1 ELSE 0 END = 0
      AND F.to_city = T.from_city
)
-- Return Transitive Closure of Roads
SELECT DISTINCT from_city, to_city
FROM RoadPaths;
```

The Roads2 CTE creates the digraph out of Roads. The RoadPaths CTE returns all possible source/target pairs (this has a big performance penalty), and it avoids returning and pursuing a path for which a cycle is detected. The outer query returns all distinct source/target pairs:

from	to	from	to	from	to	from	to	from	to
ANC	FAI	IAH	LAX	LAX	SEA	MSP	JFK	SEA	ORD
ATL	DEN	IAH	MCI	LAX	SFO	MSP	LAX	SEA	SFO
ATL	IAH	IAH	MIA	MCI	ATL	MSP	MCI	SFO	ATL
ATL	JFK	IAH	MSP	MCI	DEN	MSP	MIA	SFO	DEN
ATL	LAX	IAH	ORD	MCI	IAH	MSP	ORD	SFO	IAH
ATL	MCI	IAH	SEA	MCI	JFK	MSP	SEA	SFO	JFK
ATL	MIA	IAH	SFO	MCI	LAX	MSP	SFO	SFO	LAX
ATL	MSP	JFK	ATL	MCI	MIA	ORD	ATL	SFO	MCI
ATL	ORD	JFK	DEN	MCI	MSP	ORD	DEN	SFO	MIA
ATL	SEA	JFK	IAH	MCI	ORD	ORD	IAH	SFO	MSP
ATL	SFO	JFK	LAX	MCI	SEA	ORD	JFK	SFO	ORD
DEN	ATL	JFK	MCI	MCI	SFO	ORD	LAX	SFO	SEA
DEN	IAH	JFK	MIA	MIA	ATL	ORD	MCI		
DEN	JFK	JFK	MSP	MIA	DEN	ORD	MIA		
DEN	LAX	JFK	ORD	MIA	IAH	ORD	MSP		
DEN	MCI	JFK	SEA	MIA	JFK	ORD	SEA		
DEN	MIA	JFK	SFO	MIA	LAX	ORD	SFO		
DEN	MSP	LAX	ATL	MIA	MCI	SEA	ATL		
DEN	ORD	LAX	DEN	MIA	MSP	SEA	DEN		
DEN	SEA	LAX	IAH	MIA	ORD	SEA	IAH		
DEN	SFO	LAX	JFK	MIA	SEA	SEA	JFK		
FAI	ANC	LAX	MCI	MIA	SFO	SEA	LAX		
IAH	ATL	LAX	MIA	MSP	ATL	SEA	MCI		
IAH	DEN	LAX	MSP	MSP	DEN	SEA	MIA		
IAH	JFK	LAX	ORD	MSP	IAH	SEA	MSP		

Here as well, you can use loops instead of a recursive CTE to optimize the solution, as demonstrated earlier with the BOM scenario. Run the following code to create the *RoadsTC* UDF, which returns the transitive closure of Roads using loops:

```
IF OBJECT_ID('dbo.RoadsTC') IS NOT NULL
  DROP FUNCTION dbo.RoadsTC;
GO

CREATE FUNCTION dbo.RoadsTC() RETURNS @RoadsTC TABLE (
  from_city VARCHAR(3) NOT NULL,
  to_city   VARCHAR(3) NOT NULL,
  PRIMARY KEY (from_city, to_city)
)
AS
BEGIN
  DECLARE @added as INT;

  INSERT INTO @RoadsTC(from_city, to_city)
    SELECT city1, city2 FROM dbo.Roads;

  SET @added = @@rowcount;

  INSERT INTO @RoadsTC
    SELECT city2, city1 FROM dbo.Roads
```

```
   SET @added = @added + @@rowcount;

   WHILE @added > 0 BEGIN

     INSERT INTO @RoadsTC
       SELECT DISTINCT TC.from_city, R.city2
       FROM @RoadsTC AS TC
         JOIN dbo.Roads AS R
           ON R.city1 = TC.to_city
       WHERE NOT EXISTS
         (SELECT * FROM @RoadsTC AS TC2
           WHERE TC2.from_city = TC.from_city
             AND TC2.to_city = R.city2)
           AND TC.from_city <> R.city2;

     SET @added = @@rowcount;

     INSERT INTO @RoadsTC
       SELECT DISTINCT TC.from_city, R.city1
       FROM @RoadsTC AS TC
         JOIN dbo.Roads AS R
           ON R.city2 = TC.to_city
       WHERE NOT EXISTS
         (SELECT * FROM @RoadsTC AS TC2
           WHERE TC2.from_city = TC.from_city
             AND TC2.to_city = R.city1)
           AND TC.from_city <> R.city1;

     SET @added = @added + @@rowcount;
   END
   RETURN;
END
GO

-- Use the RoadsTC UDF
SELECT * FROM dbo.RoadsTC();
GO
```

Run the following query to get the transitive closure of Roads:

```
SELECT * FROM dbo.RoadsTC();
```

To return all paths and distances, use similar logic to the one used in the digraph solution in the previous section. The difference here is that the distance is not just a level counter—it is the sum of the distances along the route from one city to the other.

Run the following code to return all paths and distances in Roads:

```
WITH Roads2
AS
(
  SELECT city1 AS from_city, city2 AS to_city, distance FROM dbo.Roads
  UNION ALL
  SELECT city2, city1, distance FROM dbo.Roads
),
```

```
RoadPaths AS
(
  SELECT from_city, to_city, distance,
    CAST('.' + from_city + '.' + to_city + '.' AS VARCHAR(MAX)) AS path
  FROM Roads2

  UNION ALL

  SELECT F.from_city, T.to_city, F.distance + T.distance,
    CAST(F.path + T.to_city + '.' AS VARCHAR(MAX))
  FROM RoadPaths AS F
    JOIN Roads2 AS T
      ON CASE WHEN F.path LIKE '%.' + T.to_city + '.%'
              THEN 1 ELSE 0 END = 0
      AND F.to_city = T.from_city
)
-- Return all paths and distances
SELECT * FROM RoadPaths;
```

Finally, to return shortest paths in Roads, use the same logic as the digraph shortest paths solution. Run the following code to return shortest paths in Roads:

```
WITH Roads2
AS
(
  SELECT city1 AS from_city, city2 AS to_city, distance FROM dbo.Roads
  UNION ALL
  SELECT city2, city1, distance FROM dbo.Roads
),
RoadPaths AS
(
  SELECT from_city, to_city, distance,
    CAST('.' + from_city + '.' + to_city + '.' AS VARCHAR(MAX)) AS path
  FROM Roads2

  UNION ALL

  SELECT F.from_city, T.to_city, F.distance + T.distance,
    CAST(F.path + T.to_city + '.' AS VARCHAR(MAX))
  FROM RoadPaths AS F
    JOIN Roads2 AS T
      ON CASE WHEN F.path LIKE '%.' + T.to_city + '.%'
              THEN 1 ELSE 0 END = 0
      AND F.to_city = T.from_city
),
RoadsMinDist -- Min distance for each pair in TC
AS
(
  SELECT from_city, to_city, MIN(distance) AS mindist
  FROM RoadPaths
  GROUP BY from_city, to_city
)
-- Return shortest paths and distances
SELECT RP.*
FROM RoadsMinDist AS RMD
```

```
    JOIN RoadPaths AS RP
      ON RMD.from_city = RP.from_city
     AND RMD.to_city = RP.to_city
     AND RMD.mindist = RP.distance;
```

You get the following output:

```
from_city to_city distance    path
--------- ------- ----------- -------------------------
ANC       FAI     359         .ANC.FAI.
ATL       IAH     800         .ATL.IAH.
ATL       JFK     865         .ATL.JFK.
ATL       MCI     805         .ATL.MCI.
ATL       MIA     665         .ATL.MIA.
ATL       ORD     715         .ATL.ORD.
DEN       IAH     1120        .DEN.IAH.
DEN       LAX     1025        .DEN.LAX.
DEN       MCI     600         .DEN.MCI.
DEN       MSP     915         .DEN.MSP.
DEN       SEA     1335        .DEN.SEA.
DEN       SFO     1270        .DEN.SFO.
IAH       LAX     1550        .IAH.LAX.
IAH       MCI     795         .IAH.MCI.
IAH       MIA     1190        .IAH.MIA.
JFK       ORD     795         .JFK.ORD.
LAX       SFO     385         .LAX.SFO.
MCI       MSP     440         .MCI.MSP.
MCI       ORD     525         .MCI.ORD.
MSP       ORD     410         .MSP.ORD.
MSP       SEA     2015        .MSP.SEA.
SEA       SFO     815         .SEA.SFO.
FAI       ANC     359         .FAI.ANC.
IAH       ATL     800         .IAH.ATL.
JFK       ATL     865         .JFK.ATL.
MCI       ATL     805         .MCI.ATL.
MIA       ATL     665         .MIA.ATL.
ORD       ATL     715         .ORD.ATL.
IAH       DEN     1120        .IAH.DEN.
LAX       DEN     1025        .LAX.DEN.
MCI       DEN     600         .MCI.DEN.
MSP       DEN     915         .MSP.DEN.
SEA       DEN     1335        .SEA.DEN.
SFO       DEN     1270        .SFO.DEN.
LAX       IAH     1550        .LAX.IAH.
MCI       IAH     795         .MCI.IAH.
MIA       IAH     1190        .MIA.IAH.
ORD       JFK     795         .ORD.JFK.
SFO       LAX     385         .SFO.LAX.
MSP       MCI     440         .MSP.MCI.
ORD       MCI     525         .ORD.MCI.
ORD       MSP     410         .ORD.MSP.
SEA       MSP     2015        .SEA.MSP.
SFO       SEA     815         .SFO.SEA.
SEA       ORD     2425        .SEA.MSP.ORD.
SEA       JFK     3220        .SEA.MSP.ORD.JFK.
ORD       SEA     2425        .ORD.MSP.SEA.
ORD       DEN     1125        .ORD.MCI.DEN.
```

ORD	IAH	1320	.ORD.MCI.IAH.
ORD	LAX	2150	.ORD.MCI.DEN.LAX.
ORD	SFO	2395	.ORD.MCI.DEN.SFO.
MSP	IAH	1235	.MSP.MCI.IAH.
SFO	IAH	1935	.SFO.LAX.IAH.
SFO	MIA	3125	.SFO.LAX.IAH.MIA.
MIA	LAX	2740	.MIA.IAH.LAX.
MIA	SFO	3125	.MIA.IAH.LAX.SFO.
LAX	MIA	2740	.LAX.IAH.MIA.
LAX	ATL	2350	.LAX.IAH.ATL.
SFO	MCI	1870	.SFO.DEN.MCI.
SFO	MSP	2185	.SFO.DEN.MSP.
SFO	ORD	2395	.SFO.DEN.MCI.ORD.
SFO	ATL	2675	.SFO.DEN.MCI.ATL.
SFO	JFK	3190	.SFO.DEN.MCI.ORD.JFK.
SEA	IAH	2455	.SEA.DEN.IAH.
SEA	MCI	1935	.SEA.DEN.MCI.
SEA	ATL	2740	.SEA.DEN.MCI.ATL.
SEA	MIA	3405	.SEA.DEN.MCI.ATL.MIA.
MSP	LAX	1940	.MSP.DEN.LAX.
MSP	SFO	2185	.MSP.DEN.SFO.
MCI	LAX	1625	.MCI.DEN.LAX.
MCI	SEA	1935	.MCI.DEN.SEA.
MCI	SFO	1870	.MCI.DEN.SFO.
LAX	MCI	1625	.LAX.DEN.MCI.
LAX	MSP	1940	.LAX.DEN.MSP.
LAX	ORD	2150	.LAX.DEN.MCI.ORD.
LAX	JFK	2945	.LAX.DEN.MCI.ORD.JFK.
IAH	SEA	2455	.IAH.DEN.SEA.
ORD	MIA	1380	.ORD.ATL.MIA.
MIA	JFK	1530	.MIA.ATL.JFK.
MIA	MCI	1470	.MIA.ATL.MCI.
MIA	ORD	1380	.MIA.ATL.ORD.
MIA	MSP	1790	.MIA.ATL.ORD.MSP.
MIA	DEN	2070	.MIA.ATL.MCI.DEN.
MIA	SEA	3405	.MIA.ATL.MCI.DEN.SEA.
MCI	MIA	1470	.MCI.ATL.MIA.
JFK	IAH	1665	.JFK.ATL.IAH.
JFK	MIA	1530	.JFK.ATL.MIA.
IAH	JFK	1665	.IAH.ATL.JFK.
SEA	LAX	1200	.SEA.SFO.LAX.
MSP	ATL	1125	.MSP.ORD.ATL.
MSP	JFK	1205	.MSP.ORD.JFK.
MSP	MIA	1790	.MSP.ORD.ATL.MIA.
MCI	JFK	1320	.MCI.ORD.JFK.
LAX	SEA	1200	.LAX.SFO.SEA.
JFK	MCI	1320	.JFK.ORD.MCI.
JFK	MSP	1205	.JFK.ORD.MSP.
JFK	SEA	3220	.JFK.ORD.MSP.SEA.
JFK	DEN	1920	.JFK.ORD.MCI.DEN.
JFK	LAX	2945	.JFK.ORD.MCI.DEN.LAX.
JFK	SFO	3190	.JFK.ORD.MCI.DEN.SFO.
IAH	MSP	1235	.IAH.MCI.MSP.
IAH	ORD	1320	.IAH.MCI.ORD.
IAH	SFO	1935	.IAH.LAX.SFO.
DEN	ORD	1125	.DEN.MCI.ORD.
DEN	ATL	1405	.DEN.MCI.ATL.

DEN	MIA	2070	.DEN.MCI.ATL.MIA.
DEN	JFK	1920	.DEN.MCI.ORD.JFK.
ATL	MSP	1125	.ATL.ORD.MSP.
ATL	DEN	1405	.ATL.MCI.DEN.
ATL	SEA	2740	.ATL.MCI.DEN.SEA.
ATL	SFO	2675	.ATL.MCI.DEN.SFO.
ATL	LAX	2350	.ATL.IAH.LAX.

To satisfy multiple requests for the shortest paths between two cities, you might want to materialize the result set in a table and index it, like so:

```
WITH Roads2
AS
(
  SELECT city1 AS from_city, city2 AS to_city, distance FROM dbo.Roads
  UNION ALL
  SELECT city2, city1, distance FROM dbo.Roads
),
RoadPaths AS
(
  SELECT from_city, to_city, distance,
    CAST('.' + from_city + '.' + to_city + '.' AS VARCHAR(MAX)) AS path
  FROM Roads2

  UNION ALL

  SELECT F.from_city, T.to_city, F.distance + T.distance,
    CAST(F.path + T.to_city + '.' AS VARCHAR(MAX))
  FROM RoadPaths AS F
    JOIN Roads2 AS T
      ON CASE WHEN F.path LIKE '%.' + T.to_city + '.%'
              THEN 1 ELSE 0 END = 0
      AND F.to_city = T.from_city
),
RoadsMinDist
AS
(
  SELECT from_city, to_city, MIN(distance) AS mindist
  FROM RoadPaths
  GROUP BY from_city, to_city
)
SELECT RP.*
INTO dbo.RoadPaths
FROM RoadsMinDist AS RMD
  JOIN RoadPaths AS RP
    ON RMD.from_city = RP.from_city
    AND RMD.to_city = RP.to_city
    AND RMD.mindist = RP.distance;

CREATE UNIQUE CLUSTERED INDEX idx_uc_from_city_to_city
  ON dbo.RoadPaths(from_city, to_city);
```

Once the result set is materialized and indexed, a request for the shortest path between two cities can be satisfied instantly. This is practical and advisable when information changes infrequently. As is often the case, there is a trade-off between up to date and fast. The following query requests the shortest path between Los Angeles and New York:

```
SELECT * FROM dbo.RoadPaths
WHERE from_city = 'LAX' AND to_city = 'JFK';
```

This query generates the following output:

```
from_city to_city distance    path
--------- ------- ----------- ----------------------
LAX       JFK     2945        .LAX.DEN.MCI.ORD.JFK.
```

A more efficient solution to the shortest paths problem uses loops instead of recursive CTEs. It is more efficient for reasons similar to the ones described earlier; that is, in each iteration of the loop you have access to all previously spooled data and not just to the immediate previous level. You create a function called *RoadsTC* that returns a table variable called *@RoadsTC*. The table variable has the attributes *from_city, to_city, distance,* and *route*, which are self-explanatory. The function's code first inserts into *@RoadsTC* a row for each (*city1, city2*) and (*city2, city1*) pair from the table Roads. The code then enters a loop that iterates as long as the previous iteration inserted rows to *@RoadsTC*. In each iteration of the loop the code inserts new routes that extend the existing routes in *@RoadsTC*. New routes are added only if the source and destination do not appear already in *@RoadsTC* with the same or shorter distance. Run the following code to create the *RoadsTC* function:

```
IF OBJECT_ID('dbo.RoadsTC') IS NOT NULL
  DROP FUNCTION dbo.RoadsTC;
GO
CREATE FUNCTION dbo.RoadsTC() RETURNS @RoadsTC TABLE
(
  uniquifier INT         NOT NULL IDENTITY,
  from_city  VARCHAR(3)  NOT NULL,
  to_city    VARCHAR(3)  NOT NULL,
  distance   INT         NOT NULL,
  route      VARCHAR(MAX) NOT NULL,
  PRIMARY KEY (from_city, to_city, uniquifier)
)
AS
BEGIN
  DECLARE @added AS INT;

  INSERT INTO @RoadsTC
    SELECT city1 AS from_city, city2 AS to_city, distance,
      '.' + city1 + '.' + city2 + '.'
    FROM dbo.Roads;

  SET @added = @@rowcount;

  INSERT INTO @RoadsTC
    SELECT city2, city1, distance, '.' + city2 + '.' + city1 + '.'
    FROM dbo.Roads;
```

```
      SET @added = @added + @@rowcount;

  WHILE @added > 0 BEGIN
    INSERT INTO @RoadsTC
      SELECT DISTINCT TC.from_city, R.city2,
        TC.distance + R.distance, TC.route + city2 + '.'
      FROM @RoadsTC AS TC
        JOIN dbo.Roads AS R
          ON R.city1 = TC.to_city
      WHERE NOT EXISTS
        (SELECT * FROM @RoadsTC AS TC2
          WHERE TC2.from_city = TC.from_city
            AND TC2.to_city = R.city2
            AND TC2.distance <= TC.distance + R.distance)
        AND TC.from_city <> R.city2;

    SET @added = @@rowcount;

    INSERT INTO @RoadsTC
      SELECT DISTINCT TC.from_city, R.city1,
        TC.distance + R.distance, TC.route + city1 + '.'
      FROM @RoadsTC AS TC
        JOIN dbo.Roads AS R
          ON R.city2 = TC.to_city
      WHERE NOT EXISTS
        (SELECT * FROM @RoadsTC AS TC2
          WHERE TC2.from_city = TC.from_city
            AND TC2.to_city = R.city1
            AND TC2.distance <= TC.distance + R.distance)
        AND TC.from_city <> R.city1;

    SET @added = @added + @@rowcount;
  END
  RETURN;
END
GO
```

The function might return more than one row for the same source and target cities. To return shortest paths and distances, use the following query:

```
SELECT from_city, to_city, distance, route
FROM (SELECT from_city, to_city, distance, route,
        RANK() OVER (PARTITION BY from_city, to_city
                      ORDER BY distance) AS rk
      FROM dbo.RoadsTC()) AS RTC
WHERE rk = 1;
```

The derived table query assigns a rank value (*rk*) to each row, based on *from_city, to_city* partitioning and *distance* ordering. This means that shortest paths are assigned with the rank value 1. The outer query filters only shortest paths (*rk = 1*).

When you're done querying the RoadPaths table, don't forget to drop it:

```
DROP TABLE dbo.RoadPaths;
```

Conclusion

This chapter covered the treatment of graphs, trees, and hierarchies. I presented iterative/ recursive solutions for graphs and also solutions in which you materialize information describing a tree. The main advantage of the iterative/recursive solutions is that you don't need to materialize and maintain any additional attributes—the graph manipulation is based on the stored edge attributes. The materialized path solution materializes an enumerated path and possibly also the level for each node in the tree. You can either maintain your own custom materialized path or use SQL Server 2008's built-in HIERARCHYID data type. In the materialized path solution, the maintenance of the additional information is not very expensive, and you benefit from simple and fast set-based queries. The nested sets solution materializes left and right values representing set containment relationships and possibly the level in the tree. This is probably the most elegant solution of those I presented, and it also allows simple and fast queries. However, maintaining the materialized information is very expensive, so typically this solution is practical for either static trees or small dynamic trees.

In the last section, I presented solutions to transitive closure and shortest path problems.

Because this chapter concludes the book, I feel I should also add some closing words.

If you ask me what's the most important thing I hope you carry from this book, I'd say that it is giving special attention to fundamentals. Do not underestimate or take them lightly. Spend time on identifying, focusing on, and perfecting fundamental techniques. When you are faced with a tough problem, solutions will flow naturally.

"Matters of great concern should be treated lightly."

"Matters of small concern should be treated seriously."

— *Hagakure, The Book of the Samurai* by Yamamoto Tsunetomo

The meaning of these sayings is not what appears on the surface. The book goes on to explain,

"Among one's affairs there should not be more than two or three matters of what one could call great concern. If these are deliberated upon during ordinary times, they can be understood. Thinking about things previously and then handling them lightly when the time comes is what this is all about. To face an event and solve it lightly is difficult if you are not resolved beforehand, and there will always be uncertainty in hitting your mark. However, if the foundation is laid previously, you can think of the saying, 'Matters of great concern should be treated lightly,' as your own basis for action."

Appendix A
Logic Puzzles

Logic is at the heart of querying problems. SQL is logic, and each query problem in essence is a logic puzzle. The toughest part of solving a querying problem is usually figuring out its logical aspects. You can improve your SQL problem-solving capabilities by practicing pure logic puzzles.

A while back, I provided a couple of logic puzzles in my T-SQL column in *SQL Server Magazine (www.sqlmag.com)*. I wanted to show the strong relationship between SQL and logic. Originally, I planned on providing only those couple of puzzles. But the puzzles raised so much interest with readers—interestingly, even more than the T-SQL puzzles—that for a while we published a new logic puzzle every month. I'd like to thank *SQL Server Magazine*, which kindly allowed me to share the puzzles from my column with the book's readers. The puzzles you will see here are a compilation from my column.

I'd also like to thank Gabriel Ben-Gan, Dejan Sarka, Adi Dafni (Didi), Adam Machanic, Marcello Poletti (Marc), Clifford Jensen, Ron Talmage, and Nicolay Tchernitsky, who originally introduced some of the puzzles to me.

Puzzles

The following section introduces logic puzzles. You can find the puzzle solutions in the section that follows this one.

Someone once said, "A puzzle is its own reward." Enjoy!

Puzzle 1: Remainders

Find the smallest integer (n) that yields a remainder of $i - 1$ when divided by i, for any i in the range 2 through 10. That is, $n \% 2 = 1$, $n \% 3 = 2$, $n \% 4 = 3$, …, $n \% 9 = 8$, $n \% 10 = 9$, in which the percent sign (%) signifies the T-SQL modulo operator.

Puzzle 2: Round Manhole Covers

Why are manhole (maintenance hole) covers typically round? You might find this a strange topic for a puzzle, but the answer lies purely in logic.

Puzzle 3: Shaking Hands

My wife and I were at a party recently with four other married couples. All the people who didn't know each other shook hands. Of course, each person knew his or her spouse. I asked each of the nine other people at the party how many hands they shook and received all possible answers ranging from 0 through 8. Each person shook a different number of hands. What was my wife's answer?

Puzzle 4: Then There Were Five?

This puzzle involves a mix of logic and English. Can you think of a sentence that contains the word "and" five times consecutively ("and and and and and")? The sentence must make sense. In other words, I'm not aiming for a sentence such as "Five times *and* is *and and and and and*." Rather, the sentence should make sense without such silly tricks.

Puzzle 5: Arranging Soldiers in a Row

A commander decides to discipline his platoon after they misbehave and also check their logic. He gives them these orders:

1. You will enter a room one by one.

2. At the entrance to the room I will place a hat on your head. The hat will have either a circle or a square sign. You will not know what your sign is, but you will be able to see the signs on the hats of all those that have already entered the room.

3. Don't remove your hat or in any way check what the sign on your hat is.

4. Arrange yourselves in a row, with all soldiers with a circle on their hats on the left and all soldiers with a square on their hats on the right.

5. Don't communicate with each other verbally or by any other means; rely solely on your sight and logic to form a row in compliance with these instructions (all circles to the left and all squares to the right).

Assume you're one of the soldiers who entered the room. Your commander placed the hat on your head. You're facing none, one, or several soldiers arranged in a row. You don't know what sign is on your hat, but you can see the signs of the others. What logic should you follow to comply with your commander's instructions?

Puzzle 6: Crossing the Tunnel

Four people—let's call them persons A, B, C, and D—need to cross a dark tunnel. Only two people at a time can cross the tunnel, and because the tunnel is very dark, a flashlight is mandatory. Person A can cross the tunnel in 1 minute, person B can cross in 2 minutes, person C can cross in 4 minutes, and person D can make it in 5 minutes. The group has one flashlight, containing batteries that last only 12 minutes. What strategy will enable all members of the group to cross to the other side in 12 minutes, before the flashlight's batteries run down?

Puzzle 7: Escaping a Cave

While hiking a mountain, you enter a cave. Suddenly, rocks fall and block the cave's entrance. You turn on your flashlight and start walking deeper into the cave. After a while, you find another opening. Unfortunately, the opening gives way to a sheer rock wall 60 feet above a climbable surface. You figure that 10 feet is the greatest distance you could jump down without sustaining serious injuries (also taking your own height into consideration).

You look around the cave and find that the ceiling is very high—40 feet above the floor. After a while, you find a 40-foot rope hanging from ceiling to floor. A few minutes later, you find another 40-foot rope hanging from ceiling to floor. You have your hiking knife with you. Can you think of a plan that will let you get out of the cave and down the climbable surface without jumping down more than 10 feet?

Puzzle 8: Free Tuna

You go to the grocery store and grab eight cans of tuna from the shelf. You go to the cash register to pay. Because he's in a good mood, the store owner hands you three plastic bags and says, "If you can arrange the eight cans in these three plastic bags so that each bag contains an odd number of cans, you can have them for free." Can you think of a way to get that free tuna?

Puzzle 9: Naming an Heir

A mighty king had three sons and wanted to declare the wisest of them as his heir. He decided to give them a logic puzzle to test their wisdom. He placed the sons in a triangular room, each in a different corner, and placed a hat on each son's head. The king said, "You need to determine the color of your hat. You can't take your hat off to look at it, and you can't communicate in any way. The hat on your head is either green or red. At least one of you is wearing a green hat. I'll be waiting outside the door and will ring a bell every five minutes. You can't leave the room until you know the color of your hat. If you know the answer, you must wait for the next bell and then come tell me the answer." At the third bell, one of the sons opened the door and told the king the answer. The king said, "You're correct, and I'm naming you my heir. However, I'm disappointed in you. You still have much to learn." What was that son's answer, and why was the king disappointed?

Puzzle 10: The Next Element in a Series

Given the following series of elements, can you determine the next element?

1, 11, 21, 1211, 111221, 312211, ?

Puzzle 11: Same Birthday

What's the probability that in a group of 23 randomly chosen people, at least 2 of them will have the same birthday?

Puzzle 12: Catching a Train

Two trains race toward each other on a railway segment that's 100 miles long. The trains are traveling at 100 mph. A mosquito flying at 200 mph flies from one train toward the other, and as soon as it arrives at the other train, it flips its direction and flies back toward the first train. The mosquito continues bouncing back and forth between the trains until the trains crash. What's the total distance that the mosquito covers until the moment of the crash?

Puzzle 13: Prisoners and Switches

A prison warden meets with 23 new prisoners when they arrive. He tells them, "You may meet today and plan your strategy for the challenge I'm about to propose. But after today, you'll be in isolated cells and will have no communication with one another. In the prison is a switch room, which contains two switches labeled A and B, each of which can be in either the On or Off position. The switches aren't connected to anything. I'm not telling you the switches' present positions. After today, from time to time, whenever I feel so inclined, I'll select one prisoner at random and escort him to the switch room. This prisoner will select one of the two switches and reverse its position. He must move exactly one of the switches: He can't move both switches, and he can't move no switch at all. Then, I'll lead the prisoner back to his cell. No one else will enter the switch room until I lead the next prisoner there, and I'll instruct him to do the same thing. I'm going to choose prisoners at random. I might choose the same prisoner three times in a row, or I might jump around and come back. However, given enough time, everyone will eventually visit the switch room as many times as everyone else. At any time, if you're 100 percent certain, any one of you can declare to me, 'We have now all visited the switch room.' If that person is correct, I'll set you all free. If that person is wrong, and somebody hasn't yet visited the switch room, I'll feed you all to the alligators." What strategy can the prisoners use to obtain freedom?

Puzzle 14: Probabilities in China

Is it possible to prove statistically that at least two people in China must have the same number of hairs on their heads? Try to stick to pure probability and not to assumptions such as, "There must be many bald people in China." Also, is it possible to prove statistically that at least two people in China are missing exactly the same set of teeth (for example, the upper left bicuspid, the lower inner incisor, and the two lower wisdom teeth)? Again, try to stick to pure probability and not to assumptions such as, "There must be many old people with no teeth, or people with no missing teeth."

Puzzle 15: Two Mathematicians

Two mathematicians (let's call them M and N) who were once good friends meet after a long time to have a drink together. M asks, "Are you married? Any kids? Do you still live in that old apartment building?" N replies, "Yes, I'm married with three kids, and we live in a house now." M asks, "How old are your kids?" N replies, "Let me answer with a riddle: The product of the ages of my kids is 36. Now, see that bus over there? The sum of my kids' ages is equal to that bus number." M thinks for a moment, then says, "I don't have sufficient information to solve the puzzle." N replies, "Oh, yes, you're right, I forgot to mention that one of my kids was born before we bought the house." Soon after N provides this last bit of information, M solves the puzzle and tells N the correct ages of the kids. Can you figure out the solution? Also, how would the solution change if N's additional piece of information was that one of his kids was born after he bought the house?

Puzzle 16: Crazy Sequence

This puzzle requires that you determine the next number in the following sequence:

0,

1,

2,

2601218943565795100204903227081043611191521875016945785727541837850835631156947382240678577958130457082619920575892247259536641565162052015873791984587740832529105244690388811884123764341191951045505346658616243271940197113909845536727278537099345629855586719369774070000370043078375899742067678401696720784628062922903210716166986726054898844551425719398549944893959449606404513236214026598619307324936977047760606768067017649166940303481996188145562519559256691883082551494294759653727484562462882423452659778973774089646655399243592878621251596748322097602950569669992728467056374713753301924831358707612541268341586012944756601145542074958995256354306828863463108496565068277155299625679084523570255218622235813001670083452344323682193579318470195651072978180435417389056072742804858399591972902172661229129842051606757903623233769945396419147517556755769539223380305682530859977441675784352815913461340394604901269542028838347101363733824484506660093348484440711931292537694657354337375724772230181534032647177531984537341478674327048457983786618703257405938924215709695994630557521063203263493209220738320923356309923267504401701760572026010829 28

80423356066430898887102973807975780130560495763428386830571906622052911748225105366977566030295740433879834715185526028053338663571391010463364197690973974322859942198370469791099563033896046758898657957111765666700391567481531159439800436253993997312030664906013253113047190288984918562037666691644687911252491937544258458950003115616829743046411425380748972817233759553806617198014046779356147936352662656833395097600000000000000000000000000000000000000000000000000000000000000000000000000000000000000000000000000000000000000000000000000000000000000000000000000000000000000000000000000000000000000,

?

Puzzle 17: Minimum Number of Weights

Can you determine the minimum number of weights required to measure any integer weight in the range 1 through 100 pounds using a scale? Also, can you generalize your answer for a range 1 through *n* pounds?

Puzzle 18: Counting Triangles

Can you figure out how many triangles Figure A-1 contains? Can you think of a methodical approach or formula to calculate this number?

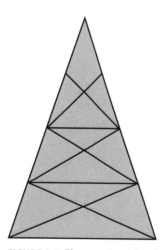

FIGURE A-1 The counting triangles puzzle

Puzzle 19: Counterfeit Coins

Suppose you have 10 stacks of coins, with 10 coins in each stack. One stack consists of 10 counterfeit coins, and the other 9 stacks each consist of 10 legitimate coins. Each legitimate coin weighs exactly 1 gram. Each counterfeit coin weighs exactly 0.9 grams. You have a digital scale that's graduated in tenths of grams. Using the scale to take only one reading, determine which stack has the 10 counterfeit coins. You can weigh any number of coins from any number of stacks, but must you weigh them all together. (In other words, you can take only one reading from the scale.)

Puzzle 20: Too Clever by Half

A chicken and a half lay an egg and a half in a day and a half. How many eggs would one chicken lay in three days?

A builder and a half build a house and a half in a year and a half using a tool and a half. How many houses would one builder build in nine years? Can you generalize your calculation to solve both equations?

Puzzle 21: A Cat, a String, and the Earth

This puzzle is quite simple, but I like it because it's so counterintuitive. Suppose you lay a string on the ground all around the earth right over the equator. The length of the string would be equal to the earth's equatorial circumference—40,075.02 kilometers. Suppose you add 1 meter to the string and suspend the string directly above the equator, with an even distance from the ground all the way around. Would a cat be able to pass from one hemisphere to another below the string?

Puzzle 22: Josephus Problem

The Josephus problem is an ancient puzzle that involves a group of 41 men standing in a circle. Going around the circle, every second standing man is executed (one skipped, one executed) until only one man is left standing. Assuming that the positions are numbered 1 through 41, which position should Josephus (one of the men) choose if he could so that he would be the only one to remain standing? Can you generalize the solution for *n* men? Write a T-SQL solution that returns the position based on the input number of men @*n*.

Puzzle 23: Shipping Algebra

The combined age of a ship and its boiler is 42. The ship is twice as old as the boiler was when the ship was as old as the boiler is now. How old are the ship and its boiler?

Puzzle 24: Equilateral Triangles Puzzle

Examine the drawing in Figure A-2.

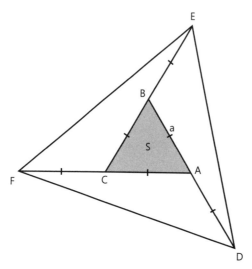

FIGURE A-2 The equilateral triangles puzzle

The triangle ABC is an equilateral triangle with an area *S* and a side length *a*. The line CF is a continuation of the line AC, AD is a continuation of BA, and BE is a continuation of CB. The length of all continuation segments (CF, AD, and BE) is *a*—the same as the length of triangle ABC's sides. The puzzle is to calculate the area of the triangle DEF.

Puzzle Solutions

This section contains solutions to the logic puzzles.

Puzzle 1: Remainders

When solving such a problem, try first to relax the limitations and simplify the problem. Then add complexity layers. For example, first ignore the requirement to find the minimum integer *n* that qualifies. Try to find a solution for any integer *n* that would yield the remainder *i* − *1* for any *i* value. Obviously, if you multiply all *i* values (2 × 3 × 4 × 5 × 6 × 7 × 8 × 9 ×10) and subtract 1, the result meets the puzzle's requirement (except for the requirement to find the minimum *n*). You can express the same result as the product of the prime factors of the various *i* values: (2 × 3 × [2 × 2] × 5 × [2 × 3] × 7 × [2 × 2 × 2] × [3 × 3] × [2 × 5]) − 1. Next, tackle the minimum requirement. Of course, you'll have to keep at least one occurrence of each prime number (2, 3, 5, 7). The distinct prime factors already cover the *i* values: 2, 3, 6, 5,

7, and 10. You'll need to add occurrences of some of the prime numbers to also cover 4, 8, and 9. It's sufficient to have 3 occurrences of 2 to get 4 and 8, and it's also sufficient to keep 2 occurrences of 3 to get 9. So, the minimum integer n that qualifies can be expressed as $2 \times 2 \times 2 \times 3 \times 3 \times 5 \times 7 - 1 = 2519$.

Puzzle 2: Round Manhole Covers

Manhole covers are typically made round as a safety measure. Any way you turn the round cover, it cannot fall into the round manhole because of its geometrical properties. With other geometrical shapes (rectangle, square, and so on), if you turn the cover in a certain way, it can fall into the manhole and endanger the people working there.

Puzzle 3: Shaking Hands

Let's start with the person who shook eight hands (call that person P8). All those who shook the hand of P8 (including myself and excluding the spouse of P8) shook at least one hand. Therefore, the spouse of P8 must be the person who shook zero hands (call that person P0). Now, take P8 and P0 out of the equation. You know that the remaining six people shook a known number of hands (exactly one) from the being-excluded couple. So you subtract one from the answers of all remaining individuals. Simply imagine that you're now facing the same puzzle, but with four couples and with the seven individuals besides me replying to my question with the answers 0 through 6.

You'll quickly conclude that the five couples, including me and my wife, shook hands in the following chiastic manner: 8/0, 7/1, 6/2, 5/3, 4/4. Because I asked nine individuals how many hands they shook and I got nine unique answers, my wife and I must be the couple who shook four hands each. Hence, my wife shook four hands.

Puzzle 4: Then There Were Five?

I've seen several versions of solutions to this puzzle, but they're essentially all the same. Here's one with a bit of SQL in it: Given the filter expression *col1 = 1 and col2 = 3*, there are spaces between 1 and and and and and col2. Another version of the solution refers to a restaurant sign that says "fish and chips," and the owner wants to replace the spaces between fish and and and and and chips with hyphens.

Puzzle 5: Arranging Soldiers in a Row

The key to the solution is that each soldier can put himself between the correct pair of (placed up to then) soldiers without knowing what's on his hat. Assuming you're one of the soldiers, here's the logic you would follow:

- If you enter the room first, simply position yourself somewhere in the room so that the next soldier can see the sign on your hat.

- If you're not the first one in the room, look at the hats of the soldiers that are already there. If all soldiers have the same sign, stand to the right of the rightmost one in case that sign is a circle and to the left of the leftmost one in case the sign is a square.

- If some soldiers have a circle and some have a square, squeeze yourself between the two with the different signs.

Puzzle 6: Crossing the Tunnel

Most people try to solve this puzzle by letting person A walk from start to end with each of the others, then walk back alone to pair with the next person. Intuition says that this approach must be the fastest because person A is the fastest. But if you calculate the total time it takes all four people to get to the end, you get 13 minutes. Of course, the pace is dictated by the slowest in the pair. Person A would need to go from start to end three times: with B (2 minutes), C (4 minutes), and D (5 minutes). These walks amount to 11 minutes, plus the two times that person A needs to walk back alone (1 minute per walk), and you get 13. The trick to solving the puzzle is to figure out that you can save most time by letting the two slowest people walk together. Here's the strategy that gets all the people across in 12 minutes:

- Persons A and B walk first from start to end (2 minutes)

- Person A walks back (1 minute)

- Persons C and D walk from start to end (5 minutes)

- Person B walks back (2 minutes)

- Persons A and B walk from start to end (2 minutes)

Puzzle 7: Escaping a Cave

First, climb one of the ropes and cut it at the halfway point. You now have 20 feet of rope in your hand, you're hanging on to the 20-foot rope anchored to the ceiling, and you're 20 feet above the floor. Make a knot at the edge of the hanging rope to form a small loop. (For the purpose of simplification, we'll assume that knots don't affect the length of the rope.) Slide the 20-foot rope through the loop to its middle point (the 10-foot mark). Now, you have a 20-foot rope hanging from the ceiling, plus another 10-foot segment (20 feet, doubled up), amounting to 30 feet in total. You can now shimmy down the rope, and when you reach the end of the doubled-up segment, let go of one end of it and let it slide through the loop as you jump down. You now have a 20-foot rope in hand.

Next, carrying this 20-foot rope, climb the second rope and cut it when you're 10 feet from the ceiling (or 30 feet above the floor). Tie the resulting 30-foot rope to the end of your 20-foot rope to form a 50-foot rope. Again, make a loop at the end of the hanging 10-foot rope and slide the 50-foot rope through the loop to its middle point. In total, you have 35 feet of rope made by the two segments (10 feet of hanging rope plus 25 feet made by the doubled-up 50-foot rope). You can now shimmy down the rope, and when you get to the end of the rope (5 feet above the floor), hold one of its ends and jump down. You now have a rope that's 50 feet in length, and you can use it to get down from the cave to the climbable surface.

Puzzle 8: Free Tuna

Obviously, you can't divide the eight tuna cans into three separate plastic bags so that each holds an odd number of cans. However, nothing in the puzzle dictates the arrangement of the bags around the tuna cans. The sum of three odd numbers $x+y+z$, where each number is considered only once, naturally amounts to an odd number. However, taking one of the odd numbers into consideration twice allows for an arrangement in which one of the elements is even (say, y)—for example, $(x+(y))+(z) = 8$. The use of parentheses is intentional—each pair of parentheses represents a plastic bag. For example, let x equal 1, y equal 2, and z equal 5: You place 1 tuna can in plastic bag A, 2 tuna cans in plastic bag B, and 5 tuna cans in plastic bag C. Then, place plastic bag A in plastic bag B. You end up with 1 tuna can in bag A, 3 in B ($x+y$), and 5 in C.

As an aside, if you like trying to solve open puzzles, the tuna cans puzzle reminds me of a mathematical conjecture that so far hasn't been proven. The conjecture, which is called *Goldbach's conjecture*, is named after its creator. The original conjecture says: Every integer greater than five can be expressed as the sum of three prime numbers. Euler simplified the conjecture to this form: Every even number greater than two can be expressed as the sum of two prime numbers.

Puzzle 9: Naming an Heir

That son's answer was green, based on the following logical deduction:

- If there were two red hats and one green hat, the son with the green hat would have realized it immediately (by seeing both his brothers wearing red hats) and approached the king at the first bell ring. Because this didn't happen, there is—at most—one red hat among the sons.

- If there was one red hat and two green hats, each of the two sons wearing green hats should have seen his brothers wearing one red and one green hat; therefore, both these brothers could have deduced that they were wearing green hats (because no one approached the king after the first bell, and there's at most one red hat in such a case) and thus approached the king at the second bell.

- The son who ultimately figured out the answer reasoned that his brothers weren't stupid, so if no one approached the king at the second bell, they must all be wearing green hats. Of course, this tells you that he saw both his brothers wearing green hats. So, he approached the king at the third bell to say that he was wearing a green hat.

Why was the king disappointed in his son? The answer involves true wisdom. The son should have reasoned that any setting in which (at minimum) one of the hats is green and not all of them are green is an unfair contest. If at least one hat is green and not all hats are green, different sons can figure out their own hat color at different points in time.

For example, if two of the hats are red, the son who wears a green hat can figure out the answer immediately and approach the king at the first bell, while the other two must wait to see whether someone approaches the king at the first bell (in which case it will be too late for them). Similarly, if one of the hats is red, the two sons wearing green hats can know the answer after the first bell and approach the king at the second bell, while the son with the red hat must wait to see whether someone approaches the king at the second bell (in which case it's too late for him).

If the king had favored one of the sons, he would have named that son his heir without a contest. Because he wanted to put their wisdom to test, you would expect the contest to be fair. The only way for the contest to be fair while having a minimum of one green hat is to have three green hats. The king expected one of his sons to approach him at the first bell with this logic.

Puzzle 10: The Next Element in a Series

Each element describes the previous element by counting the number of consecutive occurrences of each digit from left to right. For example, to describe the element 1, you would say that there's one occurrence of the digit 1, or "1 1," resulting in 11. To describe 11, you would say that there are two occurrences of the digit 1, or "2 1s," resulting in 21. The description of 21 is "1 2, (then) 1 1," resulting in 1211. The description of 1211 is "1 1, 1 2, 2 1s," resulting in 111221. Following this logic, the next few elements are 312211, 13112221, and 1112213211.

Puzzle 11: Same Birthday

The answer to this puzzle might seem strange. Most people intuitively assume that the probability is very low. However, the probability that two people in a group of 23 have the same birthday happens to be greater than 50 percent (about 50.7 percent). For 60 or more people, it's greater than 99 percent (disregarding variations in the distribution and assuming that the 365 possible birthdays are equally likely). The tricky part of the puzzle is that you need to determine the probability that any two people share the same birthday—not a specific two. For the exact solution and some interesting information about the birthday paradox, check out the Wikipedia entry at *http://en.wikipedia.org/wiki/Birthday_paradox*.

Puzzle 12: Catching a Train

Some people try to solve the puzzle by doing infinity-related calculations—that is, attempting to calculate the distance the mosquito covers in each leg from one train to the other before turning around. However, a solution based on time and speed is much simpler, although I should constrain the term *simpler* to most mere mortals (and not to mathematicians who might find infinity-related calculations to be a natural way of thinking). Naturally, the trains will meet halfway in a half hour. The mosquito's speed is 200 mph, so in a half hour, the total distance it covers is 100 miles.

Puzzle 13: Prisoners and Switches

The solution is to put one prisoner in charge of counting and notifying the warden when the count is complete. We'll call him Charles. Charles should follow these instructions each time he enters the room:

- Toggle switch A.
- If you just turned the switch Off and you also turned the switch Off on your previous visit to the room, increment the count of prisoners who visited the room.

The prisoners who aren't in charge of counting should follow these instructions:

- If switch A is Off and you have never switched it to On yourself but you have previously *seen* it On, turn switch A to the On state.
- In any other case, toggle switch B.

The logic is that the only prisoner who can turn switch A to Off is Charles. The other prisoners can turn switch A to On, but each can do so only once and only after seeing it in the On state previously. This means two things: First, when a prisoner who isn't in charge (say his name is Paul) and who has seen switch A On at some time in the past sees that switch A is Off, he knows that Charles visited the room before him and was the one who turned it Off. (Paul saw the switch On in the past, but it is now Off, and Charles is the only prisoner who ever turns the switch to Off). Paul will then turn switch A to On. Second, Paul knows that switch A will remain On until Charles subsequently turns it off knowing that another prisoner (not Charles himself) turned it on, and Charles will count that prisoner (Paul) in his tally.

Puzzle 14: Probabilities in China

The answer to the first puzzle is yes. China has more than a billion people, and a human head has fewer than a billion hairs. Because there are fewer hairs on a human head than people in China, it's impossible for every person in China to have a different number of hairs. Therefore, at least one number must occur twice; in other words, at least two people in China have the same number of hairs on their heads.

The answer to the second puzzle is no. It can't be proven that at least two people in China are missing the same set of teeth. Humans have as many as 32 teeth. You can represent any set of (missing) teeth from these 32 with a 32-bit bitmap, using a 0 to represent missing and a 1 to represent not missing. The number of distinct 32-bit bitmaps is 2^{32}, or more than 4 billion. Because the number of subsets of human teeth is greater than the number of people in China, it's possible that all Chinese people are missing a different set of teeth.

Puzzle 15: Two Mathematicians

A good way to start solving this puzzle is to first list all groups of three integers whose product is 36, then calculate each group's sum:

$1 + 1 + 36 = 38$

$1 + 2 + 18 = 21$

$1 + 3 + 12 = 16$

$1 + 4 + 9 = 14$

$1 + 6 + 6 = 13$

$2 + 2 + 9 = 13$

$2 + 3 + 6 = 11$

$3 + 3 + 4 = 10$

M knows the sum of the kids' ages (equal to the number of the bus N pointed to). Notice that all sums arise in one way except for the sum 13, which arises from two different groups of three integers. Had the bus number been something other than 13, M would have immediately known the answer. Because M said that he doesn't have sufficient information to solve the puzzle, the bus number must have been 13. Now, the question remains, which of the two age variations is the correct one? Notice that in both cases (1, 6, 6 and 2, 2, 9), there are twins. The additional piece of information N provided was, "One of my kids was born before we bought the house." The implication is that one of the kids is older than the other two, so of the two variations, the correct one is 2, 2, 9. Now, how would the solution change if N's additional piece of information had been that one of his kids was born after he bought the house? In this case, one of the kids is younger than the other two, so the correct answer would be 1, 6, 6. Interestingly, you can solve this puzzle with a T-SQL query, like so:

```
WITH
  L0 AS(SELECT 0 AS c UNION ALL SELECT 0),
  L1 AS(SELECT 0 AS c FROM L0 AS a CROSS JOIN L0 AS b),
  L2 AS(SELECT 0 AS c FROM L1 AS a CROSS JOIN L1 AS b),
  L3 AS(SELECT TOP(36) 0 AS c FROM L2 AS a CROSS JOIN L2 AS b),
Nums AS(SELECT ROW_NUMBER() OVER(ORDER BY (SELECT 0)) AS n
          FROM L3),
Divisors AS
(
  SELECT C1.n AS age1, C2.n AS age2, C3.n AS age3,
    COUNT(*) OVER(PARTITION BY C1.n + C2.n + C3.n) AS cnt
  FROM Nums AS C1
    CROSS JOIN Nums AS C2
    CROSS JOIN Nums AS C3
  WHERE C1.n * C2.n * C3.n = 36
    AND C1.n <= C2.n AND C2.n <= C3.n
)
```

```
SELECT age1, age2, age3
FROM Divisors
WHERE cnt > 1
  AND age3 > age2; -- One born before others (before house);
```

To solve the version where N's additional piece of information is that one of his kids was born after he bought the house, change the last predicate in the outer query's filter to *age1 < age2*.

Puzzle 16: Crazy Sequence

Let *n* be the zero-based position of the number in the sequence (0, 1, 2, 3, …). The given numbers are what you get if you begin with the number *n*, then take the factorial *n* times in sequence—that is, 0, 1!, 2!!, 3!!!, and so on. The lengthy last number in the sequence is 3!!!, so the next number in the sequence is 4!!!!. It is probably prudent not to include the actual number in this space because it wouldn't leave space for anything else.

Puzzle 17: Minimum Number of Weights

The puzzle doesn't restrict you to placing the item you're weighing on one side of the scale and the weights on the other. Therefore, you can place weights on both sides. To simplify the solution's explanation, first assume that there was a restriction to place the item you're weighing on one side of the scale and the weights on the other.

Given a set of weights, to measure some item's weight (call it *w*), you need to use a subset of the weights you have—that is, each weight from your set of weights will be either used or not used to weigh the item. So any *w* in the range 1 through *n* must be representable with a binary system, where each bit represents a different weight from your set of weights, and only the bits of the participating weights will be turned on. The best strategy is to use the positional values of binary representation. For example, to represent any integer in the range 1 through 100, you need 7 bits (1, 2, 4, 8, 16, 32, and 64). Notice that you get a geometric sequence (also known as a geometric progression) with a common ratio 2 (1×2^0, 1×2^1, 1×2^2, 1×2^3, and so on). To use any set of weights, their total weight must be at least the largest weight you need. The simplified formula for the sum of the geometric sequence in our case is $2^{num\_weights} - 1$, and this sum must be greater than or equal to *n*. Hence, the minimum number of weights required is *ceiling(log$_2$(n+1))*.

Next, remove the restriction to place weights only on one side of the scale. Now each weight from your set of weights can assume one of three roles: first, placed on the same side of the scale as the item you're weighing (a negative value); second, placed on the other side of the scale (a positive value); and third, not used (a 0 value). If you think about it, just like you can represent numbers using a binary system where each bit represents a different power of 2, you can represent numbers using a ternary system where each *trit* (ternary digit) represents a different power of 3. A ternary system where each trit can be –1, 0, and +1 is known as a *balanced ternary system*. As an example, in this system the number 150 is represented as $1 \times (0) + 3 \times (-1) + 9 \times (-1) + 27 \times (0) + 81 \times (-1) + 243 \times (+1)$. Though very cumbersome, such a system provides the optimal solution in terms of the number of weights required to weigh any object. With a set of weights that are consecutive powers of 3 starting with 1 and on (1, 3, 9, 27, 81, ...) whose sum is s, you can express any number in the range $-s$ through s. In our case, only the positive numbers are relevant. So in order to be able to weigh any w in the range 1 through n, you need the sum of the values represented by the trits to be greater than or equal to n. This time, the common ratio of our geometric sequence is 3. The simplified sum of the geometric sequence is $(3^{num\_weights} - 1) \div 2$. To represent any integer in the range 1 through n, the minimum number of weights required is $ceiling(log_3(2 \times n+1))$.

Puzzle 18: Counting Triangles

To follow the explanation of this puzzle's solution, examine Figure A-3, in which the points in the diagram are marked with letters.

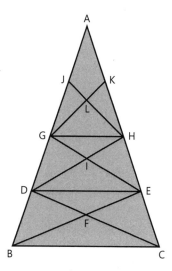

FIGURE A-3 The counting triangles puzzle solution

To find a methodical approach for solving the puzzle, you must identify a repeating pattern in the diagram. Note that the diagram contains a repeating pattern of floors or levels. Each floor except the top one consists of two lines crossing each other as well as a ceiling.

To create a formula for counting the triangles, you must determine the effect of adding each floor. You can start by drawing only the outermost triangle (ABC). So far, your count is 1. Add the ceiling of the first floor (DE), and the triangle ADE adds 1 to the count. Next, add the lines crossing each other within the first floor (DC, BE). The new triangles formed as a result of adding these two lines include 4 one-celled triangles (DBF, FBC, EFC, DFE), 4 two-celled triangles (DBC, BCE, CED, EDB) and 2 three-celled triangles (ABE, ADC), thus adding 10 new triangles to the count. So adding the first floor (including the ceiling and the two lines crossing each other) adds 11 to the original count of 1.

Add another floor by marking the lines GH, DH, and GE. This adds 11 new triangles (the first floor is also added), plus 2 new four-celled triangles (GBE, HDC). In other words, the first floor adds 11 to the count, and every additional floor beyond the first adds 13 to the count.

Although the top floor doesn't have a ceiling (no line exists between points J and K), you can imagine the floor as if there were a ceiling (namely, add 13 to the count), then subtract the triangles that are eliminated by removing the floor. Four triangles are eliminated (AJK, JLK, JGK, JHK). So the total number of triangles you get is 1 + 11 + 13 + 13 – 4 = 34.

The general formula for n floors when the top floor has no ceiling is $1 + 11 + [(n – 1) \times 13] – 4$. If you simplify the formula by expanding the parentheses $(1 + 11 + (n \times 13) – 13 – 4)$, you get $(n \times 13) – 5$. So for 3 floors you get $(3 \times 13) – 5 = 34$. Now you can easily calculate the number of triangles for any given number of floors.

Puzzle 19: Counterfeit Coins

Take 1 coin from stack 1, 2 coins from stack 2, and so on. Weigh the stack of 55 coins. If all the coins were legitimate, the scale would show 55 grams. If stack 3 is the stack of counterfeit coins, the scale will show 54.7 grams because the pile of coins you weighed contains 3 counterfeit coins and is therefore 0.3 grams light. More generally, if stack n is the stack of counterfeit coins and w is the weight the scale shows, $n = (55.0 – w)/0.1$.

Puzzle 20: Too Clever by Half

The intuitive yet incorrect answer to the chicken-and-eggs puzzle is that one chicken lays three eggs in three days, while the correct answer is that one chicken lays two eggs in three days. Our brain plays a trick on us and makes us think that if a chicken and a half lay an egg and a half in a day and a half, one chicken lays one egg in one day. But if you express the relationship between chickens, days, and eggs mathematically, you get this equation:

3/2 chickens × 3/2 days = 3/2 eggs × k chicken-days per egg

For the purposes of solving this puzzle, the factor *k chicken-days per egg* can be ignored. Under reasonable assumptions—that the number of eggs is directly proportional to the number of chickens and directly proportional to the number of days and that the same number of chicken-days is required for every egg—*k* will be a constant, and I can safely manipulate the equation without writing down the factor *k chicken-days per egg*.

Reducing the number of chickens from 3/2 to 1 is achieved by dividing the original number by 3/2. For the equation to be true, you also need to divide the number of eggs (3/2) by 3/2, giving you this equation:

1 chicken × 3/2 days = 1 egg

Reducing the number of days from 3/2 to 1 has a similar effect on the number of eggs; namely, you need to divide 1 (egg) by 3/2, giving you this equation:

1 chicken × 1 day = 2/3 egg

If you increase the number of days from 1 to 3, the effect on the number of eggs is a factor of 3 as well:

1 chicken × 3 days = 2 eggs

So the correct answer to the puzzle is that one chicken lays two eggs in three days.

In a very similar manner, you can express the relationship between builders, houses, years, and tools with the following equation:

3/2 builders × 3/2 years × 3/2 tools = 3/2 house

To reduce the number of builders, years, and tools to one each, you need to divide the number of houses by 3/2 three times; in other words, by $(3/2)^3$:

1 builder × 1 year × 1 tool = 3/2 ÷ 3/2 ÷ 3/2 ÷ 3/2 houses

This gives you the following equation:

1 builder × 1 year × 1 tool = 4/9 house

Thus, one builder with one tool will build four houses in nine years.

To generalization the equation, you need to divide the right side of the equation by 3/2 n times for n elements in the left side of the equation. Or, if you want to express the calculation as a multiplication instead of division, multiply by $(2/3)^n$. For example, take our last equation:

3/2 builders × 3/2 years × 3/2 tools = 3/2 houses

The left side of the equation contains three elements; therefore, you get this equation:

1 builder × 1 year × 1 tool = 3/2 × $(2/3)^3$ houses

This is equal to:

1 builder × 1 year × 1 tool = 4/9 house

Puzzle 21: A Cat, a String, and the Earth

As I said, although this puzzle is quite simple, I like it because it's so counterintuitive. It probably seems inconceivable that adding only 1 meter to such a large circumference would make any noticeable difference in the radius, let alone allow a cat to pass below the string in the space that was added. But if you do the math, you realize that the actual circumference has no significance in determining how the radius would be affected when extending the circumference. Instead, only the addition is significant. The circumference can be expressed as $C = 2\pi r$ (2 times π times the radius). Hence, the original radius can be expressed as $r_{original} = C/(2\pi)$. Adding 1 meter to the existing circumference would change the equation to $C + 1 = 2\pi r_{new}$. Isolating r_{new}, you get $r_{new} = (C + 1)/(2\pi)$. Expanding the parentheses, you get $r_{new} = C/(2\pi) + 1/(2\pi)$. Because the original radius was $C/(2\pi)$, the new radius is $1/(2\pi)$ greater, which is about 16 centimeters (a bit more than 6 inches) greater. That's enough for a cat to go under and move from one hemisphere to the other.

Puzzle 22: Josephus Problem

An easy way to find a generic solution to this puzzle with any number of men is to first solve it with very small numbers of men (1, 2, 3, and so on) and to look for a pattern in the results. If you solve the puzzle for small numbers, you get the results shown in Table A-1, where n is the number of men and p is the position of the only man left.

TABLE A-1 Results of the Josephus Problem

n	p
1	1
2	1
3	3
4	1
5	3
6	5
7	7
8	1
9	3
10	5
11	7
12	9
13	11
14	13
15	15
16	1

The pattern you can identify is that p is an increasing sequence of odd integers that restarts from 1 when n is a power of 2. You express n as $2^a + b$, where $b \geq 0$ and $b < 2^a$. That is, a is the highest power of 2 such that 2^a is smaller than n, and b is n minus 2^a. Then, p can be expressed as $2b + 1$. For example, for $n = 41$, express n as $2^5 + 9$. Since $b = 9$ and $p = 2b + 1$, you get $p = 19$.

Of course, this is just an observation of a pattern based on the cases that were tested. To ensure that the pattern holds for all cases, you need a mathematical proof. You can find one at *http://en.wikipedia.org/wiki/Josephus_problem*. The following T-SQL statement calculates and returns *p* for a given *@n*:

```
DECLARE @n AS INT = 41;
SELECT 2 * (@n - POWER(2, CAST(LOG(@n)/LOG(2) AS INT))) + 1 AS p;
```

Puzzle 23: Shipping Algebra

Here's the algebra I used in my solution to the problem:

Let s = current age of ship, b = current age of boiler, and y = years passed since the age of the ship was equal to the current age of the boiler. You can translate the statements in the puzzle to the following three equations:

1. $s + b = 42$
2. $s = 2 \times (b - y)$
3. $s - y = b$

From equations 2 and 3 you get the following equation:

$s = 2 \times (b - s + b)$

This gives us equation 4:

4. $3 \times s = 4 \times b$

From equations 1 and 4 you get the following equation:

$3 \times s = 4 \times (42 - s)$

When you solve the equation for *s*, you get 24. And now that the age of the ship is known, you can solve equation 1 for *b*:

$b = 42 - 24 = 18$

The solution is that the ship's current age is 24 and the boiler's current age is 18.

Puzzle 24: Equilateral Triangles Puzzle

You can solve this puzzle in many ways. I provided this puzzle not because it is tough but rather the contrary—it is pretty simple. However, some of the solutions are simply beautiful. I'll first provide an ordinary solution and then a more creative one. To explain the first solution, examine the drawing in Figure A-4.

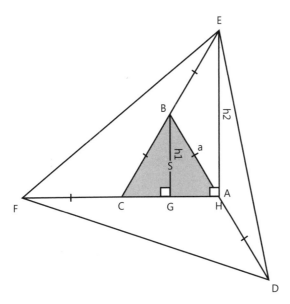

FIGURE A-4 Solution 1 to the equilateral triangles puzzle

The segment *h1* has the same length as the altitude of the triangle ABC, and the segment *h2* has the same length as the altitude of the triangle CEF. G is the point where *h1* intersects CA, and H is the point where *h2* intersects the same line. It is fairly easy to prove that H is the same point as A but not really necessary for our purposes. The triangles GBC and HEC are similar because they have two corresponding angles that are equal (both have a right angle and share another angle). |CE| is twice |CB|; therefore |HE| (which is |h2|) is twice |GB| (which is |h1|). The area of a triangle is ½bh (half base times altitude). Because the bases FC and CH of the triangles CEF and ABC have equal lengths but |h2| is twice |h1|, the area of CEF is twice the area of ABC. In other words, the area of CEF (as well as DEB and DAF, which are congruent to CEF) is 2S. Therefore, the area of the triangle DEF is 3 × 2S + S = 7S.

The second solution is more creative. Examine the drawing in Figure A-5.

You draw the lines EG and GF parallel to CF and EC, respectively, to form the parallelogram CEGF. Next, draw the lines BG, BH, and CE. We know that |FC| = |CB| = |BE| = |EG| = |GH| = |HF| = |HB| = |a|. Triangles ABC, CHF, and BGH are congruent because corresponding sides and the angle between them are equal. This means that |HC| = |BG| = |a|. This means that the four triangles BEG, BGH, CBH, and CHF enclosed by the parallelogram and ABC are congruent; therefore, the area of the parallelogram is 4S. The triangle CEF has exactly half the area of the parallelogram; therefore, the triangle's area is 2S. Therefore, the area of the triangle DEF is 3 × 2S + S = 7S.

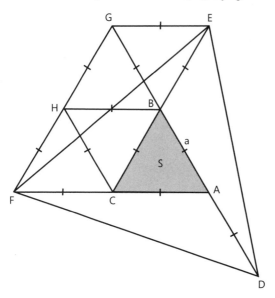

FIGURE A-5 Solution 2 to the equilateral triangles puzzle

Conclusion

I hope that you find logic puzzles challenging, fun, and a great tool to improve your logic and SQL. And if you're still looking for a reason to practice them, here's one:

> *"Crime is common. Logic is rare. Therefore it is upon the logic rather than upon the crime that you should dwell."*
>
> —*Sir Arthur Conan Doyle, 1859–1930, The Adventures of Sherlock Holmes,*
> *"The Adventure of the Copper Beeches"*

Index

Symbols and Numbers

A

X

Y

About the Authors

Itzik Ben-Gan

Itzik Ben-Gan is a mentor and cofounder of Solid Quality Mentors. An SQL Server Microsoft MVP (Most Valuable Professional) since 1999, Itzik has delivered numerous training events around the world focused on T-SQL querying, query tuning, and programming. Itzik is the author of several books about T-SQL. He has written many articles for *SQL Server Magazine* as well as articles and white papers for MSDN. Itzik's speaking engagements include Tech Ed, DevWeek, PASS, SQL Server Magazine Connections, various user groups around the world, and Solid Quality Mentors events.

Lubor Kollar

Lubor Kollar is Group Program Manager in Microsoft Corp. He has been working in SQL Server development organization since 1996. Prior to joining Microsoft, he was developing various DB2 engines at IBM. Currently Lubor is leading SQL Server Customer Advisory Team (SQL CAT) working on the most challenging SQL Server deployments around the world. SQL CAT is responsible for maintaining tight connections between the users and creators of new SQL Server releases. Another goal of SQL CAT is to spread the wisdom learned from the most advanced SQL Server deployments. One of the major channels easily accessible to the widest audience is the *www.sqlcat.com* Web site.

Dejan Sarka

Dejan Sarka focuses on development of database and business intelligence applications. Besides projects, he spends about half of his time on training and mentoring. He is a frequent speaker at some of the most important international conferences, including PASS, TechEd, and SqlDevCon. He is also indispensable at regional Microsoft events—for example, the NT Conference (the biggest Microsoft conference in Central and Eastern Europe). He is the founder of the Slovenian SQL Server and .NET Users Group. Dejan is the main author, coauthor, or guest author of seven books about databases and SQL Server. Dejan also developed two courses for Solid Quality Learning: Data Modeling Essentials and Data Mining with SQL Server 2008.

Steve Kass

Steve Kass holds a Ph.D. in mathematics from the University of Wisconsin, and he is a professor of Mathematics and Computer Science at Drew University, where he has taught since 1988. An SQL Server Microsoft MVP since 2002, he has written for *SQL Server Magazine* and spoken at SQL Server Magazine Connections events and to user groups in the New York City area. Steve's mathematical work has appeared in *Complex Systems* and the *Journal of Algebra*.

Best Practices for Software Engineering

Software Estimation: Demystifying the Black Art
Steve McConnell
ISBN 9780735605350

Amazon.com's pick for "Best Computer Book of 2006"! Generating accurate software estimates is fairly straight-forward—once you understand the art of creating them. Acclaimed author Steve McConnell demystifies the process—illuminating the practical procedures, formulas, and heuristics you can apply right away.

Code Complete, Second Edition
Steve McConnell
ISBN 9780735619678

Widely considered one of the best practical guides to programming—fully updated. Drawing from research, academia, and everyday commercial practice, McConnell synthesizes must-know principles and techniques into clear, pragmatic guidance. Rethink your approach—and deliver the highest quality code.

Agile Portfolio Management
Jochen Krebs
ISBN 9780735625679

Agile processes foster better collaboration, innovation, and results. So why limit their use to software projects—when you can transform your entire business? This book illuminates the opportunities—and rewards—of applying agile processes to your overall IT portfolio, with best practices for optimizing results.

Simple Architectures for Complex Enterprises
Roger Sessions
ISBN 9780735625785

Why do so many IT projects fail? Enterprise consultant Roger Sessions believes complex problems require simple solutions. And in this book, he shows how to make simplicity a core architectural requirement—as critical as performance, reliability, or security—to achieve better, more reliable results for your organization.

The Enterprise and Scrum
Ken Schwaber
ISBN 9780735623378

Extend Scrum's benefits—greater agility, higher-quality products, and lower costs—beyond individual teams to the entire enterprise. Scrum cofounder Ken Schwaber describes proven practices for adopting Scrum principles across your organization, including that all-critical component—managing change.

ALSO SEE

Software Requirements, Second Edition
Karl E. Wiegers
ISBN 9780735618794

More About Software Requirements: Thorny Issues and Practical Advice
Karl E. Wiegers
ISBN 9780735622678

Software Requirement Patterns
Stephen Withall
ISBN 9780735623989

Agile Project Management with Scrum
Ken Schwaber
ISBN 9780735619937

For C# Developers

Microsoft® Visual C#® 2008 Express Edition: Build a Program Now!

Patrice Pelland

ISBN 9780735625426

Build your own Web browser or other cool application—no programming experience required! Featuring learn-by-doing projects and plenty of examples, this full-color guide is your quick start to creating your first applications for Windows®. DVD includes Express Edition software plus code samples.

Microsoft Visual C# 2008 Step by Step

John Sharp

ISBN 9780735624306

Teach yourself Visual C# 2008—one step at a time. Ideal for developers with fundamental programming skills, this practical tutorial delivers hands-on guidance for creating C# components and Windows–based applications. CD features practice exercises, code samples, and a fully searchable eBook.

Learn Programming Now! Microsoft XNA® Game Studio 2.0

Rob Miles

ISBN 9780735625228

Now you can create your own games for Xbox 360® and Windows—as you learn the underlying skills and concepts for computer programming. Dive right into your first project, adding new tools and tricks to your arsenal as you go. Master the fundamentals of XNA Game Studio and Visual C#—no experience required!

Programming Microsoft Visual C# 2008: The Language

Donis Marshall

ISBN 9780735625402

Get the in-depth reference, best practices, and code you need to master the core language capabilities in Visual C# 2008. Fully updated for Microsoft .NET Framework 3.5, including a detailed exploration of LINQ, this book examines language features in detail—and across the product life cycle.

Windows via C/C++, Fifth Edition

Jeffrey Richter, Christophe Nasarre

ISBN 9780735624245

Jeffrey Richter's classic guide to C++ programming—now fully revised for Windows XP, Windows Vista®, and Windows Server® 2008. Learn to develop more-robust applications with unmanaged C++ code—and apply advanced techniques—with comprehensive guidance and code samples from the experts.

CLR via C#, Second Edition

Jeffrey Richter

ISBN 9780735621633

Dig deep and master the intricacies of the common language runtime (CLR) and the .NET Framework. Written by programming expert Jeffrey Richter, this guide is ideal for developers building any kind of application—ASP.NET, Windows Forms, Microsoft SQL Server®, Web services, console apps—and features extensive C# code samples.

ALSO SEE

Microsoft Visual C# 2005 Step by Step
ISBN 9780735621299

Programming Microsoft Visual C# 2005: The Language
ISBN 9780735621817

Debugging Microsoft .NET 2.0 Applications
ISBN 9780735622029

Collaborative Technologies— Resources for Developers

Inside Microsoft® Windows® SharePoint® Services 3.0
Ted Pattison, Daniel Larson
ISBN 9780735623200

Get the in-depth architectural insights, task-oriented guidance, and extensive code samples you need to build robust, enterprise content-management solutions.

Inside Microsoft Office SharePoint Server 2007
Patrick Tisseghem
ISBN 9780735623682

Led by an expert in collaboration technologies, you'll plumb the internals of SharePoint Server 2007—and master the intricacies of developing intranets, extranets, and Web-based applications.

Inside the Index and Search Engines: Microsoft Office SharePoint Server 2007
Patrick Tisseghem, Lars Fastrup
ISBN 9780735625358

Customize and extend the enterprise search capabilities in SharePoint Server 2007—and optimize the user experience—with guidance from two recognized SharePoint experts.

Working with Microsoft Dynamics® CRM 4.0, Second Edition
Mike Snyder, Jim Steger
ISBN 9780735623781

Whether you're an IT professional, a developer, or a power user, get real-world guidance on how to make Microsoft Dynamics CRM work the way you do—with or without programming.

Programming Microsoft Dynamics CRM 4.0
Jim Steger *et al.*
ISBN 9780735625945

Apply the design and coding practices that leading CRM consultants use to customize, integrate, and extend Microsoft Dynamics CRM 4.0 for specific business needs.

ALSO SEE

Inside Microsoft Dynamics AX 2009
ISBN 9780735626454

6 Microsoft Office Business Applications for Office SharePoint Server 2007
ISBN 9780735622760

Programming Microsoft Office Business Applications
ISBN 9780735625365

Inside Microsoft Exchange Server 2007 Web Services
ISBN 9780735623927

microsoft.com/mspress